Second City

To Ralph

Best wishes

Rich

RICHARD VINEN

Second City

*Birmingham and the Forging of
Modern Britain*

ALLEN LANE
an imprint of
PENGUIN BOOKS

ALLEN LANE

UK | USA | Canada | Ireland | Australia
India | New Zealand | South Africa

Penguin Books is part of the Penguin Random House group of companies
whose addresses can be found at global.penguinrandomhouse.com.

First published by Allen Lane 2022
001

Text copyright © Richard Vinen, 2022
The moral right of the author has been asserted

Set in 10.2/13.87pt Sabon LT Std
Typeset by Jouve (UK), Milton Keynes
Printed and bound in Great Britain by Clays Ltd, Elcograf S.p.A.

The authorized representative in the EEA is Penguin Random House Ireland,
Morrison Chambers, 32 Nassau Street, Dublin D02 YH68

A CIP catalogue record for this book is available from the British Library

ISBN: 978-0-241-45453-4

In memory of W.F. ('Joe') Vinen
Professor of Physics, University of Birmingham, 1962–97

Contents

CONTENTS

List of Illustrations

List of Tables

List of Maps

Introduction: The 'Wrong Kind of Vulgarity'

When I was growing up in Birmingham in the 1960s and 70s, history was something that happened somewhere else. On school trips, we would pile into coaches to visit the castles at Warwick and Kenilworth but I never knew that the remains of a real castle could still be seen in the middle of the Weoley Castle council estate, a short walk from my house. Birmingham did not feature in the kind of history that I learned from Ladybird books. It had no obvious links with monarchy or aristocracy. Since my youth was haunted by images of the Second World War, I was also struck by Birmingham's absence from military history. On three occasions England's fate hinged around a 'battle of Birmingham'. The first of these came in 1897 when patriotic defenders fought a valiant rearguard action against Russian troops around 'the high crest on the Hagley Road'. The second took place in 1940 during 'Operation Victor' as German paratroopers attacked the city. The third came in 1984, when the Warsaw Pact dropped a nuclear bomb over Winson Green prison – thus reducing the whole of Birmingham to a radioactive ruin which, after the war had been brought to a halt, was preserved as a memorial 'Peace City West'. These three battles, though, were all fictional. The first occurred in William Le Queux's 'invasion scare' novel of 1894, *The Great War in England in 1897*. The second was part of an official exercise when 'battle raged on paper for three days'.[1] The third featured in General Sir John Hackett's novel *The Third World War: The Untold Story* (1982). All of these fictions felt immediately implausible. Indeed, one suspects that Birmingham featured in the work of Le Queux and Hackett precisely because the notion of a battle there seemed so incongruous and also, perhaps, because Hackett might have assumed that the sacrifice of Birmingham was a price his fellow generals would be willing to pay.

There was a sense, of course, in which I was right to assume that my home town had no history. Though the word 'Birmingham' first appears in the Domesday Book of 1086, it referred to nothing more than a tiny hamlet. Weoley Castle was for much of the Middle Ages part of a separate entity that was more important than Birmingham itself.[2] It was not formally assimilated into Birmingham until 1911. In 1928, a journalist visited the city and commented on the effigies of the old Lords of the Manor of Birmingham in St Martin's parish church: 'They lie, inexpressibly remote in the silence, deserted, forgotten, the men who pegged out the claim had no idea that they had founded anything larger than a green village.'[3] Rodney Hilton, one of the great historians of the Middle Ages, spent most of his professional life at Birmingham University, but when he wrote about the 'West Midlands' he was referring primarily to places such as Evesham and Pershore.[4] Birmingham was still a village, albeit a large and prosperous one, until the end of the sixteenth century.

In more recent times, the very pace of Birmingham's growth and the accompanying social and economic upheaval sometimes discouraged its inhabitants from dwelling on the past. The motto the city adopted on its incorporation in 1838 was 'Forward'. In 1835, the Frenchman Alexis de Tocqueville wrote that the town's inhabitants lived as though 'they must make their fortunes today and die the next day'.[5] Until recently, making one's fortune did not entirely exclude concern for the past. Some nineteenth-century Birmingham industrialists were sufficiently interested in history to devote much energy to correcting the first historian of the city – William Hutton – who had himself made a modest fortune. After 1945, however, it sometimes seemed that Birmingham was seeking to obliterate its own past. The poet W.H. Auden came to Birmingham in 1967 to receive an honorary degree from the university at which his father had been a professor. He had not set foot in the city since the 1930s and remarked that it seemed less associated with its own past than any other place that he had seen in his travels:

> [N]o city was more striking in the changes it had made in itself, not even New York. New York City rebuilt more, but you could always discern the old city behind or beneath. In Birmingham they seemed simply to have cleared away the whole thing and started again.[6]

The campaign against old buildings in Birmingham was notoriously epitomized by the words of Herbert Manzoni, the city's engineer:

I have never been very certain as to the value of tangible links with the past. They are often more sentimental than valuable ... As to Birmingham's buildings, there is little of real worth in our architecture. Its replacement should be an improvement ... As for future generations, I think they will be better occupied in applying their thoughts and energies to forging ahead, rather than looking backward.

Future generations have, as it turns out, applied Manzoni's words more quickly than he might have hoped and many of the structures that were most associated with his period of influence have now themselves been demolished.

Birmingham lacks old institutions as well as old buildings. Unlike Hamburg or Barcelona, it was never a 'second city' in any formal sense. It is not the centre of a regional government or of regional patriotism, and even institutions such as courts of law have only existed in Birmingham for a relatively short time.[7] London, by far the largest city in England as well as its political capital, its financial centre and, since the editor of the *Guardian* left Manchester in 1964, the base for every national newspaper, overshadows Birmingham as it overshadows every provincial city.

There was a brief period when Birmingham seemed, in the eyes of contemporaries and later historians, to enjoy a special status. This came in the nineteenth century – especially its latter half. This was the time when the city had a distinctive civic culture – particularly associated with the mayoralty of Joseph Chamberlain from 1873 to 1876 – and it was also a period when some believed that Birmingham incarnated a particular kind of society – one that was often held up as a contrast to the social divisions of large-scale capitalism seen in Manchester. In a characteristically gnomic passage, G.M. Young contrasted:

Manchester, solid, uniform, pacific, the native home of the economic creed on which aristocratic England had always looked, and educated England at large was coming to look, with some aversion and some contempt: Birmingham, experimental, adventurous, diverse, where old Radicalism might in one decade flourish into lavish Socialism, in another into pugnacious Imperialism.[8]

The most influential academic historian of Birmingham – Asa Briggs – was primarily a historian of the Victorian age. Briggs, a spectacularly energetic academic entrepreneur, was fascinated by the dynamism of Birmingham's politicians in the nineteenth century. He also developed the most systematic elaboration of a social interpretation of nineteenth-century Birmingham. It was one that fitted neatly with the political climate of the early 1950s when Briggs's work was published, in which the city's social structure, supposedly revolving around small business, elasticity of trade and social mobility, was presented as a challenge to Marxism. Briggs wrote the volume of the official history of Birmingham that covered the years 1865 to 1938. His work, however, acquired a curiously elegiac quality. It was commissioned by the last members of the great bourgeois dynasties who had once run Birmingham, but at the very moment when the vestiges of their power were ebbing away. It seemed that the days of Birmingham's political importance had not been sustained after the death of Joseph Chamberlain and that its social distinctiveness had not been sustained after the arrival of the large factories that came with the twentieth century. Indeed, by the time the final volume of the official history of Birmingham was published, two decades after Briggs's work, some scholars assumed that, if Birmingham was significant at all, then it served merely as an English 'middle-town' providing sociologists and political scientists with an object of study that was statistically representative, rather than providing historians with an object of study that might be interesting.[9]

It is odd that historians should so often regard Birmingham as becoming less significant at the moment when it became England's second city (1911) and at the beginning of a period when it was to see an increase in its population and in its economic importance. In part, Birmingham's very success served to remove it from view. Inter-war writers set out to 'discover' provincial England. The conservatives among them were often seeking the deep, rural roots that they believed to underlie their country. It was a vision most famously expressed in a speech that Stanley Baldwin made in 1924, during a brief period when he was not serving in, or leading, a Conservative government:

> The sounds of England, the tinkle of hammer on anvil in the country smithy, the corncrake on a dewy morning, the sound of the scythe against the whetstone and the sight of a plough team coming over the brow of a hill, the sight that has been seen in England since England was a land and that may be seen in England long after the Empire has perished and every

works in England has ceased to function, for centuries the one eternal sight of England.

Similar images were found in H.V. Morton's bestselling *In Search of England* (1927), which finishes with the author telling a country parson in Warwickshire 'You have England' but does not even mention the nearest big city. In fact, both Baldwin and Morton were closely associated with Birmingham – the former was a Midlands industrialist partly educated at Mason College (the institution that would later become Birmingham University) who had close political and business ties to two Birmingham families – the Chamberlains and the Kenricks. As for Morton, he had grown up in Birmingham and written his first articles for the Birmingham newspaper that his father edited.[10] However, the urbanization of Britain fostered a nostalgia for rural life – Tolkien's first evocation of 'Middle-earth' was published in 1937 and owed much to his upbringing in Sarehole, then an independent village but absorbed into Birmingham in 1911. In practical terms, the middle class who discovered rural England in the inter-war years largely did so because of the cheap Austin Seven cars that rolled off the production line at Longbridge in Birmingham.

Commentators on the left were not as culturally removed from Morton and Baldwin as they might have liked to think. George Orwell and J.B. Priestley were both fascinated by the countryside: the latter wrote that the Cotswolds was the 'most English' part of the country. Both men, however, were also interested in the poverty of the North in the 1930s. Birmingham, which had relatively low unemployment, did not fit into their vision. Indeed, as far as Priestley was concerned, the city had 'the wrong kind of vulgarity', by which he seemed to mean that its 'miles of ugliness [and] squalor' lacked the romance of real slum streets.[11]

Birmingham dropped out of the conventional picture of Britain in a literal way. Bill Brandt's photographs of working-class life in the 1930s and 40s are so ubiquitous that they probably influence even those who have never heard his name. They feature on the front cover of the Penguin edition of Orwell's *The Road to Wigan Pier* and on those of innumerable history books. Brandt's famous photographs were of London and the North – as though the working class were always either cockneys or natives of Yorkshire. During the Second World War, though, Brandt worked for a time for the Bournville Village Trust, which had been established by the Cadbury family, taking photographs of Birmingham domestic life. Some of them were used for a book published by the Trust, but most were simply forgotten until a sharp-eyed researcher dug them out of the archives in 1993.[12] Perhaps the notion that the Birmingham working class might be a matter of interest never crossed any publisher's mind; perhaps Brandt himself felt that there was something awkward or incongruous about the subject.

The study of British cities was fashionable for a time from the early 1950s until the mid 1970s (Asa Briggs was himself an important influence on this fashion). But urban history has changed in revealing ways. It began life as a pushy, parvenu sub-discipline – largely based, as far as its British practitioners were concerned, in Leicester. Now, it sometimes seems that academic historians of the city have risen so far from these humble origins that they mingle with a more established and patrician variety of urban specialist – John Julius Norwich or Jan Morris. There is less talk of sewers and statistics, and the cities that attract most attention are those – London, Salonika, Venice, Constantinople – that are ancient and/or beautiful. There have been at least a dozen histories of Paris, alone, in the last twenty years.

Two, partly related, historiographical shifts began in the late 1960s and 70s that served to occlude British provincial cities in general and Birmingham in particular. First, historians turned their attention towards the twentieth century. Second, they were less interested in industrialization and the organized working class. Increasingly, they focused on marginality, crime, 'deviant cultures' and sexuality. Often, these interests brought them back to London, where society seemed most variegated and subject to rapid change. Indeed, anyone who based their knowledge of male homosexuality on publications with titles such as *Capital Affairs*[13] or *Queer London*[14] might suppose that anything but the most conventional form of sexual activity was unknown outside Zone One of the London Transport network. They might also be surprised to hear that the authors of these works spent a significant part of their careers at the University of Birmingham.

Curiously, the shifting academic culture of the period was particularly associated with the Centre for Contemporary Cultural Studies (CCCS) at the University of Birmingham – so much so that anyone carrying out an internet search about class or race in Birmingham is as likely to come across studies of how class and race have been perceived through the prism of theories developed in the CCCS as they are to come across work on how class and race were experienced at the Dunlop factory or in the streets of Alum Rock. Sometimes, though, it looked as if the only subject that did not interest the CCCS was the society of the city in which it was based. When Kieran Connell, a historian from, and of, Birmingham, interviewed veterans of the CCCS, he asked them what role the city had played in their thinking. Some gave interesting answers but some appear never to have considered the matter.

Why then do I think it worth writing the history of a city that so many of my most distinguished colleagues find uninteresting? Partly the answer to this question is simply that the history of Britain is so extraordinarily focused around London that seeing it from another perspective is worthwhile. And partly it lies in a desire to explore the identity that a city might have. Writing an introduction to a monograph on the sociology of Auxerre in 1950, the historian Lucien Febvre remarked that, though the population of the city had been transformed by industrialization and migration, it seemed, like one of the regiments whose soldiers were slaughtered and replaced during the First World War, to preserve a certain continuous identity.[15] I feel the same way about Birmingham. Though the powerful personalities who attract most attention are concentrated in the late eighteenth and nineteenth centuries, I feel that the city itself has a kind of personality which can be discerned at different times – though sometimes, rather like Virginia Woolf's *Orlando*, it assumes very different guises in its successive incarnations.

Partly in search of continuities, I have written a history that goes back to the earliest times, but there is obviously a sleight of hand in this since Birmingham has grown so much in recent years that the number of people who have lived in the city since 1900 must be greater than the number who lived there in the whole of history before 1900. My book, therefore, focuses on relatively recent times and especially on the twentieth century. Indeed, a key argument of this book is that the history of Birmingham in the twentieth century should not be treated as merely the postscript to a Victorian golden age. Birmingham, more than anywhere in Britain, perhaps more than anywhere in Europe, illustrated the social transformation that went with mass production from the early twentieth century until the mid 1970s. It also exemplifies in particularly stark form the painful transition that came when there was no work to be had in a city that had been founded on work.

Birmingham forged modern Britain in a literal sense. It was a great centre of metalworking, engineering and, for most of the twentieth century, motor manufacture. More generally, Birmingham was at the centre of many of the greatest dramas of modern British history. Moving to Birmingham – first from surrounding counties, then from other parts of the United Kingdom, especially South Wales, and finally from overseas – changed hundreds of thousands of lives. One consequence of this was that, especially during the 1960s, Birmingham was recognized across the world as a cauldron of racial hostility. Questions about labour relations (why unions were weak in the 1930s and why strikes, often not led by unions, were so common in the 1970s) or politics (why sections of the working class have so often voted Conservative) can be answered partly with reference to Birmingham. As for military matters, there never was a real 'battle of Birmingham', but the Battle of Britain in 1940 was won as much in the Spitfire factory at Castle Bromwich as it was on the aerodromes of the Home Counties.

I will finish with a personal note. The first words that I learned to write, after my own name, were 'Middle Park Road, Selly Oak, Birmingham, B29 4BJ'. I grew up in this street and finished writing this book at my parents' house there in the summer of 2021. This does not mean that I have some special understanding of the city in which I spent the first eighteen years of my life. My parents, like so many Birmingham residents, were migrants who came to the city when my father got a chair at the university shortly before my birth. Like many of their generation, they navigated the strange world of the middle class with the help of books – my father taught himself to write with the help of *Fowler's Modern English Usage* and my mother's dinner parties owed much to Elizabeth David. There were times when my sister and I might just as well have been growing up in London, or even – since our house had a large garden and the grand family that sold it to us still referred to the most distant part of this as 'the paddock' – in the countryside. I only once came across a reference to my own street in my researches for this book. Listening to an interview with Albert Bennett, a retired car worker and trade unionist, I heard how he had sprinted up Middle Park Road in the 1920s, on one of the occasions when Herbert Austin had kept the Longbridge factory open late to try to prevent his workers from voting in a municipal election.[16] The detail reminded me of how little I knew about one of the largest factories in Birmingham – even though, when I look back on it, I realize that I must have gone to primary school with children whose fathers worked there. I make no claim to being an insider who is uniquely equipped to explain Birmingham to the world. Rather I regard myself – as I suspect many people who live, or have lived, in Birmingham might – as a curious stranger trying to make sense of this extraordinary place.

City Limits: A Note on Geography

French scholars, especially those who wrote during their country's period of relative social stasis from 1870 to 1940, make much of natural features. André Siegfried wrote that the politics of the west of the country could be explained in terms of a difference between areas of granite and areas of limestone. It would be hard to do this with Birmingham. Anyone looking at Spaghetti Junction or the Rotunda, or for that matter Corporation Street, would understand that this is a place where people make the landscape rather than vice versa. Roy Fisher, born in 1930, was the poet of post-war Birmingham and his poems are about a universe 'centred ... just beyond the garden path of Seventy-Four Kentish Road Handsworth'. He writes of buildings and roads and buses. His references to the natural landscape are mocking. The title of his most famous work – 'Birmingham River' – is a joke because the rivers in Birmingham have long been culverted.

Among the many artificial things in Birmingham are the city limits. One rarely knows when one enters or leaves Birmingham. Approaching the city from Coventry in 1933, J.B. Priestley came across a Birmingham Corporation sign saying 'This is Birmingham' in the middle of what seemed to be 'russet tranquillity'. Passing through Edgbaston or Bournville, one can feel as though one is in the countryside while still in Birmingham. The expansion of Birmingham in the twentieth century blurred the distinction between countryside and city. In the early 1950s, 9 per cent of Birmingham's area was covered by working farms and 40 per cent of these lay in the relatively built-up areas of the town: there were two working farms in Handsworth as late as the 1930s. There could be odd juxtapositions. Purely residential areas, especially in the prosperous suburbs of South Birmingham, could feel like villages. On the other hand, working farms sometimes looked like depressing urban wasteland. Their soil had often been damaged by industrial pollution, and farmers were discouraged from investment in their land and buildings by the fact that their tenure was insecure – the corporation owned the freehold for many farms and usually had plans to build on them.[1]

Birmingham has expanded over the centuries. At first, it was one 'manor' among eighteen on the site of what is now the city. Then it was a parish – taking in most of what is now the centre of the city. Then it became a parliamentary borough taking in other parishes, notably that of Edgbaston. As Birmingham came to be defined as a 'city' in 1889, it continued to annex new areas. The last major acquisition – Sutton Coldfield – happened in 1974. For most of the post-war period a 'green belt', at first only informally recognized, constrained the city's further expansion, but even this was sometimes encroached on.

Birmingham is partly bounded by farming country. To its north-west is an area that has been industrialized for as long as Birmingham itself. A shallow, and thus easily mined, seam of coal underlay the prosperity of an area around Dudley and was exploited extensively from the eighteenth century. Iron manufacture also developed, partly as a result of accessible coal. The area centred on Dudley, and including places such as Rowley Regis, Halesowen, Smethwick and Brierley Hill, came, from the 1840s, to be known as the 'Black Country'. This area was sometimes contrasted with Birmingham. It had a more homogeneous economy and one that in the inter-war period seemed less prosperous than that of Birmingham. However, parts of the Black Country blend into Birmingham without any obvious break.

I have adopted a common-sense definition of the town. I have excluded places – such as Coventry or Wolverhampton – with a clear civic identity of their own. And I have included places, – such as Smethwick and Solihull – that adjoin Birmingham and intertwine with its history, even though they have never been, formally speaking, part of it. Doing otherwise would generate peculiar results with regard to some of Birmingham's most famous inhabitants. It would mean that Samuel Boulton was part of the city's history when he first established his works on a site in Snow Hill, but ceased to be so when he moved to Handsworth, outside the city limits then, but inside them now, or when he moved on to Smethwick, which is outside them even now. It would mean that the Kenrick family were part of Birmingham's history when they were at home in Edgbaston or in the Council House (three members of the family were mayors or lord mayors of Birmingham) but ceased to be part of its history when they commuted to their factory in West Bromwich.

I should, however, admit that a 'common-sense' definition is not always a good guide to how things are commonly sensed. The expansion of Birmingham and the spectacular changes that its fabric has undergone mean that even those who have lived there all their lives sometimes have trouble orientating themselves. Henry Green left Oxford and went to work at his father's factory – it made beer-bottling machines – in Yardley in 1926. He found that his workmates would often argue about the location of 'a certain Stoney Lane that, soon after the war [i.e. the war of 1914–18], had been obliterated in a clearance scheme in the district'.[2]

Birmingham's transport network makes it particularly hard to get a sense of the city as a whole. William Hutton published the first history of Birmingham in 1781 and began it with a description of a walk around the town – he regarded carriages as a symbol of aristocratic frippery. In 1807, the street commissioners, who provided much of Birmingham's municipal government at the time, began to 'perambulate' the boundaries of the towns that they were to administer.[3] Now, however, Birmingham has become one of the least walkable cities in Britain – not just because it is large but because it is cut up by busy roads that divide its different quarters. A few years ago, a sociologist interviewed young people from the Alum Rock Road. One of them, Ashfaq, recalled having walked five or six miles to the west to the Bristol Road. It felt like alien territory and 'when we got back to Alum Rock and saw the Saltley Viaduct bridge we started praying and thinking "Thank God, we're back home."'[4] A little later another sociologist, studying young Muslim men in Birmingham, conducted 'walked interviews with his subjects'. He found that walking triggered interesting conversations as men saw places that had been important to them when growing up or met people they knew. 'This was this road for many years ... I used to go every day ... So it's a case of these roads (being) special to me. Every road I look at I've seen them develop. I've seen them change. It's part of my personal history.'[5] But they walked only in a narrow area. A man who had moved to Kingstanding, a mainly white council estate, chose to come into the city centre for his interview. Different parts of Birmingham can feel sharply divided from each other. Those studying children at a primary school in Small Heath in the 1970s concluded that they were more familiar with 'David Attenborough's Borneo', which they had seen on television, than with neighbouring districts.[6]

If Birmingham people have any sense of their city as a whole, it often derives from buses – hence the special part that the No 11 (outer circle) route plays in the public imagination. John Taylor, the bass player from Duran Duran, regarded himself as a 'Birmingham flâneur' during his youth in the 1970s, but he saw the city through the windows of a Midland Red bus:

> Past the Maypole and Bates' Toy Corner, through Kings Heath with its massive Sainsbury's supermarket where I now worked a weekend job, past Neville Chamberlain's old residence in Moseley [he is actually referring to Joseph Chamberlain's residence, which the family gave up during the First World War] and the Edgbaston Cricket Club and past the ABC cinema (now a McDonald's), peeling off at the Albany Hotel, taking a right at the Crown pub and past the Jacey cinema, where Mum and I used to watch cartoons and shorts, but by then showed twenty-four-hour porn. Then, in a moment, out of the daylight and into the depths of the bus depot. [7]

Roads sometimes tie in with more complicated psychological frontiers in Birmingham that only partly relate to formally defined areas. Birmingham University organized a conference in 2014 revolving around photographs of Varna Road, 'the wickedest street in Britain', that had been known for prostitution before it was demolished to make way for the Belgrave Middleway in the 1970s. Varna Road is usually described as being part of Balsall Heath, a famously rough neighbourhood, but a member of the audience at the conference said that he had always considered the road to be part of Edgbaston, the eminently respectable suburb in which the university is located. Edgbaston is one of the most clearly defined parts of Birmingham because, in the eighteenth and nineteenth centuries, it was largely controlled by a single aristocratic family: the Calthorpes. Even Edgbaston, however, is blurred around the edges. Eric Dodds came to Birmingham in the 1920s and lived first in George Street 'between opulent Edgbaston and the adjacent slumland'.[8] The architectural historian Nikolaus Pevsner first lived in Birmingham in the 1930s and recalled later that Duchess Road, where he lodged, was in Edgbaston but 'on the wrong side of the Hagley Road'.[9]

On the edges of Edgbaston runs the Bournbrook. This tiny stream is now mainly underground and invisible but it has marked frontiers for centuries. Once it was the border between Worcestershire and Warwickshire and, from at least 1291 until the establishment of a cathedral in Birmingham in 1905, between the dioceses of Worcester and Lichfield. There may even have been a time when it divided the Anglo-Saxon kingdoms of Hwicce and Mercia.[10] More recently, it has come to mark the boundary of Edgbaston and Selly Oak: an important frontier because the industry that the Calthorpe family excluded from Edgbaston concentrated on the edge of Selly Oak, so that the leafy campus of Birmingham University was once bordered by factories. The factories are gone now but somehow the division persists. The Bournbrook Hotel was once a rough pub frequented by bikers – a brief attempt at gentrification that entailed renaming it 'The Old Varsity Tavern' seems to have failed.

Sometimes Birmingham residents imbued natural features that might seem almost unnoticeably small to an outsider with a significance that derives from social history as much as from physical geography. Longbridge in Birmingham and what was until recently rural Worcestershire are divided by a small hill. It is not much of an obstacle, and in the 1930s a Birmingham student could still cycle past Longbridge to pick apples in a Worcestershire orchard. However, for trade unionists trying to organize the car plant at Longbridge, the workers who commuted in from Worcestershire came from a different world, in which the notion of social class counted for less. The trade unionists talked with exasperation of 'brow people' – meaning those who lived over the brow of the hill.[11]

Even the recent landscape of Birmingham – that which derives from buildings rather than hills or streams – can be interpreted in unexpected ways. The Sentinels, the two high-rise buildings that loom over the inner ring road, were intended as a symbol of pride in the new modernistic city that was built after the Second World War. However, they soon acquired a significant population of gay men – who valued them for their proximity to the city centre – and became known in the more louche Birmingham clubs as the Fairy Towers. Things turned darker during the AIDS epidemic of the 1980s – when they were sometimes called 'the pearly gates'.

I should perhaps finish by saying that Birmingham cannot be defined with exclusive reference to its own immediate area; the city has colonized other places. Birmingham's water comes from reservoirs in Wales and these are in an odd kind of way outposts of the city. There were once Birmingham Corporation signs around the dams, and the buildings associated with them were constructed in what locals referred to as 'Birmingham baroque' – though they were built of Welsh stone rather than red brick. Birmingham policemen were sent to guard the dams at the outbreak of the First World War. In the 1950s and 60s, the council paid for houses to be constructed for Birmingham residents, some of whom then commuted back to work in Birmingham, in satellite towns that included Daventry, which is sixty-eight miles away.

Most importantly, Birmingham has always been a migrant city. Those people who are most likely to be presented as quintessentially local are usually, in fact, the children or grandchildren of someone from somewhere else. The family of Enoch Powell, born in 1912, were from the Black Country a generation previously and from Wales a generation before that. In his father's factory in the late 1920s, Henry Green was struck by the accent and idioms of the workers. He thought such vivid turns of phrase as 'eyes started out of his head like a little dog's testicles' were characteristic of Birmingham working-class speech.[12] Perhaps some men did indeed speak a local patois but the whole factory and a large part of its workforce had moved from London in the comparatively recent past. After 1945, migration to Birmingham came from ever more distant lands, and a history of the city needs to take account of ways in which the partition of the Punjab or the construction of the Mangla Dam in Pakistan displaced people who would end up in Birmingham. It also needs to allow for the way in which remembered, and misremembered, pasts structured how people related to the city in which they lived – even if their links to those pasts amounted to nothing more than a picture of St Kitts on their grandmothers' tea towels.[13]

Modern Birmingham, showing the city and district boundaries

N

City Boundary

SUTTON COLDFIELD

PERRY BARR

ERDINGTON

HODGE HILL

LADYWOOD

YARDLEY

EDGBASTON

HALL GREEN

SELLY OAK

NORTHFIELD

| 0 | 1 | 2 | 3 miles |
| 0 | 1 | 2 | 3 | 4 km |

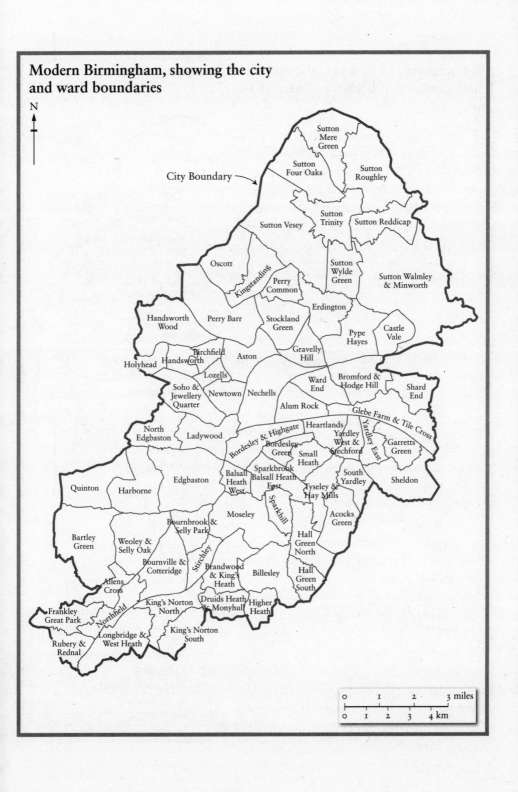

Modern Birmingham, showing the city and ward boundaries

N

City Boundary →

Sutton Mere Green
Sutton Four Oaks
Sutton Roughley
Sutton Vesey
Sutton Trinity
Sutton Reddicap
Oscott
Kingstanding
Perry Common
Sutton Wylde Green
Sutton Walmley & Minworth
Handsworth Wood
Perry Barr
Stockland Green
Erdington
Pype Hayes
Castle Vale
Holyhead
Handsworth
Birchfield
Aston
Gravelly Hill
Bromford & Hodge Hill
Shard End
Lozells
Soho & Jewellery Quarter
Newtown
Nechells
Ward End
Alum Rock
Glebe Farm & Tile Cross
North Edgbaston
Ladywood
Bordesley & Highgate
Heartlands
Bordesley Green
Small Heath
Yardley West & Stechford
Yardley East
Garretts Green
Quinton
Harborne
Edgbaston
Balsall Heath West
Balsall Heath East
Sparkbrook
South Yardley
Sheldon
Tyseley & Hay Mills
Bartley Green
Weoley & Selly Oak
Bournbrook & Selly Park
Moseley
Sparkhill
Acocks Green
Hall Green North
Bournville & Cotteridge
Stirchley
Brandwood & King's Heath
Billesley
Hall Green South
Allens Cross
Frankley Great Park
Northfield
King's Norton North
Druids Heath & Monyhull
Higher Heath
Rubery & Rednal
Longbridge & West Heath
King's Norton South

0   1   2   3 miles
0 1 2 3 4 km

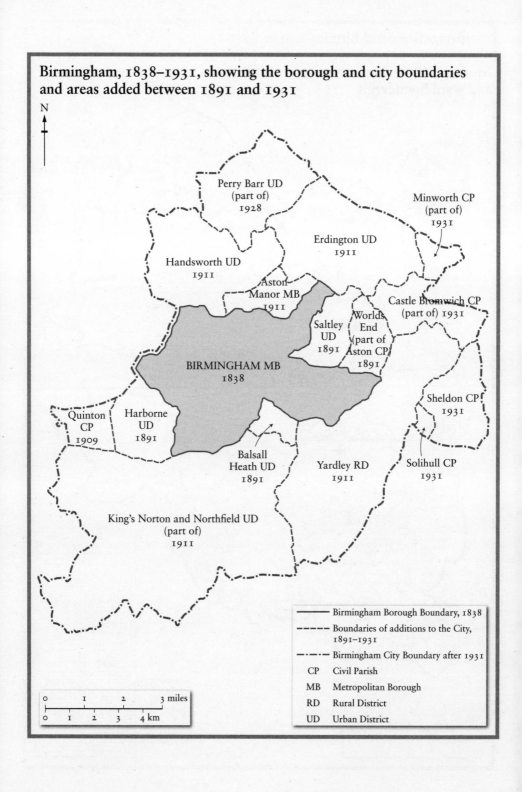

Birmingham, 1838–1931, showing the borough and city boundaries and areas added between 1891 and 1931

N

Perry Barr UD
(part of)
1928

Minworth CP
(part of)
1931

Erdington UD
1911

Handsworth UD
1911

Aston
Manor MB
1911

Castle Bromwich CP
(part of) 1931

Saltley
UD
1891

Worlds
End
(part of
Aston CP)
1891

BIRMINGHAM MB
1838

Sheldon CP
1931

Quinton
CP
1909

Harborne
UD
1891

Balsall
Heath UD
1891

Yardley RD
1911

Solihull CP
1931

King's Norton and Northfield UD
(part of)
1911

—————	Birmingham Borough Boundary, 1838
- - - - -	Boundaries of additions to the City, 1891–1931
—·—·—	Birmingham City Boundary after 1931
CP	Civil Parish
MB	Metropolitan Borough
RD	Rural District
UD	Urban District

0   1   2   3 miles

0   1   2   3   4 km

Settlements around Birmingham in 1686

N

STAFFORDSHIRE

WARWICKSHIRE

WORCESTERSHIRE

○ Sutton

○ Witton ○ Erdington

Handsworth ○

○ Aston

Smethwick ○

○ Birmingham

○ Yardley

Edgbaston
Harborne ○ ○

○ Moseley

○ Selly Oak

Bartley ○

Frankley ○

Northfield ○

Tessal ○

○ Norton

Lindsworth ○

Rednal ○

○ Cofton

0	1	2	3 miles
0	1	2	3	4 km

Settlement	Population in households
Aston	44
Bartley	5
Birmingham	9
Cofton	19
Edgbaston	10
Erdington	14
Frankley	11
Handsworth	10
Harborne	5
Lindsworth	6
Moseley	6
Northfield	33
Norton	6
Rednal	6
Selly Oak	12
Smethwick	5
Sutton	26
Tessal	6
Witton	5
Yardley	9

Birmingham's foundation myth. The name Birmingham seems, originally, to have meant 'the land of Beorma'. Some date the town's origins from the arrival of Anglo-Saxons led by a man of this name in the seventh century. In 2002, the Beorma Arch, designed by Stephen Field, was built in Gooch Street, near the river Rea. The inscription under it reads 'Near this river crossing an Anglian tribe led by Beorma founded Birmingham'.

I

Minute Beginnings

Towns as well as everything in nature, have exceedingly minute beginnings.

William Hutton, *History of Birmingham*, 1781

Why does Birmingham exist? It is not explained by any natural feature. It has no navigable river and no hill that would make defence easy. There are no valuable natural resources there. Planners in the 1960s, concerned to move industry to the 'development areas' of the North, were sometimes perplexed as to why Birmingham had been settled in the first place.

There was a time quite recently when Birmingham schoolteachers told their pupils that in the seventh century Beorma led 'a small group of axe-wielding Anglo-Saxons' who cleared a space in woodland near the river Rea and established the settlement that became Birmingham. It is curious that some in Birmingham have made so much of the city's Anglo-Saxon roots at a time when much of its population is not of Anglo-Saxon descent and when its economy depends so heavily on investment from abroad. In 2002, a Beorma arch was constructed in Deritend by the river Rea – in reality little more than a stream. The inscription under it reads: 'Near this river crossing an Anglian tribe led by Beorma founded Birmingham.' There are, or were, plans for a 'Beorma quarter' to be constructed around a high-rise office block devised by a Kuwaiti company.

In fact there is not much evidence that Birmingham's existence can be traced back to a single event and certainly not one that involved an Anglo-Saxon tribe. One historian counted only seven written references to the Birmingham area (and none to a place called 'Birmingham') in the whole

Anglo-Saxon period.[1] Indeed, historians who study the Midlands before 1086 often depend on surviving objects, or on conclusions that they draw from the landscape, rather than documents. Birmingham's Roman past was disinterred only in the twentieth century – because new construction, especially around the medical school, went with an increasingly sophisticated approach to archaeological finds. But Birmingham, unlike say Chester or London, never felt like a place with a Roman past. William Hutton, writing the first history of Birmingham in the eighteenth century, assumed that the Roman fort at Metchley, which was partly visible in his day, had been built by the Danes – those 'pilfering vermin'.

The first written record of Birmingham's existence comes with the Domesday Book of 1086. The entry read:

> From William, Richard holds four hides in Birmingham. There is land for six ploughs, in the demesne, one. There are five villagers and four small-holders with two ploughs. The woodland is half a league long and two furlongs wide. The value was and is twenty shillings. Wulfwin held it freely in the time of King Edward.

Richard was a sub-tenant for William Fitz Ansculf, who held Dudley castle. William was a Norman, though from a family that had settled in England before the conquest, from which they greatly benefited. A 'hide' was a unit of measurement (usually around 124 acres) considered sufficient to support a household – though in practice most ordinary people did with much less. The term 'demesne' referred to the land directly controlled by Richard, rather than by his tenants. Wulfwin had been the independent lord of Birmingham before the conquest – though some sources suggested that Richard was himself an Anglo-Saxon.

The manor called 'Birmingham' was only one, and not the most important, of the manors in the area of what is now Birmingham. There were six in Warwickshire, nine in Worcestershire, one in Staffordshire, one that stood on the boundary between Warwickshire and Staffordshire one that stood on that between Worcestershire and Warwickshire. One of the Warwickshire manors, Aston, covered a sprawling area that included several villages. The largest compact settlement was Northfield, in Worcestershire, a few miles south of what is now Birmingham city centre, which had thirty-three residents. Its value was several times that of Birmingham.

The first nobleman who is known for sure to have borne the name of Birmingham is William in the twelfth century and it is unclear whether he was related to the family that had occupied the manor at the time of the Domesday Book. His son, Peter, obtained a charter to establish a market at Birmingham in 1166 and the degree of care with which this market was laid out suggests that it may have been a deliberate creation rather than simply a recognition of a long-established fact.

The Birmingham family had a tumultuous history which often involved conflict with their feudal overlords at Dudley. They fought for Henry II when Dudley rebelled against the king in 1173–4, but against the king when Dudley stayed loyal to him during the rebellion of Simon de Montfort – William de Birmingham was killed in the Battle of Evesham of 1265.[2] The Birminghams were, though, never particularly important and in any case never wholly attached to the village that bore their name – the part of the family that migrated to Ireland was probably more significant.[3] The last male member of the family, Edward, was born in 1497, was imprisoned in the Tower of London from 1533 to 1537, apparently the result of another quarrel with the Dudley family, and died shortly after this.

The death of Edward de Birmingham might be seen, at least in retrospect, as marking a kind of social revolution. His second wife, Elizabeth, was the daughter of a wealthy Worcestershire lawyer and was described by her relations at court as a 'poor gentlewoman' who was 'like to go a begging'. She may, though, have been less vulnerable than her defenders suggested. She survived her husband by over twenty years and contrived to have the pension the king had granted her husband doubled to £40 per year. She also married two more times and the second of these marriages was to a prosperous miller, Thomas Askrigge.

Elizabeth's second marriage illustrated a broader change. Noble families who could trace their lineage back to the Norman Conquest were less important to the life of Birmingham. By the late eighteenth century, William Hutton, a keen believer in the virtues of social mobility, could claim that: 'The families of those ancient heroes, of Saxon and Norman race, are, chiefly by the mutations of time, and of state, either become extinct, or . . . reduced to the lowest verge of fortune.'[4] They were being replaced by 'yeomen' – the Rastells, the Veseys, the Smalbrokes (or Smalbrooks) and the Colmores – who had risen through their own enterprise or good fortune.

Charitable foundations preserve some traces of these families. In 1526, William Lench, a cattle grazier who had no children, left his money to help the poor (the charity that bears his name still administers alms houses in Birmingham) and to repair roads. Wealthy men also endowed guilds. The assault on religious foundations that began under Henry VIII and took its most severe form under Edward VI spared Lench's charity, which had aims that went beyond religion. The Guild of the Holy Cross was dissolved along with the Guild of St John in Deritend. However, Richard Smalbroke managed to persuade the authorities that the Guild of the Holy Cross should be transformed into an educational foundation – though curiously it was the Guild of St John that had until that point supported a school. The result of these manoeuvres was the establishment of King Edward VI's grammar school in 1552. Its charter declared that it was to be governed by 'twentie honest and discrete men inhabitants of the town and parish of Birmingham or the manor of Brymychan to the same town adjoining'. The governors of King Edward's School were a self-appointing group who chose the successors for members who died or left the area. They were an oligarchy who continued to exercise power, and arouse resentment, into the nineteenth century. They seem, however, to have been drawn from tradesmen rather than nobles or from those who were recognized at the time as gentlemen. The first twenty included William Ascrigg (presumably a descendant of the miller who had married the widow of Edward de Birmingham). They also included Richard Smalbroke and two members of the Colmore family.

In spite of the injunction that they should be honest and discreet the governors were soon divided among themselves. One source of friction was the bitter mutual hostility of the Smalbroke and Colmore families – a hostility that seems to have been exacerbated, rather than appeased, by inter-marriage. The conflict was waged on every front and with every possible weapon. It involved not only expensive libel suits, but also an apparent attempt to murder Thomas Smalbroke in 1604 and the subsequent siege of the Smalbroke family home by the Colmores. Only the intervention of Sir Thomas Holte, owner of Aston Hall and one of the few individuals in the area whose power exceeded that of the Colmores, brought this violent episode to a close.[5]

Three broader points can be drawn from the study of the notable families who emerged in sixteenth-century Birmingham. First, they were growing rich. In 1566, William Colmore left £300 to each of his five children.[6] The family eventually came to own the Newhall estate on which much of modern central Birmingham is built. Even those more modest families who were still tied to particular trades could have substantial fortunes. The wealthiest of the sixteen tanners for whom an inventory of possessions at his death exists left goods with a value of around £235.

Secondly, their wealth derived from both agriculture and trade. Often, they made money from milling or weaving that involved the processing of agricultural goods. Occasionally they practised more than one trade. Thus Thomas Rastell was, like other members of his family, described as a draper but his belongings at his death in 1591 included sixty-seven cheeses, a balance and lead weights and six loads of hay.[7] Henry Greisbroke, who died in 1557, was a butcher but his possessions included three spinning wheels.[8] Men who themselves had more than one source of income sometimes bequeathed different kinds of resources to different sons. When Richard Smalbroke died in 1575, his will endowed his younger son Thomas with the more obviously mercantile part of his property – leases, land, shops, building timber, half a ton of iron and weights and scales – while his older son, Richard, inherited 'things belonging to husbandry'.[9]

Thirdly, despite all the mutual accusations of criminal behaviour, the families aspired to gentility. Sometimes the term 'gentlemen' was applied to men who still lived in the town and still practised a trade. Becoming a gentleman sometimes involved acquiring property in the country – which often meant simply that urban merchants returned on a larger scale to the agricultural lives their families had lived just a generation or so previously.

Sometimes 'gentility' meant education, which led to the Church or the law. At least fifty Birmingham men who passed through King Edward's School between 1566 and 1692 subsequently went to the universities of Oxford or Cambridge, and most of these were then ordained or called to the Bar. Some came from families that had already escaped from mercantile origins. At least eight had fathers in holy orders, four had fathers with titles (three baronets and a baron) and a number of fathers were described as 'gentleman'. However, there were also five Colmores on the list (as well as two members of the Porter family who were related to them) and three Smalbrokes (as well as four members of families related to them). Many of the names on the list were the sons of ironmongers or mercers or, in two cases, bakers. One was the son of an innkeeper.[10] Thomas Rastell, who was admitted to Christ Church Oxford in 1644, was only a generation or two away from his namesake the draper and, from Dorothy Rastell, who had been fined in 1571 for selling wine at an excessive price, having already been fined a little earlier for committing the same offence with regard to fish.[11]

John Vesey (probably born in the mid fifteenth century) went to Oxford, became an associate of Cardinal Wolsey and was eventually appointed Bishop of Exeter. He established Bishop Vesey's grammar school in Sutton Coldfield. Sir Richard Shelton, whose father, John, had been a mercer in Birmingham, was admitted to the Inner Temple and attracted the support of the king's favourite, the Duke of Buckingham. He became solicitor general, but his career ended in the mid 1630s – according to Clarendon he was 'old, illiterate and useless' – and was thus spared from direct involvement in the Civil War. Clement Colmore (1550–1619) was the son of William Colmore from Birmingham and, having studied at Oxford, became a judge at the ecclesiastical court in the diocese of Durham.[12] Richard Smalbroke (1672–1749) went from Oxford to become chaplain to the Archbishop of Canterbury and then Bishop of Lichfield.

THE ECONOMY OF EARLY MODERN BIRMINGHAM

By the early fourteenth century, the manor of Birmingham had become the most important of the settlements in the area that would eventually become the city of Birmingham. In 1327 it had seventy-five inhabitants whose goods were worth more than 10 shillings and it paid tax of £7 6d. Among neighbouring manors, only Edgbaston, Duddeston and Erdington paid more than £1. Edgbaston was the next most important with nineteen inhabitants whose property was valued at more than 10 shillings. Aston, which had been larger than Birmingham in 1066, was now known as 'Aston juxta Birmingham' and paid just under 15 shillings of tax. Villages in the West Midlands – such as Solihull and Stratford – were, however, not far behind Birmingham. All of these places were still overshadowed by the more established towns in the region. Worcester and

Lichfield – administrative and ecclesiastical centres – were bigger than Birmingham, and Coventry, an industrial and commercial town, was six or seven times its size.

Industry, such as existed in Birmingham, sprang at first from agriculture and involved leather and wool, the latter being treated in a number of mills that drew water from the river Rea. As textiles declined, metal-working industries, with which Birmingham was to be so associated, rose – though the rise was probably less dramatic than casual visitors, their attention drawn by the sparks and noise of workshops, assumed. The prosperity of Birmingham at this stage did not derive from natural resources (though it benefited from the relative proximity of coal and iron ore in Staffordshire and charcoal from the Forest of Dean) nor from access to the sea. Mainly the town seems to have grown because of its relation to other places. It stood at a point where a number of roads, none of them very important in themselves, converged, and it provided a relatively easy place to cross the Rea by ford. This mattered because the Rea, though small, was often an obstacle to travel when it was in flood and because, at many points, it was surrounded by marsh-land that made it hard to approach. Cattle being driven east from south Wales crossed the Rea at Birmingham.

Birmingham was an entrepôt – a place where things were traded but also where finished goods were made from raw materials supplied else-where. Of course, simply being close to other places does not in itself explain economic success. Perhaps, curiously, it was the very absence of a single obvious advantage that made Birmingham what it was. It became a place where other regions traded the various commodities in which they specialized. It also became a town that gave a high added value to products – increasingly it made things that were light, easily transported and relatively valuable. In the eighteenth century, Hutton would write with disdain of the primitive rural hinterland in Stafford-shire where production revolved around simpler goods – nails in particular – that depended on easy access to raw materials rather than skill and sophistication.

The population of Birmingham probably reached 1,500 in the middle of the sixteenth century, and there were around then forty baptisms per year – which rose to seventy per year by the first decade of the seventeenth century. But one should keep all this in perspective. At the end of the sixteenth century, Birmingham was still a large industrial village – less developed, as one of its twentieth-century historians was to point out, than the Suffolk town of Lavenham.[13]

RELIGION

Birmingham had no cathedral or abbey, or, until after the Reformation, any notable school. There is no evidence that the dissolution of religious foundations in Birmingham in the mid sixteenth century produced great suffering or evoked much protest. The town did have one unusual feature in that the congregation of St John's chapel at Deritend had enjoyed the right to select their own priest since its foundation in 1380. It is tempting to suggest that this made them sympathetic to reform of the Church in the sixteenth century. John Rogers, born in 1505, had worshipped at this church as a young man before being educated at Cambridge and ordained. He participated in Tyndale's English translation of the Bible, and in 1555 became the first Protestant to be burned during the Marian persecution. There is no evidence, however, that Rogers had acquired his Protestant inclinations in Birmingham – he had been radicalized during his time as chaplain to the Merchant Adventurers in Antwerp.

It is hard to discern a social pattern behind support for, or opposition to, the Reformation in Birmingham. Some country gentlemen in Warwickshire – such as the Throckmortons and the Catesbys – remained Catholic and, indeed, supported the Gunpowder Plot against James I in 1605. Meanwhile, the Earls of Warwick and Leicester were strongly Protestant. It is possible that the kind of families who were rising in Birmingham in the sixteenth century – those with links to trade, a propensity for making up their own minds and, increasingly, a taste for book learning – may have provided fertile ground for Protestantism, though it may be more likely that they simply found it prudent to align themselves with the religion of the state. Some prominent figures in Birmingham, including some with links to trade, opposed the Reformation. Bishop John Vesey was hostile to reform – though sufficiently discreet in the expression of his opinions to die in his bed. The Middlemore family, lords of the manor of Edgbaston, were staunch Catholics: Humphrey Middlemore, a Carthusian priest, was executed for treason in 1535 after refusing to recant his belief in papal supremacy.

POLITICS

During the Civil Wars of the 1640s, Birmingham was considered to be on the side of Parliament. Clarendon later wrote that the town had 'as great fame for hearty, wilful affected disloyalty to the King as any place in England'. The town appears, though, to have been governed by a hard-headed realism rather than religious or political conviction. Some prominent families, such as the Smalbrokes, remained mainly interested in their businesses. Even the Colmores, those most involved on the parliamentary side, were careful to take no stand, especially after the execution of the king, that was likely to be held against them later. The exception that proved the rule was John Sanders of Harborne. He was a radical visionary who combined calls for peaceful restoration of the monarchy and reform of the Church with the suggestion that the nail-makers of Birmingham should cease work for a month as a means to extract money from their oppressive employers. Sanders was treated as mad by his own family and especially by that of his wife – who beat him, arranged to have him arrested and seized his property.[14]

Birmingham was not an important centre of the English Civil War. King Charles stayed at Aston Hall as a guest of Sir Thomas Holte, a Royalist, for a single night in October 1642. There was to be much inconclusive discussion of whether Kingstanding, later the site of Europe's largest council estate, had been so named after a spot on which Charles had stood to review his troops. Birmingham itself was directly affected by the Civil War only in April 1643, when supporters of Parliament improvised defences to try to prevent Prince Rupert's forces from passing through and thus provoked the Battle of Camp Hill and subsequent pillaging of the town by Rupert's men. Clarendon remarked that but for the death of Lord Denbigh, killed in fighting with the Royalists on this occasion, he would not have mentioned 'an action of so little moment as this of Birmingham'.

William Hutton, writing in the late eighteenth century, suggested that, for Britain as a whole, the accession of Henry VII in 1485 marked the divide 'between ancient and modern' – or between 'medieval and modern' as historians of a later generation would put it. Hutton added, however:

But the ancient and modern state of Birmingham, must divide at the restoration of Charles the Second. For though she had before held a considerable degree of eminence; yet at this period, the curious arts began to take root, and were cultivated by the hand of genius. Building leases, also, began to take effect, extension followed, and numbers of people crowded upon each other, as into a Paradise.

The Restoration of 1660 might simply be an arbitrary moment in political history that happens to coincide with a moment when Birmingham's economy and society began to change for reasons that were only indirectly related to politics. There were, however, some respects in which the Restoration, or, at least the period between the Restoration of 1660 and the accession of William and Mary in 1689, mattered. This was not so much because of what happened as because of what did not happen. Old structures in Birmingham had gone in the mid sixteenth century when the local branch of the Birmingham family had become extinct and the religious institutions had been dissolved. At the same time, families basing their wealth on trade had begun to assume new importance, but this new importance was not accompanied by the creation of bourgeois institutions (or at least not ones that would be recognized by the bourgeoisie of the nineteenth century). Indeed, the bourgeois liberals of the nineteenth century were offended by the institution that had best incarnated the power of the Birmingham elite of the sixteenth century – the governing board of King Edward's School.

The Restoration might have brought change in either direction. It might have produced a counter-revolution by which the Birmingham families would have been subordinated to the country gentry in the surrounding area while political and religious orthodoxy was restored. Certainly, the king's ministers urged Sir Charles Holte, the most prominent local notable, to supress Nonconformist ministers in the areas. Equally, the Restoration might have brought a more modern form of municipal government that went with incorporation – the Royal Borough of Sutton Coldfield (later to be a suburb of Birmingham) had its municipal charter confirmed by Charles in 1664, thus attaining a formal status that Birmingham would not match until the early nineteenth century. As it turned out, however, there was no dramatic change in Birmingham after the Civil War.

In the last years of his reign Charles II sought to extend monarchical power, a project that was continued by James II when he succeeded in 1685. Among other things, this entailed revising many municipal corporations. Perhaps partly because Birmingham did not have a corporation, the governing board of King Edward's School became a political battlefield. In 1684, the school was given a new charter and a new board of governors. The requirement that governors reside in Birmingham was abolished. This meant in effect that country gentlemen were given authority that had formerly belonged to townsmen. Lord Digby and Sir Charles Holte were the most important figures behind the move, but the old governors resisted it and continued to meet at the Red Lion Inn in Birmingham. In 1689, the attorney general brought an action against the old governors – arguing that they had been corrupt and inefficient. The action was stalled by the deposition of James II and, after the accession of William and Mary, some expensive litigation restored the old governors.

If the attempt to depose the old governors had been a reactionary policy, their restoration was not a revolutionary one. The important families of Birmingham had already begun to move away from radicalism even before the restoration of Charles II. This was reflected in another piece of litigation relating to King Edward's School. In 1650, Captain Robert Girdler, a sword cutler and parliamentarian from Birmingham, brought an action against the governors of the school – arguing that the headmaster and a number of governors (including two Smalbrokes and a Colmore) had failed to honour the legal obligation to swear allegiance to the Commonwealth. The recalcitrant governors then swore the required oath – though their initial reluctance suggested they were a group of men primarily concerned to avoid taking any stand that might later be held against them. William Colmore had been the most prominent parliamentarian from the town, but he argued that he had held no office after the execution of the king. His son, also called William, sat in Parliament from 1689 to 1695 – and he did so as a Tory.

A BIRMINGHAM TOAST,

A PIG'S-STYE
a View from Hackney·

I have not drank so glorious a Toast since I was Parson of Brentford & kept it up with Betty & Mrs Laun·

Hear our Prayer & consume as one King & Whores of Babylon

Put eternity between us & the wicked and bring down the heads of all Tyrants & dissenters quickly to our Lord, Amen we pray

O grant the wishes of their worshippers

Amen! Amen!

──── on the 14ᵗʰ of July by the ──────── Revolution Society·

A cartoon showing the dinner of July 1791 designed to celebrate the anniversary of the fall of the Bastille. It provoked the Church and King riots that effectively ended the Birmingham Enlightenment.

2

Enlightenment Birmingham

I consider my settlement in Birmingham the happiest event in my life.[1]

Joseph Priestley

The town was large, and full of inhabitants, and those inhabitants full of industry. I had seen faces elsewhere tinctured with an idle gloom void of meaning, but here, with a pleasing alertness: Their appearance was strongly marked with the modes of civil life.[2]

William Hutton describing his first arrival in
Birmingham in 1741

What has come to be called the Birmingham or Midlands Enlightenment brought together an unusually curious and energetic group of men (they were all men, though their wives and daughters were often shrewd and well-informed commentators on their activities). Joseph Priestley and William Hutton epitomized the atmosphere of optimism, uninhibited enquiry and material prosperity some associated with Birmingham in the eighteenth century. The former was a minister of religion, though mainly known to posterity as a scientist; the latter was a well-to-do bookseller, though mainly known to posterity as a writer, particularly as the author of the first history of his adopted city. Both men, however, came to have less happy memories of Birmingham than those implied by the quotations above because both their houses were burned down in the Church and King riots of 1791.

DEMOGRAPHY

Priestley and Hutton were typical of Birmingham. Both were immigrants –
having been born respectively near Batley in Yorkshire and in Derby.
Hutton first came to Birmingham as a runaway apprentice in 1741 but
then returned to settle in the city in 1750. Priestley came to Birmingham
in 1780 to serve as the senior minister at the New Meeting House. Both
men were partly drawn to the town by what they took to be its tolerant
and open atmosphere. Hutton was, like Priestley, a Dissenter and
believed that religious dissent was made easier by the fact that Birmingham was not an incorporated town and was thus free from the provisions
of the 1665 Act that had forbidden Nonconformist ministers from living within five miles of a town from which they had been expelled.*
Hutton and Priestley were also drawn by Birmingham's prosperity.
Priestley's stipend of £100 per annum at the New Meeting House was
relatively modest but was supplemented by the subsidies that local businessmen provided to his scientific ventures. The commercial opportunities
of Birmingham made Hutton a wealthy man.

Birmingham grew rapidly in the eighteenth century as new arrivals
came seeking employment – though most, unlike Hutton and Priestley,
had not travelled far. The majority of those who arrived in the period up
to 1757 came from the counties of Warwickshire, Worcestershire and
Staffordshire – about a quarter of them from places that would become
part of Birmingham by 1937.[3] In 1700, Birmingham's population probably stood at between 5,000 and 7,000 (Hutton with characteristic
exuberance estimated it at 15,000); it reached over 23,000 by the middle of the century and then tripled again in the second half of the
century.

Birmingham's growing population was contained in a relatively small
area. At the time Hutton wrote his history of the town, which was first
published in 1781, most of Birmingham's population still lived within a
quarter of a mile of his shop. An act of Parliament in 1746 allowed the

* There is not much evidence that Birmingham Dissenters were treated very differently from
their co-religionists in, say, Coventry, and the notion that Birmingham had been especially
welcoming to Nonconformists only seems to have become widely accepted in the late
nineteenth century – i.e. at the time when its municipal government was largely in the hands
of Unitarians and Quakers.

development of the Colmore estate and thus opened up fresh territory for building in the north of the town, as well as making the Colmore family even richer than it already was. For various reasons the other major owners of property around Birmingham were unable or unwilling to permit building on their land. In any case, the direction of Birmingham's travel was north, where reserves of coal and iron ore lay.

The town of Wolverhampton was expanding almost as fast as Birmingham and places such as West Bromwich moved quickly from being villages to being centres of industry. Some observers talked of the roads (and soon canals) leading from Birmingham to Staffordshire as being so built-up that they looked like a single town. The county and cathedral towns around Birmingham – Lichfield and Worcester – remained important as cultural and political centres but they expanded less fast, which was partly why they were seen as more genteel.

A French visitor was told in 1784 that six tenths of the houses in Birmingham had been built in the previous twenty years.[4] In 1700, there were 2,500 houses in Birmingham, spread over 28 streets; by 1731 there were 3,756 houses and 51 streets; in 1781, there were 9,556 houses and 133 streets and by 1791 there were 12,681 houses over 203 streets.[5] Most of the new houses were relatively cheap – having a rateable value that was too low to make them liable for the Poor Rate, which became a problem as time went on. Many of Birmingham's houses were owned by people of comparatively modest means who rented them out. In 1765 Henry Gough, a 'bricklayer' (presumably a builder rather than a labourer), had eight houses that were insured for a total of £390.[6]

ECONOMY

The Birmingham economy flourished partly through the production of light goods – ones that were comparatively cheap to transport and derived their value largely from skilled workmanship. Such goods were known as 'toys' though they were nothing to do with children's playthings. Most manufacturers specialized in working a single metal – steel or brass – and often produced a single item, such as buckles. A letter from a particularly ambitious industrialist, however, captures the range of products that were on offer in 1772:

Snuff Boxes, Instrument Cases, toothpick Cases – gilt, glass and steel Trinkets, Silver filigree Boxes, Needle Books etc etc – all manner of plated Goods, as Tea Kitchins, Tankards, Cups, Coffee potts, Cream Juggs, Candlesticks – sauce boats, Terrines etc etc – Bronz'd Tea Kitchins and Tea Kettles as well plated as Tin'd inside, Saucepans, Cheese Toasters etc etc etc.[7]

The Birmingham economy was changed by increasingly efficient means of transport. The speed and frequency of stagecoach travel increased. In 1731, there were weekly carriages to London, and the time taken to reach the capital was cut from two and a half days to fourteen hours between 1750 and 1782. A traveller could get to Paris in six days.[8] Speedier travel meant that information circulated more quickly and that Birmingham came to feel part of a wide world – connected to other provincial towns and to the continent as well as to the capital. Sometimes commercially significant events in Europe were known in Birmingham before they were known in London.

CANALS

Travel by water was slower than travel by road but it permitted the movement of heavy goods. Canals had a particular impact in Birmingham because it had no natural navigable rivers. In 1769 the first cargoes on the new canal, whose construction had been overseen by James Brindley, were unloaded in Birmingham. The canal linked Birmingham to Staffordshire and reached Addersley near Wolverhampton in 1772. The most dramatic effect of the canal was to lower the price of raw materials, particularly coal. The price of coal from Wednesbury dropped from 13 shillings per ton just before the opening of the canal to 7 shillings in 1772.

From the late eighteenth century onwards, Birmingham industries were often grouped around canals, and, since they followed the contours of the land, the railways that came in the nineteenth century were often built parallel to them. As well as bringing raw materials in, canals provided a means of getting finished goods out of the town. The latter became particularly important in 1772, when the Birmingham Canal linked up to the Staffordshire and Worcestershire Canal to provide access to the sea.

The development of canals was associated, as cause and effect, with the development of the steam engine. Canals brought coal but also provided water, which was not always easily available from natural sources on the plateau to the north of Birmingham, for engines.[9] The industrialist Matthew Boulton had his own pond at the Soho works (of which more below), and initially feared that the construction of a canal might deprive him of this water. However, he soon appreciated the opportunities that canals opened up. The need to pump water for locks meant that canals provided a market for steam engines. One of the first steam engines that Boulton and his partner James Watt sold was to provide a pump for the locks at Smethwick, and it was at Smethwick that they later built their forge to make steam engines. Matthew Boulton later wrote:

> To . . . produce the most profit, my idea was to settle a manufactory near to my own, by the side of our canal, where I could erect all the conveniences necessary for the completion of engines, and from which manufactory we would serve all the world with engines of all sizes.[10]

Local men invested in the construction of canals and this in itself created new habits and associations. Those who wanted to promote new canals needed to garner public support in more than one town, negotiate with landowners across whose property the canals would pass, arrange for bills in Parliament and, of course, raise money. Canal investment was profitable: shares bought for £140 in 1768 could be sold for over £1,000 a decade later. Boulton was able to extract himself from the threat of bankruptcy in 1772 by using ten canal shares as security for a loan of £3,000.[11]

TOWN GOVERNMENT

At first glance, Birmingham's new economic status was not matched by a new political one. The town was not to be represented in the House of Commons until 1832. In 1715 there had been riots there, linked to the wider disorder that occurred across the country as mobs who thought of themselves as Tories and Anglicans attacked Presbyterians. The Old Meeting House in Birmingham was partly burned down. Afterwards, some citizens petitioned that the town should be incorporated, which would have allowed more local and efficient means of keeping the peace.[12]

The petition failed and, at least in the early part of the century, Birmingham was indeed governed by agencies 'nearly the same as the Saxons left', as Hutton put it, that might more usually have operated in a large village. There were officials with picturesque titles – the 'high' and 'low' tasters inspected food and drink. There were also two bailiffs (high and low). The bailiffs were the most powerful figures and the low bailiff had special power because he nominated the 'Leet' jury, which in turn chose the next bailiffs. At some point after the Glorious Revolution, to limit conflict a compromise emerged in Birmingham by which the high bailiff was always an Anglican and a Tory and the low bailiff was always a Whig and a Nonconformist. Because of the particular powers of the low bailiff this also meant that the Whigs controlled the town for many years – though the Tories attempted to pack the leet jury in 1722 and again in 1792. In 1726, paying two constables to maintain some semblance of order cost £100. Surveyors of the highways accounted for £200 and church wardens £250. By far the greatest item of expenditure in the parish was relief of the poor, which cost £1,300 or 70 per cent of the total budget.[13]

Some reform was undertaken later in the century. An act of Parliament in 1752 established a Court of Requests to deal with small debts. In 1769, an 'Act for the laying open and widening certain ways and passages within the Town of Birmingham, and for cleansing and lighting the streets, ways, lanes, and passages there, and for removing and preventing nuisances and obstructions therein' (commonly known as the 'Lamp Act') provided for the establishment of 'street commissioners'. These fifty unpaid citizens of the town, drawn from among those who owned property with a rateable value over £15 were responsible for maintaining the streets and in theory had some power of policing, though in practice they lacked the money to do much about this. Policing rarely meant more than trying to suppress the more obvious kinds of disorder and, especially during the Church and King riots at the beginning and end of the century, not everyone was confident that all local magistrates were enthusiastic about doing that. More sophisticated criminals seem to have prospered along with the rest of the town – men who had learned their trade as button-makers found it relatively easy to transfer their skills to counterfeiting coins, and it was said that the imprisonment of Birmingham men was particularly expensive because their experience of handling tools made them adept at picking locks.[14]

All local government was hampered by the fact that it depended on the willingness of the relatively wealthy to volunteer their services for no reward, and they, particularly those who were keen to devote their time and energies to the acquisition of greater wealth, were often reluctant to make this sacrifice. This was true of new officers, such as the street commissioners and the judges in the Court of Requests, but true also of the bench of magistrates. As Birmingham expanded, sitting on the bench in its environs became a more time-consuming exercise. Joseph Carles, the magistrate for Handsworth in Staffordshire, was in awkward financial straits, and a number of Birmingham men, including some who would later resent his activity, or inactivity, during the riots of 1791, sought to obtain for him one of the general receiverships for Warwickshire in the hope of easing his circumstances.

Birmingham's political life is best understood in parallel with that of the surrounding area. There was much dispute over who was to pay the expenses incurred as people moved into the town, but in fact town and country were never completely divided. The propertied had moved into Birmingham as well as the poor. This meant that, even though Birmingham itself had no parliamentary representation, many Birmingham men were electors in the places from which they came and in which they still often owned property. Equally, men from the town bought property outside it. Hutton, perhaps because of his humble origins, became addicted to the purchase of land. Social clubs drew men in from outside Birmingham. This was most famously true of the Lunar Society (of which more below). Less well known, but perhaps politically more important, was the Bean Club, which gathered together townsmen and country gentlemen of a Tory disposition.

In a 1774 Warwickshire by-election, Sir Charles Holte (the sixth baronet and owner of Aston Hall) stood for the seat and won. This seemed a challenge to the power of the grander aristocrats who had usually dominated the politics of the area. Holte, though, represented 'independent' county interests rather than the interests of the town of Birmingham, and his election may actually have upset the calculations of local industrialists, who were in any case unlikely to have forgotten that the Holte family had often in the past acted against the interests of prosperous Birmingham merchants. The election did not make a great difference – Holte was ill, he never spoke in Parliament and resigned in 1780. However, it seems to have been agreed that from this time on one of the county seats around Birmingham should effectively be chosen by the town to represent its interests.[15]

THE CULTURE OF EXPANSION

Most of all, Birmingham's expansion in the eighteenth century was associated with the activities of a group of men who might be described as entrepreneurs in the broadest sense of the term – in that not all their enterprises were commercial and that, indeed, commerce for them was not always separate from culture, science and even religion. The first and most striking of these figures was Matthew Boulton, born in Birmingham in 1728. His father (also Matthew) was a 'toy'-maker specializing in steel buckles. Boulton joined his father in business at an early age and emerged as the dominant figure in the company even before his father's death in 1759. He married a distant cousin, Mary, and when she died married her sister Anne. Marrying a deceased wife's sister was a brave move because it was forbidden under ecclesiastical law, though not illegal in civil law. The marriage illustrated a willingness to challenge the authority of the Anglican Church – though Boulton was not, unlike many of his associates, a Dissenter and, also unlike some of his associates, he was wary of challenging authority unless there was something clear to be gained. Something was certainly gained by marriage because both sisters were heiresses and between them they brought Matthew Boulton £28,000. He could have retired with the fortunes of his two wives and lived the life of a country gentleman. Instead, he invested in his businesses. In 1762, he acquired the means of making 'Sheffield plate', which had been invented a few years earlier and involved fusing and rolling sheets of silver and copper. From this he moved to making silverware.

Boulton's formal education had finished at an early age and most of what he knew had been picked up in the course of his working life. He was, however, anything but a crude provincial. He understood the uses of political contacts and first appeared before a committee of the House of Commons representing the buckle-makers of Birmingham, Warwick and Wolverhampton in 1760. He had an acute sense of style and an interest in those sections of society that did most to influence fashion. He took care to observe the correct forms of address when writing to a duke and duchess or a member of the gentry.[16] During a single visit to London in 1770 Boulton called on Lord and Lady Shelburne, the Duke and Duchess of Northumberland, the Earl of Dartmouth, the dowager Princess of Wales and the Queen.[17] Like other Birmingham industrialists, he understood that public events – royal birthdays and even elections – would have an influence on what people wore and what objects they displayed. A death at court, which would plunge fashionable society into mourning, was always a risk to business. In 1773, Boulton was one of the men who lobbied successfully for an Assay Office in Birmingham. When the office was established, five peers of the realm were included among its thirty-six guardians.[18]

Boulton also had good contacts outside Britain. His father had been involved in trade with Thomas Winkelmann of Brussels since around 1748, and by 1772 Boulton's firm was trading with every country in Europe. He had a hard-headed view of the different markets that he might serve and wrote:

> [I]t is not necessary to attend to elegance in such articles of my manufacture as are destined for Siberia and America, or even some parts of Germany. Fashion hath much to do in these things, and that of the present age distinguishes itself by adopting the most Elegant ornaments of the most refined.[19]

Boulton decided that his father's old premises in Snow Hill were no longer sufficient to accommodate his business. In 1761 he bought the lease for a new site at Soho – the name was said to come from a hunting cry – on Handsworth Heath, which was still a relatively sparsely populated area about two miles from Birmingham proper. The site encompassed about thirteen acres and contained a house and a 'slitting mill', designed to cut metal into strips. To power the mill, a pond had been formed by damming Hockley Brook. Boulton spent several years overseeing the construction of a bigger manufactory on the site of the mill. He created a second mill pond to provide a more reliable flow of water and eventually the two ponds were merged to create a lake; the use of steam would later turn the lake into an ornamental feature.[20]

Soho House did not always live up to the colossal ambitions of its owner. Boulton's plans in the 1780s to rebuild it with rooms for

'Wet Chymistry, Dry Chymistry, Natural History, Botany-Green House, Astonomy' came to nothing. It was initially inhabited by Boulton's mother and one of his sisters and then by his business partner before Boulton took it for himself in 1766. The 'manufactory' encompassed a mill and numerous workshops as well as accommodation for some workers. Boulton claimed that it employed almost 1,000 workers – though, even at its peak in the early 1770s, this was probably an exaggeration. The de la Rochefoucauld brothers, who were among the many foreign visitors to Soho, reckoned it to be the largest factory in the world. It was not designed simply with a view to industrial efficiency. Boulton was a good, if authoritarian, employer. He made sure that his works were well ventilated and whitewashed the walls to make rooms as bright as possible and to ensure that they were kept clean. The Soho works were expensive. They cost £10,000, which was five times the initial projected budget and did not include the cost of later additions.

Soho was built to impress. The factory was designed in Palladian style by architects from the Wyatt family, men whose acquaintance was useful to Boulton because they had introduced him to their clients from landed families. The grounds were landscaped and partly turned into gardens. Boulton acquired short-term tenancies on another twelve or so acres of land in the late 1760s and by the end of the century owned the freehold of an area of over eighty. On this land he created a park. Making the grounds around Soho fit for horticulture required large amounts of manure, which Boulton acquired even though, as ever, his finances were stretched. Anyone approaching the manufactory would have the sense that they were visiting a country house – 'the stately palace of some duke' as an American visitor put it – rather than a place of work.[21] Eminent people from around the world were encouraged to visit Soho; Catherine the Great's favourite, Count Orloff, the Baron de Montesquieu and the Earl of Shelburne were among those who did so. At first Boulton was relaxed about the fact that some of these visitors, such as the improbably named Baron Richagenius, were industrial spies; Boulton had himself obtained secrets of French brass manufacture through bribery. Many who came did so as a part of a regional tour that took in sites of industrial interest along with grand houses and places of historical importance. Everything about the Soho site – which came to include an aviary, a menagerie and a tea room – was calculated to attract the curious and Boulton insisted that some visitors, especially the grandest, should join him for dinner. About half of Soho's recorded visitors seem to have come from abroad: 21 per cent came from France, 11 per cent each from Russia and the Italian states, 5 per cent each from Prussia and America, and the remainder from Switzerland, Scandinavia, Spain, Portugal, Poland, various parts of Germany, the Dutch provinces, Canada and the Ottoman Empire.[22]

Boulton entered into partnership with John Fothergill in 1762. Born in Russia and apprenticed in Königsberg, Fothergill epitomized the cosmopolitanism of many Birmingham businessmen and did much to foster Boulton's international trade. Fothergill was a more conventional and cautious person than Boulton and became alarmed at the fact that their enterprises were so often constructed on rickety foundations of improvised short-term credit. The differences between the two men were illustrated by the fact that, when Fothergill inhabited Soho House, he failed to maintain the grounds because 'his love of money was greater than for a garden' and that consequently 'the land is much impoverished having not received the assistance of one L[oa]d of muck'.[23] Fothergill died in 1782.

Boulton's second and most important business partner was James Watt. Like Fothergill, and indeed like most people, Watt was more cautious than Boulton. He had been born in Greenock, Scotland in 1736. His father was a shipwright whose financial reverses meant that the young Watt lived for a time in poverty. He had moved to Glasgow and worked as a scientific instrument maker. He managed to acquire practical skills from an attachment to a London craftsman – though he was never formally an apprentice and therefore never considered to be fully qualified – and he also acquired a good deal of scientific learning while making instruments at Glasgow University. In 1759 he began to work on steam engines and eventually produced an improvement to the Newcomen engine that was then in widespread use. Initially, he developed this device in partnership with Dr John Roebuck, a physician turned industrialist, but Boulton, who met Watt when he came to visit the Soho manufactory in 1768, expressed the desire to exploit the machine that Watt had patented. Roebuck was willing to sell his interest in the new steam engine but only for the counties immediately around Birmingham. Boulton replied: 'It would not be worth my while to make for three counties only; but I find it very well worth my while to make for all the world.'

The matter was resolved when Roebuck went bankrupt and Boulton, who was one of his creditors, acquired his share. Boulton and Watt formed a new partnership in 1775 and Boulton arranged for a parliamentary bill to extend Watt's patent so that the two of them would enjoy exclusive right to build the machines until 1800. He could now sell, as he put it to James Boswell, 'what all the world desires: power'. He did, indeed, sell it to the world. Cornish mines were one of his clients and he devised a special tariff so that mines which used the new machine were charged a rate that amounted to a third of the coal they saved. Eventually, and partly because Boulton knew that London would provide a shop window for his sales, he established steam-driven mills for brewers in the capital. Charging clients, some of whom had previously driven their machines with horses, required a new unit of measurement and the invention of 'horsepower' to describe the capacity of engines. Boulton and Watt also sold their machines abroad. Their first target was France, which they visited in 1786, seeking to acquire contracts for pumping water at a variety of locations including the palace of Versailles. In 1792 Lord Macartney, undertaking a diplomatic mission to China, promised that he would also try to sell steam engines.

Alongside engines, Boulton and Watt provided the mechanics to erect and sometimes maintain them. It was an awkward business because the export of both technology and expertise was supposedly forbidden.[24] Watt noted that one engine had been stopped by customs in 1781 until 'by a proper dose of the golden powder the eye-sight had been cleared'. Boulton and Watt soon realized that it was a dangerous game to send their most skilled men abroad because of the frequency with which they found more lucrative or attractive positions. One employee disappeared in 1793 having been sent to Holland. Watt thought that he might have made his way to Spain: 'What confirms this opinion is his having always expressed a desire to be employed from home, probably that he might be a proper distance from his wife whose excess of affection for him sometimes carried her to violent lengths.'[25]

At first, Boulton and Watt built engine parts at the existing Soho works but in 1796 they opened a new Soho foundry (about a mile from the original Soho works, which continued to operate) that built entire machines. This spectacular undertaking was inaugurated with a feast – an occasion made even more expensive by the fact that many of the guests (presumably men who understood the value of metal) stole the cutlery. Construction of the foundry pushed Boulton and Watt into difficulties again, partly resolved by a savage campaign of litigation as Boulton sued those who had infringed the patent that he and Watt owned on their steam engine.

For all his energy and ability, it was not always clear that Boulton's enterprises turned a profit, but his most spectacular project involved making money in a literal way. He was aware that many industrialists were constrained by an absence of ready cash and, having acquired a surplus of copper from the Cornish mines in which he had an interest, he sought to resolve this problem. He established a mint at Soho that struck coins for private enterprises (such as the East India Company) and foreign governments, as well as making tokens that could be used as a substitute for money by British industrialists. His production, based on steam power and mechanisms that gripped coins (which meant that they could stamp their edges), was more efficient than that of the Royal Mint in London. Eventually he acquired contracts producing British currency, as well as selling coins and minting machines around the world.[26]

Boulton was extraordinary, but a bit less extraordinary in Birmingham than he would have been elsewhere. This was because the town contained a group of men with wide interests and an uninhibited curiosity. The most famous incarnation of this spirit was the Lunar Society, which met at Soho House at full moon, so that members could find their way home. It is tempting to present these men as a coherent group marked by their mutual association but also by religious dissent (which meant exclusion from the English universities), by a culture that was urban rather than rural, by an interest in the modern world of 'natural philosophy' rather than the ancient one of classical literature, and by support for progressive, perhaps even revolutionary, politics. There were exceptions to all of these generalizations. Perhaps the most important feature of the notable men from Birmingham was not so much that they belonged to a category as that they transcended existing divisions between Anglicans and Dissenters, between scholars and practical men or between different kinds of academic discipline (even at a time when academic disciplines were less clearly marked than they were later to become).

Boulton illustrated some of this capacity to transcend categories. He was a businessman who revelled in the making of money, but his apparently mercenary motives did not mean that he was exclusively interested in profit. He often embarked on enterprises that risked bringing great losses and his business interests were so complicated (he came to be engaged in thirteen different partnerships) that he may not even have known whether he was making money or losing it. His interest in industrial processes was more than a matter of simple investment. He was a self-taught engineer – prone to be suspicious of both book learning and purely manual skill but capable of learning from people who had both. James Keir, who had managed part of the Soho works at one time and, like many of Boulton's associates, had become nervous about his uncertain finances, wrote after his death: 'Mr B is proof of how much scientific knowledge may be acquired without much regular study, by means of a quick and just apprehension, much practical application and nice mechanical feelings.'[27]

Joseph Priestley was an even more complicated figure. He was interested in science and is now mainly remembered for the chemical experiments by which he sought to isolate the component elements of air. He was also a theologian and classical scholar – capable of alluding to his work in several different domains in the course of a single breathless passage:

> I have made many observations on human nature with a view to the illustration of Hartley's theory ... I am satisfied that my argument for Peter not being one of the two disciples going to Emmaus was not well founded. I think to print the Greek Harmony this winter ... The sparry adi is an acid contained in what the chymists call flour. In Derbyshire it is called spar, and they make vases and ornaments for chimney pieces out of it. The acid air is procured by pouring upon hot oil of vitriol.[28]

Priestley had been born into a Calvinist family and educated largely for the ministry. Because of his fragile health it looked as if he might not be able to withstand the rigours of theological study and he had for this reason devoted part of his education to preparation for a commercial career. This meant that he understood French, Italian and Dutch as well as the ancient languages. It also meant that his apparent unworldliness sometimes coexisted with flickers of interest in practical matters. Even after his ordination, he considered putting his scientific knowledge to commercial use and suggested that his brother (also a minister of religion) might provide the manual dexterity that he himself lacked.

In his youth, Priestley was haunted by the fact that his failure to experience a moment of spiritual rebirth made him think that he might be damned, while his poor health made it seem likely that he would soon find out whether or not this was the case. Eventually, his own beliefs became less austere and this was to have an effect on both him and eventually Birmingham. He also began to move towards Unitarianism – the belief that God was a single entity rather than a Trinity and that Jesus had simply been a good man rather than an incarnation of divinity. Once he entered the ministry, he moved several times because congregations were either unsympathetic to his views or unable to provide for him financially. For a while, he worked as a librarian and travelling companion for the Earl of Shelburne. He visited France with Shelburne, met a number of French scientists and enjoyed a frisson of disapproval because he concluded that, beneath their Catholic orthodoxy, many Frenchmen did not believe in God.

In 1780, Priestley was summoned to become minister at the New Meeting House in Birmingham. It was attractive to him because much of the town's dissenting population had moved away from the dour and venerable certainties of Calvinism – the Calvinists had broken away from other Dissenters to set up their own meeting house in Carrs Lane in 1747. In theory, Priestley's Unitarianism was illegal until 1813 – another Unitarian remarked that men of his belief were 'theological negroes'[29] – but Priestley's beliefs, or perhaps his tolerant attitude to other people's beliefs, were attractive to many Birmingham Dissenters. Catherine Hutton, the daughter of William, wrote on Christmas Day 1780:

> The celebrated Dr Priestley has taken up his residence among us for the sake of facilitating his philosophical experiments, and Mr Hawkes, one of the preachers at the New Meeting, having resigned his place, it has been offered to the Doctor and it is generally believed he will accept it. If he does so you may expect to hear of my becoming a convert to his religion, for I am very weary of Calvinistic monotony and nonsense.[30]

Religion mattered to Priestley, and to part of the audience for enlightened ideas in Birmingham, but not all of his associates were religious. Indeed, the most striking thing about the Lunar Society was not so much that it brought together men of different religious beliefs as that it brought together men such as Priestley, who was deeply if unconventionally pious, with men who had no religious beliefs at all. Erasmus Darwin, a doctor at Lichfield who attended the Lunar Society, made little attempt to hide his atheism – a fact which would seem so shocking to Victorian convention that his grandson, Charles Darwin, omitted some of his remarks when he edited his writings.

What united men such as Darwin and Priestley was a wider belief in rationality. This involved the excitement of natural science and a willingness to experiment in all aspects of their lives. Sometimes these experiments involved objects: they were early enthusiasts for ballooning. Sometimes they involved people: Jean-Jacques Rousseau had met some of the Lunar Society when he was in England in 1766 and the younger members of the group were entranced by his ideas of naturalness, particularly with regard to the education of children.

Thomas Day, born in 1748, took Rousseauian experiment to extreme lengths. He acquired two orphan girls (one aged eleven from an orphanage in Shrewsbury, whom Day named Sabrina Sidney, and one aged twelve from the London Foundling Hospital founded by Thomas Coram, whom Day named Lucretia). He planned to raise them according to Rousseau's principles and then marry whichever one of them turned out better – promising to make sure that the other was placed in an appropriate position. He took them to Avignon and began their education, which meant, first, teaching them to read. From Day's point of view, the experiment was a disaster. Attempts to train Sabrina to withstand pain and fear – by dropping sealing wax on her neck and firing a pistol into her petticoats – seem to have been the last straw. The older members of Day's circle – men more influenced by Voltaire than Rousseau – probably derived amusement from the episode and may have noticed the pleasant irony that the girls themselves came out of it well. Lucretia was apprenticed to a milliner and, with a dowry from Day, married a linen-draper. Sabrina was sent to boarding school and, having turned out beautiful and charming in spite of the pistols and sealing wax, married a barrister, again with a dowry, and after she was widowed became a housekeeper and lived to a ripe old age.

The members of the Lunar Society were interested in France. They visited the country and corresponded with its scholars. Boulton referred to Soho House as his 'Maison d'amitié sur Handsworth Heath'. Their admiration was qualified, though. Priestley and Day did not much enjoy their time in France. Boulton described the country as a world of papier mâché, a revealing analogy from one whose production so often involved ornamentation. Interest in things French accompanied certain attitudes to politics. Some Birmingham men followed the French Revolution with sympathy. The sons of Matthew Boulton (Matthew Robinson Boulton) and of James Watt (James Watt junior) were both educated partly on the continent and both witnessed the beginnings of the revolution. Watt's son became involved in Jacobinism in the early 1790s in ways that caused his ever-cautious father great anxiety. Edmund Burke, who a few years previously had described the Soho works as a 'palace of enchantments', now alluded to the links between Birmingham scientific enlightenment and the French Revolution in mocking terms: 'The wild gas, the fixed air is plainly broke loose; but we ought to suspend our judgement until the effervescence is a little subsided, till the liquor is cleared, and until we see something deeper than the agitation of a troubled and frothy surface.'

Matthew Robinson Boulton returned from France and gave a memorable account of what he had seen. But even the most radical figures in Birmingham were not really political revolutionaries. Their admiration for France was expressed during the early stages of the revolution before the execution of the king and the Terror. They were emphatic that this was not a model that they wanted Britain to follow and, on the contrary, insisted on their loyalty to the king. They had mostly interpreted events in France as illustrating what happened in regimes, unlike Britain, where monarchs and aristocracies were not wise enough to compromise with reform in due time. During the French Revolution, Birmingham Dissenters were looking back with satisfaction to the Glorious Revolution of 1688, the anniversary of which they had just celebrated. In Britain, they looked forward to modest reform and particularly to the repeal of the Test and Corporations Act which imposed civil disabilities on Dissenters.

In any case, Birmingham's most prominent men had complicated and sometimes contradictory political attitudes. Watt was repelled by the prospect of radical change. Boulton was guided by a hard-headed sense of his own interests. His odd mix of radicalism and conservatism was illustrated when he began to mint coins. The mere fact that a private individual might create money was revolutionary and some of the coins that he struck for industrialists portrayed their own heads rather than that of the monarch. All the same, when he ran off a collection of sample coins, he stamped on their sides the slogan 'Give unto Caesar the things that are Caesar's'.

Of all the Birmingham men, only Priestley left Britain after the French Revolution and this was not really a matter that he decided for himself. His son was granted French citizenship in 1792 and Joseph Priestley senior could have had a political career in France but he declined the chance. James Watt junior did become involved in the revolution for a time but his father went to great lengths to get him safely back in 1793.

Nothing illustrated the contradictions of Birmingham attitudes better than slavery. There was a very small population of black people in the West Midlands – one study suggests just 246 in the whole period before 1918. At first these were mainly men who had been acquired as slaves in America and brought back to work as servants in country houses. It is not clear how free or otherwise these people were once they got to Britain – the last slave sale in the area took place at the Baker's Arms in Lichfield in 1771. By the beginning of the nineteenth century, black people in the area were more likely to have been born free. Jane Harry, the daughter of a Jamaican Grand Court judge and a black woman, worked as a governess for the fifteen children of Sampson Lloyd in Sparkbrook between 1779 and 1782, at which point she married a white surgeon. The Lloyd family were Quakers and influential proponents of the abolition of slavery, though they seem to have used a black slave in their Digbeth mill in 1749.[31]

Priestley preached against slavery in strong terms.[32] Thomas Day co-wrote a poem, 'The Dying Negro', against slavery. When the former slave Olaudah Equiano published his autobiography, sixty-three of the subscribers who subsidized the publication came from Birmingham (of whom seven were members of Priestley's congregation).[33] Birmingham, unlike Liverpool and Bristol, was not directly involved in the slave trade and it is possible that Matthew Boulton's ever fertile mind might have considered the possibility that the end of slavery would create a bigger market for the kind of machines that he built – though in the short term he was happy to talk to slave owners about how machines might replace *horses* on their West Indian plantations.

Nothing was clear-cut. Priestley's condemnation of slavery was eloquent but brief. The topic did not absorb much of his energy and he maintained cordial relations with powerful Dissenters who defended slavery and profited from it. This was an era in which hard-headed commercial attitudes to slavery were so common that the owners of the slave ship *Zong* claimed insurance money after a shortage of drinking water had caused the ship's crew to throw 131 valuable slaves overboard in mid-Atlantic. Edward Thomason was apprenticed to Matthew Boulton at the age of sixteen in 1795, before establishing himself as a maker of medals in his own right. Though he was a staunch Tory and Anglican, he was 'in common, I believe with most of my townsmen, a strong advocate and great admirer of the principles which actuated Mr Wilberforce's philanthropy' (i.e. opposition to slavery). But this did not prevent Thomason from maintaining cordial and, one assumes, profitable relations with the governor of Tobago – a fierce opponent of 'canting abolitionists'.[34]

Birmingham also had important indirect links with the slave trade. It manufactured guns, and Africa was an excellent market for these, particularly for cheap, poor-quality weapons. Lord Shelburne claimed in 1765 that Birmingham produced 150,000 guns per year and half of them 'from the manner in which they are finished are sure to burst in the first hand that fires them'. He was exaggerating – not least because the poor-quality guns were accompanied by poor-quality gunpowder which rarely produced large explosions.[35] These guns were given to West African chieftains in exchange for slaves. A history of the Birmingham gun trade published after the Second World War breezily recalled the days 'when a Birmingham-made Musket costing 7s 6d together with a couple of horse pistols and bottle of gin, could be exchanged for a West African slave'.[36] The biggest of the Birmingham gun makers was Samuel Galton, who was said to have amassed a fortune of £43,049 by 1785. He was a Quaker, one of those who met the former slave Equiano on his visit to Birmingham in 1790. In the same year, the Society of Friends required that 'none among us make means of war'.[37] Samuel Galton retired and passed his business to his son in 1796. The following year, the Birmingham meeting of the Society of Friends refused to accept Galton junior's participation but when he in turn handed his business to his son in 1804, he was taken back and eventually buried in the precincts of the Quaker meeting house.[38] When the British slave trade was abolished in 1807, the Board of Ordnance allowed the Galton firm to raise its prices on the grounds that it no longer had a means of disposing of inferior guns.

THE RIOTS OF 1791 AND THE END OF
THE BIRMINGHAM ENLIGHTENMENT

The Birmingham notables felt comfortable in the 1780s. They were prosperous, approved of the political regime in their country, and hoped for modest reform within that system. Their own town was, they believed, a model of political and religious harmony, which had left the tumults of the previous century behind it. Shrewd observers might have noticed some ominous signs. First, though the leaders of the Birmingham Enlightenment were radical in many things, they were conservative when it came to property, especially their own property. William Hutton was public spirited enough to volunteer his time in adjudicating the disputes that came before the Court of Requests, but resisted an extension of rates to the many small properties he owned. His objections to the extension revolved around the claim that landlords such as himself provided a service to the community by housing workers who contributed to industrial growth.[39] Similarly, Matthew Boulton boasted of the benefits provided by his construction of the Soho works:

> I founded my manufactory upon one of the most barren commons in England, where there existed but a few miserable huts filled with idle beggarly people, who by the help of the common land and a little thieving made shift to live without working.[40]

No one reading these lines would have guessed the 'idle beggarly people' might have considered that their own property had been annexed.

Second, the attitudes of some prominent Birmingham figures to religion aroused resentment. The problem was not that the leaders of Birmingham religious Dissent were intolerant and sectarian – rather the reverse. Priestley insisted on the importance of toleration for all religious beliefs – indeed he wanted a form of toleration that would extend beyond all Christian denominations to take in Muslims and Jews. He prided himself on his willingness to work with Anglicans, particularly in the denunciation of the slave trade. There was, though, a suffocating condescension in the toleration of such men. This was particularly evident in their attitude to Catholics. They wanted the legal disabilities under which Catholics, as well as Nonconformists, laboured to be abolished but they were prone to assume that Catholicism, with its

38

subordination to the 'Bishop of Rome', was so obviously absurd that no intelligent person could sincerely subscribe to its tenets. It was typical of Priestley that he expected a cordial debate with the French Jesuit and natural philosopher Boscovich – even though he had, in the publication in which he discussed Boscovich's work, described the pope as the anti-Christ and though, in subsequent correspondence with Boscovich, he wrote: 'the Church of Rome of which you are a member . . . I consider as properly antichristian, and a system of abomination little better than Heathenism'. [41] It is hardly surprising that a Birmingham Catholic responded coldly when Priestley invited him to a political dinner: 'We Catholics stand better with the Government than you Dissenters and we will not make common cause with you.'

The combination of complacency about the virtues of religious toleration with dismissal of Catholic beliefs was not unique to Priestley. It could be found too in the writings of William Hutton. He condemned both 'the tedious reign of the Romish priest [who] substituted mystery for science' and the 'absurdity of reducing a nation to one faith, vainly attempted by Henry VIII'. But his attitude to Catholicism was governed by the certainty that it was an irrational religion and for this reason condemned to decline. Priestley, though, had a special gift for exasperating his opponents. This sprang partly from his own certainty that he was right and capable of persuading others. Catherine Hutton recognized the danger that he posed:

> A circumstance which particularly rendered Birmingham a likely theatre for mischief was the zeal of Dr Priestley, fervent though not intemperate. Having fully assured himself of the truth in religion, he conceived it his duty to go abroad into the world and endeavour to persuade all mortals to embrace it, an idea which has done more mischief than any which ever entered the erring mind of man. He sometimes, too, in his sermons, glanced at politics—a subject that should never be mingled with religion; and this treasured up wrath. [42]

Even Priestley's courtesy could be exasperating. He purported to take the arguments of his opponents seriously to expose them, and the scalpel of his irony could be more wounding than the cudgel of a cruder polemicist would have been. Men with a conventional university education felt humiliated to be outmanoeuvred by the product of a provincial Dissenting academy. If Priestley had been in London, or if he had been crossing swords with antagonists in a different place, as he had crossed swords in religious terms with Boscovich a decade earlier, then his barbs might not have done much harm. But he was now often up against clerics from Birmingham itself. The number of religious texts published in the city increased markedly during the 1780s – and Priestley alluded, with the disarming expression of regret that often preceded his attacks, to the risk of 'public controversy with a person residing in the same place with one's self'. In truth, Priestley enjoyed controversy and assumed that his opponents entered into it with the same relish – he collected hostile prints of himself. Indeed, he considered that taking him on was a recognized route to preferment in the established Church and continued hostility to him sprang from the fact that 'He had already made two Bishops and there were several heads which wanted mitres.'

For some in Birmingham, the Enlightenment ended in July 1791. A Constitutional Society in the town announced that a dinner would be held on 14 July (the second anniversary of the storming of the Bastille) at the Royal Hotel for 'any friend of liberty'. Around eighty men turned up to the dinner. Priestley was not there, because his friends had persuaded him that his presence would be unwise, nor was Hutton, because he did not like such dinners. James Keir chaired the meeting at which there were repeated toasts to 'King and Constitution', the 'Rights of Man', the 'National Assembly of the Patriots of France'. There was reference to revolution in Poland and to the English traditions that could be traced back to Hampden in the seventeenth century. Keir insisted later that he had not conceived that the meeting 'could be misinterpreted as being offensive to a government, whose greatest boast is liberty'.[43]

Hostile crowds gathered and attacked the hotel – though the guests had gone by this time. The mob went to the New and Old Meeting Houses and set fire to both buildings. After this they attacked Priestley's house, then that of the merchant John Ryland, and the house and bookshop of William Hutton. Hutton's tenure on the bench of the Court of Requests had made him many enemies. It is easy to imagine that a man from such humble origins had enjoyed the exercise of power in the court and he had often finished cases with the words 'thee will pay sixpence'. Now the crowd shouted the same words. Some property owners were able to bribe the rioters with drink and/or scare them with hired men.

Boulton and Watt protected the Soho works with cannon. Boulton said that he would let the attackers destroy his house – perhaps he would, since he had dreams of rebuilding it on a grander scale – but would fire on them if they attacked his factory. Eventually, troops arrived and the disturbances were suppressed.

Many were suspicious about the origins of the riots. Magistrates had not looked unduly eager to put down the disorder and some of them had in fact been present when it started. Anglican clergymen were said to have incited trouble. There were trials at Warwick and Stafford but many rioters were acquitted, even when the evidence against them seemed strong. Perhaps some in authority had not been sorry to see the Dissenters attacked, and it is certainly true that the juries at Stafford and Warwick were reluctant to convict. But this does not mean that there had been a conspiracy to incite the riots. William Grenville, the Foreign Secretary, said: 'I do not admire riots in favour of the government much more than riots against it.'[44] Juries were often reluctant to convict in cases such as this – partly because the penalties for those found guilty were likely to be so harsh. Three men were hanged. At least one was killed by those defending William Withering's property at Edgbaston Hall. Eight men died while drinking in the cellar at Priestley's house when fire caused the roof to fall in.

The riots came as a surprise to their victims: 'Party spirit has been gradually declining for an age, and seemed totally annihilated in Birmingham, where trade had mingled all its votaries in one mass.'[45] Priestley refused to believe that the attack was happening and it was difficult to persuade him to move away to safety. On 19 July, he wrote to the people of Birmingham:

> In this business we are the sheep and you are the wolves. We will preserve our character and hope that you will change yours. At all events we return you blessings for curses, and hope that you shall soon return to that industry and those sober manners for which the inhabitants were formerly distinguished.

However, afterwards some came to interpret the event as not simply a political one that might have been manipulated from above but as a general disorder that was both a consequence and a cause of the coarsening of society. Catherine Hutton recalled that her family's coachman insulted his employers as he drove them away from their burning house: 'the riots had loosened every tie of subordination and the greatest blackguard was the master'.[46] William Hutton said that the riots had more to do with 'thirty-nine bottles than thirty-nine articles'. Boulton associated them with a return of habits such as bear-baiting to the streets of Birmingham. Even the defences that the rioters offered seemed to mock the values of reason and morality that mattered so much to men like Hutton and Priestley. William Rice produced as an alibi a man who swore that he and Rice had visited a prostitute on the night in question and 'been occupied all evening'. Bartholomew Fisher's father appealed for clemency on the grounds that his son had been drunk.[47]

Catherine Hutton continued to live in Birmingham until her death in 1846 but wrote: 'I have for ever quitted Birmingham as a home.'[48] Her letters were edited by her cousin Catherine Hutton Beale, who recalled the riots of 1791 with bitterness and associated their memory with a longer view of radical Dissent that went back to the seventeenth century. But, after 1791, Catherine Hutton herself often expressed a hard-headed conservatism. She described a Society for the Abolition of War as 'chimerical':[49] 'Men and horses, dogs and cocks, doves and red-breasts, have always shewn a disposition to fight each other.' When asked about equality of property, she replied: 'I laugh at the idea.'[50] Such remarks might suggest that she was simply explicit about a conservatism that had been implicit in the writing of her father, but she was also exasperated by the naivety of both her father and Priestley before the riots, and her defence of aristocracy – 'a proper barrier between the power of the sovereign and the upstart wealth of his plebeian subjects'[51] – sounds remarkably like an attack on the milieu of her father.

The material damage of the riots was limited. William Hutton some-times reproached himself for an irrational wish to buy land ('this desire after dirt'), but land did not burn as easily as paper and so he managed to keep a part of his fortune. In addition to this he, like all the victims, was paid compensation. Many lost no property at all. Boulton and Watt's greatest enterprise – the construction of the Soho foundry to build steam engines – was undertaken after the riots. But the mood changed. The first Soho works had been an elegant building open to the public; the foundry was more utilitarian and closed. Boulton and Watt handed over the management of the business to their sons and though – or perhaps because – these men had flown so close to the flame of revolution in France they were careful and well organized in their business dealings. The Lunar Society ceased to meet. Boulton died in 1809. His son lived on to 1842 but withdrew from the business. The Galton family remained important gunmakers, though the grandson of the company's founder – Samuel Galton the third – gave up all pretence of being a Quaker. His son gained a sinister fame as the father of eugenics, and Erasmus Darwin's grandson became even more famous as the author of *On the Origin of Species*.

At the time, the Priestley riots seemed to mark an end to a period of turbulence, but they were not followed by stability. On the contrary, nineteenth-century Birmingham would become a place of political upheaval. Unitarianism and even to some extent republicanism would prove to be highly influential.

The Curzon Street station. The railway came to Birmingham in 1838 – the same year that the town was incorporated. The Curzon Street station, first called just 'Birmingham', was a little way east of the centre of town and was soon replaced by Grand Central (which was itself quickly renamed New Street station). However, the elegant classical façade of Curzon Street station survived and, in recent years, has been exposed once again by the demolition of buildings around it to make way for the HS2 rail line.

3

Revolutionary Birmingham?

Eric Hobsbawm described the late eighteenth and early nineteenth centuries as being marked by a 'dual revolution'. By this he meant the political revolution in France and the industrial revolution in Britain. At first glance, Birmingham fits neatly into this analysis. It was a centre of industry but one without much political significance – until 1832, it was not represented in Parliament. A second glance suggests a more complicated picture. It was true enough that Birmingham was a centre of industry but it was not a centre of industrial revolution, or even of that more limited economic mutation that recent historians, wary of the term 'revolution', might discern in some northern cities. The population and economy of Birmingham grew in the eighteenth century; in 1750, it was the third largest town in England. All of this stalled in 1793 after the outbreak of war with France, and there may even have been a period in which the population of Birmingham fell. Thereafter it grew again, but until the second half of the nineteenth century, it did so less fast than other industrial towns, particularly Manchester.

As for politics, Birmingham was marked, at least for a time, not so much by quiescence as by confusion and turbulence. In the first couple of years after 1789, prominent figures in Birmingham had regarded the French Revolution with optimism. The Church and King riots of 1791 in Birmingham, and the beginning of war with France in 1793 changed all this and in Birmingham, as elsewhere, those who admired the French Jacobins were well advised to keep quiet for the next few years. After the end of the revolutionary wars in 1815, however, a new kind of radicalism came from Birmingham, which was seen in its most spectacular form in the Birmingham Political Union founded in 1829. This radicalism was marked by calls for parliamentary reform and, along with this, for parliamentary representation of Birmingham. Birmingham's new radicalism left strange legacies. The town was 'incorporated' in 1838 – that is to say, for the first time it had a mayor and council – but incorporation sometimes appeared to entrench the privileges of the propertied classes and the Bull Ring riots of 1839 saw violent conflict between those classes and the plebeian groups who had been their allies in earlier movements for reform.

BIRMINGHAM AND THE REVOLUTIONARY WARS

Between 1793 and 1815, Britain was almost continuously at war with France. The immediate effect of this was to disrupt trade and damage the economy of Birmingham. There were, however, ways in which parts of the town's industry gained from the wars in the longer term. Though Birmingham was important for the gun trade and for ironware of a more general kind that might be used for military purposes, none of this meant that the revolutionary wars were a time of contentment for Birmingham industry. On the contrary, Birmingham was mainly known, particularly in the later part of the period, for bitter complaint. In the 1809 edition of his *History of Birmingham*, William Hutton wrote: 'the ruinous war with France has been the destruction of our commerce, caused 500 of our tradesmen to fail, stagnated currency and thinned the inhabitants'. This was particularly so when orders in council from 1807 to 1811 sought to shut off France's external trade and thus restricted the outlets for British industrialists. The coming of peace in 1815 produced another burst of complaint as wartime orders dropped off.

It is possible that the Birmingham economy lost from both the beginning and end of war (perhaps because its economy had been restricted to military demands) and possible that different people gained and lost from war and peace – though it also seems likely that businessmen would have complained whatever happened. Catherine Hutton – bitter at her native city after the riots of 1791 and more sceptical than her father, the historian – wrote:

> I like Mr Galton and Mr Attwood as much as you do; but I like the town
> of Birmingham rather less. Its inhabitants may petition the Government
> against Orders in Council, because the war silenced their hammer and

stopped their lathes; but I never heard any objection they had to the property tax or the American War. War has been their principal amusement for
twenty years. No pleasure was ever equal to beating Bonaparte.[1]

It may indeed be that the culture of complaint was itself the most
important legacy of the wars for Birmingham. Since war was an activity
that was so obviously associated with the decisions of government,
a protracted conflict fostered the sentiment that the government must
be responsible for the economic problems of the town. Complaint came
from its business elite but it also had a wider resonance, which is partly
why the business elite became confident that they spoke for the 'indus-
trious' classes. In the eighteenth century there had been riots in
Birmingham but, though these had usually involved attacks on wealthy
people, they had been accompanied by a conservative rhetoric of patriotism, monarchism and loyalty to the established Church. During the
wars with France, things changed. James Bisset (1762–1832) was an
industrialist, poet and collector. He had been deputy chairman of the
dinner to mark the anniversary of the fall of the Bastille in 1791, the
dinner that provoked the violent Church and King riots. His politics
were hard to decode. He himself expressed patriotic opinions during the
Napoleonic Wars and, indeed, made money partly by issuing medallions
celebrating martial valour. He was proud of the fact that Nelson had
visited his private museum. All the same, he drew attention to the damage to trade caused by war. He also noticed something new. The slogans
chalked and painted on walls were less likely to be patriotic and loyalist
and more likely to condemn the government.[2]

The writers of graffiti may have reflected a more general turn against
war and perhaps eventually against established authority. James Luckcock (1761–1835) was a successful jeweller, on the way to becoming 'a
man of notoriety and public business'. In 1811, he published a pseud-
onymous pamphlet, 'An Appeal to the British Nation, on the Folly and
Criminality of War'.[3] Luckcock, however, combined anti-war sentiment
with a social and moral elitism. He wrote that there 'must be inequali-
ties of condition ... the only thing at which we should aim is to be
satisfied with our lot, and to be true to the station and duties assigned
to us'. He believed that the Priestley riots of 1791 had been caused by
the failure of the superior classes to provide the poor with proper
leadership.[4]

Luckcock and Bisset were both self-made men of reasonable, but not exceptional, prosperity who combined their business with a wider set of cultural interests (among other things Luckcock accumulated a collection of buttons). They were both Dissenters and both identified themselves as progressives in politics, though Luckcock's expression of his opinions, at least under the cover of anonymity, was less inhibited than Bisset's.

The most prominent exponent of Birmingham opinion, however, came from a different milieu. Thomas Attwood (1783–1856) was the son of a wealthy ironmonger who had moved into banking in partnership with Isaac Spooner (1735–1816). Attwood acquired an additional fortune from an advantageous marriage. He began his political life as a Tory and became high bailiff of Birmingham, a post by custom reserved for Tories and Anglicans, at the age of twenty-eight in 1811. Attwood's first political initiative involved protest against the orders in council that had limited international trade. He was joined in this activity by Richard Spooner (1783–1864), who was the son of Isaac and who had himself succeeded Attwood as high bailiff of Birmingham.

Attwood came to believe that the economic problems of Birmingham – indeed economic problems in general – were rooted in one thing: currency. This was a belief that owed something to the time. The government had suspended cash payment (that is to say it had issued paper notes that could not be exchanged for gold) in 1797, and had in effect printed money to pay for the war. Now it sought to restore the value of the currency and to underwrite its value once again with gold. The consequence was a sharp contraction in the money supply. An interest in currency was also linked to place. Birmingham had a mint and was the centre of the jewellery trade, in which gold was continuously being melted down and recycled. It was also a place where industrialists had often lived on credit, sometimes rather precariously, and were thus vulnerable to a reduction in the money supply.

Shortage of ready cash was a persistent complaint in Birmingham. What appears to have been the earliest petition to Parliament from 'the inhabitants and tradesmen of Birmingham' had concerned the 'scarcity of milled money'.[5] There was an interesting distinction between the ways in which an earlier generation had treated monetary questions and the way that Attwood did so. Matthew Boulton had minted coins for the Treasury but also produced tokens with which manufacturers could conduct transactions. He had effectively circumvented the government and created his own money. Attwood, by contrast, placed his hopes in the government and believed that only a change in policy could rescue the economy. He advocated paper money to counter depression. He expressed himself in lurid terms, comparing the economist David Ricardo and the politician William Huskisson, both defenders of gold, to 'Sin and Death guarding the gates of Hell'.[6]

Attwood's early political intervention did not cause him to question his Toryism. In 1825, at a time when he believed that the government might be sympathetic to his ideas, he wrote to his wife: 'I will have no contact with the Radicals, unless things take a strange turn.'[7] But as time went on, his interest in radical economics began to tie in with an increasingly radical political vision. Others too thought that Birmingham's economic interests would be better looked after if the town was granted a more explicit political representation. One driving force for political reform in Birmingham was George Edmonds (1788–1868). Edmonds, the son of a Baptist minister, earned his living at various times as a button burnisher, schoolteacher and eventually lawyer's clerk. He sometimes represented people, usually the poor, in court, though he was not formally accepted as an attorney until he was fifty-nine years old. He never became rich, but he was a person of great energy, who is remembered, among other things, for his efforts to create a universal language. His curiosity and moral courage would have seemed familiar to Joseph Priestley or Erasmus Darwin. Like Priestley, he also had a sharp tongue and gift for mockery that often enraged his opponents: he once advised British aristocrats to take lessons as dancing masters so that they could sustain themselves in political exile.[8] He had supported the campaign against the Orders in Council. In 1816 he formed Birmingham Hampden Club – harking back to the seventeenth-century radical parliamentarian. When the high bailiff of Birmingham refused his request to hold an open-air meeting on 22 January 1817, he went ahead regardless and organized what turned out to be the first of many large-scale meetings on Newhall Hill.

On 12 July 1819, Edmonds – with Major John Cartwright and Thomas Wooler, the publisher of the radical journal *Black Dwarf* – organized another meeting on Newhall Hill. Like many political meetings in Birmingham in this period, it took place on a Monday. The town's workers often observed 'Saint Monday' – that is to say, they took

Monday off and sometimes used the occasion to drink. Some may also have noticed that this date was close to the anniversary of the fall of the Bastille. A magistrate wrote to the Home Secretary to warn him of the impending meeting:

> Your lordship will not fail to observe the day and the hour fixed for this meeting, both of which are well calculated for the collection of a crowd of persons, many of whom will be fast approaching to a state of intoxication, and therefore more easily inflamed to acts of violence, by the speeches which will no doubt be addressed to them.[9]

It is an illustration of the complexity of Birmingham politics that the magistrate in question was Isaac Spooner junior – the brother of Richard Spooner, who was allied with Thomas Attwood, who, in turn, would later become allied with Edmonds. The meeting was not, as it happened, as disorderly as the magistrate had anticipated it would be. Isaac Spooner, who had observed events from a rooftop, estimated that 10,000 people, of whom many were women and children, had been present and conceded that it was 'attended by no breach of the peace'.[10]

The meeting approved a proposal that Sir Charles Wolseley (1769–1846) – a Staffordshire baronet who had associated himself with the cause of reform and even hinted that he might as a young man have assisted in the storming of the Bastille – should be made 'legislative attorney' for Birmingham. This meant that the people of Birmingham would circumvent normal electoral law and take the initiative in sending a representative to Parliament. The organizers of this initiative were prosecuted for conspiracy at the Warwick Assizes. Edmonds was sentenced to nine months' imprisonment. It was characteristic of him that even while on bail for this offence, he addressed another meeting at Newhall Hill to protest against the killing of radical protesters at Peterloo near Manchester. He told his audience: 'Murder has been committed under peculiar and aggravating circumstances – under the authority of the Guardians of the Law.'[11]

A more prudent attempt to secure parliamentary representation for Birmingham was made in 1827 when Sir Charles Tennyson (1784–1861) sponsored a proposal to transfer parliamentary representation from the borough of East Retford, a notorious centre of corruption, to Birmingham. This move failed. Attwood and Joshua Scholefield (1775–1844), an iron manufacturer and banker who had been high bailiff in

1819, now proposed a political union for the protection of public rights, and on 25 January 1830 they held a meeting attended by around 30,000 people, which inaugurated the Birmingham Political Union (BPU). The BPU played a role in the wider campaign for parliamentary reform. At first, its membership was relatively small – probably just 6,000 in August 1830 – but the advent later that year of the government of the Whig Lord Grey, which was committed to parliamentary reform, gave it new life.

Attwood addressed large audiences at meetings across the country. His programme at this stage was relatively moderate. He did not yet support universal male suffrage or annual parliaments. On the other hand, he did flirt with a violent rhetoric that evoked the possibility of bloodshed. For all their sometimes apocalyptic tone, the Birmingham supporters of reform chose their words carefully. Possessing arms was not an offence and might imply that they were seeking merely to defend themselves, or a reforming government, rather than rebel. Edmonds distinguished between the subversive act of arming in secret and the legitimate one of arming in public. The lawyer Joseph Parkes (of whom more below) scrutinized the public statements of his allies to make sure they observed the letter of the law – in 1831, he said that he had allowed Edmonds and Attwood to adopt a 'tone just up to the mark and not beyond'.[12]

In 1832, the Duke of Wellington attempted to form a government after Tories in the House of Lords had blocked a Reform Bill that had been passed by the Commons, but he failed, in the face of popular agitation and a run on the Bank of England. Lord Grey returned to office and eventually the Reform Bill was passed. The act extended the franchise to a larger group of male property owners. The electorate of England and Wales increased from about 350,000 to 650,000 – that of Scotland grew more and that of Ireland less. The bill also redistributed parliamentary constituencies – suppressing some that had few inhabitants and granting representation to towns that had expanded. One beneficiary of the act was Birmingham, which, for the first time, was to be represented in Parliament.

Some attributed the Reform Bill to the Birmingham Political Union. The Irish politician Daniel O'Connell wrote: 'It was not Grey and Althorp who passed the [Reform]Act but the brave and determined men of Birmingham.' Attwood himself claimed: 'In less than three years, they [the council of the Union] had accomplished the greatest political change recorded in the history of the world.'[13] The sense that the Birmingham Political Union had defeated Wellington was particularly important. The journalist Eliezer Edwards recalled his arrival in Birmingham in 1837:

> This is the town which, five years before, had vanquished the Conqueror of the Great Napoleon! This is the place which, for the first time in his life, had compelled the great Duke of Wellington to capitulate! This is the home of those who, headed by Attwood, had compelled the Duke and his army—the House of Lords—to submit, and to pass the memorable Reform Bill of 1832![14]

The Liberal MP John Bright (of whom more below) arrived in Birmingham more than a quarter of a century after the first Reform Bill but he too looked back to 1832 as a heroic moment in the history of his adopted town:

> Am I not in the town of Birmingham, England's central capital; and do not these eyes look upon the sons of those who, not thirty years ago, shook the fabric of privilege to its base? . . . Shall their sons be less noble than they? Shall the fire which they kindled be extinguished with you? I see the answer in every face. You are resolved that the legacy which they bequeathed to you, you will hand down . . . to your children.[15]

Popular pressure – from Birmingham at least – played a smaller part in the passage of the act than many liked to imagine. Radicals had discussed some sort of armed movement – though in this case it would have been a movement in favour of the government rather than against it. The Grey government would certainly not have welcomed such support. Birmingham was a centre of arms manufacture, but it is hard to believe that a rising there would have done more than destroy local property – probably that belonging to the very men who led the Political Union. The Scots Greys were garrisoned in the town and 'rough sharpened' their swords at the height of the dispute – thereby ensuring that they would inflict the nastiest kinds of wounds on rioters. A few soldiers seem to have been supporters, perhaps even members, of the BPU. There was a single sad incident when a soldier in the Scots Greys – Alexander Somerville – wrote to a radical newspaper to say that his comrades would not act against supporters of reform. But it seems unlikely that many members of the regiment would have taken the risk of breaking with military discipline. A few of them did manage to smuggle a bottle of rum to Somerville in the hope that this would make it easier to endure the 200 lashes to which he was sentenced. A cussed man, he refused to drink it.[16]

Attwood and Joshua Scholefield were now triumphantly elected as the first Birmingham MPs. However, the results of this were not happy ones from their point of view. The problem for Attwood and Scholefield was partly that the Reform Bill did not, in itself, transform Parliament. Much still revolved around the enforcement of the Bill's terms and the elimination of corruption in elections. In addition, Attwood was an ineffective parliamentarian. The oratorical style that he had developed to address large meetings was not well received in the House of Commons. Furthermore, his obsession with currency reform evoked irritation from his allies and ridicule from his opponents.

The entry of Birmingham into parliamentary politics intertwined with the party system in complicated ways. Attwood, who had been a Tory, now defined himself as a 'Radical' – meaning that he supported dramatic reform of Church and state. Though he had worked with a Whig Prime Minister in support of parliamentary reform in 1832, he retained a suspicion of the Whigs in his later career. He explained his own isolation from both parties thus:

> The House of Commons is divided into two great parties: the Whig and the Tory. To the former I had been mainly instrumental in assisting to do a favour too great for a proud man ever to forgive; and to the latter I had been instrumental in assisting to do an injury . . . I was obnoxious to them as a tradesman – I was obnoxious to them a forward leader in political matters; and above all things I was obnoxious to both parties as having for twenty years denounced and exposed the errors and crimes they were committing.[17]

Scholefield was more favourable to the Whigs and had kept relations with the government open in 1832 – perhaps preventing physical violence by doing so. Richard Spooner, Attwood's ally, stood as a Tory candidate for Birmingham in 1835 and 1841 and served as Birmingham's first Conservative MP between 1844 and 1847. The journalist Eliezer Edwards believed that Spooner had moved to the right: 'Like many others who in their later years have become "rank Tories", he began his political life as a Liberal, contesting the town of Stafford unsuccessfully in that interest.'[18] This is unfair. Spooner had been opposed at Stafford by the successful Whig candidate. Spooner had Tory beliefs, particularly with regard to the defence of the Church of England, and there was no moment, even during his flirtation with Radicalism, when he ceased to think of himself as a Tory – though aristocratic families regarded his attempt to have himself elected to Parliament as an example of the 'last touch of his Brummidgan impudence'.[19]

Nevertheless Radicalism in Birmingham was often such an influential current that it transcended differences between Whigs and Tories. Furthermore, political divisions at national level, often revolving around the established Church, counted for less at local level, especially when, after the incorporation of Birmingham in 1838, candidates for office were merely required to swear that they would not damage the Anglican Church, rather than that they would uphold it. In municipal elections, Richard Tapper Cadbury (a member of the Quaker family that would be strongly identified with progressive causes for much of the century) stood as a Tory.

Often Radicalism in Birmingham seemed as much a matter of style as of support for specific policies. This was illustrated by the extraordinary figure of George Frederick Muntz (1794–1857). Muntz's family were of Polish extraction and driven by political persecution to France, where they became aristocratic landowners. After the French Revolution, George Muntz's father, Philip Frederick, left France and eventually settled in Birmingham where he became a business associate of Matthew Boulton. George Frederick took over the family metalworks and became wealthy partly by exploiting a form of metal compound that was of special use in the manufacture of ships' hulls. Muntz then joined Attwood in pushing for reform of the currency and political system. Muntz's politics were an odd mixture. He had been brought up an Anglican, but with characteristic perversity he joined the Baptists – moving in the opposite direction from most men who tended to go from Nonconformism to Anglicanism as they grew more prosperous. When he succeeded Attwood as a Birmingham MP in 1840, Muntz sat with the Whigs in Parliament, but as far away from the ministers as possible in 'the darkness of the backbench under the gallery'.[20] Some observers regarded him as a 'Tory Radical'. He also claimed to be a republican in spite of his 'innate aristocratic' style. Edwards considered him a 'living contradiction' and believed that he was motivated by an egotism that bordered on clinical insanity as well as by 'the hereditary aristocratic tendencies of his mind'. An ally claimed that his speeches could not be published verbatim because 'no printing office in the world would have capital I's enough'.[21]

What most marked him out was his gift for striking gestures and phrases. Apparently it was he who first coined the phrase (often attributed to the London Radical Francis Place) 'to beat the Duke go for gold' – meaning that men should provoke a run on the banks to bring down the Duke of Wellington's government. In 1847, when he had become an MP, Muntz was denounced at a meeting in Birmingham for having refused to form an electoral alliance that would benefit the Liberals. The audience were first disconcerted and then amused when Muntz himself appeared at the back of a meeting, stood on a chair, ostentatiously eating oranges and spitting out the pips, and defended his conduct.

The behaviour of Birmingham's first representatives in the House of Commons illustrates an interesting change. In the eighteenth century, prominent Birmingham men, Matthew Boulton in particular, had been content to exercise political power indirectly. They lobbied MPs and worked through the members for counties adjacent to Birmingham but they did not seek to sit in Parliament themselves or to occupy the front of the political stage in any other way. Their political manoeuvres were conducted on narrow grounds devoted to the promotion of their business interests. Attwood and Muntz, by contrast, were rarely happy when they were not the centre of attention, and framed their campaigns in the widest possible terms. Their politics were not directly related to their business interests. Attwood – having been born rich – died in 'almost Spartan poverty'.

The awkwardness of these political crusaders presented a revealing contrast to the style of Joseph Parkes (1796–1865). Parkes did not start out wealthy – his father had lost money in a business venture, forcing Joseph to abandon his hopes of a career at the Bar and to work as a Birmingham solicitor. He became an expert on electoral law. He was a Whig – though he had worked for Spooner when he contested the Stafford by-election against the Whigs. Above all, he was a fixer – concerned with the best way to get things done rather than with grand declarations of principle. Much of his energy was devoted to trying to impose discipline on Muntz and Attwood, persuading the former to form useful electoral alliances and the latter to abandon his self-defeating obsession with monetary questions. He wrote of Attwood in 1838: 'He is determined to run his head against the post . . . you might as well argue with a born idiot.'[22]

Attwood became convinced that the solution to his problems lay in more parliamentary reform, and he was now converted to universal male suffrage. Birmingham politics were also polarized by the activities of Tories, or more particularly those Tories who thought of themselves as clear opponents of radicalism. A Loyal and Constitutional Society was formed at Dee's Hotel in December 1834, and in 1837 a Conservative parliamentary candidate, Augustus Stapleton, contested Birmingham. The candidate stood no chance but did succeed in provoking a violent response that continued even after the election.

In 1837 Attwood resurrected the Birmingham Political Union, which now worked for a time in alliance with a new movement, Chartism, which emerged from the London Working Men's Association, founded in 1836. A 'Charter' of six points, presented in May 1838, called for universal male suffrage, secret ballots, removal of property qualifications for Members of Parliament, payment of MPs, redistribution of parliamentary constituencies to provide a fair reflection of their populations and annual parliaments. In August of that year a petition for the Charter was launched in Birmingham. Newhall Hill having become too built-over, the event took place at Holloway Head, between the centre of town and Edgbaston. A 'convention' of Chartist delegates met from February to September 1839. Its meetings generally took place in London, but from 14 May to 6 July it met at the Lawrence Street chapel in Birmingham.[23]

All of this coincided with changes in the local politics of Birmingham. The town's government was archaic. Some of its institutions – including the high and low bailiff – dated back to the Middle Ages. The Improvement Act (or Lamp Act) of 1769 had created street commissioners who were, as their name suggests, responsible for maintaining the streets (see chapter 2). They were also a self-perpetuating oligarchy who appointed their own successors. Alongside the street commissioners stood parish authorities who were responsible for the administration of poor relief until the 1834 Poor Law Amendment Act, which established a board of guardians bringing together a number of parishes.

The guardians were elected, by all who paid the poor rates, in triennial

elections. The areas that adjoined Birmingham but were not yet technically part of the town had their own forms of administration. In the mid
1830s, there were street commissions for Deritend, Bordesley, Duddeston and Nechells. The last two also had 'surveyors', whose functions
partly overlapped with those of the commissions. It was said that commissioners controlled footpaths while surveyors oversaw roads so that
'when one party scraped the mud in the middle of the street, the other
scraped it back again'. Edgbaston too had its own surveyors and guardians of the poor.

The Municipal Incorporation Act of 1835 made it possible, among
other things, for towns such as Birmingham to petition for corporate
status, which would turn their government over to a council elected by
ratepayers. In October 1838, Birmingham was one of the first towns,
along with Bolton and Manchester, to be granted this status. The council equipped itself with a motto – 'Forward'.

Incorporation closed a chapter in Birmingham's history. There must
have been some present at the celebratory dinner to mark incorporation
for whom the liberty cap, prominently displayed above the mayor's
chair, recalled the dinner of 14 July 1791 that had provoked the Church
and King riots. Now, however, those who thought of themselves as
friends of reform were in a more powerful position. Fourteen of the
forty-eight councillors had previously been members of the council of
the Birmingham Political Union. Men who had helped the BPU, notably
George Edmonds who was made clerk to the justices of the peace, were
given office. Birmingham acquired a quarter sessions court of its own
and appointed its first recorder. It also now had a coroner and, unusually,
appointed a doctor rather than a lawyer to this position. This decision,
which fitted with the scientific traditions of Priestley, allowed the town to
displace John Welchman Whateley, who had been the county-appointed
coroner and was a Tory.

The triumph for those who thought of themselves as reformers was not
an unqualified triumph for democracy. The propertied elite of the town
exercised considerable power over elections. Indeed, a group of such men
met to set out how elections ought to be conducted and who should be put
forward as a candidate. They justified this on the grounds that

> To leave to the desultory efforts of the electors generally the nomination
> of proper and fitting men, would be to hand them over, in their weakness

and uncombinedness a sacrifice, trimmed and ready, to the public enemy . . . It seems therefore but natural that in such a case some popular body should assume a task which otherwise might be indifferently done, if not unsuccessfully attempted.[24]

Some saw incorporation as a moment of betrayal when propertied men, who had presented themselves as friends of reform when it suited them to oppose aristocratic and county interests, now relished their own authority. Apart from the obvious fact that the electorate for the council was composed exclusively of ratepayers, the council also had the right to appoint sixteen aldermen who would serve for longer than ordinary councillors. Two of those so appointed had not been elected to the council at all, and two had not been elected by the wards to which they were appointed. Father Thomas McDonnell, a radical Catholic priest who was later to be ejected from his Birmingham parish by Cardinal Wiseman, commented on Birmingham's middle-class radicals thus: 'although they carried the Reform Bill from a conviction of the truth of that principle, yet they had hardly thought of applying the benefits of their labour to their own town'.

Opposition to Birmingham Council came from the Tories, who protested against the ways in which electoral boundaries had been drawn to benefit the Radicals. Since the Tories still controlled parish vestries, responsible for raising rates, they could deny the council money. Opposition also came from those who thought of themselves as Radicals – particularly those who came from areas on the edge of the town that had formerly enjoyed some measure of independence. The Duddeston and Nechells Reform Society (established in 1839) opposed attempts by the town council to take the powers then exercised by the Duddeston and Nechells street commissioners, and also complained that councillors had been refused appointment as aldermen on the grounds that they did not uphold the established Church.[25]

Most of all, the middle-class leaders of the new Birmingham Council came into conflict with the Chartists with whom some of them had recently been allied. A group of middle-class men from Birmingham resigned from the Chartist Convention in March 1839 – though Attwood still supported the Charter and presented a petition to Parliament based on its principles in June 1839. Chartists in the North were now in open conflict with those who had once been their allies in

Birmingham. *The Northern Star and Leeds Advertiser,* a Chartist news-paper, published an 'Address to the Working Men and Women of Birmingham' in which it was alleged that 'The middle classes panted for an opportunity of deserting you.' Some suggested that the split arose over the fact that northern Chartists now advocated violence as a means to achieve their aims. In fact, the divisions on this question were com-plicated and did not always align neatly with class boundaries. Attwood had talked in violent terms before the passage of the Reform Bill in 1832; on the other hand, George Edmonds, from a humbler background and a man who had been imprisoned, opposed violence in the late 1830s, as did John Collins, the only working-class man from Birming-ham to be a delegate to the Chartist Convention.[26] The division between working-class Chartists and their former allies in Birmingham seems to have sprung from the fact that the Birmingham men were now them-selves in power in their own town. Edmonds, who had endured so much for his beliefs in the earlier part of his career, was now understandably relieved to have been given employment as clerk to the justices and reluctant to jeopardize his new position.

In July 1839, there were riots in the Birmingham Bull Ring, where Chartists had taken to gathering. William Scholefield, the mayor, had tried unsuccessfully to arrange for them to hold their meetings in the more controlled circumstances of the Town Hall. Shopkeepers, who were to play an important role in Birmingham politics in the mid nine-teenth century, appear to have become fearful that their property might be damaged. Birmingham, though now incorporated, did not yet have its own police force, partly because of Tory resistance to the payment of rates, so policemen were sent from London. Their arrival – like the Chartist delegates, they were early passengers on the London to Bir-mingham train – enraged the crowds in the Bull Ring. A riot erupted, pitting defenders of property, including those middle-class men who might usually have been in favour of reform, against the Chartists. The mayor requested outside help to suppress the disorder; one of the mag-istrates with whom he worked was Philip Muntz, the brother of George, who had chaired the first meeting of the BPU. Charles Geach (1808–54), who had come to Birmingham from Cornwall, personified the dynamism and forward thinking on which the Birmingham elite often prided itself. He was, effectively, the founder of the Midland Bank. In politics, he was a Liberal and was eventually elected to Parliament for this party. However, in 1839 his preoccupation was the preservation of property. It was he who galloped through streets filled with rioters to alert the magistrates and he who placed his staff on the roof of the bank ready to hurl missiles at the crowds below.

Conflict between the Birmingham political elite and the working classes was not as open and violent after 1839 as it had been during the Bull Ring riots. The government now provided Birmingham with a police force – initially under the control of the Home Office but devolved to the council as it acquired the means to raise rates. Birmingham Council also began to expand its influence and, in 1851, it took over the powers previously exercised by the street commissioners. Men who had been opposed to the council's power were assimilated into it. Henry Hawkes, one of the figures behind the Duddeston and Nechell's Reform Society, became mayor of Birmingham in 1852. Indeed, the council itself took on the qualities of its opponents. Power passed down the social scale – not to the working classes but to shopkeepers, who made up a large proportion of ratepayers.

The period from 1852 until the late 1860s is often seen as one of stagnation in Birmingham's local politics and there was an element of truth to this caricature. Birmingham Council sometimes showed a remarkable lack of enterprise in the middle of the century – on two occasions in the 1850s, it tried to reject gifts of land to create parks on the grounds that their maintenance would be too expensive.[27]

But curiously it was during this period of apparent municipal stagnation that Birmingham was transformed by the great new technology of the nineteenth century: railways. Rail came to Birmingham in 1838, when Curzon Street station was opened – slightly east of the town centre. For a while, it was the terminus for all the railway companies, which meant that trains coming from the west curved around Birmingham, though the different companies operated different platforms and one opened the Lawley Street station, almost next door to Curzon Street. The notion of linking the station to the town centre by building a wide road was discussed, but eventually it became clear that new stations were needed and the lines approaching them were run through tunnels into the centre of the town. New Street station (still, at the time of writing, Birmingham's main station) was opened in 1846. It was originally called 'Grand Central', and Snow Hill (demolished in the 1970s but then resurrected as a smaller operation in the late 1980s) came a little later. Curzon Street ceased to be a significant station for passenger trains in 1856.

Struggles between the rival rail companies made some Chancery QCs rich and produced some picturesque episodes. When the Shrewsbury and Birmingham Company tried to run a train into Birmingham New Street in December 1851, the London and North Western Company loaded its own train with solicitors and officials and sought to block access. The two locomotives faced each other, their boilers hissing like angry cobras. An entire viaduct was built at Duddeston as a gambit during negotiations about lines. It still exists but no train has ever run over it and, indeed, no track was ever laid on it. But in general railways in Birmingham were relatively well planned and executed, with few of the false starts and aborted projects that were seen in, say, Liverpool.[28]

Railway companies were ruthless enterprises. They cut up Birmingham in ways that often disadvantaged its poorest inhabitants (few of whom could afford to travel on trains) and that sometimes anticipated the way that motorways would cut up the city in the late twentieth century. Inhabitants of Saltley found that the network of railway lines around their area made it harder for them to get into central Birmingham. Housing was cleared to make way for new lines and the moralism of slum clearance sometimes turned out to overlap conveniently with the commercial interest of rail companies whose supporters claimed they would erase 'a collection of houses and streets that it would be advantageous to Birmingham to get rid of, both physically and morally'.[29] It was when dealing with railways that the claims of Birmingham notables to be disinterested servants of the public good (see chapter 4) were least plausible. Perhaps this was because publicly quoted companies imposed the logic of the market more ruthlessly than those that were owned by individuals or families, or perhaps because the age of railway development in Birmingham came just before the moral rigour that was to be brought to public life by the powerful Unitarian and Quaker families after the 1860s. Street commissioners in the early nineteenth century had an influence over railway routes and it is notable that the ten local directors of the London to Birmingham Railway line included eight street commissioners.[30] Magistrates and MPs – such as Richard Spooner or Philip and George Muntz – intervened on behalf of railways in which they had interests.

Railways were good for the Birmingham economy. They supplemented the canals in providing a town with no natural navigable waterways with an easy means to transport finished goods. The fact that Birmingham expanded in the late nineteenth century meant that it was built around railways rather than forcing railways to find a way into an existing urban fabric. The manufacture of rolling stock itself became an important industry in eastern Birmingham. Rail also brought social and political change. The journey time to London was cut so dramatically that, for the first time, a man might begin his morning with some brisk business in the town council and finish it sitting in the chamber of the House of Commons.

In the short term, however, few exploited the new chance to combine Westminster and local politics. The middle part of the century was marked by a kind of divorce between national and local politics in Birmingham. This was illustrated by the career of John Bright (1811–89). Bright had been born in Rochdale and made his reputation as a leader of the Anti-Corn Law League that campaigned for free trade. He had been an MP for Durham and then Manchester but his opposition to the Crimean War caused him to lose his Manchester seat in 1857 and the following year he was elected for Birmingham. For a time, Bright was the single most famous name associated with Birmingham and one of the town's principal streets was named after him, but he never really presented himself as a Birmingham man and referred in his speeches to 'your city'.

While Bright talked of national and international affairs, the council seemed to retreat into itself. The dominant figure on it, though he never became mayor, was Joseph Allday, a butcher's son whose wife kept a tripe shop on Union Street and who was himself editor of a scurrilous newspaper. He had been imprisoned in 1831, having libelled George Edmonds and Joseph Parkes. His attacks on Edmonds had made much of his alleged social pretensions and the impropriety of someone who was not of gentle birth seeking to set themselves up as a lawyer. Allday himself made no pretence to gentility and seemed on the contrary to relish his plebeian origins and manners. His politics were marked by suspicion of large-scale spending projects and by the rumbustious tone that he and his cronies adopted during their meetings at the Woodman Tavern. Allday was also opposed to a certain kind of moralistic modernity that was incarnated by the new Birmingham prison established in

1849 – an institution that sought to reform its inmates with regular work on the crank but which drove a fifteen-year-old boy to hang himself.[31]

Allday is now almost forgotten in Birmingham. His name is recalled, if at all, by people who seek to contrast his regime of penny-pinching 'shopocracy' with the more ambitious and expansive form of local government that would come after him at a time when Birmingham's local politics fitted once more into national initiatives. The man who would become associated with this new mood arrived in Birmingham at the age of eighteen in 1854. His name was Joseph Chamberlain.

"I HOL

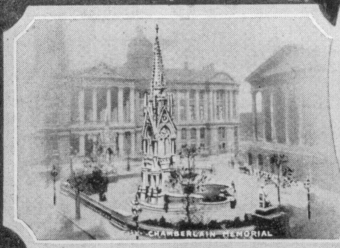

CHAMBERLAIN MEMORIAL

Mrs CHAMBERLAIN.

In Comme
OF THE SEVENT
The Rt. Hon Jose
AND HIS THIRTY
F
BIRMI

(TENEBO FIRME)
(I HOLD FAST)

HIGHBURY

SCOTT SERIES Nº 1054

...MORATION
...ETH BIRTHDAY OF
...H CHAMBERLAIN
...EARS MEMBERSHIP
...R
...GHAM

Rt.Hon. AUSTEN CHAMBERLAIN.

Postcard celebrating the thirtieth anniversary of Joseph Chamberlain's election to Parliament. The card shows the Chamberlain Memorial and Highbury, Chamberlain's house in Moseley. It also shows his third wife. His first two wives had both been intelligent and forceful members of the Kenrick family (themselves important Birmingham notables). His third wife came from Boston and was younger than Joseph's oldest child. Unlike most of the Birmingham ruling families, she liked London high society. There is something about her photograph that spells trouble. The card also shows Joseph's oldest son and designated heir Austen Chamberlain. Conspicuously absent is his younger son Neville, who seemed in 1906 still destined for a business rather than a political career.

4

Chamberlain's Birmingham

*Though the English have built the greatest towns that the world
has ever seen, they have always exhibited a singular inability to
organize, or even to understand, the true municipal life. What they
have established have been huge agglomerations of houses rather
than cities . . . The only place in England or America which appears
to form a striking exception to this rule is Birmingham. In spite of
the fact that in many ways it is intensely English, the midland
metropolis has developed something of the spirit which marked
the cities of Greece and Rome and of mediaeval Italy and France.*

The Spectator, 3 January 1891

Did Joseph Chamberlain make Birmingham or did Birmingham make
him? Chamberlain is the single name most associated with the city. Its
central square, which contains the Chamberlain Memorial Fountain, is
named after him as is the clock tower of the university, modelled on a
building in Siena, that dominates the skyline of part of the south of the
city. This formal commemoration of a great man is unusual in Britain.
There are few buildings named after Gladstone or Lloyd George and
Conservative politicians – Salisbury, Disraeli (Beaconsfield), Churchill –
are mainly remembered in the names of pubs.[1] Chamberlain's admirers
argued that the whole city was his monument. They associated Chamberlain's period as mayor, from 1873 to 1876, with a new dynamism in
municipal government – one that transformed the centre of the town by
slum clearance and the construction of Corporation Street and that
transformed the lives of the town's inhabitants. John Thackray Bunce,
editor of the *Birmingham Post* from 1862 to 1898, wrote of Chamberlain's effect:

All that was wanting is now provided: public buildings, parks ... baths, libraries, education institutions, common schools, the streets are thoroughly drained, perfectly kept, and well lighted ... and the pebble pavement ... replaced with stone or asphalt or brick ... the sewage no longer pollutes the streams but is employed to fertilize the land; courts and houses are carefully inspected, with the consequent removal of causes of disease. The gas, cheapened to the lowest point, is in the hands of the Corporation and the water supply ... is constant and unrestricted, alike to the poorest and to the wealthiest in the town.[2]

Strictly speaking, Birmingham was a town rather than a city until 1889 but by this time it was larger than many places that had enjoyed city status since the Middle Ages. More importantly, Birmingham thought like a city. The resonances of the word – biblical, classical and evocative of Italian city states – seemed to fit a place in which there was a strong sense of public life.

Many also attributed a transformation in Birmingham politics to Chamberlain. When he first entered politics, Birmingham was – as John Bright put it – 'Liberal as the sea is salt'. Only once and briefly had the town been represented by a Tory MP. Chamberlain himself was a Liberal and at first strengthened the association – both by the force of his personality and the ruthless organization of his supporters. However, when Chamberlain broke with Gladstone over Home Rule for Ireland in 1886, he effectively broke with Liberalism, and the new party that he eventually helped form – the Liberal Unionists – were allies of the Conservatives. After some hesitation, Birmingham followed Chamberlain on this. There was never a point between 1886 and 1914 when the Liberal Unionists held fewer than five of the seven Birmingham seats. With many reservations, even among Chamberlain's closest associates, the Birmingham Liberal Unionists followed him again in 1903 when he broke with Liberal traditions of support for free trade. After the 1906 election, when the Liberal Unionists had won all seven seats in Birmingham at a time when orthodox Liberals enjoyed such success elsewhere, Chamberlain issued a postcard celebrating his victory with the slogan 'Well done Birmingham. We are seven.'

Joseph Chamberlain continued to haunt Birmingham politics after his death in 1914, after the death of his youngest son (Neville) in 1940 and even after the Conservative/Unionist Party lost its grip on the city in 1945. In 1925, Norman Tiptaft (born in 1883 and himself to be Lord Mayor of Birmingham during the Second World War) published a novel that evoked the continuing power of 'Radermain' (Chamberlain) in Brassville (Birmingham):

> Fifty years ago it had a statesman, and ever since progress in Brassville has been regulated by the ideas of the early seventies. No Conservative politician (needless to say, Brassville is solidly Conservative) need be at a loss, at a Brassville public meeting, to evoke cheers from his audience . . . all he has to do . . . is . . . remind his audience – not of the future, not even of the present, but of what 'Your most distinguished citizen, alas, no longer with us, the Right Honourable Benjamin Radermain said in 1871.'
>
> What it was the Right Honourable Benjamin Radermain said in 1871 no one ever hears, owing to the prolonged applause.[3]

As a Labour candidate who opposed Neville Chamberlain in 1924, Sir Oswald Mosley was drawn to Birmingham by the mystique that was still attached to Neville's father. A Communist shop steward in a Birmingham car factory, born in 1909 and interviewed in the 1980s, referred to the Chamberlain tradition in general and the Liberal Unionist slogan of 1906 in particular, when he explained the Conservatism of Birmingham before the Second World War.[4] In 1964, when Roy Hattersley sought to overturn a small Conservative majority in Birmingham Sparkbrook to win the seat for the Labour Party, Roy Jenkins (then MP for Stechford) told him that his 'real opponent' would be Joe Chamberlain.[5]

CHAMBERLAIN'S PERSONALITY AND CAREER

There are good reasons why Chamberlain should be remembered because he was the most extraordinary British politician of the nineteenth century. Winston Churchill would later write that Chamberlain had 'made the weather' in the politics of his time.* The cabinet roles that he held in the early part of his career – responsible for trade and

---

* Though he regarded Joseph Chamberlain as important, Churchill did not consider his influence on British public life to have been benign. During the war, he told his private

local government – were relatively minor ones and, when his position would have been strong enough to ask to be Chancellor of the Exchequer, he preferred to become Secretary of State for the Colonies. In spite of this, historians accord him an importance that exceeds that of many Prime Ministers. His two sons spent their entire lives trying, and failing, to live up to their father's example, even though both held great offices of state and one of them was Prime Minister. Chamberlain radiated power. A Frenchman wrote of his appearance: 'one senses that an order can and must come from that firm mouth ... one guesses that it will be short, clear, precise.' He quipped that the nannies of British aristocrats would threaten their infant charges with Chamberlain when they mis-behaved.[6] A French visitor to London noted his paradoxical mix of intimidation and charm:

> The reality of him is less terrible than his name, and during the London Season one encounters not a few people who, having expected to find in Mr. Chamberlain some fierce and aggressive person, profess their aston-ishment at discovering him to be a very agreeable gentleman with a large stock of conversational subjects, appreciative of humour and light in hand.[7]

Chamberlain attacked the aristocracy when it suited him to do so – mocking its apparent idleness and claiming at one point that the House of Lords had 'protected every abuse and sheltered every privil-ege'. However, when the time came, Chamberlain worked well with the man who seemed to revel in his own image as the epitome of aris-tocratic reaction: the third Marquess of Salisbury. Chamberlain was amused at the idea that he might be offered a title but not tempted to accept. He appeared to assume that his own superiority over rivals, however well born, was too obvious to require elaboration – his atti-tude puts one in mind of Lady Bracknell's distinction between those 'born in the purple of commerce' and those who had risen 'from the ranks of the aristocracy'.

Chamberlain was supremely 'unclubbable'. When his brothers were blackballed from the Reform Club, he threatened to sue. This was not because he really cared about the matter but simply because he wished

---

secretary, John Colville, that Joseph Chamberlain and Baldwin were the men who had done most to damage Britain.

to cause his enemies as much trouble as possible: 'if money and labour can do it, we will bring their grey hairs with sorrow to the grave'.[8] Some suggested that he lacked the discipline he might have acquired from a public school education. It would be fairer to say that Chamberlain had his own conceptions of discipline (he regarded physical exercise as a frivolous waste of time) that were so strong that they would have resisted any outside intervention. Chamberlain sent his sons to Rugby but insisted the school adjust to his family rather than his family adjust to the school. In particular, he threatened to withdraw his eldest son rather than let him endure corporal punishment. He wrote: 'The ready appeal to physical force is a mental preparation for the rowdy jingoism which is a characteristic of many educated, middle-class Englishmen.'[9]

Chamberlain grew orchids and the orchid in the buttonhole became (along with the monocle) part of his public persona. It was a revealing hobby. An aristocrat, or a self-made man who aspired to live like an aristocrat, might have planted oak trees to be enjoyed by his grandchildren. Chamberlain's natural milieu was the hothouse. He wanted quick and spectacular results and he was competitive in everything he did. He was said to have once purchased a single orchid for 500 francs on the Quai aux Fleurs in Paris. The seller assured him that it was the only example of its type in France and then watched in horror as Chamberlain shredded it in his hands. He already had the orchid in his collection and had merely wanted to ensure that his possession would preserve its rarity value.[10]

Chamberlain's career involved some extraordinary volte-faces. He was never an Anglican and, after the death of his second wife in 1875, not a religious believer of any kind. Opposition to the established Church was a central element of his early politics and he proposed disestablishment in 1885, but a few years later he had become the ally of men who would have claimed that the defence of the Church of England was one of their principal political aims. He was a republican in the 1860s, albeit one who took no action to depose the monarchy, and yet he became the last minister to see Queen Victoria before her death in 1901. Twice in his career he effectively incited his supporters to riot. The target on the first of these occasions (at Aston Hall in 1884) was the Tory Randolph Churchill and the target of the second (at Birmingham Town Hall in 1901) was the Liberal Lloyd George. One key to understanding

Chamberlain lies in the fact that he was above all a Radical and that for him, as for Attwood and Spooner earlier in the century, Radicalism was a spirit that transcended the gap between the main established parties. There was something 'unEnglish' about Chamberlain – he often retreated to France in moments of emotional crisis – and his third marriage, attended by the president of the United States, was to Mary Endicott of Boston. A journalist wrote to Lord Rosebery in 1910: 'Almost every Englishman has a touch of the essential Whig about him and a liking for moderation and the Via Media. Joe has none. Once a Jacobin always a Jacobin.'[11]

In fact, Chamberlain was not exactly a 'Jacobin' and his numerous admirers in France and the United States understood, better than Chamberlain's own compatriots, that his Radicalism was that of a Clemenceau or a Lincoln – men who constructed a new order after the old order had been overthrown. A Frenchman wrote of what he described as Chamberlain's 'state socialism':

> If he is the friend of American democrats, he is the student of French democrats, a student who, in many respects, outpaces and corrects his teachers. For a long time, people have taken, or pretended to take, him for a revolutionary. In reality, he is a born legislator, an organizer, a constructor of societies. In this, he is the man of the hour; he marks the second age of democracy, when, after having destroyed, its mission is to rebuild.[12]

The reconstruction that Chamberlain effected was seen first in local government when he became mayor of Birmingham and pioneered a new degree of municipal activism that made Birmingham seem, as an American journalist put it, 'the best governed city in the world'. It was seen too in party organization when he worked with a caucus that imposed a new degree of discipline on Liberals in Birmingham and that became a model for party management in all democracies. The Tory Randolph Churchill, who watched Chamberlain's early political moves with a mixture of horror and admiration, talked of Birmingham as being dominated by a 'Tsarist despotism' and alleged that 'the whole government power of Birmingham is in the hands of the Caucus ... which owns the gasworks, owns the water supply, they control the lunatic asylum, the grammar school ... as well as the drainage farm'.[13]

CHAMBERLAIN AND BUSINESS

Chamberlain was not simply a powerful man who happened to find an outlet for his power in Birmingham. There were good reasons why the town suited him and why he suited it. Business was what first drew him to Birmingham. He had been born in Camberwell, south London, into a Unitarian family. His father, also called Joseph, was a cordwainer (or shoemaker). The business had become prosperous partly by supplying boots for soldiers – perhaps because of this, the family were marked by a degree of martial ardour that was unusual in Nonconformists. His religion excluded him from Anglican institutions but Joseph was well educated at University College School. He left at the age of sixteen and was apprenticed to his father's firm, briefly working as a craftsman before moving to deal with the accounts.

In 1854, when he was eighteen, he moved to Birmingham. He worked for a company established by his father and his father's brother-in-law, John Sutton Nettlefold, to exploit a patent that they had acquired for a new American method of producing wood screws. The new company – in which Joseph Chamberlain *père et fils* were partners of Nettlefold and his son Frederick – established a factory at Smethwick. The firm prospered. Nettlefold concerned himself with production; Chamberlain handled accounts and marketing. In business, Chamberlain displayed qualities that would later mark his political career. He was audacious, innovative and aggressive. He travelled extensively to promote the business and dealt with the firm's employees in a paternalistic, if authoritarian, fashion. Chamberlain and Nettlefold eliminated their competitors. First, they bought out the two significant Birmingham firms that made screws, having threatened them with ruinous undercutting on price if they did not sell. When this was done, Chamberlain applied the same tactics more aggressively to smaller firms – so that some men who had been owners of their own small enterprises became instead employees of Chamberlain and Nettlefold.

Chamberlain's success in business came partly from the fact that he was not always in conventional terms very businesslike. His actions were sometimes driven by an almost atavistic desire to win and to dominate rather than by rational calculations of profit and loss. His style was revealed when a group acquired a patent for the production of screws that was supposedly superior to that held by Chamberlain and Nettle-fold. The group established a factory in Smethwick, almost next door to that of Chamberlain and his associates, and planned to float shares with which to fund their venture.

At first Chamberlain was pessimistic about the chance that his own company stood of beating the new enterprise, which was called the Birmingham Screw Company, but he eventually devised a strategy that would involve raising prices to accumulate money during the period when his rivals were setting up their own operation and then cutting prices ruthlessly in order to drive them out of business once they started production. He talked repeatedly of 'smashing' his competitors and feared that delay would make it 'simply impossible to kill them'. His language suggested a military conflict as much as a business dispute:

> I feel certain that to let the [new] company get fairly in the market would be to abdicate forever our position as Screw Kings. I do not mean to say that we might not do very well as regards money ... but for a certainty, our sole supremacy would never be re-established.
>
> Of course in such a matter as this our decision is partly a Speculation. But I give my vote for the bold game and believe it will pay in the long run the better of the two.[14]

Chamberlain won. The promoters of the Birmingham Screw Company – beaten down by Chamberlain's threats of undercutting, by his efforts to prevent skilled workmen from joining them and even by his preemptive purchase of land that they planned to use – withdrew from the field. But he was also lucky. The outbreak of the Franco-Prussian War in 1870 cut his competitors off from the supplies they needed, and their decision to fund their operations by floating shares made them vulnerable to nervous shareholders. Things might have been very different. Josiah Mason, who stood behind the Birmingham Screw Company, had already made a fortune in pen manufacture. He was a very rich man and the fact that he gave away almost half a million pounds in the course of his life reflected both his wealth and his willingness in certain circumstances to subordinate the making of money to other considerations. This last quality was dangerous in the game of bluff that Chamberlain was engaged in, but on this occasion Mason seems to have decided that conflict was not worthwhile.

In different times or a different place, Chamberlain's business practices might have led him to the bankruptcy court or worse. He was
lucky that he started out in the mid Victorian boom and that he moved
from business to politics as that boom ended. He was lucky too in his
family. They provided him with the contacts and capital to start out.
They also helped limit the damage that might otherwise have been done
by his impetuousness. He was a gambler by nature – if he had been born
into a grander and less pious family one can imagine him betting the
family estate on a spin of the roulette wheel – and one who lived for
drama. His relatives, including eventually his younger son, Neville,
brought more prosaic qualities to the family enterprises.

CHAMBERLAIN AND THE
BIRMINGHAM FAMILIES

Because he was so solitary, and so good at making enemies, Chamberlain benefited from the unconditional loyalty that sometimes went with
family and from the fact that his arrival in Birmingham introduced him
to a network of powerful and interlinked families. The Nettlefolds had
provided his first contacts in the town. His relations with his uncle Nettlefold were not very good and Chamberlain's brother, Arthur, had to be
set up in a different company after a brief and unsuccessful period
working for Chamberlain and Nettlefold. All the same, the ties between
the families were never entirely cut.

The most important family to become associated with the Chamberlains was one that Joseph encountered after his arrival in Birmingham:
the Kenricks. Like the Chamberlains, they were Unitarians. Their origins were in Denbighshire, but they had moved to Shropshire and then
to Birmingham. Archibald Kenrick established a hardware manufactory at West Bromwich in 1791. Joseph Chamberlain's first wife was
Harriet Kenrick, whom he married in 1861. Harriet Kenrick's brother,
William, married Joseph's sister, Mary, in the following year. Chamberlain's first wife died after childbirth in 1863, and he then married her
cousin, Florence Kenrick, in 1868. Joseph's brother, Arthur, was married to Florence's twin sister, Louisa. In later life, respectable families
from outside Birmingham – the Potters of London and the Endicotts of
Boston and Washington – did not welcome the prospect of having

Joseph Chamberlain as a suitor for their daughters, even though he was by this stage a wealthy and successful man. The Kenricks, however, embraced Joseph, provided him with emotional support after the death of both his wives and helped to bring up his children. For a time Chamberlain effectively lived with the parents of his first wife – keeping a cottage on the edge of their property to which he could retire to smoke cigars.

Chamberlain was left distraught by the death of his second wife, Florence, in 1875, but his relationship with the Kenrick family remained central to his life. In 1882 he got to know Beatrice Potter (later to be Beatrice Webb), who was gripped by a strange mixture of fascination and horror at the force of his character. She wrote of him in her diary:

> He recognizes no distinctions of class, and in this, as in all matters, he is supported by the powerful clan to which he belongs. The Kenricks and Chamberlains form the aristocracy and plutocracy of Birmingham. They stand far above the town society in social position, wealth and culture; and yet they spend their lives, as great citizens, taking an active and leading part in the municipal, political and educational life of the town. There is one eternal refrain in a Chamberlain-Kenrick household: Birmingham society is superior in earnestness, sincerity and natural intelligence to any society in the United Kingdom! Apparently, the conviction remains unshaken by wider social experience, for the Cabinet Minister and his womenkind repeat with warmth the same assertions in the London drawing room. Certainly, as far as my own experience went of the family and its immediate surroundings, earnestness and simplicity of motive were strikingly present.[15]

The Chamberlain/Kenrick 'clan' was closely linked to two other Unitarian families. The first were the Beales, who had been merchants in Birmingham in the eighteenth century. William John Beale (1807–83) was a solicitor and in 1842 formed a partnership with Thomas Colmore – presumably one of the last representatives of the family that had been so influential in Birmingham in the sixteenth and seventeenth centuries still to be resident in the town. A few years after this, Colmore disappeared from the scene and the Beale Colmore firm became the Beale Marigold firm. The Beale family earned their living mainly as lawyers: three of William John Beale's four sons were lawyers, though, as the years passed, increasing numbers of them were called to the Bar

Chamberlain, Kenrick and Martineau family tree

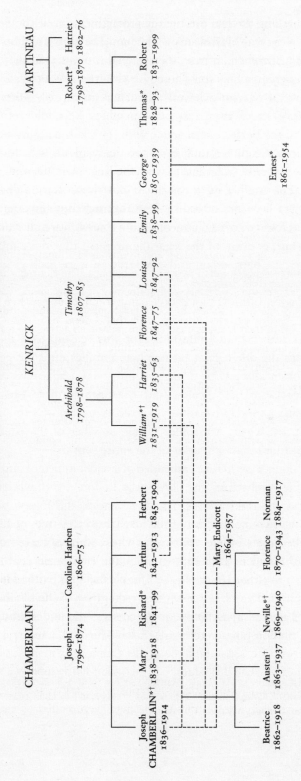

Only individuals relevant to the text are included.

* Mayor of Birmingham
† MPs for a Birmingham constituency

Source: Andrew Reekes, *The Birmingham Political Machine: Winning Elections for Joseph Chamberlain* (Alcester, 2018)

rather than pursuing the less prestigious profession of solicitor. Similar to the Beales were the Martineaus – of Huguenot origin – who were associated with Birmingham from the eighteenth century. Robert Martineau (1798–1870) and his son Thomas (1828–1893) both lived there. Like the Beales, the Martineaus were a largely professional, rather than industrial, family and many of its male members were lawyers.* The Martineaus and the Beales intermarried with the Chamberlains and the Kenricks: Joseph Chamberlain's first two marriages made him the brother-in-law of, first, Thomas Martineau, and then Charles Beale (1843–1912). The families were associated in other ways too. When the Kenrick business was formed as a private limited company, the most important directors (who held almost all the shares) were all members of the family but, because of the legal requirement that there must be seven directors, a Chamberlain and a Martineau were each given one share and appointed as directors.

The last of what Birmingham people came to know as the 'five families' were the Cadburys. First grocers and then cocoa producers, they were Quakers rather than Unitarians. For this reason, they did not intermarry with the other great Birmingham families until the 1920s,† though they often allied with them in commercial, philanthropic and political enterprises. Three Beales, four Martineaus, three Chamberlains, three Kenricks and two Cadburys served as mayors of Birmingham between 1841 and 1941. A member of one or other of these families was mayor for more than a quarter of the entire century.

The five families were in turn embedded in a wider milieu of families – the Rylands, the Pembertons, the Lloyds, the Taylors – with whom they mixed, married and did business. Timothy Kenrick and Joseph Chamberlain were the two most active of the non-family directors of Lloyd's Bank after it became a public company in 1865. Some of these families had been established in Birmingham since the eighteenth century or before. They were either Unitarians or Quakers and all had made their money in business. They were sometimes richer than the five families – Louisa Ryland gave away £180,000 in her lifetime and left around three quarters of a million pounds to charity when she died, unmarried and

---

* The best-known member of the family (Harriet) was not really a Birmingham figure – though she was buried, along with many Birmingham notables, in Key Hill Cemetery.
† In 1925 Laurence Cadbury married a Unitarian (Joyce Matthews).

childless, in 1889. None of them, however, was as tightly woven into the inner circle of the five families and none of them was as prominent in the public life of the city.

The great Birmingham dynasties were not always united. Samuel Kenrick had broken with his uncle Archibald in 1827 to found a rival business. Neville Chamberlain would recall that his father and uncle (he meant Arthur Chamberlain rather than his Kenrick uncle) competed like 'rival terriers'. Sampson Lloyd (1820–89) was a Quaker and a member of the banking family. Everything about his background suggested that he should have been a Liberal and a supporter of Nonconformist rights (as his brother George Braithwaite Lloyd was), but Sampson contested Birmingham, unsuccessfully, as a Conservative in the parliamentary elections of 1867 and 1868 (he was eventually elected for Plymouth in 1874) and sat with the 'ecclesiastical' party on the Birmingham School Board. Nonetheless, personal relations softened the violence of these conflicts. Tacit agreements about the distinction between family, politics, business and philanthropy were often observed and direct confrontation was avoided when possible.

Money mattered to the Birmingham families. All of them were comfortably off and all of them, even those whose primary income derived from law, had some association with business. There were times when contacts and influence helped their business, and even the Unitarian families might be tempted to profit from such contacts. Samuel Beale (1803–74) was both a director of railway companies and a member of the Paving Committee, which was consulted about railway construction. He left a fortune of £350,000.[16]

Oddly, though, some of the political and social influence of the Birmingham notables derived from the fact that they were not entirely mercenary. Philanthropy was an important part of their life. Some Birmingham manufacturers gave away the greater part of their fortune. Joseph Gillott, the penmaker, left £350,000 when he died in 1874 but was reckoned to have given away almost half as much in the course of his life. Josiah Mason, also a penmaker, left £56,000 when he died in 1881 but had given away almost ten times as much as that sum. His largesse launched Mason College – the institution which eventually became Birmingham University. Joseph Chamberlain gave £1,000 (1 per cent of what he would get from selling his interest in the family business) to the city art gallery in 1874.[17] Only in the 1890s, by which time he had lost a good deal of money and acquired an expensive third wife, did he begin to reduce the scale of his gifts.

Birmingham notables gave their time to a wide variety of projects – Sunday School teaching, campaigning, municipal government – that were not remunerated. Their political influence in the locality derived partly from the perception that they might be disinterested servants of the public good. Writing in the late 1960s, a historian of the Kenrick company was to argue that excessive involvement in public life had distracted directors from their commercial concerns and partly accounted for the decline of the firm. Foreign observers – especially those accustomed to Tammany Hall – commented on the altruism of those who served on the Birmingham Council: 'No opportunity is afforded for jobbery or corruption because the work is done under the immediate personal supervision of the Water Committee, composed of eight of the best businessmen on the council, serving without a penny of remuneration.'[18] The Franco-Russian political scientist Moisei Ostrogorski wrote:

> The group of men who were associated under the lead of Mr Chamberlain, and who thus contributed their personal services, contributed money as well, and with equal readiness. Their names always appeared at the head of subscription lists and for considerable sums. Every public-spirited effort was assured in advance of their sympathy and attention. Thus they furnished a brilliant proof of the fact that social leadership, such as had been the glory of old England, could still be exercised for the public good by others than landlords and without the spirit of paternal condescension characteristic of the aristocracy.[19]

Some of this altruism may have derived from religion. Some may have sprung from a particular quality of Birmingham: the fortunes of even its wealthiest inhabitants were not huge. The comparison was striking with London, where bankers were much richer than most provincial businessmen. But it was also marked in relation to other provincial towns. Among men who died in the last twenty years of the nineteenth century (whose wealth would, in general, have been amassed rather earlier), there were two millionaires and fifteen half-millionaires in Manchester, four millionaires and eleven half-millionaires in Clydeside and eight of each in Merseyside. In the West Midlands there were two millionaires (of whom one was from Birmingham) and three half-millionaires (of whom two were from Birmingham).[20] There were fewer very rich people in Birmingham partly because the city's expansion in the nineteenth century had not given time for fortunes to accrue and partly because manufacture provided a harder route to great wealth than trade or shipping, businesses that were obviously concentrated in port cities.

There was also a cultural dimension to Birmingham's relation with wealth. A large fortune could own a man as much as he owned it. The very rich were sometimes consumed by the desire to extend and preserve their wealth. Birmingham businessmen, by contrast, often saw the primary purpose of business as being to provide them with enough money to do other things. Joseph Chamberlain sold out of his business before he was forty. Even men who stayed in business often had comparatively limited financial ambitions. The world of Birmingham Nonconformity did not encourage spectacular spending. As better roads, railways and finally motor cars made transport easier, the city's *grande bourgeoisie* sometimes bought houses with land on the outskirts of the city – or just outside its limits – that allowed them to combine rural calm with easy access to their offices and factories. But their acquisitions were usually modest. In the nineteenth century, only fourteen Birmingham men purchased estates of more than 1,000 acres, three bought more than 3,000 acres and one acquired a property of 25,000 acres. Most rural properties that belonged to Birmingham men were smaller. Some wanted to buy places where they could run 'hobby farms',[21] but often country houses seemed to go with an extension of middle-class habits rather than an attempt to ape aristocratic manners. The life of the big houses near Birmingham revolved around tennis, croquet and gardening rather than riding to hounds; men were more likely to shoot rabbits than grouse. It seemed appropriate that Edgbaston Hall, once the seat of an aristocratic family, would end up as a golf club in the twentieth century.

The notion of establishing an ancestral seat from which they would influence the surrounding countryside, and which would be passed down the generations, would have mystified many in Birmingham. Houses were bought and sold without much regard for sentiment. The Kenricks and the Cadburys reserved their emotional attachments for their firms. Richard Cadbury bought Moseley Hall and George Cadbury bought The Manor in Northfield; together the brothers acquired several hundred acres of poor-quality farmland in the Lickey Hills.

None of these properties stayed in the family for more than a generation. All of them were given away – the first for a children's convalescent home, the second to the University of Birmingham and the third to the Corporation of Birmingham to provide its citizens with outings in the fresh air. The Birmingham families attached so little importance to the ownership of real estate that they sometimes became tenants of charities they themselves had established. Josiah Mason gave his own Norwood House with its thirteen acres of gardens to the orphanage he had set up. The Cadbury family swapped the freehold of their house in Hole Lane for the lease of a few extra acres from the Bournville estate.

The expansion of Birmingham itself discouraged its inhabitants from becoming too attached to any particular property as areas that had been havens of rural tranquillity were absorbed into the town. The Galton family acquired an estate in Duddeston, when it was still outside the city, in the eighteenth century. Mary Anne Galton described the journey there through 'sequestered lanes, whose banks were rich in flower, or over-arched with dark umbrageous trees ... various animals, and ragged children who tended them, added to the wild and picturesque effect'. By the mid nineteenth century, Duddeston was built up and the family sold the estate. Part of it became a private lunatic asylum and Samuel Tertius Galton remarked briskly that now 'no one in their right senses would want to live there'.[22]

Once they had enough to run a large house in Somerset Road and, by the end of the century, to send their sons to Rugby, the interest of many Birmingham businessmen in making more money declined. Prestige among the Birmingham middle classes often went with achievement that could not be measured in monetary terms and a sense that the right to move in powerful circles did not depend on wealth. This was particularly true of ministers of religion (of whom more below). George Dawson left only £3,000 when he died in 1876 and the Unitarian Henry Crosskey left £5,500 when he died in 1893. But both these men mixed with and influenced those who were richer than themselves.

EDGBASTON

Relations between the powerful families of Birmingham were facilitated partly by the fact that often they lived close to each other. The district of

Edgbaston, which covered 2,500 acres, or about a third of all the land inside the boundaries of Birmingham as set in 1838, played a paradoxical role in the life of the town. In some respects, this was a centre of aristocratic power. The Gough family bought the Edgbaston estate in 1717. The Gough money derived from the East India trade but the acquisition of land went with increasing gentility, and by the early nineteenth century Edgbaston was owned by the branch of the family that had been raised to the peerage with the name of Calthorpe. The Calthorpes owned over eight tenths of the freeholds in Edgbaston. They themselves had moved from Edgbaston to Suffolk in the late eighteenth century and on at least one occasion considered selling their urban holdings in order to buy more land around their rural estate – a decision that would have been, even allowing for the fact that they did not always exploit Edgbaston as efficiently as they might have done, very financially disadvantageous. The third Lord Calthorpe (1787–1851), who inherited the title and properties in 1797, developed Edgbaston as a residential estate – one from which industry would be in large measure excluded and on which most property would be held in the form of ninety-nine-year leases.

The Calthorpes had been a Whig family, and were sometimes Liberals in the nineteenth century. Generally, however, they drifted to the political right. Their Conservatism was on the whole restrained and pragmatic – their agent, the solicitor John Whateley, was more politically engaged than they were – and they sought to maintain good relations with the town.[23] Nonetheless, they were aristocrats and defenders of Anglican interests. As such, they were to come into conflict with Chamberlain in the early part of his political career. He used one of his first political speeches in 1869 to denounce absentee landlords. In 1880, Augustus Calthorpe presented himself as a Conservative parliamentary candidate. His diffident manner and reluctance to speak (satirists labelled him 'the Sphinx') provided a painfully sharp contrast with the manner of Chamberlain, who was the most prominent of the Liberal candidates. The contrast was made more awkward by the fact that Calthorpe shared the Conservative ticket with the eccentric, brave and extrovert adventurer and soldier Frederick Burnaby. Calthorpe came bottom of the poll.

Curiously the effect of aristocratic control of Edgbaston was to make it into a haven for the upper-middle classes, who were at least at first often Liberal and Nonconformist. The fact that most property in Edgbaston could only be leased (rather than acquired by freehold) may have suited the unsentimental view that the city's businessmen took of residential property; not surprisingly, hard-headed businessmen often made more money subletting the properties they leased than they paid in ground rent to their landlord. The Calthorpe family provided Edgbaston with paved and drained roads before Chamberlain's municipal administration brought these things to the rest of Birmingham.* The population of Edgbaston increased in the nineteenth century. It stood at 1,180 in 1811, had risen to 17,442 by 1871 and to 26,398 by 1911, but building there was strictly controlled so that overcrowding and industrial development were prevented. The elevation and usually the direction of the wind protected it from factory smoke. It was, and is, possible for someone walking down the leafy streets of Edgbaston to imagine that they are in a distant suburb or even the countryside. But, in fact, Edgbaston was not far from the industrial centres of the West Midlands. An office boy at the Kenrick factory in West Bromwich recalled that George Kenrick, vice chairman of the company, travelled from his house in Somerset Road in Edgbaston by bicycle – his relatives and fellow directors occasionally came by horse-drawn coach.[24] One hundred and forty-seven people from Birmingham left a fortune of more than £100,000 between 1775 and 1924; of these, forty-seven were usually resident in Edgbaston.[25]

Chamberlain himself lived in Edgbaston or its fringes for much of his time in Birmingham, as did his political allies Jesse Collings and George Dixon – the latter represented Edgbaston when it was created as a separate parliamentary constituency in 1885. The Edgbaston electorate was not always Chamberlainite – some middle-class voters did not follow Chamberlain when he broke with Gladstone and/or broke with free trade. All the same, a significant proportion of Edgbaston notables were allied with Chamberlain and that meant that his party was well organized in the constituency. It was the only one in Birmingham that the Gladstonian Liberals did not bother to contest in 1892 and was the

---

* The salubrity of Edgbaston, at least early in the nineteenth century, was only relative. Richard Tapper Cadbury complained in the 1840s that the ditches around his house in the Hagley Road were 'reeking with the contents of the water closets of the finest neighbourhoods of Birmingham'.

constituency to which Neville Chamberlain would retreat in 1929 as the Labour Party advanced in more plebeian quarters of the city.

Joseph Chamberlain's main residence was in Birmingham at Highbury Hall, which was completed in 1880. A Venetian Gothic house, it was set in thirty acres of grounds landscaped by Edward Milner.[26] It was a place of 'ponderous luxury' and, towards the end of Chamberlain's life, filled with the relics that he had acquired as Colonial Secretary. It was located in Moseley, still an easy walk from Edgbaston and a slightly more energetic one from the town centre. Joseph's brother Arthur lived next door. Highbury also adjoined the house built by Richard Cadbury. Neville Chamberlain, already displaying the snobbery that would mark his attitude to his native city, referred to the neighbouring house as 'the cocoa palace'.

Edgbaston was becoming a less attractive area for the rich by the end of the nineteenth century – partly because advances in transport had made more distant locations more accessible and partly because the smoke from Birmingham industry was now beginning to reach this suburb, to such an extent that plants in the botanical gardens were wilting. Shortly before the First World War, a tram service was even established on the Hagley Road. The university that Chamberlain had helped establish brought professors to the area in the twentieth century and some of them were amused by the relics of upper-middle-class life they found in their houses. Oliver Lodge, arriving as the first vice chancellor in 1900, bought a property that had once required six gardeners for the upkeep of its grounds – though fortunately the vendors kept the stable yard, the kitchen garden and the glasshouses, leaving Lodge with just a 'flower garden and a paddock'.[27] When he was professor of Greek in the 1920s, E.R. Dodds bought a couple of 'small late Georgian houses in Sir Harrys Road'. They came with a stable, a walled pleasure garden, a walled fruit garden, a heated glasshouse and a small lake, in which Dodds bred trout.[28] Rudolf Peierls – a thirty-year-old German Jewish refugee who arrived as professor of physics in 1937 – had only an acre of garden attached to his house in Carpenter Road, though the property did have a butler's pantry and a set of rooms for the 'coachman' above the garage.[29]

Even after its greatest days were past, however, Edgbaston still contained a high proportion of Birmingham's most notable families. In 1882, a number of people subscribed to support the publication of a history of the Old Meeting House there – which had been an important centre of Nonconformism and latterly of Unitarianism. Included among the numerous Edgbaston residents in the list were one Beale, one Crosskey, four Martineaus, three Kenricks, two Oslers, two Pembertons and one member of the Ryland family.[30] Around the same time, twenty-two of forty-eight Birmingham councillors lived in Edgbaston. By 1901–2 this had declined to fifteen out of fifty-three, though over half of aldermen (more established and usually older than ordinary councillors) still lived there even then.[31] Adrian Boult, who arrived to conduct the City of Birmingham Orchestra in 1924, believed that 'Edgbaston was responsible for the good government of Birmingham' because its grand houses and gardens meant that some of the wealthy businessmen stayed in the city and concerned themselves with public affairs while their counterparts in, say, Liverpool set up homes out in the country.[32] Even those who moved from Edgbaston rarely went far; some simply further down the Bristol Road to Northfield, still a rural area, or a little further into Worcestershire. South-west Birmingham remained the centre of power for the Birmingham elite until at least the Second World War. The Cadbury family built their factory estate at Bournville, where, more or less next door to Edgbaston, they created a twee version of its semi-rural charms. Edgbaston became a state of mind as much as a place. The journalist Godfrey Winn recalled meeting Neville Chamberlain's wife in the late 1930s, by which time she had been resident in Downing Street for almost a decade: '[S]he would also ask after my Aunt Edith as though we were all still living cosily together in the smaller parishes of Edgbaston.'[33]

RELIGION

The milieu around Chamberlain was partly welded together by religion. It was widely assumed that Birmingham's unincorporated status in the seventeenth and eighteenth centuries had protected it from the provisions of the 'Five Miles Act', which forbade Nonconformists from preaching within five miles of a corporation from which they had been excluded. In fact, in the nineteenth century and in purely statistical terms, Birmingham was not a Nonconformist town; in 1851, about half of its inhabitants were Anglicans. This was roughly the same as the total for

England as a whole and much higher than in most northern industrial towns. Wesleyanism in particular was weaker in Birmingham than in most northern towns. It was, though, true that religious Nonconformity remained important to the image that some Birmingham citizens had of themselves. It was also true that some relatively small denominations – the Unitarians, who made up 3.7 per cent of the town's population in 1851, and the Quakers, who amounted to 1.2 per cent – exercised an influence that was disproportionate to their numbers.

When he became mayor, Chamberlain could depend on the support of forty-two members of the town council. The religion of thirty-five of these is known: two Baptists, seven Anglicans, five Quakers, seven Congregationalists and fourteen Unitarians.[34] The figures are striking in view of the fact that such a tiny proportion of the population were Quakers or Unitarians. Nonconformists in Birmingham had two advantages. First, the Unitarians and the Quakers contained a disproportionately large number of wealthy families, something that set them apart from, say, the Wesleyans or the Baptists. Between 1775 and 1924, the religious affiliation is known for 117 of the 147 people who died in Birmingham with a fortune of £100,000 or more. Of these, sixty-four were Anglicans, twenty-eight were Unitarians and twelve were Quakers. All the other Birmingham Nonconformist denominations together counted for only thirteen of the great fortunes. Second, Nonconformists in Birmingham, Unitarians especially, enjoyed stable leadership. Until 1905, Birmingham had no cathedral and any ambitious Anglican cleric was bound to see a living there as temporary. For certain kinds of Nonconformists, by contrast, Birmingham was the pinnacle of their careers. It had the distinction of association with Priestley and it offered wealthy congregations. It also attracted ministers who defined themselves by their refusal to conform to the dour standards of certain kinds of Victorian Nonconformity.[35]

John Vincent has written about the politics of nineteenth-century Nonconformity: 'The dissenters above all were formed in a historical culture of almost Judaic narrowness ... and their politics were grafted onto an interpretation of seventeenth century politics.' This was only partly true of the most important Birmingham Dissenters. The Quaker Richard Tangye had the country's largest collection of objects relating to Oliver Cromwell at his house in Yardley – though the fact that he kept this collection in his billiard room hints at a flexible notion of

Puritanism.[36] More common than direct reference to the Civil War was a conception of the ways in which seventeenth-century history had itself been at stake in the Priestley riots of 1791. Unitarianism was generally an optimistic, forward-looking religion – perhaps, as Priestley had shown in 1791, naively so. The rapid expansion of Birmingham meant that the town did not easily lend itself to the cultivation of memories of past conflicts. Many of its prominent Nonconformist families were relatively recent arrivals. The Old Meeting House, which evoked memories of a time when the expression of Nonconforming religious beliefs could be dangerous, and which had itself been rebuilt after being partially destroyed by a mob in the eighteenth century, was by the mid nineteenth century frequented mainly by artisans. The upper-middle classes worshipped at the Church of the Messiah, built in the 1860s.[37] Henry Crosskey, who preached there, spoke in terms that suggested the importance he attached to the present and the future:

> The rightful discharge of social and political duties depends upon the sacredness we attach to the history of our own age. If we imagine that the age is poor and mean – that it is best managed for paltry designs . . . then we may put great principles aside as too good for daily use – the Lord God will simply put us, with any influence, wealth or status we may possess, on one side, as insignificant and unworthy triflers.[38]

Indeed, the striking thing about the most prominent religious Dissenters in Birmingham was that they wore their theological orthodoxy lightly and were, partly as a consequence, rarely closed in on themselves. The memorial to George Dawson (1821–76) – who arrived in Birmingham to preach at the Baptist Mount Zion Chapel in 1844 but then moved to the more liberal Church of the Saviour in 1845 – read: 'In religion, his teaching was free from the limitations of creed and full of reverence for all forms of sincere faith being inspired by a firm belief in the fatherhood of God and the brotherhood of man.' As a preacher, he praised Voltaire and implied that non-believers might be the most interesting interlocutors for Christians. When the Archbishop of Canterbury called for a day of fasting as a response to an outbreak of cattle plague, Dawson remarked that 'piety will not save you from the results of stupidity'.[39] Robert Dale (1829–95), the Congregationalist who was minister of the Carrs Lane chapel from 1854, was more theologically orthodox but equally disdainful of traditional clerical dress or even titles. William Crosskey (1826–93) combined his ministry at the Church of the Messiah with a distinguished career as a geologist, a significant fact at a time when geology challenged the literal truth of the Bible.

All of these men argued against two things. The first of these was the privilege of the established Church. This is not to say that they were against Anglicans or Anglican theology but that they were against the special status that the Church of England enjoyed, especially in education. They supported freedom of worship for all – Catherine Hutton Beale (a woman who was old and well-connected enough to have heard first-hand accounts of the Priestley riots) drily compared the Anglican campaign against Anglo-Catholicism in the late nineteenth century with that against Puritanism in the seventeenth century.[40] The second and less explicit of their targets was Calvin – and particularly Calvinist notions of predestination and original sin. One might almost say that a whole strand of Birmingham Nonconformity defined itself in opposition to the theologian who had exercised the greatest influence on British Nonconformity in the seventeenth century.

The Birmingham Nonconformists also emphasized the duties of Christians in the public world. Crosskey wrote:

> I have always held that in becoming a minister of Religion I did not cease to be a citizen … Politics have meant for me Methods of just Government, or in other words, the Methods of Government which will promote the establishment of a Kingdom of God on earth and by consequence the development of a righteous civilization.[41]

WOMEN

One of the revealing paradoxes of Joseph Chamberlain's character concerned his relations with women. During their curious semi-courtship, Beatrice Potter discerned that he was 'anxious to ascertain whether I yielded to his absolute supremacy', and her humiliation at finding herself in love with him was exacerbated by his patronizing assurance that her feelings were 'purely womanly'. After watching him make a speech in Birmingham she noted in her diary that the crowd listened so attentively that 'it might have been a woman listening to her lover'.

This obsessive masculinity sat oddly with the fact that Chamberlain accorded women a degree of political respect that would have surprised his cabinet colleagues in London – though not his fellow councillors in Birmingham. All three of his wives came from families that were accustomed to playing a public role, and his second wife in particular had a strong private influence on Chamberlain's views and helped to draft his public statements. His relation with Beatrice Potter revealed a man who appreciated the company of a strong and intelligent woman.

Women of the Birmingham elite played a greater role in public life than their sisters in any other part of the country. The fact that, at least at first, so many men in this elite had not been to public school or university meant that the gap between them and their female relatives was less marked than it would have been in other parts of the upper-middle class. The tightness of the family links among the Birmingham elite also gave women a special role. The gulf between home and public life was less sharp when a woman felt comfortable in the houses of half a dozen influential relatives, in which powerful men were likely to be cousins with whom the women had played as children. The migration of the great Birmingham families from the centre of the city to Edgbaston in the early nineteenth century often meant that women were removed from the family business – until this time some of them had lived next door to the factory. But this did not mean a retreat into purely domestic life. Hannah Cadbury, born in 1830, was a 'Lady Guardian' of the poor, her sister Elizabeth (born in 1832) a temperance worker, her sister Sarah (born in 1836) a prison visitor, her sister Caroline (born in 1838) headed the Friends Mission to Syria and her sister Emma (born in 1844) was a pioneer of the Young Women's Christian Association.[42] Indeed, the Cadbury family had their own view of the separate spheres that the sexes should occupy. By the early twentieth century, the great matriarchs of the family, particularly Dame Elizabeth (1858–1951), appeared to be most active in local politics as well as charity and educational work, while their husbands and brothers concentrated on the more mundane matter of making money.

This was a culture that produced assertive women. Chamberlain's eldest son was sent to boarding school partly to get him away from the power of his older sister's personality – though the move does not seem to have imbued much iron into the character of Austen or to have diminished the capacity of his sisters to exercise influence. Neville

Chamberlain still wrote to one of his sisters almost every day when he was Prime Minister.

The civic gospel of Birmingham Nonconformity also offered middle-class women roles outside the home. The attempt by Birmingham women to reform or rescue prostitutes does not seem to have had a great effect on the lives of prostitutes (or women who were on the edge of prostitution), but it did offer those who did the rescuing a chance to display energy and enterprise. Mrs Hallowes visited brothels – always smartly dressed, with a new pair of gloves and a collection of interesting magazines and periodicals – always between 3 p.m. and 4.30, which was, she understood, the time when the women working there had recovered from their labours of the night before but not yet begun to receive clients.[43]

The fact that municipal politics were so important in Birmingham meant that public life often involved issues that were, in the literal sense of the word, domestic. Some women voted in municipal elections before they could vote in parliamentary ones, and in 1880 the 74,600 voters in Birmingham council elections included 10,000 women.[44] The fact that education played such a large part in the politics of Nonconformist Birmingham was important because women were recognized as having a special interest in the welfare of children; the Unitarian Caroline Kenrick succeeded the Quaker Eliza Sturge on the Birmingham School Board in 1876. Women were also elected to the town council in Birmingham. In theory, only unmarried ratepayers were eligible but the returning officer apparently turned a blind eye to this requirement and allowed Mrs Hume Pinsent, who had made her reputation with work concerning the 'feeble minded', to be elected. In 1902, there were twenty-six members of the Birmingham Liberal Association Management Committee. Most of them were businessmen but, almost twenty years before female enfranchisement in national elections, two gave their occupation as 'woman'.[45]

Women of the Birmingham elite sought education for themselves as well as extolling its virtues for the population as a whole. The Ladies Education Association was founded in 1871 and incorporated into the Birmingham Higher Education Association in 1875. Edgbaston High School for Girls was founded the following year. It was so successful that some Birmingham families continued sending their daughters there even in the mid twentieth century, when King Edward's High School for Girls provided an equally good education for free. The Cadbury family were so attached to the school that Adrian Cadbury (born in 1929) was sent there for a short time – presumably to provide him with the intellectual rigour that he was unlikely to get from his subsequent time at Eton. The Birmingham Nonconformists of the nineteenth century would have been delighted that the most famous alumna of Edgbaston High in the twenty-first century should be Malala Yousafzai, who campaigned for girls' education in Pakistan.

Birmingham was a centre of the campaign for women's suffrage. In 1909, the city's Winson Green prison was one of the first places where suffragettes on hunger strike were force fed.[46] Crosskey was a supporter of women's suffrage and presided over the Birmingham Women's Suffrage Society (founded in 1868) for almost the whole period from 1876 to 1890. A male president of a society for female suffrage may seem incongruous to modern eyes but many Birmingham women, especially from Crosskey's own Unitarian congregation, were also active in the society. At a meeting in support of their campaign in Birmingham in 1881, thirteen of the women on the platform, a third of the total, were Unitarians. Crosskey's wife, Hannah, briefly replaced him as president of the society and explained her own politics thus:

> I received my baptism of fire in Manchester when our beloved member John Bright and his illustrious colleague Mr Richard Cobden waged their brilliant crusade against the protectionist Corn Laws. Monster meetings were held in Manchester, largely composed of women, and much of the material help which brought that struggle to its glorious issue was due to the exertions of women.[47]

Much of female involvement in the civic life of Birmingham revolved around campaigns for suffrage or access to education and was sometimes expressed in terms that a modern feminist might recognize. Catherine Osler – a Unitarian who campaigned alongside her husband and parents for female suffrage – wrote:

> It is no more unwomanly for a woman to take part in politics than it is unmanly for a man to nurse a baby. All that is strong and manly we need in the government of a child, and just as much, all that is pure and womanly we need in the government of men.[48]

However, movements that might be seen as anti-feminist could draw Birmingham women into public life as much as those that would now be seen as feminist. Chamberlain's second wife, Florence, was a supporter of female suffrage but Beatrice, Chamberlain's daughter from his first marriage, was an energetic campaigner *against* giving women the vote.* Joseph Chamberlain himself voted in favour of female suffrage when he first became an MP but had reversed his position by the 1880s.[49]

MUNICIPAL POLITICS

Birmingham was strongly associated with Liberalism by the time Chamberlain arrived there in 1854. Party divisions were not always clear-cut, though, and this was particularly so at the local rather than national level. At its foundation in 1865, the Birmingham Liberal Association defined its aims with regard to parliamentary politics and made no reference to municipal affairs. The alliances in the town council often cut across Liberal/Tory divisions.

The important division in the council was not that between Liberals and Tories but that between 'Old Radicals' and the rest. Old Radicals were marked by a reluctance to spend public money, and some associated this with the fact that they tended to represent small businesses – the 'shopocracy': 'in their private lives they were not accustomed to deal with big transactions and high figures ... spending very large sums of money, if proposed, filled the brewer, the baker and the candlestick maker with alarm'.[50] Old Radicals were increasingly in conflict with a different group of notables. These men were often drawn into municipal government by those who preached the civic gospel. Their businesses, though rarely large by national standards, were substantial enough to give them a sense of the benefit that might be derived from investment, and indeed of the way in which municipal investment in education or infrastructure might in the long term bring private profit to Birmingham business. The first of these new men to make an impact was George Dixon (1820–98), a prosperous merchant. He became councillor for Edgbaston in 1863 and was mayor from 1866 to 1867 before entering Parliament in a by-election. Henry Wiggin (1824–1905) was a metal

---

* Joseph's son Austen also campaigned against female suffrage, presumably because his sister had instructed him to do so.

manufacturer who joined the council in 1861 before becoming mayor in 1864. But the rise of men such as Dixon and Wiggin did not instantly disperse the Old Radicals; John Saddler, the leader of the Old Radicals, was elected mayor in 1871.

Joseph Chamberlain played almost no part in political life before the by-election of 1867, in which he spoke in favour of Dixon. Thereafter, he was elected to the council in 1869 and became mayor in 1873. He sought election to Parliament in 1874 (in Sheffield) but failed and was eventually returned unopposed for Birmingham in succession to George Dixon in 1876. Chamberlain was to remain a member of Birmingham Council, as an alderman, until 1880. His period as a member of the council amounted to just eleven years (compared to the thirty-eight that he spent in Parliament) and his time as mayor was only three years (compared to the twenty or so during which he was a commanding figure in national politics). All the same, Chamberlain's period in local government came to be regarded as enormously important. It seemed to anticipate a degree of state intervention that was not to be carried out at national level until after 1945. It was remembered favourably even when Chamberlain's later views (for imperialism or against Irish Home Rule) had become embarrassing.

Under Chamberlain, gas and water companies were bought up by the council. Characteristically he threatened that he would buy the gas company with his own money if the council failed to act. Providing piped water was one of the means by which Chamberlain hoped to persuade people to stop drinking from polluted wells. Drainage in the town was improved. Commentators made much of the way in which, before reform, excrement had piled up in the streets and in the courts around which slum houses were grouped. Chamberlain once said 'sanitary engineering is a hobby of mine', one of those remarks that only he could have made without being laughed at.

Sanitation came to be strongly associated with a certain image of Birmingham and Chamberlain. Ostrogorski wrote in 1893:

> In their minds ideals and the means of attaining them lay confused in a vague sort of way behind the catch-word 'improvement', which they applied to the state as well as to sewers. Amelioration, improvement, progress, liberalism were so many notes which on their lips blended into a single chord.[51]

Some of the manufacturers who were most active in Birmingham politics were associated with the manufacture of brass and hollow metals used in pipes and bathroom fittings. Godfrey Winn, who was born to a family of prosperous businessmen in King's Norton in 1906, recalled his milieu:

> The Midlands in those days, and the environs of Birmingham especially, were full of men of brass. That was the admired thing to be. Not so much a man of property with many acres to your name, as a man of brass. Make your pile, and then indulge in such fancy pursuits as winning prizes for your grapes at horticultural shows, or naming the orchids in your hothouses after each new addition to the family. But you had to be sure of the brass first. While the fact that almost every bathroom in every new house built in the suburbs of Birmingham had at that time the label 'Charles Winn and Co' inscribed upon its taps was in no way a handicap to social grace. On the contrary.[52]

Sometimes it seemed that sewage had become a weapon in a class war between the bourgeoisie on Birmingham Council and the aristocratic landowners in the countryside around the town. Charles Adderley sued Birmingham Corporation on the grounds that the town's sewage works at Saltley was a 'nuisance' to his country house at Ham Hall on the river Tame. He won his case but the dispute rumbled on. Gladstone visited Ham Hall in 1895, by which time he was a bitter enemy of Chamberlain. He later said: 'Ham fills – shall I say – a fragrant place in my recollection.'[53]

The most ambitious of Chamberlain's municipal projects came about when he took advantage of the Artisans' and Labourers' Dwellings Improvement Act of 1875 to buy up property in the centre of the city – ostensibly to clear slums and at the same time build 'a great street, as broad as a Parisian boulevard', to be named Corporation Street. The reconstruction of Birmingham in Chamberlain's time saw a new level of flamboyance in buildings. The architect J.H. Chamberlain (1831–83) had no blood relation to Joseph though the two men became associated in professional terms. J.H. Chamberlain designed public buildings, most notably the Birmingham School of Art, which was completed in 1885. He also built private houses for some of the great Birmingham families – including Chamberlain's house at Highbury. Chamberlain was a disciple of Ruskin, and his style was Venetian Gothic, which underlined the sense that Birmingham embodied a civic spirit present in early modern Italy – though Ruskin himself had complained that Venice was disfigured by 'gas lamps on each side [of the Rialto bridge], in grand new iron posts of the latest Birmingham fashion'.

Municipal achievement under Chamberlain was not all that it appeared. A three-year tenure as mayor was a short time to bring large-scale public works to a conclusion and much was unfinished when he moved the centre of his attention to Westminster in 1876; some of it was still unfinished when he died in 1914. Chamberlain was good at giving an impression of efficacy that was not always matched by concrete achievement. He was also good at denigrating his predecessors and opponents and thus enhancing his own credit. Some felt that burnishing his own image was his principal accomplishment. An article in the Tory *Gazette* in 1874 described the failure to prevent a lethal fire:

> Our corporation is so exclusively political that such small matters as the safety of the lives of the people will always be a secondary matter to passing votes of censure on a Conservative Government. It seems a pity to touch the rates of the borough for any benefit of the inhabitants when they can be so much better employed in the excessive ornamentation of our streets, or in the development of gigantic plans for the glorification of some ambitious politician.[54]

Some of the most impressive features of nineteenth-century Birmingham predated Chamberlain. The town hall was the most striking building in the city centre – though it was a venue for concerts and meetings rather than a hub of local government. A journalist in the 1920s wrote that the building was the 'great thrill' of the city: 'It stands there as if attempting to make up its massive mind to walk down Hill Street and catch the last train back to Rome.'[55] The very classicism of the building revealed that it had been built in the early, rather than the late, nineteenth century. In fact, it dated to 1834 – before Birmingham was incorporated and before Joseph Chamberlain had set foot in the place.

In any case, the plan to redevelop the centre of the town ran into problems that were characteristic of Chamberlain's impetuosity and propensity to seize on any expedient that might help him get what he wanted. The council sought to borrow government money on advantageous terms and to issue compulsory purchase orders, but its capacity to do both hinged on demonstrating that this was a scheme to improve housing for the poor, when it was really just designed to improve the appearance of the town and to provide new commercial opportunities. The council ran into legal difficulties over the purchase. Its proposal to buy only freehold property and to leave leases to expire was successfully challenged in the courts: the scale of its debts was made manageable only by a fall in commercial lending rates in the 1870s. With his usual ebullience Joseph Chamberlain had promised that the rents from the new properties in Corporation Street would make the whole venture profitable, but they did not do so until almost thirty years after his death, by which time his youngest son was Prime Minister.[56]

Chamberlain and his allies were interested in working-class housing but they did not really expect the council itself to provide it. Rather they looked to private construction and to the possibility, made increasingly likely by new means of transport, that working-class people could be moved away from the centre of town altogether. Corporation Street was eventually finished in 1904 but the fact that the council had planned to use money intended for slum clearance to build it always limited their resources. In 1882 the new street was still only half its intended length and Augustus Calthorpe, Chamberlain's opponent in the 1880 parliamentary election, described it, in an uncharacteristically eloquent moment, as a 'crooked abortion'.[57]

The entry of Chamberlain and some of his associates into national rather than municipal politics was due at first to education. The civic gospel preached by the Birmingham ministers laid a heavy emphasis on schooling – Chamberlain himself had taught at the night school attached to the Church of the Messiah. He was also one of the Birmingham industrialists who understood that good schooling might provide them with a more efficient workforce. Most importantly, though, education mattered in Birmingham because it intersected with religion. Dissenters resented the privileges accorded to Anglican schools – though the first politician to mobilize this discontent was George Dixon, an Anglican. Dixon's Birmingham Education Society, which provided funds for educational endeavours, evolved into the Birmingham Education League, established in 1867 to campaign for state provision of education, and which in turn became the National Education League in 1869.[58] The National Education League was designed to be a popular movement but not a democratic one. The council of the League was to contain all

members who were MPs, all who had contributed more than £500 to
its fund and one 'reporter' from each branch. This added up to 300
people. Not surprisingly, the real business of the League was conducted
by an executive committee of forty members – including George Dixon,
Jesse Collings, another of Chamberlain's associates, and John Jaffray,
the proprietor of the *Birmingham Post* – and by an even smaller 'inner
committee', which met once a week. Chamberlain chaired both the
executive committee and the inner committee. Chamberlain and his
immediate family also provided a tenth of all subscriptions to the
League in the years up to 1877. Almost half the forty-nine members of
the executive committee and all the officers came from Birmingham.
Not surprisingly, those from other towns complained that Chamberlain
was 'sole dictator' of the League.[59]

The League became increasingly radical in its opposition to the Elementary Education Bill introduced by the Liberal William Forster in 1870.
The bill created school boards, which would be chosen by election to
administer schools in particular areas. It did not satisfy the League
because it allowed money from the rates to be paid to denominational
schools, which meant in effect that Nonconformist ratepayers would
subsidize Anglican schools. The League's own position shifted too in
that it had begun by campaigning for education to be non-denominational
but moved towards campaigning for it to be entirely secular. Some of
the Birmingham ministers had argued that an education that confined
itself to Bible readings with no denominational bias would simply
encourage scepticism about all religion. Chamberlain himself was on
the way to the complete loss of faith that he would experience in 1875
but this did not prevent him from tormenting schoolteachers with questions about how they would explain particular passages in the Bible.
The League was not successful. It never achieved its aims and its supporters were humiliated when – due to bad management – they failed to
secure control of the Birmingham School Board in 1870, even though
they had obtained more votes than their 'ecclesiastical' opponents.

Parallel to the National Education League ran a more general reorganization of Liberalism in Birmingham. The Birmingham Liberal
Association (BLA) was established in 1865. The novelty of the BLA
became apparent as it sought to live with the consequences of the 1867
Reform Bill, which had extended the franchise and increased the number of parliamentary seats granted to Birmingham from two to three. In

a bid to preserve some presence for the weaker party in those boroughs with three seats, each voter in them was given two votes. The hope was that supporters of the most popular party, which in practice meant the Liberals, would give both their votes to the most popular Liberal candidate and thus allow the Conservative to secure the third seat by concentrating their votes on a single candidate. Liberal organizers sought to counteract this with a new level of organization. They created a 'caucus' in which voters were instructed on which candidate they should vote for in order to give the greatest chance of securing all three Birmingham seats for Liberals. This also meant creating a large committee to endorse candidates – though it was so large that it became unwieldy. In practice, the caucus, like the National Education League, was directed by a smaller inner group.

The power of the Birmingham Liberal Association was greatly enhanced by the work of William Harris (1826–1911), an architect and journalist who served as the Association's first secretary, and Francis Schnadhorst (1840–1900), a draper who succeeded him. The latter in particular displayed an extraordinary capacity for organization. When Randolph Churchill failed in his attempt to win a seat in Birmingham in 1885, he attributed his defeat to 'the dark and evil deeds of Mr Schnadhorst'. Characteristically, Chamberlain presented the Birmingham Liberal machine as a model to be imitated by Liberals across the country. In 1877, the first meeting of the National Liberal Federation was held in Birmingham and addressed by Gladstone – the glass roof of the Bingley Hall was dismantled to enable the audience of 30,000 to breathe. The Federation's early history was dominated by Birmingham men. It was chaired first by William Harris (from 1877 to 1882) and then by William Kenrick (from 1882 to 1886). Its first treasurer was John Skirrow Wright (1822–80), who had been chairman of the Birmingham Liberal Association from 1868.

The consistent theme in Joseph Chamberlain's career as a national politician was inconsistency. This became clear after the Third Reform Bill of 1884. The Bill enfranchised rural householders and this expanded the electorate to include about 60 per cent of the male population. It had particularly dramatic consequences in Ireland. At first, the House of Lords looked minded to reject the Bill and this had provoked Chamberlain to talk of confrontation between people and peers. The following year, another law redistributed seats and abolished most multi-member constituencies. This meant that Birmingham ceased to be a single constituency that elected three MPs. Instead it was divided into seven constituencies, each of which elected one. Chamberlain took care that the arrangement of Birmingham constituencies suited the Liberals and he was himself, from then on, a candidate in West Birmingham.

Chamberlain also launched an 'unauthorized programme', so called because it went beyond the stated aims of Gladstone, his party leader. The programme entailed: free primary education; full local government for the counties; 'home rule all round', by which was meant home rule for the constituent parts of the Empire; a graduated tax system; land reform that would make the acquisition of small rural property easier; disestablishment of the Church of England; universal manhood suffrage and the payment of Members of Parliament.

The programme enraged the aristocratic Whig faction in the Liberal Party but it was not as dramatic as it seemed. Much of it had already been presented, more discreetly, through articles in the *Fortnightly Review*, a couple of years earlier. Chamberlain distinguished between immediate objectives, such as the provision of free primary education, and more distant ones, such as disestablishment of the Church of England; by this time he was sufficiently reconciled with the established Church to educate his own sons at Anglican institutions. A writer for the *Wolverhampton Express and Star* captured the ambiguities of Chamberlain's position well:

> Radicalism is not a formulated principle or group of principles. It does not admit of codification. It has no necessarily unchanging principles in the ordinary acceptation of the term. It acknowledges in politics that government should be 'by the people, of the people and for the people', and it asks the popular vote to interpret that principle, and then it demands all of practical embodiment that interpretation admits of.[60]

Chamberlain's call for the redistribution of land in a way that might provide every resident of the countryside with 'three acres and a cow' was designed to appeal to agricultural labourers who had just been enfranchised. Some found it incongruous that Chamberlain – who was so strongly associated with a city – should have concerned himself with such matters. Perhaps, though, Chamberlain's radicalism sprang precisely from the fact that his view was so urban. His idea of property was rooted in the leasehold houses of Edgbaston and the factories of

Smethwick. He could not understand the emotional charge that the aristocracy might attach to their own inherited lands. This was also a time when Chamberlain seemed most violently opposed to the aristocracy. He talked of a class who 'do not toil nor do they spin', and in one of his most explosive moments asked, during a speech in Birmingham in January 1885: 'what ransom will property pay for the security that it enjoys?' It was a typical Chamberlain formulation. Thinking in terms of economic interest came naturally to him and his own business career had often been based on demanding that other enterprises pay a ransom to avoid his savage competition. All the same, the phrase, which appeared to imply the prospect of violence, aroused indignation in much of the political class.

Chamberlain served briefly in the government that Gladstone formed after his electoral victory of 1885. But the two men, and eventually their party, were divided by the proposals that Gladstone put forward for Home Rule in Ireland, proposals that would have devolved power to a separate Parliament in Dublin, leaving Westminster with control of foreign and military policy. Chamberlain resigned from the government in March 1886. His resignation placed him in an odd position. His allies in opposing Home Rule for Ireland were the Conservatives and the aristocratic Whigs in the Liberal Party – people with whom he had little in common and who had been offended by his unauthorized programme the previous year. He had written recently in private that he would 'do anything and everything that may be disagreeable to the Whigs'.[61] He was now part of a Liberal faction of whom the other leading member was Lord Hartingdon, the heir to the Duke of Devonshire.

Why did Chamberlain care about Ireland so much that he was willing to throw his party into confusion and risk his own political career? Birmingham did not have a very large Irish population and this population had diminished in the years leading up to 1886. It may be because of this that Chamberlain was late in appreciating the significance that Ireland would assume for British politics. For most of his career, he had expressed a vague sympathy for the Irish desire to enjoy greater political autonomy and he had sought in office to expand and centralize the power of local councils in Ireland. The branch of Nonconformist Protestantism to which he belonged was not anti-Catholic – though it had often exasperated Catholics with its condescension towards them. Chamberlain's disagreement with Gladstone was framed in quite narrow terms at first. He claimed that he feared the damage that would be done to imperial unity if Irish MPs withdrew from the Westminster Parliament.

Perhaps Chamberlain's position on Home Rule for Ireland owed more to personal considerations than he would have cared to admit. The majority of Liberal leaders – especially the aristocratic Whigs – could not rival Chamberlain for dynamism or charisma. Gladstone could. Chamberlain had already sought to distinguish himself from Gladstone in the early 1870s through education. His private correspondence suggested that he tried to do the same with Home Rule in 1886. Initially, he anticipated either that Gladstone's proposal would fail and that the Prime Minister would therefore be forced to resign, or that Gladstone would succeed and then take an honourable retirement. Chamberlain was not quite fifty at the moment of his resignation and had been in Parliament for a decade; Gladstone was seventy-six and had been in Parliament for over fifty years. It was reasonable to assume that the future belonged to the former rather than the latter. Opposition to Home Rule would not have affected Chamberlain's long-term relations with the Liberal Party if the issue had been resolved quickly one way or the other. As it was, Home Rule remained a central issue in British politics until the First World War and Gladstone remained the central figure in the Liberal Party until 1894.

The National Liberal Federation, which he had done so much to create, did not follow Chamberlain in his break with Gladstone and Schnadhorst remained with the Gladstonians. Many assumed that the two factions of the Liberal Party would reunite. Indeed, some of those loyal to Chamberlain – notably the Nonconformist minister Robert Dale – were keen that the Liberal Party should not be divided. Chamberlain formed a National Radical Union, a move that was designed to mark his distance from the Whig Unionists, who had formed a Liberal Unionist Council, as much as his distance from the Gladstonian Liberals. However, negotiations designed to reunite the Liberal Party failed in early 1887. The Birmingham Liberal Association's formal split came in March 1888, and the following month Chamberlain formed the Birmingham Liberal Unionist Association. Liberal Unionism was significant because it worked in close alliance with the Conservatives – to such an extent that it was eventually to blend into the Conservative Party. In 1885, Birmingham had returned seven MPs, of whom one described himself as 'Labour-Liberal' and six described themselves as 'Liberal'. The following year, it returned one Conservative and six Liberal Unionists. No orthodox Liberal would win a Birmingham seat again until 1969. As for the Labour Party, which began to replace the Liberal Party after the First World War, its advance was slower in Birmingham than elsewhere. The effect of all this was that an industrial city, with a primarily working-class population, would elect mainly or exclusively MPs who were, in practical terms, Conservatives for the whole period from 1886 until the Second World War.

Why did Birmingham follow Chamberlain? There was no obvious reason why the electorate of the town should have been particularly moved by the question of Home Rule. Indeed, one might have expected the strength of Unionism to come in those places – particularly Glasgow and Liverpool – where large Irish populations were matched by a strong movement of Orange politics. There was neither in Birmingham. There had been anti-Irish riots (the Murphy riots) in 1867 but there was no sense that these fitted into a longer-term political project. In fact, some of those who stayed loyal to the Gladstonian party in Birmingham did not support Home Rule and sometimes expressed their mystification that it should have become considered so important – in 1906, the Birmingham Liberals issued a pamphlet entitled 'Home Rule: Who Raised the Issue?'[62]

Chamberlain benefited from discreet Conservative support, or at least from a willingness on the part of Conservatives not to challenge his candidates in Birmingham. Chamberlain's personal appeal partly underlay his success in bringing Birmingham over with him. He also benefited from the family links of the Birmingham elite. His own family followed him, as did the Kenricks and most of the Martineaus. One critic claimed that Chamberlain led the party of 'his brothers, his brothers-in-law, his whips and his henchmen'.[63] The Beale family were mainly Gladstonian Liberals and Sir William Beale stood against the Unionist candidate in the Central Birmingham by-election of 1889. The Cadbury family remained loyal to Gladstonian Liberalism but even they were muted in their criticism of Chamberlain. George Cadbury gave discreet help to a Gladstonian candidate in North Worcestershire but avoided direct confrontation with the Liberal Unionists in Birmingham itself.

Chamberlain's eventual recognition that reconciliation with the

Gladstonian Liberals was impossible meant accepting that he would have to work in alliance with the Conservatives. In 1895, he accepted office in Lord Salisbury's administration. The ministry he asked for and obtained was that of the colonies. It marked another departure in his career. Up until this stage, his political concerns had seemed primarily domestic. He was later to suggest that his experience of Empire had placed these concerns in a new perspective:

> When you are 6,000 miles away from the House of Commons, it is perfectly extraordinary how events and discussions and conflict present themselves in different – I think I may even say in truer – proportion. You are excited at home about an Education Bill – about Temperance Reform – about local finance. But these things matter no more to South Africa, to Canada, to Australia than their local affairs matter to you. On the other hand, everything that touches Imperial policy, everything which affects their interest as well as yours, has for them, as it ought to have for us, a supreme importance.[64]

The departure was not as radical as it first seemed. Chamberlain had been interested in Empire even when a member of the Liberal Party – he had been much influenced by the historian John Seeley's book *The Expansion of England* that was published in 1883. It was a concern for imperial unity that partly underlay his opposition to Irish Home Rule. In addition to this, his vision of Empire was a curiously domestic one. The exoticism of India seems to have moved him little. He was primarily concerned with the settler colonies and almost exclusively with their white populations. His biographer wrote contemptuously of his predecessors as 'negrophilist pedants'[65] and no one could have accused Chamberlain of being sympathetic to the indigenous inhabitants of Africa.

The Colonial Office was the Birmingham of government departments – relatively new and unglamorous. Unlike the Chancellor of the Exchequer or the Foreign Secretary, the Colonial Secretary was required to involve himself in the details of administration rather than just the Olympian heights of policy – there were numerous letters to be signed and appointments to be agreed. Chamberlain modernized the department itself and his admirers regarded it as typical of him that he installed electricity to light the offices.[66] There were times when it looked as if his vision of Empire was a constellation of Birminghams, in which hard-working men made their own way. This was a world without aristocracy or ancient universities and one in which the power of the established Church was more limited than in England. Chamberlain had no interest in the societies that might have preceded white settlers and he valued Empire because of the sense that a world was being built from scratch. It often seemed that the modernity of this world was like that of a Victorian city. Chamberlain cared about trade, railways, telegraph lines, sewers and the treatment of tropical disease. Characteristically, he once tried to ensure that the profits derived from the Suez Canal should be spent on imperial projects – rather as he had once spent the profits of the Birmingham Gas Department on municipal improvement. His Empire was that of the office rather than the explorer and he sometimes seemed disdainful of the men of 'rough fibre' to be found in outstations.[67]

The Empire was changing in this period in ways that particularly attracted Chamberlain's attention. Economic possibilities, most spectacularly diamond mines in South Africa, came into view. But it was also increasingly clear that exploiting such resources was going to require new levels of spending – particularly in the provision of transport. The Boer War in South Africa between 1899 and 1902 was a product of imperialism, but the expense incurred because of the conflict provided a new incentive to exploit imperial resources. Enoch Powell, born in Birmingham in 1912 and intermittently fascinated by Joseph Chamberlain, was later to say that

[T]he British Empire, as we know it ... was an invention ... invented at a specific time, definable to within a very few years: and if it be an exaggeration to ascribe the invention to one person alone, there is one person who has as good rights in the matter as most of those who take out patents ...

The Colonial Secretary of the day was a specialist in 'unauthorized programme', and this one the Tory party had to adopt, because they needed the support of that same Colonial Secretary and of the Liberal Unionists whom he brought into their camp.[68]

Empire led Chamberlain to a break in his career, which was also a break in British politics. In 1903, he spoke in favour of tariff reform that would give Britain preferential trading relations with the colonies but impose barriers to imports from other countries – which meant particularly Germany. He attempted to present this policy as fitting with a tradition that earlier Liberals might have recognized but he also talked of a 'Birmingham School' of economics that differed from the 'Manchester School' of unrestricted free trade. Perhaps tariffs coincided with some Birmingham interests because the city's engineering industries were particularly threatened by foreign competition. Perhaps, too, tariffs fitted with a wider view – prone to place the interests of industry above the rigid operation of a free market – that had produced the currency reformers earlier in the century. It would, however, be hard to argue that Chamberlain's support for tariff reform was simply a reflection of the interests of Birmingham industry. The *Birmingham Post* had supported Chamberlain when he broke with Gladstone over Home Rule but followed his move on tariffs only in 1905, after Chamberlain's allies had managed to evict the editor. George Dixon, the MP for Edgbaston, died in 1898, but it is hard to believe that he could have supported tariffs since one of his objections to Irish Home Rule was the belief that an independent Irish Parliament might abandon free trade.[69]

Chamberlain himself had opposed tariffs in the days when he had been an active businessman because his experience in dealing with American competition convinced him that they were unnecessary. The Kenricks – the Birmingham industrialists who were so closely connected to Chamberlain – remained strong supporters of free trade. In the short term this might have been because ironware proved to be one of the few industries in the Midlands that survived the late Victorian economic downturn well (Kenrick exports peaked shortly before the First World War). But the Kenricks continued to be free traders even when their own business declined and even after their cousin (Joseph Chamberlain's son Neville) had finally moved the country away from free trade in 1932. On a visit to the Birmingham Chamber of Commerce in 1960, Harold Macmillan was amused by the fact that W.E. Kenrick made a 'reactionary, witty, "laissez-faire" kind of speech'.[70]

The Cadbury family also remained committed to free trade and opposed to Chamberlain's vision of Empire. George Cadbury bought the *Daily News* in 1901 partly to provide a paper that would oppose the Boer War and support free trade. Though there was never a direct political confrontation between Chamberlain and Cadbury in Birmingham, there was a legal case – in effect, a political battle. A Conservative newspaper, *The Standard*, accused the Cadbury family of hypocrisy because they took cocoa from parts of Portuguese Africa that were cultivated by labourers who enjoyed so little freedom that they might as well have been slaves. The Cadburys brought a libel action that involved the most celebrated and politically engaged barristers of the day – Edward Carson (who had cross-examined Oscar Wilde to devastating effect and who was to become one of the most aggressive spokesmen for Ulster Unionism) represented the defendants. On the Cadbury side were Rufus Isaacs and Sir John Simon (both soon to be appointed as Liberal law officers before going on to grander offices). Cadbury won his libel action – though the Birmingham jury awarded only a farthing in damages.[71]

The reasons for Joseph Chamberlain's conversion were national and political more than local and economic. He wanted to strengthen the Empire, he hoped (without much reason as it turned out) that tariffs might provide a means of financing social reform. The fact that tariff reform was sure to enrage the Whig aristocrats was certainly no disadvantage in Chamberlain's eyes. Above all, he was simply a man who needed new and dramatic causes. His taste for drama was illustrated in the celebrations of 1906 in Birmingham that marked his seventieth birthday. There was a parade of eighty motor cars (a harbinger of the role that these vehicles would play in Birmingham for the rest of the century), a banquet and speeches. Chamberlain spoke fondly of his adopted city. He also justified the frequent changes in his own political position. 'People talk of a change in opinion as if it were a disgrace. To me it is a sign of life. If you are alive you must change. It is only the dead who remain the same.'[72] A few days after this speech (and perhaps as a result of the strain that the celebrations had inflicted on him), Chamberlain suffered a severe stroke. He survived but was paralysed.

Paralysis struck Chamberlain (and his associates) in a political as well as literal sense. The politics of the family and of those who regarded themselves as Chamberlain's heirs became frozen around the last of the causes that their master had adopted: tariff reform. The authorized biography of Joseph Chamberlain seemed to symbolize the crushing weight that the old man imposed on his successors. Leo Amery, the Unionist MP for Birmingham South, was the first to be approached, in 1915, to write the biography but proved too busy. The task was then taken up by James Louis Garvin, editor of the *Observer*, but he did not produce his first volume until 1932. Garvin finally abandoned the work in 1946, having written four volumes. The last volume (entirely devoted to the tariff reform campaign) was produced by Julian Amery (the son of Leo) in 1969.

During the last years of his life, Joseph Chamberlain was often represented by his oldest son, Austen, who had been in the cabinet since 1902 and was Chancellor of the Exchequer from October 1903. Austen was placed in an impossible position since his father expected him to put filial loyalty above the collective responsibility that he owed to his ministerial colleagues. In spite of the fact that Austen was a milder character than his father – or perhaps because of it – this was a period in which the Conservatives sometimes seemed particularly hostile to the Chamberlain family, and this was often expressed with reference to Birmingham. Lord Salisbury wrote in 1910 that Birmingham meant 'the caucus and the wire-pullers – and what is called the discipline of party'.[73] The Conservative journalist and MP Thomas Gibson Bowles claimed of Austen that 'another Birmingham mind ... would run an Empire on the principles of the retail trade'.[74] Balfour said that 'Birmingham influence ... was pursuing things which by no stretch of the imagination can be described as Conservative'. Not surprisingly Garvin (the journalist closest to the Chamberlains) thought that a 'curious lot of old Tory and Anglican feeling against Birmingham and Unitarianism was coming out'.[75]

Joseph's younger brother Arthur was one of the many members of the family who sometimes sought to save Joseph Chamberlain from the consequences of his own impetuousness. Arthur was an early proponent of systematic management, and helped to establish the influential department of commerce at Mason College, the institution that later became Birmingham University. He wrote a 'Book of Business' in 1899, which was privately printed and circulated to his own family. It contained a sentence that summed up the problems that Joseph Chamberlain created for his associates. A well-run business, Arthur wrote, was one that 'can support the unexpected absence of the principal'.

Workers at a Birmingham pen factory. One of the problems of interpretations of nineteenth-century Birmingham that emphasize benign relations between masters and men is that they ignore that substantial proportion of the working population who were not adult men. Many workers in pen factories were women and two of Birmingham's largest fortunes – those of Josiah Mason and Joseph Gillott – partly derived from their labour.

5

Classes without Conflict? Social Relations in Birmingham in the Long Nineteenth Century

If Engels had lived not in Manchester but in Birmingham, his conception of 'class' and his theories of the role of class in history might have been very different.

Asa Briggs, *Victorian Cities*, 1963

Asa Briggs summed up a social interpretation of nineteenth-century Birmingham and a provocative suggestion of how that interpretation might challenge the most influential analysis of society advanced in the nineteenth century. Four things underlay Briggs's analysis. First, 'the exceptional elasticity to the trade of the town' that came from the diversity of trades practised there. Second, the multiplicity of small workshops rather than large factories, which meant that 'Relations between "masters" and "men" were close . . . if not always good.' Third, a high proportion of workers in Birmingham were 'skilled and therefore well-off economically'. This in turn meant that there was less fear of women and children's work, more dependence on friendly societies rather than trade unions and an emphasis on education. Finally, there was a high level of social mobility 'or at least considerable local optimism about the prospects of "rising in society"'.[1]

Briggs was a work of social history in himself. Born to a comparatively humble family in Yorkshire in 1921, he died as a member of the House of Lords in 2016. Close to Denis Healey, whom he had known since they were schoolboys, and Roy Jenkins, with whom he served in the war, Briggs supported the right-wing of the Labour Party. He believed in 'progress' while opposing Marxism and assumed that social mobility, especially associated with education, would go with political

consensus. These qualities meant that he fitted neatly into British, perhaps especially Birmingham, politics in the early 1950s – though he
never lived in the city and does not seem to have been specially
attached to it. He was not the first person to identify peculiarities in its
society and he drew on earlier writers. The Franco-Russian political
scientist Moisei Ostrogorski had sought to explain the harmonious
class relations that he associated with the hegemony of Chamberlainite Liberalism:

> [O]f all the great manufacturing cities Birmingham possessed conditions
> the most favourable for the establishment of such relations. Thanks to the
> special character of its industrial life, Birmingham did not exhibit in clear
> contrast and opposition the immense fortunes of employers and the mis-
> ery of the manufacturing proletariat; it did not have the 'two nations'
> spoken of in Disraeli's *Sybil*.[2]

Ostrogorski drew on the writing of Léon Faucher, who was to become
first minister of France and had discerned in Birmingham during the
1840s:

> [A]n industrial democracy within a vast city, this being true even in
> the workshops where steam is the motive power. While in Great Brit-
> ain fortunes tend to concentrate, in Birmingham they are distributed more
> and more. Industry in this city, like agriculture in France, is subdivided
> among many small enterprises ... This form of industrial organization is
> connected with the nature of the occupations pursued. At Birmingham
> labour is wholly manual. Machines are used as aids in manufacturing, but
> everything depends on the skill and intelligence of the workman.[3]

Similarly, Alexis de Tocqueville wrote in 1835:

> At Manchester a few great capitalists, thousands of poor workmen and
> little middle class. At Birmingham, few large industries, many small
> industrialists. At Manchester workmen are counted by the thousand, two
> or three thousand in the factories. At Birmingham, the workers work in
> their own houses or in little workshops in company with the master him-
> self. At Manchester there is above all need for women and children. At
> Birmingham, particularly men, few women.[4]

Briggs, Faucher and Tocqueville were all influenced by the first author
to write about Birmingham in a systematic way: William Hutton, who

published his history of the city in 1781. His vision revolved around the notion of social mobility. He was proud of his own rise from humble origins and regarded Birmingham as a place in which such transformations, and also spectacular social decline, were common.

Simply citing these authors draws attention to some problems. For one thing, the presentation of Manchester as a city of large-scale industry with which Birmingham can be contrasted is not one that many recent historians would recognize. In this context, the problem is not that Engels ignored Birmingham – he had read Faucher's work on the city – but that he misunderstood Manchester. Ostrogorski and Faucher made only relatively brief visits to Birmingham. Both presented the city in terms that were designed to support broader interpretations of English society. Both were artists of the still life. Neither paid much attention to change over time or the possibility that the industrial activity they admired might itself have wrought long-term social and economic changes. Hutton's work on Birmingham was more of an essay in interpretation, with a good deal of focus on his own time, rather than a narrative. In any case, the first edition of his book was written before the industrial growth of the city.

The very range of Briggs's interests contributed to a curiously static interpretation of nineteenth-century Birmingham. His ideas were expounded as though the Birmingham of the period after 1865 (of which he wrote the official history) was much the same as that of the 1820s and 30s, on which he had done most of his primary research. His work contributed to the sense that Birmingham had a single social character across the whole of the period stretching from the late eighteenth century, as described by Hutton, through the 1830s and 40s, described by Faucher and Tocqueville, and the 1880s, described by Ostrogorski, until the First World War.

ECONOMIC STRUCTURE

Briggs was right to say that there was an 'elasticity of trade' in Birmingham in the sense that the town did not depend on a single industry and that consequently it enjoyed a degree of protection from certain kinds of downturns. In the mid nineteenth century, directories listed a little over 200 trades practised in Sheffield and around 500 in Birmingham.

The latter included manufacturers of artificial limbs, billiard tables and dog-collars.[5] Change over time was important. The Birmingham economy did not simply swing from a trade when it turned down and then swing back again as it recovered. Rather, the metalworking trades that were so important in the town (what would have been called 'toy' manufacture in the late eighteenth century and 'light engineering' in the twentieth) were flexible. They depended on skills that could easily be transferred from one industry to another and lent themselves to changes that fitted in with the more general evolution of the British economy. For example, when the buckle trade, in which his father had made his money, collapsed in the late eighteenth century, Edward Thomason moved into the manufacture of tokens and medals. One should stress, however, that Birmingham's flexibility and diversity of manufacture contrasted more sharply with those small towns of the North that revolved entirely around textile manufacture than it did with Manchester.

What of the suggestion that the Birmingham economy was dominated by a 'multiplicity of small workshops'? Judging by census returns, in which employers were asked to say how many people worked in their enterprises, during the second half of the nineteenth century, Birmingham apparently had fewer large enterprises than Manchester; both cities had more large enterprises per head of population than the country as a whole. But the difference was not as marked as one might suppose from much contemporary writing on the topic. In 1871, there were more businesses employing four or fewer people in Manchester than in Birmingham and more employing five to nineteen in Birmingham than in Manchester. In both cities, the average size of enterprise increased across time. Eventually, there were more businesses employing between 250 and 499 workers in Birmingham than in Manchester – though the latter still dominated among enterprises that employed more than 500.

Table 1. Firms by Number of Employees in Birmingham and Manchester, 1851–81

No of employees	1851		1861		1871		1881	
	Birmingham	Manchester	Birmingham	Manchester	Birmingham	Manchester	Birmingham	Manchester
1	358	267	349	230	204	212	384	327
2–4	768	570	712	566	495	537	949	883
5–9	375	272	417	316	340	301	596	477
10–19	248	140	250	215	203	191	397	287
20–49	183	89	177	133	179	153	344	212
50–99	51	19	58	37	73	60	130	84
100–199	21	13	22	22	29	34	55	52
200–249	3	2	7	4	12	5	3	15
250–499	4	4	5	21	11	8	32	22
500+	5	5	3	14	3	15	8	15
Total	2016	1381	2000	1558	1549	1516	2898	2374

Source: Harry Smith, Robert J. Bennett and Carry van Lieshout, 'Entrepreneurship in Birmingham and Manchester, 1851–1911: A Tale of Two Cities?', *Midland History*, 45, 3 (2020) pp. 357–80

The number of large enterprises increased further in the late nineteenth century, and by 1914 the largest firms were all incorporated companies. At this point the largest Birmingham companies were as follows:

Table 2. Size of Largest Companies in Birmingham in 1914 by Number of Employees

Name of company	Number of workers
Cadburys (chocolate)	6,000
Dunlops (tyres)	4,000
Austin Motors	2,000
Nettlefolds (screws)	3,000
Buttons	2,000
Elkingtons (electro-plating)	2,000
Perry and Co (pens)	1,500
Metro Railway Carriage (rolling stock)	1,100
Brown, Marshalls and Co (carriage works)	1,100

Source: Eric Hopkins, 'Industrial Change and Life at Work in Birmingham 1850–1914', *Midland History*, 27, 1 (2002), pp. 112–29

The most spectacular novelty of the Birmingham economy at the beginning of the twentieth century sprang from the rapid growth of the industry that would come to dominate Birmingham: motor manufacture. Herbert Austin arrived in Birmingham at the age of thirty-five in 1901 to work at the Wolseley plant. Austin was an engineer who had, while working in Australia, become associated with Wolseley's sale of agriculture machinery. In 1905, he broke with Wolseley and founded his own company to make motor cars in a former print works at Longbridge, which was then still outside the city limits. He employed fifty people and had sold twelve cars by the end of 1906. By 1914, he was running a publicly quoted company that employed 2,000.

In spite of Ostrogorski's argument quoted above that the power of Chamberlain rested on the predominance of small businesses, Chamberlain and his political allies were industrialists who operated on a relatively large scale and often defined themselves in contrast to the 'shopocracy' they had displaced from the town council. Chamberlain was explicit about the way in which he thought Birmingham was changing. In 1866, he recognized that Birmingham industry fifty years previously had been 'more like the chamber masters of London than the great manufacturers of Leeds or Manchester'. Now, however, a

> revolution . . . is taking place in the principal hardware trades, and . . . is assimilating the town to the great seats of manufacture in the North, and depriving it of its special characteristic, viz, the number of its small manufacturers, which has hitherto influenced its social and commercial prosperity as well as its politics.[6]

The proportion of owners of large businesses on the Birmingham Council was larger in 1892 than ever before. Thereafter it declined slightly – mainly because the expansion of the city brought in areas in which those with small businesses were powerful.[7]

Studying the size of businesses and the implications of that size is harder than it seems. Large factories attracted the interest of competitors, clients and even foreign tourists. Their owners provided evidence to official enquiries, and by the end of the century they were subject to formal inspection. They took out insurance policies that required them to state the value of their property. Even so, simple questions about how many people such enterprises employed could be hard to answer and it was not always obvious that the owners themselves knew, which means that the census data itself may be open to question. The Kenricks founded a company that lasted until the twenty-first century and were noted for careful organization of their accounts. But the company's historian, writing in 1968, had to depend on the recorded memories of a single employee to estimate how many people the company employed during its first years of existence. He thought that eighty to one hundred men worked for the company in the early nineteenth century and that this increased to 'between 250 and 400', 'though, in 1836, a year of booming activity, it is likely that an even larger number may have received payment on account of production'. We reach firm ground only in the 1870s when the company employed about 700.[8]

Small businesses, by contrast, were hardly likely to keep records of any kind. Many of them existed in private houses or in some small corner of residential property – 'garret masters' were seen as particularly characteristic of Birmingham. Given that children were sometimes used as porters and messengers, it is possible that bigger companies had only a vague idea about the scale or whereabouts of their subcontractors. Such businesses could live or die without leaving any legacy except memories among those who had worked there or who had lived in their vicinity.

Small workshops – for example, in the gun trade – could be part of an integrated system of mass production as components were moved from one shop to the next. Equally, the 'factory' might encompass many different kinds of unit within its walls. Complicated systems of sub-contracting operated inside companies. 'Masters' might be rewarded according to how much they produced and were left free to hire their own labour and engage their own apprentices. A subcontractor might operate inside a factory that belonged to someone else. An official enquiry of 1843 reported: 'Many superior workmen also become small masters by renting from a manufacturer a part of his shop, each of whom employs a certain number of Adults and Children, occasionally as many as fifty.'[9]

Kenricks provides a sense of how things worked – though also a sense of how limited the sources can be. Some employees were paid by the day, others at piece rates. The works were partitioned into shops. These were divided by function, but at first sometimes also identified by the name of subcontractors who paid their own assistants. In 1814, there was Aaron's shop, Wright's shop, Steven's shop, etc. However, Kenricks was relatively centralized by Birmingham standards. Apprentices were hired directly by the company rather than by each individual master and the company employed foremen who exercised some control over the pieceworkers.[10] In other Birmingham firms, pieceworkers rented their shops and equipment so that they were effectively running autonomous businesses within a larger factory.

A SKILLED AND PROSPEROUS WORKING CLASS?

The belief that Birmingham was characterized by its numerous small businesses often went with the belief that its working class had a special quality. Briggs suggests that it was characterized by high levels of skill and high wages. For him, much production in Birmingham still depended on the practised manipulation of tools rather than the raw power of steam engines, and this meant that workers had a high degree of autonomy and power over their own wages and working conditions. The implied contrast is again with Manchester, where large factories employed unskilled, poorly paid hands, many of whom were women.

It is true that, at least in the early part of the nineteenth century, unskilled workers seemed to constitute a relatively small part of the Birmingham population. One might add that Birmingham contained a small but significant Irish minority – it was at its nineteenth-century peak in 1861 when the Irish-born made up just under 4 per cent of the town's population.[11] The Irish were mainly poor and largely concentrated in labouring occupations. They were crowded into particular quarters and often described by the authorities as criminal, dirty and prone to spread disease. Some of them spoke no English. The division between a 'respectable' and 'non-respectable' working class often overlapped with the division between the English and the Irish, and this may have made it easier for observers to ignore the latter.

Even as far as the English-born and relatively well-off workers were concerned, the implications of their good fortune could be complicated. Skill and prosperity might go with a desire for respectability and self-improvement. It might, though, equally go with insubordination by workers who knew that they were too valuable to sack. Men who earned money with relative ease might choose to spend it on hard drinking rather than saving to set themselves up in business. The persistence of rough sports in Birmingham suggested a working-class culture that rebelled against the values of the urban middle class, even if it did not do so in a way that implied political radicalism. The Fighting Cocks pub in Moseley was first recorded as a venue for sporting contest between 'Gentlemen of Worcestershire and Gentlemen of Warwickshire' on Boxing Day 1759; in the 1980s it would become a venue for earnest punk bands. Cock-fighting and bear-baiting survived in the city until driven underground by legislation in 1836. Many employers complained that their workers would put in long hours for much of the week when they needed to earn money but then observe 'Saint Monday' while they slept off hangovers. In the late eighteenth century, even such a large employer as Matthew Boulton could not prevent his men from taking Monday off. In 1855, an old man recalled the Birmingham workers of his youth in colourful terms:

They lived like the inhabitants of Spain, or after the custom of the Orientals. Three or four in the morning found them at work. At noon they rested, many enjoyed their siesta; others spent their time in workshops eating and drinking, these places often being turned into taprooms and the apprentices into pot boys.[12]

Working hours became more regular in large enterprises in the late nineteenth century but small employers might still find that their skilled workers took Monday off.

Walter Allen (born in 1911) was the son and grandson of Birmingham workers. His paternal grandfather had been a metal worker, illiterate and a hard drinker who had regularly taken Monday off and regularly been sacked on Tuesday. His skill was so great, though, that he was invariably rehired on Wednesday. Allen added: 'He was – naturally – I am tempted to say, a Radical and Mr Gladstone was the only God he recognized.' Allen's father was also a skilled worker though with more education – he had a year of grammar school that had given him the elements of Latin. In his youth, he was a member of the Independent Labour Party.[13] Walter recognized his background as one that bred intense class consciousness, but suggested that there were at least three different ways in which consciousness might manifest itself. It might, as in the case of his grandfather, involve an ostentatiously 'non-respectable' rebellion against the discipline that an employer sought to impose – though the grandfather combined this with the more formal, and usually 'respectable', politics of Gladstonianism. As in the case of his father, it might involve a formal political organization by men who were relatively educated and 'respectable'. Finally, class consciousness might involve seeking the independence that went with owning one's own workshop – which one of Walter Allen's uncles did. In an autobiographical novel, Walter Allen suggested that, far from being a source of harmonious class relations, the predominance of small workshops might be a product of acrimonious ones:

I cannot see how any working man, brought up in the kind of society in which I was reared, could fail to be class-conscious. It is as plain to me now as it was fifty years ago that my boss – any man who employs me, whom I am dependent on – is my enemy; he stands in my way; his power curbs me and robs me of my freedom of choice. So my ambition was always to escape his domination. I wanted to be my own boss. I mean just that: I did not want to be anyone else's.[14]

Skill was declining by the end of the century. Traditionally, Birmingham was a town without guilds. Consequently, formal apprenticeships were comparatively rare and this may have made the shift away from skilled work easier (though perhaps also less well recorded) than it would have been in other places. Boys seem to have been increasingly attracted to the short-term earning they might acquire from working with machines rather than the skills they might acquire from learning a trade. Hand-operated devices (such as those for stamping) might remove skill from production even before the arrival of power-operated machinery. By 1896, one observer believed that there were fewer than twelve apprentice plumbers and fifty apprentice bricklayers in the whole city. He added that among iron founders 'few are born here', and it may be that such skilled trades as survived in Birmingham did so largely by importing adult workers who had served apprenticeships elsewhere.[15]

By the end of the nineteenth century, if not before, social hierarchies had become more complicated in ways that undermined a simple division between skilled and unskilled. At the top of the hierarchy were those workers with regular and reasonably well-paid employment whose style of life often resembled that of white-collar employees, but there were also people whose lives revolved around insecure employment, frequent changes of lodging and, when they happened to have money, heavy drinking. One resident of Sparkbrook described a subtly graded social hierarchy that was based on streets and types of houses rather than employment as such (though clearly there was a close relation between employment and housing). The eight-part division – ranging between 'dog rough' and 'beautiful' – is all the more striking because it involved a few streets within a single working-class neighbourhood.

> Studley Street was rough. Queen Street was roughish. That was the difference between Highgate Road and Studley Street; the dog rough and Highgate Road . . . Alfred Street was reasonable. Colville Road was a bit better. You're moving away from that area. Better houses. Water on. Gas on. Electric on. Services were laid on. Colville, Leamington, Brunswick were all about the same. Gradually getting to Church Road. No back houses. Brighton Road was beautiful. Bay windows. Clifton Road not so bad. Runcorn Road a touch better. It was like in a wave. Runcorn Road was always a nice road and Brighton Road was even nicer again. Towards Moseley. They had servants. White Street was pretty low. Kept pigs in one

of 'em. Roughish. Ombersley Road? Nice. Oldfield Road not so good. Highgate Road, back houses. Turner Street and Tillingham Street? Pretty reasonable.[16]

Often the gradations inside the Birmingham working class were hard to discern because the poorest inhabitants of the city were simply invisible to those parts of the middle class who were most likely to leave written accounts. The densely packed housing in the centre of the city meant that slums were even less apparent to an outsider than they would have been in other cities. Houses were often constructed around 'courts', which meant that they were set back from the street. A clergyman wrote in 1898: 'One may casually pass for a lifetime along the Saltley tram route and never become acquainted with the awful character of the neighbourhood.'[17]

SOCIAL MOBILITY

The belief that Birmingham was a place of small enterprises and highly paid skilled workers went together with the belief that it was a place of high social mobility in which masters and men might regularly change places. A Birmingham industrialist wrote in 1865: 'In no town in England is comfort more common or wealth more easily diffused. If millionaires are few, absolute poverty and wretchedness are also rare.'[18] Levels of absolute poverty do seem to have been higher in many other towns and the number of millionaires was certainly higher elsewhere – eight times as high in Merseyside (see chapter 4). It was theoretically possible that one of the workers in Chamberlain's screw factory might become as rich as his boss while not even the most optimistic miner in one of the pits owned by the Marquess of Bute (at one time the richest man in the world) could have imagined there was the faintest chance that he might rise to the level of his master.

Statements about such mobility were more than simply observation of facts; they implied a political vision. If masters and men might easily change places, it could be argued, their interests were easy to reconcile. This point was made as an objection to the extension of the franchise – but it was also made by those, in the early nineteenth century, who sought to unite the middle and working classes in favour of reform.

Talk of social mobility might also have a moral dimension. William Hutton presented his own life as a fable about virtue rewarded – though we have only his own word for the scale of his economic ascent, and his description of the extreme poverty of his youth sometimes puts one in mind of Gradgrind's claim to have been 'born in a ditch'. However, the moralization of social mobility might cut across its supposed role as a force for social cohesion. If everyone could rise, then those who failed to do so were at fault. For William Hutton, it was obvious that sloth, drunkenness and 'vice' were the causes of persistent poverty in Birmingham. He celebrated the man who began life 'at the lowest ebb; without property, or any advantage but that of his own prudence' but who 'quits the precincts of servitude and enters the dominions of command'. He was anything but an egalitarian, though, and considered a 'world consisting only of masters . . . like a monster consisting only of head'. He wrote about success and failure in terms that attributed an almost sub-human status to the latter. He compared those suited for 'drudgery' with the feet of a body and those suited for 'direction' with its head; he distinguished one 'directing the bridle' from one who 'submits to the bit'.[19] Similar thinking could be discerned among the Birmingham Nonconformists in the nineteenth century. The charitable emphasis that such people placed on improvement, temperance and education accompanied an uncharitable assumption that the failure of their social inferiors to make more of their lives must be rooted in their own conduct and character rather than their economic circumstances.

Men who prided themselves on having made their own way often expressed distaste for those who had failed to do so. The French writer Paul de Rousiers described a toolmaker, Joseph Brown, who ran a workshop in his own house in Nechells. He employed ten men – though this number sometimes rose as high as twenty-two. He claimed to have established his business 'without a penny from my parents or my wife's parents'. He worked alongside his men – 'he stayed a worker in becoming a boss' – but, as Rousiers put it, he did not seem a 'tender employer'. He recognized that his workers had valuable skills but he despised them. He believed them incapable of saving money or working except when compelled by hunger. His only service to his men consisted in preventing his son from lending them money with which to gamble.[20]

Those who had risen in the world were not always regarded with favour by those they had left behind, and the association of education, self-control and restrained manners with social status was not universally accepted. George Edmonds was an intelligent and educated man and one who succeeded in rising from relatively humble origins to become an attorney, though he never made much money and did not achieve formal recognition as a lawyer until he was almost sixty. But he came up against Birmingham Tories, claiming to speak for the mass of the population, who insisted that social station was a matter of birth and upbringing rather than effort or achievement. Some implied that plebeian manners were in fact desirable on the part of one from his background. An anonymous journalist wrote of Edmonds in 1817: 'Master Orator I should ha' got on much fast with ye' hadn't it been for your stuffing in so many o' your hard words ... Why don't you speak plain, common Brummagen English as I do?'[21]

In any case, the mechanisms of social mobility were more complicated than those who lauded it allowed. Occasionally, a single individual might make a great fortune in a single lifetime. Charles Geach started his working life (at the age of fifteen in 1823) as a draper's clerk and finished it thirty-one years later as a wealthy banker and MP. Generally speaking, though, the acquisition of great riches in a lifetime was rare and this is illustrated by the backgrounds of the very men who celebrated such acquisition most. Boulton claimed that 'all the manufacturers I have known began ... with very little capital', but he had himself inherited a modest fortune from his father and substantial fortunes from each of his two wives. As for Philip Muntz – who said in 1841 that 'Half the masters in Birmingham had been working men'[22] – he was the descendant of Polish and French aristocrats.

More common was a relatively slow ascent that took place over more than one generation. The history of the Cadbury family would extend from the moment that the draper Richard Tapper Cadbury arrived in Birmingham in 1794 through several generations of increasing prosperity until the family firm, by now a limited company, was the largest employer in Birmingham in 1914. The company was floated on the stock exchange in 1962 – at which point the various trusts that represented the interests of the branches of the family no longer involved in running the business were able to extract a fair price for their shares.

Social descent was also slow and complicated. The Kenricks had arrived in Birmingham, like the Cadburys, in the late eighteenth century. Their business grew for almost the whole of the nineteenth century and

declined for most of the twentieth. Ideas of déclassement were important in Birmingham but often for reasons that bore only a very tangential
relation to reality. Walter Allen wrote of his own family's belief that they
were descended from nobility. He added: 'I doubt if there is a working-
class family in England that does not cherish similar legends of
aristocratic connections.'[23] Perhaps such 'legends' flourished in Birmingham partly for the simple reason that the only aristocratic notables to
exercise much influence in the town after the sixteenth century – the
Holtes of Aston Hall – had a relatively common name.[24]

The Middlemore family – once lords of the manor of Edgbaston –
reveal interesting aspects of the myth of aristocratic decline. They had
been Catholics and supporters of the king in the Civil War and, perhaps
for this reason, Hutton, a Nonconformist who dated Birmingham's
greatness from the Glorious Revolution, described their falling prosperity with ill-concealed satisfaction:

> We have among us a family of the name of Middlemore, of great antiquity,
> deducible from the conquest; who held the chief possessions, and the
> chief offices in the county, and who matched into the first families in the
> kingdom, but fell with the interest of Charles the First; and are now in
> that low ebb of fortune, that I have frequently, with a gloomy pleasure,
> relieved them at the common charity-board of the town. Such is the tot-
> tering point of human greatness.[25]

Other accounts suggest that the decline of the Middlemore family
stopped a long way short of the precipice that might have led to absolute poverty. A historian of the family, writing in the early twentieth
century, noted wistfully that, but for their support for the king in the
Civil War, they might have founded 'a great territorial family'.[26] As it
was, two daughters of the family inherited Edgbaston manor and sold
it to the Gough family in 1717 (see chapter 4). The estate then was
worth less than it would be 150 years later but it was still a substantial
possession and the daughters appear in any case to have been well provided for – one of them married a baronet.

Even cadet branches of the Middlemore family were enterprising
enough to make their own way in the world. One of them established a
leather business, which prospered in the nineteenth century – perhaps
the embrace of bourgeois values was assisted by the fact that, having endured so much for their faith in the sixteenth and seventeenth

centuries, most Middlemores had converted to Anglicanism, or even the Baptist creed, by the nineteenth. Far from being recipients of charity, the Middlemores were responsible for two large charitable bequests – one medical[27] and one that founded a children's home[28] – in the Victorian age. The family even clawed their way back to political influence and the foothills of the aristocracy. John Throgmorton Middlemore was elected as Liberal Unionist MP for North Birmingham in 1889 – he succeeded a Kenrick – and was created baronet of Selly Oak in 1919.[29]

The most important form of social mobility may have been that which is hardest to study: the moves that saw workers acquire enough capital to set themselves up on a small scale and hire a few men. Were the small employers in Birmingham mostly men who had previously been employees? Even if they were, there is no knowing what happened to men who had become small employers. A few rose further to greater prosperity or to found industrial dynasties. Joseph Lucas described himself as an electroplating journeyman in 1855 (though, like many people in Birmingham who had such status, he had not in fact served his indentures). He had fifty-eight employees by 1880; by 1892 Lucas was a limited company with a value of £170,000 and a Chamberlain on the board.

Success such as this was unusual. Most small employers stayed small. Some failed and, indeed, if we are to assume that masters and men frequently changed places, then failure must have been common. Many must have been reduced to their original status after years of work. The key question is how those involved felt about the process. It may be, as Briggs suggests, that they were optimistic about their chances of rising, or it may be that small masters saw themselves, like Sisyphus, condemned to endure repeated reverse. One should note that the celebration of social mobility came almost entirely from rich men in Birmingham and that the very terms in which they spoke implied that they knew their words would seem implausible to those beneath them.

CLASS RELATIONS AT WORK

Those who believed in and celebrated a society of small enterprises and social mobility also believed that this produced a benign intimacy between employers and workers. John Thackray Bunce (the editor of the *Birmingham Post*) wrote:

In the ordinary workshops ... masters and men often worked at the
bench together, and so were comrades rather than masters and servants.
Ranks were not so sharply divided as to exclude real companionship and
intercourse ... it was not uncommon for workmen to address their
employer ... by his Christian name.[30]

There was no automatic relation between size of enterprise, level of
social mobility and nature of relations between employers and workers.
There were times when relations might be intimate in even large
firms. The motor manufacturer Herbert Austin (1866–1941) worked
alongside one of his own apprentices, as did Oliver Lucas, the heir to
the family engineering business, who was born in 1892 (see chapter 6).
Members of the Cadbury family were set to work in the factory before
moving into management. But intimate relations were not always the
same as good relations. Lucas and Austin were noted for ruthless discipline on the factory floor. Cadbury was more benign – though the mailed
fist of scientific management could sometimes be discerned underneath
the velvet glove of Quakerly informality.

Joseph Chamberlain knew some of the workers at his screw factory
well. He persuaded important skilled men not to desert to a rival – while
making it brutally clear that those who did so would never be re-
employed. His workers may have regarded him with grudging respect
but it seems unlikely that knowing him made them like him – any more
than it made his cabinet colleagues like him in the later part of the
century.

An even starker example of the ways in which close relations could
be bad ones was provided by Charles Shaw. His father had made a fortune as a curry-comb maker. Charles Shaw had little formal education
but was set to make himself useful in the business from an early age, 'his
daily associates being the working people of the place'. He grew up with
coarse manners and though, like many members of the Birmingham
bourgeoisie of his era, he could display 'the most inflexible ideal of honour, honesty, and rectitude' in public life, he was 'grasping in business'.
He seemed to cherish his reputation as 'the hardest man in Birmingham'
and one of his associates who regarded himself as more or less a friend
concluded:

Probably no Birmingham man occupying a prominent position was ever
so unpopular as Charles Shaw. He was generally disliked and somewhat

dreaded. He was unscrupulous and regardless of truth, where truthful-
ness and his interests were antagonistic.[31]

It was Shaw who chaired the magistrates when striking glass workers
were imprisoned in the 1840s.[32]

MASTERS AND MEN?

The phrase 'masters and men', often used to describe the apparently
benign relations between the classes, is itself a revealing one because it
implies that class relations in Birmingham concerned male adults.[33] It is
true that in the early period of industrialization factories that relied on
women and children were less common in Birmingham than in parts of
the North. Hutton's account of his own life revolved around a contrast
between his beginnings as an 'apprentice' stocking weaver – which
apparently meant a factory hand – who started work at the age of seven
in Derby, and his life as an adult man in Birmingham.

However, the key difference between Birmingham and the North was
not that women and children did not work but that their work was less
visible. A significant minority of those who owned businesses in Birmingham were women. In the second half of the nineteenth century, the
proportion of entries in Birmingham trade directories that referred to
businesses owned by women varied between 4.4 and 8.2 per cent. A
woman such as Ann Alford, who died in 1883, left an estate worth over
£2,000, which included a pub, three cottages in Herefordshire as well as
the equipment, stock and goodwill of her business, which made parasols
and umbrellas.[34] George Holyoake recalled that his mother had a horn
button workshop attached to her house in Inge Street – though her husband had a secure job at the Eagle foundry. He added, 'There were no
"Rights of Women" thought of in her day, but she was an entirely self-
acting, managing mistress.'[35]

More commonly, though, women's businesses were hand-to-mouth
affairs usually run in a family house and usually employing family
labour. Such concerns were means of survival rather than stairways to
social ascension. Emma Page illustrated this. She had been born in Walsall in 1840 and had a house on Smith Street. It was relatively large by
the standards of the area and contained one room downstairs and a

pantry while there were two bedrooms and an attic upstairs. Her grandson, whose account provides all that we know about 'Grandma Page', reckoned that her rent would have been around 3s 6d per week. She and her husband, Tom, had seven children, of whom five survived to adulthood. Tom Page ran his own soldering business, which required little equipment beyond a set of bellows, but at some point he moved to Sheffield. He never returned – though he sent his wife money and also constructed a workshop in one of the washhouses in the collective courtyard at the back of the house. It was in this workshop that Emma Page ran her business. She employed her daughter Kitty ('from the cradle' until Kitty's marriage) and a female neighbour, Adie Hewitt. For at least part of the time, she employed other women. Emma Page's business involved soldering brass caps onto nails for coffins and also attaching pins and clips to military badges. She subcontracted for two larger enterprises and seems to have helped them evade regulations on hours and conditions of work – in theory it was forbidden for government contracts, such as those for military badges, to be subcontracted. Emma Page was paid according to the amount that she produced and she paid her workers on the same basis. By dint of twelve-hour working days (those in factories were limited to ten and a half hours), the women made a reasonable income.

Emma Page was a tough woman but there was little chance that she could have risen beyond the station that she occupied or established a larger enterprise. She could never have obtained credit, and one assumes that the larger enterprises that found her services useful would have had no difficulty in cutting her out of commercial networks if she had expanded to the point where she might have competed with them. The chances of falling into destitution were more real than those of rising to prosperity. She often tottered on the edge of desperate circumstances. Her son, his wife and their four children came to live with Emma Page at one point but all but one of them were suddenly taken with consumption and died. Emma Page herself performed crucial tasks that required precise measurement of expensive materials until she was almost blind.[36]

Towards the end of the nineteenth century, as factories became larger in Birmingham, women's labour was more visible, if only in the sense that employers now exerted an overt discipline that had been less necessary in the era of home working. In 1895, Joseph Lucas bought his daughter Louisa a diamond bracelet to reward her for her help in supervising women workers at his plant – though he also employed a woman (nicknamed 'Polly closet') who exercised a cruder control by preventing female workers from spending too much time in the toilet.[37] Harry (the son of Joseph) wrote a note that illustrated how women were supervised, and also how an intimate knowledge of their workers did not necessarily imply benign feelings on the part of employers:

> Annie Rice has been rather erratic lately. She got her eye blacked the other
> week by her sweetheart for talking to Cook's chap who did the gas fitting,
> so she stopped away till it got better, and yesterday and today she is away
> on the drink.[38]

The Cadburys would not have written in such brutal terms, but the prosperity of their factory depended partly on the labour of young, unmarried women. The hierarchies of sex and age were conspicuous at Cadbury: the company had separate structures for male and female employees until the 1960s.

Almost every kind of economic organization in late nineteenth-century Birmingham was run by, and for, men. This was particularly true of those trade unions that preached class cooperation. The Birmingham Brassworkers' Union did not admit women until the First World War. The Bedstead Workmen's Union did not admit them until 1919 – and did not change the 'Workmen' in its title to 'Worker' until 1924. The benign conditions that some people believed were enjoyed by male workers in Birmingham were to some extent rooted in the employment of women. Some trades had a heavily female workforce. It was said in 1849 that the steel pen industry employed 1,550 women but only 300 men and boys.[39] The 'elasticity' of the economy, to which Briggs drew attention, derived partly from the fact that women were often employed in different industries from their menfolk and that consequently households were protected from a downturn in any particular sector.[40]

Birmingham children, even more than their contemporaries elsewhere, worked from a young age, particularly in the early nineteenth century. Parish apprentices – that is to say children of paupers who were sent to work from a young age by the parish authorities – were comparatively rare in the Birmingham workforce. However, many children were sent to work by their own parents and some families seem to have come to Birmingham from surrounding areas specifically because it offered work to their children.[41] In 1841, large numbers of children started work at eight or nine though Samuel Jones had begun as a stamper at five. Even in the 1860s, some children were industrial veterans. Samuel Enfield was ten when he was interviewed at Josiah Mason's pen factory. He had been there nearly four years and had previously 'worked at umbrellas'; Charles Walters, also aged ten, had been employed at a gun works. William Thorne (1857–1946) had begun work as a ropemaker in Duddeston at the age of six; he worked at weekends for an uncle who was a barber. After the death of his father in 1864, he went to work for an uncle at a brickworks (presumably his uncle was a subcontractor rather than the proprietor of the business) but was dismissed for sleeping during a late shift. He then worked as a plumber's mate and collecting cow and pig hair from butchers. Finally, at the age of fourteen, he got a job at a metal works, which involved dealing with hot bars and acid. Thorne, who eventually became a trade unionist and Labour MP, later wrote: 'I can never forget the horror of my childhood days and the misery and suffering I have seen.'[42]

Children were subject to a hierarchy within the working class as well as a hierarchy of the classes. The poorest families often depended on money brought in by their children. In many instances it was small masters, working as subcontractors for larger enterprises, who hired children – so that the limited autonomy enjoyed by a male subcontractor might itself depend on the subordination of juvenile labour. The fact that children worked in comparatively small units and were often subordinate to subcontractors meant that their work was less visible than it was in the textile mills of the North, which also meant that it was regulated later. Sometimes investigators in Birmingham stumbled across details that suggested that businessmen did not always reveal, and perhaps did not even know, how the children under their nominal aegis were treated. Managers at Gillott penmakers said they did not employ children under the age of thirteen but the Children's Employment Commission found two aged twelve in Gillott's factory in 1862.[43]

The social effects of this elicited complicated and contradictory responses among those respectable adults who commented on the economy. Some congratulated themselves on the fact that children were too busy to get into mischief. Some saw the employment of children as undermining paternal authority because children were rendered financially independent – though they were often, in fact, put to work under the aegis of their fathers. Some noted that the comparative ease of obtaining work meant that children, by which they mainly meant boys, were less likely to undertake apprenticeships – the relative scarcity of formal apprenticeship was to be a feature of Birmingham throughout the nineteenth century, and even such apprenticeships as existed rarely involved residence with, or substantial social control by, the master.[44]

Children could be treated harshly. They were sometimes beaten or had their pay withheld. Injuries at work were common though, at least in the 1840s, these were limited in severity by the comparative rarity of powered machinery.

The spread of compulsory education eventually limited the number of children employed in Birmingham – though working-class families were still dependent on the incomes they derived from their younger members. Most such families enjoyed brief periods of prosperity when their children left school and began to bring in an income, which was handed over to their parents. Even in the 1920s, raising the school-leaving age was unpopular in the poorest quarters of the city (see chapter 7).

RATIONAL RECREATION, NIGHT CLASSES AND SUNDAY SCHOOL

The social relations between employers and employees changed for reasons that were only partly to do with the changing sizes of enterprises. Large employers were able to impose more regular working hours on their employees towards the end of the nineteenth century. Joseph Chamberlain reduced the working day in his factory to nine hours – though he also took steps to ensure that the pace of work was steady within that working day. Employers who sought to encourage regular work habits were assisted by the cult of 'rational recreation' that was often sponsored by the city's Nonconformist Churches. The Bournville estate that the Cadbury family built around their factory in 1900 epitomized the new culture. Workers could no longer send out apprentices to fetch beer (none was sold on the estate) or stage rough games in the workplace. Instead they clocked in promptly (there were bonuses for good timekeeping). They were encouraged to go home for lunch and to spend their leisure time (Saturday afternoons and summer evenings) on the cricket pitches and bowling greens that surrounded the factory.

Part-time education – at night or on Sundays – was important in Birmingham. Different institutions provided education for different purposes. The radical George Holyoake recalled that five years of Sunday school at Angell James' Carrs Lane chapel had taught him nothing but hymns, the Bible and to be content with his own station. Holyoake acquired a different kind of education at the Mechanics Institute, where he himself eventually became a teacher. The institute refused to provide education for women in 1840. Eventually they got classes from the explicitly political Owenite Hall of Science.[45]

Part-time education became more available in the later nineteenth century and even that which was sponsored by religious institutions (especially by the Unitarian George Dawson) became more secular. It did not necessarily encourage good relations across the classes – Joseph Chamberlain was a harsh and sarcastic teacher. It was, however, increasingly likely to provide its recipients with the means of advancing in their careers or questioning the political judgements of their social superiors. Perhaps more than the economic structure of the city itself, part-time education may have promoted social mobility in Birmingham. Joseph Brown, the toolmaker and small employer described by Paul de Rousiers, had little formal education but had studied at night school. The second wife of Joseph Lucas, founder of the engineering firm, stated:

> I have heard many times my husband say that whatever good there was
> in him was owing to the teaching and ministry of George Dawson, whose
> school he went to as a young man and whose Church later on he was a
> member of as long as it was in existence as such.[46]

It was, presumably as a result of Dawson that Lucas was literate (his first wife signed the marriage register with a cross) and that he gave up drink shortly before he founded his business. His first wife drank herself to her grave.* In the late 1920s, Henry Green spent two years working – in the storeroom, then as a pattern maker and then in the moulding room – at the Birmingham factory of Pontifex that was owned by his father. He was impressed to discover that 'almost everyone of the age

* Joseph Lucas died of cholera after drinking contaminated water in Naples.

I had reached who was not a labourer went to night school to learn more of whatever trade he was in'.[47]

One should note, once again, that the prospect of social mobility was more celebrated by those at the top of the scale than those seeking to fight their way up. Joseph Brown did not think that any of his own employees were attending night school or were likely to rise in professional terms. As for Henry Green, his autobiographical reflections on a Birmingham factory suggested a world in which highly skilled men could expect (unless their family was afflicted with illness) to achieve economic security and a degree of independence with regard to factory management. He recalled men whose skills were so highly regarded that they were allowed to keep their pet dogs by them on the factory floor or to insist that notoriously insubordinate labourers to whom they were close should not be disciplined. All the same, Green's own educational career (he had idled his way through Eton and Oxford) offered a quicker route to a senior position in the factory than any amount of night school. He also noted that the happiest men in the factory seemed to be old labourers – men whose children had grown up and who had abandoned all illusion that they might improve their situation.

BEYOND THE FACTORY

In some ways, the focus on direct contact between workers and employers in the workplace is deceptive. Each workplace was part of a wider web of class relations, and this web became more extensive and more complicated as time went on. Furthermore, a significant part of the Birmingham population did not work in industry at all. In 1881, 6.6 per cent of the city's population were employed in finance, commerce and business services (the comparable figures for Manchester and London were 8.9 per cent and 8 per cent respectively). The elegant arcades of central Birmingham would look incongruous to twentieth-century visitors (and provoke some excited study by earnest readers of Walter Benjamin) but they illustrated the extent to which the city had been a centre of the retail trade, often drawing customers from surrounding towns. The largest shop in the city employed 500 people by 1885.[48] The Birmingham Law Society was formed in 1818 by nineteen of Birmingham's fifty-seven attorneys. It worked to establish the law as a profession which would be regulated and to which entry would be controlled. Both Birmingham and Manchester were regional centres that provided services to the surrounding area and sometimes to small towns (in the case of Birmingham, those of the Black Country) that were more exclusively industrial. In Birmingham, the Beale and the Martineau families (primarily lawyers) were almost as influential as the Chamberlain, Kenrick and Cadbury families (primarily industrialists). Pictures of the Birmingham economy that revolve around 'masters and men' sweating in workshops should be supplemented by a recognition of the more general power that was exercised – particularly when it came to credit, fundraising and eventually the formation of limited companies – by men in frock coats who worked at desks. The Beale family in particular derived considerable wealth from businesses they did not own, and after the First World War two members of that family (both lawyers) were successively chairman of GKN, by that time one of the largest industrial companies in the country.

Banking was important in Birmingham. Some of the city's most prominent citizens in the nineteenth century – Spooner, Attwood and Geach – were primarily bankers, though banking and industry were never entirely separate. Given the frequency with which interpretations of the British economy suggest that London-based financial interests acted to the detriment of provincial industry, it is worth remembering that two of the five big national clearing banks – Midland and Lloyds – had first been established in Birmingham. Far from being a distant and ruthless agent of financial discipline, Lloyds went on providing one of Birmingham's industrial dynasties with generous credit after it had ceased to be prudent to do so.[49] The fact that access to credit was associated with perceptions of respectability as well as with family or personal contacts operated a brake on how fast any individual was likely to rise or fall.

As well as helping to create a particular kind of capitalist, banks also created a particular kind of worker, though one unlikely to define themselves as working class. A significant proportion of the Birmingham population were clerks – working for banks, or for the corporation of the town itself, or for large firms that became increasingly bureaucratized. Clerks had a special kind of status. They were (until the twentieth century) mainly male – in 1841, there were 1,369 clerks in Birmingham of whom only five were women.[50] They were not always 'masculine', though. Their work did not involve physical strength or manual dexterity. Their workplace was more likely to be under the direct control of their employer than a workshop or factory floor. They were required to be deferential, clean and well spoken. The eagle eyes of Joseph Chamberlain, who had begun his own career keeping the accounts of his family firm, noted how the two worlds collided. He wrote that the offices of the large bureaucratized firms that were coming to dominate Birmingham reflected their 'piecemeal' origins in private houses: 'furniture of the old dwelling-house may frequently be seen in the counting-house or warehouse'.[51]

The peculiar social status of clerks in Birmingham, and in most British cities, was revealed in the First World War. Men who thought of themselves as middle class did not want to serve in the ranks alongside manual workers but they, unlike those who had public school and university educations, were unlikely to be commissioned as officers. The solution was to establish special city battalions, known colloquially as 'pals' battalions' (three from Birmingham were attached to the Warwickshire Regiment). A significant minority of those who joined these battalions were eventually commissioned, but the majority of clerks who survived finished the war in the same social no man's land in which they had started it – too refined to think of themselves as ordinary soldiers but not patrician enough to become officers.[52]

Intervention by agencies of the state changed relations between employers and workers – making them more regular, formal and structured. These changes were felt strongly in areas where the state itself was an employer, such as the Post Office, but also in those, such as the railways, where the state acted as a regulator. The city of Birmingham regulated some enterprises (such as tram companies),[53] but it was also an employer in its own right. Birmingham had begun the nineteenth century as a manor that employed a handful of quaintly titled officials; it finished the century as a city with whole departments of administration. One effect of this was to create a section of the Birmingham bourgeoisie that was not directly involved in business. In 1890, the city's thirteen most important officials ranged from the Town Clerk (with a salary of £2,200 per year) to the Chief Inspector of Nuisances, who earned £130 per year. By 1914, the Chief Inspector of Nuisances had disappeared but the city had now added a Tramways Manager, Gas Engineer and Chief Librarian. Each of these men had many employees beneath them.[54]

*

The attempt of Asa Briggs to discern a pattern to class relations in Birmingham runs up against three general, and related, problems. First, it assumes a unity of the whole 'long nineteenth century'. Alongside the explicit comparison with Manchester, his interpretation of nineteenth-century Birmingham involves an implicit comparison with the period after 1914, which he sees as being marked by industrialization on a new scale. This is strange because most of the large companies that were to dominate Birmingham in the first half of the twentieth century – Austin, Cadburys, Lucas – already existed, and were already operating on a large scale, before 1914.

Secondly, Briggs's analysis assumes that relations between employers and workers involved direct encounters between individuals. This ignores the role of municipal regulation and of intervention by lawyers or bankers. It also ignores the fact that both employers and workers were more organized by the end of the nineteenth century than they had been at its beginning. There was an interesting paradox here. Those who celebrated benign relations between the classes in Birmingham in the first half of the nineteenth century made much of individual relations and an economy that involved vigorous competition between small enterprises. However, in at least one respect, class relations in Birmingham were worst at the time when small business was most predominant. Prosecutions under the Master and Servant Act, which was used until 1871 against workers who attempted to organize in ways that might be construed as a breach of contract with their employers, were more common in Birmingham than in Liverpool, Sheffield or Manchester.[55]

By the end of the century, class cooperation in Birmingham was likely to involve trade unions (notably those that represented the brass and coffin furniture trades) whose leaders argued that the interests of their members (by which they meant established male workers) were best served by cooperating with employers – usually, by now, quite large-scale employers – to keep wages high and suppress competition between firms. But the 'alliance' that emerged from these arrangements did not last much beyond the end of the century.[56]

Thirdly, if we are to assume that a particular pattern of politics was associated with a social structure in Birmingham, then we do not see a unified 'long nineteenth century' that was followed by a new order after the First World War. Rather we see a succession of dramatic changes in the nineteenth century – often towards the end of the period, associated with the twists and turns of Joseph Chamberlain's stance. In particular, one should note that Chamberlain may always have had some working-class support but this did not mean that the same kind of worker always supported him. Until 1885, parts of the skilled and 'respectable' working class voted for Chamberlain. But this group were often hostile to the shifts in Chamberlain's later political stance and W.J. Davis, the leader of the brass workers' trade union, who had once seemed to epitomize inter-class cooperation, came close to standing against Chamberlain in the 1906 election.[57] In the early twentieth century, support for Chamberlain's candidates in Birmingham apparently came largely from the north, central and Aston constituencies – all of which were poor.[58]

Just as the nineteenth century was not marked by continuity, the First World War, which Briggs sees as marking the end of Birmingham's nineteenth-century social structure, was not accompanied by a sharp change in the city's politics. Chamberlainite Unionism (and, indeed, members of the Chamberlain family) dominated Birmingham from the late nineteenth century until the outbreak of the Second World War.

None of this means that there is no substance to arguments about the peculiarity of Birmingham's social structure. Elasticity of trade was an important feature of the city's economy (though one rooted in the different jobs that men and women did as well as the capacity of workers to move from one trade to another). Businesses do seem to have been smaller than in some northern towns, and social mobility was widely talked about in Birmingham, even if it was celebrated more by those at the top of the ladder than by those trying to get their foot on the first rung.

Most of all, perhaps, looking at class relations in Birmingham in the long nineteenth century illustrates two things. First, that such relations increasingly meant something more than just relations between workers and their own employers. Both industrialists and workers existed as part of larger structures that influenced their activities and adult education may have had more impact on ideas of social mobility than the purely economic structure of Birmingham. Secondly, confrontation, or cooperation, between classes took place in many settings and in many different ways. Two institutions illustrate the possible ambiguity of class relations. The first of these is the much vaunted small enterprise. As has been argued, small enterprises might be a means of social ascent and hence imply a consensual notion of class relations (though those who had ascended might be all the more disdainful of those who had failed to do so) but it might also be, as Walter Allen suggested, a means for a worker to assert their independence in ways that implied hostility to any potential employer. One might note in this context that Dick Etheridge – the Communist convenor at the Longbridge factory from the Second World War until the 1970s – seems to have been free of deference to his employer partly because he had spent his formative years working in his father's small shop (see chapter 9).

The second institution that illustrates the ambiguity of class relations in Birmingham is Saint Monday. This was associated with a certain sort of rebellion by skilled workers but it is usually assumed that this was an informal, non-political and archaic rebellion that revolved around heavy drinking and rough sports. It might also imply a rebellion against the notions of respectability and bettering oneself that mattered so much to part of the Birmingham bourgeoisie. Monday had two other meanings, though. For women it was often a day on which they did housework and shopping – activities that their social betters would have regarded as signs of 'respectability'. Monday was also the day when political meetings were usually held in Birmingham and the authorities were sometimes disconcerted by the sobriety and order of these meetings.

KINGS ROAD

KINGSTANDING

A postcard showing Kings Road, Kingstanding. Kingstanding was a large council estate, built in 1929–30 at a time when council houses tended to be reserved for the most prosperous and 'respectable' sections of the working class. Note the large trees – deliberately kept from open country on which the estate had been built.

6

New Society, 1911–38

[S]he [the city of Birmingham] is vitally concerned with the visitor who prefers to see history in the making, to witness with his own eyes the twentieth century being hammered into shape in great forges, to behold and understand a city where every nerve strains eagerly forward beyond the forefront of progress and industrial achievement.

Statement by City of Birmingham publicity department, 1934[1]

Between 1910 and 1938, Birmingham's population grew faster than that of any other British city. This was partly a product of administrative change: in 1911, Northfield, King's Norton, Yardley, Handsworth, Erdington and Aston were brought inside the city limits, and it was this that made Birmingham for the first time the second most populous city in England. In the 1920s, Perry Barr was also annexed. Parts of Castle Bromwich and Sheldon were brought into Birmingham in 1931. In addition to this, the city expanded because new factories and new housing estates were built on its outskirts on what had previously been mostly farm land. Finally, Birmingham sucked in people. About 3 per cent of the entire working-age population of Wales moved to the Midlands between the two world wars and Birmingham was by far the most common single destination.[2] What brought people to the city was work. After a faltering start, the Birmingham economy did well in the 1920s and 30s and this became particularly important in the latter decade as companies closed and unemployment rose in many other industrial parts of the country. There were still areas of poverty in Birmingham, particularly in the centre of the city, but overall, more than anywhere else in the country, it epitomized a new kind of world, in which a significant

147

number of people had money to spend and spent it on new kinds of goods produced in Birmingham's own factories. The breezy vulgarity of this new world often aroused disapproval from those who looked at Birmingham from outside or, indeed, from the city fathers whose own culture was still rooted in high-minded, Victorian Nonconformity.

THE FIRST WORLD WAR

At first, war seemed likely to slow Birmingham's growth rather than speed it up. Unemployment increased as exports fell. Men joined the armed forces – either because they had been thrown out of work or because they wanted to see action and feared that the war would be over before they could reach the front. A total of 15,000 Birmingham men joined up in the first two weeks of September 1914. Overall, around 150,000 Birmingham men (a little over half the male population of military age) served in the forces. Of these, 35,000 were disabled and 13,000 were killed. Some men had extraordinary experiences. James Adams, a private with the London Scottish, was captured on the Italian front. He found himself in Bohemia during the revolutionary upheavals of 1918 and escaped from a prison camp with another soldier. They managed to get back home via Prague and Genoa.[3] Just as it took Birmingham men far away to fight, the war also brought some people to Birmingham from far away to work. Won Fan, a Chinese sailor who had been stranded in Britain, found his way to a Birmingham munitions factory and, in July 1917, died of tuberculosis in the city's hospital.[4]

The influential Birmingham Nonconformist families had come to terms with the values of the officer corps by 1914. Ernest Martineau, the Lord Mayor of Birmingham, was a colonel in the territorial army who took his regiment abroad early in the war. Neville Chamberlain had married the daughter of a cavalry officer in 1911. Two of Joseph Chamberlain's nephews (John and Norman Chamberlain) were killed in action. Even the Quaker Cadburys did nothing to prevent their employees from joining up; they kept jobs open for those men who had done so. Egbert – the youngest son of George and Elizabeth Cadbury – became a naval pilot and won the Distinguished Flying Cross.[5] In total 2,148 men from the Bournville works served in the war and 218 of them were killed.[6]

After the early disruption, war increased industrial activity in Birmingham. Field Marshal Sir John French said that the First World War was a battle 'between Krupps [the German armaments manufacturer] and Birmingham'. The Birmingham Small Arms Company – the combine established in an attempt to overcome the limitations of small-scale arms production – had begun to move into the manufacture of bicycles by 1914. The war brought it back to its origins. Early in the conflict, it made 134 Lewis machine guns per week; by its end, it was 2,000 per week. It had produced over 145,000 by the end of the war. William Mills (1856–1932) converted the Atlas Aluminium Works in West Birmingham into the Mills Munitions Factory in early 1915. It was here that he produced 'Mills bombs', i.e. hand grenades. Of the 75 million used by the allied armies during the war, 4 million were made in Birmingham. Kynoch, at the peak of its production during the last spurt of 1918, made 30 million rifle cartridges in a single week. Kenricks, the hardware manufacturer, converted to armaments production to such an extent that by 1918 military contracts made up 80 per cent of its sales, which amounted to £348,379.[7]

A NEW CAPITALISM?

The war and its aftermath brought changes to Birmingham industry. Production took place on a larger scale and with higher levels of mechanization. The Austin motor factory moved from employing 2,000 people in 1914 to employing 20,000 in 1918. A special station was built to serve the factory at Longbridge and eventually 10,000 people per day passed through this. Not all expansion was sustained after the war – companies that had directed their production to the war effort were sometimes in an awkward position as orders dried up – but in general factories were larger after 1918 than they had been before 1914. Business became more organized. The Federation of British Industries (soon renamed the Federation of British Industry) was founded in 1916. It was closely linked to industry in the Midlands and owed its foundation largely to the influence of Frank Dudley Docker, who had made his own fortune with the Birmingham Small Arms Company. A wave of mergers brought Birmingham companies into larger corporate structures that operated at national level. Lucas took over four firms in two years in the mid 1920s. By 1935, GKN was the second largest employer in Britain, with 50,000 people on its payroll. It was still largely a Birmingham company and its board was chaired from 1928 to 1947 by members of the Beale family. Lucas, ICI, Vickers, London, Midlands and Scottish Railways and General Electric were also among the thirty largest employers in Britain. They were all based, at least partly, in Birmingham. Three of the best-known factories in Britain (the Cadbury works at Bournville, the Austin works at Longbridge and Fort Dunlop in Erdington) were in Birmingham. Cadbury, Austin and Dunlop were, respectively, the twenty-ninth, seventeenth and thirteenth largest employers in the country.[8]

The fact that companies grew in size does not mean that they were all large or that the majority of Birmingham workers were employed by large concerns – one historian estimates that by the late 1920s only one in five Birmingham workers were employed by companies with more than 2,000 employees. Birmingham moved from being a city of workshops to one of factories. In 1895 there were 4,868 of the former and 5,321 of the latter; by 1931 the relative figures were 2,545 and 5,856. This was partly a matter of administrative change: workshops had been defined as those concerns that employed fewer than fifty people, but by the 1930s they were defined by the non-use of electrical power.[9]

In any case, there was no automatic relation between size of enterprise and 'modernity' of management style. Modernization could mean several different things in inter-war British business. It could mean a change in management structure as companies associated with a particular individual or family merged into larger combines with more formal corporate structures and with a greater degree of separation between ownership and management. Birmingham companies were affected by such changes – though even large firms sometimes remained under the control of families. This was true of Lucas and of Cadbury, even after their merger with Fry put them under the nominal aegis of the British Cocoa and Chocolate Company. Energetic individuals – such as Dudley Docker – still exercised much influence inside conglomerations. Modernization might also mean simply the deployment of new technology as a means of production or as a product. This was widely seen in the Birmingham motor industry.

Modernization could also mean 'scientific management'. This was associated with the ideas of the American Frederick Winslow Taylor

(1856–1915), who published a series of books on the topic. Taylor timed workers, broke their tasks down into a succession of simple movements and devised piece rate payments to encourage efficient work. Charles Bedaux (1886–1944) established a consultancy and claimed to have devised a system that could measure work in terms of 'B units'. Bedaux was a louche figure. A friend of Pigalle gangsters and the Duke of Windsor, he eventually killed himself in an American prison while awaiting trial for treason after he had collaborated with the Nazis in occupied France. His interventions also aroused resentment among workers. Perhaps for these reasons, he did not always figure in celebratory histories of scientific management – though he had exercised much influence in interwar Europe.

Birmingham looked an unpromising place for scientific management. Taylor had spoken in the city in 1910 and not been well received. Birmingham factories, even after the expansions that occurred during the First World War, were small by American standards. The city had a large engineering industry but engineers of the kind that would have been recognized by Taylor – i.e. university-trained people with a strong sense of their professional authority – were rare. Craft skills, acquired by apprenticeship, or by trial and error through on-the-job experience, were still important in Birmingham industry. Men who had learned a wide range of metalworking skills in the manufacture of sporting guns, a trade that had been in decline for decades, sometimes moved into large factories. Independent, cussed and capable of turning their hand to many things, such men were highly valued in factory toolrooms, but they were the opposite of the interchangeable and disciplined workers who featured so large in Taylor's thought. Those who ran factories, such as Herbert Austin (of whom more below), were also often self-taught engineers whose skills owed more to conversations with skilled workers than to the university laboratory.

For all this, scientific management (sometimes disguised by other names) did influence some Birmingham companies. Tom Brindley (born in 1908), a drill operator at Rover in Tyseley, recalled how his company was reorganized. When he started in 1922, it was run by 'rate setters' who were 'charge hands cum foremen'. In 1929, the company was close to bankruptcy and was rescued by managers who brought in the Bedaux system. The system seemed attractive and men could double or triple their pay with bouts of ferociously hard work. But in early 1932, the factory gates were suddenly shut. Brindley was without work for a couple of days and then invited to return with a new contract that converted 'Bedaux time' into money. Unsurprisingly, this meant a sharp drop in pay. Brindley was not bitter. He stayed with the company for many years and had a rueful admiration for its management but he still recalled: 'we'd sold ourselves really'.[10]

The most conspicuous example of failure to modernize in Birmingham industry was that of the Kenrick hardware firm. The Kenricks were still political notables – powerful in municipal politics and closely linked to the Chamberlain family. In spite – or perhaps partly because – of this, their company was in decline. The number of workers employed by Kenricks dropped from something over 900 during the war to about 500 by 1934. The proportion of sales that came from exports dropped from 30 per cent in 1923 to 7 per cent in 1933. The company was reluctant to cut prices even as it faced increasing competition from manufacturers who used aluminium. It moved into the production of baths (a good business to be in at a time of building by the middle classes) but its prices were too high. Family control as such did not damage the company. Indeed, a cadet branch of the Kenrick family formed a separate company (Kenrick and Jefferson) specializing in stationery that was highly successful. Kenrick and Jefferson were innovative in their management techniques and this seems to have sprung partly from the fact that they embraced managers from outside the family, thus creating a new sub-dynasty descended from managers who had been given shares in reward for their competence.[11] Furthermore, a member of a different associated dynasty (Arthur Baldwin, the son of the Conservative politician and Prime Minister) was a director of Kenricks. He repeatedly, and unsuccessfully, pressed for a new approach to management.

The problem for the Kenricks lay, first, in the family piety that made younger members of the family reluctant to challenge their elders, even when they understood the problems their company faced. It also lay in the fact that senior Kenricks were so involved in public life. Byng Kenrick (1872–1962), who had first joined the company in 1895, became a director in 1896 and chaired it from 1934, when his cousin George (1850–1939) retired, until his own retirement in 1951. Byng Kenrick had considerable abilities – he was skilful at negotiating to keep the peace among members of his family, which may be why his younger

relatives were reluctant to depose him. He was also an important figure
in business associations, which, by controlling prices, sometimes served
to conceal how uncompetitive Kenricks had become. However, he
lacked a good grasp of management accountancy. Indeed, at times he
appeared indifferent to the notion of profit and to believe that sustain-
ing a company was an end in itself rather than a means of making
money. This unworldly attitude went with a highly developed public
spirit. He sat on Birmingham City Council from 1914 to 1949. He
chaired the education committee from 1922 to 1928 and again from
1931 to 1943, and was Lord Mayor in 1928–9. He arrived at the West
Bromwich works of his company almost every morning but rarely
stayed there for the whole day. A management consultant's report of
1937 noted: 'The present chairman, Mr W. Byng Kenrick, is, we understand, largely occupied with public duties.'[12]

Other Birmingham companies managed to combine family control
with prosperity and efficient management. Cadbury was one example
and also illustrated the complicated relation that some Birmingham
industrialists had with 'scientific management'. Edward Cadbury had
conducted a public debate with Frederick Winslow Taylor in 1913 and
1914. Cadbury recognized virtues in Taylor's system but also expressed
doubts about its rigidity and its effect on workers. Laurence Cadbury,
who would become chairman of the company in 1944, had met Henry
Ford when visiting the United States. Cadbury was a benign employer (of
which more below) who avoided the labour disputes that often accompanied the implementation of scientific management. The company also
sometimes covered its innovations with a veneer of self-deprecating
Quaker informality – men who were described as 'rate-fixers' at Bournville learned to present themselves as 'time-study engineers' if they applied
for jobs elsewhere.[13] Nonetheless, the company's consideration for the
interests of its workers was accompanied by a close attention to extract-
ing the maximum value from them. Cadbury measured the output of its
workers, especially women. Those whose production was judged inadequate were helped, first with advice and then, if necessary, medical care,
but if their work rate did not pick up they were sacked.[14]

Cadbury was so concerned with efficient management of time and
work that its managers devised a 'decimal hour', divided into ten units
of six minutes – so that the working day sometimes started at 7.42
rather than a quarter to eight.[15] It was also one of the first industrial

companies in the 1930s to train graduates for management positions. Chocolate bars – neatly divided into squares – lent themselves to production-line techniques. Cadbury had introduced 'dairy milk chocolate' in 1905, and in 1920 the bar was given its distinctive blue packaging that endures to the present day. The company concentrated on a small number of products – it introduced the Flake in 1920 and the Fruit and Nut bar in 1926. It also brought prices down sharply between the two world wars. It charged 2 shillings for a bar of Dairy Milk in 1920 and 1 shilling four years later. Cadbury cut its costs and overheads by 56 per cent in real terms between 1924 and 1938. Its return on capital was five times greater around this time than that of its rival Rowntree, which was based in York. Cadbury's Dairy Milk bars accounted for 420 of the 700 tonnes of milk chocolate sold per week in 1936, and the company reckoned that 90 per cent of the population, 'of all classes', ate its chocolate.[16]

Nothing illustrated the paradoxes of industrial modernity better than the chocolate box. Cadbury decorated its boxes with pictures. Richard Cadbury (1835–99) painted scenes depicting the children of his own family that were used for this purpose. 'Chocolate-box art' was to become one of the great symbols of inter-war middle-brow culture. It portrayed scenes of domesticity or rural calm, but much calculation lay behind these apparently innocent pictures. Frank Lockwood, a painter and lithographer who worked for the Cadbury design studio, painted a watercolour of a harbour in Devon in 1929 that was used by his employer. He noted in his diary: 'it is suggested that I add a few more flowers – brighten up the flowers . . . generally make it more chocolate-boxy looking'.[17] Cadbury also paid considerable attention to the visual image of its own factory. Though it was surrounded by gardens and playing fields, it was not as bucolic as was implied by the pictures that the company published – some of which might have given the impression that workers relaxing in their lunch hour were attending a village fête. Photographs and paintings of the production line itself were almost invariably of women (or, since the majority of its female employees were young, girls) rather than men. They also rarely included machinery and were sometimes cropped to give the impression that production took place in small workshops rather than in a large factory. Pictures showed bright rooms with large windows – though such rooms were rare because chocolate melted if exposed to too much sunlight.[18]

Lucas Industries, like Cadbury, was still managed by descendants of the founder, Joseph Lucas, who had set up the company in the 1870s. Family piety, however, had never been a feature of the company's management. Harry Lucas (born in 1855) had scolded his father: 'If you ever get us into such losses as you have this twelve months or more, I shall go clean off my head.'[19] Those who ran the company in the twentieth century took a similarly hard-headed attitude. Harry's son Oliver (born in 1892) joined the board in 1921. He worked in tandem with Peter Bennett (born in 1880), who had been the co-owner of a magneto manufacturing firm that Lucas had bought in 1914. Bennett and Oliver Lucas came from similar backgrounds – both had been educated locally at King Edward's School. This may not have made much difference to what they learned (the curriculum at King Edward's was as traditional as that of any public school) but it probably saved them from the high-minded distractions that increasingly occupied the Kenrick family. Lucas and Bennett were still rooted in the workshop culture of nineteenth-century Birmingham. The former had been set to work with Jack Orme, a craftsman of his own age. The latter kept his own workshop in the factory and sometimes worked in overalls. This did not, however, mean that either man was attached to the past. Oliver was a frequent visitor to the United States and sought to introduce the techniques that he observed there. In particular, he brought in experts on time and motion from the Bedaux consultancy. Protests by workers eventually forced the management into an apparent retreat on the employment of Bedaux, but in practice the system was introduced under a different name and Fred Garner (still on the Bedaux payroll) became an influential figure in Lucas management.[20] The workers more or less understood what was going on. One of them recalled: 'Lucas was on the piece-work system, the bedder system ... That was what they called "Lucas points".'[21]

The greatest dramas of inter-war Birmingham business were seen at the Austin car factory at Longbridge. Herbert Austin, who had established the company in 1905, remained the largest shareholder and ran the company until his death in 1941; he signed off designs for post-war models of cars just minutes before he died. The company's fortunes fluctuated in revealing ways. Having expanded so quickly during the First World War, it adjusted badly to the coming of peace. The number of its employees dropped by more than half between 1918 and 1919. It had trouble paying its debts and tottered on the edge of extinction; a receiver was appointed in 1921. This crisis may have done the company good. It forced Herbert Austin to accept the appointment of managers imposed by his creditors and meant that Austin's own powerful personality was partly contained thereafter by formal structures. C.R. Engelbach (1876–1943), who became works' director at Austin in 1921, was the most important architect of the Longbridge plant's reorganization. Leonard Lord, who had resigned as managing director of Nuffield in 1936, moved to Austin in 1938, the year that Engelbach retired, and eventually became managing director of the company.

It was in the aftermath of his company being put into receivership that Herbert Austin pulled off his most spectacular industrial coup. He converted the billiard room at Lickey Grange, his Worcestershire home, into a workshop and summoned a single seventeen-year-old apprentice (Stanley Edge) from the drawing office at Longbridge. Edge, who had worked at the Austin works since he was fourteen, was given the free-hand drawings that Herbert Austin had produced himself and told to turn them into a design for a new car. They worked through a variety of ideas – some 'ridiculous and interesting' – before hitting on the small car that became the Austin Seven. Herbert Austin was not a nice man but it is hard not to be moved by the thought of him and a boy young enough to be his son (Austin's real son, Vernon, had been killed in action in 1915) huddled over the table in their shirtsleeves as they drew up the plans that would save the company. Austin and Edge fitted into a social pattern that some had discerned in nineteenth-century Birmingham – a world in which rough, self-made men worked alongside sharp-witted lads who reminded them of their younger selves.[22]

The design for the new car – the 'Baby Austin' as it became known – was turned into a prototype in the few weeks between Easter Monday and Whit weekend 1922. It was a gamble. A wheel fell off a model as Herbert Austin himself took it round a sharp bend, and Edge was so nervous that he could not watch when the car was shown to the public for the first time. Austin's son-in-law Arthur Waite, a racing driver, took the car racing at Monza in Italy, in the hope that no one in Britain would notice if it failed. As it turned out, the Austin Seven succeeded. Austin had wanted a car that was cheap enough to compete with the motorcycle and sidecar, and eventually the price of the Austin Seven came down to £100. In 1922, Austin sold 2,600 cars, of which 178 were Austin Sevens. In total it had just 4 per cent of the UK market. By 1935,

Austin sold over 75,000 cars, of which more than 27,000 were Austin Sevens. Between 1929 and 1939, Austin had at least a fifth, and some-times a quarter, of the UK market.[23] The Baby Austin was to the middle classes what Cadbury's Dairy Milk was to the working classes – a cheap and mass-produced version of what would once have been a luxury.

SOCIAL CHANGE IN INTER-WAR BIRMINGHAM

Those who commented on standards of living in inter-war Birmingham were oddly divided. Some cited examples of picturesque poverty. Frank Price, born in Hockley in 1922 and Labour mayor of Birmingham after the war, claimed that some of the families with whom he grew up put a single Oxo cube on the altar at harvest festival.[24] Oswald Mosley, when a Labour candidate in Birmingham in the 1920s, talked of mothers who were so starved that they could produce no milk for the babies at their breast.[25] Many historians interpret Birmingham in more optimistic terms, though, and associate this with a more optimistic interpretation of inter-war Britain – one that emphasizes the relative prosperity of the Midlands and the South East rather than the poverty of Wales and the North. Historians have often pointed out that the 1930s were a good time for some in Britain because new industries provided both employ-ment and new kinds of consumer goods. Nothing illustrates this better than the success of the Baby Austin and it is significant that Austin, almost bankrupt after the First World War, paid a dividend in 1930 – for the first time in twelve years.

In part, these varied interpretations sprang from the fact that Bir-mingham's expansion had really created multiple cities. In the inter-war period, more than ever before, Birmingham was marked by a division into three rings. The inner ring was the oldest and most crowded part of town. Factories and houses were close together and many of the trad-itional industries – jewellery, gun-making – in this part of the city were in decline. The slums of central Birmingham often seemed familiar to those who migrated to the city in search of work – as though this was a town that had been transplanted from the North. Conditions in the middle ring were better. Comparing overall mortality rates is deceptive (because the inner ring had a disproportionate number of old people) but infant mortality figures are revealing. In 1931, they stood at 96 per 1,000 live births in the inner ring, 75 in the middle ring and 55 in the outer ring. Overall, infant mortality across the city dropped for most of the inter-war period (it increased briefly in the late 1920s). It stood at 60 per 1,000 across the city in 1937 and 1938 (it had been 214 in 1898). There was, however, a slight increase in the outer ring in the early 1930s. This may have been partly because the new council estates built on the outskirts of the city were more crowded than the housing that had previously been there, though much less crowded than the housing most of the inhabitants had left. It may have been because some of the families on the new estates had only just arrived from less salubrious areas.[26]

The outer ring itself was changing as new areas were annexed by the city and as people moved into neighbourhoods that had previously been sparsely inhabited. Modern estates were built on what until recently had been farmland. The working-class ancestors of the historian Alison Light were 'rural migrants who were drawn to Birmingham as the city reached out to them'. She was surprised to find that her own father, who regarded himself as a 'Brummy', had actually grown up in the 1920s in Cleeve Road in Billesley Common, at a time when it was still an area of farms and woods only just beginning to see the growth of housing estates.[27] The artist Frank Lockwood moved to Acocks Green in the late 1920s. During the run-up to the Second World War it was to become one of the major centres of the aircraft and motor industries, but Lockwood's early paintings are nostalgic – depicting the world of barns, carts and village greens that was disappearing, rather than the world of giant factories and arterial roads that was coming into existence.[28]

For some time the policy of Birmingham Corporation had been to encourage house building further from the centre. More than 100,000 houses were built in inter-war Birmingham, the majority of them in the outer ring,[29] in areas such as Acocks Green and Weoley Castle. The Kingstanding estate was for a time the largest municipal estate in Europe. However, most new houses were private rather than controlled by the council. In the twenty years to January 1939, the council built 50,268 houses, which accommodated 200,000 people; during the same period, private developers built 54,536 houses. The balance of public and private construction varied sharply over time. Almost 33,000 council houses (over half the inter-war total) were built between 1924 and

1931. After the Depression of 1931, public building slowed markedly, though it picked up slightly in the late 1930s.

Council housing was not designed to accommodate the poorest. Alison Light's grandfather built council houses, but his wages as a bricklayer were too irregular for him to live in one. Rents were relatively high. They were around 10 shillings per week for most council houses and could be as high as £1 a week for the best houses in Kingstanding, at a time when houses in central Birmingham could be had for less than 5 shillings per week.[30] To start with, housing on the estates was specifically built for the 'respectable' – though families displaced by slum clearance were being moved into such places by the end of the 1930s. Indeed, respectability was almost built into new houses. They had front gardens – tenants felt obliged to tend these semi-public spaces, though they were not useful as places for children to play or housewives to dry washing. The council gave prizes for well-tended gardens. The Lord Mayor, presenting such a prize, told his audience that the two most beautiful things in the world were 'music and flowers' and that 'a tenant who allowed weeds to grow rampant was a nuisance to the whole neighbourhood'.[31]

Houses often had front parlours, which were also kept fit for public viewing, though they were hardly used, except, one suspects, when working-class families received the middle-class social investigators who occasionally descended on them. The majority of tenants – 7,495 of the 11,224 applicants for council housing in 1935 – did not want houses with parlours, because they were more expensive.[32] Often, however, they were forced to choose between having this surplus room and not getting a house at all. Parlours illustrated the paradoxes of working-class respectability. In theory, at least on the Kingstanding estate, tenants were allowed to use their parlour as an extra bedroom but few chose to do so. Parlours went with a more general sense that 'keeping house' was in itself a full-time job. Married women on the new estates rarely did paid work. The big engineering and motor factories employed more women than their counterparts in northern cities but women, and especially married women, were still only a minority of their employees. Cadbury sometimes took married women for short bursts of seasonal work before Christmas and Easter but kept few on long-term contracts. In 1938, the company employed 4,664 full-time single women but only 222 married ones.[33] The firm regarded it as desirable that at least some of its employees should return home for lunch, which presumably meant a lunch that had been cooked by a wife or mother. On the whole, the full-time jobs for married women, such as they were, were in the old workshops in the centre of town. Women who moved to the new estates were usually moving away from steady, paid employment. They some-times found work as cleaners – the estates in the south west of the city were close to the large houses of Edgbaston and Moseley, which, after the First World War, were less likely to have live-in servants. Generally, though, tenants on the new estates apparently regarded the non-working wife as another symbol of respectability.

The career of Lily Thomas provides a good example of how new housing matched new definitions of respectability. Her parents were nail-makers (a notoriously rough trade) and worked in a workshop at the back of the small family house. Lily had seven siblings, one of whom died in infancy. Her family was too poor to send her to grammar school (though she passed the entrance examination) and she was obliged to work part-time from the age of twelve. For about six years she worked at the Austin factory – at first commuting in the back of a lorry. In 1933, she was married and gave birth to her first child, in the back bedroom of her sister-in-law's council house in Halesowen, which she shared with her new husband. Soon after this, the couple and their child moved up in the world because they were able to buy a house for £350 in Sunbury Road.[34] Lily's husband, Dick Etheridge, eventually was employed at the Austin works himself where he became convenor. He believed that his union (the AEU) had made a mistake by not accepting women workers, but insisted that Lily give up work.

There was another shift in family life associated – as cause and/or effect – with moving to the new estates. Working-class families became smaller. Twelve women who moved to new estates in south west Bir-mingham between the wars had twenty-one children between them; their mothers had had fifty-seven children, of whom six had died in infancy.[35] Middle-class observers took a keen interest in family size. They noted that large families often lived at levels that were 'below suf-ficiency'. A third of all families fell into this category. Among those with one child, only 13 per cent were below the 'minimum standard'; among those with two, the proportion rose to 45 per cent and, among those with six or more children, it was 96 per cent.[36]

Some could not sustain their lives on the new estates. Florence

Lutwich's family seemed particularly out of place in Kingstanding. Her mother was illiterate and had given birth to her first child on her sixteenth birthday, which was also her wedding day, on a sheet of newspaper in a poor house in Hockley. The family had four children by the time they moved to Twickenham Road in Kingstanding (they had nine eventually) but they had moved back within months. Florence believed that it was because her father could not tolerate the fact that there was no pub within easy reach of his house – though it may have been for professional as much as personal reasons because he was a newsvendor who made part of his money from acting as a 'nark' or lookout on behalf of illegal bookmakers.[37] Of the hundred residents of Jervoise Road in Weoley Castle estate between 1929 and 1939, only half stayed. About a quarter of them moved back to cramped districts of central Birmingham – three of them returned to the very houses they had left.[38]

Even for those with adequate incomes, the estates were not always easy places to live in. There was little attempt to match new housing with new factories. Many men travelled long distances to their work, sometimes catching three separate buses or trams. Buses replaced trams as Birmingham spread out. In the year ending March 1927, trams had carried 238 million passengers against 43 million carried by buses. By 1938 the figures were 174 million and 225 million. By this time, Birmingham Corporation owned the largest fleet of buses in the world.[39] Not surprisingly, public transport became an obsession for many. The outer circle, which was opened in 1926, was 25 miles long and took over two hours to complete. The city circle (number 19) opened in 1932 and was just under 7 miles long while the inner circle (number 8) opened in 1928, and was 11 miles long. There is a small literary genre devoted to Birmingham bus routes. One of Roy Fisher's post-war poems alludes to the illuminated bus that emerged from the Kyotts Lake Road depot to celebrate the centenary of Birmingham's incorporation in 1938. The writer William Bloomer, visiting Birmingham around the same time, described the destination of the 12A, 'World's End via Lakey Lane', as 'pure Auden'.[40]

Even Cadbury, which had constructed the Bournville estate specifically to accommodate its workers, employed some people who lived far away. Only a minority of workers at the Longbridge car works lived in its vicinity. Women who lived on new estates – often young mothers – were less likely to work but they found shopping difficult. Some of them remained emotionally tied to older, more central areas of the city, especially when their own mothers still lived in them. Until the late 1930s, estates were often built with little concern for collective amenities. The Kingstanding estate had roughly the same population as Shrewsbury but had only one church and one hall at first, while Shrewsbury had thirty churches, twenty halls and two cinemas. A woman who moved to the Billesley estate in the 1920s recalled that bus conductors used to call out 'Siberia' when they arrived at the terminus that served her home.[41]

Standards of living in Birmingham varied over time as well as from place to place. Birmingham industry contracted sharply after the First World War. In 1921 there were 64,129 people in Birmingham without work of any kind and the city was said to have more unemployed than 'Manchester and Liverpool combined'.[42] The National Unemployed Workers' Union was sufficiently active in Birmingham to attract the attention of the Home Office. There was also much short-time working. Kenricks hardware put part of its workforce on a three-day week in the early 1920s. Declining trades, such as jewellery, were prone to adopt short-time working – though so too were some of the modern industries, notably motor manufacture (see chapter 7). Some estimated that there were times when a quarter of the entire Birmingham workforce was on short-time.

However, Birmingham became more prosperous in the late 1920s and the Depression of the early 1930s was less severe and less long lasting in Birmingham than in much of the country. The comparison was especially marked with respect to Wales, Scotland and the North. Birmingham and Glasgow had roughly the same population, but in October 1931 unemployment in Birmingham peaked at around 70,000; in Glasgow, it was over 125,000. A year later, the number in Birmingham had dropped to just over 50,000; in Glasgow it had risen to around 127,000. By October 1934, there were around 30,000 unemployed in Birmingham and 107,000 in Glasgow.[43] The Board of Trade carried out enquiries about factories that opened and closed in various parts of the country. In Wigan, in the three months to September 1935, five factories employing more than twenty-five people closed. One, employing forty workers, moved to Bolton; the others, employing a total of 880, had 'given up'. In Birmingham, during the same period, new factories opened and those that closed almost invariably reopened at another site in the city.[44]

Birmingham unemployment was also lower than that of the immediately adjacent areas in the Black Country, where the economy still revolved around older industries. At the worst moment of the Depression in 1931, the unemployment rate in Birmingham was 17.7 per cent. In Dudley, it was 38.8 per cent and, out of fifteen Black Country towns, only Smethwick had an unemployment rate below 20 per cent.[45] The gulf between Birmingham and the Black Country is even more striking when one remembers that a significant proportion of those who were employed in Birmingham commuted from places such as Willenhall and Walsall. When Birmingham established schemes to provide work and training for the unemployed, these were only authorized by the government on the understanding that a substantial proportion of places (at first a half and then a quarter) should be reserved for people from areas where unemployment was worse.

MIGRATION

In the 1930s, even more than previously, Birmingham became a magnet for immigrants from parts of Britain where the economic climate was less benign. Some found their own way to the city. An unemployed miner from the Rhondda walked to Birmingham in 1936. When he arrived, he went to the police station and asked for directions. They told him that the nearest collieries were around Coventry, but they put him up overnight in the cells and had a whip round to pay his onward fare.[46] The police also recorded 300 'lorry girls' who had hitched lifts to Birmingham between 1930 and 1935 – almost all of them were from the economically distressed areas of the North.[47] Some workers came to Birmingham because they were sent to one of the training centres there and subsequently obtained jobs. Some were sent directly by local labour exchanges and some were guided by family contacts or local networks. A single worker who moved from Heywood in Lancashire subsequently encouraged between eighty and a hundred people from his home town to move to his new factory in Birmingham.[48] Different communities of migrants concentrated in particular parts of the city – some from Wales lived in Tyseley; some from Oldham in Washwood Heath. Many of those who came to Birmingham were very young. Juveniles – cheap and relatively easy to control – were attractive to employers. Most migrants

SECOND CITY

were working class and driven by unemployment but even middle-class
people moved. Grace Holte, born into the post-war Birmingham working class, remembered being taught at William Cowper School in
Newtown in the 1960s by teachers who had come, or whose parents
had come, from the Welsh mining valleys – 'Big Mr Jones, Little Mr
Jones . . . Miss Jones'.[49]

Coming to Birmingham was not always easy. This was true even of
those who lived within commuting distance. Among the workers at the
Austin factory, 300 lived in Wolverhampton – which must have involved
them in about three hours of travel every day. Arthur Bate grew up
around Dudley in the Black Country. After six months of unemployment, he cycled from his home to get a job at the Austin works in
Longbridge.[50] Phil Blewitt started work at the Austin plant in Longbridge around 1938, when he was twenty-one. He lived in Oldbury in
the Black Country. At first, he paid a neighbour who worked in the
same factory for a lift in his car. After a while, a local company provided
transport from Oldbury to Longbridge – first in lorries covered with
tarpaulin and then in coaches. Blewitt got his journey free in return for
acting as a conductor and collecting the fares of his fellow passengers.
Those who came from nearby towns sometimes found they were treated
as outsiders in Birmingham. This could be just banter but it could be
intimidating, especially for a young worker: Blewitt recalled that, even
though his own father had worked at the Austin factory, his colleagues refused to speak to him for the first two or three weeks of his
employment.[51]

For those from further afield, the move to Birmingham was even
harder. Leslie Jones was born in the Rhondda in 1921. He left school in
August 1935 and, after a few weeks of unemployment, the labour
exchange found him a job in a Midlands foundry – in Halesowen, where
unemployment was worse than in Birmingham though better than in
south Wales. Jones found the accent hard to understand and the job
hard to master. He felt homesick and begged to leave. He was then sent
to the Midlands again, this time to work as a scullion at the public
school in Bloxham. Finally, he went to Birmingham. His two older
brothers had been trained as welders in the centre set up for the
unemployed in Garrison Lane in Bordesley. Leslie started work in a
New Street hotel for 10 shillings per week (he was now seventeen) and
began to explore the city – which was known to the Welsh for its 'pubs,

164

pictures [i.e. cinemas] and pawnshops'. Finally, wanting to have his evenings free, he got a job at BSA in Waverley Road and was now paid 18s 4d per week. For the next few years, as Birmingham entered the dizzy economics of rearmament, he was able to change jobs frequently, pushing his wages up by a 'few coppers' each time. He moved through Reynolds Tubes, the Singer Motor Company and then back to another BSA works. Finally, he had a lucky break when one of his brothers got him a job at Britannia Tubes, where he was able to learn gas welding and thus acquire a trade. He moved to AJ Homer in Balsall Heath where his wages reached £3 a week before disaster struck and he was conscripted into the air force, on 14 shillings per week.[52] Bryn Charles was also Welsh and had started work in the mines at the age of fourteen but he left when he became unemployed and went to Birmingham. He started digging ditches at the Cadbury grounds and was accommodated in a railway carriage alongside the factory until he could be found lodgings. Then a relative, a second cousin whom he had never actually met until he arrived in Birmingham, got him a job at Briggs Motors.[53]

Ernest Taylor was born in 1920 in Sunderland. He left school at fourteen and worked in a succession of jobs – as a grocer's errand boy, at a butcher's and in the stables in which a brewery kept its horses. He soon discovered, like many boys of his generation, that keeping a job beyond the age of eighteen, when he would become more expensive to employ, was hard. He was sent (presumably by the labour exchange) to Birmingham and put on a scheme designed to train him to be a semi-skilled machinist working on a capstan lathe. The course was meant to last for six months but, when the war broke out, he left and returned home to join the Durham Light Infantry. Instead of enjoying five years of relative prosperity as a worker in the Birmingham war economy, he fought his way across North Africa before being captured. It was as a prisoner of war at Siemens that he finally submitted to factory discipline.[54]

As striking as the migration into Birmingham, was the fact that migration out of the city stopped. The Middlemore Homes had been founded in 1872 in Birmingham to prepare children from poor backgrounds – 'gutter children' as it was put at the time – for emigration to the British Empire. At first, they took such children largely from Birmingham.[55] By the 1930s, though, fewer children in the Middlemore Home in Weoley Park Road came from Birmingham. Of the fifty-four boys and twenty-four girls who arrived in 1936, almost all came from the 'Special Areas of the North of England' (largely from Newcastle). The charity's trustees believed that Birmingham children were mainly 'well-nourished'.[56]

Relatively low unemployment did not mean that everyone in Birmingham was spared. Women, who had made up a large part of the Birmingham workforce, were often first to lose their jobs. Big employers systematically got rid of married women. The effect of such practices was to ensure that a high proportion of the workforce was made up of young girls on low wages. During the Depression, girls could sometimes find that they were forced to support their families. Women were also more likely than men to be turned down for public assistance, which meant that they sometimes did not even bother to register as unemployed and consequently disappeared from the statistics altogether. There was poverty in parts of the city. In 1935, 30,212 families were said to be living in conditions 'detrimental to good health'.[57]

SPENDING MONEY IN INTER-WAR BIRMINGHAM

Overall, though, Birmingham was a prosperous city between the wars, and especially towards the end of this period. Its inhabitants enjoyed the new amusements of the time. Norman Tiptaft, the Birmingham municipal politician, believed that the decline of the jewellery trade, which had once been so closely identified with the city and in which he had made his own money, sprang from the fact that people now spent money on less tangible items.[58]

Nothing epitomized the prosperity and modernity of inter-war Birmingham better than the pub. The grand public houses of the city centre or the beer shops of the poorest quarters were increasingly replaced by large establishments – parodies of a country coaching inn – which were constructed by the breweries in the developing areas on the edge of the city, where space was easiest to come by. This was part of a more general process. Ever since the beginning of the century and across the country, brewers had been encouraged to adopt a 'fewer and better' policy, which meant giving up licences in the centres of cities in return for being allowed to construct a relatively small number of large pubs in the suburbs. This policy began to have a marked effect in the inter-war period and in the most prosperous areas: London and the Midlands.

There was a specifically Birmingham dimension to this change. The Nonconformist families who exercised such power in the city favoured temperance. The Cadburys had excluded pubs from the Bournville estate, which meant that a ring of such establishments formed just outside the area that they controlled. Joseph Chamberlain had taken a subtler approach. He did not seek to prevent the consumption of alcohol but rather to regulate it. He had tried to create independent inspectors, who would be less prone than the regular Birmingham police to take bribes from publicans for turning a blind eye to breaches of licence conditions, and he had considered municipal control of drink sales. He said, characteristically, that he wanted 'to treat the drink question as we have treated the gas question'.[59] Chamberlain's brother, Arthur, who until 1904 presided over the committee of city magistrates that granted licences, was not a complete prohibitionist but he hoped to prevent the expansion of pubs in the new areas that the city was annexing.

Elsewhere in England, the politics of drink were fairly simple in the early twentieth century: Tories, who were close to brewers, came up against Liberals, who had associations with temperance campaigners. In Birmingham, the Unionists, while being Conservatives in all but name, preserved traces of their disapproving attitude to drink. A few local brewers remained hostile to the Birmingham Conservative Party, though sympathetic to the national one, right up to the 1950s.[60] There were also Birmingham brewers who recognized that they needed to reach an accommodation with the authorities. The largest of them – Mitchells and Butlers of Smethwick – were sympathetic to the idea that they should sell their beer in a smaller number of outlets and with a higher degree of regulation. They also probably appreciated that such a policy might give them an advantage over their smaller competitors. In 1900 there had been twenty-three brewers in Birmingham, of which seventeen were 'public' (i.e. quoted on the stock exchange) and six were private; by 1940 there were just seven brewers, all of them public. Mitchells and Butlers did particularly well out of the process and its total value reached £5 million – the next largest Birmingham brewer, Ansells, was worth about £1,350,000. Nine of the pubs that M&B built in Birmingham proper were worth over £20,000 each – though, in view of the ways in which 'reformed pubs' seemed to be allied with modernity, it was appropriate that the most expensive of M&B's new operations was at Elmdon Aerodrome, which was eventually to become Birmingham airport.

Table 3. New Pubs in the Different Parts of Birmingham, 1905–39

	Inner	Middle	Outer	Total
1905–14	15	9	4	28
1919–29	12	10	41	63
1929–39	18	13	68	99

Source: David Gutzke, *Pubs and Progressives: Reinventing the Public House in England, 1896–1960*, p. 86

A new style of pub underwrote a compromise between brewers and the local authorities. It marked a move away from spit and sawdust bars (banishing spittoons and laying down linoleum were important parts of the new order) in which the closing-time punch-ups had been the only distraction from drinking. Large, well-lit and built on main roads, usually close to new housing estates, the new pubs were orderly places – 'easily supervised by the manager, his staff and the police'. The moral tone that lay behind slum clearance often also underlay the new policy on licencing – in both cases much attention was given to light, ventilation and hygiene.

The new pubs offered a wide range of attractions other than drinking. Birmingham pubs were the first in the country to introduce rooms for children. Toilets – with 'Ladies' and 'Gentlemen' carefully positioned at opposite ends of the building – seemed fancy at a time when most residents of central Birmingham still shared outside privies with their neighbours. Architects came to specialize in pubs – Bateman and Bateman designed ten in Birmingham. Bateman had, in the nineteenth century, built the Church of the Saviour on Edward Street and the firm's buildings were intended to impress. Among M&B's inter-war pubs, four were influenced by the Jacobean revival style, two were neo-Georgian, one Arts and Crafts and one Moderne – the latter category encapsulating those buildings that were intended to look as though they had been built in the inter-war period. The Court Oak in Quinton (another M&B pub) was Hispano-Moorish in style. Long before the majority of

Birmingham's inhabitants owned cars, the new pubs had areas for parking – partly because some aimed to cater for 'charabanc parties'. Some were surrounded by extensive and well-tended grounds, with hedges, gardens and bowling greens. It seemed almost as though the brewers were mocking the Cadbury family by creating miniature versions of Bournville Village around each of their pubs.[61]

The most spectacular of Birmingham inter-war pubs was the Black Horse in Northfield, built in 1929. Its proprietor, Davenports (a comparatively small brewery), hailed its opening thus: 'This half-timbered, gable surmounted, mullion windowed, Tudor doorwayed building – a pleasant version of merrie England – is surely some stately baronial hall bequeathed to us by Elizabethan days.' The architect (Francis Goldsbrough of Bateman and Bateman) had insisted that a 'Tudor' pub should involve some authentic material and craftsmanship – the building featured stonework by Sidney Smith and decorative woodwork by Jean Hahn. A mantelpiece was left unfinished because, it was said, the old stonemason, who had been given an unexpected chance to display his skill, died, having expressed the wish that his last work should be left as it was.[62] As well as two smoking rooms (one reserved for 'gentlemen'), bars and a bowling green, the Black Horse had assembly rooms designed to look like the great hall of a manor house. It was made a listed building in 1981 on the grounds that it was 'the grandest of the post-First World War "reformed pubs", built on a vast scale in a highly successful, picturesque, high Vernacular Revival'. Its location was significant. It stood on what was then the edge of the city and on the main road that would have taken coach parties towards the Lickey Hills. It was close enough to Bournville to be within reach for workers from the Cadbury factory who wanted to refresh themselves with something other than malted milk. It was also close to the Austin car works. The pub's huge rooms would have provided a convenient place for trade unionists to meet. Perhaps it is significant that one of the people who signed the visitors' book in 1931 – describing it as 'one of the most beautiful houses I have seen' – was Margaret Bondfield, the Minister of Labour in the Labour government of 1929–31.[63]

There were other signs of prosperity in inter-war Birmingham. The number of radio licences trebled in the 1930s to reach almost 300,000.[64] Radio began to blur regional and social distinctions. Henry Green arrived, fresh from Eton and Oxford, to work at his father's factory in

Yardley in 1926. He recalled: 'At the time I went there when hardly any-one had more than a crystal set, the announcers of the BBC had not got going with their BBC English so that I sometimes had trouble to make my accent understood or to understand theirs.'[65] Ten years later, he would have found communication easier – though the Birmingham working classes were more likely to have picked up the slightly Ameri-canized tones of band leaders and comedians rather than the patrician accents of newsreaders.

A dog-racing track at King's Heath opened in 1927. It offered dis-traction to many and an income for an enterprising few. Edward Sturman had been born in 1912 between Birmingham and Dudley. His life was hard because his mother died of tuberculosis and he himself caught diphtheria, which kept him off school for two years. He finished his education at St Paul's in Balsall Heath; he remembered that most of his classmates had no shoes and that he would deliberately dirty his new sweaters to avoid standing out. He had the good fortune, however, to be raised by his grandfather, who was a bookmaker and noticed that the boy was a good judge of form. By the age of seventeen, Edward himself was 'making a book'. He spent his illegal gains on joining the Midland Aero Club, where he had flying lessons for 30 shillings an hour, and on paying a tutor to coach him in mathematics and navigation. He eventu-ally joined the Air Transport Auxiliary and spent the war ferrying Spitfires around the country.[66]

Some observers, especially from the political left, disapproved of commercialized spectator sport in Birmingham. One of the characters in an autobiographical novel by Norman Tiptaft says: 'the rulers of Brassville admit, if watching football does not require the highest type of brain, neither does it make revolutionaries'.[67] This was unfair. It is true enough that Birmingham did not have many revolutionaries but those who grew up watching the three main professional teams with followings in Birmingham – Aston Villa, Birmingham City and West Bromwich Albion – probably voted Labour, and at least one Villa fan, Denis Howell, would become a Labour MP. In any case, watching sport did not preclude playing it and there were still hundreds of teams attached to Birmingham factories in the 1930s – though it was only Cadburys who gave their workers the resources to play squash or bad-minton. Curiously, the miners from south Wales who flooded into Birmingham factories did not bring their game with them and rugby remained almost exclusively the sport of those who attended the schools of the King Edward's Foundation.

Birmingham was also a cinema city. The Futurist in John Bright Street showed the first talking picture in Birmingham – *The Singing Fool* – in 1929. The queues for the five daily performances were so long that police were sent to contain them and 100,000 people were said to have seen the film in four weeks.[68] It was at the Futurist that John Hampson Simpson, the homosexual novelist, and Therese Giehse, the German Jewish actress, spent their one afternoon of 'honeymoon' after their marriage of convenience on 20 May 1936 (see chapter 12).[69]

A survey of almost 1,500 Birmingham schoolchildren showed that only a tiny minority never went to the cinema; over half did so at least once a week. Oscar Deutsch – who had started as a scrap metal merchant – opened the first of his Odeon chain of cinemas in Perry Barr in 1930. He would go on to open 300 of them across the country (thirty-seven in 1937 alone) and he remained based in Birmingham until 1939. By this time there were around a hundred cinemas in the city. New cinemas in the 1930s were sited particularly in the new estates – Kingstanding got its cinema in 1935 – and they were often the first institutions to provide centres of collective life in such places.

Films saturated every corner of Birmingham life. As a pupil at King Edward's School in the late 1930s, Kenneth Tynan subscribed to *Film Pictorial* and *Picturegoer*.[70] When the Birmingham police uncovered a network of homosexual men in the 1950s, they were struck by the pseudonyms that their suspects operated under – Marlene, the Duchess, Garbo, Rita, Jezebel – all sure signs of men who had grown up on a diet of pre-war Hollywood.[71] Cinema became a cultural battleground in the 1920s and 30s. A part of the town's middle class disapproved of films. They believed that they went hand in hand with cheap thrills and Americanization. 'We do not,' said the deputy chair of the city magistrates, 'want children to say "Oh yeah" and "OK kid".' Films were also feared to encourage violence – though children's favourites were comedies, and one suspects that the boy who said he valued cinema 'because it shows me how to strangle people' may have had a sharper sense of humour than his interviewer.[72]

A Birmingham Cinema Committee was established, under the chairmanship of the vice chancellor of the university, to investigate the effects of films. Birmingham had been particularly associated with the promotion of 'rational recreation', i.e. recreation that was also 'improving' in moral and educational terms, that often accompanied the 'civic gospel' preached by the city's nineteenth-century ministers. Those who regarded themselves as guardians of this tradition found it galling that the Mount Zion chapel, in which George Dawson had once preached, had become the Lyric cinema, having briefly served as a music hall and venue for boxing matches. The rational recreationalists were particularly opposed to the Sunday opening of cinemas but they failed in their campaign against it and, in 1930, between 40,000 and 50,000 people in Birmingham went to the cinema on a single Sunday. Even the members of families most associated with the civic gospel sometimes recognized that cinema might have some improving qualities. Neville Chamberlain presided over the opening of the first Birmingham cinema to specialize in newsreels and was himself an accomplished performer in such films.

Social change went with a new sense of class. A large proportion of the Birmingham working class no longer lived near their workplace and did not socialize with their workmates. Working-class life was increasingly likely to revolve around the home rather than the factory. Leisure was not often explicitly marked by class. Until the Second World War, there was little reference to the life of factories on the radio and discussion of class was most likely in programmes that were primarily aimed at the middle class.[73] A section of the middle class may have disapproved of cinema or the frequenting of pubs but neither the new-style pubs nor the cinemas were exclusively working class. The cinema was, above all, escapist. J.B. Priestley wrote, after visiting Birmingham in 1933: 'Why were the newest and largest buildings ... either picture theatres or pubs? Because both of them offer escape ... either the confectionery drama of the films or a few quick drinks.'[74] The big, glamorous Birmingham cinemas were built to seem as unlike daily life as possible. Bernard Loftus, born in Aston in 1923, recalled:

> The thing that struck me with cinemas, you left the world outside, you went into another world ... At Lozell's Picture House I remember ... there'd be a young lad in uniform with a great big cylinder on his shoulder ... he used to squirt perfumed air out and that smell I'll never forget ... the lovely feel of carpets ... you'd sink into the seats and you were lost for two hours.[75]

The poet Louis MacNeice was a long way from Bernard Loftus's social world but he too understood the attractions of unreality. He recalled the time that he and his wife spent in Birmingham in the late 1930s:

Four or five times a week we went to the cinema, going solely for entertainment and never for value, holding hands like a shopgirl with her boy-friend. The organist would come through the floor, a purple spotlight on his brilliantined head, and play us the 'Londonderry Air' and bow and go back to his tomb. Then stars would return close-up and the huge Cupid's bow of their mouths would swallow up everybody's troubles – there were no more offices or factories or shops, no more bosses or foremen, and no more unemployment, and no more employment, no more danger of disease or babies, nothing but bliss in a celluloid world where the roses are always red and the Danube is always blue.[76]

The great majority of films concerned the wealthy and/or the American. The thing most conspicuously absent from Birmingham cinema was Birmingham. Even when cinemagoers at the Odeon in Perry Barr or Kingstanding saw films in which Gracie Fields, George Formby or Dick Van Dyke impersonated the English working classes, they could be sure that they would never hear a Birmingham accent or catch a glimpse of their own city.

Austen Chamberlain campaigning. Austen Chamberlain inherited his father's West Birmingham seat in 1914. Unlike his father, he did not have much taste for popular politics but, unlike his younger brother Neville, he was too honourable to abandon his working-class seat even when, in 1929, his majority shrank to almost nothing.

7

Old Politics, 1911–38

The dramatic social changes of inter-war Birmingham raise questions: why did a new capitalism not create a new socialism? Why did a city that contained some of the largest factories in the country remain 'an inviolate citadel'[1] of Conservatism or, strictly speaking, of Chamberlainite Unionism? There were ninety parliamentary elections in Birmingham between 1918 and 1944 and Unionists/Conservatives were elected on eighty-two of these occasions. This statistic looks even more startling in view of the fact that six of Labour's eight electoral victories occurred in 1929, and that every one of these victories was overturned in 1931. The Labour Party, by now the main opponent of the Conservatives, did not even contest seats on eighteen occasions.

Some had explained the politics of nineteenth-century Birmingham as a product of consensual relations between workers and their employers in small workshops. This explanation was less plausible in the twentieth century because there were more large factories. In any case, there was a bitterness to class relations in the inter-war period – sometimes most vehemently expressed by those who defended property and order. The General Strike of 1926 was relatively well observed in Birmingham at first – particularly among transport workers – but it provoked a vigorous response. Neville Chamberlain, as Minister of Health, had reminded local authorities of their duty to maintain essential services in the event of a strike; 10,000 volunteers worked to keep buses and trains running. Some of them were drawn from the university. Dodds, the professor of Greek, managed to ensure that students who supported and those who opposed the strike were treated in an even-handed manner. There were earnest appeals by churchmen and middle-class women's associations for 'compromise', but the aftermath of the strike saw local trade unionists and Labour leaders lose their jobs and face prosecution – even though Oswald Mosley, at that time nursing a Birmingham constituency for the Labour Party, was away in London when the police raided the strike headquarters and consequently was denied his chance of a well-reported arrest.

THE POLITICS OF SLUMS

There was a strange relation between a certain kind of class consciousness and a certain kind of politics. The central wards were the poorest areas of Birmingham and also the neighbourhoods in which people's lives were most intimately associated with work, in that they lived close to the factories that employed them. These areas, however, did not always vote for the left. Labour won only thirty-two out of ninety-one municipal elections in the inner ring during the inter-war period. In fact, the slums were often Conservative to an extent that perplexed the most prominent Conservatives – perhaps particularly so because Birmingham Unionism had once been associated with notions of respectability and improvement, though parts of the 'respectable' working classes seem to have deserted Joseph Chamberlain after his break with Gladstone and embrace of imperialism (see chapter 5). Austen Chamberlain wrote to his sister in 1922: 'But why anyone who lives in such slums should not be a Socialist, a Communist or a Red Revolutionary I am at a loss to say.'[2] The persistence of Conservatism in the poorest parts of inner Birmingham was sustained by social continuity. These were the oldest parts of the city and, therefore, the ones in which loyalty to the politics of the Chamberlain dynasty had the deepest roots. They were disproportionately inhabited by the old, which may have had a similar effect. Jewellery, though by now a small part of the overall Birmingham economy, was still important in one central quarter and people who lived from the sale of luxury items may have felt that they had interests in common with the wealthy. Those who made sporting guns, another declining industry in central Birmingham, may have had similar feelings.

The Labour Party's emphasis on improving the lives of workers could seem patronizing and intrusive to the least privileged. The terms in which some Birmingham left-wingers described their failures said much about the reasons why they might exasperate part of their potential electorate. In 1925, Norman Tiptaft, who was then still a socialist, put these words into the mouth of a character in an autobiographical novel about Birmingham:

> That is the damnable fact about your average slum dweller. He is living below a decent human standard, and he believes the Almighty put him there. He doesn't want to get out. All he wants is food, drink and amusement. What is the use of talking about the 'New Jerusalem in England's green and pleasant land' to people like that? Amuse the men and promise the women a ride in a car. That, in the twentieth century, is the way to get votes in many parts of highly civilized England.[3]

Slum clearance itself could be offensive to slum dwellers. Frank Lannon, a working-class Conservative candidate, told his electors: 'Housing: the socialist policy is slum clearance. (They refer to your house as a slum.) This means house hunting and removal.' Education also lost Labour votes in the slums. Raising the school-leaving age would have taken away wages that some working-class families needed. This point was also hammered home by Lannon: 'Did you know that the present Socialist Government intend raising the school-leaving age to 15? Did you ask them? Of course you did not!' George Sawyer, the Labour MP for Duddeston from 1929 to 1931, publicly denounced his own party's policy on the school-leaving age.[4]

Charity might also encourage the poor to vote Conservative. Smedley Crooke, Conservative MP for Deritend, spent half his parliamentary salary on 'relieving distress'. The *Birmingham Daily Mail*, which was closely associated with the Conservative Party, gave away clothes and boots to poor children – the items were stamped with the letters 'DM' to prevent families from pawning them. The political implications of accepting such largesse must have been underlined by the fact that it was sometimes distributed at police stations.

Those who lived in the outer part of Birmingham, and particularly those on the council estates that were constructed there, presented an interesting contrast with those of inner Birmingham. In some respects, they were 'less working class' than the relatives they had left behind in the central wards. Their houses were set wider apart and they were more comfortably off. They did, however, often vote Labour. The Conservatives blamed voters on council estates for their loss of Erdington in the 1929 general election,[5] and it may be significant that the greatest swing to Labour came immediately after the greatest burst of council house construction. There were some obvious reasons why council estates were likely to vote Labour. They contained a relatively large number of young people, especially couples with children, who were in all areas more likely to vote Labour. At first, there was little communal life on the new estates, and this itself may have helped to break the political traditions associated with Conservatism, but, when new institutions were established, they provided an opening for new kinds of political organization. The informal solidarity of slum streets was now replaced by a more explicit and large-scale mobilization. Residents of the Weoley Castle estate helped, in some cases with their own hands, to build a Community Hall at Shenley Fields in 1934. Community Associations were often linked with left-wing causes. Their newsletters carried reviews of books on fascism and appeasement and celebrated 'Dusty' Bennett, who left Kingstanding to fight with the International Brigade in Spain, where he was killed.

Council housing did not transform Birmingham politics overnight. Not everyone who moved to the new estates stayed (see chapter 6) and it took time to construct a new political culture. But such a culture was becoming visible by the late 1930s. The mere fact that residents of council estates had a single landlord made it easier to organize them – there was a rent strike by Birmingham council tenants in 1939.

POLITICS AND WORK

Political change (or its absence) in inter-war Birmingham was linked to work as well as housing. The development of new housing on the edge of the city was matched by the establishment of new factories, or the rapid growth of ones that had existed before 1914. To the south west of the city centre were Austin and Cadbury, to the north were GEC, Fort Dunlop and the Birmingham branch of the Cincinnati Machine Tool Company. One might expect large factories to bring a new level of unionization, class consciousness and left-wing power. One might also expect class politics to be strongly associated with the industry that was coming to dominate Birmingham: motor manufacture. In the second half of the twentieth century, many centres of worker militancy in Europe – the Renault works at Boulogne-Billancourt, the

Fiat works in Turin and the Austin/British Leyland works at Longbridge in Birmingham – would be car factories.

The link between large factories, especially car factories, and labour militancy was not an automatic one. Overall, unionization in Birmingham was low. Walter Lewis of the electrical trade union said that Birmingham was 'absolutely stinking with non-unionists'.[6] Dunlop insisted that negotiations between workers and management be conducted via 'works councils', which meant that trade union membership was largely restricted to craft unions. Membership of some unions in Birmingham dropped – that of the Amalgamated Engineering Union from 8,745 in 1920 to 5,371 in 1928. Trade union strength and support for left-wing parties were closely related to each other and it was particularly difficult for workers who were known to be associated with the left to get jobs in many Birmingham factories. Industrialists were usually Conservatives, and two of the most fiercely anti-union employers in the city were Conservative MPs: Herbert Austin represented King's Norton from 1918 to 1924 and Walter Higgs represented West Birmingham from 1937 to 1945. Jim Simmons was working as an inspector at a motor factory in 1924 when he first stood as the Labour candidate in Erdington. After the campaign, he lost his job.[7] Robert Dennison won the parliamentary seat of King's Norton from Austin in 1924 with the memorable slogan 'sack the boss'. However, the Conservatives won the seat back in 1929, at a time when the overall movement was in favour of Labour, and were said to owe their success partly to the fact that Austin had threatened to close his works if Labour won again.

Working-class activists were weakened by the fact that factories that were modern in terms of the things they produced or the machinery they deployed could seem archaic in their rhythms of work. This was especially true of the car industry. The image of motor manufacture was often tied to the pitiless regularity of the production line. In reality, production was uneven. Sales of cars depended on the season. They were highest in the run-up to the annual motor show, which was in October, and around Easter; they were lowest in midwinter and the early summer. A worker at Wolseley recalled that the business he entered in the 1920s was 'very seasonal . . . if you worked three months it was a luxury'.[8] The Midlands Divisions of the Factory Inspectorate reported that the bicycle and motor trades worked an average of fifty-five hours a week in the most active six months and forty-eight hours in the other half of the year.[9] Sometimes the pace slackened in more dramatic ways. The Austin factory was a steadier employer than most of the Birmingham motor factories, which was partly why it paid lower wages, but it often worked short time. Occasionally, it resurrected a joyless and compulsory form of Saint Monday as workers were told not to return to work at the beginning of the week.[10] It also laid workers off when demand reduced and this provided it with an easy means to get rid of agitators. Just after a strike in March–April 1929, there was a brief moment when unions got a foothold at the Austin works (even though the strike had been unofficial). By December of that year, though, the number employed at the Austin works had dropped from 10,000 to 3,000 and many of those dismissed were shop stewards. Dick Etheridge, who would be the convenor at Longbridge during the very different period after 1945, said of the 1930s: 'The breaking of the shop stewards plus the seasonal form of employment meant that no one could get established. Unemployment was deliberately used to undermine the union.'[11]

The effects of unstable employment could be seen in the career of McHugh, a semi-skilled worker said to have been a Communist. McHugh was hired at the Austin factory in 1928 and worked there for twelve of the next twenty years. He left his employment seven times: twice of his own volition and five times because he was discharged.[12] Austin sometimes deliberately looked for quick labour turnover – disposing of experienced workers who had shown themselves ill-disciplined and picking up fresh recruits. Each bout of rehiring in the motor industry was accompanied by ostentatious displays of managerial authority. Foremen would be sitting 'in all their splendour'[13] at the labour exchange when men went to enquire about work.

There was a special dimension to labour relations at the Austin factory at Longbridge. Though it was the most modern factory in Birmingham, it was built on the outskirts of the city in almost rural surroundings. Men who went there from more industrialized parts of the Midlands were astonished to find that they had to walk up what seemed to be a cart track to get into their workplace. Because of this, many of Austin's first workers were recruited from the small towns and countryside of Worcestershire. Such men had no previous experience of industry, or of trade unions – though some of them were drawn from the village of Great Dodford, in which the Chartists had once established a 'settlement'.[14] One of their colleagues recalled: 'A great number of the workers at the Austin also came from rural areas – Bromsgrove etc – and they were less conducive to challenging the management, ... you know lack of trade union tradition really.'[15]

Migration into Birmingham also weakened trade unionism, at least in the short term. Even when unemployment in the city itself was relatively low, Birmingham workers knew that people might be imported from less fortunate areas. Alf Allen recalled the paint shop manager at Longbridge telling workers who might be tempted to strike: 'if you don't want to come into work tomorrow you needn't. I 'ave got five hundred Black Country people ready to come in.'[16] Some also blamed the Welsh for holding down wages. There was, however, a double edge to the use of workers from elsewhere. Migrant workers could seem cheap and docile when they first arrived, but men from outside Birmingham, and especially from mining areas, often brought traditions of militancy with them. Bryn Charles spent most of his life working in the Birmingham motor industry but his political culture owed much to his early life in south Wales: 'Once you're a miner – and being in the Miners' Federation – you're brought up and taught the meaning of the trade unions and so forth.'[17] The unofficial strike at Austin in 1929 was led by a Welshman, Tegfryn Bowen, who would become Lord Mayor of the city in 1952. Mostyn (Moss) Evans was born, the son of a miner, in Wales in 1925 and moved to Small Heath when his father came to Birmingham in search of work in 1937. Evans, having risen through the union hierarchy of Birmingham engineering factories, would end up as general secretary of the Transport and General Workers' Union in 1978.

The instability and insecurity of the industries associated with the motor trade was to some extent counterbalanced by employment that was sheltered from the full operation of market forces. Joseph Chamberlain's municipal activism had created a substantial group of public employees who would be the political opponents of his sons. Bus workers were almost all members of the Transport and General Workers' Union; the gas, water and electricity industries were also highly unionized. The railways were private enterprises, with an authoritarian management, but this was a tightly regulated sector that offered secure jobs and in which workers were often politicized by the obvious link between government policy and their interests. The National Union of Railwaymen, the Associated Society of Locomotive Engineers and

Firemen and the various clerks' associations were powerful in the Birmingham railways. It was said that only twenty Birmingham rail workers did not join the General Strike of 1926. Between 1918 and 1931, railwaymen in Birmingham made up almost 10 per cent of Labour councillors and candidates for the council at a time when they accounted for only 1 per cent of the city's workforce. Of eighteen women councillors and candidates for the council in the same period, at least six were the wives of railwaymen.[18] Rolling stock production was another relatively stable and highly unionized business concentrated in east Birmingham.

Cadbury was the most benign employer in the city – and perhaps the country – though it was paternalistic and patriarchal in its assumption that permanent workers would be men. It provided its employees with a mini welfare state of playing fields, concert halls and medical treatment. About 40 per cent of them lived on the Bournville estate that the Cadbury family had built. Cadbury recognized trade unions as legitimate interlocutors. Where other companies used their works councils as means to circumvent trade unions, Cadbury insisted, at first, that members of the council should also be members of their trade union – though, with a mix of business sense and apparent generosity that was typical of his family, George Cadbury, a member of the Labour Party, suggested that foremen could represent workers better than trade unions.[19] The company provided a refuge for trade unionists who could not get work elsewhere and this refuge was especially important because Bournville was close to the ferociously anti-union Austin factory at Longbridge.

The Cadbury family itself was divided by politics. Sir George Cadbury (1878–1954) joined the Labour Party in 1922. However, his half-brother Laurence Cadbury (1889–1982) seems to have moved to the political right, partly as a result of his distaste for the 'well-manured' consciences of the pacifists that he encountered during his wartime service in the Friends Ambulance Unit.[20] Thereafter, he lost his Quaker faith and, like many people who have lost their faith, felt most at home in the Church of England. He sent his sons to Eton rather than to the Quaker public school he had attended and, in 1930, he sold the *Daily News* (the radical paper his father had bought to campaign against the Boer War). From this point on, the senior men of the Cadbury family, who were most directly associated with running the business, seem to have been discreetly Conservative in outlook, but the public interventions of the family, often conducted by women, continued to be associated with progressive causes. Dame Elizabeth Cadbury even challenged Herbert Austin in his King's Norton constituency when she stood as a Liberal parliamentary candidate in 1923.

Even those Cadburys who were most deeply immersed in business rarely felt the morbid fear of the left that was common among industrialists. William Adlington Cadbury (1867-1957) was one of the few people willing to defend Sir Roger Casement when he was convicted of treason for seeking to help Irish nationalists in 1916. As Lord Mayor of Birmingham in 1921, he said that his Quakerism prevented him from acceding to a government request that he encourage ex-sevicemen to join a 'Defence Force' to protect men working during a strike. The cabinet, chaired in the absence of the Prime Minister by Austen Chamberlain, decided that this duty would be undertaken by the deputy mayor.[21] Sir Adrian Cadbury (1928-2015) was to be a pillar of the Confederation of British Industry, but he maintained friendly relations with Eric Hobsbawm – the Communist historian who had taught him at Cambridge.

Partly because of the Cadbury family's protection, Bournville became a refuge for active members of the Labour Party. When George Cadbury sat as a Labour councillor from 1922 to 1927, six of his colleagues, a substantial portion of the entire Labour group, were employees of his family's company, and Bournville, which accounted for about one in thirty of the Birmingham population, provided a quarter of all the city's Labour councillors. Support from the Cadburys was not an unqualified advantage for the Labour Party in Birmingham. The influence of Cadbury money was a source of dispute in the party. In addition to this, the Quakerly morality of the family and the fact that the Bournville estate was designed to attract, and promote, the most respectable elements of the working class reinforced the association between the Birmingham Labour Party and an improving turn of mind that repelled some working-class voters.

LABOUR DIVIDED

The limited success of the Birmingham left was partly due to the divisions in the Birmingham labour movement. The city's trade unions had often developed in industries that laid a heavy emphasis on inter-class cooperation, and the men who had been formed by this tradition remained powerful, even when the industries from which they came diminished in importance. In addition to this, Birmingham had been, between 1914 and 1918, a centre of pro-war labour leaders while the shop stewards' movement, which incarnated rebellion in the factories against wartime regulations, was weaker in Birmingham than in other industrial centres. In June 1918, trade union 'patriots' led by John Beard, Eldred Hallas and W.J. Davis had seceded from the Trade Council to establish the Birmingham and District Trade Union Industrial Council, which was to be run on 'entirely non-political lines for the specific purpose of safeguarding and promoting Trade Union interest'. They claimed a membership of 100,000 against the 20,000 of the Trade Council – though the very fact that they seceded from, rather than took over, the Trade Council suggests that they were actually in a minority. Eldred Hallas made his first entry into parliamentary politics as a candidate for Duddeston in 1918 for 'Coalition Labour' – meaning that he supported the coalition under Lloyd George that had been formed during the war, though his support for Lloyd George did not, as it turned out, last long.

Some working-class leaders in Birmingham supported the Chamberlainite version of Conservatism. Alfred Jephcott (1853–1932) was a member of the Amalgamated Society of Engineers and one-time leader of the Birmingham Trade Council. He sat as Conservative MP for Yardley from 1918 to 1929 – though he admitted that his position on industrial, as opposed to constitutional, matters was not very different from that of the Labour Party. Two important local politicians moved from Labour to the Conservatives. Percival Bower was the first Labour Lord Mayor of Birmingham in 1925, and was at first regarded by the right as dangerously extreme.[22] However, he angered many of his colleagues when he kept municipal administration running during the General Strike of 1926. He finally left the Labour Party in 1932, having refused to follow the party line that Neville Chamberlain, responsible for cutting unemployment benefit, should not be granted the freedom of the city. The following year, he joined the Conservatives.

Norman Tiptaft had been a Labour candidate in municipal elections in Handsworth before the First World War and an independent 'progressive' councillor and parliamentary candidate, immediately after it.

In 1935, he joined the Conservatives, and stayed with the party, as councillor and mayor, until his cussedness and thwarted vanity took him out of it again, this time becoming an extreme opponent of state intervention, in 1945. Even those who were not tempted by Conservatism, sometimes apparently echoed the tone of municipal improvement that was associated with the memory of Joseph Chamberlain. Percy Shurmer stood for the council in 1921 as a Labour candidate on a manifesto that read 'Vote for Shurmer. His next work: gas and taps in all houses.'

There was also an important group in the Birmingham Labour movement that stood on the extreme left. Jim Simmons, Labour MP for Erdington from 1929 to 1931 and again in 1945, wrote in his memoirs: 'It is sometimes forgotten with what joy the British people welcomed the October Revolution.' Simmons himself represented a political interpretation of the First World War that was very different from that of, say, Eldred Hallas. A private soldier, he had lost part of one leg at Vimy Ridge and subsequently been imprisoned for opposing the war – during his first period in Parliament, one of his colleagues acidly asked the Speaker what rank a man had to have held before he earned the right to be referred to as 'gallant' by other parliamentarians.

Sometimes internal animosities threatened to break the Birmingham Labour Party entirely. Dr Robert Dunstan (a former captain in the army medical corps subject to savage right-wing attacks for allegedly favouring the Germans) had left Labour to join the Communist Party. In 1929, he fought West Birmingham (Austen Chamberlain's seat) as a 'Workers' candidate' who opposed the official Labour candidate, though he had had, at least for a time, support from prominent figures in the Labour Party. Joseph Southall – an artist, Quaker and member of the Independent Labour Party – attacked 'two rich men who control the local Labour Party'; he was referring to George Cadbury and his cousin Harrison Barrow, another wealthy notable. Southall was expelled from the party in 1927 but two constituency associations (Edgbaston and Moseley) then rebelled against the central party in opposition to this expulsion. Two other rich men – Oswald Mosley and John Strachey – also caused division. Glamorous and wealthy outsiders, they could fund their attempts to win Birmingham constituencies from their own resources. They aroused the resentment of more plebeian local Labour leaders. Mosley's 'Birmingham Proposals' of 1925 were designed to break with the economic orthodoxies of both parties and their attitudes to currency must have reminded some of Thomas Attwood. Matters were made more complicated in the early 1930s when Mosley and, for a time, Strachey left Labour to found the 'New Party'. The venture attracted a certain amount of support from Birmingham left-wingers – though few from Birmingham followed Mosley when he established the British Union of Fascists, partly because Birmingham had a small Jewish population and little anti-Semitism.

POLICING POLITICS

The interventions of the police created further difficulties for the Birmingham left. The Home Office supported, and drew information from, 'moderate' elements of the labour movement. In 1921, an official examining 'revolutionary' organizations wrote:

> My Birmingham correspondent reports that the task of the moderate men, who are attempting to counteract the exploitation of the unemployed by extremists is becoming increasingly difficult ... There is dissension among the unemployed committee in Birmingham owing to the effort of the communists to oust the 'moderate' members of the Independent Labour Party.[23]

After a national police strike in 1919, in which the participation of men from the Birmingham force had been relatively high,[24] police pensions and pay were reformed in ways that made policemen less likely to challenge authority. Though working class in terms of origins and pay, the city's policemen were often isolated figures in working-class communities. They found allies elsewhere. Mervyn Pugh was prosecuting solicitor in Birmingham, and the only provincial agent of the Director of Public Prosecutions, from 1924 until 1958. He spent much of his time in the company of senior policemen and was, almost needless to say, a freemason. A sympathetic biographer wrote that 'He was a man's man and a policeman's man.' He himself said: 'I've got one job in life. This is to protect the police.'[25] In turn, the police devoted much energy to the surveillance of the left – two detectives were once assigned to report on a Labour meeting that turned out to be concerned with the organization of a children's outing.

Charles Rafter, the Chief Constable of Birmingham from 1889 to 1935, had been born in County Cork and began his career in the Royal Irish Constabulary, a force that took a particular interest in countering 'subversive' threats. As Ireland became independent and teetered on the brink of civil war, Rafter recruited veterans of the Irish police to serve in Birmingham – the most important of these, Cecil Moriarty (1877–1958), was to succeed Rafter as chief constable. For Rafter, a keen flautist, even the police band seemed to be an instrument of the class war and he once proposed, to the annoyance of the Musicians' Union, that it might supplement the city orchestra.[26]

In Birmingham, perhaps even more than elsewhere, Labour leaders were caught in an awkward dilemma. They faced a hostile police force and were sometimes prosecuted but were themselves mostly respectful of legality. The Watch Committee, which supervised the Birmingham police, met in secret and was dominated by Conservatives but it did contain some Labour councillors. George Sawyer and Percy Shurmer were members of the Watch Committee and deferential to the chief constable,[27] even though both had been prosecuted for criticizing the police and special constables during the General Strike of 1926. They might have been disconcerted to be told that some Birmingham men served as special constables while they were themselves on strike from their regular jobs.[28] Even the left-winger Jim Simmons came to regard the policemen who followed him with a weary affection. In his memoirs he recalled Detective Sergeant Freedman, who took notes at his meetings and then occasionally bought him a cup of tea afterwards.[29]

THE CHAMBERLAIN TRADITION

Birmingham between the wars was more than ever associated with the Chamberlains. Joseph Chamberlain's two sons were both MPs for Birmingham. In addition to this, the city attracted politicians who considered that their support for a certain kind of imperialism made them heirs to Joseph Chamberlain. The most eminent of these was Leo Amery, who represented Birmingham constituencies from 1911 to 1945 (of whom more below).

The apparent continuity of the Chamberlain tradition in Birmingham was rendered all the more intriguing because continuity had been the very characteristic that Joseph Chamberlain had most lacked; indeed, Chamberlainism after Joseph Chamberlain was marked by a stable and understated quality that had been conspicuously absent in Birmingham politics in his heyday. The change was partly a matter of personalities. Joseph Chamberlain's designated heir was his eldest son, Austen (1863–1937). The journalist George Dangerfield talked of Austen Chamberlain having a 'father-haunted mind'. It was one of Austen's many misfortunes that the peak of his career coincided with the moment when commentators became interested in Freudian psychology. He adopted the external mannerisms – the monocle and the orchid in the buttonhole – but in every important respect was his father's antithesis. Whereas Joseph Chamberlain had been self-made and raised outside the Anglican establishment, Austen was educated at Rugby and at the grandest of Cambridge colleges – one suspects that only Austen would not have seen the joke in a member of the country's most eminent Unitarian family matriculating at Trinity.

Austen Chamberlain was trained for statesmanship as his father had been trained for business and by the time he was twenty-five had met Clemenceau and Bismarck. He had finished his education in Paris at the École Libre des Sciences Politiques, which was particularly concerned with the education of diplomats. Foreign policy was the most important aspect of Austen's political career and the single office in which he exercised most influence was that of Foreign Secretary, which he held from 1924 to 1929. Austen's world was one of conciliation where his father's had been one of confrontation and dramatic breaches.

Joseph's iron will had made itself felt even when he was paralysed after 1906; Austen, by contrast, sometimes seemed unable to impose himself even when he held a great office of state. He was lazy, melancholic and frequently ill. His most striking physical capacity lay in his ability to sleep for long periods. He wrote to his sister in March 1933, the month in which Hitler came to power: 'The world is hollow and my doll is stuffed with straw. In fact I am at the moment horribly depressed. Perhaps I shall feel better after lunch. If not, I shall feel tempted to take to my bed again and drink.'[30]

There was also a formality about Austen that sometimes seemed to turn him into a fossilized parody of his father. Joseph had hated corporal punishment, partly because he blamed himself for having beaten Austen as a child. Austen circumvented his inherited objections to such violence by insisting that, when he stood in for the Home Secretary, his deputy should authorize the birching of criminals. Similarly, Austen Chamberlain once asked his father about a French novel (presumably one that might have offended the morality of Birmingham Nonconformity) that was locked in a glass cabinet. When Joseph offered to take the book out and let his son read it, Austen refused. The young Joseph would have insisted on reading it and asked one or two awkward questions about how his father had come to acquire it.

Harold Macmillan once wrote 'there was not much of Birmingham about Austen Chamberlain'. His relations with the city were, like so many things in his life, dutiful and courteous. When his father died, Austen replaced him as Member of Parliament for West Birmingham, in accordance with 'the binding force of father's wishes',[31] though this meant leaving his Worcestershire constituency where he had been happy. He rarely visited the new constituency and lived 'at home' (i.e. at his father's house in Birmingham) until he moved into Number 11 Downing Street as Chancellor of the Exchequer at the age of forty. Thereafter he lived in London and at his country house in Sussex. He barely mentions Birmingham in his autobiographical writings. He never worked in business and never had much association with those Birmingham men who did – his rigid insistence, as Chancellor, on repayment of debt to the government was one of the reasons why Herbert Austin almost went bankrupt after the First World War. Even the loyal Conservative correspondent of *The Times* injected a note of sarcasm into his report of Austen Chamberlain's visit of Birmingham factories during the 1922 election: 'a proceeding unique in his experience'.[32] Frank Price, who would become a Labour councillor after the war, recalled Austen Chamberlain's visit to his constituency in a chauffeur-driven car and noted that he did not remove his white gloves when shaking hands with working-class constituents: 'Rumour had it that when he returned home he had his servant remove his glove to be burned.'[33] The story is implausible but the mere fact that it could be repeated by someone who would himself become Lord Mayor of Birmingham is revealing.

The qualities that Austen most valued were those of a 'gentleman'. He believed in loyalty, selflessness and good manners. There was a touch of Birmingham in this – though it was the Birmingham of his Kenrick mother more than that of his father. Austen wrote to his stepmother (the third of Joseph's wives and the first not to be a Kenrick) in 1911: 'I have a good deal of the Kenrick in me by nature. Left to myself, I don't think I should have done much ill to anyone; but if I work and persist and fight with political beasts at Ephesus or elsewhere it is because I am his son and *"Noblesse oblige!"*.'[34] Just as the Kenrick family neglected their business so that they could devote themselves to public service, so Austen Chamberlain repeatedly sacrificed his political career to what he considered to be the interests of his party, his country or simply 'good form'. Austen might have become leader of the Conservative Party, in succession to Arthur Balfour, after the Conservative defeat in the 1910 general election. Though Birmingham MPs continued to describe themselves as Unionists, they were now effectively part of the Conservative Party, and the two groups were formally merged at national level in 1912. The obvious candidates to succeed Balfour were Austen Chamberlain and Walter Long, a Tory, though one whose moderate support for protection ran parallel to the policy of the Chamberlains. Long and Austen both stood down to avoid splitting their parliamentary group and thus allowed the third candidate – Andrew Bonar Law – to become party leader.

The First World War meant, eventually, the creation of a coalition government under first Asquith and then Lloyd George. Coalition suited Austen's temperament and he was willing to forgive the attacks that Lloyd George had made on his father during the Boer War. He served as Secretary of State for India – characteristically, he felt obliged to resign over deficiencies in a military campaign that had been launched under his nominal aegis in Mesopotamia. He returned to the cabinet without portfolio in March 1918 and became Chancellor of the Exchequer in January 1919. In March 1922, he became leader of the Conservative Party when Bonar Law fell ill. It was one of the rare occasions in British political history when someone could claim with plausibility that office had been thrust upon them.

The second of Joseph Chamberlain's sons was Austen's half-brother Neville (1869–1940). He was raised with very different ambitions in mind. Where Austen had been trained for politics, and particularly for diplomacy, Neville was destined for business. He had been educated in practical subjects at Mason College in Birmingham. At the age when Austen had been presenting his card to grand figures of French politics, Neville had been packed off to Andros Island in the Bahamas where his father had decided that it would be possible to restore the family fortunes through the cultivation of sisal. After enduring six years of loneliness and relentless hard work, Neville conceded defeat and returned to England, having lost £50,000. The venture was so unprofitable that Neville eventually sold the whole of Andros Island for a sum that he spent on buying a single French cabinet. Thereafter, it seemed that his career would revolve around business in Birmingham which, like many of his relations from the great Birmingham Nonconformist families, he might combine with municipal politics. He first held elected office as a Birmingham councillor in 1911. He was over forty and his half-brother had been a cabinet minister for almost a decade.

Neville Chamberlain's life was changed by the First World War. He became Lord Mayor of Birmingham from 1915 to 1917. In some respects, the war fitted neatly with the municipal activism that had been pioneered by Joseph Chamberlain. In 1916 Neville established a municipal bank in which factory workers could be encouraged to save their money. He recalled its foundation in terms of filial piety: 'The idea of a bank backed by the municipality flashed across my mind when crossing Chamberlain Place.' He emphasized the value of state intervention but also of ensuring that state interventions were managed by 'practical men', which largely meant men with experience in business. Neville's own politics were rooted in a culture of public service that can be traced back to the civic gospel of the nineteenth century. He believed that labour should be directed in the best interests of the war effort but also that businessmen should be prevented from making excessive profits during the war. His patriotic view of this matter resembled that of Stanley Baldwin, another Midlands businessman and later Chamberlain's political ally. One should note that Neville Chamberlain was beginning to demonstrate an ability – not always possessed by his father or half-brother – to combine convincing expressions of concern for the public good with actions that advanced his own commercial or political interests. Neville Chamberlain's first experience of public office – as Director of National Service in 1917 – was not a happy one but it drew him into national politics and, in 1918, he was elected as MP for Birmingham Ladywood.

Neville Chamberlain supported the continuation of the wartime coalition government led by Lloyd George, though he did not like or trust Lloyd George and did not accept office in his government. He had himself been elected as an MP without having to deploy the 'coupon' issued by the coalition that would have protected him from a degree of electoral competition. He was glad when the bulk of the Conservative Party withdrew its support for Lloyd George and brought his government down – thus bringing Bonar Law to power as Prime Minister. Neville was in Canada when this happened and did not, therefore, play an active part in supporting Bonar Law. This was convenient because his half-brother still supported Lloyd George and because Bonar Law's propulsion into the premiership meant Austen's eviction from leadership of the Conservative Party. Austen hastened to assure the Birmingham Conservatives 'how little attraction a return to office has for me'.[35]

Alongside the political realignments at national level, the Conservative and Liberal Unionist parties merged in Birmingham after the First World War. They dropped the words 'Conservative' and 'Liberal' so that they became simply 'Unionist'. Sceptical commentators might have asked why the word 'Unionist' mattered so much at a moment when Southern Ireland was about to be granted its independence, something far beyond what Gladstone had envisaged in 1885, and when Northern Ireland still seemed firmly locked into the United Kingdom, though with an independent Parliament in Belfast. In fact, Unionism now implied a position with regard to the politics of mainland Britain. It meant the policy of tariff reform, the rhetoric of social reform and, above all, the reality of control by the Chamberlains and their allies. Neville Chamberlain wrote, with characteristic cynicism: 'The decision to unite practically places the direction of Unionist politics in my hand. I am not quite sure whether all those present perceived this: I did not mention it.'[36]

Neville was appointed as Postmaster General by Bonar Law and then brought into the cabinet as Minister of Health. This was not a prestigious ministry but it was an important one – it oversaw much of housing policy, in which Neville had a particular interest, as well as purely medical matters. In August 1923, Stanley Baldwin, who had succeeded Bonar Law as Conservative leader and Prime Minister, made Neville Chancellor. Five years after his entry to Parliament, Neville now had matched the highest ministerial appointment of his brother and exceeded that of his father. But his tenure was brief because the Conservatives lost the election of December 1923. When they returned to power in 1924, Neville was again appointed Minister of Health. He was a cabinet colleague of his brother, who had returned to office as Foreign Secretary, and of Leo

Amery, who was Colonial Secretary. Three of the twelve Birmingham MPs were now in the cabinet.

Austen Chamberlain's reputation was at its highest in the late 1920s – his role in negotiating the Locarno Treaty won him the Nobel Prize for Peace in 1925. Quietly, however, Neville was pulling ahead of his half-brother. He became Chancellor again in 1931, and this time would last in that position until he became Prime Minister six years later. He also managed to fulfil what he saw as being his father's wishes by introducing tariffs. He remarked, in terms that might yet again have interested Freudians, that 'Like Hamlet, I have been haunted by my father's ghost. Now the ghost can rest in peace.'

Neville seems indeed to have freed himself of family ghosts during the 1930s. After the Conservative election defeat of 1929, Austen did not hold ministerial office again – except for a brief spell as First Lord of the Admiralty. Neville was now his own man in a way that his older brother had never managed. His political position seemed secure. After 1931 the Unionists held every parliamentary seat in Birmingham. Neville Chamberlain regarded the National Government, instituted in response to economic crisis in 1931 and drawing together a fraction of the Liberal and Labour parties in alliance with the Conservatives, as being the natural incarnation of 'Unionism': indeed, he expressed the hope that 'Toryism' might disappear. The centenary of Joseph Chamberlain's birth was celebrated with much pomp in 1936. Predictably, Neville presided over events in Birmingham, where a wreath was laid on the Chamberlain memorial. Austen spoke at the Albert Hall in London, where he read a message from the king and unveiled a portrait of his father that was almost large enough to stretch to the top of the building.

The frequent reference to Joseph Chamberlain was a sign of weakness. It showed that the Conservative Party was living on its past and this past could be dangerous because Neville and Austen were so conspicuously different from their father. The contrast had been illustrated in 1924 by Oswald Mosley's intrusion as Neville Chamberlain's Labour adversary in the Ladywood constituency. He came within seventy-seven votes of defeating Chamberlain. Mosley was elected as Labour MP for Smethwick in 1926. He was a forceful, ambitious man who took a cavalier attitude to party loyalty and there were many who recognized that his character bore marked resemblances to that of Joseph Chamberlain. Mosley's biographer rubbed in the comparison. He claimed that:

old men went up to him [Mosley] saying, 'Back to Joey, back to the great tradition!' One old man said 'I have heard Bright, Joseph Chamberlain, Lloyd George and all the giants of the past at the summit of their powers, but never anything like this meeting. The only thing comparable with this was Joe at the very height and vigour of his manhood.'[37]

Chamberlain's victory over Mosley in the 1924 election was a pyrrhic one because his majority was so slim. In the following election he retreated to Edgbaston – Birmingham's most bourgeois constituency and one in which the local constituency association was, conveniently, controlled by his cousin Byng Kenrick.* It was a humiliating move in view of the fact that Birmingham Unionism had once made so much of its capacity to transcend class divisions. Mosley recalled the 1924 election as though it had been a defeat for Chamberlain:

A downpour of rain and hundreds of motor cars enabled the Unionist candidate to scrape home and the lifeless body of the last of the Chamberlains has been washed back to Westminster. The Labour campaign of six weeks had killed a tradition of sixty years, and the Chamberlain majority fell to vanishing point. Birmingham had said they no longer wanted a name but something greater than a name.[38]

In spite of not having been trained for statesmanship – or perhaps because of it – Neville Chamberlain relished his increasing eminence, while Austen had been too modest to take pleasure in such a role and Joseph had been too arrogant to care. In private, Neville often sneered at his native city. When an acquaintance told him there were few interesting people in Glasgow, he replied: 'I found the same thing in Birmingham and I fear it is common to large provincial towns. Do all the people of cultivation go to London or what is the explanation?' When his wife complained about the 'degenerate aspect' of the 'greasy' Birmingham students to whom Neville (as chancellor of the university) was presenting prizes, he replied: 'they don't come from the same class as Oxford and Cambridge and have no idea of how to dress or how their hair should be cut'.[39]

Neville Chamberlain's appointment to succeed Baldwin as Prime Minister in 1937 evoked, at least in retrospect, much sneering about his

---

*Characteristically, Austen Chamberlain refused to desert his West Birmingham constituency – though his majority dropped to just forty-three.

provincial background and aldermanic manner. It seems obvious now that a man who had spent his whole life concerned with business, municipal administration and domestic politics was poorly qualified to lead the country at a time when its future depended on its foreign policy. Things did not seem so clear at the time. Chamberlain's policy – and particularly his appeasement of Hitler at Munich in September 1938 – was popular not just with the country at large but with its aristocratic ruling class. Lord Dunglass (later Earl of Home), who accompanied Chamberlain to Munich, and John Colville, a young member of the diplomatic service, who became private secretary to the Prime Minister, admired Chamberlain.

Far from being made in Birmingham, Chamberlain's foreign policy often brought him into conflict with those in the city who had formerly been his allies. His most significant opponent was Leo Amery, who had been elected as MP for South Birmingham in a by-election in 1911 and moved to represent Sparkbrook in 1919. Though his background was comparatively humble, Amery's intellect and energy had marked him out from a young age. He made his living and gained his early reputation from journalism and concentrated especially on foreign policy and the empire. More intellectually sophisticated than Neville and more dynamic than Austen, Amery must sometimes have felt that he was Joseph Chamberlain's real heir.

The Joseph Chamberlain centenary appears to have meant more to Amery than to either of the great man's sons and he tried to use it to launch a fresh campaign around the Empire and imperial preference. Above all, though, Amery was an opponent of Neville Chamberlain's foreign policy. He was responsible for two of the most famous remarks made in the House of Commons and both were attacks on Neville Chamberlain. The first came when the Labour MP Arthur Greenwood began to denounce Chamberlain's policy on 2 September 1939, the day before war broke out. Seeking to inject more passion into Greenwood's speech, Amery shouted from the Tory back benches 'Speak for England, Arthur!' Secondly, on 7 May 1940, as the Chamberlain government entered its death throes, Amery quoted Cromwell: 'Be gone, you have sat here long enough.'

The second Birmingham Unionist with whom Neville Chamberlain came into conflict was Ronald Cartland. Cartland had been elected as MP for King's Norton in 1935 (at the age of twenty-eight he was the youngest member of the House of Commons). Like Amery, he was elected with the support of the Chamberlains but, like Amery, he disagreed with Neville over appeasement and became famous for the savagery of his parliamentary attacks. He accused the Prime Minister of having 'ideas of dictatorship' when he tried to override parliamentary opposition in the summer of 1939. Chamberlain was furious. He wrote to his sister:

> As for Master Cartland I hope that he has effectually blotted his copy-book in Kings Norton and I am taking steps to stimulate local opposition. He has always been a disloyal member of the team and his constituents have already had him on the mat more than once. But this time he made a personal attack on me which will I am sure annoy the local people even more than a difference on policy. We may lose the seat as a result but I would rather do that (temporarily) than have a traitor in the camp.[40]

Cartland had also said in the speech that so offended the Prime Minister: 'Within a month we may be going to fight and we may be going to die.' Cartland was, indeed, killed in action at the end of May 1940 – weeks after Chamberlain resigned as Prime Minister. Cartland's sister, the romantic novelist Barbara Cartland, published a biography of him in 1942 with an introduction by Winston Churchill.

Neville Chamberlain's third opponent was his own half-brother. Austen died in March 1937, two months before Neville became Prime Minister. We cannot know how he would have responded to Munich – it seems all too likely that he would, as so often, have put loyalty above every other consideration. There was no doubt, though, that Austen was bleaker in his view of foreign policy than Neville and less inclined to give dictators the benefit of the doubt. Having worked with the politicians of the Weimar Republic, he regarded Hitler with unqualified distaste. It also probably mattered that he was six years older than his brother – slightly more remote from, and less haunted by, the generation that had endured such suffering in the First World War.

Even before he became Prime Minister, Neville Chamberlain was irritated by the way in which Birmingham MPs opposed government policy towards Hitler. In 1935, he complained of Oliver Locker-Lampson, Unionist MP for Handsworth from 1922 to 1945: 'his election address, which said nothing about Government policy, but declared that he stood for "putting Hitler in his place", created an intense feeling of anxiety ... among our supporters'.[41] In the same year he wrote: 'I had to rebuke Amery.' He had been told by the Unionist chief agent in Birmingham that Amery's criticism of government policy was unpopular in the city's Unionist Party – though tolerated in his own constituency.[42] Less than a year later (in the middle of the centenary celebrations for their father) he complained that 'Austen is getting ... in with Winston's crowd.'[43]

The last two years of the 1930s seemed to belong to Neville Chamberlain. He was Prime Minister and every single Birmingham MP was from his party and, indeed, from the Unionist sub-group of his party that was so closely associated with his family name. His popularity in the city and the country seemed to reach new heights at the time that he signed the Munich accord with Hitler in September 1938. Sir Charles Petrie published his book *The Chamberlain Tradition* in 1938 and it looked at that stage as if Neville himself might be the most illustrious representative of this tradition. It was also in 1938 that Birmingham celebrated the centenary of its incorporation with a pageant in Aston Park that featured, among other things, a sixty-foot, fire-breathing model dinosaur called Egbert. The pageant also included more predictable references to the city's industrial traditions and to Joseph Chamberlain – though one suspects that Joseph and his industrialist allies might have regarded the most significant feature of the event as being the fact that it lost money.[44]

In retrospect, it is clear that Neville Chamberlain's triumphs were less complete than they appeared. The Labour vote in the late 1930s was higher than it had been in the early 1920s and the swing towards Labour was greater than in the country as a whole – though the party's advance, at both national and local levels, was partly masked by the success of the electoral coalition behind the National Government from 1931. Birmingham by-elections in 1937 and 1939 both saw further advance in the Labour vote. The high levels of employment in Birmingham during the 1930s and especially during the latter part of the decade, as the effects of rearmament were felt, laid the way for a stronger trade union movement. Anti-fascism during the Spanish Civil War seems to have had particularly powerful effects in Birmingham that helped to create a more united left.

Most importantly, the prominence of Neville Chamberlain and the political persona he adopted during the 1930s diminished the appeal that his family name had once had to some working-class voters and politicians. Stanley Baldwin associated National Government with a broader political emollience that reached out even to those Labour politicians who opposed it. Neville Chamberlain took the opposite stance. Having collaborated well with working-class Labour men in Birmingham, he attacked their leaders in Westminster. When Baldwin rebuked him for treating the opposition 'like dirt', he replied that 'intellectually, most of them are dirt'. Perhaps his feelings sprang partly from his own resentment at being driven out of his Ladywood constituency by the advance of Labour; perhaps he found it easier to deal with former trade unionists who could be patronized than with the grander figures of the Labour Party's national leadership, who might be prone to patronize him. Maybe it was precisely because he saw the National Government as being the continuation of Liberal Unionism, rather than just a veil for Conservatism, that he resented those socialists who opposed it. Anyway, Chamberlain aroused such rancour on the opposition benches that in May 1940 Labour leaders preferred to serve under Churchill, the reactionary grandson of a duke, rather than under the progressively minded son of a Nonconformist businessman. National feelings transmitted themselves back to Birmingham and by March 1938 the left of the city could unite under the slogan: 'Chamberlain must go'. Birmingham Conservatives by this time were divided and the issue that caused the greatest division among them was the policy that was from then on to be most associated with the Chamberlain name – not Unionism or empire or tariff reform but 'appeasement'.

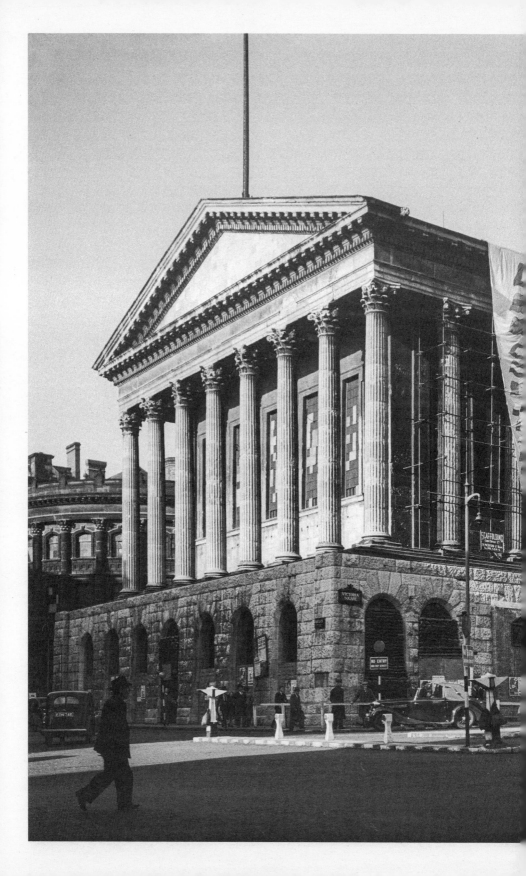

Birmingham Town Hall was built in 1834 and designed by Joseph Hansom, who also designed the Hansom cab. It predates Birmingham's incorporation and serves as a venue for concerts and meetings rather than a seat of local government. A journalist wrote of its classical façade that it was the great thrill of the city and 'It stands there as if attempting to make up its massive mind to walk down Hill Street and catch the last train back to Rome'. The wartime publicity to promote the construction of warships is less incongruous than it might seem. In spite of the city's inland location, Birmingham factories did much work for the Admiralty.

8

The Second World War
in Birmingham

*Germany invaded Poland this morning. Hitler says he will only
bomb places of military importance. Sez him. Went for a walk to
Perry Barr. AA guns manned.*
Diary entry by Eric Armstrong, seventeen-year-old at
Handsworth Grammar School, 1 September 1939[1]

*In 1939 when the war started they moved us to what was called
The Dangerfields, you know ... that was making the ammunition, the bullets and like, that's why they called it 'the dangerfields'
because it was dangerous like.*
Daisy Stanford, wartime worker at Kynoch in Witton[2]

After September 1939, Neville Chamberlain was pilloried for having
sought to stop Britain going to war against Germany. War, though, came
to his home city before the formal declaration of hostilities because,
from the late 1930s, Birmingham was a centre of war production –
particularly of aircraft. This, and the war itself, transformed its social
and economic life and also finally broke the hold that Chamberlain's
political party had exercised over the city for so long.

THE ECLIPSE OF BIRMINGHAM
NOTABLES

The collapse of the Chamberlain tradition intertwined with the
eclipse of the kind of local government in which Joseph and then

Neville Chamberlain had first made their names. The old Birmingham families lost influence. In 1940, as in 1914, the Lord Mayor of
Birmingham was a member of the Martineau family – between these
two men, the mayoralty had been held by a Kenrick and a Cadbury
and, of course, by Neville Chamberlain himself. However, Sir Wilfrid
Martineau (1889–1964), who served as Lord Mayor in 1940 and
1941, would be the last member of his family (or any of the big Birmingham families) to hold this post until the 1980s. Byng Kenrick
resigned as chair of the council's education committee (a position that
he had held almost without interruption for over twenty years) in
1943.

The city council mattered less during the war. The fire brigade was
'nationalized' (i.e. brought under the control of central government
rather than the local authority) between August 1941 and 1947.[3]
This saw the humbling of another Birmingham dynasty. Alfred Robert Tozer was the son, grandson and great-grandson of firemen. He
succeeded his father as chief fire officer of Birmingham in 1906 but
he had to resign in November 1940, when the Birmingham Fire Brigade failed to control fires sparked off by bombing raids.[4]

The council was circumvented by other bodies. The offices of the
Midland Civil Defence Region were established 'because it was felt that
under the stress of heavy raiding, different parts of the country might be
cut off from the Central Government in London'.[5] In practice, bombing
never did such dramatic damage and Birmingham never risked being cut
off from London. Indeed, the Civil Defence Region, which answered to
the Home Office, increased the power of central government. The Civil
Defence Region encompassed Warwickshire, Herefordshire, Shropshire
and Staffordshire, but the parts of this area that mattered most for the
purposes of war were the industrial towns – Wolverhampton, Coventry
and, above all, Birmingham, which became, more than ever before, a
kind of regional capital. The frontiers of the Birmingham war industry
were not quite the same as those of the Birmingham local authority.
Most people treated the factories at Castle Bromwich, Solihull and
Smethwick as part of Birmingham – though all of these were strictly
speaking outside the city limits.

THE WAR ECONOMY

Birmingham gained from rearmament spending in the late 1930s. Some politicians had wanted to use the armament industries to help revive the 'distressed areas', mainly in the north, where unemployment was worst. But Birmingham's strengths in engineering and automobile manufacture lent themselves to military use. Particularly significant for Birmingham was the 'shadow factory' scheme. Shadow factories were intended to enable the rapid increase of aircraft production in wartime. New plants were established that 'shadowed' existing factories. The idea had first been discussed in the 1920s – though the term 'shadow' and the first concrete proposals apparently dated from the report of the Weir Committee on munitions production in 1934. The government owned the shadow factories but private companies managed them in return for a fee. Initially, the firms involved were mainly civilian car manufacturers – though aviation factories were brought into the scheme from 1938. The idea was to bring experience of mass production methods into aircraft manufacture and to provide civilian companies with experience of armament production, which would be useful once war started.

Wolseley, Daimler, Standard, Singer and Rover were involved in the scheme, but the most important participant was Austin. Herbert Austin chaired the Shadow Aero Engine Committee, established in 1936 to bring together industrialists involved in the programme. Austin was largely responsible for the particular form the shadow factory scheme took – with most firms making components while Austin itself and the Bristol Aeroplane Company assembled complete motors. Austin drove a hard bargain. Neville Chamberlain, so bruised that he refused to attend meetings with contractors, talked of negotiations being conducted like a 'poker party'.[6] Lord Nuffield, based in Oxford, was the other prominent figure in the motor industry but he quarrelled with the air ministry and withdrew his firms – Singer and Wolseley – from the scheme for a time. He was brought back in when he was given the task of making planes at the giant plant in Castle Bromwich, but then withdrew again.

There were four shadow factories in, or close to, Birmingham. The Cofton Hackett factory was built next to the Austin works at Long-bridge. The Castle Bromwich factory was run by first Nuffield and then

Armstrong Vickers. Rover did not have enough space to expand around its main base in Coventry and so established two plants: one in Acocks Green and one in Lode Lane in Solihull. The new factories were big and were all built at least partially on land that had formerly been used for agriculture – to an even greater extent than before, large-scale production in Birmingham now took place on the outskirts of the city. The new construction at Longbridge was accompanied by a tunnel, 25 feet wide and 600 feet long, which served as a component store and later as an air raid shelter. Even building on this scale sometimes proved inadequate, though. The Cofton Hackett factory at Longbridge had been designed to produce light, single-engine bombers that were pretty much obsolete by the beginning of the war. After May 1940, Longbridge switched to making four-engine Stirling bombers. These were too heavy for the initial configuration of the factory. It was extended and a new railway siding was built because the access roads proved inadequate for the transport of components.

The next group of shadow factories were built on an even more ambitious scale. Their average cost was £2 million. The Castle Bromwich factory covered a site of 345 acres, on which buildings that covered 52 acres were erected. By late 1944, it employed 25,000 people and visitors remembered hangars so large that they could hardly see to the other side of them.[7] As they were built from scratch, the factories were modern. To the exasperation of the Treasury, high-quality materials were used (particularly ones that would resist fire) and the sheer size of the new buildings made large production lines easier to run – though such lines were sometimes interrupted by walls designed to contain bomb blasts.

Aircraft were the most important single item to be manufactured in Birmingham during the war. Castle Bromwich would eventually become the main centre for the production of Spitfires, which increased fast. Not a single plane had been produced there by May 1940, when Nuffield lost control of the plant. Thereafter ten planes were made in June but 1,800 had been built by the end of 1941. In all, more than 12,000 Spitfires (about two thirds of all those produced in the war) came from Castle Bromwich. The Spitfire – a fast, manoeuvrable, single-seater plane that jousted with Messerschmitts over the Home Counties – was a glamorous plane, but Castle Bromwich was not a glamorous place – the shadow factory had been built partly on top of an old sewage works.

All the same, those who knew about the war recognized that the Spitfire factory was important. Roy Deeley worked as an office boy at Castle Bromwich from the moment he left school, at the age of fourteen in 1940, to the moment in 1944, when, infuriated by the refusal of the authorities to draft him into the RAF, he volunteered to work in a coal mine as a 'Bevin boy'. He remembered the curious drama of the factory. He carried the reports that gave directors the weekly production figures, and consequently he himself was the first person in England to know this important and highly secret piece of information. He saw the King of Norway, the Duke of Kent, Eleanor Roosevelt and Winston Churchill when they walked around the factory.[8]

Alex Henshaw was the chief test pilot at the factory – there were usually four or five of them and twenty-five such pilots passed through Castle Bromwich in the course of the war. Henshaw had been a racing pilot before the war, but was persuaded to work for Armstrong Vickers rather than fly in combat. He tested up to twenty planes per day (and may have tested a tenth of all Spitfires). Apart from his expertise as a tester, Henshaw was also a public figure. Visiting dignitaries watched his aerobatics and were then introduced to him. To the alarm of his co-pilot, he would turn a barrel roll in a heavy Lancaster bomber or fly a Spitfire upside down at a height of fifty feet. Peter Ayerst, who became a test pilot at Castle Bromwich after having flown in combat almost continuously since 1939, believed that Henshaw was the best pilot he had ever seen.[9]

For all his courage and skill, Henshaw was a cautious and modest man. At the request of his wife, whose first husband had been killed in an aircraft accident, he gave up flying after the war. Birmingham was a difficult place to test planes because there was little open space on which to land if something went wrong and because the city was ringed by barrage balloons that were designed to impede German bombers. Two test pilots from the Spitfire factory died in accidents. Henshaw discouraged his pilots from unnecessary risks and his own most spectacular stunt – flying low up Corporation Street – was undertaken to demonstrate his irritation at being asked to put on what he regarded as an unnecessary display for the benefit of the mayor and a party of visitors. Henshaw also showed a touching enthusiasm for helping the war effort in unspectacular ways. He arranged to keep pigs at the aerodrome, which were fed on scraps from the factory canteen. Sometimes he commuted from his home at Tanworth-in-Arden in a small training plane, but other times he came by bicycle in the hope that this might underline the importance of saving petrol.[10]

Smaller factories in Birmingham, often ones that had previously sub-contracted for the motor industry, now provided components for aircraft. Around three quarters of carburettors installed in Spitfires and Hurricanes came from the Birmingham firm of SU. By the end of 1944, 470 firms in the Midlands made parts for the aviation and/or motor industry (the latter by then almost entirely dominated by military need) and around half of these employed fewer than fifty workers. By the end of 1941, the Midlands was the area that took the largest share of employment provided by the Ministry of Aircraft Production and was also equal with London and the South East in the overall share of munitions employment that it took. More surprisingly, 15.5 per cent of those employed on Admiralty contracts were from the Midlands, a proportion exceeded only in Scotland and the South East.[11]

A post-war report summed up the range of production thus:

> In the Midland Defence Region almost every item of war equipment was poured from the factories, e.g. precision components of microscopical smallness accurate to 1/5000,000th part of an inch, and forgings for giant shafts 80ft in length weighing nearly as many tons; revolver cartridges and shells for 15 inch guns; small incendiary bombs and 12,000 block busters; midget motor cycles for paratroops and 50 ton tanks; Spitfire fighters and giant Lancaster bombers; rayon as fine as a spider's web and steel hawsers for the great battleships.[12]

Alongside aircraft Birmingham factories continued to produce motor vehicles. Before 1941, when it switched mainly to aircraft production, the Austin works built trucks and cars for military use, including 3,000 Bedford troop carriers.[13] The Birmingham Railway Carriage and Wagon Company in Smethwick turned its experience of heavy engineering to making tanks – it also produced military gliders. The Midlands Railway Company turned its factories at Saltley and Washwood (in Birmingham) and at Wednesbury (in the Black Country) to tank production. Norman Edwards had been sales manager of the company. This became a redundant position at a time when the War Office bought everything it produced, but Edwards had been a tank soldier in the First World War and was now set to costing production and obtaining material. It was he who hunted down the rubber the company used for the inflatable floats on a 'swimming tank'. He listened to his boss trying to explain to an official from the War Office that there was not much point in trying to maintain secrecy by surrounding the factory with barbed wire because the workers would still gossip in the pub each evening and also because prototype tanks would be driven through the streets to be tested in a large pond on a nearby farm.[14] The Birmingham Small Arms Company returned to its military vocation after 1939. In 1936, it had made 10,900 rifles; by 1940 the figure was 68,200. It also made Browning .303 machine guns, with which aircraft were armed. Overall about seven tenths of Browning machine guns produced in the war came from the Midlands.

All sorts of companies were converted to war production. In 1942, the Home Office sent out a questionnaire about bomb damage to factories. Some companies sent terse replies saying that they were too busy to fill such documents. Those who did respond gave statistics about their clients. One of the Rover factories sent 100 per cent of its production to the air ministry. At W.T. Avery, based in the Soho foundry that had once belonged to Matthew Boulton, 15 per cent of production was for the Admiralty, 55 per cent for the ministry of supply, 5 per cent for the air ministry and 5 per cent for other government departments. At Triplex Glass in King's Norton, 2 per cent of production went to the Admiralty, 47 per cent to the ministry of supply, 45 per cent to the air ministry and 1 per cent to other government departments.[15] The Cadbury sheet metal and moulding department, previously used to maintain chocolate production lines, sub-assembled aircraft landing gear – though Cadbury's more conventional production was also important to wartime morale. The physicist Rudolf Peierls (of whom more below) took time out from inventing the atom bomb to work as a volunteer firefighter. He recalled that one night, at the height of the Birmingham Blitz, two girls in steel helmets hopped out of a Cadbury van and served cocoa to his exhausted colleagues.[16] Gaskell and Chambers, which had made beer pumps for pubs, turned to producing fuses for sea mines. As time went on, production was dispersed so that the destruction of a single factory would not wipe out an entire category of munitions. Spitfire production was spread around twenty-three locations. The Vickers factory at Castle Bromwich, once solely devoted to the Spitfire, produced around 300 Lancaster bombers, as did the Longbridge factory. Longbridge also made 300

Hurricane fighters, marine engines, components for tanks, military trucks, jerry cans and steel helmets.

Ernest Withers experienced the improvised economy of wartime Birmingham. He had been born in 1922 and was not called up until late 1941. For a year, he worked in Oldbury near Birmingham for a firm, originally based in Birmingham, which had previously made pen nibs but now made belts for the Browning machine guns that were installed in Spitfires and Hurricanes. As different kinds of war work came into the factory, Withers, who was employed in packing, found that he was handling 'all sorts of bits' without really knowing what they were or where they were going.[17]

Birmingham's most dramatic contribution to armaments involved a tiny group of people working in secrecy. Two Jewish physicists – Rudolf Peierls, originally from Germany, and Otto Frisch, originally from Austria – had come to Birmingham University in 1937 and 1939 respectively. Because they were strictly speaking 'enemy aliens' they were not allowed to work on the scientific problem that seemed of most pressing importance – the development of radar. Instead, they pursued their interest in the apparently more abstract questions of nuclear physics and, in March 1940, they drafted a memorandum on the possible military uses of their research. The memorandum gave rise to the so-called 'Maud Committee' (it was named after the housekeeper of one physicist), which investigated the potential of nuclear material for civilian and military use. The committee included Mark Oliphant and Philip Moon (both from Birmingham University).[18] Frisch, Peierls, Oliphant and Moon all moved to the United States during the later stages of the war and helped develop the first atomic bomb. In old age, Moon would entertain academic dinner parties in Birmingham with his accounts of how the scientists at the Los Alamos site were instructed to tell anyone who enquired about the base that it was a hospital for American servicewomen who had fallen pregnant.

WORKERS

Unemployment in Birmingham was already low before the outbreak of the war and everyone understood that labour was going to be needed in factories. Unlike in 1914, there was not a period when men were laid off as export markets were lost, and quite rapidly almost everyone was sucked into the war economy. SU Carburettors even found that it could employ blind people as inspectors – relying on their sense of touch to detect faults in production.[19] By October 1944, 400,000 people in Birmingham worked in munitions industries.[20] Wages varied. They were highest in the factories that worked for the air ministry – in one, in 1942, the average bonus was almost four times the basic pay.[21] Conscription into the armed forces was matched by creation of a schedule of reserved occupations – trades from which men of a certain age could not be called up and which they could not leave even if they wished to. Birmingham was under-represented among those who went into the forces during the Second World War because so many men were held back in factories.[22]

Though labour markets across the country became tighter after the outbreak of war, Birmingham still drew workers from outside the city. A report on an ICI plant in Birmingham noted that there had been 3,816 male and 2,281 female workers in August 1937; by August 1941 there were 6,696 male workers and 5,249 female ones. They came from the North, parts of Scotland, Northern Ireland and Eire.[23] One company talked of drawing 'foreign labour' from 'as far as Dundee, Belfast, London etc'.[24] Even workers from other areas with high demand for labour sometimes migrated to Birmingham during the war. E.A. Dorking had been born in London in 1930. He was evacuated to first Eastbourne and then Pembrokeshire and seems to have started work before the official school-leaving age. By 1945, he had reached Birmingham. His education certificates had been lost in the move but he was able to find work – indeed, once in a reserved occupation, he found it impossible to escape from it.[25]

With the outbreak of war, Irish migration, already speeding up in the late 1930s, became more controlled. Irish citizens needed to get permission to come to Britain. At the same time the authorities also sought to promote migration, and Austin and ICI sent recruiters to Ireland.[26] Lucas Industries had problems because 3,000 of its workers had been called up. In its battery factory it needed men who were physically strong but not skilled, and therefore not exempt from conscription. It solved the problem by recruiting first in Belfast (there was no conscription in Northern Ireland) and then in Dublin. The head of personnel at Lucas Industries recalled times when he went to New Street station at nine o'clock every evening of the week to receive fifty Irish workers, who had to be found food and places to stay before they could start work.[27] The majority of those who came were men – though a growing proportion (reaching almost 40 per cent by the end of the war) were women.

The Irish in Birmingham were in a strange position. They were sometimes the object of hostility – the IRA had bombed Birmingham and, with more lethal consequences, Coventry in 1939. Two Irish men – probably not the bombers – were hanged in Winson Green prison in February 1940. The British government treated Irish workers who had been brought directly over from the Free State as 'mobile', which meant that it claimed the right to move them around to suit its purposes. Irish people could also have more freedom than the English. Those who had been in the country for less than two years were exempt from conscription. An Irish person could always escape from British officialdom by the simple expedient of returning home and Irish men (this was less true of Irish women) sometimes led rough and ready lives that would have been hard for anyone to control. Leslie Jackson had been born in Birmingham, in Balsall Heath, apparently the illegitimate son of a wealthy Mancunian Jewish textile manufacturer. Jackson deserted from the artillery in the early stages of the war and joined a group of itinerant Irish building workers. When one of them – John Kenneally – returned to Ireland, Jackson took his identity card and joined the Irish Guards. It was under this new name that Jackson – who had never set foot in Ireland – won the Victoria Cross in North Africa.

The war also saw the beginnings of non-white immigration to Birmingham. Conditions in the Lucas die-casting shop were unpleasant and unlikely to be endured by men who had much choice with regard to their employment. The company solved the problem by engaging Arabs who had jumped ship in Liverpool and were in effect prisoners.[28] The Birmid foundry in Smethwick (another company that needed men to work in harsh conditions) recruited Indians from the Punjab in 1942.[29]

Women were being drawn into Birmingham factories in larger numbers than ever before. Jennie Bellenie-Tullock, who was from Sunderland but had been drafted to BSA in Birmingham in 1941, lodged with four other girls – three from Scotland and one from Scarborough.[30] Megan Llewellyn's family had migrated from south Wales to Erdington in 1936.

Her father was one of those numerous Welshmen who had come to Birmingham in search of work. Once the war began, Megan had no trouble finding employment. She moved from the Valor factory (at that stage still making stoves) to Dunlop and then to the Vickers factory at Castle Bromwich. There she spent three years working on the starboard wings of Spitfires – measuring and drilling holes that were then riveted by her colleague Albert.[31] Marjorie Powers also went to work at Castle Bromwich and she too drilled holes in the wings of Spitfires – in her case riveted by Fred. She thought there were six women working with Fred. Overall, however, the factory was primarily staffed by men. A woman might get £7 per week at Castle Bromwich, which was almost certainly more than she would have earned previously, but men often earned double this.

Women were rarely recognized as skilled workers – though they had some qualities that were particularly valued, such as having hands sufficiently small to be squeezed into the narrow recesses of a Spitfire. For women, even more than for men, war work was a lottery. Employment in a shadow factory meant good money and many benefits in kind – which might range from meals in the canteen to having a well-known band perform to the night shift at midnight. Jobs in smaller factories were less desirable but few people had much choice where they went. Evelyn, born during the First World War, had started work at BSA, been sacked on her marriage in 1938 (because the company gave preference to men over married women) and then re-engaged as the war economy began to heat up in November 1938. She stopped working when her daughter was born in 1940 but then volunteered to work for a couple of hours per day in the canteen at Lucas while her mother minded the baby. Now she was stuck. Wartime regulations kept her at Lucas when she returned to full-time work even though Rover was closer to her home. She made machine gun turrets from 1941 until the end of the war.[32]

A few Birmingham women achieved fame as Stakhanovites – Evelyn Duncan, a capstan lathe operator, broke the world record for shell production.[33] Most achievements attracted less attention. Gwendoline Stewart, born in 1925, was evacuated from Birmingham to Ashby-de-la-Zouch but she was unhappy at her exile. On her way to school one day, she saw a Midland Red bus with 'Birmingham' indicated as its destination and hopped on board, walking the last three miles from Birmingham city centre to her home. Her Birmingham grammar school was now closed and she went to work (aged fourteen and a half) in a small factory making parts for submarines. Her boss noticed that she had a sharp eye for detail and taught her the elements of draughtsmanship. She kept pencil and paper beside her telephone and worked on plans between answering calls.[34]

The war did not draw young people into the Birmingham economy – those between the ages of fourteen and eighteen had usually worked and because they were cheaper to hire had often held their jobs even when their elders were unemployed. It did, however, mean that they worked longer hours and could expect to be better rewarded for their labours. Middle-class observers were alert to the danger that war might corrode the moral fibre of the young. An organizer of the YWCA believed that 'In districts where many young people had to spend continuous nights in public shelters, there was a serious increase in drinking, illicit intercourse and petty thieving',[35] and one from the Birmingham University settlement in Summer Lane reported that 'The increase in bad language is noticeable even in this tough quarter.'[36] Observers were worried about the young – particularly those who had come in from outside the city – having too much money or being freed from the control of their parents, a consideration apparently especially important with regard to girls. Youth workers, though, stressed that those involved in youth organizations were the least delinquent and one was able to assure her correspondent: 'The question of petty crime, increased drinking or loose living does not affect the Girl Guide movement in Birmingham.'[37]

In fact, the amusements of the newly prosperous young workers in Birmingham seem to have been mainly innocent. On Saturday nights, they scrubbed the oil from under their fingernails, dressed up (boys in suits and ties) and went to the Embassy Ballroom in Edgbaston. Boys and girls courted. When Jennie Bellenie-Tullock started going out with Phil, who worked with her at BSA and whose hands were dirty from handling rusty rifles, her friends teased her because she had brown marks on her legs after dates.[38] The young drank more alcohol – though this was partly because soft drinks were harder to get.[39] There was an increase in juvenile crime – because of the opportunities for theft offered by bomb damage – though many offences were minor and fifty-one of the 1,787 cases brought before the juvenile courts involved 'the theft of fruit'.[40]

BOMBING

The bombing of Birmingham began in earnest after the fall of France in 1940. The authorities had expected daytime raids – presumably aimed at the important factories – but in fact the raids happened at night and were less well directed. The first one was on 9 August, but bombing was at its worst after 7 November 1940, when Goering ordered attacks on the aircraft industry. The Luftwaffe dropped 762 tonnes of bombs on Birmingham, including 166 bombs weighing 1,000 kg each and 1,563 small incendiary canisters. But Birmingham was a hard target to hit. There were no obvious landmarks. Crucially, the blacked-out city, unlike so many German targets, was not on the coast or on a large river. Some believed that the Grand Union Canal was the bombers' main route to the city centre.[41] Captured German aircrew told their interrogators that they had tried to orientate themselves with reference to reservoirs but these were too numerous to be easily identifiable and in any case were rarely close to factories.[42]

The fact that important factories were located on the outskirts of the city made them all the more difficult for bombers to locate. Donald Thompson (born in 1923) was an army cadet who lived in Hall Green and ran messages for air raid wardens. He reckoned that the Germans knew of the existence of aero factories in Solihull and Shirley (presumably he meant Acocks Green) but had no idea where they were and frequently dropped their bombs on open country. Castle Bromwich – surrounded by a distinct grid of roads – would have been easiest to identify. Henshaw recalled that 'the Germans seemed to find the factory at Castle Bromwich almost every time'. Around 200 bombs dropped on the site and at least eleven people were killed there. Some who worked in, or lived near, the factory remembered gruesome stories of how victims had been blown up into the rafters of the roof – presumably such incidents reflected the efficiency of blast walls in ensuring that the effect of explosions was directed upwards rather than spreading the length of a workshop. Given that the factory employed up to 25,000 people, the number of casualties was relatively low. High winds, which blew off the roofs of some buildings in May 1943, apparently impeded production at Castle Bromwich more than any single bombing raid.[43]

Longbridge was the hardest target. Looking down in the dark from a height of several thousand feet, it would have been difficult to tell that the Austin factory (with Worcestershire farmland on one side and the greenery of Bournville and Edgbaston on the other) was in a town at all. The newest factories were large, which meant that a single bomb might not hit anything valuable. They had been designed to stand up to blast and particularly to avoid fire. In July 1942, 500 incendiary canisters were dropped in the precincts of the ICI/Kynoch factory, apparently without starting a serious fire.[44]

Central Birmingham was easier to hit. Buildings were denser. Large numbers of small factories crowded together and were surrounded by slum housing. Old factories and workshops – often built with wooden roofs – burned easily. Successive waves of German bombers homed in on the fires that had been started by the first incendiary bombs. Edward Ashill was acting station officer of the fire brigade posted to Selly Oak in late 1940. The Longbridge works was a little way from his station but his crews were repeatedly called in the other direction to central Birmingham.[45]

The most important factory in central Birmingham was BSA at Small Heath. It was bombed on 18 November 1940 and a six-storey building collapsed. The archaic structure of the plant made things worse – in order to get to shelters, workers had to run across narrow bridges over a canal in the middle of the night. After the raid, there was a period when discipline at the factory collapsed.

> It was reported that following the early and heavy bombing of the BSA Small Heath works, when the whole plant was brought to a complete standstill, the workers presenting themselves for their wages took over and controlled the entrance to the factory. Their attitude, in the words of management, was both ugly and menacing, and was due, or so it was averred by them, to delay and difficulties which were entirely avoidable in paying out the wages which were outstanding. The authorities were powerless to control the temper of several thousand workers and relief was only gained when an air raid alert was sounded, which heralded the approach of an enemy reconnaissance plane.[46]

Things were made worse at BSA by rumours that bodies had been buried under rubble and never recovered. Almost two years after the raid, an official noted: 'The bombing of the BSA works, where casualties were very high, proved very disturbing to public opinion and it was, and still is, believed that all the casualties were neither recovered or accounted for.'[47] These rumours affected the workers at other Birmingham companies too. The managers of Harris and Sheldon in Stafford Street wrote:

> In connection with the disturbance created by gossip about casualties, it is noteworthy that the effects of the incident at BSA when a number of workers were killed, were very much increased by the crop of rumours which exaggerated the incident. It is said that the combined effects of the incident and the subsequent rumours was to set up a great reluctance among workers of this firm to go on night shifts.[48]

Rumours flourished in wartime Birmingham. A graduate student carrying out interviews in the 1970s was told that Birmingham fire tenders had been sent to Coventry at the height of German bombing and simply disappeared.[49] The authorities had to deny that bomb shelters had been sealed up with the corpses of those killed still inside them.[50]

Even in central Birmingham, the damage caused by bombing was spectacular, though not very significant as far as the war effort was concerned. After the raid of November 1940, one official believed that two more raids of comparable severity would have rendered it 'uninhabitable'.[51] But that never happened and even the raid of November 1940 did not have a dramatic effect on war production: 'The remarkable feature of the raid is that in such a severe raid so little material damage of national importance has been reported, the main damage has been to residential and shopping property and some small factories.'[52] There had been severe damage to 'fifty shopping premises and about thirty small factories'. Small Heath, Sparkbrook, Balsall Heath, Ladywood and Saltley (all densely populated areas in the city centre) had suffered worst. Northfield, Harborne, Weoley Castle, Selly Oak, King's Norton, the east of Sheldon and the new Kingstanding estate (all on the outskirts of the city) had escaped. In the long run, casualties in the Midlands were relatively low. The worst year was 1940, when 2,592 were killed by bombing; in 1941 the figure was 1,141. By 1942, the RAF and the United States Air Force were taking the war to Germany and the Luftwaffe was increasingly occupied with defence – only 248 people in the Midlands were killed by bombs in that year. In 1943 the figure was zero.[53]

There was a sharp difference between British and German reports on the effectiveness of raids. German aircrew saw fire and smoke (the latter often hiding much of what was really happening on the ground) and assumed that they had done severe damage. Their superiors reckoned: 'The most important foundation of the British armaments industry is to be regarded as severely shaken.'[54] However, even in the city centre where damage was worst, production continued. Of 200 factories in the area, 22 per cent suffered serious damage but their tools were mostly intact.[55]

Deliberate deception played a part in the inaccuracy of German bombing. The Civil Defence Camouflage Establishment created over 10,000 decoy targets, which were estimated to have attracted 5 per cent of all German bombs. The Establishment was staffed largely by cinema technicians – used to working at a frantic pace in difficult circumstances. They created decoy sites near Birmingham. Gangs of local authority workmen were drafted to distribute drums of oil across open fields, which were ignited to give the impression of a city on fire.[56] Not surprisingly, those who lived near the decoys did not welcome measures to attract bombers. A post-war report noted drily: 'At one period the correspondence from people living near these sites became voluminous.'[57]

Though direct hits on valuable targets were rare, bombing had an effect on morale and efficiency in Birmingham. The following casualties were recorded simply as a result of the sirens being sounded in August 1940: two heart failures, one death from falling downstairs, two broken arms, one head wound, one foot badly cut on broken glass, one attempt at suicide by gas asphyxiation.[58] Donald Thompson recalled his mother arriving home at 9.30 a.m. in November 1940. There was no public transport after the bombing raid and she had walked home from her night shift in a munitions factory. She heard that his grandmother's house in Smethwick had been bombed and so the two of them set off to find out what had happened. The journey would normally have taken an hour and a half but, because transport was so disrupted, they did not reach Smethwick until 3 p.m., only to find the street they were seeking cordoned off because a German parachute mine had become tangled in the tram cables outside Smethwick town hall.[59]

Many people left their homes – either because their houses had been damaged (it was estimated that 7,600 houses in Birmingham and a further fifty-six in West Bromwich were destroyed), because there were unexploded bombs nearby or simply because they feared what might happen. About 10 per cent of Birmingham inhabitants moved within the city during the war.[60] Occasionally, this meant that they disappeared from the eyes of officialdom. One man, born in the 1930s, was able to evade conscription for a time after the war because his family had been bombed out and had no fixed address at which he could be tracked down.[61] Sometimes moving meant simply finding a house in a better location but sometimes it meant moving at short notice and imposing on reluctant acquaintances. Theresa Bothwell recalled her family's move. The police called at 7 a.m. and told them they had half an hour to leave their house because their whole estate had been scattered with bombs with time-delay fuses. They went to the home of a woman they knew from church but she could put them up only for a night because she was herself planning to move from the city. Then they went to a cousin of her mother's who ran a pub in Dudley, where they stayed for a time, though 'Auntie Kittie' made them feel 'like lepers'.[62] Those who were forced to take refuge with strangers to whom they were allocated by the billeting office had an even harder time. Some sent to Handsworth were not allowed to turn on the gas or brew tea.[63]

Some left the city entirely. A few relatively prosperous people simply went to safer places outside the city limits, even though they may have continued to work in the city. Some moves involved migrant workers who returned home. It was reckoned that between a third and a quarter of those from Ireland went back quite soon. About 1 per cent of the population 'trekked', that is to say left the city on the nights of raids.[64] The authorities often associated trekking with a general breakdown of order as refugees left cities to sleep in nearby fields. However, the traffic manager of the Midland Red Bus Company depicted a more orderly process. The city's size, in contrast to that of Coventry, made it hard for people to leave on foot. Rather they travelled on public transport and found short-term refuge between ten and thirty miles away in Bromsgrove, Droitwich or Worcester: 'In fact the usual bank holiday resorts.'[65] Coach companies advertised services that would take Birmingham residents to the country for the night.[66] Many returned the following morning to work – sometimes pausing at their houses to pick up the milk.

Some children were evacuated from Birmingham early in the war – though the number who went was smaller than the authorities had anticipated (80,000–90,000) and smaller than the proportion evacuated from London, Liverpool or Newcastle. In total, probably about

25,000 elementary school pupils and 5,000 students from secondary schools along with a little over 4,000 teachers went in September 1939. Many returned home by the end of 1939, though more left the city when serious bombing started; 50,000 children were probably evacuated at one time or another.[67] Four of the Fewtrell brothers (children of an Aston taxi driver) were split up. Eddie went to a reasonable house in Gloucester, Frankie and Donald were sent to a much rougher family near him, where they were made to do agricultural labour. John, aged four, was sent to Aberdare. He returned speaking Welsh. Their youngest brother (born in June 1940) stayed behind with his parents. Their sister Phyllis, aged sixteen, was 'doing ammunition' at a factory in the Aston Road and being bombed at night.[68]

The fact that some of the most highly paid, and therefore skilled, workers lived in estates on the edge of the city meant that casualties among them were relatively low, but workers did not necessarily live close to their places of employment – even when those factories were on the outskirts of the city. This meant that keeping people working meant keeping buses running. Electricity and gas were also important. The Longbridge factory itself was not hit in November 1940 but damage to electricity pylons slowed production there.[69] Herbert Manzoni, the city's chief engineer and a man whose post-war schemes would, as wags often pointed out, do more damage to Birmingham than the Luftwaffe, responded to bombs with his favourite material: concrete. He sought to erect crude 'hutments' in parks and other public spaces. These could then be used to accommodate both those who had been bombed out of their houses and a mobile army of labourers who would be brought into the city to repair bomb damage.[70]

The effects of bombing were seen through political prisms. On the one hand, the left reproached the city authorities for having failed to provide enough efficient shelters. On the other hand, the government and its local informants distrusted much of the Birmingham working class. One official wrote:

> The loss of time for personal reasons is high in relation to weight of attack when compared to other cities. This may be partly because in November 1940 raids were still a new experience and partly because there is an unusually large proportion of unskilled workers. Many of these are not attached to their firms by any strong link (they are often

engaged for a particular job and dismissed when completed) and may be expected to lose time on little provocation.[71]

Outright rebellion by workers, of the kind seen at BSA in November 1940, was rare. What worried the authorities was absenteeism. They saw workers as prone to stay away – particularly, since bombing occurred at night, from night shifts – or to cease work too quickly when air raid sirens sounded. Civil servants wrote reports on the views of 'the common man' and 'the common people', which commented that 'Those suffering from intensive air raids see little of the general perspective.' There were strangely few references to the fact that a large proportion of the wartime workers in factories were women, sometimes with husbands away fighting, who had to combine paid work with domestic chores. A woman working at Tube Investments in Aston said:

> I am going home to do an evening's scrubbing. First I've got to do my bit of shopping on the way home. I have to queue for it because they make no allowances for me in the factory all day. My two little boys are in school all day. They have their dinners there, and the teachers keep them till 6 o'clock when I call for them. But I have to get a meal ready, and there's always some washing and mending to be done every night. I never get to bed before 12. I wish I had a daughter about 14 years old. My friend's got a daughter of 14 and she is such a help.[72]

It is hardly surprising that a mother who had left a child alone in an Anderson shelter might not have had her mind entirely focused on the production line. There were particular features of life in Birmingham that made life harder for working women. A move to a new estate had often separated young women from their mothers who might normally have provided help with child care, and the distance of some estates from both shops and workplaces, which was an annoyance in peacetime, could be a serious problem in war. The concentration of bomb damage in the town centre meant that some shops were out of action and, on 17 November 1940, in an effort to avoid congestion at the time when bombing might start, all shops were ordered to close at 4 p.m. and the bus terminus was moved half a mile out of town.

Some attributed absenteeism at work to lack of 'factory background'[73] – though others pointed out that recent migrants to the city seemed more strongly motivated than those who were established there. Irish women in particular often turned out to be better educated than would have been normal for factory work and were sometimes promoted to supervisory positions.[74] On 4 September 1940, the cabinet discussed the effects of air raid warnings at Castle Bromwich. Ministers were told that 700 men had left the factory without authorization at lunchtime on 31 August and another 700 had done so at 5 p.m.; 3,500 had stayed 'but there was a marked disinclination on the part of men to continue at work after an air raid warning had sounded'. Ministers agreed that air raids were less destructive than had been expected and that workers should no longer be encouraged to take cover as soon as sirens sounded. The cabinet recognized that it would be a 'grave decision to apply compulsion to skilled workers in the aircraft industry'. They did, however, suggest further consideration of the possibility that protection from service in the forces might be withdrawn from workers.[75] Since the country needed Spitfires more than it needed untrained private soldiers, one assumes that the 'consideration' did not take very long. In practice, the most useful measure to prevent unnecessary interruption of work during air raids involved using spotters to give precise warnings about the imminence of a raid on a particular plant, which could then be relayed by telephone so that entire factories did not shut down every time a single German reconnaissance plane flew over the city.

Birmingham was a good place to be during the Second World War: casualties were low, wages were high and a substantial proportion of men were excused from military service. For all this, memories of the period 1939 to 1945 were often marked by anger – perhaps precisely because some had seemed to escape the most malign effects of the war. Two sociologists working in the 1960s were surprised to find that simply mentioning the war to inhabitants of a working-class district could evoke a ferocious response:

[W]e heard bitter comments even from young people who could hardly have remembered the events, about those who left the area during the 1940–45 War, leaving the others to look after their houses and face the bombing. ('Everyone deserted during the War, all rushed to the country, and they'll do the same thing next time. Yes, they'll clear out. Alf look after me house will you?') Similarly, the fact that some husbands and sons avoided conscription whilst other families lost all their menfolk was frequently remarked upon. These particular points of conflict are still very close to the surface and if they were not mentioned spontaneously, we could easily start our respondent off on quite heated descriptions of what 'went on' by asking a simple question about what it was like in the War.[76]

THE POLITICAL CONSEQUENCES
OF WAR

All the Birmingham MPs in 1939 were Conservatives. During the war, there were by-elections at Edgbaston, King's Norton and Aston (all resulting from the deaths of incumbents) but the major opposition parties did not contest these. This continuity masked a growth in support for the left which had already been discernible in elections of the late 1930s, though it had not been sufficient to unseat any MP. There had also been an important mobilization of the left in the summer of 1939, just before the outbreak of war, when the city's council tenants protested against the level of their rent by withholding it altogether. The rent strike was important because it involved a high level of participation by women and suggested that the arena for working-class mobilization might not be confined to the workplace.

The war itself was a cause of dramatic political change, which began in the factories. Trade unions had been weak in inter-war Birmingham and employers had been ruthless in firing troublesome workers. The balance of power between the two sides was changed partly by the ever-tightening labour market of the late 1930s. Employment was more stable. The seasonal downturns that had given men like Herbert Austin a chance to purge trade unionists did not happen once rearmament was under way. The shadow factories were easier places for trade unionists than the private concerns with which they were associated. Strictly speaking, the new factories were owned by the government. The industrialists who managed them had less incentive, and fewer opportunities, to get rid of militants.

When Arthur Bate arrived at Longbridge in the 1930s, he could not discern a union organization there at all. However, he was contacted by a colleague from the toolroom (often a centre of skilled work and labour militancy), and by 1941 he was himself a shop steward.[77] The career of Albert Bennett illustrated the changes brought by the war. He had lost his job in 1926, a month after getting married. He had walked all over the city in search of work and even cycled to Coventry on a second-hand bike that his mother had bought from a rag-and-bone man. After signing on at the labour exchange in Selly Oak he would walk or, if he had a few coppers, take the tram to Longbridge where he would have to fill out a form and then hang about to see if there was any work: 'You'd stop all night.' Eventually he got a job but understood all too well what the company required:

> [A] docile sort of chap ... We were a little bit frightened to know any-thing about it [trade unionism] because, how circumstances were in them days, you kept your nose clean ... they were frightened to death, in case, if they joined the union and the boss – the gaffer – or the foreman found out – that they'd get their cards.

Men who were members kept their union badges hidden on the inside of their lapels.

The arrival of the aircraft factories began to change things and Ben-nett reckoned that, by 1938, a quarter of men were unionized. Early in the war, he became a shop steward himself. The new arrivals in the factory were relatively easy to recruit. Only the established workers held out:

> But by dint of hard work and discussion and, in some instances with threats, begun to change their minds ... we started putting the pressure on them, knowing that the management couldn't get rid of us because of the war restrictions and we went in and told the management: look we ain't having anybody in this shop who wouldn't join a trade union. We didn't say it was a closed shop because it would have caused a battle if we would have done, which we didn't want at that particular time, but we were told; we're not having anybody here that won't join a trade union.

Sometimes the tactics that shop stewards used seemed remarkably like the tactics the 'gaffers' had used against them in the 1930s: 'I'm com-ing back tomorrow about 12 o'clock for this form [to join the union]; if you ain't filled it up, you're out.'[78] With Labour ministers, especially Ernest Bevin, in government, the climate for trade unions was more benign after May 1940. In a curious way, the fact that strikes were made illegal in July 1940 increased the power of unions, as they were often called in to resolve disputes or to smooth things over when an unofficial strike broke out. Trade union leaders found that even the arrival of workers with no tradition of conventional organization could help their cause because the occasional outburst of spontaneous rebellion put more pressure on bosses.

The pen industry had always had a large female workforce even before the war and at the factory where Ernest Withers worked, now turned over to munitions work, there were 500 women and only about sixty men. The women were not unionized (or at least did not belong to a national trade union) and they had to work hard to earn reasonable money on piece work. All the same, they walked out when a new director tried to install new working practices and returned only when the management backed down.[79] A shop steward at Longbridge recognized that the Irish who came during the war brought a quality that was different from politically disciplined workers from south Wales who had already arrived in such numbers in the 1930s: 'Irish lads are particularly rebellious. I don't know whether it is necessarily trade union rebelliousness, but they're in for a fight, they weren't like the mass of Brommies who were very acquiescent.'[80]

Even when employers wanted to sack trade union organizers, they now found it impossible to do so. The Essential Works Order of 1941 prevented men from leaving jobs that were defined as important to the war effort but it also prevented their employers from getting rid of them. Denis Howell, born in 1923 and later to be a Labour minister, was an office boy at Hercules Cycles at the beginning of the war – hammer toes prevented him from being called up. He joined the Clerical and Administrative Workers' Union and became the first person to organize a union at the plant. After two years, he left and was hired at Higgs Motors. This he recalled as a 'traumatic experience' because Walter Higgs was an authoritarian boss and a Conservative MP. The experience was probably even more traumatic for Higgs because Howell established a union branch at Higgs Motors. In peacetime, an office boy who set up a union at such a firm would have been sent on his way with a clip round the ear. In wartime, Higgs needed to get workers transferred via the Ministry of Labour. The ministry sent the transfer application to Howell and asked for his observations. He wrote: 'Mr Walter Higgs is the Conservative MP for West Birmingham. I am the secretary of the West Birmingham Labour Party. That is the reason for this application.' The application was refused. Higgs had to wait until the 1945 Labour government repealed the Essential Works Order to sack Howell.[81]

Most Birmingham trade unionists were, like Denis Howell, supporters of the Labour Party. Support for Communism in the city was microscopic. Arthur Bate reckoned that there were forty Communists in the main Austin factory and about 400 in the 'Aero' – i.e. what had been the shadow factory[82] – this would have meant that they constituted not much more than one in a hundred of all workers there. Immediately after the war, a social survey of Aston deemed it worthy of note that Communists had become more numerous than Spiritualists.[83] But Communists acquired an influence in the trade unions that was disproportionate to their numbers. In particular, it was during the war that Dick Etheridge – the Communist shop steward who would dominate industrial relations at Longbridge for decades – came to prominence. No doubt the Communists owed their success partly to dedication and ruthlessness. But, at least after June 1941, they also fitted well into the British war effort. From the moment that the Soviet Union was invaded, British Communists sought to promote the war against Nazi Germany. A couple of militants spent most of a night painting 'Open a second front now' on the side of Rubery hospital – the graffiti was still visible years after the war. [84] The Clarion singers, founded in 1940 by Dr Colin Bradsworth, who had been a military doctor with the Republicans in Spain, sang in factory canteens.

Most importantly, Communists sought to speed up production rather than to slow it down. In September 1941, the Birmingham and District Shop Stewards Council complained that men in one factory had spent a whole night shift playing darts. They blamed this on the uneven flow of material due to poor management. The Austin shop stewards issued the following declaration in April 1944:

> above the searching for holes in agreements, above the dodging, the jiggery-pokery, the slick manoeuvring, and the sharp practice, lies the dominant fact of our obligations to those of ours who have pumped their life blood on the beaches of Dunkirk, Salerno and Anzio.[85]

Under these circumstances, portraying the left in general as 'bolshevik' – the tactic that had worked so well for Birmingham Conservatives after the First World War – was unlikely to be effective in 1945.

The Labour Party also gained from local politics. The regional commissioner for civil defence was the Earl of Dudley, a descendant of men who had once been the feudal overlords of Birmingham. He was a Conservative notable, a director of various industrial concerns, son of the former governor of Australia and a well-known figure at point-to-point races. His aristocratic style brought him into conflict with the middle-class men who controlled Birmingham Council – particular offence was given when the Lord Mayor and his wife were not shown due respect on the occasion of a royal visit to the city in 1942. This seems, at a time when the national government was reeling from the fall of Singapore, to have been the main concern of the city notables.[86] The Lord Mayor, Norman Tiptaft, was moved to attack the regional commissioner and the London authorities, to whom he answered, in extraordinary terms. He told the Rotary Club:

> The menace to the city does not, in war-time, come solely from Germany. It comes from nearer home, it comes from gentlemen in London and their local organization, who, with the excuse that there's a war on, would impose on Birmingham and other cities a form of government which is irresponsible, anonymous, and not as efficient as the municipality itself can produce.[87]

Since both the regional commissioner and the leaders of the council were Conservatives, this squabble between them was bound to damage their party. While they quarrelled among themselves, Labour representatives on both the council and the commission gained credit. The Labour councillor Albert Bradbeer made himself spokesman for those who had been rendered homeless by bombing. And in the commission, two of the four subcommissioners were George Archibald and George Lindgren, who had at one time or another been Labour parliamentary candidates. Both men took a special interest in welfare – the area most likely to bring them into close and sympathetic contact with voters.

Bombing helped the Left. Councillor Norman Tiptaft headed the city's civil defence committee. If his autobiography is to be believed, he was a man of exceptional energy and prescience. He had undertaken a course in German in Hamburg in 1938 and taken the opportunity to inspect German measures of protection against bombing. Perhaps disarmed by his aldermanic manner and association with Chamberlain's city, the German authorities tolerated his investigations. He once ordered tear gas be released on the streets to encourage Birmingham residents to carry their gas masks.[88] However, Birmingham shelters and civil defence provision seemed inadequate and this reflected badly on the Conservative municipal administration and especially on Tiptaft, who had been a Conservative since 1935. The debate on shelters in Birmingham became bitter – partly because it involved two particularly intemperate and vain men. The Bishop of Birmingham believed that civil defence was inadequate and that concrete manufacturers were profiteering from their contracts – an allegation that got him sued for libel. Tiptaft alleged that the campaign for 'deep shelters' was a 'subversive display associated with Communism'.[89]

The Labour Party made much of shelters and hinted, in terms more careful than those used by Bishop Barnes, that contractors were benefiting from their relations with the council. The working class – especially the part of it that lived close to the factories of the city centre – felt more vulnerable than the middle class, which lived mainly in the suburbs. Victims of bombing seized control of the social club room at the Tyburn Road transport depot in August 1940, when they felt that they had not been provided with 'immediate relief in the way of suitable alternative housing or billeting accommodation, feeding, and the alleviation through the distribution of money grants and clothing, of hardship and distress'.[90]

The authorities tended to regard protests as signs of 'disorder' but in fact they sometimes seemed to portend a new order. Birmingham residents looked to political organizations to channel their discontent:

> Public agitation, in the form of deputations from established and responsible organizations, such as the Labour Party and Trade Unions, and from tenants of housing estates in the city, waited on the council with proposals for a more effective ARP policy for the civil population. In particular, after care and treatment for the victims of air raids was stressed, together with the plea that the city should be regarded as a vulnerable area with facilities for the organized evacuation of women and children from target areas.[91]

The *Town Crier* (the city's Labour newspaper) made an issue of air raid precautions. The Labour Party again became a means of transmitting popular discontent after the raids of November 1940. In the factories too, responses to bombing sometimes accompanied a growth in the power of unions, or simply of shopfloor organization: 'the organized workers were not, for the most part, consulted as to their views on factory or workshop ARP and this was a source of considerable grievance'. In some cases, workshops elected their own aircraft spotters (the people charged with warning of raids) to replace those appointed by managers.[92]

The extent to which Labour had strengthened its position in Birmingham was revealed in the 1945 general election. All twelve seats had been won by the Conservatives in the 1935 general election, the last to be held before the war. Even on the day of the election, a correspondent for *The Times* thought that 'there is still a chance that it will remain solidly Conservative'.[93] As it turned out, Labour won ten of the Birmingham seats, of which there were now thirteen. The swing was more marked than in any other city in the United Kingdom. Partly this was the product of a larger and more unionized industrial working class, partly it was due to popular dissatisfaction with the way the Unionist council had prepared for civil defence and to popular approval of the way in which Labour had associated itself with welfare measures during the war.

The 1945 election had a special twist in Birmingham for two reasons. First, a vote for Labour after the war was often seen as a vote against unemployment before it. One might suppose that citizens of Birmingham – where employment levels had been relatively high in the 1930s – would be less influenced by memories of the inter-war Depression than voters from other parts of the country. Curiously, though, the extraordinarily tight labour market of the war years seems to have made Birmingham people – particularly the young who can have had almost no memories of the economic crisis of the early 1930s – nervous about the future. It may be that the migration of workers from the North to Birmingham during the war brought stories of unemployment to the city. Boys and girls at a Birmingham youth club explained their wartime behaviour thus: 'Aw well, we get good pay now and we spends it. After the war we shall not have the chance – then back on the dole – if we aren't killed before that.'[94]

Secondly, Conservatives in other parts of the country were shocked by the fact that the election result seemed to be a rejection of the wartime Prime Minister, Winston Churchill. In Birmingham, though, the Conservative Party was strongly associated with Churchill's predecessor and the architect of pre-war appeasement, Neville Chamberlain. The association between Birmingham and Chamberlain was so strong that the Luftwaffe had codenamed their worst bombing raid on Birmingham in November 1940 'Operation Umbrella' – after Chamberlain's famous accoutrement. The only member of the Chamberlain family to contest a seat in the 1945 election was Austen's son-in-law, Colonel Arthur Maxwell, who stood unsuccessfully for Acocks Green – though perhaps the break with the Chamberlain tradition might have been illustrated even more brutally if pregnancy had not caused Elizabeth Pakenham, Austen Chamberlain's granddaughter and Neville's great niece, to stand down as Labour candidate for King's Norton.*

The association of appeasement and Birmingham Conservatism was unfair because so many Birmingham Conservatives – notably Leo Amery, who lost his seat in 1945 – had opposed appeasement, but it was nevertheless strong enough to overcome all objections. Denis Howell celebrated the election result by planting the red flag on the Chamberlain clock in the jewellery quarter. After the First World War, the Right had made capital of the fact that many Labour candidates had been pacifists or opponents of the war. An appeal based on patriotism or militarism cut less ice in 1945 – partly because the Labour Party had been represented in the wartime government and partly, perhaps, because a large proportion of the Birmingham electorate had themselves been kept out of the armed forces by their work in industries useful to the war.

Generally speaking, the 1945 election in Birmingham was a victory for local candidates. Two of the three Conservatives elected (Sir Peter Bennett and Sir Patrick Hannon) were incumbent candidates. The third, Harold Roberts, was a former city councillor and Lord Mayor. Eleven of the thirteen Labour candidates (and eight of those elected) were from Birmingham. Two of Labour's successful candidates – Jim Simmons and Fred Longden – had previously been elected for Birmingham seats in 1929. Four of them (Simmons, Percy Shurmer, Edith Wills and Julius Silverman) had been councillors. Most of them were relatively old – some having been active in Birmingham politics since the end of the First World War. The national leadership of the Labour Party imposed

---

* In 1956, Elizabeth Pakenham's daughter, Antonia, married the Conservative MP Hugh Fraser. Neville Chamberlain's widow, Anne, summoned her to express her satisfaction that a member of the family had returned to the Conservative fold. Anne died in 1967 and did not, therefore, see Antonia Fraser's second marriage to the playwright Harold Pinter.

two younger candidates from outside the city – described by Simmons as 'wonder boys from Transport House'. They were Captain Raymond Blackburn, who would be imprisoned for fraud in 1955, and Woodrow Wyatt, who would turn out to be fraudulent in a more general sense of the word and who finished his career as a columnist on the *News of the World*, lucratively rewarded chairman of the Tote, and counsellor to Margaret Thatcher.

Herbert Manzoni (*left*), the City Surveyor and Engineer from 1935 until 1963, acquired an almost diabolical status in the minds of conservationists because of the damage that he did to Birmingham's Victorian fabric. But, like many men who pride themselves on being hard-headed realists, he was a romantic and his vision of Birmingham as the epitome of Americanized modernity was, in its way, as fantastical as the notions that the nineteenth-century notables had entertained that they might model their town on the Italian city states. He is seen here with the City Architect. The two men did not have easy relations.

9
Motor City, 1945–75

Morris took the newly opened section of the Inner Ring, an
exhilarating complex of tunnels and flyovers ... From here you
got a panorama of the whole city and the sun came out at that
moment, shining like floodlighting on the pale concrete facades
of the recent construction work, tower blocks and freeways,
throwing them into relief against the sombre mass of nineteenth-
century slums and decayed factories. Seen from this perspective
it looked as though the seeds of a whole twentieth-century city
had been planted under the ground a long time ago and were
now beginning to shoot up into the light, bursting through the
caked, exhausted topsoil of Victorian architecture. Morris found
it an oddly stirring sight, for the city that was springing up was
unmistakably American in style – indeed that was what the local
blimps were always beefing about – and he had the strange feel-
ing of having stumbled upon a new American frontier in the
most unexpected place.

David Lodge, *Changing Places* (1975)

Morris Zapp is a professor from California who spends a six-month
sabbatical in the English city of 'Rummidge'. His understanding of Birmingham (though not his approval) would have been shared by many.
Indeed, those who did not live in the city (and such people rarely found
any reason to visit it) often came to identify it exclusively with a complicated interchange of motorways – the Gravelly Hill (or 'Spaghetti')
junction that they were compelled to navigate as they travelled between
more attractive parts of the country. 'Spaghetti' (in 1970s Britain the
word whispered the enchantments of an exciting cosmopolitanism)

Junction was finished in 1972. *The Times* reported that the Queen conducted the opening ceremony 'in an atmosphere normally reserved for the independence days of an emergent African state'. At roughly the same time, two new buildings – the Sentinels – were completed on the Holloway Head. At thirty-one storeys, they were the highest structures in the city and were said to have been designed to be just higher than the tower blocks that had recently been opened with much fanfare in Glasgow. High-rise building and road construction were the Siamese twins of Birmingham's modernity – the Sentinels overlooked the inner ring road, which had been opened, also by the Queen, in 1971. The Lord Mayor described the ring road as 'the largest single undertaking in the city's history'.[1] It was the culmination of years of work; it had first been suggested in 1917.[2] As early as 1944, a group of city councillors had concluded a meeting on the topic with the words: 'The road nothing but the road'[3] – a phrase that might have served as a motto for post-war Birmingham.

Birmingham made cars. The total number of vehicles produced in Britain peaked in 1972 at 2.3 million (though Britain had, in 1960, ceased to be the second most important manufacturer of motor vehicles after the USA). A large part of this production was concentrated in Birmingham. In 1961, 14 per cent of workers in the city were employed directly in motor manufacture and it was reckoned that between a fifth and a quarter of both workers and capital in the city were devoted to the motor industry in a broader sense.[4] For a time at least, the Birmingham car industry was efficient. Productivity increased fast during the 1950s. There was also a sense in which cars made Birmingham and this was a matter of conscious design rather than just a response to social change. The city was built around the convenience of drivers long before the majority of its inhabitants had a car.

This modernist city of skyscrapers and motorways did not spring to life fully formed after 1945. The historian David Cannadine was born in 1950 and must have left Birmingham in the same year that Morris Zapp arrived. He recalled that he had spent his youth in Victorian buildings and in a city that would have been 'instantly recognizable to Joseph Chamberlain'. When David Lodge arrived to teach English at Birmingham University in 1960, he too discovered a Victorian world, though perhaps because he was arriving rather than leaving, he expressed less affection for this world than Cannadine. Lodge found a Birmingham that was pre-Chamberlainite in that the arts faculty of the university had not yet moved to the Edgbaston campus, which Joseph Chamberlain had helped acquire. It was still based in Edmund Street, in the centre of the city, in a building 'that had a worn, neglected aspect and smelled faintly of drains and gas inside'.[5]

Wartime bombing in Birmingham had not been sufficiently spectacular to require great works of reconstruction. There was no Birmingham equivalent of the South Bank Centre, Coventry Cathedral or the Guards Chapel.[6] The public buildings of the city were more or less intact. About a third of houses had been damaged by bombing. Frank Lockwood painted a watercolour to which he gave a variety of titles – 'Survivors of the Blitz', 'Bombed Houses' and 'Bombed Area' – in the early 1950s. It showed a scene in Great Brook Street, Ladywood. A couple pass an area of such desolation that, as one art historian has pointed out, the scene might have represented central Europe.[7] Bomb damage, though, was concentrated in the poor and densely populated neighbourhoods where houses and small factories were close together, and these areas were the least visible to outsiders. The city authorities had long-term plans for slum clearance and a quarter of destroyed houses were actually in places marked for clearance. In spite of this, some bomb sites ('pecks' in Birmingham argot) remained untouched for many years. Children growing up in Small Heath in the early 1970s (some of them from families that had not even come to Britain until after 1945) played on the pecks even though their parents had warned them of the dangers. One of them told researchers: 'they see it as a castle or a good hiding place'.[8]

War lingered in Birmingham in strange ways. There were still almost 200 unexploded bombs around the city in October 1946.[9] Tony Green, born in 1943, claimed that he found an incendiary bomb in a playground sandpit in Quinton sometime in the 1950s.[10] Prefabricated houses were thrown up quickly during or immediately after the war to replace bombed-out buildings or accommodate the increased population drawn in by war industries. In 1947, the family of Joan Hart, whose father was a metal shearer, moved into such a house, said to have been built by Italian prisoners of war, in King's Heath. The houses had been designed to last for ten years. Joan's family was still there thirteen years later.[11]

A few of Birmingham's post-1945 residents had searing memories of the war. Broseslaw Smojkis had been born in Vilnius and sent by the

Germans, at the age of fourteen, to work in an iron ore mine in France. At the liberation, he joined the Polish army and ended up in a displaced persons camp in Staffordshire. Unable to return home – his native city was no longer even part of Poland – he became one of the 3,000 Poles who went to Birmingham, where he married a local woman. He later found that his mother had been deported to Siberia, where his brother died. His daughter met her Polish grandparents only once, on a brief visit in the 1970s. Broseslaw rarely talked about his past and his new workmates, unable to pronounce his name, christened him 'Barry'.[12] The gentile East Europeans who arrived in the late 1940s – some of whom had good reason to be discreet about their activities between 1939 and 1945 – were a less visible presence than the Jews who had come in the 1930s, and many Birmingham inhabitants were mystified when they happened to catch site of the dome of the Serbian Orthodox Church built for Yugoslav exiles in Hole Lane on the Bournville estate.

Some young men in Birmingham were more likely to be conscripted after 1945 than before because so many of them had been kept in factories by the needs of war production. Grace Holte (born in 1963) described how post-war military service bit into the lives of her family. Grace's parents married on 23 December 1953 because that was when her uncle was able to obtain leave from his unit in Germany. Until the package holidays of the 1960s, none of Grace's family had been abroad except when they had been posted there with the armed forces.[13] Less affectionate memories of conscription came from 300 workers at Enfield Rolling Mills in Ladywood who went on strike in 1964 because they objected to the foreman's use of 'army language'.[14]

MANZONI

The restructuring of post-war Birmingham owed much to one man. Herbert John Baptista Manzoni was born in 1899 in Birkenhead. His father was a sculptor from Milan who had left his native land, apparently for political reasons. Manzoni joined the army during the First World War and won a commission. Perhaps because of his war experiences, he came to feel uneasy with the 'artistic temperament' that he believed he had inherited and decided to counter this by training as an engineer. He arrived in Birmingham in 1923 and became an assistant in the Sewers and Rivers Department – an important institution in a city that was still influenced by a Chamberlainite interest in sanitary engineering. He became head of this department in 1927 and rose to be city engineer and surveyor in 1935. He was an energetic, forceful man – a great one for sitting on committees, presiding over societies and writing reports. His influence was felt as far away as Kenya; the authorities there asked him to produce a report on the Public Works Department. But, above all, he dominated Birmingham in the thirty years after 1945, almost as much as Joseph Chamberlain had done in the last thirty years of the nineteenth century.

Manzoni's hegemony coincided with a broader change. Until 1940, Birmingham had been ruled by the notables and especially by those who belonged to the 'five families' (see chapter 4). Their experience of local government stretched back over generations, they drew on networks of mutual support and they had the financial security to devote time to municipal affairs. This style of local politics would have ended anyway as business and municipal administration were both becoming more complicated and time-consuming. The days when it was possible to spend the morning at the company office and the afternoon in the Council House were gone. However, the increased power of the Labour Party in Birmingham Council made the change even more dramatic. Suddenly councillors of the ruling party were men with relatively little experience and formal education. They were still obliged to earn their living and often to do so in comparatively menial employment, which did not leave them with much free time. In such circumstances, a confident full-time administrator who arrived at every meeting with detailed plans and a clear sense of 'what needed to be done' exercised great power.

Manzoni retired in 1963 and died in 1972 but his influence was felt most sharply in the period immediately after his death. Two Victorian buildings – the one designed by Edward Barry that housed the Birmingham and Midland Institute, and the one designed by J. H. Chamberlain that housed the central library – were demolished. In their place the architect John Madin proposed to erect a new library. This would be a 'brutalist' building of concrete but clad with stone to match the nearby town hall. It would form part of a larger complex of buildings – encompassing offices and the music school, with a bus interchange located underneath. As it turned out the scheme was conceived at the moment (1969) when the Birmingham economy began to downturn. By the time the library was built in 1974, there was no money for stone cladding or for the larger complex of buildings.

As fashions turned against modernist architecture in the 1980s, Manzoni acquired an almost diabolic status.[15] The denunciation was not entirely fair. Manzoni's position was more complicated than it seemed and he sometimes changed his mind over the course of his long career. Like many men who think of themselves as hard-headed, Manzoni was a romantic. His vision of Birmingham as the epitome of American-style modernity looks as fantastical in retrospect as the late Victorian notion that Birmingham would become a latter-day Italian city state. Manzoni's ideas for how Birmingham might be transformed dated back to at least 1939. His ambitions seem to have increased during the war, which showed how a determined official might cut through the usual procedures to get things done. Strangely, the focus on short-term survival often went side by side with projects for spectacular transformation when peace came.

POST-WAR HOUSING

As it turned out, the return of peace did not immediately open up the chance of grand transformation. Money was tight and Birmingham did not feature much in the plans of the post-war Labour government. The city council had acquired a good deal of land in the inter-war period and it now used this to build new houses. Between January 1945 and September 1954, 25,000 new homes were constructed. Of these, 20,000 were built by the council: 4,625 were temporary bungalows (in practice the bungalows were often still in place until at least the 1970s).[16] The fact that much construction involved houses – particularly the slightly improved version of council houses that were known, after the Minister of Health, as 'Bevan houses' – rather than flats, was significant. It marked continuity with Birmingham's sense of its identity as being 'not flat-minded' that dated back to the late nineteenth century. The development at Kent Moat in 1946 seemed daring in that it contained a small number of three-storey buildings divided into flats for 'bachelor girls'.[17]

Things began to change in Birmingham when the Conservatives won a majority of seats on the council in the 1948 election. They believed that slum clearance would require a shift to building flats – or maisonettes – along with houses. They established a house-building committee, independent of the existing public works committee, which was chaired by Charles Burman, a civil engineering contractor. Burman's father had been MP for Duddeston, and Burman himself had been a councillor since 1934 and Lord Mayor from 1947 to 1949. He was, however, different from the pre-war Birmingham notables. Unlike them, he did not seek consensus in municipal politics. He was close to building firms, such as Laing, Wimpey and Wates, and he became a director of Tarmac in 1955. Manzoni also worked with Wimpey who demonstrated the economic advantages of simple design with the six-storey block of flats they constructed at Tile Cross in the early 1950s.[18]

Manzoni was fascinated by novelty and scale and saw high-rise flats as fitting into a broader vision for the city that revolved around the motor car (of which more below). There was also a political dimension to building. In the 1950s and 60s both parties were desperate to demonstrate their capacity to build houses. Harold Macmillan owed much of his reputation to his success as Minister of Housing and Local Government from 1951 to 1954. The fact that Birmingham Council swung between Labour and the Conservatives made it important for both sides to demonstrate their success in providing houses. Central government granted subsidies for house building and eventually for 'high-density' (i.e. high-rise) building. It also bent the rules to ensure that Birmingham benefited from these subsidies even when it was building on cheap, previously unused, land that ought not to have attracted support.

For the next twenty years, much council construction in Birmingham involved multi-storey, low-quality concrete buildings. Estates were built on the edge of the city rather than in the neighbourhoods where slums were due to be demolished – six out of seven of the estates projected in 1952 were on the outskirts of the city. By the early 1970s, Birmingham had built 464 high-rise blocks of flats of which almost two thirds were on or beyond the city's outer ring road. A new cityscape came into view. Until 1945, housing away from the city centre had been less dense and almost invariably more desirable than housing in the centre. Now the houses and greenery of what had previously been the city's outer ring were contained within a new ring that was made up of high buildings. The Labour councillor Albert Bradbeer talked of the city being surrounded by 'forts'; David Eversley, who campaigned against the new

style of housing, wrote in 1957 of a 'saucer city' because it rose at its
edges and then again in its centre.[19]

There was bitter dispute over the nature of Birmingham's building
projects. Alwyn Sheppard Fidler was appointed as the first city architect
in 1952. He was not opposed to modern design or building techniques
but he favoured high-quality work and estates that would mix different
styles of building, houses as well as flats. But he found that his powers were limited – particularly when he came up against Manzoni's
engineers:

> When I went to Birmingham you could have called it Wimpey or Wates
> town. The Deputy Chief Engineer came into my office the very first day I
> arrived, showed these plans on my desk, and said 'Carry on with these!'
> He was letting contracts as fast he could go, didn't know what he was
> doing, just putting up as many Wimpey Y-shaped blocks as he could! This
> rather shattered me ... in Birmingham the House Building Committee
> could hardly care about the design as long as the numbers were kept up.[20]

Sheppard Fidler's desire for high-quality work brought him up against
a powerful coalition of the city's engineer, councillors from both sides
of the political divide and British building firms. When he tried to get
the French firm Camus to build one estate, he was overruled by those
who insisted on the British company Bryant. Sheppard Fidler – driven
to desperation by the construction of buildings that he regarded as
'mud-pies' – resigned in 1964.

Judged against what came after him, Sheppard Fidler looked good. He
was not on the take and he cared about the quality of buildings. His tenure, however, was not always remembered as a golden age by those who
had to live in his buildings. Like many architects who take their job seriously, he was influenced by fashion and curiously slow to recognize that
building styles that worked in, say, southern France might not be appropriate to a rainy town in the English Midlands. Though the very tallest
constructions in Birmingham came after him, the overall proportion of
high buildings on council estates peaked under Sheppard Fidler: 85 per cent
of blocks built on council estates in 1963 had more than six storeys. This
proportion declined thereafter – partly because of changing fashions and
partly because central government subsidy for high-density housing was
withdrawn in 1967. The project that best epitomized Sheppard Fidler's
style – the Lyndhurst estate in Erdington – won a prize for its design, but

it was not popular with residents and was eventually recognized as a site of 'hard to let' housing.

Sheppard Fidler was succeeded, on a temporary basis, by his deputy, J.R. Sheridan-Shedden, who was described by one colleague as 'an appalling medieval baron of an architect, a man of zero architectural quality, a primeval creature who could have gone to work for Wimpey or some other contractor'. Sheridan Shedden was then replaced by Alan Maudsley in 1966. The power of the city architect's department was now reduced. For most of the 1960s, the council pressed for rapid, cheap construction. They were helped in this aim by the increasing use of 'system building', which meant that floor and wall panels were made in factories and brought to the site for assembly. Three large estates constructed in the mid 1960s – at Castle Vale, Bromford Bridge and Chelmsley Wood – used system building.

There was also a cruder dimension to council construction in Birmingham. Local politicians and officials had business interests that overlapped with those of builders – indeed a small but significant proportion of Birmingham councillors (just under 4 per cent in the 1960s) were builders. Alan Maudsley went to prison in 1975 having admitted that he had a corrupt relation with a local architectural practice. Three directors of the Bryant building firm (including the managing director) were subsequently convicted of having improperly provided gifts to councillors. Bryant, of which the Labour Alderman W.T. Bowen was a director, had won two thirds of all Birmingham council contracts between 1966 and 1968. No elected politician went down, but there were plenty of rumours. George Brown, the Labour minister, performed the topping out ceremony at one new building. Having enjoyed the lavish hospitality that building firms provided on such occasions, he shouted to the assembled dignitaries: 'You are all in Chris Bryant's pocket.'[21]

Denis Howell was a councillor from 1945 to 1956, Member of Parliament for Birmingham All Saints from 1955 to 1959 and then for Small Heath from 1961 until 1992. In between his stints in Parliament, he established a public relations consultancy, which worked for Bryant. He was worried that his name would come up in the Bryant trial.[22] Frank Price, Lord Mayor of Birmingham in 1964–5, and a long-standing chair of the city's public works committee before then, was indignant when *Private Eye* accused him of having accepted 'kick backs' – though, like Howell, he refrained from issuing a libel writ[23] – but his autobiography evokes the world of post-war municipal government in which a man who had been born poor and drew no official salary could enjoy chauffeur-driven cars and generously subsidized 'study trips' to foreign cities. Price moved from the public works committee to become a director of a property company.

THE CHARMS OF NEW ESTATES

New estates could seem soulless, especially to those who lived in tower blocks, and in the 1980s some acquired terrible reputations for crime, vandalism and squalor. In view of this, it is hard now to recapture how exciting and attractive they could seem to their first residents. Carol Davis was born in 1943 to a family who lived in a prefabricated house in the Maypole and then 'we moved to what we thought was a very posh estate at Lickeys in Rednal'.[24] People used to narrow streets and outdoor toilets marvelled at the wide open spaces between blocks of flats and the modern amenities of their new homes. One newcomer to Castle Vale said that a flat with an indoor toilet 'seemed like Utopia'.[25] Paul Hill, born in 1959, recalled his family's move:

> we were offered a new house on Castle Vale, which we took because it was like a holiday camp. There was grass ... there was an indoor bathroom ... at Nechells we always had to go to the end of the yard ... we had a metal bath which we all had to pile in to use the same water.[26]

Birmingham residents often remembered getting an inside toilet for the first time. The comedian Frank Skinner, who grew up in an Oldbury council house that had an outside toilet until the 1970s, memorably remarked, while interviewing Tony Blair, that the 'piss bucket in the bedroom' was a symbol of working-class identity.[27] In terms of hot water, bathrooms and inside toilets, owner-occupied properties were better equipped than council ones and, even more strikingly, private renters were worse off than council tenants. One might add that there were considerable divisions within each of these categories – related to areas of the city – and this in turn was often related to concentrations of immigrants. Old housing near the centre of the city was usually of poor quality. It was here that private renting was most common but council houses were also often of low quality – many of them were 'patched houses', that is to say old buildings in slum areas that had been renovated rather than demolished. Not surprisingly, those who rented from private landlords or who lived in the inferior quality council houses usually jumped at the chance to move.

A resident of Castle Vale, Tracy, recalled a terrible episode (it must have been in the mid 1970s) that captured the ways in which new buildings could conjure up images that were simultaneously promising and sinister:

> While I lived there, some of the mothers in summer used to sit out, put blankets on the grass, sit out with children. It was nice. I remember this one girl, a blonde girl. She had a Cockney accent, she was from London. I said to her, 'where do you live?' and she went, 'I live in Cosford Tower.' I went, 'so do I', and she said, 'how long have you lived here?' I think my daughter must have been eight years old then and I said, since she was nine months old so it's been seven years ... and she said, 'I've lived here three years since my little boy was born' ... she asked 'where [in the building] do you live and I pointed to mine there, the fourth one up, and she said 'well, I'm six on top of you.'[28]

Later in the day the blonde cockney's son fell from her flat and was killed. Tracy felt unable to help and sensed vaguely that things (community spirit as well as the safety of children) might have been easier in old-fashioned housing.

Jill Campbell also recalled the snakes and ladders of Birmingham council housing and the ways in which tenants sometimes valued aspects of their housing that might not have been apparent to an official. She spent the first seven years of her life in her grandmother's house in Small Heath in the 1950s. Though her father was in regular work at BSA, they could not afford a place of their own. Her parents got a maisonette in Hall Green, which still seemed almost rural – the children played in corn fields and picked blackberries by the railway embankment. When Jill married, at the age of eighteen, she moved back to Small Heath and took a council flat in Pritchett tower, on the eighteenth floor. The flats had originally been built for private tenants and were, therefore, comfortable, but it seemed an unnatural place for their daughter to grow up. There was nowhere for the child to play because the neighourhood was 'very concretified' and her daughter, used to the silence of her high flat, was frightened by the noise of traffic. Jill's husband arranged a swap with another council tenant who lived closer to his own workplace and got a place in a three-storey building. This seemed to work better and Jill got to know her neighbours – one of whom minded her daughter when she returned to work.[29]

Getting the right kind of council house in the right kind of area was tricky. No one could apply until they had lived in the city for five years. A part of the white working class did well from this system. Along with the advantages they derived from long-term residence in itself, they understood how to work the system. Young white couples seeking council houses were often the children of council tenants and resident with their parents or in-laws at the moment they applied. Many knew councillors who could be persuaded to have a word in the right ear. This created an ethnic hierarchy in which long-term residents were placed above immigrants and immigrants themselves were divided by date of arrival – generally, the Irish had come first, followed by West Indians and then Asians. In addition to this, needs were assessed according to a number of criteria, which included 'war service', something else that would generally have advantaged the British-born. War service was still a criterion for the allocation of council housing – one that counted for more than whether potential tenants lacked an inside toilet or had to cook on an open fire – until 1976. For the purpose of council house allocation, common-law relationships, frequent among West Indians, were not counted as being the equal of conventional marriages until the couple had lived together for five years.[30] A Barbadian bus driver was blunt about the allocation of housing: 'Only white people had houses, black people lived in maisonettes or tower blocks.'[31]

Later, when large numbers of immigrants had lived in the city for long enough to acquire the right to council houses, the Birmingham housing department made an active effort to disperse non-white tenants. In the late 1960s, it sought to ensure that not more than one in every six tenants in any building or any street was black. The policy had the effect of moving some black tenants to predominantly white neighbourhoods, such as Northfield, that were in the outer part of the city. It also disadvantaged non-white people (especially West Indians) because they primarily asked to be housed in the inner neighbourhoods, notably Handsworth, that were established sites of non-white settlement and in which black housing was now effectively rationed.

West Indians were likely to find that they were refused their first choice of council house. Asians, who were less likely to ask for council housing in the first place and who were also more likely to have been displaced by slum clearance (which gave them automatic preference when being considered for rehousing), fared better. The Birmingham housing policy was ruled as discriminatory by the Race Relations Board in 1975.[32]

Even when they were officially encouraged to move to new estates, non-white people rarely found life easy there. Castle Vale, one of the last big estates to be built, was almost exclusively white. This became an attraction for some working-class residents who saw themselves as having 'escaped' from areas of high immigration. Those few non-white families who came to Castle Vale were not welcomed. One resident recalled an Asian family who moved from Ladywood:

> The removal van turned up and . . . a crowd gathered round and started calling names. They were not just little kids, they were grown men and women. They [the Asian family] said to the removal van, 'stop, put our stuff back on we're going' and they left.[33]

Those in the lowest-quality housing were allocated the highest priority. But this did not mean that they were always given the newest houses and flats that the majority of council tenants regarded as most desirable. Council 'visitors' assessed families and, though council houses were no longer deliberately priced to be accessible only to the skilled and respectable working class, in practice many families believed that visitors would reserve the best housing for those whom they regarded as clean and tidy. This made life difficult for the very poor in slum housing where cleanliness was not easily achieved. Anita Stanton, who was born in 1947, the daughter of an Irish building worker, and grew up in Duddeston, recalled: 'the clean people were moved to better areas such as Alum Rock and Erdington and the others would be sent to Aston'. She described surreal scenes as linen was passed from house to house so that successive families could show the visitors impeccable bed clothes.[34]

With the new estates came a new degree of separation between city and countryside. At least at first, the big post-war council estates could be surprisingly green places. There were large expanses of grass between the tower blocks, and mature trees were left in place. Those who lived high in the towers on the estates on the edge of the city could see out to surrounding counties, though there was no way that the new estates could be considered rural. It was not possible, as it was in parts of Edgbaston or Bournville, to find places where one could look around without seeing a single building. The ring of concrete created by the estates also marked a frontier that was visible even before a formal green belt was instituted in 1975. Conservative Agriculture Ministers recognized that containing Birmingham's growth was one of their duties.

MOVING INDUSTRY OUT OF BIRMINGHAM

The post-war decades were the age of the planner, and planners did not like Birmingham – at least they did not like the city in the form it currently took. Central government policy was driven by the belief – which had been expressed in the Barlow report of 1940 on industrial location – that the major towns were overpopulated. It was also driven by the desire to move industry away from the most prosperous areas, which meant the Midlands and the South, towards Wales and the North, which had been defined as 'distressed areas' before 1938 and were now designated 'development areas'. The government provided subsidies for companies that moved to these areas and they also sought to squeeze industry out of places such as Birmingham through the use of industrial development certificates. Any company wishing to build a factory of more than a certain size (or to expand an existing one) was required to obtain a certificate from the Board of Trade, which pressed firms to move to where employment was less plentiful.

Birmingham businesses did move, or at least established new branches, in development areas. Such moves, however, were not very successful. A study of thirteen Birmingham companies that relocated part or all of their operations to south Wales showed the managers of all but one of them would have preferred to stay in Birmingham but for the inducements they had been offered to move. Within not much more than a decade, three of the plants had closed and five would have done so if their managers had been able to find premises to move back to in Birmingham.[35] Companies, particularly those in metallurgy, valued the networks of subcontractors and clients that they had built up,[36] and, in spite of their frequent complaints about labour in Birmingham, found it hard to get skilled workers elsewhere. Measures to encourage industry to move to 'development areas' were probably more important in persuading companies who might otherwise have moved to Birmingham not to do so and this had the effect of freezing the city's economy – ensuring that it remained concentrated in metalworking, engineering and especially motor manufacture. The consequences of this concentration were to be felt in the late 1970s.

SATELLITE TOWNS

Alongside attempts to move industry to the North and to Wales, efforts were made to move people to locations that were nearer at hand. Immediately after the war, Birmingham's own planners believed that the city could not reasonably accommodate more than 990,000 people and this meant that it needed to lose about a tenth of its population. Projects to demolish slum housing near the centre of town meant that some residents would have to be relocated and this project was part of a general drive to reduce the density of population. Simple expansion of the city into surrounding areas was now discouraged and an attempt by the City of Birmingham Corporation to build an estate at Wythall (about seven miles to the south of the city) was rejected by a planning enquiry in 1959.

A law of 1946 allowed the Treasury to subsidize 'new towns' that would take population from overcrowded cities. However, at first this was only used to relieve London. Birmingham indulged in a more limited form of urban colonization, which was permitted under existing legislation. This involved negotiation with other towns that agreed to take 'overspill'. Most overspill towns were in the three counties adjacent to Birmingham – Worcestershire, Warwickshire and especially Staffordshire – though some discussed the prospect that Birmingham firms might move to Weston-super-Mare, a Somerset seaside town of fading gentility that was remote from Birmingham in every sense of the word.[37]

Birmingham Corporation subsidized the building of council houses in 'reception towns' on the understanding that these would be reserved for people from the city. A special waiting list was opened for residents who wanted council houses and were willing to accept them outside Birmingham. Many of those who put their names on the list seem to have been people whose existing accommodation was relatively good and who would consequently not have stood much chance of being rehoused within Birmingham. By 1956, Birmingham Council had agreements with seventeen local authorities to rehouse its population. Fourteen of these authorities were in neighbouring counties (ten of them in Staffordshire) but three were in more distant counties – Northamptonshire, Shropshire and Radnor.[38]

In the 1950s, some in Birmingham had campaigned for the creation of new towns in the Midlands that would relieve the pressure of population in the city. In the early 1960s, new legislation did permit the establishment of two new towns designed to serve Birmingham: Redditch (relatively close) and Dawley (in Staffordshire). Dawley replaced an original proposal to build in Swynnerton, which was overruled by Conservative grandees who wanted to protect good agricultural land.[39] Dawley was initially intended to take 50,000 people from Birmingham, but in 1968 it was extended to take in a number of surrounding industrial hamlets, rechristened 'Telford' and designated as the destination for 100,000 Birmingham residents, which, with migration from elsewhere, was expected to produce a total population of around 250,000. By this time, the authorities reckoned that they would need to move 350,000 people out of Birmingham into the overspill areas by 1981.

All of these projects involved a curious attempt to turn back time. Some of the overspill towns – Tamworth, Lichfield, Worcester – had been administrative or ecclesiastical centres when Birmingham had been a village. The Roman roads bringing salt from Droitwich had passed over the land that was later Birmingham before it was inhabited at all. Telford brought together places – including Coalbrookdale and Telford's Iron Bridge – that had been important industrial centres. The fate of Telford was particularly poignant. In any age when local authority brochures promised light, airy surroundings, Telford suffered because its landscape was so obviously scarred by slag heaps and disused mines. Only with the growth of 'industrial archaeology' in the 1970s did it begin to attract worthy middle-class visitors from Birmingham, who had come to see it as a *lieu de mémoire*.[40]

Attempts to relocate the Birmingham population – whether to overspill areas or new towns – failed. Telford's population, which was meant to have reached 250,000 by 1981, is only just over 140,000 today. Some local politicians disliked the policy. They thought that Birmingham people should be able to live and work in the city from which they came. Labour councillors were particularly prone to be hostile. This is hardly surprising because the kind of people who were moved, relatively prosperous workers who lived, or wanted to live, in council houses, were also those who were most likely to vote Labour. Local authorities elsewhere were also often hostile. The Worcestershire County Plan of 1952 referred to the 'great urban mass of Birmingham and the Black Country', which was 'forcing its tentacles of development south'.[41] Above all, persuading employers to move proved more difficult than persuading individuals and families to do so. In 1968, the West Midlands Economics Planning Council estimated that they would need to move 80,000 jobs if they were to meet their target of relocating 350,000 people; current progress suggested that they would actually move 17,000.[42] Industrialists who had refused the blandishments of the development areas were reluctant to move to places that were sometimes only thirty or forty miles closer to Birmingham.[43] Sometimes the government exercised its powers to refuse industrial development certificates in overspill towns on the grounds that they were part of the West Midlands and therefore amply provided with employment.

The result was that those who had left Birmingham sometimes commuted back to work in the city. This could involve long journeys – Daventry, in which some from Birmingham were resettled, is sixty-eight miles away. It exacerbated another feature of post-war planning in Birmingham: the important role that it ascribed to the motor car.

CARS

Cars had been a symbol of Birmingham for the whole twentieth century. In the 1920s, the Labour Party had campaigned to have the use of cars banned in elections because they provided such an advantage to Conservative candidates,[44] but everyday travel by car was rare until after 1945. In 1943, when he was over seventy, Byng Kenrick, the industrialist and former Lord Mayor, still got around Birmingham by bicycle.[45]

Manzoni, though, saw cars as key to the future of Birmingham from an early stage and in 1943 he was already planning how the city would be restructured around them. This meant, first, the construction of three ring roads – inner, middle and outer – that would encircle the city. Other means of city travel were discounted. The Labour Alderman W.T. Bowen campaigned without success for an underground railway. The closure of tramlines began in 1947 – the last went in 1953. Buses remained but even their routes were disrupted by post-war road building. The number 8 bus, which had been known as the 'workman's special' because it passed so many factories in the inner part of the city, changed its route to take account of new roads that cut across it.

Making Birmingham into a car city was a conscious imitation of America. In 1955 Manzoni said: 'I see no reason why traffic in this country should not reach the proportions of traffic in America ... one vehicle for every adult'; a year later he added: everybody wants a car, and if there are a few who don't, there are others who want two ... This is quite obviously every family's ambition.'[46] Manzoni led a delegation to examine roads in Chicago, Pittsburgh, Philadelphia, Washington and New York in 1956.

By 1967, Birmingham's debt, per inhabitant, for road construction was twice that of any other provincial city.[47] Underpasses ensured that pedestrians did not impede traffic – though, in practice, by the 1970s some pedestrians preferred to take their chances with the speeding traffic on the surface rather than with the muggers in the underpasses. The post-war townscape might have been different if Manzoni had achieved his initial ambition to put cars into tunnels and leave pedestrians on the surface.

The most dangerous roads were often built through the inner-city neighbourhoods, whose inhabitants were least likely to drive – fewer than a quarter of residents in high-density council estates in central Birmingham had driving licences in 1972.[48] The *British Medical Journal* published a study of the 183 deaths caused by road traffic accidents in and around Birmingham in 1960. Unsurprisingly, the majority of deaths involved pedestrians hit by cars. More revealing was the fact that the most common victims were not, as road safety campaigners often supposed, children, but the old.[49] The authors of the paper said that the fact that fifty-seven of the ninety-seven pedestrians killed were over the age of sixty-five made their actions in walking across busy streets 'difficult to understand'.[50] Old women in particular were less likely to drive than those in early middle age – in 1968, fewer than one in 300 women aged over fifty-nine in Birmingham had a driving licence.[51] Perhaps it is not too fanciful to suggest that those who had lived in the same neighbourhood since the early part of the century regarded road construction schemes in the same way that eighteenth-century agricultural populations might have regarded land enclosure – as something that deprived them of their traditional access to the area around their own homes. Road building inflicted the long-term effects of pollution on the inhabitants of the inner city as well as the constant awfulness of noise: those near the Aston Expressway barricaded their houses with mattresses and hardwood in an attempt to insulate themselves from what one woman described as the 'brainwashing noise'.[52]

Spaghetti Junction brought motorways right through the centre of the town. Mini ghettos were created as roads cut across parts of the inner city – laying down barriers as impassable as a fast-flowing river. Newtown in Aston had been a centre of slum clearance in which a number of tower blocks were constructed. It was relatively close to the city centre but effectively boxed in to its own world by the busy roads that surrounded it. In 1971, a journalist wrote: 'Birmingham is dominated by the motor car. Strangled by a concrete collar of ringways, flyovers and interchanges, it is as if it has been enslaved by its own creation.'[53]

Existing divisions were exacerbated by cars. The first of these was social. Ownership of cars in Birmingham increased fast – from 60,306 in 1952 to 184,980 in 1965 – and it was unusually high by national standards but, in 1972, this still only meant that 42 per cent of households had a car; in the least privileged neighbourhoods this figure was 20 per cent.[54] Often the very workers who built the motor city did not drive. The labourers who worked on Spaghetti Junction and its attached motorway system were mainly Irish. One of them summed up their means of travel thus: 'The Wimpey coach would pick you up on the Coventry Road and drop you on the way back six days later.'[55] Many workers got to factories on bicycles. In the early 1950s, Cadbury provided its employees with vast bike sheds, and one man was given a full-time job fixing punctures.[56] The characteristic cyclist in post-war Birmingham was a middle-aged man in overalls on his way to work – fifteen out of the sixteen cyclists killed on Birmingham roads in 1960 were men.

Frank Skinner recalled growing up in Bristnall Hall Road in Oldbury.

Our side of the road, the council house side, had barely a car parked on it; there was the odd motorbike and side-car and Mr Feraday's massive lorry, but that was it. The opposite side was all private houses, with cars parked on the street, and in the driveways, where people had had their front gardens tarmacked over for that specific purpose.[57]

As time went on, the social divisions around cars increasingly cut across the working class. By 1972, the proportion of skilled workers and foremen who had driving licences (75.4 per cent) was actually higher than the proportion among professional, managerial and other non-manual workers (71.2 per cent). This was partly because the middle classes were better placed than workers to buy houses close to their workplace and partly because a strand of the Birmingham bourgeoisie still regarded driving as vulgar and occasionally sent their children to expensive private schools in taxis. Among unskilled and semi-skilled workers, however, only 34.4 per cent had driving licences.

Car factories themselves illustrated the social stratification that went with transport. An unusually high proportion of car workers were drivers – partly because they were relatively well paid and partly because they got discounts on their company's products. In a characteristic sleight of hand, Birmingham Corporation used figures relating to employees of motor factories to justify their claim that travel by car was more common than travel by bicycle.[58] Even for car plants, though, the statistics ignored the division between workers and managers. Most workers at the Longbridge factory lived in Birmingham, but only a fifth of managers did.[59] A large proportion of those who ran Longbridge commuted from outside the city – particularly from Solihull. Solihull, technically outside the city limits (and of which more below), and Sutton Coldfield, outside the city limits until 1974, were the places in England where people were most likely to travel to work by car.[60] They were also, in 1979, the two safest Conservative seats in the country.

There were sharp differences in how and when people from different classes acquired cars. Some of the most privileged drove almost as soon as they were old enough to take the test. A sociologist studying the education of girls in the 1970s was struck by the fact that some sixth formers at King Edward's School – the most academically demanding but by no means the most socially exclusive of Birmingham schools – travelled to school by car.[61] The Birmingham Young Conservatives were so 'motor minded' that, in 1954, they created the only political associ-ation to be affiliated with the Royal Automobile Club. Since two thirds of Birmingham Young Conservatives lived with their parents, one assumes that few of them bought cars with their own earnings.[62] By contrast, Leslie Jones had been working full-time since the age of four-teen, partly in car factories. He was thirty-five by the time he was able to buy his first car – a second-hand Austin Cambridge – in 1957.[63] Grace Holte's father could get a discount on a car (an Austin A40) because her uncle Bert worked at the Austin. Even then, he could not afford the purchase until he was in his mid thirties, though he too had been working since the age of fourteen.[64]

The greater part of the population still depended on public trans-port. Most residents – especially women, children and the old – built their lives around bus routes. An elderly working-class white couple in Sparkbrook disliked their neighbourhood – 'litter . . . immigrants, mug-gings' – but conceded that it was 'handy for buses'.[65] In 1950, the Labour group on the city council achieved a rare victory when they managed to introduce free bus travel for old age pensioners; thirteen years later, an independent 'ratepayer' councillor won a case in the High Court to have this ruled illegal. The city's political elite lived in a differ-ent world from many of those whose lives they influenced. In 1975, most members of the council transport committee had not used public transport in the previous four months.[66]

At first, immigrants were unlikely to have cars or driving licences. Many of them came from rural areas in their home countries and were, therefore, particularly discomfited to find a city that was built around the convenience of drivers. An Irishman recalled:

Another thing I hadn't seen until I came – cos we were only in the country – I'd never seen traffic lights. I remember going across the road, and I wouldn't budge off the path . . . I could see all the traffic coming and I nearly left it too late, then I made one mad dash.[67]

Manzoni was prone to use the phrases 'a car for every adult' and 'a car for every family' as though they meant the same thing, and his sta-tistics suggest that he actually anticipated a city in which every *male* adult had a car. Working-class women were unlikely to drive even if their husbands did and even when middle-class women began to do so. In 1972, only 8 per cent of women in council houses had driving licences.

Housewives spent much time negotiating buses, escalators and pedestrian bridges. Some of them remarked that planners, who had devoted such attention to the interests of motorists, seemed to have given no thought to how one might get a pram around the new shopping centres,[68] or even over the steep kerbs by pedestrian crossings.[69] One woman recalled her life as a young mother in the early 1960s: '[Women] didn't have access to cars, not in the circles we mixed, ordinary working-class women; women didn't have ownership of a car. I couldn't take the children into town. I couldn't get on the bus with a twin pram.'[70] The general restructuring of Birmingham around the car also had marked effects on the journey times of women who worked. Among a sample of men who moved from the centre of the city to outlying districts between 1952 and 1960, the proportion who lived within ten minutes of their work dropped from 54 per cent to 5 per cent; among women, it dropped from 75 per cent to zero.[71]

Differences of age, sex and class intersected to create a hierarchy that revolved around access to cars. Middle-class men acquired cars first but their wives, and even their teenage children, got them at times when the majority of residents in some parts of the city still relied on public transport. In the early 1960s, a bemused newcomer to the city found that women in the grandest houses could tell him nothing about bus routes: 'we are all two-car families in this part of Moseley now'.[72] The Birmingham car factories could almost have divided their production lines by sex and age: at Solihull, Rovers were built for middle-aged, middle-class men, while, a little later, the Mini, built at Longbridge, was designed for women and the young. In Birmingham, even more than elsewhere, big and powerful cars were associated with macho showmanship. Manzoni had been an amateur racing motorist before the war and the city council embarked on an unsuccessful bid to run a grand prix race around the city centre in the 1970s.

SOLIHULL VERSUS EDGBASTON

Some of the changes in post-war Birmingham can be illustrated by comparing Solihull and Edgbaston. Both areas had once belonged to the estates of the Middlemore family and been sold in the eighteenth century. In the nineteenth century the latter had become the natural home of Birmingham's economic elite (see chapter 4). Between 1895 and 1924, twenty-nine residents of Edgbaston each left an estate of £100,000 or more when they died; the comparable figure for Solihull was three.[73] Even then, however, some discerned a drift of the wealthy away from Birmingham. The *Birmingham Daily Mail* wrote: 'Like the Arab, they are folding their tents and stealing away in the direction of Knowle and Solihull, where the octopus tentacles of expanding Birmingham are as yet in the distance.'[74]

After 1945, the migration became more marked. Now, the Birmingham economy revolved largely around national or international companies, and the wealthy were more likely to be managers – 'executives', as they liked to say – rather than owners. The most important of the Edgbaston families had left the city altogether. Charles Beale, born in 1913, was a relic of Victorian Birmingham. He was a solicitor and, like his grandfather, pro-chancellor of the university. He and his wife, a Crosskey with Kenrick and Nettlefold ancestors, still lived in Edgbaston, in a lugubrious house that was known, on account of a peculiarly shaped window, as 'coffin corner'. But most of his relations now lived in London. Beale, Marigold and Beale had opened its first London office in 1865, and in the 1970s the firm finally severed its links with its original Birmingham base. The Martineaus and Chamberlains were also now mainly London families. The two most prominent members of the latter – Harriet Harman* and Lady Antonia Fraser – are quintessentially metropolitan figures.

The Edgbaston families became victims of their own success. Their children were increasingly likely to go to public school. Often this meant being sucked towards London and the South East. When he arrived at Birmingham University in the early 1960s, Richard Hoggart looked for houses around Edgbaston, which provided him with 'a fascinating social cameo'. What he found '[m]ost haunting were the children's bedrooms; the overlapping pop-star posters seeming both lonely and public, the children away at boarding school'.[75]

On some of its frontiers, Edgbaston teetered on the edge of the precipice into which Handsworth had already fallen as large houses were divided up into bedsits for the poor and especially for immigrants. But Edgbaston was sustained by a deliberate decision of the town council to

---

* Harman's husband, Jack Dromey, was Labour MP for Erdington.

keep it as a kind of memorial and game reserve for the *grande bourgeoisie*. After the war, the council decreed that the population density in the inner part of the city should be between 75 and 120 persons per acre. In the outer part it was 50 per acre. However, Edgbaston, though close to the centre, was treated as a special case. Its population was not expected to exceed 30 per acre.[76] In the 1960s, many of the leases in Edgbaston came up for renewal – the aristocratic Calthorpes still owned the freeholds, although they had ceased to have any real association with the city. The council could then have built estates in Edgbaston, but Frank Price, the Labour leader of the council, chose to leave Edgbaston as an enclave of private houses – to prevent even more of the middle classes being siphoned off by Solihull and Sutton Coldfield. It was characteristic of Birmingham that the Bristol Road – a busy dual carriageway – was used as the new frontier to mark Edgbaston off from council house development.[77] Bournville, near Edgbaston, was also largely spared from the effects of development. This was partly because the area was still controlled by the 'Village Trust' that had been established by the Cadbury family and partly because Bournville was the natural home of Labour councillors, such as Frank Price and Clive Wilkinson.

Solihull after 1945 came to serve the function that Edgbaston had served in the nineteenth century. It too offered Birmingham businessmen a haven in which they could be comfortably remote from the industries that provided their money. Birmingham had more jobs than people – 111 jobs for every hundred residents in 1951. Solihull, by contrast, was a commuter town – there were only fifty-one jobs for every hundred residents.[78] The people most likely to commute were the most prosperous. In 1966, just under half of business employers and managers, and just over half of professionals, who worked in Birmingham lived outside it.[79] Solihull's population expanded rapidly to accommodate them – it stood at around 60,000 in 1940 but had roughly doubled by 1960 and almost trebled by 1980. New houses sprang up, mainly on what had previously been agricultural land. Unlike the new houses built in Birmingham, those in Solihull were mainly private developments, which were then sold to owner-occupiers, rather than becoming council houses. The houses in Lady Byron Lane, Solihull's smartest address, were not as grand as the best in Edgbaston but they were large and well appointed – one of them was rumoured to have a toilet decorated with gold-plated dolphins. Even a boy at school in Edgbaston might recognize Lady Byron Lane as the natural home of those he described as 'Percival Jones' types.[80] Solihull was a place where money trumped social prestige: Dave Hill – the heroically vulgar guitarist with Slade, who parked his Rolls-Royce with a personalized number plate that read 'YOB 1' outside his house in Brueton Avenue[81] – epitomized the spirit of the area.

Bill Dugdale, the Conservative leader of Warwickshire County Council, described Solihull as a 'pro-Tory village',[82] but its village-like qualities were eroded in the years of post-war expansion. It became a municipal borough in 1970 and then a county borough in 1974. It was thus largely freed from the power of Warwickshire Council. Local residents still referred to the shopping centre as 'the village', though it had been transformed by demolition and new building in the 1960s to the point where central Solihull looked like a cleaner version of central Birmingham. Conservatism – Solihull people never paid much attention to the 'Unionist' label that mattered so much in Birmingham – was strong in Solihull. Until 2010 the town always returned Conservative MPs – Percy Grieve, a London QC, held his seat with ease from 1964 to 1983, even though he once campaigned with the Betjemenesque slogan 'Grieve for Solihull'. Even Conservative MPs with Birmingham seats – Leslie Seymour, who sat for Sparkbrook from 1959 to 1964, or Anthony Beaumont-Dark, who sat for Selly Oak from 1979 to 1997 – sometimes came from Solihull. Sir Charles Burman, who had presided over much of post-war Birmingham's reconstruction, lived in Sir Harrys Road, Edgbaston while he was mayor but retired to a manor house in Tanworth-in-Arden, which is just beyond Solihull.

Solihull is east of Birmingham – closer to London and neatly plugged into its transport networks. Birmingham airport might more accurately be called 'Solihull', as might the grandly named Birmingham International station, which was opened in 1976, the same year as the National Exhibition Centre that it existed to serve. The NEC eventually became famous mainly as a venue for showbusiness events, but it was conceived at a time when it seemed possible that the Midlands might become a hub of the European economy. The International Motor Show – previously held at Earl's Court or Crystal Palace in London – was held in the National Exhibition Centre from 1978 until 2004, thereby giving the motoring press a ringside seat from which to watch the death throes of the Birmingham car industry.

The Cadburys were the last of the great families who had dominated nineteenth-century Birmingham to retain much connection with the city. Their main factory was still at Bournville. Sir Adrian Cadbury (1929–2015) ran the business from 1965 until 1989. He had been born at his family house in Hole Lane just off the Bristol Road, which was, as he recalled, 'within smelling distance' of the chocolate factory. His Cadbury grandparents lived across the road in Northfield Manor House and his maternal grandparents lived a little way north in Edgbaston. Adrian began his working life commuting to the factory on a bicycle and recalled wistfully that the atmosphere of Bournville village was somehow associated with this mode of transport. However, by the time he became chairman of the company in 1965, he had moved to Solihull. Soon he had merged his firm with Schweppes, which meant that company headquarters were at Marble Arch. His daily commute now involved a car to Birmingham International station followed by the train to Euston.[83]

Edgbaston still had a few advantages. It was the centre of Birmingham's cultural life. The Barber Institute of Fine Arts, or the arts centre in Cannon Hill Park, where one could see a Buñuel film at a time when most Birmingham cinemas were still showing *Emmanuelle* ('now in its second fantastic year'), were in Edgbaston. Most importantly, Edgbaston had the edge over Solihull when it came to schools. Solihull School and King Edward's School, Birmingham, had both been founded in the sixteenth century and begun as grammar schools – for much of their early life they would both have been known just as 'the grammar school'. The frontier between grammar schools and what became known as 'public schools' was not always clear; several times King Edward's had come close to crossing it. It might have done so if the local gentry had wrested it from the control of town merchants in the seventeenth century and it might have done so again later, when there were plans to move it out of the city, introduce boarding houses or closed scholarships to a college at Oxford or Cambridge, and, at one time, merge it with Bromsgrove School.

None of these plans came to anything. In a curious way, the school was saved because it did not have very good relations with the city's nineteenth-century elite. Though its origins were associated with men who had been parliamentarians during the seventeenth century, the school became a bastion of Anglicanism. This did not make it an appealing choice for Unitarians and Quakers, who sent their children to

Dissenting academies first and then, as they became richer, to Rugby. Even after the oligarchic power of the governors was broken by the city council in the 1860s, Birmingham's wealthiest inhabitants rarely sent their sons to the school. Strictly speaking, several schools around Birmingham now belonged to the King Edward Foundation, but in practice the original school remained the most prestigious and powerful. It was next to New Street station – which kept it clear of public school frippery and ensured that boys could escape quickly, many of them going home for lunch.

King Edward's was a centre of academic distinction and also a place that conferred on its pupils the mad confidence that came from the belief that their school was not really comparable to any other institution. It was this confidence that marked the career of the school's most distinguished twentieth-century alumni. George Painter (1914–2005) started life as a classical scholar and poet before working at the British Museum, where he became an expert on early printed books. In his spare time, he wrote a famous biography of Marcel Proust. A gentle man who had been a conscientious objector during the war, he was possessed of extraordinary intellectual self-assurance and remained unperturbed when lesser scholars produced evidence that many of his conclusions were wrong. Field Marshal Lord Slim began his working life as a clerk and fought his way, via a commission in the Great War, to be chief of the Imperial General Staff. Enoch Powell was commissioned in the Second World War and he too could have been a field marshal if he had not returned to civilian life and politics. His career – almost as much as that of Joseph Chamberlain – was marked by a capacity to make the weather that was often unrelated to holding any particular political office or even belonging to any particular party. Kenneth Tynan also exercised an influence that looked disproportionate to any conventional achievement. He was a theatre critic and eventually producer who changed British drama more than any late-twentieth-century playwright. Most Englishmen who came in from the cold of the provincial middle class either attacked the establishment or tried to join it. Slim, Powell and Tynan just laughed at it. Powell once explained that he had put his unborn child down for Eton because some of the Etonians that he had met at university knew almost as much as himself.*

* Powell's child turned out to be a daughter.

Around the time of the Second World War, both Solihull School and King Edward's refashioned themselves – in opposite ways. Both acquired headmasters who had served with distinction in the Second World War – though both men were so flamboyantly odd that they sometimes seemed to have emerged from one of the pre-war novels of Evelyn Waugh. Ronald Lunt – an Etonian who had been a chaplain in the Coldstream Guards and the Special Air Service and won the Military Cross – presided over King Edward's from 1952 to 1972. He was the kind of man who would have impressed almost any board of governors – though he was not taken entirely seriously by parents or pupils, while arch hostesses of Edgbaston dinner parties would tell their guests 'the boys have a very naughty name for him'. At Solihull, Harry Butler Hitchens arrived as headmaster in 1947. He was only thirty-six years old but had held the rank of brigadier in the army, been director of intelligence in Austria and south eastern Europe and had supporting references from Field Marshal Montgomery and Dwight Eisenhower. He had more of an impact on his school than Lunt had on his – though it ended abruptly in 1963. Having been arrested for gross indecency, he committed suicide after writing his letter of resignation to the governors, in a final Waughesque gesture.

Solihull School tried, and failed, to be recognized as a 'direct grant' grammar school, which would have given it government support while allowing it the freedom to manage its own affairs. After this setback the school's governors decided it should become a 'public school'. The invented traditions that mark most public schools were particularly late and blatant at Solihull. Though football had been the school game until 1930, the rugby team became the object of a quasi-religious cult. It was only after 1945 that prefects were called 'benchers' and that the fourth form was christened 'Shell'. The school's most famous alumnus was John Curry, the Olympic figure-skater, but it did not advertise its links with a man whose sexuality was the object of much newspaper speculation.[84]

The main King Edward's School succeeded in obtaining direct grant status – its satellite schools were given the less prestigious status of 'voluntary aided' schools, subject to a greater degree of control by the council. Success in this domain owed something to the fact that the first post-war headmaster (Charles Morris) had been a wartime civil servant and was able to lobby the relevant minister. King Edward's shed its traditions at the very moment when Solihull was inventing its own: the 'Usher' was briskly renamed the 'Second Master'.

Most importantly, King Edward's had moved to Edgbaston just before the war. This gave it more space and grander buildings but, strangely, the change worked precisely because of Edgbaston's social decline. The school was now adjacent to the university and the medical school – both of which expanded in the 1950s and 60s. Large numbers of academics bought houses in Edgbaston – doing something to sustain its gentility and a good deal to speed its economic descent. These were the perfect parents for an academically pushy school. Among the hundred or so boys admitted in a single year was one whose father would go on to win the Nobel Prize in physics and another who would himself win the Fields Medal for mathematics.

FULL EMPLOYMENT

The Birmingham economy boomed during the twenty-five years after 1945. There was not the burst of unemployment and underemployment that had accompanied demobilization after the First World War. In 1955, the city's unemployment level stood at 0.5 per cent – half the national figure, which was itself considered unnaturally low by many economists. Some recalled a jobs market that was almost oppressively buoyant. In March 1953, there were 4,657 adult men unemployed in Birmingham and 2,227 unemployed women. However, almost half of these had been out of work for less than a fortnight. Only ninety-two men and twenty women had been jobless for more than a year.[85] Jill was offered work as a secretary at Eagle Star Insurance on the Hagley Road on the Friday before she left school – in spite of the fact that she had missed her bus stop and been an hour late for the interview. Almost all her friends had job offers before her.[86] When Grace Holte's father left his job at BOC, he read an advertisement seeking workers for Tucker Eyelets in Perry Barr. He rang from a call box and was told to start on Monday. Labour exchanges might find work for a new arrival within a matter of days, but in practice most people got jobs through their own initiative – indeed, many in the white Birmingham working class regarded simply going to a labour exchange as an admission of failure. The worst moment in the Birmingham economy in the first two post-war decades came in 1956 when the British Motor Corporation sacked 5,000 men. It was such a surprising event that an economist likened it to 'a sudden collapse of confidence on the Stock Exchange', but, even in these circumstances, only 15 per cent of the dismissed men resorted to the labour exchange.[87] Most found jobs quickly and just over half were back with their old employer within a few years.[88]

Informal networks often drew workers into employment – for most people such networks were composed of family, friends and friends of friends – though even the Communist Party had a quiet word in a convenor's ear when it wanted to put one of its members into a factory.[89] Immigrants, who lacked contacts, could be at a disadvantage, but even new arrivals from Ireland usually preferred to navigate the job market without recourse to the labour exchange. Among a group of Irish workers in Sparkbrook, twenty-five found their first jobs in Birmingham through friends or family; twenty-three 'just walked around' until they obtained employment; only four men and two women took more than a fortnight to find work.[90]

While it lasted, the buoyant Birmingham job market produced a particular kind of culture. Full employment went with stability. It was easy, and often financially advantageous, to move jobs but surprisingly few people did so. Those who arrived in the city would often move around for a few months or a few years, but eventually fix on a single employer with whom they would stay. Leslie Jones had first come to Birmingham in the mid 1930s to escape unemployment in the Rhondda. As the Midlands economy had heated up with rearmament, he had repeatedly changed jobs and run through at least a dozen employers, but in the 1950s he got taken on at the Rover plant, where he worked for twenty-eight years, finally accepting redundancy in 1982.[91] An Irishman started at the Dunlop factory but found it 'terrible hard with dirty fumes and all the rest. So I tried Fisher and Ludlows and I got started there and I worked in it for 24 year.' Another Irishman had four different jobs in six weeks but 'ended up at Dunlop' where he stayed.[92] In the 1980s, Steven Tolliday interviewed men who had worked in Midlands car factories. Most of them had been shop stewards – the kind of men who would have lived in constant fear of the sack until the mid 1930s. There were still sackings until the mid 1950s but a competent man who was shrewd enough to avoid having unnecessary rows with management and to keep the support of his union could usually survive. Tolliday's interviewees had mostly worked at the same plant, and sometimes in the same workshop, from the armaments boom of the late 1930s until some point in the 1970s. They liked the stability. Even – and perhaps especially – union militants were attached to the particular factories where they worked. They liked their mates – they often asked Tolliday about their former colleagues – and sometimes came to regard management with a weary and exasperated affection.

Starting a new job could be an anxious process. Workers had to learn new skills – perhaps particularly awkward when their job was defined as an unskilled or semi-skilled one that did not require formal training – and they had to reach an accommodation with colleagues who did not always welcome a newcomer. Men sometimes remembered their first weeks or months in a job as particularly difficult and, not surprisingly, they did not want to start over again if they could help it. Staying with an employer for years or decades also brought advantages. Some men rose into supervisory posts or positions in the trade union that conferred more real authority than that enjoyed by managers. Even a man who simply worked on the same machine for his whole career acquired seniority in the eyes of his colleagues and at the very least the right to be treated with courtesy. A car worker on an assembly line summed up the advantages of long service:

Actually, the foreman, the gaffer, don't run the place, the men run the place. See, I mean you get one of these chaps says, 'Alright, you're on so and so today.' You can't argue with him. The gaffer don't give you the job, the men on the track give you the job, they swop each other about, tek it in turns. Ah, but I mean the job's done. If the gaffer had gid you the job you would ... They tried to do it, one morning, gid a chap a job you know, but he'd been on it, you know, I think he'd been on it all week, and they just downed tools ... There's four hard jobs, actually, on the track and there's dozen that's, you know, a child of five could do, quite honestly, but everybody has their turn ... That's organized by the men. Especially like the man who, the one who's on the track longest, you know, who knows what rotation it is see

INTERVIEWER: He's the foreman or the supervisor?

He's nothing, he's nothing.

INTERVIEWER: So why do the men recognize his authority?

Well, they don't recognize his authority. They just . . . he's been on the track longest.[93]

Secure employment sometimes meant entering a whole world associated with a particular factory. Those who worked at Fort Dunlop (there were over 10,000 of them in the 1960s) remembered that it seemed like a city state. A corridor that linked up the production departments was a third of a mile long. The factory had its own fire brigade, its own water supply (drawn from wells) and its own transport system, which involved railway locomotives to move goods around the plant. It also had its own class system. The canteen was divided into sections for 'top brass, staff and workers'. Junior employees were meant to use only particular entrances. New entrants to the apprentice school were told 'craft people to the left and technical to the right'. There were sexual hierarchies too. Most girls were recruited as clerical workers, but even those who did manual work recalled men milling and machining at one end of the corridor while women assembled, tested and packed at the other end. Many entered the Fort at fifteen and stayed for decades. Boys generally began with a year at the plant apprentice school (which had about forty students at any one time) before spending several years being trained in trades. For many, the Fort was a family affair. Graham Whitefoot was there from 1969 to 1980. His father had worked there as did two of his brothers, his uncle and his cousin and eventually his father-in-law.[94]

A steady job made it possible for men to get married, to have children and sometimes to allow, or force, their wives to give up work. After 1945, most new houses in Birmingham, and the great majority of those that provided attractive homes for working-class people, were council houses. Getting a council house in a reasonable location was hard even for white working-class families that were well established in the city – it was, until the late 1960s, pretty much impossible for those who did not belong to this group. Before the war, families in private lodgings had sometimes moved frequently – among the poorest section of the working class, moonlight flits had once been common when rent was due – and even the first council house residents had not always stayed long. After 1945, those in council houses stayed put. The new regime of full employment meant families could be pretty much sure of being able to pay the rent so, once they got a house that was within a tolerable distance of their workplace, men were reluctant to move.

Grace Holte recounted the quest of her parents for a council house that would balance the needs of their family and her father's work. They started their married life, in their early twenties, living with 'grandad Hatfield' while her father worked for BOC and her mother for Cadbury. In 1956, her grandfather died and her parents had to move out of his council house. Her aunt was able to pull strings with a local politician to get them a council flat on the top floor of a building in Northfield.[95] Northfield is not far from the Cadbury factory in Bournville, where Grace's mother had begun her working life, but she bitterly resented the separation from her own mother – 'it's like the dark side of the moon and a two-bus journey ride from Ladywood'. Shortly before Grace's birth, her mother returned to her own mother in Guildford Street. Her father now caught three buses to get to work, then went to his mother-in-law for supper before returning home to sleep in Northfield. When his wife went into labour, he caught the outer circle bus to see her and the baby at Dudley hospital before going home again. Then, suddenly, a stroke of luck. A council house became vacant on Guildford Street – just yards from Grace's grandmother. The family moved in and never left – even though Guildford Street, from which one could smell the HP Sauce factory in Aston, was just the kind of location that urban planners assumed people would wish to leave.

Children also made men reluctant to move jobs. Schooling required stability. The school-leaving age rose to fifteen after the war and then to sixteen in 1972. The days when some working-class parents had resented the school-leaving age and wanted their children at work as young as possible were over. The most ambitious working-class families wanted their children to have a formal academic education. There is much debate about how far Enoch Powell's 'Rivers of Blood' speech in 1968 reflected the real experience and opinions of the white working class in the Midlands for whom he claimed to speak. One part of the speech, however, rings true. Powell said that he had recently spoken to a constituent, 'a middle-aged quite ordinary working man employed in one of our nationalized industries' who had told him: 'I have three children. All of them been through grammar school.'

For a small number of Birmingham working-class children, passing the eleven plus might mean a chance of going to university. In fact, the proportion of children who attended grammar school in Birmingham was not high by national standards but the Labour Party in the city was reluctant to oppose educational selection even when the national party began to do so. Perhaps this was partly because in a time of full employment the consequences of not having an academic education were not as severe as they would be in, say, the 1980s. Perhaps, too, it was because a small proportion of working-class parents – especially those whose own educational advance had been blocked by their family's poverty – particularly valued grammar schools. One Labour councillor suggested that every grammar school place abolished would take 'four or five votes with it'.[96] For many, especially before the university expansion of the 1960s, education simply meant the prospect of getting some 'O' levels or Certificates of Secondary Education (the less prestigious qualification available at secondary modern schools) that would open the door to a white-collar job – not necessarily one that would pay better than manual employment but one that would offer more security and, in the eyes of their parents, greater dignity.

Roger Evans was born into a working-class Birmingham family in 1939. He passed the eleven plus, gained six 'O' levels and finished his education with a 'miserable six months' in the sixth form at King's Norton grammar school. After this, he 'stoically stuck' fifteen months of employment at Lloyds Bank before joining the West Midlands Gas Board which, with an interruption for National Service in the air force, was to employ him for the rest of his working life. He hated office work and spent his spare time fixing up his motorcycle (the RAF had trained him as a mechanic) but his whole life seems to have been dominated by the desire to live up to the hopes of his beloved mother.[97] Grace Holte had a happier experience of education and social mobility. She remembered that her parents put aside money to pay for education – this did not mean paying school fees but paying for those quite small expenses (particularly the uniform) that had sometimes prevented working-class people, including her own father, from taking up places at grammar school. The ambition to have children in white-collar jobs could be a powerful motive and sometimes the prospect of achieving this made life in a blue-collar job seem more bearable.

Even, perhaps especially, if they did not escape the factory floor, the young – young men at least – were confident. In 1964, the Ministry of Labour and the Birmingham Joint Recruitment and Training Committee for Engineering established a three-month course to prepare teenagers for semi-skilled jobs in factories. Seventeen boys were brought from Gateshead to join the scheme. But the boys from the North East felt that they lacked the 'instinctive feel' that their Birmingham contemporaries appeared to have for engineering work. A representative of one firm said: 'They look subdued to me, they do not have the cockiness of Birmingham boys who have never had it so good.'[98] 'Cockiness' did not translate into rebellion, though. Young men settled down on the assumption that they might work for the same firm for the rest of their lives.

Tighter labour markets made workers more powerful. Before the war, many Birmingham employers had found it relatively easy to keep unions out of their factories. The war and its aftermath gave unions and the Labour Party new power. Birmingham employers did not reform overnight. Many of them were still hostile to unions and to the Labour Party and some tried to use the rundown in production at the end of the war to get rid of troublesome workers. Frank Price found it hard to keep his job as a toolmaker when his boss heard that he had been elected a Labour councillor in 1949.[99] Jack Farrell lost his job because he took time off to support Denis Howell's campaign to be elected to the council – though Howell's own employer, a Conservative, was more sympathetic.[100] Employment in the motor industry was still unstable; whole groups of workers were laid off if business slowed down or if a model ceased production.

But things were changing, as was shown by a strike at the British Motor Corporation in 1952.* On the face of it, this dispute apparently fitted into a pattern that stretched back to the late 1920s. It was sparked off by a round of redundancies when the company ceased making the Austin Atlantic or A90 model and more specifically by the fate of McHugh, a troublesome worker who had been employed at, and dismissed from, the Austin works a number of times since 1928. McHugh was made redundant, with a large number of other men, in 1952. He was a shop steward for the National Union of Vehicle Builders and the NUVB called a strike in protest at his dismissal. The company responded by sacking strikers and putting other workers on short time. Leonard Lord, who had worked for Austin since the 1930s and succeeded Herbert Austin as managing director of the company in 1941, said:

* The British Motor Corporation was formed by a merger of Austin and Morris Motors in 1952. Many Birmingham people, however, still referred to the factory at Longbridge as 'The Austin' even in the 1980s when it had undergone several more corporate upheavals.

Presumably employees discharged will report to their own labour exchanges, and when we have to fill any vacancies that might arise the exchanges will be notified in the usual way. The strikers have all been discharged. No dispute now exists. Therefore, the 3,000–4,000 employees who are still suspended in consequence of the strike will be paid by the company for the guaranteed week of 34 hours from Monday.[101]

The NUVB claimed that redundancies had been used as a means to get rid of around fifty shop stewards. Edwards, the works manager, denied this, though he admitted that the company kept a list of workers it did not wish to re-employ.[102]

Beneath the surface, the McHugh strike revealed ways in which the pattern of labour relations had changed. The mere fact that Edwards was willing to talk to the unions was one sign of these changes. There was an official enquiry – organized by the Ministry of Labour – which concluded that McHugh had not been discriminated against and that the NUVB had improperly sought assurances that the jobs of shop stewards would be preserved. In practice, shop stewards seem to have enjoyed privileged treatment in subsequent rounds of dismissals. Most importantly, the buoyancy of the labour market meant that the threat of dismissal was less alarming than it would have been in, say, 1931. One Trotskyist militant recalled: 'If you got the sack and really wanted a job, you could get one anywhere you liked. A lot of the fear of the bosses was destroyed on that basis.' He compared the change in attitude by managers that came with full employment with the change in attitude that he had seen among army officers when units moved to the front line and they knew that the men behind them were carrying live ammunition.[103]

Many of those who left the Austin factory after the McHugh strike obtained better-paid work at the Armstrong Whitworth aircraft factory in Coventry. Eventually, McHugh himself was found a job there. It seems that the union, the Ministry of Labour and possibly Midlands engineering employers had cooperated to obtain the job for him. One official minuted that the NUVB 'gave the impression apart from the Communist element . . . [that] the dispute payment to Mr McHugh had gone on long enough'.[104]

Things changed further in 1956 when Leonard Lord handed the running of Austin to his deputy, George Harriman. The company instituted meetings with shop stewards and Harriman was ostentatiously friendly to the most powerful of them – Dick Etheridge. Shop stewards benefited from sheer longevity. Etheridge had been a steward since 1941 and, according to the company, four of the five men who had been elected to that position in 1940 were still there in 1952.[105] Etheridge was briefly displaced by his own union colleagues in the late 1940s, but, other than that, he remained in place until 1975. When the British Motor Corporation transmuted into the company that eventually became British Leyland by taking over Pressed Steel in 1965, Jaguar in 1966 and then Leyland Trucks in 1968, Etheridge helped create the Combined Shop Stewards Committee (it was later called the Combined Trades Union Committee – though it was not recognized by any union) that drew together shop stewards from all of the company's plants across the country.

Etheridge was a stocky man with thick spectacles whose brusque manner concealed a sharp intelligence and a charm that sometimes seduced even his political opponents. His robust style sprang partly from the fact that he came from outside the working class. He had left school at sixteen and begun work as a laboratory technician – so he had more schooling than most of his comrades and he had supplemented this with a good deal of reading. He had rebelled against his first employer and spent some time working for his father who ran a small shop. He did not arrive at Longbridge until early in the war and had therefore never endured the humiliations meted out to workers during the 1930s. He was a Communist. This sometimes brought him into conflict with other trade unionists and sometimes aroused hostility from his fellow workers – particularly during the last years of Stalin's bloodthirsty reign and again in 1956, when the Soviet Union invaded Hungary – but it did not have much effect on his relations with management. He had spent the early part of his union career – during the period of Anglo-Soviet alliance – seeking to push up production. Thereafter his attitude was often marked by pragmatism. He appreciated that only a tiny number of the workers in the factory shared his political beliefs and that 'I was convenor in spite of being a Communist not because of it.' In 1953, he arranged for the Whitsun holiday to be moved so that his colleagues could enjoy the Coronation.[106] He disliked direct confrontation: 'Because I knew the tactics of the management was if they got you into a ... frontal position of any consequences, then they'd chop everybody.'[107] He sometimes resisted automation, which brought him into conflict with his own son who was briefly employed as a production engineer at Longbridge. On the other hand, he was not opposed to reorganization. This flexibility sometimes set him at odds with the craft unions in the 1950s. Etheridge recognized that workers and managers at Longbridge might have the same interests. In 1963, the company sought to expand its plant at Cofton Hackett in ways that would have impinged into the leafy areas to the factory's south. A planning enquiry was held and one of those who opposed the expansion suggested that the meetings should be held in the evening so that local residents could express their objections. Etheridge announced that, if evening sessions were held, he would bring '15,000 BMC workers to give evidence on the other side'.[108]

Longbridge more or less stopped employing non-union workers in 1964 but, even before the formal institution of the 'closed shop' (meaning that workers were required to belong to a union), managers were often complicit in enforcing union membership. Phil Blewitt was a shop steward whose work station was next to the supervisor's office. When a new man was hired, the supervisor would ask him whether he was a member of the union and, if he said no, he would be sent to see Blewitt who, in his own words, 'more or less bullied or tried to convince them'.[109] Not surprisingly most of them signed up. When men refused, the company itself could be hypocritical. In January 1974, a worker resigned from his union. The personnel manager knew that keeping such a man would be more trouble than it was worth. He went through his record with the foremen:

> Unfortunately nowhere could we find evidence of him doing bad work . . .
> All in all we could find nothing to substantiate a letter saying we were
> dissatisfied with his work, so we came to the conclusion in the end . . .
> that we would sack him on grounds of incompatibility with other
> employees.[110]

Right-wing commentators would later complain that the unions had come to run the Birmingham car industry and particularly Longbridge. But the truth was that management often turned to union leaders to sort out unofficial strikes. The Austin management eventually installed a phone (in a soundproof booth) next to Etheridge's place on the production line so that he could be contacted whenever his help was needed.

Etheridge himself believed that management valued 'a stable secure set-up and someone they could talk to'.[111]

In the 1970s, workers at Longbridge held a succession of small strikes in protest against the Industrial Relations Bill of the Heath government (which would have imposed legal restrictions on union power). It was widely assumed that the strike was a symptom of Communist influence at the plant. However, in private, Etheridge worked with managers to avoid the most damaging effects of a strike. He rang Ron Savage, one of the personnel managers at Longbridge, to discuss safety cover during a strike on 1 May 1973, and Savage wrote in his diary a couple of days later: 'I spent all morning with Etheridge ... sorting out the arrangements for passes for 1 May [i.e. passes for employees who would be authorized to work on that day].'[112]

POLITICS

In the early years of the twentieth century, Birmingham was a Conservative town. After 1945, the balance was sharply reversed. In the Macmillan landslide of 1959, the Conservatives won seven of Birmingham's thirteen seats. This was the only occasion on which they gained a majority of Birmingham seats and even then their margin of victory was smaller than that in the country as a whole. Heath's win in the election of 1970 came with six Birmingham seats. The Thatcher victory of 1979 brought six Conservative MPs, including the one from Sutton Coldfield, which was now incorporated into the city. Other than this, they won four seats in each of the three elections between 1950 and 1955, three in February 1974 and two in the election six months later. Labour support in the city was wide but not deep. Many in the car factories were what sociologists came to label 'affluent workers' with an 'instrumental' view of politics. They voted Labour because the party seemed most likely to advance their interests but they did not have the ancestral loyalties to socialism that marked some northern constituencies. This may also explain why the turn against Labour in the 2019 general election was not as marked or as bitter in Birmingham as it was in much of the North.

Political change reflected a change in Birmingham's social structure. An official of the Conservative Party in the West Midlands wrote in

March 1951: 'In Birmingham we hold only 4 seats out of 13; in 1935 we held the lot although that is unlikely to happen again because the Birmingham of today is very different from the Birmingham of the Chamberlains.'[113] Six months later, after a general election that the Conservatives had won at national level, another explained: 'I am afraid that we have to face the fact that here in the West Midlands with its over full-employment attributed to Socialism, makes our seats difficult to win.'[114] Birmingham was becoming a more working-class city. This was partly a question of numbers. The proportion of the male Birmingham population that belonged to social classes IV and V increased from 27.3 per cent to 32.3 per cent between 1951 and 1966 while that belonging to the top three social classes declined from 62.7 per cent to 57.7 per cent. Middle-class workers in Birmingham were increasingly likely to live outside the city limits.[115] The working class was more assured, more confident, particularly with regard to security of employment, and more unionized than it had been before 1939.

Social change ate into the leadership of the Birmingham Conservative Party itself. Before 1939, this had been controlled by those whose business interests and political power bases were both in the city. Funding for the party had come from local industrialists – so much so that its leaders had never much bothered with the fêtes and raffles that often dominated the life of Conservative constituency associations elsewhere.[116] The decline of the great Birmingham families accompanied a decline of Birmingham-based political notables. After 1945, the names Chamberlain and Martineau still lingered in documents relating to the Birmingham party but this was because a few grand old ladies still played a part in the women's organizations of the party – though, in the case of Neville Chamberlain's widow, it was a part that must have been limited by the fact that she lived in London. Male members of the great families, however, were almost entirely absent between 1945 and 1975.[117]

After 1945, companies were increasingly likely to work at national rather than local level and in any case it would have been harder to combine a serious business career with even the modest demands on time that would have been made of a backbench Conservative MP. Simply finding people who were willing to contest Birmingham seats was hard. In May 1950, to the fury of Conservative Central Office, the following advertisement appeared in the *Birmingham Post*:

A vacancy for a Parliamentary Conservative candidate exists in a local industrial division [the constituency was Aston]. Will those interested supply full particulars to the undermentioned box number and such information will be treated in a confidential manner.[118]

The very notion of the Birmingham notable came to seem like a contradiction in terms. Conservative Central Office took it for granted that its best candidates would be national rather than local figures – Birmingham's distance from London (which would have seemed substantial only to those who spent their whole life in the Home Counties) was cited as a disadvantage for ambitious politicians. Between the defeat of Leo Amery in the 1945 election and the arrival of Norman Fowler in 1979, there was not one Birmingham Tory who stood a chance of senior ministerial rank. Edward Boyle, who represented Handsworth from 1950 until 1974, was an intelligent and liberal-minded man, shrewd enough to take the young Margaret Thatcher under his wing, but his heart was never really in Conservative politics – he had managed to resign from ministerial office (over Suez) at an age when most of his contemporaries were still condemned to fighting hopeless seats.

The problems of Birmingham were the problems of all big cities – Conservatives retreated from them in the post-war period. But there was a special dimension to Birmingham that came from the particularity of its Conservative tradition or, more precisely, from the fact that Birmingham had been Unionist rather than Conservative. Birmingham Conservatives preserved their pride in their tradition long after they had lost the political strength that underlay that tradition. They had been so well funded and powerful that they had considered themselves independent of the usual Conservative regional structure. The chief agent in Birmingham was paid more than the chief agent of the West Midlands who was nominally his superior. Birmingham Conservatives resented attempts to 'nationalize' the party by increasing central control. However, within the city, the Conservative Party itself was centralized – the last legacy of the kind of discipline once exercised by Chamberlain's caucus. The Unionist headquarters in Empire House in the centre of town was often at odds with individual constituencies. Most agents were based at Empire House. The party was riven with squabbles.[119]

Messy alliances emerged. Charles Burman was close to Conservative Central Office but was pitched against the Birmingham Chief Agent Eric Tranter and Tranter's patron, Geoffrey Lloyd, who had been MP for Ladywood from 1931 to 1945 and for King's Norton from 1950 to 1955 and was now president of the Birmingham party, though – almost needless to say – he did not live in Birmingham. Lloyd caused acrimony because he seems, perhaps because of his pre-war contacts, to be the last man who could raise money in Birmingham.[120]

Eventually, the Birmingham Conservative/Unionist Party conceded defeat. Party organization in the city lost its autonomy. From the early 1970s, it was subordinated to Central Office, which in turn delegated power to the West Midlands regional organizer. In the mid 1970s, Douglas Hurd, then an aide to Edward Heath, visited Birmingham. He recalled a meeting held under portraits of three Chamberlains but, perhaps without realizing it, he recorded the ways in which the grip that the Chamberlains had exercised over Birmingham was now loosened. By the 1970s, power lay with Jack Galloway, who was chief agent for the West Midlands rather than Birmingham: 'Not a parliamentary candidate was selected, not a local by-election was arranged, not a mouse stirred without Jack's sardonic approval.'[121] One wonders what Joseph Chamberlain would have said about the Birmingham party taking orders from someone whose office was in the twee spa town of Leamington.

In contrast, for Labour success bred success in post-war Birmingham. After 1945, the city was established as a reservoir of safe seats, which meant that it was attractive to candidates. It also meant that Labour politicians sometimes took the city for granted. Christopher Price was selected to fight Perry Barr for the party in 1966 – he later recalled that he had no idea where Perry Barr was but understood that it was 'inhabited by lots of council estates'.[122] The two most distinguished Labour MPs in Birmingham were Roy Jenkins, elected for Stechford in 1950, and Roy Hattersley, elected for Sparkbrook in 1964. Neither was particularly attached to the city. Jenkins never lived there. He stayed overnight with a long-suffering party worker when he had to visit his constituency. An essay he wrote in retirement on Birmingham looks as if it was based on a single day's visit and conceded that it 'is not a city which easily clutches at the heart strings'.[123] Hattersley distinguished between his constituency, for which he felt affection, and the city as a whole, for which he did not much care. He remained a professional Yorkshireman and, like many professional Yorkshiremen, felt happiest in his smart central London flat.

Labour was also the ruling party at local level for most of the post-war period. Before 1939, it had suffered from boundary divisions that disadvantaged its candidates and from the 'winner's bonus' that meant that the most successful party tended to get a share of seats on the council greater than its share of votes. After 1945, the balance of power was reversed.

Labour politicians in Birmingham were a mixed group. It is hard to imagine two men further removed from each other than Roy Jenkins and Jim Simmons – MP for Erdington, Birmingham West and then Brierley Hill. Jenkins was the clever, well-educated son of a Labour MP. He was also the most liberal Home Secretary in British history and took pride in the way in which his tenure had laid the way for the 'permissive society'. His patrician drawl, taste for good Burgundy and propensity to sleep with the wives of his friends all contributed to the impression that he was an eighteenth-century Whig, and he was indeed close to the Duke of Devonshire.[124] Simmons was a devout Christian of working-class origins who feared that Socialism might become too close to 'materialism' and believed that the writers of the 1960s were prone to 'peddle lavatory scribble or wallow in filth'.[125] There was, though, less acrimony in the Birmingham Labour Party than there was among the Conservatives – Roy Jenkins wrote an introduction to Simmons's autobiography.

Furthermore, the Birmingham Labour Party had a particular identity after 1945. Almost all prominent Birmingham Labour politicians were on the right of the party. In some cases, they were so far to the right that they eventually left it entirely (see chapter 13). More generally, the Birmingham party was marked by an enthusiasm for social democracy rather than democratic socialism and by a distaste for the extreme left. The high point of Communist electoral support probably came when the party pushed the Liberals into third place in a single ward in a municipal election in 1965 – in practice, the Communist leaders of Birmingham trade unionism were never that extreme. More threatening were those left-wing tendencies or groups that sought to operate in the Labour Party itself. Frank Price allied with Denis Howell to work against 'undercover trots' on the council.[126]

FALLING THROUGH THE CRACKS OF MODERNIZATION

Not everyone was directly affected by the modernization projects of post-war Birmingham. Aside from the high-rise buildings and motorway flyovers, sometimes literally in their shadow, were parts of the city that remained much as they had been in the 1930s. The very flamboyance of Birmingham's plans for modernity created a curious in-between quality for many of the city's residents. The new world of tower blocks, wide open spaces and motor cars served to remind many that they themselves did not live in such a world and suggested that their own lives were archaic or marginal. Nineteenth-century buildings – dilapidated small houses rather than the grand public structures that would later attract the interest of the Victorian Society – were still common, but they did not fit in with the image of the city that was propagated by planners. The anticipation that such areas would be 'cleared' sometimes meant that they were less likely to be well maintained in the short term and also engendered a sense of embarrassment among their inhabitants.

The poet Roy Fisher had been born in Handsworth and grew up in Birmingham. Critics sometimes commented on the extent to which Fisher seemed American in his approach (he was fascinated by jazz) and one wrote that his evocation of urban life was 'nearer Dos Passos' Manhattan than those woodcut Christmas cards of romantic Wigan that were circulated in the 1950s'. However, Fisher's fascination with America – focused on the bleak underside of modernity – was very different from that of Herbert Manzoni.[127] Fisher despised 'the civic authority' of 'limited means' which preserved a 'superficial order'. His Birmingham was one of demolition sites rather than new buildings:

> When destruction comes, it is total: the printed notices on the walls, block by block, a few doors left open at night, broken windows advancing down a street until fallen slates appear on the pavement and are not kicked away. Then, after a few weeks of this, the machines arrive.[128]

Those who interviewed children in the run-down neighbourhood of Small Heath noticed the frequency with which they said 'slum', 'in spite of the attempts by both central and local government to delete the word

from the English language'.[129] Children compared the residential quarters of the inner part of the town with both the commercial centre of the
city and the more spacious new estates that had been built on the
outskirts:

> As the bus is going through town, I notice very clean streets and clean
> shops. We go into Digbeth I notice the City getting dirtier and as we enter
> Small Heath it looks like a slum area . . . the bus goes down Belchers Lane
> and the area starts getting better as we approach the Fox and Goose
> Shopping Centre and then we enter Castle Vale and there the land is green
> and beautiful.[130]

Children might once have taken the grime of local factories for
granted – until the late 1940s, most would have been destined to enter
those factories at the age of fourteen. But by the early 1970s, there was
a sharp contrast between their perception, derived from school and television, of how the world ought to be and the reality of how their own
world was: 'Dirt, grime and smoky fuel has changed the whole aspects
of the world.'[131] Occasionally, though, children drew an interesting distinction between their area and their own houses: 'These back-alley
houses look terrible and old and should be completely pulled down but
from the inside they are completely different. They are clean and tidy
and the habitants are happy there.'[132]

It is hard to look back on post-war Birmingham without being haunted
by our knowledge of what happened next. The new council estates that
had seemed so attractive in the 1960s would look like scenes from a film
of dystopian science fiction by the late 1980s. The new buildings in the
city centre, which had appeared so enticingly modern on the drawing
board, were out of fashion before they were finished. Birmingham roads
became a by-word for traffic jams and pollution. Indeed, the 'Americanization' of Birmingham's road system was at its most feverishly
intense at the moment in the late 1960s when Ralph Nader, who
intruded unhelpfully into the life of Morris Zapp, was beginning to
challenge the hegemony of the car in California. The attempt to build a
middle ring road in the early 1970s would have taken the problems of
traffic into the more middle-class areas of the city and unsurprisingly it
was at this point that resistance to road building became serious.[133]

There was something uncomfortable about Birmingham politics too.

Local politicians seemed divorced from the preoccupations of a new Left that had emerged from the late 1960s. The success of the post-war trade unions and Labour Party in Birmingham had been built on white male industrial workers. But the Left invested less hope in such people than it had done once and, as the election of 1979 was to show, such people did not always invest much hope in the Left.

In retrospect, it is obvious that prosperity, particularly in the car industry, created a complacency and an attachment to established ways of doing things that would make industrialists too slow to respond to what was happening in French, German and, eventually, Japanese factories. It is obvious too that the efforts of central government to move industry out of the city would fail, but that their attempt to prevent new industry from moving in would succeed and that this would have catastrophic consequences as new industries acquired greater importance. It is especially poignant that some of Birmingham's plans in the 1960s for dealing with an overheated economy focused on preparing for 1981 – a year when, as we now know, Birmingham would experience recession and a rise in unemployment that was even sharper than in any other part of the country.

Father Dan Cummings served as chaplain to the 'floaters and drifters' of the Birmingham Irish Community. Here he is shown (in a hard hat) with workers (almost all Irish) building Spaghetti Junction in 1972. The photograph is by Brendan Farrell of the *Irish Post*.

10

Birmingham Irish, 1945–74

The Irish were the first immigrants to arrive in large numbers from overseas in twentieth-century Birmingham. The city had had a big Irish population in the mid nineteenth century but few new migrants came between the 1860s and the late 1930s. The great majority of the 36,000 Irish-born residents of Birmingham in 1951 had arrived in the previous few years. The number of births to Irish couples peaked in 1965 when 4,525 babies were born of two Irish parents and 2,707 had one Irish parent.[1] The second group were a source of concern to priests who worried that children would not be brought up as Catholics.

The status of Irish immigrants was complicated. A substantial minority came from the north of Ireland and were therefore British subjects – though the Catholics among them did not always feel British. Those who originated from the south of Ireland were foreign. Indeed, the fact that the Republic of Ireland withdrew from the Commonwealth in 1949 made them, strictly speaking, more foreign than those from India, Pakistan or the West Indies. Hostility to the British state was often central to Irish politics: an early twentieth-century migrant to Birmingham was the equestrian statue of George I, which had become an embarrassment in Dublin and was acquired in 1937 by the director of the Barber Institute of Fine Arts.[2] The Irish, who had settled in so many parts of the world before they came to Birmingham in such numbers, also sometimes thought of politics in transnational terms – subscriptions from the Irish community paid for a mosaic depicting John F. Kennedy to be placed outside St Chad's Cathedral in 1968.

In practice, Irish citizens could travel to and work in the United Kingdom without restriction after wartime controls were lifted at the end of 1946. Once there, they enjoyed the rights and duties of British subjects.

Irish men, if usually resident in mainland Britain, could be conscripted until the end of 1960 – the Connolly Association, a left-wing Irish group in Birmingham, recruited members partly by campaigning against conscription.

The Irish had things in common with non-white immigrants to Birmingham. They lived, at least at first, in the same areas. They were often excluded from the best jobs and almost always excluded from the best housing. The most savage burst of ethnic violence in post-war Birmingham was probably that directed against Irish people after the IRA bombings in the city in 1974. By the early 1970s, sociologists and left-wing activists – there was, especially at the Birmingham University Centre for Contemporary Cultural Studies, a substantial overlap between the two categories – sometimes thought that the Irish might be treated as honorary black people. One wrote of his Irish subjects:

> Like many of the Irish families in the area they had developed close ties with black neighbours by sharing the same survival strategies, living spaces and supportive child-care networks. (The parallel experiences of Irish and black migrant workers generally was an important foundation of much of the interaction between the two communities.)[3]

In fact, and perhaps partly because they so often lived in the same neighbourhoods, the Irish were frequently in conflict with the non-white population. One of the offences for which Gerry Hunter had been arrested before he was charged with the Birmingham pub bombings involved a brawl with Asian men. West Indians, interviewed in the early 1960s, often believed that the Irish were better treated than themselves, and sometimes implied that they were less deserving of good treatment.[4] One West Indian said that the English were more hostile to the Irish but less able to identify them by colour.[5]

There were also sharp differences among the Irish themselves in Birmingham. A significant minority were middle class – 10 per cent of British doctors in the 1950s were of Irish origin. The majority were working class. Within this group there were divisions between Dubliners and 'culchies', those who came from the countryside. The latter lived mainly in Sparkbrook and Sparkhill. Those from Dublin lived mainly in the south west of the city. The former worshipped at the English Martyrs church; the latter at St Anne's. The two were divided by mutual stereotyping – Dubliners were seen by those from the country as too smooth and glib; while 'culchies' were regarded by Dubliners as slow-witted.[6] The split between urban sophistication and rural simplicity partly overlapped with the division between those who had been in Birmingham for a long time and recent arrivals. Dick Etheridge, the convenor at the Longbridge car works, said that he sometimes heard long-established Irishmen tell their compatriots to 'go back to the bog'.[7]

Tinkers were a separate subgroup. They made a living by dealing in scrap or old furniture. There were still groups who lived in caravans around Birmingham in the 1960s, who were regularly moved on by the authorities. Some tinkers had come to live in houses in Sparkhill, but their neighbours claimed they were undomesticated people who chopped up furniture for firewood, slept in their vans and conducted their social life in the street. In their study of racial division in Spark-brook, John Rex and Robert Moore claimed that the tinkers were 'an explosive element' and that hostility to them from all parts of the community might have channelled animosities that would otherwise have split whites and 'coloured'. Rex and Moore highlighted different groups in the tinkers themselves, pointing to an 'elite' of horse dealers among them.[8] One assumes that this elite cannot have conducted its operations in central Birmingham and may for this reason have been spared some of the conflict that often governed the lives of less privileged tinkers.

Rex and Moore also believed that there was a small subgroup of Irish population in Sparkbrook who lived by theft and social security fraud. Even Irishmen who stood on the wrong side of the frontiers of respectability, or the law, could be oddly precise about where those frontiers might lie. In 1963, a television reporter interviewed a group of Irish scrap metal merchants. The Irishmen played up to their rough image – saying that they could not read and abusing an Indian neighbour whose family had erected barbed wire to protect their house. When the reporter asked whether they were tinkers, they denied it. 'Tinker', they seemed to suggest, was a formal status that should not be confused with a simple lack of respectability.[9]

Large-scale twentieth-century Irish migration to Birmingham began with the rearmament boom of the late 1930s. During the war, the Ministry of Labour controlled the recruitment of Irish labour to the mainland and had often acted as a recruiting agent (see chapter 8). The number in Birmingham hired via the ministry fell after 1945: in 1948 it was 9,600, by 1950 it was 3,400. Now some private companies recruited workers directly in Ireland. An engineering firm in Smethwick engaged 450 Irish women in 1948 – enticing them with, among other things, two travel warrants a year to return home. Nettlefolds and Lucas (Birmingham firms in engineering and motor parts respectively) opened recruitment offices in Dublin.

Birmingham Corporation hired Irish labour for its public transport system in the early 1950s. It took on, for example, fifty-one Irish people from April to June 1952 and paid them £155 in expenses. By the middle of the decade, when this direct recruitment ended, a third of transport employees in the city (mostly women) were Irish.[10]

Most importantly, individuals could simply cross the Irish Sea in search of work. Oliver Reilly, from County Kildare, investigated migration to Birmingham on behalf of the Catholic organization Muintir na Tire. In June 1957, he bought a ticket – 'Second class return. Dublin to Birmingham ... £5 2s (no sleeping)' – and caught the ferry *Cambria* at 8.40 p.m. from Dun Laoghaire to Holyhead. He and his fellow travellers arrived at New Street station just after five the following morning. Finding lodgings was hard but getting work was easy. The labour exchange found him a job at P.H. Parsons – a factory employing about 200 people – where he was paid £8 14s per week.[11]

Migrants enticed others to follow them. A twenty-two-year-old woman returned home on holiday with 'a wardrobe of clothes and £98'.[12] Another migrant told of a relative:

> After the war ... they came over looking for recruits in Dublin. She came over with a crowd of them on the boat ... and they put her in digs when she came to the country. The digs weren't very good but she enjoyed it ... and she was always writing home to say how it was, and the money was so good.[13]

A farmer's son from Longford, who had left school at fourteen and worked at a local turf-cutting plant, remembered his decision to leave:

> My brother ... he was the first one to come here and he came to Birmingham in 1962 ... he stayed, he came here in July and he stayed here 'til Christmas and came home for a holiday at Christmas time, anyway ... I saw he had lovely clothes, a nice new watch, well dressed 'n everything like that, and I decided to take the emigrant boat along with him.[14]

Once one member of a family had moved to Birmingham, it was easy for their relatives to join them. The city often acted as a receiving centre even for those who finished up in other parts of the country. Georgina Mullen was born in Birmingham in 1942. Her father had arrived from Ireland in 1937 and then served in the Royal Engineers during the war. Georgina's mother felt isolated because of the war 'and the IRA' and the children were often sent to live with their grandparents. Nevertheless, her mother's fifteen siblings all eventually came to Birmingham.[15] A single house or a few rooms in a house might become an entrepôt for waves of Irish migrants. One in Claremont Road, Sparkhill was owned by a Pakistani who lived in West Bromwich. The ground floor contained a kitchen, living room and bedroom and was rented by an Irish couple and their two young children. At various times the house had also been inhabited by the husband's parents, his four brothers and his three sisters. The wife's sister and mother had lived in the house and her father had died there.[16]

Eamon de Valera, who served three terms as Prime Minister and was then President of Ireland from 1959 until 1973, described his vision of his country thus:

> the home of a people who valued material wealth only as a basis for right living, of a people who, satisfied with frugal comfort, devoted their leisure to the things of the spirit – a land whose countryside would be bright with cosy homesteads, whose fields and villages would be joyous with the sounds of industry, with the romping of sturdy children, the contest of athletic youths and the laughter of happy maidens, whose firesides would be forums for the wisdom of serene old age.

Birmingham – an English industrial city – was the antithesis of everything that de Valera believed to epitomize truly Irish qualities. In 1951, Maurice Foley, a trade union official who later became Labour MP for West Bromwich and a junior minister with responsibility for immigrants, wrote a report on 'The Irish Worker in Birmingham', which caught de Valera's attention and informed a speech he made in Galway in August 1951. For de Valera 'the saddest part of all this is that work is available and at home, and in conditions infinitely better from the point of view of both health and morals'. De Valera thought, as a British diplomat put it, that working in Britain was 'a danger inter alia to morals and religion'.[17]

How did Irish people explain their move to Birmingham? The availability of well-paid work was important. Among a group of Irish living in Sparkbrook, twenty-three of forty-five men and thirty-one of forty-four women said they had come for reasons related to employment. There was a subtle difference between the sexes in that seventeen men said they sought to 'earn money' and six said they sought to 'find work'; among women, fifteen wanted to 'earn money' and sixteen wanted to 'find work'. Some came to join their family (six men and sixteen women), while two men and one woman wanted to escape their family. Thirty-two gave less clear-cut reasons for the move. They wanted a 'better life', to travel, or had come for 'no particular reason'. Some positively wanted to get away from the kind of society that de Valera had created. They saw Ireland in the 1950s as a place of joyless puritanism. Some women had special reasons for wanting to get away (of which more below). Many regarded the crushing weight of religion in Ireland as something to be escaped. Those from the north often thought of themselves as fleeing from religious conflict and, in the case of Catholics, from discrimination: Catholic communities in Northern Ireland sometimes had unemployment rates of 10 per cent at a time when the rest of the United Kingdom experienced near full employment. Those from the south had a more complicated position. Few thought of their society as divided – most believed that relations with Protestants were better than in the north. Few were in all-out rebellion against Catholicism. Most still went to mass at least on some occasions, and many sent their children to Catholic schools.

Birmingham – the city of Cardinal Newman – was, in terms of institutions, a good place for Catholicism: between 1945 and 1972, the archdiocesan authorities presided over the construction of seventy-two new Catholic schools (fifty-three primary, fifteen secondary and four grammar).[18] However, priests in Birmingham were less powerful than in Ireland and they were less able to intrude into the private lives of their flock. This was partly a matter of numbers. It was also because the notion of parish meant less in Birmingham than it did in a solidly Catholic country. Furthermore, the kind of men who chose to minister to Birmingham Catholics were different from those who stayed in Ireland. An Irish priest was a village notable who could expect to see the best china set out when he invited himself to tea. In contrast, priests in Birmingham were outside the local establishment and ministering to the poor. Religious practice among the Birmingham Irish was sometimes most marked among those – the tinkers in particular – who were in other ways, least respectable. Father Daniel Cummings, who exercised a non-parochial ministry to the 'floaters and drifters' among the Birmingham Irish, had been toughened up by service as a wartime chaplain in the Irish Guards.[19]

The Irish in Birmingham sometimes relished and propagated an image of themselves as rough and hard-drinking. The writer Tom Murphy was born in Galway. He had four brothers and two sisters, all of whom went to work in Birmingham. One of his brothers told him about a famous Birmingham Irish brawler who carried part of a man's ear in a matchbox. Tom Murphy later recalled 'an oral culture, stories, a mythology about fighting men and fighting prowess. And a new pocket of vocabulary fanciful, to be enjoyed … I saw little violence but I heard a lot about it.'[20] Even middle-class Catholics who were worried about the moral welfare of Irish workers in Birmingham described drunken evenings in pubs and street fights with something that bordered on approval – as though Guinness and fisticuffs were as much a part of the national culture as Gaelic football. Of course, a certain kind of Irish person – young, boisterous and male – was particularly visible in Birmingham. This visibility was conferred by working outdoors and by spending much time in the street or in pubs. The latter was sometimes a product of confined and squalid lodgings which offered no recreational possibilities but merely a bed to sleep in – occasionally it was claimed that Irishmen on the night shift slept in the beds that had just been vacated by those who rose to work on the day shift.

Many Irish men laboured on building sites. A group on the ferry from Dublin to Liverpool answered the question 'Why are you coming?' with one word: 'Wimpey' – the name of a large building firm.[21] The burst of construction – of both buildings and roads – in post-war Birmingham sucked in labour. A foreman in a factory suggested that the Irish preferred 'to work with the builders where there is a lot of overtime and Sunday work. The Sunday work, you know, is the beer money.'[22] Working outdoors may have seemed natural to men who had grown up in agricultural communities. There were other reasons why Irishmen congregated in the construction industry. The fact that so much employment was temporary meant that it was easier for a newly arrived man to get a foot in the door. The fact that there were already many Irishmen in the trade drew others in. Factories could seem forbidding to 'foreigners', but construction sites, where sometimes nearly all workers were Irish, could seem like the 'thirty-third county'.

Building work was highly paid and probably attractive to men who may have assumed at first that they would eventually return or who were sending money to families in Ireland. But the instability of the building trade could create its own grim routine. Men were often away from their families and – unless they wanted to join earnest Irish dancing groups in church halls – they did not have obvious things to do outside work. The culture of the post-war English affluent workers – revolving around television and domesticity – did not mean much if 'home' was a room shared with half a dozen other men. Not surprisingly, Irish workers often spent their wages on drink.

Men could be well paid but unable to save. When Dan Cummings took Cardinal Conway, Archbishop of Armagh, to see Irishmen on an Erdington building site, they muttered in response to the cardinal's well-meaning enquiries that their money 'seems to slip away and vanish'.[23] Some men worked for subcontractors. This could mean that part of their pay (up to half) was skimmed off. It could also mean that they worked 'on the lump', taking jobs in which they were not officially registered and paid no national insurance. Some lived peripatetic lives. Birmingham was the nearest thing they had to a permanent home but they took short-term jobs across the Midlands as and when they came up. The Mermaid pub in the Stratford Road served as an informal labour exchange in which such men could be hired. A journalist described how a working day might start:

> You can see at seven in the morning outside the monolithic Highgate Hotel in Birmingham – a five hundred bed hotel differing from a doss house only in price (65p a bed) and the fact that there are single rooms, hardly big enough to hold a bed. Subcontractors roll up in vans, pick up their men and take them off to sites all over the Midlands at £4 to £7 per twelve-hour shift with no insurance or tax.[24]

Generally speaking, the Irish took jobs which were either too hard (such as building work) or too poorly paid (such as hotel work) to be attractive to people established in Birmingham. The Birmingham-born working-class population was most attracted to factory work – which offered stability, reasonable pay and the simple advantage of being indoors in winter. But Irishmen were never entirely absent from factories and, as they became more established, they were increasingly likely to move from outdoor work to the production line. It was said that, by 1974, the Irish made up a sixth of the workforce at the Longbridge car works.

Irish men were highly visible, but the Irish were unusual migrants in that large numbers of women came. Although the Birmingham Irish population was more male than that of other cities – perhaps because jobs in the service sector were less common – women made up a significant minority of the Irish in the city. This was partly because there was not always much of a place for women in rural Ireland and partly because certain kinds of women – those regarded as mentally or morally deficient or those who had borne children out of wedlock – were encouraged to leave. Women worked in factories but also became bus conductors and nurses. Nursing was particularly attractive as it often offered the prospect of accommodation: one Irish-born woman recalled that she had earned 12 shillings a week as a nanny in Dublin and then £3 a week, even after deduction had been made for her accommodation, as a nurse in Birmingham.[25] The fact that they did not conform to the conventional image of their compatriots sometimes made Irish women invisible and there were times, particularly after the Birmingham pub bombings, when they actively sought invisibility.

Those who concerned themselves with the welfare of the Irish in Birmingham were particularly worried about sexual morality. One commentator wrote in 1956:

> It is disheartening to find some who have decided to live as putative man and wife, without any attempt to marry; worse still when they go before the Civil Registrar. Irish girls have been found living in concubinage with Poles, with coloured men and with married men; Irish boys with divorced women and with landladies.[26]

The report of a mission to Irish immigrants in Balsall Heath in 1961 talked of 'a number of Irish girls living in concubinage with coloured men'.[27] Given that young Irish women often lived in the same neighbourhoods as other immigrants, and given that some of the Irish women who came to Britain may have been seeking to escape the moralism of de Valera's Ireland, it is hardly surprising that they should form relations of which Catholic commentators disapproved. Often, the mundane realities of life in Birmingham could seem troubling to those who regarded themselves as guardians of Irish morality. Crowded lodging houses were very different from the 'cosy homesteads' of de Valera's imagination.

Sometimes Irish life in Birmingham was as squalid as de Valera and the priests imagined. Billy Power had been born in Ardoyne in Belfast. He had spent three months in Borstal for persistent truancy from school. He had left Northern Ireland in 1963 to escape unemployment but had not proved very good at holding down a job in Britain either. He had drifted in and out of employment in London. Eventually he came to Birmingham and set up with Nora from Cork, with whom he shared a single room in Handsworth. They had a child together but Nora backed out of marriage three times. When they finally did marry, they did not have enough money for a drink. After the ceremony, Billy went to the betting shop and Nora went home to change the baby's nappy. Marriage to Power brought Nora terrible heartache because in 1974, just after the couple had obtained a modern council house in Cranwell Grove, Erdington, he was arrested by police who claimed that he had planted bombs in Birmingham pubs. He was to spend the next seventeen years in prison.[28]

Often, however, Catholic commentators were disconcerted to encounter Irish people in Birmingham who were clearly moral and 'family minded' but whose conception of morality and the family was different from that of the Church. During his brief stay in Birmingham, Oliver Reilly shared a room with a 'grand lad from Mayo' who worked as a bus driver. The lad's girlfriend, also from the west of Ireland, lived in the room next door. The couple shared their food and she washed his shirts. Both of them sent money home to their parents. They proposed to get married 'sometime'. Reilly told them: 'But it is not exactly right living like this.' He was also concerned to discover that even married couples could not have children in lodgings: 'Hence birth control is practised freely.' [29]

Irish priests often assumed that women would be their natural allies in ensuring that children were given a Catholic upbringing. In Birmingham, though, things were more awkward. Women worked and earned money. Couples enjoyed (or at least admitted to) greater sexual freedom than they had in Ireland. A survey of fertility in Sparkbrook in 1964 revealed two different statistics that would have worried the Church – Irish women were more likely than their English counterparts to conceive children before marriage (though they were also more likely than the English to marry before the birth) and they were less likely than the English to conceive a child within the first two years of marriage.[30] It seems probable that women might have particularly resented the questioning about these matters in the confessional. Some Irish women lost interest in religion more quickly than their husbands. Perhaps one or two of them had come to suspect that there was a link between the Church and the pub and that both were characterized by singing, sentimentality and a constant call on the wallet – it was said that the Old Ship in Camp Hill was packed with an Irish clientele after mass on Sunday.[31] Among the Irish in Sparkbrook in 1964, ten men, out of a total of thirty-nine, had not been to mass in the previous month; twenty-five had been four times or more; of the forty women, eleven had not been to mass at all and twenty-two had been four times or more.[32]

By the early 1970s, the Irish were the best established of the immigrant groups in Birmingham. They had been there longest and, not being distinguished by language or colour, had found it easiest to blend with their neighbours. At first, the Irish had settled mainly in the areas inhabited by other immigrants. In 1961, 17.3 per cent of the population of Sparkbrook was Irish, as was 16.8 per cent of that in Sparkhill and 17 per cent of that in Small Heath. However, they began to move away from the centre of the city and spread out mainly to the north and east to Hall Green, Fox Hollies and Acocks Green.[33] Irish people were eligible for council housing once they had lived in the city for the requisite five years and they seem to have been less affected than nonwhite people by informal exclusion from such housing. Perhaps access to council housing was eased by the fact that Irish people made up a large proportion of members of the Labour Party in some areas of the city and that there were nine councillors of Irish origin by the late 1960s.

Establishing themselves in Birmingham sometimes aroused awkward feelings in people from Ireland. Many returned on holiday and took their children to see relatives who had stayed behind, but the experience could be uncomfortable. Tom Murphy remarked of his own family: 'they were people who didn't quite belong in England but they found they didn't quite belong here either'. He wrote a play about a man who returns to visit his Irish family with his 'bastard accent' and an English wife. Children born of Irish parents in Birmingham had an odd relation with the city. When a sociologist asked them to identify themselves according to various categories, he was struck that 'of those that did adopt the Brummie label, only two did so with any warmth or conviction'. One recalled:

> Brummie was used as a derogatory term around where I grew up, a very derogatory term among second-generation kids. I always sensed among the Irish, our parents' generation, they viewed the Brummies as a specifically miserable bunch and it was a sort of jokey thing but it had negative connotations and I guess that's something that always sort of stuck with me.[34]

The unease that Irish people felt about Birmingham was increased by the 'Troubles' that began in Northern Ireland with the civil rights campaign of 1968 and then the formation of the Provisional IRA in 1969. Initially, British troops were sent to Northern Ireland to protect the Catholic population. The government instituted internment without trial for terrorist suspects in August 1971 and, on 30 January 1972 in Londonderry, soldiers from the Parachute Regiment shot and killed thirteen unarmed protesters demonstrating against internment. At first, violence in Northern Ireland seemed detached from anything that was happening in Birmingham. In many ways, Irish Catholics enjoyed more rights in mainland Britain than they would in Londonderry or Belfast. Many from Northern Ireland had migrated precisely because discrimination kept them out of the most desirable jobs in the place of their birth. But some had also moved because they disliked sectarianism of any kind. In the late 1960s, some families in Belfast encouraged young men to move to Britain because they wanted to prevent them from being drawn into violence. James McDade, who was accidentally to blow himself up with his own bomb in Coventry in 1974, had been sent to Britain by his family, at the age of sixteen, because they hoped to get him away from conflict in Belfast.

At the same time, people who had not previously thought of themselves as politically committed were mobilized by what was happening in Northern Ireland. Johnny Walker had lived in England since 1952 (when he was seventeen). A hard-working man, popular with his colleagues and the father of six children, he was well established in Birmingham. He had done his National Service in the British army, in which his brother was a regular sergeant. A visit to Londonderry in 1972 to attend his father's funeral appears to have transformed him. He believed that his father's death had been hastened by exposure to tear gas, and he brought a British plastic bullet (of the kind fired at republican crowds) home as a souvenir. The incongruous relation between Walker's background and his politics was reflected in the fact that he collected money for Irish republican prisoners at the Kingstanding ex-servicemen's club. Collecting money for the republican cause was legal. In fact, being a member of the IRA or, after 1969, the Provisional IRA, was not originally a criminal offence. In August 1969, Padraig Yates was interviewed on Midland News. He said that he was recruiting around Birmingham for the IRA and that he expected the number of volunteers to reach three figures.[35]

One assumes that expressing support for the IRA did not always make the Irish popular with their colleagues or neighbours, but there was no reason for Birmingham to be particularly hostile to Irish republicanism. Unlike Liverpool or Glasgow, it had no tradition of Orange Protestantism. Even those Birmingham people who voted Conservative would probably have been hard pressed to say why their party still described itself as 'Unionist'. As for those on the left in mainland Britain, they were often sympathetic to at least part of the republican case – they disliked discrimination against Catholics, unfair electoral arrangements, internment and army brutality.

Everything changed on 21 November 1974 when bombs exploded at the Mulberry Bush – a pub built into the Rotunda building on the corner of New Street and St Martins Circus – and at the Tavern in the Town, 300 yards away on New Street. A third bomb was found and detonated in a controlled explosion at a bank in the Hagley Road. Twenty-one people died in the bombings – including two young men who had been passing the Rotunda and were buried in the rubble. Two hundred and twenty people were injured. Anthony Gaynor was driving the number 90 bus close to the Rotunda when the first bomb exploded. Many of the windows on his vehicle were blown out and he thought at first that someone had crashed into him from behind. Others understood immediately what had happened. Ian MacDonald Lord was in the Mulberry Bush. He was thrown in the air by the force of the explosion and recalled that he shouted 'bastards' before he even landed. A woman in the Tavern in the Town described what happened:

I went over to the bar with my girlfriend and was just about to buy a drink when there was a bang and everything started falling upon us. The lights went out and there was screaming and moaning everywhere. I flicked on my light and saw my friend next to me had lost her foot. I thought I was dead and my spirit was just carrying on.[36]

Someone with an Irish accent had telephoned a warning but it was insufficiently clear and there was no time for the pubs to be evacuated. There was no way either pub could have been described as an official or military target.

Within hours of the bombings, five men of Northern Irish origin who lived in Birmingham were arrested as they were about to board the ferry to Belfast. A sixth was arrested in Birmingham. Four of the six confessed to having planted the bombs. The police explained that the confessions had been signed because the killers had been overcome with remorse. The men themselves said that they had signed confessions because the police had beaten the shit out of them.* All six were convicted of murder and given twenty-one life sentences. They were eventually released in 1991 after their convictions were judged unsafe.

Years of arguing, often with people who have never set foot in Birmingham, have taught me that those who still believe the Six to be guilty are not going to change their minds. For those interested in the matter, I have laid out the evidence in appendix IV.

Roy Jenkins, MP for Stechford and Home Secretary, came to Birmingham on the day after the bombing. He recalled his visit:

[T]he atmosphere in the unusually deserted centre of the city hung heavy with some not wholly definable but unforgettable and oppressive ingredients. Others felt it as strongly and physically as I did. Partly no doubt it was the lingering scent of the explosions, but there was a stench of death and carnage and fear. Maybe this was all in the imagination, but what was certainly physically present was a pervading atmosphere of stricken, hostile resentment such as I had never previously encountered anywhere in the world.[37]

The Irish, like most residents of the city, were shocked by the brutality of the bombing. Irish people had been killed in the pubs. An Irishman,

---

* This is not just a distasteful turn of phrase. One of the arrested men soiled his trousers during his interrogation.

John Reilly, was asked to identify the body of his son, Eugene, but was shown instead that of his other son, Desmond, whom he had not known to be in the city. It turned out that Desmond had come back to Birmingham and met Eugene for a drink at the Tavern in the Town, where both men died. The Birmingham Irish were also victims of their neighbours who sought revenge. Attacks were indiscriminate. Few sought to distinguish between those who came from the north and the south of Ireland. The Irish centre in Digbeth was firebombed. Catholic churches and schools were attacked. The National Front organized a demonstration in the city calling for the return of the death penalty. A convoy of fourteen lorries from British Road Service drove to the Birmingham Council House and delivered another petition calling for the return of hanging.[38] Staff at Birmingham airport refused to deal with flights to Ireland and those in the city's market refused to deal with Irish produce. Bridget Reilly, the mother of Eugene and Desmond who had been killed in the bombings, was refused service by shopkeepers when they heard her Irish accent.

Many of the Birmingham Irish were scared in the aftermath of the bombings. Their situation was painful. Some had left Ireland (and especially Northern Ireland) partly because they wanted to get away from the crushing legacy of past conflicts: 'we had to live here and we didn't know what we'd be letting ourselves in for. And, in any case, really and truly it was a generation before us.' Some remembered being 'ashamed to be Irish'. Even in hospital, anti-Irish feeling was expressed. A woman who gave birth hours after the bombs exploded was told by a fellow patient: 'Another Irish bastard is born.' An Irish nurse remembered:

> The time of the Bombings here it was desperate in the hospital. I tell you, that was the worst time here ... there were loads of us that were Irish working that night and that night we heard it on the news, what happened, and it was the IRA. And from midnight, when the news came out, not one English nurse would work with us. That is the Gospel truth, they were so bitter. So that went on for days, nights but we still had to work. That never disappeared, they were bitter for a long time after that.[39]

One woman said that she chose a check-out in Sainsbury's that was operated by a friend of her daughter's 'because I knew that she being of Irish parents would understand'. A child described being refused service at the local butcher by people with 'strife on their faces'. Women suffered much verbal abuse but men often worked in places where physical violence was common. A union leader said that 'bricks might start falling accidentally on building sites', though one assumes that men with anti-Irish feelings probably kept quiet on those sites where most of their colleagues were Irish. A child recalled: 'I feared for my dad more than any of us . . . dad had a lovely brogue . . . out there working in the community.' Another said: 'I think maybe Dad was getting a lot of stick at work.'[40]

Factories were dangerous places for Irishmen after the bombings. Irish workers were sufficiently numerous to be visible without being sufficiently numerous to defend themselves. At Lucas, the piper who had played a lament for James McDade, the IRA bomber who blew himself up a week before the pub bombings, was suspended from work.[41] Workers at Ford in Daventry refused to handle spare parts destined for Ireland. Rumour had it that Irishmen had been beaten up at the Longbridge factory. Some believed that there had been an anti-Irish riot or that the Irish workers had had to be extracted and bused away. Frank Henderson was a Trotskyite shop steward at Longbridge. He remembered:

> I've never been so scared in all my life . . . News was only just circulating by word of mouth. Nobody was working. Tracks weren't working . . . During the course of the day all sort of vile anti-Irish things came out: really poisonous stuff. A head of steam was building for a demonstration – a real pogrom – against anyone Irish.[42]

The diary of the personnel director at Leyland also recalls a violent atmosphere after the bombings. A worker had been killed in the explosion; others expressed vigorous republican sympathies and the management feared trouble. Dick Etheridge was away in London attending a conference on pensions, so the matter was handled by more junior trade unionists. They persuaded a vociferous Irish republican to leave the factory for a time. They agreed that the company itself should collect money for victims of the bombing – to prevent such a collection being organized spontaneously in ways that might feed violence. Managers were keen that workers should not go on strike or be sent home – which they thought might arouse even more ill-feeling. There was a single demonstration during which workers left the Longbridge plant and marched up and down the Bristol Road holding a banner that read 'Hang the bastards'.[43]

The worst place of all for Irish men to be after the bombings was prison. Even those who denied that the Birmingham Six had been beaten in police custody often accepted that they had been savagely attacked in Winson Green prison. Other Irish prisoners were also victims of violence – indeed those who really were members of terrorist organizations seem to have been the only group who enjoyed a degree of protection. An 'ordinary decent criminal' of Irish origin told sociologists:

> When the Irish first came into prison they used to get really hassled by some of the cons especially from Birmingham. At that time all the Irish had to watch their backs. But the political stayed together and eventually got accepted as a group you could trust – not to do business with, you understand, but to be straight and to stand up to the authorities.

Even Irish prison officers in Birmingham had a hard time after the bombings: 'You get tired of all the Irish jokes – but if you don't laugh you're under suspicion.'[44]

Birmingham was not an easy place for Irish people to be in the late 1970s, even after the initial violence of 1974 had died down. The Prevention of Terrorism Act – introduced by Roy Jenkins – gave the police powers which they used enthusiastically. Houses in Irish areas of Birmingham were raided. One of the Irish shop stewards at the Longbridge car factory was said to be sympathetic to the IRA. Management and unions were able to protect him from the wrath of his workmates but not from the police. In January 1975, he was sacked for stealing. The personnel manager recorded how this had come about: 'The police searched his home and although they didn't find any evidence of what they were looking for, as is usual with the police they found something else and charged him.'[45]

The arrest and conviction of the six men who were accused of having planted the Birmingham bombs had complicated effects on the Irish community. In the short term, many were relieved:

> Irish people were pleased that there was somebody arrested for it. And that it wasn't anybody belonged to them. And it did, undoubtedly, serve as a safety valve – totally unfairly. They were our own, but nevertheless, that's it now. The English people will be satisfied to have people locked up. And that would be the end to all the hatred.[46]

Some Irish people must have realized, even more quickly than many English ones, that there were some disturbing features about the case that was presented against the Birmingham Six but 'people didn't trust themselves to start asking questions. The sum total was that there was a kind of fog of shame and doubt, it hung over us like a blanket.'[47] As it became increasingly obvious that the convictions of the Six were unsafe, the Birmingham Irish found themselves in an odd position. It was easy enough for English left-wingers to attack the verdicts but the more they distrusted the police the more Irish people had reason to be prudent. One young woman said that it was 'hard to be politically active'. Going on a march might have exposed her to the risk of 'being fitted up'.[48]

The children of the men accused of the bombing were horribly bullied at school. Elsewhere children with Irish parents noticed a new current of anti-Irish jokes that they realized in retrospect must have come from the parents of their schoolmates. Laura O'Reilly's grandparents had migrated to Sparkhill from the Irish Republic in 1963. They had some sympathy for the IRA – though not for all its actions. After the bombings, the family retreated into a cocoon – the wife worked in an Irish pub and the children went to Catholic schools. The latter were in a strange position: raised in England and talking with Birmingham accents, they were most conscious of their Irish origins when they moved outside their original milieu. One assumes that the experience of a daughter who went to Nottingham University in 1995 was more benign than that of a son who started work at the age of sixteen in Birmingham in 1982. Laura's grandfather also began to feel that his own position was incongruous as he tried to explain to his 'English' children why he had wanted to come to Britain when he disapproved so strongly of its policies.[49]

The Birmingham Irish and their families often felt uncomfortable after 1974 because most of them disapproved, at least to some extent, of both the IRA and the British state. Sandra Hunter was the English wife of one of the men convicted of the bombings. Her house was wrecked by looters and she moved to Belfast for a time with her three children. But she felt awkward there too: 'Word got around that their Dad was a hero of some kind. I didn't want that because their Dad was innocent and I didn't want to bury my sons when they were eighteen.' She moved back to Birmingham but her children were 'brainwashed never to reveal who we are'. She said that she felt 'on the run'.[50]

Irish migration to Birmingham declined sharply. This would probably have happened anyway because unemployment in the city increased during the 1970s. There was a new wave of Irish migration to Britain in the 1980s, but this involved mainly educated people rather than manual workers and over half of them settled in London. However, most Irish people who lived in Birmingham in 1974 stayed. Public expressions of Irish identity – such as the St Patrick's Day Parade – ceased, but the Irish still exercised a quiet influence. Raymond Carter believed that he had failed to hold the Northfield constituency for Labour in the 1979 election because he had served as a minister for Northern Ireland. He reckoned that 20 per cent of his constituents were of Irish origin and some officers in his local party resigned in protest at his association with government policy.[51]

One teenager remembered being told by an English couple 'that I had to choose between Irish or English'.[52] In fact, the situation of second-generation Irish children rarely came down to a simple choice. Unlike other racial minorities, their appearance did not identify them. Most of them spoke with Birmingham accents or at least were capable of affecting one if they found it useful to do so. They could switch from one identity to another. Philip Ullah interviewed a family with strong republican sympathies, who had endured Special Branch raids: 'they even knew the name of our dog'. One son (nineteen years old around 1990) was aware that the police kept track of his movements between England and Ireland; the other son, however, had joined the Royal Marines.[53] Rebellious young men might present themselves as Irish nationalists or as supporters of a certain kind of white, working-class violence that was also, in its way, nationalist. They might even move between the two. In the late 1970s, the sociologist Christine Griffin interviewed a Birmingham teenager, Mick. He said that he wanted to join the army or the police force: 'I wanna go to Brixton to beat up blacks or Ireland to kill paddies.' She replied: 'But you've just said you're half Irish.' He said: 'Yeh . . . it's not the same – none of *them* are British.'[54]

Photograph taken by Janet Mendelsohn in a Balsall Heath café around 1967.

I I

Neighbours? Non-white Immigrants
to Birmingham, 1945–75

I've been here a period of years. I've reconciled myself to the fact
there's a possibility that I am going to die here.[1]

> Jamaican woman, King's Heath, Birmingham,
> 8 February 1964

The British people in the past have operated a 'colour bar'
throughout the world and the majority now wish to establish
one here.

> Kenneth Clarke, Nicholas Budgen and John Lenton,
> *Immigration, Race and Politics: A Birmingham View* (1966).*

In the 1964 parliamentary election, supporters of the Conservative candidate in Smethwick, Peter Griffiths, used a notorious slogan about who
the voters might want as their neighbour. Griffiths refused to denounce
those who used these words, though he did not utter them himself and
his position on race was not actually very different from that of many
in the Liberal and Labour parties. The immigrants who aroused the ire
of some Smethwick voters were mainly Asian but those who used such
often imprecise terms of abuse could be catholic in the range of their
enmities. A former official of the Midland Immigration Control Association, which was based in Birmingham, applied the same racial epithet
that had attracted attention in Smethwick to almost all immigrants:
'West Indians, Pakistanis, Malts and Cypriots. I don't count the Greeks

---

* The authors of the pamphlet did not themselves approve of a colour bar – though they
thought that many Conservatives in Birmingham did.

as really white.'[2] In private, Enoch Powell, the Conservative MP for Wolverhampton, distinguished between those of African and Asian descent, but in his 'Rivers of Blood' speech, delivered at the Midland Hotel in Birmingham in April 1968, he talked of 'the black man' and 'piccaninnies'. The word 'black' could be confusing – especially for children. Many do not seem to have identified themselves in racial terms before they arrived at school and one literally minded West Indian boy pointed out to his classmates that his hair was black but his face might better be described as 'brown'.[3] The mixed-race children who were born in Birmingham found that the colour of their skin confounded their white classmates. Chris, who had a West Indian father and a white mother, went to school in Northfield, an almost entirely white area, and was abused in terms associated with the Indian subcontinent: 'Because I wasn't full black, because I was brown, I think they just associated brown with Pakistanis or whatever it was.'[4] Racial hostility was sometimes expressed in ways that did not involve words at all. Some West Indians, women in particular, had unpleasant memories of the frequency with which they were greeted in the street with monkey noises.

Polite people often used a term that was also imprecise: 'coloured'. The Birmingham West Indians interviewed for the documentary *The Colony* (of which more below) also usually said 'coloured'. The more politically conscious among them sometimes used the word 'negro' – though one woman recalled that a white colleague, with whom she apparently had friendly relations, rebuked her for using this word which they took to be derogatory. One man – seeking to demonstrate the ancient roots of African civilization – said that Septimus Severus, emperor of Rome and thus ruler of Britain from 193 to 211, was a 'pure blooded African negro'. West Indians, though, were not always 'pure-blooded'. Stuart Hall, the Jamaican-born cultural theorist who came to Birmingham in the mid 1960s, pointed out that the society in which he had been raised was marked by a sharp racial hierarchy that revolved in part around degrees of pigmentation.

The West Indian who referred to Septimus Severus had Irish blood and remarked: 'I'm on a very thin line where this lightness of skin is concerned with my fellow brothers from the African continent.'[5] Many Birmingham West Indians alluded to their own mixed origins. A woman of partially Scottish descent claimed that she was 'a creole in the real sense of the word'. Another West Indian said that his father could have passed for Scottish, adding: 'If he had married a woman of his complexion, I would normally have passed as an English then I wouldn't be embarrassed or have any race consciousness about me.'[6] Some insisted that they 'weren't aware of colour or any of its implications when we came',[7] but others acknowledged that there had been subtle distinctions of colour in their native countries: '60 per cent of the big jobs are held by Jamaicans, yes, but light brown, pale people'.[8]

The word 'black' began to be used in the late 1960s, as a term of approbation by those who sought to mobilize and unite non-white people. American proponents of 'black power' were sometimes surprised to find the term being used by British Asians. Those who talked of 'black unity' were right to argue that the different kinds of immigrants who came to Birmingham after 1945 had many experiences in common. All were drawn to the city by the prospect of work and almost all got jobs, though often jobs that more established Birmingham residents did not want. Houses were harder to come by than jobs. Immigration often made a mockery of attempts at urban planning. While the white working class were moved to outlying council estates, new arrivals crowded into the central areas of the city. They were excluded from council houses (reserved for those who had lived in the city for at least five years) and often, in less formal ways, prevented from obtaining mortgages or renting the more desirable kinds of property. But common experiences did not always create fellow feeling among the various immigrant groups. Even communities from the same country or region might be divided among themselves. Sociologists interviewed a Barbadian who never spoke to the Jamaican with whom he shared a room.[9]

Simply defining the various immigrant groups is harder than it seems: 'immigrant' itself could be an arbitrary term. In the mid 1960s, head teachers in Birmingham were given the following official advice:

> Whether or not to classify a child as an 'immigrant' ... must in some measure be a matter for the Head's own judgement but you are asked to use the following as a guide ... all pupils of non-European stock (one or both parents) should be regarded as 'immigrants' even if they were born here.[10]

A political scientist who interviewed Birmingham councillors in the mid 1970s found that barely one in ten of them was clear about the difference between immigrants, 'coloured people' and 'coloured immigrants'. When pressed to estimate the number of the latter in the city, councillors gave answers that ranged from 'at least five thousand' to 'not less than quarter of a million'.[11]

In recent years, the census has allowed for a large number of racial categories and invited people to identify with one of them. However, the censuses of the 1950s and 60s mainly identified people by place of birth. Up to a quarter of those who had been born in India were in fact white – though one assumes that the number of retired Indian Civil Service wallahs who settled in Birmingham was small. The partition of India in 1947 meant that people's 'birthplace' was often not the same as the country in which they had lived before coming to Britain. Some who arrived from the West Indies in the 1950s and a large proportion of those who did so from Africa in the early 1970s were of Asian origin.

WEST INDIANS: *THE COLONY*

Television came to Birmingham about the same time as the first large group of non-white immigrants, and watching clips of old television programmes captures something of the reactions that early immigrants encountered. Questions relating to the 'coloured' population were often discussed in interviews that involved only white people. Some omissions seem extraordinary. White neighbours are interviewed about the fire-bombing of a local shop. They talk of the explosion but no one mentions the name of the shopkeeper – Abdul Rahman Khan.[12] When non-white people spoke at all, they often seemed ill at ease. In the cold winter of 1963, a television reporter interviewed a group of West Indian labourers working on a railway line. The premise of the interviews was that the men would surely be happier back home in their own sunny climate. The interviewees gave very brief replies (often hard to hear because they are muffled against the cold). They all seemed nervous and perhaps exasperated by the tone of the questions.[13]

In 1964, Philip Donnellan, a Birmingham-based producer, made a television film about West Indians in the city that broke with convention in startling ways. *The Colony* begins with the camera looking out of a window towards the Chamberlain Memorial. Over this scene, a woman's voice – almost painfully precise and middle class – discusses adoption policy. She says that some children are hard or impossible to place. These include the physically and mentally handicapped. 'And then of course there's quite a big section among the coloured and half-caste children who are considered ineligible for adoption.' She adds that she is troubled by this because she is herself 'coloured'. It is only then that we see her face on the screen. She is the actress and social worker Pauline Henriques.

Almost all the talking in the film is done by black people. Some are shown in animated discussion with each other, some speak straight to camera in long monologues. Whites have a couple of walk-on parts and are shown in numerous crowd scenes. Images of the arrival of a judge at a church ceremony, where neither he nor any clergyman is heard to speak, portray their activity as an interesting but primitive ritual. Birmingham does not come across as attractive. The camera picks up dingy streets, gasometers, cooling towers and railway lines. Towards the end there are shots of high-rise buildings and new council flats (which do not look very attractive either) but there is no discussion about who might, or might not, be likely to get a council flat in Birmingham in the early 1960s. There is an implicit comparison between the grim industrial town and the West Indies, which is presented as a place of sunshine and tropical abundance – in this respect, Donnellan is closer to the clichés of television than he might have cared to admit.

The star of the show is Stan Crooke. Most of the participants are extraordinarily articulate but Crooke more than any of them has the manner of an educated man. During a discussion, someone addresses him: 'you go to university with them' (i.e. with white people), and Crooke does indeed look and sound as though he might be an academic – he has a donnish capacity to dominate the discussion with apparently innocent questions and flickers of irony. We learn towards the end of the film that he is a railway signalman.

Looking back, there are curious features in the film. Though black people speak at length, they often look to be doing so in response to questions or prompts from an unseen interviewer – presumably the white producer. Because the film has no explicit narrator, we do not learn much about the lives of the participants beyond what emerges in their conversations. In the credits at the end, some are identified in terms of name, occupation and place of origin. But not every participant is identified and, because words are broadcast over documentary footage, it is not always easy to tell who is speaking. It is also not clear whether the participants would have endorsed the way in which the film depicted them and their community. At least one of those portrayed, Pearline Neale, did not see the film until it was shown at the Drum Arts Festival in 2011.[14] The documentary included only a small proportion of the interviews the producers originally recorded. One passage that was left on the cutting-room floor might have been interpreted as a criticism of television producers themselves. One interviewee said: 'I'd rather see a documentary about West Indians in Gang Land – because it shows them as people with initiative rather than seeing them as poor unfortunate bastards who haven't got a place to lay their head.'[15]

Men do most of the talking and much of the programme revolves around discussions in an all-male group. The film shows men discussing children (at least one of them has a son who is still in the West Indies) but not women. All of them examine racial integration in terms of the relations they might have with men, particularly their work colleagues – the original transcribed interviews, rather than the ones that were broadcast, do discuss women. It is interesting that, when we see crowd scenes of white people, the camera often focuses on young women – as though the director, reluctant to ask the prurient questions that would have dominated so many programmes about the topic, nonetheless wishes to remind viewers of one reason why some white people were so exercised by immigration.

The Colony was broadcast at the end of a period of substantial West Indian immigration. It later became common for the British to talk of the 'Windrush generation', which refers to the first large arrival of West Indians at Tilbury docks aboard the *Empire Windrush* in 1948 – though only five of the 492 Jamaican passengers on the *Windrush* intended to settle in Birmingham.[16] But West Indian migration to, though not necessarily settlement in, Birmingham had begun rather earlier. West Indian men, often those who had served with the British armed forces during the war, came to the West Midlands to work. Some were accommodated in National Service hostels (initially established for those doing war work), which sometimes became sites of violent confrontations. West Indians were attacked by Irish workers at a West Bromwich hostel in 1946 and by Polish workers at the Causeway Green hostel in Birmingham in 1949.[17] As time went on, the West Indian population of

Birmingham increased and this itself attracted new immigrants who knew that they would find some kind of community in the city. One Jamaican woman came straight to Birmingham when she got off the boat in Southampton because she had an address of a 'vague contact' there. It turned out that her contact no longer lived in the house she went to but the people who did (also West Indians) took her and her small son in for a while.[18] Bill Morris came to Handsworth from Jamaica in November 1954 at the age of sixteen to join his mother – who had arrived a couple of years earlier to join her brother. The house they shared in Handsworth was frequently a stopping-off point for new arrivals in the city: 'Often complete strangers from the immigrant community would appear in the bed next to me. Sometimes it might be a friend of the family or someone who had been recommended to stay with us for a time.'[19]

West Indian immigration was made easier by the British Nationality Act, passed soon after the arrival of the *Empire Windrush*, which granted citizenship and free entry into the United Kingdom to all Commonwealth subjects. Most West Indians in Birmingham, however, arrived between 1954 and 1962 – there were 500 immigrants of West Indian origin in the city in 1951 and 17,000 in 1961. The period was framed by two pieces of legislation – one in the United States and one in Britain. In the USA, the McCarran–Walter Immigration and Nationality Act of 1952 assigned a separate immigration quota to each British colony, rather than allowing Commonwealth immigrants to enter under the general British quota. West Indians, who had previously gone to the United States in large numbers, found that the major destination for their migration was now closed and turned instead to Britain. The period of rapid West Indian migration to Britain was in turn ended in 1962 by the restrictions imposed in the Commonwealth Immigrants Act of that year. There was a burst of West Indian arrivals (particularly of women and children) in the early 1960s probably stimulated by fear that further immigration would be prevented.

Jamaicans made up the majority of Birmingham's West Indian population – about 12,000 of 17,000 in 1961 and about 19,000 of 25,000 in 1971 – and many talked as though West Indian meant the same thing as Jamaican. One Barbadian-born man recalled: 'at that time any black man was a Jamaican'.[20] Rex and Moore, sociologists working in Sparkbrook in 1964, found that the white British often described all

West Indians as 'Jamaicans' – though their own sample comprised fifteen Barbadians, fourteen Kittians, eight Jamaicans and eleven from other islands. Rex and Moore also believed that there was great hostility between Jamaicans and those from other islands – a woman from St Kitts described Jamaicans as 'all brawn, no brain, big mouths'.[21]

The Colony often seemed to equate the West Indies (or at least the West Indies in Britain's imperial past) with Jamaica. There is a shot of a map of Jamaica (drawing the viewer's attention to the number of places on the island that are named after English towns or regions) and a shot of 'Jamaica Row' in Birmingham. A significant minority of those interviewed in the film, however, came from other islands. Crooke remarked that he had had an 'insular attitude' before arriving in Birmingham and he seems to have used the word in its literal sense – meaning that he had identified with his native St Kitts and had only become conscious of himself as a West Indian after he arrived in Birmingham. A Kittian woman interviewed in the twenty-first century said that she understood why her ten children referred to themselves as coming 'from the Caribbean' though she found the term 'funny'.[22] Even those children who had learned to think of themselves as 'Caribbean' or simply 'black', retained some vague sense of different ancestry. A child born in the 1970s with a white mother and Jamaican father understood that the differences between the islands might be associated with the social differences between different areas of Birmingham: 'At secondary school they [other black children] weren't from Balsall Heath, they were from Moseley [a middle-class district] . . . their parents . . . were all homeowners. They were . . . Kittian and [from] Barbados.'[23] The Birmingham-born comedian Lenny Henry used to tell a joke about his Jamaican-born mother watching the *Black and White Minstrel Show* and saying: 'funny looking fellows; must be from the small islands'.

Coming to Birmingham could be a depressing experience. West Indians were struck by the cold weather and the grim industrial landscape. Jossett Lynch said that the 'houses looked like factories. In Jamaica we are not used to chimneys and smoke.'[24] One woman recalled that, on arrival in Britain, she saw 'smokey buildings as if they were frowning'. She cheered up as her train passed through 'meadows with flowers' but then wept when she saw Birmingham itself. Bill Morris recalled that on his first morning, he opened the curtains, saw the smoke and wondered whether the whole area was on fire.[25]

Housing was a serious problem for West Indian immigrants when they first arrived in Birmingham. Clarence came in October 1951. He had a contact from Jamaica who had been a businessman. Clarence believed that his friend had come to Britain with £600 in his pocket but, when Clarence arrived in the small hours, he was sleeping on the floor under an old coat in a room with fifteen other men. He and Clarence put a shilling in the gas meter and sat until five in the morning, talking quietly so as not to wake the other men. Clarence then lived with four men in an attic room where conditions were so bad that he caught pneumonia and had to spend three weeks in Dudley hospital. When he came out, he tried to find somewhere better to live:

[A]s soon as they saw the face the door was slammed in my face. Some of the places they see my face, they scream. I even offer half my wages if I could get a decent bed to sleep . . . nobody wouldn't have me. So eventually went back to the same house and took ill again.[26]

Clarence eventually met a white couple on a bus who offered him a comfortable lodging, where he stayed for three years. But he recalled others who had been less fortunate: 'I've seen Jamaicans stood in the phone box until daybreak, just no place to go.'

West Indians differed in an interesting way from the Irish who had preceded them to Birmingham. The southern Irish had been schooled in an intense nationalism that was, at least implicitly, anti-British. A West Indian who asked an Irish woman about the roots of Anglo-Irish hostility was mystified to be told about the 'Black and Tans'.[27] Those from Northern Ireland had more concrete reasons for distrusting the British – even if they had come to Birmingham precisely because they wanted to get away from the nationalism, with its attendant divisions and cultural conservatism, of their homeland. West Indians, on the other hand, started out – or at least claimed to have started out – with a positive view of Britain. They came from countries that were part of the British Empire until the early 1960s and members of the Commonwealth (ones that, unlike India, recognized the Queen as their head of state) thereafter. The road to independence was more peaceable than it had been for Ireland, India or Kenya. Many West Indians had fought for Britain in the Second World War. Significantly, some had served not in colonial regiments but in the Royal Air Force. In common with the white working class of Birmingham, West Indians often saw the RAF as both prestigious and egalitarian – it epitomized a world in which men might expect to be judged by their courage and/or their skill rather than by their race or class.

In fact, some West Indians looked back ruefully on what one man described as the 'English fever' that had been imparted during their early life. In *The Colony* a woman says: 'The Queen is on her throne – we are her children.' Rudolph recites a verse:

> Children of the Empire you are Brothers all
> Children of the Empire answer the call
> God Save dear old Britain

He adds: 'We believed it, you know, in all sincerity. Then you walk in and the human factor creeps in.'

One should put the disappointment that some West Indians expressed about their experience of Britain in context. Some may have been influenced by wartime propaganda about imperial unity – but this did not mean that they were unaware of the bitter labour unrest that had been seen in Jamaica in 1938. The disappointment of West Indians was hardly unique – one assumes that many British-born people thought that the society they encountered as adult workers was different from the one they had learned about at school and perhaps different from the society that some of them believed they had fought for during the war.

Whatever they may have believed about England's special qualities, most West Indians treated it as just one possible destination for migration. The fact that migration to Britain increased sharply only after the United States closed its frontiers suggests the pull of higher wages may have been stronger than that of cultural or political kinship. In their original transcribed interviews, though not in the broadcast version, the men portrayed in *The Colony* referred repeatedly to the McCarran Act and often said that, left to themselves, they would have preferred to go to the US: 'If a West Indian has to choose [he] will always go to America before coming to England. There's a certain quota you see. You see America as the land that flourishes, you know?'[28] 'Ninety per cent of West Indian immigrants that are in this country today hadn't it been for the McCarran Act would have been in America.'[29] Alongside their references to 'English fever', the interviewees gave a wide variety of reasons why their compatriots came to England, including money, desire to advance in their profession and curiosity. At least some West

Indians came to Birmingham with brutally realistic views about what awaited them. One recalled that his uncle had travelled in Britain and advised him 'go to work regular and don't talk too much, do what you're told'.[30]

One should also put the disappointment of Birmingham in context. West Indians often looked back on their homelands as places of small-town innocence and bucolic delights that seemed to underline the squalor and anonymity of the industrial city to which they had moved. Those interviewed for *The Colony* spoke of the banana trees and chicken coops of their homes. One man recalled having farmed a property of twenty acres – a vast expanse by the standards of inner-city Birmingham. Though several of them referred to ancient *African* civilization, it is interesting that they all presented the West Indies in terms of nature rather than culture. The idyllic portrayal of the West Indies owed as much to the British as to the Caribbean imagination. When the Chief Minister of Jamaica visited Birmingham in 1961, he pointed out that the number of British people who had gone to his country in the last few years was greater than the number of Jamaicans who had entered Britain.[31] Air travel made it relatively easy for the rich to take winter holidays. Anthony Eden recuperated after Suez at Ian Fleming's Jamaican house. In the next decade or so, a popularized view of the West Indies – made up of James Bond, Bounty bars and the 'totally tropical' taste of Lilt – permeated British culture. A striking photograph by Janet Mendelsohn (of whom more below) shows an Asian man standing on a drab Birmingham street in the late 1960s. Behind him is a tattered poster publicizing a dance to celebrate Jamaica Day and above that is an advertising hoarding that shows a blonde woman sipping a drink of 'tropical lemon', with the caption 'The Taste of Paradise'. The notion of the West Indies as an idyllic place against which Birmingham would be found wanting was widespread. A sociologist wrote of West Indians in Birmingham: 'The longing for "fresh fruit" and "sunshine" had a symbolic importance far greater than suggested by a literal interpretation.'[32] As was often the case, Stan Crooke, the signalman from St Kitts, subverted the sentimental view that both the British and West Indians took of the Caribbean. He warned against the danger that one might 'relapse into a realm of fantasy' and drew attention to the simple economic facts that underlay migration. Life in the West Indies was 'a kind of picnic life' but it was one 'without many sandwiches'.

RACE AND SEX

One particular kind of relation between West Indians and white people aroused attention that was almost hysterical at times. Some in Birmingham worried that white women might have sexual relations with 'coloured' men – though it was sometimes hard to tell whether those who regarded themselves as guardians of morality were concerned to protect women or to condemn them. An inter-racial marriage could be considered a matter worthy of report on the local television news. Sex underlay, or was used to justify, other sorts of hostility. A West Indian said: 'If you speak to any white person about integration they will always come to the point where they say "what about mixed marriages?"'[33] The opposition to the hiring of black bus conductors sprang partly from the fact that they might work with white women and might do so late at night. Some dance halls and pubs excluded black men because they feared fighting over white women. At work, West Indian men noticed that their male colleagues 'don't want you to go anywhere near where there's an English girl, it's like an offence. Even if one of them [a white girl] stops to speak to you, she'll be ridiculed by one of the men.'[34]

Discussion of inter-racial sexual relations almost invariably meant discussion of relations between black men and white women – though the existence of light-skinned Caribbean people illustrated the fact that sexual relations between white men and black women had once been common. Karis Campion studied mixed-race children in Birmingham born in the 1960s, 70s and 80s. Of her thirty-seven subjects, one (born in the 1980s) was the child of a mixed-race mother and a black father. The other thirty-six were the children of West Indian fathers and white mothers.[35] In 1960, a clergyman suggested – with the frisson of excitement that often characterized white people discussing West Indian sexual morality – that cohabitation between white girls and black men was the 'only form of integration that goes on at a rather deep level in a city such as this'.[36]

Given that early West Indian immigrants were mainly men, it is not surprising that some formed relations with white women. It is also possible that a large proportion of the West Indian women who eventually came to Birmingham were either already married to West Indian men or were older than the majority of male immigrants. The image of West Indian women in Birmingham often emphasized maternal, homely virtues. One of the women interviewed in *The Colony* remarked that women 'at home' had fixed career paths. If they did not become nurses or teachers, they 'went into sewing'. She added that women were strictly controlled 'when they reached the age to be engaged'. She says nothing about how women themselves might have reacted to these controls and expectations and whether migration to England might have been an escape for some of them. It is curious that hardly anyone commented on the possibility that black women had affairs with white men – though one, admittedly limited, study suggested that between a fifth and a quarter of West Indian women in Birmingham in the 1960s had done so.[37] A West Indian girl, the sister of one of the men who endured hostility when he spoke to white women at work, was conscious of complicated feelings that underlay social convention:

> When coloured people go to an English dance, the English boys don't ask for a dance ... Sometimes I think some of them would like to but it's what their friends would say that matters, not what they really feel. Some of them speak to you in the street with their friends, you know.[38]

The sexual morality of West Indians aroused much interest among white commentators. In Britain, especially provincial Britain in the early 1960s, extra-marital sex, and particularly the concrete evidence of it provided by illegitimate births, aroused disapproval. Those who studied birth control in Birmingham concluded that almost 80 per cent of West Indian women had their first child before marriage.[39] Some believed that Birmingham West Indians lived an 'easy-going, loose-knit family life, in which marriage was neither socially nor economically necessary'.[40] Others pointed to a range from 'Victorian middle-class families, men and women living in a series of temporary liaisons, stable "Common Law" marriages and single people'.[41]

Perhaps it was wrong to try to understand West Indian morality in terms of a dichotomy between the 'Victorian' and 'easy-going' family structures. The religiosity of many West Indians (especially women) could make them seem 'Victorian', as could the emphasis on certain kinds of patriarchal authority. However, both of these sat alongside a high number of births outside marriage. Migration brought separations and further complications to family life. These could be painful. A

Kittian woman, born in 1926, gave birth to her first child (outside wed-lock) at the age of nineteen – a difficult experience because of her material circumstances (her fisherman father had died when she was fourteen) and religious beliefs. She married in 1951 and had had seven further children (some of them presumably born before marriage) when her husband went to Birmingham in 1956. She joined him in 1957, leav-ing her children with her mother. Her children did not arrive in the UK until September 1960: 'It was a glorious day when my kids came.'[42] Fathers sometimes brought – or 'sent for' – children, who were taken away from their biological mothers.

Social studies – especially those of West Indians whose subsequent behaviour presented problems for the authorities – revealed the agoniz-ing effects of separation. Among sixteen unmarried West Indian mothers in Handsworth in the early 1980s (almost all in their early twenties), most said that they had 'conflicts' with their parents, and this was par-ticularly marked among those who had been born in the West Indies. These women had almost all come to Britain after their parents and the average length of separation produced by the delay was between five and seven years. Some of them had not remembered what their parents looked like.[43] Of the eleven West Indian boys from Birmingham at approved schools (i.e. schools for boys who were seen as criminal) in the late 1960s, only one had come to Britain at the same time as his parents. The rest had endured separations of between one and eight years.[44] Stanley had been born in St Kitts. His parents separated when he was six and his father went to Birmingham. However, when he was ten, his mother left for the United States with her new husband and the children she had had with that husband. Stanley stayed with his grand-mother, leaving school at thirteen and cutting sugar cane for a living. Only when his grandmother died did he go to Birmingham to live with his father (whom he hardly knew and who had a new family with young children) and to resume school. Thomas's parents separated when he was ten and he stayed with his mother, but when he was fifteen she had to go into hospital and he was sent to join his father in Birmingham.[45]

Unlike the single mothers and the delinquent boys, Lenny Henry was a textbook example of 'successful integration' – though he integrated in different ways at different times in his life. The public intellectual of his later years reflected in interesting ways on the fifteen-year-old from a secondary modern school who had gained an apprenticeship or the young man who had drawn attention as a television comic by impersonating white stars. Henry described his parents, particularly his mother, Winifred, in affectionate and admiring terms, but the circumstances in which he grew up do not sound easy. Winifred was an agricultural worker in Jamaica who had four surviving children. Her brother Clifford suggested that she join him in England and that she bring him a wife. Winifred, having saved £75 for the passage, did this and brought with her a woman that she knew from church – it is not clear whether Clifford had ever met the woman but he seemed to be happy with his sister's choice. Winifred's husband, Winston, who was thirteen years her senior, and her first four children were left behind in Jamaica. Winston was unhappy with his wife's move but unable or unwilling to prevent it. Lenny's sister Bev recalled: 'I was fifteen when Mom got on that ship; I felt the separation and cried.' At first, Winifred slept on the floor in the single room that was occupied by Clifford and his new fiancée, but eventually she moved to a room in a house owned by an Indian landlord. Winston came the following year, bringing Lenny's sister Kay. The other siblings arrived one by one – first Hylton in 1960, then Bev and her 'beau' Charles and finally, in 1961, seventeen-year-old Seymour. Winifred had three further children, the first of whom was Lenny, who was born in August 1958 in Britain. When he was about ten, Lenny was introduced to Albert Green ('Uncle Bertie'), a Jamaican man who lived in a single room in which his son Lloyd was also sometimes present. Lenny visited Bertie every Friday and did chores in return for pocket money. After about eighteen months, Lloyd blurted out that Lenny himself was also Bertie's son. He had been conceived while Winston (the man Lenny called 'Papa') was still in Jamaica. It was, Lenny recalled, 'like my world had been flipped by a cosmic spatula'.[46]

ASIANS

Some Indians had been in Birmingham since before the Second World War. Dhani Prem was born in Aligarh in 1904 and practised as a doctor in Birmingham from 1939. He served as a councillor for Great Barr from 1946 to 1950 and thereafter sometimes put himself forward as a spokesman for the Indian community. He reckoned that there were around a hundred Indian families in Birmingham by 1942.[47] An

Indian Communist, Palme Dutt, ran as a parliamentary candidate – opposing Leo Amery, the secretary of state for India, in Birmingham Sparkbrook, in 1945 – but it does not seem to have occurred to anyone that this candidacy had any significance for Birmingham itself, rather than India.

The Second World War brought more Asians to Birmingham, but the bulk of Asian immigrants to the city – 59 per cent of Pakistanis and 67 per cent of Indians – came in the 1960s. As with West Indians, there seems to have been a spike in immigration as men sought to preempt new restrictions by bringing their families to England, but the majority of Asians came after the 1962 Commonwealth Immigrants Act. Some, often Sikhs who had lost their land during the partition of India, came from the Punjab – about 40 per cent of Asians in a survey of Birmingham conducted in the 1970s were Sikhs[48] and one road in Smethwick was said to contain fifty-seven residents called Singh.[49] Others came from the Mirpur district of Pakistani Kashmir having been displaced by the construction of the Mangla Dam – the British supported the dam project and an aspect of this was the admission of immigrants whose land had been flooded. A third group of Asian migrants came in the early 1970s after having been expelled from East African countries (Kenya and Uganda) to which they or their families had migrated during the period of British rule.

Asian immigrants were, at least at first, overwhelmingly male and their motives for coming to Birmingham seem to have been mainly economic. Female migration from India and Pakistan came mainly later and occurred as wives and children joined men who were already settled. Almost all from India and Pakistan would have been born in the British Empire and many had served it – as soldiers or low-level civil servants. However, those from the Indian subcontinent, unlike those from the Caribbean, rarely expressed any sense that they regarded Britain as the 'mother country'. The East African Asians who arrived from the late 1960s were more attached to Britain, though their attachment appears to have been rooted in gratitude for having been granted a refuge rather than in positive memories of the British Empire – saying that Birmingham was more welcoming than Idi Amin's Uganda was hardly high praise.

What was life like for Asian immigrants? Dara Singh arrived in England from the Punjab in the late 1960s and went to work in a West Bromwich foundry. He worked twelve-hour days and sent around half the money that he earned home to his wife and children. He was illiterate and relied on his brother (a draper) to write letters to his family and to handle his relations with the British authorities. In 1978, he applied to bring his family over (he was now fifty-five years old) but his application was rejected on the grounds that he did not have enough money to support them – at the time that he made the application, he was unable to work because of chronic kidney disease. He appealed against the decision – demonstrating that he had saved money and that he had three bedrooms in his brother's house to accommodate his wife and children. He became very depressed and there is no record of whether his appeal succeeded.[50]

In the 1970s and 80s, Conservative commentators sometimes presented Birmingham Asians as 'successful' immigrants whose hard work and entrepreneurial attitude they contrasted with the alleged laziness, criminality and bitter hostility to the police among young West Indians. Even the Tory notable William Dugdale, a humane and good-humoured man, drew such a comparison. When the Bishop of Birmingham asked him to do something for 'ethnic' girls, Dugdale established a training scheme in office work. This was a good idea because secretarial jobs were one of the relatively attractive areas of employment from which non-white people were often excluded. The scheme seems to have been successful, but Dugdale claimed that the West Indian girls meant well but were 'poorly motivated', while the Asians took to the work with extraordinary energy and ability. One suspects that Dugdale's recollection that Asian girls arrived at work in chadors and then changed into 'the shortest of skirts, fishnet stockings and six-inch stiletto heels' may say more about him than them.[51]

It is true that a few Asians did eventually assimilate into the middle class and that those from East Africa set about restoring their fortunes with remarkable stoicism. At first, though, Asians in Birmingham were regarded by most white people as the most 'problematic' immigrants. Unlike West Indians, they were not Christian and they rarely spoke fluent English. While West Indians were seen as cheerful and sociable, Pakistanis were often described as figures of sinister mystery 'coming and going like shadows'.[52] White people often alleged that Asians were dirty. They resented the smell of their cooking and sometimes claimed that they slaughtered animals in their backyards or in the street. Often Asians were accused of carrying disease, especially tuberculosis and leprosy. Most of all, Asian family structures and relations to property aroused hostility. Pakistanis in particular tended to live in family groups even before significant numbers of women arrived. Men who had some relation of kinship (the word 'cousin' was used loosely) shared houses and helped each other with money – though this sometimes led to debts and other forms of obligation that could become crushing burdens.

Like other immigrants, Asians stood no chance of getting council houses when they first arrived and they were often excluded from the most desirable rented properties. Getting a mortgage was hard. Building societies were reluctant to lend money for the purchase of old and dilapidated property in areas such as Sparkbrook, Small Heath, Balsall Heath and Handsworth, which was likely to be the only property that most immigrants could afford to buy.[53] In addition to this, getting a mortgage still usually involved a face-to-face encounter with building society managers who had considerable discretion and were unlikely to exercise that discretion in favour of non-white people.[54] Some Pakistanis could raise money to buy relatively cheap houses by borrowing from relations and/or using bank overdrafts. To repay their debts they then had to rent out rooms in their new properties. Sometimes they took in members of their extended families and often they also rented to other marginal groups – West Indians, the Irish and white women who had given birth to non-white children. Unsurprisingly, relations between landlords, who desperately needed to collect rent, and tenants, who were not always in a good position to pay it, could be awkward. Sometimes this awkwardness was exacerbated by ethnic differences – one Catholic writer suggested that the very word 'landlord' aroused bitter ancestral memories among the Irish.[55] Houses were often crowded beyond legal limits. The Birmingham Medical Officer of Health reported in 1965: 'Examination of the records shows that of the 1,561 houses so far inspected, 950, or 61%, were owned or managed by Pakistanis or Indians, and of these 83% were overcrowded, 75% lacked sufficient facilities, and 60% were dirty and ill-managed.'[56] Since white men in suits had not helped them to buy their houses, Pakistani landlords could often not see why white men in suits should now lecture them about how they should manage those houses. All of this could create a vicious circle as houses in certain neighbourhoods became more crowded and less well maintained. White owners in such areas were terrified that their own properties might become impossible to sell. One sociologist suggested that Pakistanis in Birmingham had become 'pariah landlords' who 'will do an essential job and take the blame for doing it'.[57]

Not all relations between Asians and the rest of the Birmingham population were antagonistic. Young men who were a long way from their home communities were not unduly constrained by religious orthodoxy. Some Muslim men drank in pubs – one argued that Islam was a pragmatic religion that would eventually adjust to the surrounding culture. Some Asian men also had relations with white women. Not all of these relations were sexual – though some of the white women who frequented the poor areas in which Asians lived were prostitutes. Janet Mendelsohn, an American student visiting the Centre for Contemporary Cultural Studies in Birmingham, took a series of photographs of Balsall Heath. Particularly striking were those that concerned a working-class white woman, Kathleen, and her friend Salim. Salim's passport described him as having been born in Pakistan – though he thought that he might actually have come from Kenya. Salim was no angel – he died after being stabbed in a fight in December 1969. Mendelsohn believed that Kathleen was a prostitute and Salim was her pimp and, influenced by radical notions of race, sex and class, she may have romanticized the relationship. Kathleen denied that she had ever been a prostitute. Whatever the truth, Kathleen lived in an apparently affectionate relationship with Salim. She gave birth to their child shortly before he died, visited his mother and siblings and seems to have had better relations with his family than she did with her own mother.[58]

Later the Muslim community became more structured and exclusive – perhaps because religious organizations were established and because women came to join their menfolk and brought with them notions of respectable conduct, rather as white women had brought such notions to British settlers in nineteenth-century India. The arrival of women also stabilized the Asian population of the Midlands. When factories in Smethwick had laid off Indian workers during a downturn in 1956, most men had not bothered to claim unemployment benefit; they had simply moved to some other part of the country where they could find work.[59] Such moves became more difficult when men had wives and children with them and all the more so if they owned property.

WORK

Whatever drew them to Britain and Birmingham, almost all immigrants worked when they arrived there. Indeed, since at first few children and almost no retired people migrated to Birmingham, the proportion of the non-white population in employment was much higher than that of the white population. For most of the time, jobs were easy to find: when the job market slackened, as it did around 1958, immigration fell off too. This did not mean that immigrants got the jobs that they wanted. Many took work that was lowly paid, physically arduous, dirty and insecure. It was partly because of this that they often concentrated in the declining industries of central Birmingham, or the foundries of Smethwick and West Bromwich, rather than in the car factories in Longbridge or Solihull. Personnel managers at car manufacturers in Birmingham were awkward and defensive when faced with suggestions that some factories operated a colour bar as late as 1978. West Indians believed that jobs with the best pay and best conditions were reserved for white men.[60]

Some employers were known not to take on black people at all – often because they did not want to offend their existing workforce. Others employed black people on the shop floor but not in the office. Many immigrants were forced to work at jobs below their abilities. One told an interviewer about his visit to the labour exchange. He handed over his passport and let the woman in charge of his case record his details. When he noticed that they had put his profession down as 'labourer', he pointed out that his passport said 'joiner'. The woman told him that he was in 'an industrial belt', that only labouring jobs would be available; she added that 'you people are always asking for this and that' and told him he was 'cheeky'.[61] Kingsley said that the labour exchange put him down as a 'labourer' even though 'I never was a labourer in all my life.' When he went for a job interview, the personnel officer subjected him to a reading test – though he had filled out a written application and included a list of his diplomas.[62] Immigrants often did not have proof of having served apprenticeships. Plenty of Birmingham-born workers did not have formal proof of their time-served status either, but the absence of certificates gave labour exchanges and employers an excuse to keep black workers out of skilled jobs. The number of non-white school leavers who obtained apprenticeships in the 1960s may have been increased by the fact that some of their white contemporaries were now more likely to continue with formal education. All the same, in Birmingham the proportion of white people starting apprenticeships in the mid 1960s (30 per cent) was three times greater than that of non-white people.[63] The casual assumption that skill went hand in hand with race was reflected in a film – *The Start of a Career* – made by the engineering firm of Accles and Pollock of Oldbury.[64] In this, we see a school leaver arrive for the first day of his apprenticeship. He is shown in an engineering class, playing snooker in the recreation centre and attending an outward-bound course in Wales. He and all his fellow apprentices are white but a brief shot of the shop floor shows that many workers in the firm were black.

Highly educated, non-white people sometimes had to take manual jobs: a theology student and a nurse worked as bus conductors.[65] Earl Barrow was the son of a plantation manager in Barbados and had attended private school. Nonetheless, the first job that he got in Birmingham was as a bus conductor, a position from which he eventually rose to become a driver.[66] At first, even employing West Indians on buses had been a source of conflict. White, largely Irish, employees of the Birmingham bus company had objected to the hiring of West Indians in the early 1950s. There had been discussion of putting the matter to a vote, which came to nothing, perhaps because union leaders anticipated the embarrassment that it would cause. Eventually, West Indians were hired – though an informal quota seems to have limited their numbers.

Non-white workers were less secure than white ones. Given the buoyancy of the Birmingham labour market in the 1950s and 60s, this might seem a matter of little importance. People who lost their job could expect to be re-employed elsewhere within days. However, insecurity mattered for two reasons. First, periods of slack employment (even brief and limited ones) were likely to have a disproportionate impact on non-white workers. When the British Motor Corporation shed employees in late 1956, the small number of non-white workers in the company took much longer than their white colleagues to find other employment – two of them applied for over a hundred jobs.[67] Second, white workers valued stability of employment, sometimes more than high wages (see chapter 9). Black workers apparently had similar feelings; one of the men interviewed in *The Colony* talks about his desire not just to get but to *keep* a job. Lawrence of Handsworth said: 'Myself, I've found thirteen jobs in the country and I still haven't found a suitable job. I've done selling, I've done bus driving, twice I've done factory working, and up till now I haven't found a suitable job.'[68] Staying in the same job was useful for housing, transport and the education of children. It also made the experience of work itself more bearable. Newcomers did not know the machinery they operated – which may have contributed to a sense that they were 'unskilled' – and they did not know their workmates. Arriving at a new factory could be an intimidating experience for a white person with a Birmingham accent – how much worse for someone who knew that he would yet again have to face ostracism from his new colleagues or a round of crude jokes and intrusive questions.

Job insecurity could become a circular process. Unions negotiated deals so that redundancy affected the most recently appointed first – though white workers often argued that their 'coloured' colleagues should be made redundant first regardless of how long they had been with the firm.[69] Constantly shifting employment stopped men getting desirable jobs, for which there was a 'queue', and it cut them out of the informal networks that often allowed white workers to secure employment for their own relatives. Kenricks hardware was a long-established family firm that prided itself on the long service of some of its employees. Non-white workers came to make up 40 per cent of its employees by 1964[70] and in 1963, when the company was visited by the Jamaican High Commissioner, parts of the production line seemed to be entirely staffed by West Indians.[71] Two years later, though, the proportion had dropped to 20 per cent as the company closed its least modern and least profitable operations.

Stan Crooke, the Kittian signalman interviewed for *The Colony*, was hurt by the fact that white men who seemed to get on with him at work did not treat him as a friend after hours and did not invite him to their homes. Jack Morris, a white foreman at Midland Motor Cylinder in Smethwick, also suggested that relations between the races were better at work than away from it. He thought that his Indian colleagues were good workers and 'All of them are members of trade unions – and all of them get paid union rates.' He added:

Because I defend these men outside the factories, I get the reputation of being the coloured man's friend. But this silly tag isn't used inside the factory. There is a double standard for what a man thinks at work and at home. He may laugh and joke with the Indians in the foundry, and go home and tell people lurid stories about their toilet habits. People like to take the majority view.[72]

Tony Green was born in 1943 and grew up on a council estate on the boundary between Quinton and Harborne. He described his parents as 'mildly racist' but he remembered that his father (a bus driver who had learned to drive heavy vehicles while serving in the army in India) had good relations with Mohamed, a conductor with whom he often worked. The two men exchanged birthday presents for their children. Green thought that his father would not have wanted 'those people living next door to me' but that he recognized the need to maintain civilized relations at work. In the early 1960s, Green worked on building sites during his university holidays. One of his workmates was a ferocious racist who seemed genuinely unable to understand that there was a contradiction between his abusive language and the fact that he often went drinking with another labourer, who was Jamaican.[73]

Even at work relations were not always smooth. In the industrial areas adjoining Birmingham, factories were sites of conflict. In all factories, and perhaps especially in old industries, employees exercised a control over the organization of work that circumvented the formal hierarchies of management and, for that matter, the formal structures of trade unions. Power rested with those who had been in the factory longest and this always meant white men. One Pakistani was relieved to move from a Smethwick foundry to a Birmingham car factory because he no longer had to pay bribes in order to avoid having to do the most unpleasant jobs.[74]

Union officials were in an awkward position – torn between the need to appease their white colleagues and the purported policies of their unions, which were usually against racism. There were complicated divisions between the unions themselves. Large ones turned against racism relatively early. This was particularly true of the Transport and General Workers' Union, which recruited many unskilled workers and consequently acquired non-white members earlier than other organizations, and which was also influenced by the left-wing Frank Cousins, who served as its general secretary from 1956 to 1969. Smaller bodies that maintained craft traditions, which hinged on the control of entry to a trade, were less liberal. At Metal Closures in February 1967, white women workers walked out. A reporter asked them whether it was a 'colour bar strike'. Some denied that it was and some said 'no comment'. [75] The reporter asked, 'Who is your shop steward?' but received no reply. In fact, the shop steward was Mrs E. Law and she objected to the appointment of Sheila Nelson, a 'coloured girl', as a press operator. Mrs Law said 'we want to keep this factory white if we possibly can, but if they have got to come we want proper consultation'. She added that her colleagues and herself had nothing personal against Sheila Nelson.[76] Nigel Cook, a councillor and district secretary of the Amalgamated Engineering Union, negotiated a return to work. Interviewed on television, he measured his words carefully. The women had agreed to return to work knowing that there were 'coloured girls' in the shop. The strike was not about or 'not just' about colour. It was rather, he insisted, about not giving work to 'outsiders'. [77]

In November 1968, there was a strike at Midland Motor Cylinder in Smethwick. A hundred white workers, members of the Amalgamated Union of Engineering and Foundry Workers, had walked out and, when they returned, 200 Asian members of the TGWU stopped work. The dispute revolved around a white man: William Marshall. He alleged that Asian workers had been led out by their shop steward in protest about the fact that Marshall had been given a job. The shop steward, Johinder Singh, insisted that this was not the operation of a 'reverse colour bar' but rather that the resentment of Asian workers sprang from the fact that there was a 'queue' for the job to which Marshall had been appointed and that he had been allowed to jump it. It seems that this dispute was part of a longer-term conflict.[78] Marshall himself estimated that the factory had lost 'three or four months' of work due to it.[79] At Birmid in Smethwick there were a hundred strikes in 1968 alone and many of these were associated with racial disputes.[80]

West Indian workers, interviewed in the early 1960s, were often hostile to British trade unions – though not to trade unionism as a principle. Some disliked being pressured into joining bodies that would primarily serve the interests of their white colleagues.[81] Asian workers appear to have been more sympathetic to trade unions. This may have been partly because the linguistic and cultural elements of communities from the Indian subcontinent lent themselves to organization, or may simply be because Asian workers arrived later, at a time when some trade unions were becoming more sympathetic to action against racial injustices. Most of all, Asians probably benefited from the fact that the Indian Workers' Association, founded in Coventry in 1939, was active in Birmingham. The IWA was largely concerned with struggles in India and was close to the Communist Party but it also urged immigrants in Britain to work with, and within, British trade unions. In May 1969, a West Bromwich foundry, Newby and Son, sacked eighty Asian workers. The manager insisted that Asian workers had had good relations with both management and white workers until recently. He believed that 'a hard core of troublemakers have fermented unrest among the coloured employees'. This had resulted in 'insubordination' and 'impossible wage demands'. The Asian workers had walked out and the company had then dismissed them – though it was willing to consider re-employing them 'individually'. The rest of the workers (i.e. presumably the white ones) had 'rallied round' to keep the factory going. The Amalgamated Union of Engineering and Foundry Workers appears to have supported the dismissed Asians.[82]

The career of Bill Morris illustrated the complexity of life for a non-white worker. When he first arrived from Jamaica in 1954, his uncle found him a job at GEC, where he was put to sweeping the floor – though he had been apprenticed to a plasterer in Kingston. After a short time, he left and got a job in a small engineering factory in Handsworth that had a primarily female workforce. White men often justified the exclusion of black workers on the grounds that women needed to be protected from their attentions but Morris's new colleagues apparently displayed maternal solicitude more than fear. They clubbed together to lend him money to buy a bicycle and then a suit. There were no formal apprenticeships at the factory but Morris was able to pick up skills in metalworking – one suspects that some of the women, drawn into factory work during the war, might also have picked up skills that were never given formal recognition. Morris looked back on the eight months that he worked in this factory as the happiest of his life. When the factory moved from Birmingham, Morris got a job at Hardy Spicer in Erdington, where he was to stay for the next eighteen years. The atmosphere in his new workplace was not as warm but Morris now joined the TGWU. Two local leaders of the union – Brian Mathers and George Wright – took a friendly interest in Morris. An early attempt to become a full-time organizer – in Smethwick, shortly after the 1964 election – failed but Morris did eventually become a paid union official and, in 1992, he was elected general secretary of the TGWU. Later he looked back on how he had adapted to racism at work and on the streets of Handsworth: 'It wasn't so much that we were acquiescing, it was more a shrugging acceptance of reality.'[83]

Factories could be violent places and non-white workers were rendered more vulnerable by the frequency with which their employers assumed that violence was a natural part of their life. The official history of the Kenrick hardware company contains the following passage:

> According to William Kenrick, it was about three months before the West Indians comprehended the system of working. The episode when a slow worker was bound and threatened at knife point by the rest of the team seems to have been an indication that the relationship between earning, piece rates and team effort, had at last been learned by the majority of the workers.[84]

Larger and more prosperous enterprises were probably less dangerous – not least because the trade unions were so powerful in them. However, even the Longbridge car plant – the fiefdom of the Communist convenor Dick Etheridge – saw racial violence. On Christmas Eve 1975, a shop steward struck a 'coloured' worker. The shop steward, who bore the same name as someone who would later become prominent on the left, later apologized and insisted that he alone had been at fault.[85]

'LIAISON WITH COLOURED PEOPLE'

Alongside racism, there were genuine attempts to help non-white immigrants, though in retrospect some appear comically inept. Birmingham had traditions of relations with Africa and the West Indies that were underwritten by the missionary colleges based in the city and by Quaker activism. Often it was assumed that relations with immigrants would be best handled by people who had some previous experience of the empire – though rarely, as it turned out, the particular bits of the empire from which Birmingham immigrants came. In 1954, Birmingham became the first English city to appoint a 'Liaison Officer for Coloured People' – the job went to William J. Davis, a fifty-year-old, retired, white colonial official. He had been an educationalist in the Falklands and then in Freetown before becoming personnel officer of the Gold Coast railway. Davis was succeeded in 1956 by Alan Gibbs, who had been a police officer in Kenya. Gibbs sometimes urged integration and complained in 1959 that 'The immigrants are living in tight pockets turning in on themselves and it would seem intent on creating a "Little Jamaica" or the like within the city.' It was an odd complaint because his predecessor was reported to have handed out a list showing thirty-eight streets where 'coloured men may expect to find lodgings'.[86] The officer advised employers on how to handle non-white labour. Gibbs finished his career in quixotic style – buying a plot of land on which he hoped to train Pakistanis who wished to return to their native land and become farmers.[87]

Ernest Barnes, who was Bishop of Birmingham until 1953, held eccentric left-wing views which included a belief in eugenicism and consequently an insistence that immigration would 'damage the national stock'. Thereafter the Church was more helpful to immigrants, but it also tended to see their plight through an imperial prism. In 1959, the Bishop of Birmingham appointed Paul Burrough as a 'chaplain for coloured people'. Burrough brought the worthy assumptions of missionary work to his new post – he had, like his bishop, been a prisoner of the Japanese during the Second World War before working in Korea and would eventually end up as a bishop in Ian Smith's Rhodesia. Burrough worked from a caravan and admitted that his greatest problem sprang from the religiosity of West Indians: 'They become disillusioned when they discover that for the majority of English people the church is not a living force.'[88] Sometimes the religious enthusiasm of West Indians went with liturgical conservatism and an affection for the authorized version of the Bible, which perplexed fashionable clerics. In the 1970s, one of the Handsworth band Steel Pulse's songs was entitled 'Not the King James Version', at a time when most white churchgoers had not set eyes on a copy of the King James Bible for a decade.

THE POLITICS OF IMMIGRATION

Immigration provoked bitter political divisions in Birmingham. The National Front, formed in 1966, marched against immigration in the city – its support probably peaked in 1976 when it mobilized around the case of Robert Relf, who had been jailed in Winson Green prison after advertising his house in Leamington Spa for sale 'to an English family only'. The National Front could be frightening but only ever attracted a small number of people in Birmingham. More important were the views expressed by members of the major parties. Immigration was not, at least for most of the time, an important issue for Conservative voters. A Gallup poll of March 1964 in six marginal Birmingham seats suggested that immigration was important to 2 per cent of Tory voters and 2 per cent of Labour ones. By far the most exercised about the issue were Liberal voters.[89] This was partly perhaps because the Liberal Party, which was very small in the early 1960s, tended to attract voters who were disenchanted with the two main parties for one reason or another. It was also because of one man – Wallace Lawler, a plastics manufacturer of Irish origin. Lawler had been an independent who presented himself as being against all parties after the war but had then joined the Liberals. In 1962, he became the first Liberal councillor in Birmingham since the 1930s when he was elected for the Newtown ward. In 1969, he was elected as Member of Parliament for Ladywood in a by-election, though he held the seat only for a year. Lawler's tactics revolved around carefully targeted appeals to particular areas. In the suburbs, he presented himself to middle-class voters as an opponent of high council spending and high rates; in the central part of the city he presented himself to the white working classes as an opponent of immigration.

Race mattered not so much because ordinary voters were hostile to immigrants (or at least not because their hostility was likely to affect how they voted) but rather because it tied in with internal conflicts in the Birmingham Conservative Party. The agent, Tranter, was blamed for inefficiency and needed to explain why his party had lost so many seats in the city after its success of 1959. He did so partly by blaming immigrants. In February 1963, he wrote in apocalyptic terms, claiming that 2,100 Conservatives had left the All Saints constituency since 1959 'as a result of coloured immigration'. In Sparkbrook, he believed the number was 4,700 and in Handsworth 5,000.[90]

Conservatives who talked about race often presented themselves as speaking for the more plebeian section of their party or electorate. Edward Boyle – who had been educated at Eton and Christ Church and, indeed, done little in life other than attend Eton and Christ Church before Conservative Central Office handed him what was then the safe Conservative seat of Handsworth at the age of twenty-seven in 1951 – epitomized the mixture of patrician manners and liberal opinions that was calculated to annoy less privileged Tories. Sir Charles Burman, the chairman of the Birmingham Conservative Party, wrote in June 1963:

> Here we have a colour problem. They vote Labour, and, although there is little hostility, there is no enthusiasm for their presence. I am advising candidates to be very careful and comments such as 'We must learn to live with them' do not go down well from MPs who do not themselves have to live with them![91]

Remarks such as these, however, were rarely made in public. Ambitious Tory candidates – such as Antony Beaumont-Dark, a councillor and parliamentary candidate in the 1960s who was eventually elected as MP for Selly Oak in 1979, or John Hollingworth, who took the All Saints constituency from Labour in 1959 and held it until 1964 – knew that referring to race might go down well with their potential voters but would go down badly with Conservative Central Office.[92] The party line in Birmingham was not to talk about the matter at all. Twice Conservatives made deliberately provocative attempts to break the silence. The first of these came in 1966 and from the left of the party. Kenneth Clarke, Nicholas Budgen and John Lenton wrote a pamphlet for the Bow Group (a progressive discussion circle in the Conservative Party) about race in Birmingham. All three men were in their twenties. They were able and ambitious and probably freer in their discussion than they would have been if they had reached the stage when they were likely to be chosen as candidates for winnable parliamentary seats. They recognized that most in their party wanted to avoid discussion of the topic: 'these subjects are too dangerous to be brought into the political arena'.[93] They were sharply critical of racism in Birmingham and at least implicitly recognized that much of it came from their own party. They proposed limiting immigration but also favoured the active promotion of racial integration. They thought that such integration would involve change on both sides and believed that the sign of successful integration would be the one thing that many Birmingham people regarded with most distaste: inter-racial marriage. They placed great faith in education and social mobility and considered that universities were the only arena in which real integration had occurred. It was a thoughtful, well-informed pamphlet, though, as far as one can tell, it had been composed without talking to a single black person.

The second intervention was Enoch Powell's 'Rivers of Blood' speech on 20 April 1968. This was a construction of mischievous subtlety because Powell was careful to say nothing that contradicted the official policy of the Conservative Party and, indeed, he suggested a new limit to that policy by saying that repatriation of immigrants would become impossible once they had been in the country for ten years. It was, however, clearly designed to embarrass Edward Heath, the leader of the Conservative Party, and force him to sack Powell from the shadow cabinet. Powell must have been aware that his speech would put the Conservative notables whom he was addressing in an awkward position. Reginald Eyre, MP for Hall Green, had been due to chair the meeting but excused himself when he heard what Powell intended to say[94] – it was his telephone call to the Conservative chief whip that precipitated Powell's dismissal from the front bench. Eyre worried about immigration but refrained from commenting on the matter when asked by journalists.[95] Meanwhile, other Birmingham Conservatives recognized that Powell appealed to the grassroots of their party:

> The reason why Enoch Powell's River Tiber outburst commanded such support in the country, particularly among Conservative Associations, was that the electorate were confused as to the party's precise position. Our wishy washy tactics during the Commons debate on the Race Relations Bill did not help matters.[96]

The fact that prominent Conservatives in Birmingham refrained from public comments on race does not mean that they did not discuss the matter in private. Some of them seemed to share the concerns of their colleagues in Smethwick but feel that they were best addressed by a 'quiet talk to police and medical officers of health'.[97] Some Birmingham MPs – notably Beaumont-Dark and Jill Knight – were less liberal in their pronouncements on race when Margaret Thatcher brought a change in the tone with regard to such matters in the national party (see chapter 13). In the mid 1970s, a political scientist interviewed Conservative councillors in Birmingham about race. Most of them, especially the most senior, were careful what they said, but about a third of them, under cover of anonymity, were less inhibited. One alluded to a 'Negro pop group' on television: 'you could have put them in tribal dress and put them down in Africa . . . they are still primitives'. Others said: 'Look at all those old buggers with turbans on. They've never done a day's work'; 'the city does too damn much for the coloured'; 'My husband's a magistrate and he gets it weekly. Their moral standards are low . . . They practise prostitution in their own abodes. I don't know what the solution is, except to send them all back.'[98]

As for the Birmingham Labour Party, it was less opposed to racism than some of its leaders would later claim. Party members were mostly white. The single greatest concern of the party at local level was the allocation of council housing. This was never overtly based on race but the formal rules about allocation benefited white people for much of the 1960s. Informally many also believed that good relations with local politicians would benefit an application for council housing. When Brian Walden, who had cultivated good relations with his black constituents, stood down as Labour MP for Ladywood in 1977, it emerged that his electoral agent was linked to racist parties of the extreme right.[99]

SMETHWICK

Many in Birmingham insisted that the city itself was free of racism. They argued that Enoch Powell was MP for Wolverhampton and that his 'Rivers of Blood' speech did not really refer to Birmingham even though it was delivered there. More generally, they saw racial hostility as a feature of the Black Country towns – West Bromwich, Rowley Regis and particularly Smethwick. Harold Wilson remarked of Peter Griffiths, the Conservative who had won Smethwick in the 1964 parliamentary election, that his racist campaign would make him a 'parliamentary leper' (an interesting choice of words in view of the frequency with which Smethwick activists claimed that immigrants spread leprosy); Roger McGough wrote a poem entitled 'I'm Dreaming of a White Smethwick'; Malcolm X visited the town just days before he was assassinated in New York.

The relation between the Conservative Party and race in Smethwick was more complicated than it looked at first glance. For most of the period since 1945, Smethwick had been a safe Labour seat. Peter Griffiths was relatively young (he had been born in 1928) and entered politics through the Young Conservatives – though he could not have been more removed from the world of tennis and apolitical flirtation that was often associated with that body. He had been born into a working-class family and rose via grammar school to become a primary school teacher and eventually headmaster. He was elected to Smethwick council in 1955, at a time when only five of its thirty members were Conservatives. Griffiths brought a new degree of dynamism to the local Conservative Party and the council, becoming leader of the Conservative group in 1960. He was also adopted as the Conservative parliamentary candidate for Smethwick for the 1959 election. This marked a departure for a constituency that was usually used to blood ambitious and well-connected Conservative candidates from outside the area, who would then go on to be selected as candidates for winnable seats. Griffiths was conscious of his status as an outsider in his own party and seems to have been particularly bitter in his feelings towards Edward Boyle, whose Handsworth constituency abutted Smethwick and who was already a minister even though he was just five years older than Griffiths.

Hostility to immigrants was the force that moved Smethwick to the right and that allowed Griffiths and his allies to take control of the council. Fred Thornton won the Soho ward for the Conservatives in 1960 with a campaign that revolved around the eviction of 'coloured' people from overcrowded properties. There were disturbances on the border of Dudley and Smethwick that some had dubbed 'race riots'. Griffiths' own position was not consistent. Sometimes he insisted that he supported 'integration' and that limiting immigration was the means to bring this about; at other times, he said that the people of Smethwick (by which he seems to have meant the white people) would not accept integration. Sometimes he even presented himself as the defender of Sikhs who wished to preserve their own traditions. Some of these shifts in position were obviously governed by a search for political advantage – having won the Smethwick parliamentary seat, Griffiths became ostentatiously moderate as he sought to shake off an image that might damage his subsequent career. Sometimes, though, Griffith does look to have been motivated by a genuine, if clumsy and condescending, desire to improve relations between the races. His wife entertained Indian women to tea at her house; Griffiths talked to the leaders of the Indian Workers' Association and prided himself on promoting dialogue that would prevent 'misunderstanding'. Open racists supported Griffiths in

1964 but often, especially as he manoeuvred himself into parliamentary respectability, came to view him with distaste.[100]

As leader of the Conservative group on the town council, Griffiths had opposed further immigration but said that immigrants already in the country should be granted equal rights. In 1961, council tenants in Price Street, Smethwick withheld their rent in protest at the arrival in the street of a Pakistani family. The Labour leader of the council told them that the Pakistanis would stay and that those who did not pay their rent would be evicted – the leader of the rent strike quickly claimed that he had intended only a symbolic action. Griffiths supported the action of the council against the rent strike. A Labour councillor, Ronald Badham, was charged with talking to the tenants who refused to pay. He did so in terms that suggested that Labour Party leaders at local level had considerable sympathy for racist feelings:

> He would himself organize and take to Westminster a petition arguing that coloured immigration should be restricted for from three to five years and that immigrants committing offences should be deported . . . 'I have sympathy with you: I would not want these people living by me either,' he said.[101]

A former Labour councillor, Ken Bunch, had supported a colour bar at the Sandwell Youth Club, and the social club of the Smethwick Labour Party itself was said to operate a colour bar. In March 1962, a Smethwick branch of the Birmingham Immigration Control Association (founded in 1960) had been formed. It was chaired by Donald Finney, a planning engineer and miner's son who had voted Labour until 1959 and who subsequently became, with Griffiths' support, a Conservative councillor. Its deputy chair was Lawrence Rieper, a retired bank manager. The other twelve committee members were mostly working class. Only two were lifelong Conservatives. The Birmingham Immigration Control Association seems to have operated as a political bridge. Initially, it proclaimed itself to be apolitical and, indeed, incited its members not to vote, but by the time of its dissolution in March 1962 it had effectively rallied behind the local Conservatives.

Patrick Gordon Walker, the Labour candidate in Smethwick, was portrayed by his opponents as a remote and privileged figure (living, as they liked to remind voters, in Hampstead Garden Suburb). Given the nostalgia that some of them felt for imperial greatness, it may have

particularly offended Smethwick Conservatives that Gordon Walker
was the son of a judge from the court of Lahore and his grandfather had
been lieutenant governor of the Punjab. As shadow Home Secretary,
Gordon Walker had led the Labour opposition to the Commonwealth
Immigrants Act in 1962 but he was not particularly liberal on matters
of race and issued an electoral statement that emphasized the need for
control of immigration.

Griffiths' election was only the most widely reported of a number of
incidents. In 1963, Donald Finney, the Conservative councillor, organized
'vice vigilantes' to police an area in which he maintained white prostitutes were consorting with 'coloured men'.[102] Two years later, Finney
claimed that an eighty-four-year-old woman in Marshall Street – Edith
Batten – had been terrorized by her Indian neighbours, who had then
said 'can we take house now' when she died. He believed that the council should buy houses in the street and reserve them for white families
and that this was the 'only way to stop this black invasion from swamp-
ing us completely'.[103] The council did seek to buy houses in the street – or
at least it applied to the central government for a loan to make the purchase. Richard Crossman, the Minister of Housing, said he could do
nothing to prevent Smethwick from doing this but would not lend them
money for the purpose.

Distinguishing Smethwick, or much of the Black Country, from Birmingham was an artificial exercise. The city blended directly into many
of the surrounding industrial towns. People from the Black Country
often worked in the city – indeed, as recently as the 1930s, they had
sometimes been regarded by Birmingham workers as unwelcome
migrants. Those who discussed the matter often assumed there was no
real distinction between Smethwick and Birmingham. Peter Boyd, a
Smethwick clergyman, said: 'We don't want our Birmingham to become
another Birmingham Alabama.'[104]

Whether or not Smethwick was more racist than Birmingham, there
were reasons why racism there was more easily expressed. First, there
was an important difference between the trade unions in the two towns.
The Communist Party was the only one that never flinched in its opposition to racism and, though they were not numerous in Birmingham,
Communists were important in the city's trade unions. They did not
have the same influence outside the city limits. Furthermore, the fact
that Smethwick was smaller than Birmingham meant that a few

vociferous activists could make themselves heard. The local newspaper, *The Smethwick Telephone*, was owned and edited by Katie Billingsley, a Conservative activist, until her death in December 1962. It paid almost obsessive attention to immigration; in 1963, it devoted 1,650 column inches to the topic. It printed letters that contained passages such as this: 'With the advent of the pseudo-socialists' "coloured friends" the incidence of TB in this area has risen to become one of the highest in the country.'[105] Lawrence Rieper wrote to the paper of a 'fine race destroyed by blood poisoning' and added: 'In the event of war these coloured people will present a serious menace. Most of them would be useless in the service and white men will have to die to preserve a land fit for every colour but their own to live in.'[106]

For all of this, the racial politics of Smethwick were not completely divorced from those of Birmingham proper. When Harold Wilson attacked Griffiths in Parliament, Geoffrey Lloyd, the doyen of Birmingham Conservatives, walked out in protest. Harold Gurden, the Conservative MP for Selly Oak and secretary of the group of Conservative MPs in Birmingham, welcomed Griffiths to Parliament, though he claimed that he had had no dealings with him before his election. Wyndham Davies was elected for Birmingham Perry Barr in 1964 – like Griffiths, he bucked the national trend and, like Griffiths, he owed his success partly to anti-immigrant feeling. In 1965, Gurden and Wyndham Davies both spoke, along with Griffiths, in opposition to legislation that would have made it harder for publicans to impose a colour bar.[107]

RESPONSES TO RACISM

How did Asians and West Indians feel about verbal and physical attacks on them? At first, they were often guarded in their responses (at least in front of television cameras). Some refused to speak at all when asked about matters of racial discrimination. When a reporter on the streets of Smethwick asked people what they thought of Harold Wilson's attack on Peter Griffiths, all the white respondents condemned it. A young West Indian gave a more complicated answer – saying that Wilson had spoken too soon and too 'plainly' but adding that there was colour prejudice in the constituency. Another 'coloured' man, apparently Indian, refused to talk at all.[108]

Two welfare officers – a West Indian and a Pakistani – looked uneasy when asked about racism in 1965: 'I don't want to make an issue of anything like that . . . I wouldn't say I look out for it.'[109] Some of those interviewed by Philip Donnellan in *The Colony* had been bruised by things that had been said or done to them. But some tried to put themselves in the place of white British people. One said that he imagined that a white person coming to the West Indies might also be made to feel out of place (an odd remark since large numbers of white people *had* gone to the West Indies) and that incomers should expect to adjust to the society in which they arrived.

Some black people resented what they saw as the hypocrisy of British attitudes to race. Liberal-minded white people in Birmingham often compared their city favourably to the United States, but West Indians who had worked in the US sometimes took the opposite view:

> We prefer the situation in America because you knew exactly where you stand. In England you come and they say there's no colour prejudice, no colour bar, you just dust it under your carpet and pretend it isn't there . . . It's always there and you're never without it.
>
> Some people come to you and they want to make friends – they try so hard that it stinks. It's not natural, they are as bad as the people who actually detest you . . . You just want people to be themselves.[110]

A young Jamaican resented the smug tone of Birmingham employers:

> The one thing I dislike. You go to be interviewed. You have one of those Personnel Managers after speaking to you he says 'Oh well, I don't have any colour bar.' Well that gets me a bit embarrassed because most of the time beforehand this Personnel Manager, I forget that I'm coloured, I forget that he an English, I do go for an interview as I know that I could do the job. So I hate it when he or she mention that I have no colour bar. Then I think, there it is, that he has some colour bar, or he would interview me as another person, and not as a coloured, as someone who is unfit or fit to do the job.[111]

Matters were complicated by the double-edged nature of British responses to immigrants. The fact that British racism was so rarely expressed in unambiguous terms made it hard to confront. British people would often insist that their hostility was based on something other than race – they would not have minded a 'normal' Pakistani family but resented the fact that the house next door was said to be inhabited by fourteen people; they did not mind 'coloured' workmates so long as white people were not put out of work; they did not mind immigrants in general so long as their numbers were controlled. In Ladywood, Doreen Adkins launched a petition against non-white people being moved to her maisonette block. However, she insisted that she had good relations with the black family who already lived in the building: 'I am not a racialist and I don't mind just the one family. We have to accept her, and she is quite friendly, the trouble starts when they begin getting together.' Her black neighbour, Pearly Pinnock, told reporters that she considered the petition justified – her life might have been uncomfortable if she had said anything else.[112] Much of this must have been disingenuous but sometimes non-whites recognized that the attitudes of white people could be riven with contradictions. The Pakistani whose arrival in Price Street, Smethwick in 1961 provoked a rent strike hoped that attitudes would change when his neighbours got to know him. He had lived in Smethwick for ten years, and had previously had good relations with white people.[113]

The ambiguities of prejudice and assimilation were summed up by the career of Rudolph. He had lied about his age to join the RAF at seventeen and lived in Britain for fourteen years. He worked as a crane driver at the Austin motor works – the kind of privileged position, working on 'production' rather than labouring, that he reckoned only one or two other black men enjoyed. He said he was 'no different from the average working-class English person' – though the fact that he owned a car and house would actually have placed him at the most prosperous end of the working class. He had, against his original intentions, married a white woman though the relationship was tempestuous – 'we fight like hell verbally speaking' – and he suggested, half seriously, that 'in the back of her mind she still have got this idea more or less that we live in trees'. Rudolph had been a professional boxer for a time and oddly the boxing ring was the one workplace in which inter-racial relations were relatively amicable – 'it's just a job', said one opponent after a particularly hard-fought bout. Perhaps his prowess as a boxer also accounted for the fact that his colleagues at the Austin did not need to be told twice when he said that his name was not 'darkie' or 'sambo'. He had been deeply hurt by much of what he endured:

If I'm to be honest I never really wanted to fight anybody, I think hate is just the thing that brought me to boxing, I just wanted to beat somebody's brain out because I had a pretty rough time here. Hatred brought about by intolerance, my experience in Birmingham here as a Jamaican.[114]

One important feature of immigrant response to discrimination seems to have been the belief that they were dealing with something temporary. Quite large numbers of West Indians assumed that they would in due course return to their native countries. Of fifty-one West Indians interviewed in Sparkbrook in 1964, twenty-seven said that they intended to return permanently to their countries of origin. Those interviewed for *The Colony* expressed similar views: 'I think the majority if they get the chance they'll be heading for home. But no one want to go empty-handed. I don't think you'd find more than two of a hundred that's really contented to settle down in England till he dies.'[115] Victor Williams, the bus conductor who is seen walking around Birmingham Science Museum, was one of the few people who did go back to Jamaica, but he did not get there until 1979 and quickly returned to work again in Britain, where he died. His wife and daughters, who had also gone to Jamaica, then returned to Britain.[116]

Curiously, the sense that they did not belong may have attenuated the humiliations inflicted on them. People, men especially, worried more about their status in the societies they considered their own.[117] As for those who intended to stay – as it turned out, almost all immigrants did stay – they often assumed that discrimination was partly the product of mutual ignorance and that it would diminish with time. They believed that in time their children might expect to be fully integrated into British society. British people sometimes shared this optimism. A young couple in Sparkbrook expressed some animosity to immigrants – though they were more hostile to the Irish than to the West Indians – but they added that they

[H]oped their boys would grow up to have friends from all races and discriminate between people on grounds other than race. They also hoped that their children would settle in Sparkbrook, as they would not only learn the right lessons about race, but enjoy the improvements that were bound to come to the area in the future even though there are housing problems and rough elements present today.[118]

Even those whose actions now seem shockingly racist sometimes expected their children would grow up to be more tolerant. Seventy-five householders in Theodore Close, Rowley Regis, signed an agreement in 1964 that none of them would sell their house to a 'coloured' family in the next ten years. The following year, a black family – the Dawkinses – did buy a house. The self-appointed committee to guard the racial purity of the neighbourhood went to see Mr Dawkins to explain the situation. They claimed that they did not blame him for the purchase (apparently they blamed the vendor) and that the sale must be accepted. They were particularly concerned that older residents in the estate might leave in response to black residents moving in, but they saw the problem as temporary and explained that the ten-year rule had been imposed because 'our children will obviously grow up to accept coloured families'.[119]

What was it like for young people caught in the crossfire of racial conflict in Birmingham? Schools themselves became objects of contention. The headmaster of Golden Hillock secondary modern school refused to take five Pakistani children in September 1966 on the grounds that his school contained too many 'non-Anglophone' children.* Local officials and politicians discussed seeking to disperse immigrant children around the city and finally hit on a policy of 'friendly persuasion', which meant seeking to persuade the parents of non-white children to agree to send their children to predominantly white schools, which were often only a short distance away. In practice, however, there were sharp differences in Birmingham schools. Church schools had fewer immigrant pupils than non-Church ones (in spite of the fact that religious practice among West Indians was high) and grammar schools were overwhelmingly white. White parents objected to high numbers of immigrant children in schools because they believed that the resultant disruption would damage their own children's chances of passing the eleven plus.[120]

Jill, a white working-class girl, had almost no experience of other races until Asian children began to arrive at her secondary modern in Hall Green. She thought that the school 'did integration fairly well'. She left school at the age of sixteen in 1972 and, in the last days of full employment, spent her wages as a typist on clothes and nightclubs. After a succession of boyfriends, Jill fell in love with Lee, a boy she had known on and off

* Golden Hillock school closed in 2013. Its last headteacher was Mr Hardeep Saini.

since she was thirteen, whose father was Jamaican. Her parents told her she must give up Lee or leave home. She moved in with Lee's family and got engaged to him. Unexpectedly, her parents turned up to her wedding – Jill's younger brother had talked them round. They did not stay long at the reception (curried goat and an 'English spread'), but relations were more or less restored and the birth of Jill's daughter almost exactly nine months after the wedding seems to have made things easier.[121]

Many who grew up in the 1960s and 70s had experiences that were even harder than those of Jill and Lee. There were painful confrontations in the playground. One West Indian woman said that her daughter, Maureen, had befriended a white boy, Michael, at primary school. One day, a white girl told Maureen that she would never be able to marry Michael because he was white. 'She really cried and I had to find something to say.'[122] The fact that non-white people in Birmingham grew more numerous, and that it became increasingly obvious that they were in the city to stay, gave a sharper edge to racial conflict. Youth culture – rock concerts and football terraces – provided arenas in which racial hostility was expressed with a new degree of violence. Rock Against Racism was founded partly in response to the abuse that Eric Clapton directed at black people during a concert at the Birmingham Odeon in August 1976. Those who had hoped that children would grow up to be more tolerant than their parents had a nasty shock. Immigrants noted the frequency with which children abused them in the street and were particularly hurt by this – perhaps because they recognized that children were saying in public things that their parents said in private. The slogan that caused such a stir in the Smethwick parliamentary election in 1964 may have had its origins in something that children chanted a little earlier during local elections. Peter Griffiths had commented on this: 'We can't stop children reflecting the views of their parents. The people of Smethwick certainly don't want integration.'[123]

Racism did not fade with the passage of time. Non-white children born in Britain were sometimes more aware of it than their parents had been and white children sometimes spoke with particular brutality. White primary school pupils in a working-class area with a large immigrant population repeated remarks that they must have heard at home: 'Far too many Indians and Pakistanis, not one road without them'; 'I would be scared stiff on my own. You could hear the Pakistanis singing Yah or Eha and all that rubbish'; 'You would see a lot of dark people fighting with white people'; 'Another reason why people dislike Small Heath is all the coloured people.'[124] The working-class white boys at a Smethwick secondary modern school in the mid 1970s expressed their racism with a lack of inhibition that might have surprised even the voters of their town in 1964. Indeed, the fashionable emphasis on 'self-expression' in education released some demons. One boy began an essay with the words: 'We couldn't go Paki bashing with only four.'[125] The boys were hostile to all non-white people – though they sometimes made common cause with Jamaicans against the school authorities and they reserved particular hostility for Asians. One said that a rare aspect of his school career that he would recall with affection was 'fighting on the Pakis and fighting on the Ja[maican]s'.

Laxmi Jamdagni interviewed Asian schoolgirls in a 'large industrial town' in the Midlands around the end of the 1970s. The girls were lively and sometimes rebellious. They talked about the film *Grease* and compared John Travolta unfavourably to Bollywood stars – though at least one of them had never been to the cinema until they managed to persuade Jamdagni that taking them on such a trip would contribute to her research. They had to weave their way around a complicated maze of social and cultural constraints. Parents sometimes tried to control friendships and to isolate those that they considered to be bad influences. Many of the girls were not allowed out unless chaperoned by their brothers – though they also endured unwelcome attention from other Asian men. Most of all, the girls faced racial abuse. They were reluctant to discuss it, though, or at least to do so with those whom they did not trust. When a white teacher came into the room, they stopped talking. One of them said that she shouted back at those who insulted her in the street. Another said that 'whenever I get angry I start shouting and put two fingers up' but then added that she did these things only 'in her mind'. One wrote down her thoughts about what she endured but she did not do so in her diary, which might have been read by her sisters: 'I just write it on a sheet of paper then rip it up and throw it away.'[126]

The Black Sabbath Bridge over the Birmingham Canal. Heavy metal was the form of rock music most associated with Birmingham and, as it began to rebrand itself in the twenty-first century, Birmingham was keen to emphasize this association. The Nonconformist city fathers of the nineteenth century were remarkably open to discussion with other religions but one suspects that they would have drawn the line at celebrating men who claimed to be Satanists. The opening of this bridge in 2019 had a Spinal Tapesque quality. Two members of Black Sabbath turned up while music was played by the tribute band Sabbra Cadabra.

12

Cultural Revolutions

In any real sense of the word I was born in Oxford: I have no more connection with my early life and with Birmingham than I have with Timbuctoo.[1]

Kenneth Tynan

Kenneth Tynan was born in Birmingham in 1927 and lived there until 1945. As a critic and director, he championed the plays of the Angry Young Men in the 1950s and the foundation of the National Theatre in the 1960s. He knew Lawrence Olivier, John Lennon, Harold Pinter, Samuel Beckett, Noël Coward and all of the Hollywood stars whose pictures he had once pasted on his bedroom wall. He was also – perhaps more than any other English person – associated with the sexual revolution of the 1960s. In short, he epitomized everything glamorous in post-war Britain, but he defined his own image against Birmingham, which he described as 'the ugliest city in Europe . . . a cemetery without walls'.

Municipal worthies had always been painfully conscious that there was something incongruous about the mere association of the word 'culture' with Birmingham. Neville Chamberlain had helped found the City of Birmingham Orchestra (it became the City of Birmingham Symphony Orchestra in 1948) but even its moments of relative success seemed to draw attention to the provincialism of the city. Andrzej Panufnik, who conducted the orchestra for two years in the 1950s, recalled his bitter struggles to bring it up to the standards that he associated with the great European orchestras. He claimed the board contained a local businessman who believed that Panufnik came from Walsall (in the Black Country) rather than the capital city of Poland.[2]

When Simon Rattle became conductor in 1980, he remarked tactfully that Birmingham was 'not as ugly as Detroit or Cleveland'.

The post-war years in Britain, the 1960s especially, brought a widening understanding of what the word 'culture' might mean. It was no longer confined to concert halls and opera houses; it became more plebeian. One consequence of this was a rise in a certain kind of provincialism. Plays such as *A Taste of Honey*, novels such as *Room at the Top* and films such as *This Sporting Life* were set in provincial cities. *Coronation Street* (first broadcast in 1960 and still going strong) is set in Manchester. The Beatles came from Liverpool, David Hockney spoke with a Bradford accent. Birmingham, though, was conspicuously absent from this provincial renaissance. Newcastle was brought to the cinema screen with *Get Carter* (1971) – a film so mesmerizingly sinister that even the implausibility of Michael Caine playing a Geordie could not dent its appeal. Birmingham provided the backdrop for *Take Me High* (1973), in which Cliff Richard plays a London banker who goes to live on a canal boat in Gas Street Basin and revives Midlands cuisine with the 'Brumburger'. *Crossroads* (first broadcast in 1964) was meant to be Birmingham's answer to *Coronation Street*. The fact that it was set in a motel on the outskirts of the city captured Birmingham's obsession with a certain kind of Americanized modernity but the programme's cult status derived mainly from the fact that it was so bad.

BIRMINGHAM AS ARTISTIC AND INTELLECTUAL CENTRE: THE 1930S

There was an odd twist to Birmingham's status as the wasteland of post-war British culture because, just before the Second World War, the city had enjoyed a curious artistic and intellectual golden age. This was a period when the Birmingham Repertory Theatre, founded in 1913 by Barry Jackson, the stagestruck son of a local businessman, was a centre of innovation. Its production of *Cymbeline* in 1923 was the first major occasion on which a Shakespeare play was staged in modern dress.[3] It also put on many plays by Bernard Shaw, who had close relations with Jackson – though Shaw remarked rather ungraciously that Birmingham was 'notorious as the rottenest' of the rotten towns on the theatrical circuit.[4] It was also a time when the poets Louis MacNeice, Henry Reed

and W.H. Auden, the classicist E.R. Dodds, the literary critic Walter
Allen, the novelists John Hampson and Leslie Halward, and Reggie
Smith (who later found fame as a radio producer and a character in the
novels of his wife, Olivia Manning) were all in the city and all knew
each other. This produced some extraordinary encounters.

The most notable came in 1936 when John Hampson, a homosexual,
married Therese Giehse, a German Jewish actress who needed a British
passport. The party assembled at Snow Hill station and headed for Solihull, where the ceremony was to take place at the registry office. Walter
Allen was best man but Auden was the impresario of the event and he
funded it lavishly with money from Thomas Mann (Auden had undertaken a similar marriage with Mann's daughter, Erika, in the previous
year). After the event, everyone celebrated at a mock Tudor pub in Solihull High Street, though Auden was forbidden from playing the piano
because the pub was also hosting a funeral and a dead body was
installed in the next room. Allen and MacNeice argued about who
would have literary rights to the event. Allen, from whom this account
is taken, won.[5]

London-based commentators suggested that there was a Birmingham
school of literature. This was going too far. There was a good deal of
chance in the fact that different writers and artists happened to find themselves in Birmingham. Auden spent time in the city because his parents
lived there – his father was professor of public health at the university –
but his closest associates recognized that he had few emotional ties to the
city. MacNeice arrived as a classics lecturer (he would talk later of hearing 'Homer in a Dudley accent' echoing around the 'prison-like lecture
hall'). At first, he regarded the city with active distaste:

> that sprawling ink-blot of nineteenth-century industry. Chimneys to
> the right of us, chimneys to the left of us, someone had blundered. But
> we were not . . . the slaves of the assembly-belts, the fodder of the mills.
> Ours not to reason why and we might as well keep out of it.[6]

For five years, he and his young wife lived 'on an island', venturing out
only to go to the cinema or to drive their Baby Austin into the countryside. Only after his wife left him did he 'discover Birmingham' and
realize that the students he had been teaching were human.

Birmingham University in the inter-war years was a spectacularly
unglamorous institution. The arts faculty was still crammed into

Edmund Street in the city centre. The students lived at home with their parents – commuting on trains and trams at rush hour and leaving their lecture halls empty in the evening. The grand families who dominated Birmingham mostly sent their children to universities away from the city and could be sniffy about the institution on their own doorstep. Less sophisticated local notables still assumed that the university existed primarily to serve the Birmingham economy and occasionally asked why, for example, academics should be paid for time they devoted to their own research. In spite of all this, Birmingham University had advantages. Its student body usually totalled not much more than 1,000. Within this, the lawyers and medics were a caste apart – usually from middle-class backgrounds and assured of employment in the future. Those in the arts faculty amounted to only a few hundred and this created a certain intimacy. Louis MacNeice and Walter Allen knew each other, even though one was a lecturer in classics who had come from outside the city and the other was a local boy who was studying English. Observers sometimes mocked the earnest work ethic of students who were desperate to escape the working-class or petit-bourgeois milieu into which they had been born, but the students took life seriously. Josiah Mason, the industrialist who had founded the institution from which Birmingham University emerged, claimed that he had never read a novel and had sought to prevent the teaching of literature in his college. However, the careers of Allen, Reggie Smith and Henry Reed – their willingness to take risks, embrace new media and follow their own judgement – all hinted at a degree of entrepreneurialism that might have earned Mason's grudging approval.

One professor at Birmingham had special influence. Philip Sargant Florence and his wife, Mary, were Americans but Philip had been educated in England (partly at Rugby at a time when it was still the school of choice for wealthy Birmingham industrialists) and came to Birmingham University in 1929 as professor of commerce. This meant that he was at the Edgbaston campus, away from the arts faculty in the city centre. In practice, he had an unusually wide range of interests – being both an industrial economist and a kind of sociologist. His sister was married to James Strachey – who translated Freud into English and was himself the brother of the subversive biographer Lytton Strachey. Florence was a wealthy man and owned a large house at Highfield in Selly Park. He was one of the few professors who could sustain the retinue of servants that had once come with such houses, though he also had left-wing beliefs that attracted an unusual range of house guests. Walter Allen probably exaggerated when he said that 'Most English left-wing intellectuals and American left-wing intellectuals passed through Highfield between 1930 and 1960', and he certainly exaggerated when he claimed that William Empson had turned up at Highfield after his expulsion from Cambridge, with his toothbrush and pyjamas and stayed for six months.[7] All the same, Highfield and Florence were important. Louis MacNeice and his wife rented a stable in the grounds of Highfield (a building that was itself sufficiently large to require the labours of a full-time servant to maintain it). Maurice Dobb, A.L. Rowse, John Strachey and Naomi Mitchison came to stay. MacNeice was, or came to be, contemptuous of Florence's politics – 'the word proletariat hung in festoons from the ceilings'. MacNeice and the gardener, Robinson, who spoke in 'old Birmingham dialect', fought a rearguard action against the atmosphere of the great house that was marked by a 'gospel tent enthusiasm and quivers of prickly statistics'.[8]

Intellectuals such as MacNeice had been drawn to Birmingham by the same economic forces that sucked workers from the Welsh valleys into Longbridge and Dunlop. Birmingham was a place where one could get a job. The university was much smaller than it would become after 1945 but it expanded between the wars and it appointed new lecturers at a time when academic jobs elsewhere were hard to come by. Some refugees from the political turmoil of eastern and central Europe were also drawn to Birmingham, often because they received some support from the city's Quaker population. Francesca Wilson came to Birmingham in the mid 1920s and lived in a large house in Duchess Road in Edgbaston that she filled with 'deserving foreigners of an interesting kind'. At first the recipients of her hospitality were mainly Russians. Nikolai Bachtin, who had served in the White Guard during the Russian Civil War and then in the French Foreign Legion, came to Birmingham and eventually secured less arduous employment as a reader in linguistics at the university. E.R. Dodds believed that the Russians were 'yeast to the Birmingham dough'.[9] One assumes that it is partly through their efforts that the films of Eisenstein were shown at the film club behind Snow Hill station and partly through them that Dodds was able to meet visitors to the city who included the chess grandmaster Alexander

Alekhine and Alexander Kerensky, who had briefly led the Russian provisional government in 1917.[10]

Another generation of refugees, the most distinguished of whom was the physicist Rudolf Peierls, were driven out of Nazi Germany in the 1930s. The architectural historian Nikolaus Pevsner, who was to help make the Birmingham city engineer into a by-word for philistinism, lodged for a time at Francesca Wilson's house in the 1930s. He failed to secure a permanent academic position at the university but Florence arranged for him to be paid a grant to write a book on industrial design, the kind of topic that appealed to philanthropically minded Birmingham businessmen. Florence was one of those behind a committee formed at Birmingham to help academics fleeing from Germany and Austria.[11] Peierls and Pevsner eventually moved on to greater things but other refugees stayed. In the 1970s, during the refreshment break at the Birmingham Chamber Music Society (founded in 1946), one could still hear Mitteleuropean voices proclaiming: 'the one thing that I will never learn to tolerate in this country is the coffee'.

School teaching attracted some who, in better times, might have held university jobs. Auden, who was a teacher at a prep school in Malvern, wrote a helpful guide to the economics of teaching, in which he explained that only about one in fifty teachers was unemployed and that the salaries paid to teachers ranged from £93 per year, for an 'uncertified woman teacher in an elementary school', to £5,000 per year, for the headmaster of Harrow.[12] The great majority of students reading arts or pure science (rather than engineering or commerce) at Birmingham in the 1930s were destined to become teachers.[13] The fact that even the most socially exclusive schools in the city were day schools may have made teaching in them tolerable for people who wanted to preserve some measure of independence. One of the few Communists in the city to attract the attention of the authorities was a teacher at the Edgbaston Church of England School for Girls,[14] where one of her colleagues was Francesca Wilson.

John Hampson did not have the formal education that would have equipped him to be a teacher (he came from a family of the decayed bourgeoisie and had briefly earned his living by stealing from bookshops). However, a family of prosperous Birmingham business people (the Wilsons) hired him to look after their mentally handicapped son, Ronald. He led an idyllic life in the large house the Wilsons had bought in Dorridge (on the far side of Solihull). They treated him as a second son and when the publication of his novel *Saturday Night at the Greyhound* made him briefly famous they look to have adjusted well to the sudden arrival of houseguests such as E.M. Forster.

Birmingham's relative prosperity created opportunities for intellectuals. The city supported four daily newspapers (two morning ones and two evening ones). When he graduated from Birmingham University in 1932, Walter Allen established himself as a freelance writer – rather in the manner that the skilled workers, from whom he was descended and about whom he wrote, might have taken the plunge and set up their own workshop.[15] He managed to earn about £3 a week and for a time even formed a partnership with a local journalist who provided him with an office and touted for work on his behalf. His first article for the *Birmingham Post* was about Auden. Auden himself wrote for the socialist *Town Crier*.

It was often assumed that the Birmingham intelligentsia were 'proletarian' and this may have lent them a certain glamour in the political atmosphere of the late 1930s. In reality, they came from a range of backgrounds, which impinged on their political outlooks in complicated ways. Reggie Smith seems to have been a Communist. Leslie Halward, the only member of the group who had earned his living through manual work, probably voted Conservative. Those, such as Walter Allen, who had worked hard to escape the working class, were mystified by the sentimentality with which more patrician writers regarded their origins.

The most prominent members of the Birmingham group did not stay in the city. E.R. Dodds would later claim that his twelve years in Birmingham were the happiest in his life but this did not prevent him from leaving to become Regius Professor of Greek at Oxford in 1937. MacNeice found that Birmingham had begun to 'irk him' and left to take a job at Bedford College near London in 1936. Walter Allen also moved to the capital to be closer to influential editors and earned his living for a time as a writer of treatments for MGM – he told his employer that Samuel Beckett's novel *Murphy* was unlikely to prove profitable as a film.

The war further scattered the Birmingham writers. Auden went to the United States; Peter Chamberlain became an army motorcycle instructor; Leslie Halward was an aircraftsman. Henry Reed joined the army and was trained as a Japanese interpreter – though he became most famous as the author of a poem, 'Naming of Parts', about basic training. The life of the industrial working class, which had briefly seemed interesting to London editors in the 1930s, was now eclipsed by other matters. By the time the working class returned to fashion in the 1960s, Birmingham had fallen out of fashion and a new generation of writers – Alan Sillitoe from Nottingham and John Braine from Bradford – had risen to prominence. Charles Madge, the poet and co-founder with Tom Harrisson of the Mass Observation Project, came to Birmingham as professor of sociology in 1950. He might have been expected to revive interest in the city's working class but this never happened. Mass observers had descended on Aston – described by Harrisson as 'a great amorphous colourless, planless chunk of working-class Birmingham' in 1946. They intended their study of the area they labelled 'Blacktown' to echo their pre-war research on Bolton ('Worktown') but that on Aston was never published in book form.[16]

POST-WAR DECLINE

So what went wrong? In some ways, Birmingham became a victim of its own success. What made provincial life seem glamorous to London commentators in the prosperous Britain of the 1950s and 60s was often poverty or a picturesque working-class culture. It helped that successful young people from the provinces – from John Lennon to Shelagh Delaney – were happy to move to London. Birmingham with a booming economy and a working class that had largely been drawn from other places within the last few decades did not fit the central casting notion of what an industrial city ought to look like.

The Royal Shakespeare Company (RSC), based in nearby Stratford-upon-Avon, overshadowed Birmingham theatre and the shadow lengthened as the RSC became better known and expanded its repertoire to include the work of other playwrights. Barry Jackson's period running the Shakespeare Memorial Theatre from 1945 to 1948 helped to undermine the theatre he had established in Birmingham. The opening of a small studio theatre in 1974 (The Other Place) strengthened Stratford's position. Frank Price, who was mayor of Birmingham in 1964–5, sought to encourage theatres precisely because he knew that many people regarded the mere existence of such institutions in Birmingham as odd,[17] but aldermanic good intentions did not always fit easily with post-war fashions. Richard Hoggart claimed that a councillor, who sat on the board of the Repertory Theatre with him in the 1960s, insisted that they should pass up the chance to put on the first performance of a play by Anouilh because it was a 'kitchen sink affair' and 'to me the kitchen sink is a place of honour and dignity and I . . . will not be a party to impugning it'.[18] The highpoint of Birmingham theatre came when John Inman played the Dame in *Mother Goose* at the Alexandra; the highpoint of Stratford theatre came when Ben Kingsley played the lead in Bertolt Brecht's *Baal* at The Other Place.

Birmingham University expanded after 1945. It had 2,000 undergraduates that year, 4,000 in 1950 and 7,000 by 1970. But size did not bring prestige. The university attracted distinguished teachers and able students but, having been overshadowed by the 'ancient' universities in the pre-war period, it was overshadowed by newer creations in the 1960s – needless to say Kenneth Tynan's daughter went to the supremely fashionable new university at Sussex. Even the words that were applied to Birmingham University – 'redbrick' and 'civic' – appeared to associate it with a staid, Victorian culture. Of his own arrival at Birmingham in the 1920s, E.R. Dodds had written: 'To the traveller going north after the ancient splendours of Warwick and the eighteenth-century elegance of Leamington, the place appears the beginning of a new and sinister world, the frontier station of the land of Mordor.'

From 1965, academic travellers heading north had no need to venture into this sinister world because the University of Warwick was founded conveniently close to Leamington and was convenient too for those academics who wished to get to London fast. At least for a time, Warwick attracted some of the most famous academics in the country. Germaine Greer taught in the English department. The historian E.P. Thompson had a brief but notable career as founder of the Centre for the Study of Social History before politics brought him into conflict with the university authorities – his less flamboyant wife, Dorothy, taught at the University of Birmingham for many years.

Most importantly, Birmingham University seemed ever more removed from the city in which it was located. The transfer of all faculties to Edgbaston in the 1960s severed its links with the city centre. It was possible for students to spend three years among the elegant Italianate buildings and green spaces of their campus without having much sense that their life was different from that of their contemporaries at any other good university in the country. The nature of student intake changed. Before 1939, the university had preserved the traditions originally associated with Mason College in the nineteenth century, which meant in particular a heavy emphasis on practical subjects. Birmingham retained a strong scientific tradition but vocational degrees – in brewing or mining – became less common. The Arts Faculty, which contained 1,500 students by the late 1960s, was no longer the intimate little institution that it had been in the 1930s. The only survival of Birmingham's vocational traditions lay in the fact that the radicals of 1968 and research students ostensibly studying semiology in *Jackie* magazine were still described as students of 'Commerce' because that was the label applied to much of the social sciences. Practical subjects were now associated more with the Aston College of Science and Technology, which acquired the formal status of a university in 1966. Birmingham Polytechnic, founded in 1974, was intended to fulfil a similar function, though the students – understandably exasperated when William Kenrick, the first chairman of the new institution, said they were NCOs rather than members of the educational officer class – sometimes took rather more interest in political demonstrations than in work placements.

Birmingham became a national university – drawing its students from across the country rather than from its immediate environs. In the late 1940s, over half of those in all faculties had come from the West Midlands; by the late 1960s, this number stood at less than 20 per cent for all faculties and less than 10 per cent for some. Only one in ten students now lived at home. These changes broke the links with Birmingham still further. Most students came from elsewhere, and went elsewhere after graduation. Some – such as the theatre director Trevor Nunn – were at least as influential as Walter Allen or Reggie Smith had been in the 1930s but they almost never exercised that influence in Birmingham.

One department illustrated the new status of Birmingham University with particular force. The Centre for Contemporary Cultural Studies (CCCS) was for a time the height of intellectual fashion. It was founded in 1964 by Richard Hoggart and was associated from the beginning with the cultural changes of the 1960s. Indeed, it had roots in the inaugural event of the British 1960s since Hoggart derived part of his reputation, and some of the funds that he used to found the centre, from his role as a witness for Penguin Books in the *Lady Chatterley's Lover* trial of 1960. Hoggart was also associated with the study of working-class culture, but his own work reinforced the post-war sense that working-class culture meant northern culture. His *The Uses of Literacy* (1957) had involved much autobiographical reflection on his own upbringing in Leeds – one of his children believed that he was the model for Ken Barlow, the upwardly mobile northern grammar school boy in *Coronation Street*.[19]

Hoggart's presence in Birmingham was relatively limited. He did not move to the city until two years after his appointment and, as the CCCS became riven by political disputes, he seems to have been relieved to take a job with UNESCO and escape to the comparative tranquillity of Paris in 1968. More influential than Hoggart was his deputy, who succeeded him as acting director: Stuart Hall. Hall, from a middle-class Jamaican background, had come to Britain as a postgraduate student and fallen in with the 'New Left'. Like Hoggart, he wanted to expand the scope of university study to include a wider range of kinds of culture – though he had a more theoretical turn of mind than Hoggart and, as far as radical students were concerned, a greater charismatic appeal. Under him, the CCCS produced influential studies of race, policing and the various tribes into which young people were divided by fashion and musical taste in the 1960s. The influence of the centre spilled over into many corners of British public life. Its alumni found berths in university departments in many different disciplines, but they could also be seen writing for the *New Musical Express* or providing advice to left-wing local authorities.

Though open to the world, the CCCS sometimes seemed closed to Birmingham. Most of its members came from outside the city – often, in fact, from the new universities that looked so much more glamorous than the red brick ones. There were two particular oddities about the relations between the CCCS and the wider city. First, scholars attached to the centre pioneered the study of popular culture but often seemed uncomfortable with the culture on the streets around them. A feminist from the centre met the members of the band Slade at a screening of a film they had made. She asked the band's singer, Noddy Holder, whether their songs might be construed as sexist. That, explained Holder patiently, was the point.[20] Dick Hebdige wrote about youth groups but his work was almost entirely focused on London – on mods, the Kray twins and the criminal subcultures of Fulham – though he was well informed about rock music and reggae in Birmingham because of his friendship with the local disc jockey Mike Horseman.

Some members of the CCCS had almost no relation to the city beyond the campus. Paul Willis, who had grown up in Wolverhampton and wrote a celebrated book on working-class school leavers in Smethwick, was recognized as an exception and as the man who brought a 'breath of the city' into the CCCS – though Willis's study of 'lads' from a Smethwick secondary modern sometimes seemed to underline the gulf between the white working class in Birmingham and the world of higher education. Many of the most self-confident scholars at the centre were concerned with abstruse questions of theory. There was a revealing gender divide. Those at the centre who did empirical work on Birmingham were often women – in a couple of cases because they wanted to counter what they took to be the sexism of Willis's focus on working-class young men – and also tended to be those who were least likely, at least in the short term, to attain fame in the wider academic world. A few veterans of the centre came to a rueful recognition that there was something incongruous about the relation between the high theory they studied and the quotidian reality of their surroundings – one recalled reading Sartre's *Questions of Method* as he travelled on the number 11 bus to teach a general arts course to a class of bored, would-be plumbers at a technical college.[21]

Not surprisingly, the kind of political left fostered at the Centre for Contemporary Cultural Studies was far removed from the right wing of the Labour Party that exercised such power in the city. Stuart Hall remembered how Brian Walden had told him at Oxford that the Labour Party had no place for people such as himself, but he did not mention, perhaps did not even know, that Walden was Labour MP for Ladywood at the time when Hall was at the university.[22] However, the kind of left that flourished in the CCCS, particularly around 1968, seemed to distance intellectuals from even the most left-wing elements in the city. Frank Henderson, a Trotskyite shop steward at the Austin works was to write:

As far as I can recall May 68 didn't create much of a ripple at Longbridge. The way I recall it now, we were much more concerned with Barbara Castle at the Ministry of Labour than things as far away from Longbridge as Paris – even as far away from Longbridge as Birmingham University.[23]

In fact, Longbridge is a few miles down the Bristol Road from the university and Henderson was eventually to develop good contacts with the student members of the International Marxist Group – though not, as far as one can tell, with any of those involved in cultural studies. Fortunately, Dick Etheridge – the Communist convenor at Longbridge and a man whose views on social and cultural matters would have made Ernest Bevin look like Timothy Leary – had no contact with Birmingham University. His son graduated from Aston.

The post-war division between university and city in Birmingham owed something to the way the city changed as well as the way the university did. Full employment created a working class that was confident and self-sufficient. Those born in Birmingham in the 1930s or 40s could leave school at fifteen or sixteen and have a job within days. Young men expected to be in full-time employment until they reached retirement age. The world of young Birmingham was one of early marriage, hire purchase and, by the 1970s, package holidays in Spain. A night out meant putting on a tie and going to dance or drink – sometimes to do so defiantly at those bars and hotels that sought to keep their prices at a level that workers would not be able to afford. All this was a world away from the style of students that Birmingham people sometimes labelled 'hairy coconuts', and a sports journalist was not being entirely flippant when he suggested that the protests by Aston Villa fans after their team's defeat by Preston North End in November 1968 were Birmingham's answer to the barricades in Paris a few months earlier.[24]

The culture of the working-class young in Birmingham was reflected in its early rock and roll scene. Far from being agents of dangerous rebellion, the Birmingham bands of the 1950s were clean-cut young men. Some musicians had learned their trade in regimental bands during National Service and the names of the groups they formed – The Nig Nogs, the Red Caps – were often nods to military patois.[25] Very few men regarded music as an alternative to full-time work. Micky Bakewell left school in South Yardley in 1958 and became an apprentice at the Rover factory in Solihull. He played rock and roll at the weekends, first with the Grasshoppers and then with the cooler Modernaires, and trained with the youth team at Birmingham City on Tuesday and Thursday evenings, but he does not seem to have considered the possibility that either music or football would provide an escape from the factory and he still handed over his wages to his mother. Paul Hewitt was offered the chance to go on tour in Germany with his band – the Rockin' Berries – but 'I was at the Austin. I had a good job and I was about to get married. It had to be bye-bye Berries.' Jimmy Powell did go with the Berries to Germany – the fact that he left a job as a lathe operator at Coley Brothers in King's Norton, and pay of £7 a week, was considered sufficiently daring to be reported in the local papers.

By the early 1960s, there was a lively rock scene in Birmingham with about 500 bands in the city, but Birmingham never became a recognized centre of rock music in the same way as Liverpool in the 1960s or Manchester in the 1980s. Indeed, those who grew up in Birmingham often treated music as something that came from outside the town. Frank Skinner remembered seeing the Stones at the Odeon in September 1973; John Taylor remembered seeing Blondie at Barbarella's in February 1978. In part this was because Birmingham lacked those middle-class Svengalis who managed and manipulated bands elsewhere – such as Brian Epstein, who managed the Beatles; Kit Lambert, who managed the Who; or Andrew Loog Oldham, who managed the Rolling Stones. Generally speaking, Birmingham bands were controlled by wealthy but middle-aged and culturally conservative figures who owned the clubs in which they performed. Eddie Fewtrell was the most important of these and his tastes can be discerned from the fact that Bernard Manning wrote the introduction to his autobiography.[26]

At a time when rock stars in London could expect to be treated like the grandest of eighteenth-century dukes, Birmingham bands were just another form of light entertainment – some teetered on the painful frontier between music and comedy. Bev Bevan of the Move recalled:

> London was and still is the place to be seen. You have to go there to be seen and when you're playing at the big London clubs, you literally would see Mick Jagger, Pete Townshend, Paul McCartney, Eric Clapton et cetera in the audience, you are not going to get that in Birmingham.

Those Birmingham bands that turned professional could be hard-headed and unromantic. Steve Gibbons made a straight financial calculation about whether to give up his apprenticeship to join the Dominettes in 1959 – he reckoned that he could get as much for two or three concerts as from his day job. Bev Bevan recalled that touring Germany with Carl Wayne and the Vikings paid £30 per week as compared to £9 that he made working in a furniture shop. The band that Steve

Gibbons eventually formed under his own name often provided backing music for strippers in the early part of their career. One of its members, Bob Lamb, invested his earnings in building a studio in his Kings Heath flat.[27]

The Beatles made their first national television appearance on the show *Thank Your Lucky Stars*, which was produced in Birmingham and was famous because of the Black Country-accented catchphrase of one of its participants, Janice Nicholls, 'I'll give it foive'. The fame of the Beatles meant that almost any other provincial group tended to be seen as their potential imitators. This had particularly awkward consequences for the Plazents, a band who derived their name from the fact that they had a regular gig at the Plaza Ballroom on Old Hill. They were signed by Decca Records, which had missed out on the Beatles, but urged to change their name to the Brumbeats (in the hope that this might evoke association with Merseybeat) and then to produce an album of Beatles cover songs under the name 'The Mersey Boys'.

Even when the Birmingham bands of the 1960s and 70s became famous, there was always a faint sense that they were uncool. The Move's 'Flowers in the Rain' became the first song ever played on Radio 1 (the new national pop music radio station) in 1967, but it was hard to avoid the suspicion that this was precisely because the Move's pseudo-hippy style felt less threatening than the psychedelic experiments in which the Beatles and the Stones were indulging at that time. The Electric Light Orchestra – formed by the veterans of various Birmingham bands – sold vast numbers of records without ever taking themselves too seriously or giving the impression that they expected anyone else to do so.

The exception that proved the rule about Birmingham music was heavy metal. The origins of Led Zeppelin can be traced to the moment when the guitarist Jimmy Page first saw the singer Robert Plant perform at Birmingham teacher training college. Black Sabbath, formed in 1968, and Judas Priest, formed in 1969, also began in Birmingham. Some suggested that such music was literally rooted in the metal-bashing industries of Birmingham and the Black Country. Black Sabbath made much of their hard-scrabble youth in Aston. Ozzy Osbourne later said: 'You gotta remember, the time, 1968, was still that flower power. To us that was bullshit, living in the dreary, dismal, polluted town of Birmingham.' Perhaps, though, it would be fairer to say that the heavy metal bands of Birmingham were driven more by hostility to a certain kind of

middle-class values, particularly those of students, than by an identification with working-class ones. The only concrete link between the factory
floor and their playing style sprang from the fact that Tony Iommi, the
guitarist with Black Sabbath, had lost parts of his fingers in an industrial
accident.[28] For all the references to Birmingham industry, the big heavy
metal bands looked equally at home in California, which is where they
spent much of their time after their commercial success.

When she became a schoolteacher in the 1980s, Grace Holte, who
had grown up in a two-bedroom council house with no hot water, told
her pupils: 'I was a child in the sixties; I wasn't a child of the sixties.'
One suspects that many working-class Birmingham residents would
have said something similar. The shockwaves of political and social
upheaval that shook London were only mild tremors by the time they
reached Birmingham. There were odd ways in which the city's working class caught glimpses of a new world. Grace's family had the 'same
names passed from generation to generation' – Lillian, Emily, Ada, Florence, Nancy and Annie. Her parents had been daring in christening their
daughter after Grace Kelly, but suddenly her street was full of children
with exotic names – Michelle, Ingrid, Yvonne, Astrid and Tania. Michelle
was particularly exotic because her mother was not married to the
father, who was 'coloured'.[29]

One might argue that Birmingham exemplified dimensions of the
1960s and 70s that are sometimes neglected. The first relates to race. If
black people appear at all in standard accounts of British popular culture of the 1960s, they tend to be outsiders from the United States – hence
the attention given to Malcolm X's brief visit to the Oxford Union and
the streets of Smethwick or the glamour that surrounded Jimi Hendrix.
But actually white British culture of the period was often rooted in
black influences. West Indians interviewed in Birmingham in 1964 were
amused by this. Sylvester of West Bromwich attributed the 'general
vitality' of British culture in the 1960s to an influx from overseas: 'Take
for instance today the Beatles are top, there's so much West Indian beats
and music in those people. When I was a child the English music was a
kind of chamber music.'[30]

The relation between black music and the white working class in Birmingham was complicated. Black and white musicians in the city worked
together. In late 1963, Ian Campbell, a folk singer and father of the
brothers who would later be at the core of the white reggae band UB40,

sought to help the Stewart family, originally from Jamaica, to obtain a record contract.[31] However, it sometimes seemed that the overt sexuality of some black-influenced music would be acceptable only if it was performed with no black people present. Some West Indians recalled that dance halls were even more prone to exclude them when rock and roll became the music that was most frequently played in them. By the early 1970s, much of the music played in Birmingham clubs was black, but black music was not quite the same as music listened to by black people. Well into the 1970s, some clubs limited the number of black patrons – sometimes using black bouncers to enforce the exclusion. Jill danced at Rebecca's on John Bright Street, one of the many places owned by Eddie Fewtrell and named after one of his daughters. Jill recalled that the music played on the top floor was mainly Motown and that on the floor below was mainly disco. Reggae was played in the basement. This was where most 'coloured' patrons of the club were to be found – it was also known as the 'sin bin' and was where white couples went when they wanted to dance in an overtly sexual way.[32]

Even when they were ferociously racist, white working-class young men in Birmingham listened to soul and reggae – often because, even more than heavy metal, it was associated with a rebellion against the music that appealed to middle-class teenagers. The lads at Hammertown school told Paul Willis that the 'hard knocks' liked reggae and soul which they seemed to distinguish from the music enjoyed by 'weirdos, freaks, hippy types'.[33] Eventually some white Birmingham bands began to play music that was intended to sound black. The most notable of these was Dexys Midnight Runners, who combined an ostentatiously working-class look – they wore donkey jackets on stage – with a sound that was meant to evoke soul music. Their first hit – 'Geno' – was named in honour of the black soul singer Geno Washington.

The second dimension of the 1960s that was visible in Birmingham related to sex. The sexual revolution of the 1960s was often associated with the film and theatre of London. Kenneth Tynan – who claimed to have lost his virginity in a shop doorway in the Bristol Road in 1944 and who had once celebrated masturbation in a debate at King Edward's School on whether the young knew how to entertain themselves – was the first man to say 'fuck' on British television and produced the nude musical *Oh! Calcutta!* Back in Birmingham, though, shifts in sexual morality could seem less benign.

Male homosexuality in Birmingham attracted most attention during the 1950s – the period described by Patrick Higgins as the 'heterosexual dictatorship'. In July 1954, police arrested Kenneth Walton, a twenty-seven-year-old hairdresser who had unwisely kept a scorebook of his sexual conquests – 213 of them – from the previous three years. Twenty-one of the men were tracked down and prosecuted as part of 'a vicious clique who have infested the city for many years'.[34] The prosecution prepared a special glossary of homosexual argot to guide the jury through the case. A public toilet under New Street station – known, on account of its proximity to a ballet school of that name, as the 'Silver Slipper' – provided, in the view of the police, a 'national meeting point' for gay men. One officer remembered arresting a man who became agitated. It turned out that his anxiety did not spring from fear of prosecution or exposure but from the fact that he was a train driver who had hoped to spend a few diverting moments before taking a train out of Snow Hill station.[35]

Strangely, the legalization of homosexual relations between adult men in 1967 made homosexuality in Birmingham less visible for a time. Police raids were less likely to 'expose' men but homosexuals themselves remained discreet. Some looked wistfully to the more open, and sometimes politicized, gay scene in London. The gulf between the two cities was evident until the 1980s. Steven Bedser, born in 1965, came to Birmingham University from St Albans and considered that going to the Jester pub in Holloway Circus constituted a kind of coming out. Bedser stayed in the city and eventually became a Labour councillor for the working-class Longbridge ward, where to his surprise no one cared about his sexuality. All the same, he recalled being drawn to London in his youth. He would go to the Farringdon Gay Centre 'just to sit drinking tea and eating vegetarian quiche'.[36] During the AIDS epidemic, doctors were struck at first by the fact that rates of infection in Birmingham seemed so low. Eventually they realized that gay men travelled to London to be tested.[37]

Public discussion of sexual morality in Birmingham often seemed 'Victorian' in the most brutal sense of the word. Women who had children outside marriage were usually poor. One social worker commented that such women took full-time jobs more often than the divorced or widowed and suggested that this was partly because they felt 'undeserving'.[38] Janet Mendelsohn, who practised a kind of photographic ethnography while she was attached to the Centre for Contemporary

Cultural Studies in 1967 and 1968, must sometimes have felt that she was travelling through time as well as space when she walked around parts of central Birmingham. She interviewed and took photographs of prostitutes working in the Varna Road in Balsall Heath (see chapter 11). Her interviews captured a culture of violence, exploitation and squalor that was almost unrecognizably removed from the freedom celebrated by people such as Kenneth Tynan. Her most striking photograph showed a bare mattress on an old bed next to a broken window that looks out on the street. It was entitled 'The Bed where Kathleen turns tricks'.

The increasingly self-conscious radicalism – sexual, cultural and political – of the 1970s sometimes involved a marginalization of Birmingham. Stuart Hall left Birmingham University in 1979 and the Centre for Contemporary Cultural Studies never quite recovered from his departure. London of the 1970s – a world of squats and demos – seemed to be the centre of British radicalism. The *London Review of Books*, founded during a strike of *The Times Literary Supplement* in 1979, reinforced the sense that cultural life in Britain meant the cultural life in Camden. A succession of national conferences on women's liberation had been organized in provincial cities since 1970. It seemed uncomfortably appropriate that the last, and most acrimonious, of the series should take place in Birmingham in 1978. The local women who organized the event, in a Ladywood school, had bitter memories of feeling patronized or treated with contempt by those from more fashionable parts of the country. One recalled that she had spent her time photocopying, cooking brown rice and unblocking toilets.[39] Another said: 'there was a feeling that women in Birmingham had put a vast amount of effort into the organizing and then been shat upon'.[40]

Curiously, though, the late 1970s and the 1980s were a time of cultural rebirth in Birmingham, or perhaps a moment when a genuinely popular culture flourished. The middle-class radicalism associated with the university was getting weaker and after 1975 few academics at the university had energy for much beyond the defence of their departmental budgets. But economic downturn broke the security that had kept working-class young people in Birmingham quiet for much of the post-war period. The bands of the 1980s emerged from a world that had much to do with unemployment. Indeed, for some young people in the city, economic recession had its compensations. In the short term, it meant escape from the production line, and for a lucky few it provided

371

the springboard for new careers. The Campbell brothers from UB40 founded the Balsall Heath Claimants' Union (an association for those claiming unemployment benefit) but admitted, in parody of the Labour party slogan, that their main concern was with the 'right not to work'.

Even Duran Duran – pop stars by appointment to the Princess of Wales – had roots in the dole queue. Unemployment created a strange demi-monde in Birmingham as people who lived on supplementary benefit and black economy jobs emerged at night. Martin Degville (later to enjoy brief fame with Sigue Sigue Sputnik) shared a Walsall squat with Boy George – who would go on to achieve a more lasting reputation with Culture Club but who was at that time scraping a living by selling second-hand clothes. Barbarella's – the Birmingham nightclub most associated with punk rock – closed in 1979. Now there were two fashionable clubs. One was Holy City Zoo, owned by Andy Gray, who had once played for Aston Villa. It was here that Boy George won the prize for the weirdest person in Birmingham. The most important club, though, was the Rum Runner on Broad Street. This was a place of seedy romance – it had served as the set for some scenes in *Gangsters*, an unexpectedly edgy series that had been made in the Pebble Mill studios during the 1970s. It attracted a peculiar mixture of local celebrities – including Frank Worthington, who had played for Leicester City and seemed glamorous because he lived in the Holiday Inn – with those who had removed themselves, or been removed, from respectable society. The latter included 'Bald Bev' from Bloxwich and Patrick Black – also known as 'Lizzy Black' and 'Patsy Recline'.

Duran Duran became the house band at the Rum Runner. It brought together men from outside the city – Simon Le Bon and Andy Taylor, with John Taylor, a Birmingham art school boy, and Roger Taylor, who had worked his way up through a succession of obscure punk bands (Poison Toad, Scent Organ) while holding down a day job on the track at Rover in Solihull. Unlike his predecessors in the 1960s, he did not hesitate when offered the chance to escape the factory. Duran Duran had close links to Birmingham bands playing very different kinds of music. Steve Gibbons was, as Andy Taylor recalled, 'a shadowy, God-father figure' of the Birmingham music scene, whose appeal to younger people was enhanced by the fact that his wife, Patti Bell, ran a fashion business with the designer Jane Kahn. One of Duran Duran's earliest concerts, at the Holy City Zoo and organized by the disc jockey Mike

Horseman, saw them on the same bill as Dexys Midnight Runners, UB40 and the Au Pairs. However, increasingly Duran Duran were seen as representative of 'New Romanticism', which meant flamboyant fancy dress, make-up and ambiguous sexuality. Horseman was excited by this new movement, which he regarded as 'the last sub-culture . . . instigated by people without a marketing strategy' – though Dick Hebdige, showing the disdain for all things Birmingham that usually marked the Centre for Contemporary Cultural Studies, assured him that it was 'a load of middle-class wank'. [41]

Duran Duran became famous around the world. Less famous, but perhaps more typical of the rebellion that was rooted in unemployment, were some of the most uncompromising examples of British punk rock – so uncompromising that a few bands never showed much interest in performing numbers that anyone would listen to, let alone making records that anyone would buy. All the same, the disc jockey John Peel and his producer John Walters recalled a turning point in both their lives that came around 1977 when, bored to tears by guitar solos and concept albums, they turned up to hear the Prefects playing in support of the Clash. The unknown band introduced themselves as coming from Birmingham and then sang a song entitled 'I've got VD'. It lasted eight seconds.

Photograph of the first Mini Metros rolling off a production line at the Longbridge
Works in 1980. The Metro was the last hurrah of the Birmingham motor industry.
It was marketed with much nationalistic reference to British interests – though,
in truth, the government would have sold British Leyland to a foreign buyer if
they had been able to do so. In what seemed like a throwback to the policies of
Herbert Austin in the inter-war period, the company sought to prevent the most
militant trade unionists from working in the part of the plant that produced the
Metro.

13
Signing Off

I want to talk about the state of industry and the state of Britain, which so largely depends upon it, and where better than Birmingham to do that.

Margaret Thatcher, speech in Birmingham
Town Hall, 19 April 1979[1]

I should imagine that at the last bloody election a lot of the Austin people voted Tory.

Dick Etheridge, Communist and former convenor at the
Longbridge car factory (the Austin), in 1981[2]

In Birmingham, the Thatcher government of 1979 felt like a meteorite strike; it was as if a fast-moving object from a distant galaxy had hit the town. Birmingham did not have the worst unemployment in Britain in the early 1980s but it did see the sharpest increase in unemployment in the country. In conspicuous contrast to the 1930s, the city's unemployment was now higher than that in many of its neighbours in the Black Country.[3] The Birmingham band UB40's first album – *Signing Off* – was released in 1980; the name of both the record and the band alluded to the paperwork of dole money. Those around Thatcher felt that Birmingham was not their kind of town. When she addressed the city's chamber of commerce in 1980, her civil servants could barely disguise their disdain: 'attitudes in West Midlands industry seem very parochial; it may not go down well to quote the success of a non-Midlands automotive company'.[4] It was not just trade unionists and the Labour Party in Birmingham who felt bruised by the new government's attitudes. Local Conservatives shared the feeling and it seemed horribly appropriate that one of the last members of the great Birmingham families to be active in national politics – Jocelyn Cadbury, who had been elected as Conservative MP for Northfield in 1979 – shot himself in 1982.

The high drama of the early 1980s sometimes occludes the slower and more subtle changes that had happened in Birmingham during the previous decade. There was not an instant transition from post-war prosperity to Thatcher's recession. Indeed, the final monuments to Herbert Manzoni's vision of Birmingham as a modernist city – the central reference library, Spaghetti Junction, the inner ring road and the Sentinel towers – were all completed in the early 1970s, and the deathwatch beetles of economic slowdown were eating at their foundations before they were topped out. The most obvious problem for the Birmingham economy was the sharp decline in its car industry. In 1971, motor vehicle manufacture accounted for 150,000 jobs in the West Midlands County (most of them in Birmingham); ten years later the figure was just over 92,000, and the decline in the motor industry brought an almost equally sharp decline in the associated metal and engineering industries.[5] Until around 1978, this decline in manufacturing was partly masked by an increase in service employment but that increase stopped in the early 1980s, when it sometimes looked as if dole offices were the only employers taking on white-collar workers and it was said that the stationery firm of Kenrick and Jefferson was the only thriving business in West Bromwich because it had the contract to print UB40 forms.[6]

Though Thatcherism seemed alien and frightening to many in Birmingham it had some of its origins in the city. This was true in a literal sense because Stuart Hall wrote the first systematic analysis of Thatcherism – published in *Marxism Today* in January 1979 – while he was still at Birmingham's Centre for Contemporary Cultural Studies. It was also true in more complicated ways. Lots of people in Birmingham voted Conservative in 1979 – the largest Tory majority in the country was recorded in one of the city's constituencies. Many of these voters, like their counterparts in other places, probably did not appreciate how dramatically the economy would change under Thatcher (or perhaps how little government policies on race or crime would).

There were also two important respects in which Thatcherism defined itself in response to events in Birmingham. In 1972, the National Union of Mineworkers (NUM) struck for higher pay. There were no miners in Birmingham, but there was a large coke depot maintained by the West

Midlands Gas Board at Saltley. Pickets from the NUM sought to prevent traffic from moving in or out of the depot and succeeded partly
because of help from Birmingham workers. Men (they almost all were
men) from engineering factories and from building sites (there was also
a building strike in 1972) joined the miners. Communists – notably
Frank Watters who had arrived in the city as a full-time organizer in
1968 after having previously worked in the Yorkshire coal field – helped
organize the picket.[7] Though there were probably only around 800
Communists in Birmingham, they were energetic and efficient and willing to work with non-Communists.

The 'Battle of Saltley Gate' acquired an inflated place in the mythologies of both Right and Left. Birmingham's Banner Theatre devised a play
about this working-class victory, which was still occasionally performed
after the Tories had broken the NUM and closed the last coal mine.
Arthur Scargill – still a minor local official of the NUM – had been the
leader of the pickets at Saltley Gate and he remembered his role there in
emotional terms. He told the *New Left Review* in 1975: 'We were sta-
tioned in houses all over Birmingham. The people of Birmingham were
absolutely fantastic. The solidarity of the working class was never more
evident. On that Thursday it produced the greatest day of my life.'[8]

Equally, the 1972 strike (often conflated with the one of 1973–4
which brought the Heath government down) came to acquire great significance in the minds of Conservatives. Saltley Gate was often used by
Thatcher herself and her supporters to illustrate the dangers that might
be posed by unrestricted picketing. The two mythologies fed off each
other and copies of Scargill's interview with the *New Left Review* were
passed around the Tory front bench.

For all its resonance, the confrontation at Saltley Gate was brief. It is
hard to know how much solidarity there was between Birmingham
engineering workers and the miners – the former were still more highly
paid than the latter and the culture of a big industrial city was very different from that of the mining areas.

BRITISH LEYLAND

The most important focus of Labour dispute in Birmingham in the
1970s was not Saltley but Longbridge. Only one or two pickets from

Longbridge went to Saltley, which was on the other side of town, though the agitation around Saltley provided one of the many occasions when some production at Longbridge stopped.[9] The Longbridge works was the site that had been established by Herbert Austin at the beginning of the century. A series of mergers had brought Austin into ever larger conglomerations that finished with the formation of British Leyland in 1968, after a fusion of the British Motor Corporation and the Leyland Motor Corporation. The government sponsored this new entity – making an informal promise that its creation would not be impeded by the Monopolies and Mergers Commission and lending the company £25 million. The new group took the name of the truck maker based in Leyland, Lancashire. However, the bulk of the new company's production took place in Birmingham and Oxford, and the largest plant of all was that at Longbridge.

In the mid 1970s, Leyland was, by all realistic measures, bust. Raymond Carter was Labour MP for Northfield from 1970 to 1979. He was sponsored by the Trade and General Workers' Union and knew that the Leyland plant was 'a dominant interest' in his constituency. But he later admitted: 'In my view it should have been allowed to go bankrupt.' He thought that in private some shop stewards shared his opinion that the company was 'in possibly terminal decline'.[10] It survived because the Labour government had acquired a majority share of the company and subsequently provided it with state subsidy. In truth, the car factories, and perhaps the whole Birmingham economy, were victims of decisions that had been taken years before. The motor industry had once looked to be at the sharp edge of modernity and economic growth. Precisely because the Birmingham economy had seemed so prosperous, the government had refused to allow new industries to establish themselves there in the 1960s and this had frozen the city's economy into the structures of the 1950s. British car manufacture suffered from the fact that it had been around so long. Machinery was old. The Germans and Japanese – starting from scratch or building whole new factories after existing ones had been all but destroyed during the war – produced better and/or cheaper cars.

As Conservatives began to rethink their economic assumptions after their electoral defeat of 1974, they seized on Leyland as an example of everything that was wrong with the country. For a start, it was state-owned – it was helpful for the purposes of Thatcherite rhetoric that the company had been part-nationalized by the current Labour government. It presented an easier target for attack than those industries – rail, coal, steel – that had operated as nationalized enterprises under Tory government or those, such as Rolls-Royce, that had been bought by the state during the Heath government. Leyland also seemed to incarnate other Thatcherite preoccupations: economic decline, trade union power and frequent strikes.

It was not obvious that these different things were associated. Neither denationalization nor the weakening of union power restored Leyland's fortunes. It was widely 'known' that workers at Leyland were lazy and truculent – the topic featured in the routines of television comedians as frequently as mothers-in-law. The workers themselves, however, argued that interruption of production had more to do with mechanical breakdown than laziness and that it was often only their own skill and experience that kept antiquated machinery running.

The relation between unions and strikes at Longbridge was more complicated than it seemed. Unions became stronger during the Second World War and then again after 1961, when Leonard Lord stepped down as head of the company. Almost all employees were members of trade unions by the early 1960s. One might argue that Dick Etheridge, at Longbridge, was the most powerful Communist in post-war Britain. However, Etheridge was pragmatic in most of his day-to-day dealings with management and with those trade unionists, the great majority, who were not Communists (see chapter 9). He devoted more energy to heading off strikes than to promoting them.

The problem for Leyland management was not the trade unions but the extraordinary growth of unofficial strikes – often brief ones that involved small numbers of workers. Sometimes there could be several different walkouts on a single day. The diary of Ron Savage, personnel director at Longbridge, captures the atmosphere of the factory. On 28 February 1972, he regarded it as worthy of note that 'this is the first day that has been free from strikes for a considerable time' – though there was a lot of absence and the factory did not achieve its programme. The following day he wrote, with apparently mounting excitement: 'We have had no strikes at all this week [it was Tuesday] and production seems to be building up.' By Thursday of the same week, though, the night shift of East Works Store had walked out.[11]

Neither unions nor management found it easy to say why there were so many strikes at Longbridge. The answer may partly have been political. Car factories in continental Europe were often strongholds of the Communist Party and for this reason were also often targets for infiltration by Trotskyite and Maoist militants. Infiltration of this kind was rarer in Britain but Longbridge, one of the largest industrial plants in the country, exercised a peculiar fascination for members of radical groupuscules. Trade unionists recalled that the factory gates served as a 'magnet for pamphlets' and attracted even Jehovah's Witnesses.[12] Those groups that managed to get a foothold in the factory were often tiny – the Posadists (influenced by the ideas of the Argentine J. Posadas) were known by some as the 'flying saucer trots' because their leader was interested in the possibility of extra-terrestrial life.

But small groups of militants could hardly have been the cause of so much disruption. The key to labour relations at Longbridge was that its workers were so distant from the Marxist image of the proletariat. They were far from being a unified group who struck *en masse*; instead their action usually involved small strikes that were often accompanied by animosity between different groups of workers. Strikes which impeded production on one part of the line could have widespread effects. Sometimes strikes fed each other. Workers were dissatisfied because they had been laid off or because of a strike elsewhere in the plant or because they resented the advantages that some other group of workers had obtained. It was particularly difficult to reconcile the interests of day- and night-shift workers because their representatives did not meet in the ordinary course of events. It may also have been significant (though neither managers nor unions commented on this) that night shifts (like most unappealing forms of work) were disproportionately taken by non-white workers. Everything was complicated by the fact that there were multiple unions in the factory and multiple shops, each with its own steward. The stewards themselves were often in an awkward position – balancing loyalties to their union against their loyalties to the men in their shop. A steward might, for example, vote against a strike – i.e. an official strike – because his own shop opposed it, but then feel obliged to strike because the union as a whole had voted in favour, even though his own immediate colleagues remained at work. Most shop stewards spent much time trying to settle disputes and this was even more true of the convenor. In the early 1970s, it was common for Savage's daily diary to begin – sometimes for several days in a row – with the words: 'spoke to Etheridge first thing'.

At times the personnel manager and the union convenor seemed more like colleagues than antagonists. Savage would ask Etheridge to intervene in some part of the factory where there had been a dispute. When the whole factory went on strike on 1 May 1973 in protest at the Heath government's Industrial Relations Act, Etheridge and Savage spent a morning together producing passes for those workers who would be allowed through the picket lines to provide safety cover.

Etheridge retired in January 1975. The senior managers, including Lord Stokes, the chairman of British Leyland, attended his farewell dinner. There were speeches and back-slapping. Etheridge was given a portrait of himself; Etheridge's wife presented Lady Stokes with one of her 'famous Christmas puddings'.

Etheridge's departure came soon after other changes at Leyland. The Ryder Report in April 1975 had recommended closer integration of the various car factories within the group. It was also suggested that Lord Stokes should resign as chairman of the company. Harold Wilson, the Prime Minister, who was a friend of Stokes, thought this was unfair and arranged for him to be given the new title of 'non-executive chairman'. Most importantly, it suggested that the company needed a large amount of new investment and that this should be provided by the government, which took a 40 per cent share in the group and soon came to own over half of it. Finally, Ryder and his colleagues suggested that better industrial relations would be achieved by worker participation in management decisions. This had an odd effect. In practice, shop stewards had worked with management to try to smooth over labour disputes for some time. Now they were drawn further into the formal structures of management. Sometimes this meant they were actually removed from the factory floor and may therefore have lost some of the restraining influence they had previously possessed. They were less likely to spend their time talking to their colleagues over sweet tea and more likely to attend formal meetings at Chateau Impney – the incongruous mock Gothic stately home that Leyland used as a conference centre.

After Stokes was manoeuvred out of his position, there was a period in which no one person lasted for long at the head of Leyland. In 1977, however, the government appointed Michael Edwardes, who presented himself as marking a sharp break with the past. Edwardes was a short, pugnacious South African. He believed that he would be particularly suited to deal with trade unions because he came from outside the British class system – the Communist trade unionists whom he so despised might have asked him some interesting questions about the relations between class and race in South Africa.[13] Edwardes was keen to show how different he was from his predecessors. He insisted on being given the combined title of chairman and chief executive and ostentatiously refused to have an office in the 'monolithic headquarters' of the company at Leyland House in Marylebone – though it turned out that this meant a move to Piccadilly rather than Birmingham.

Though he had been appointed by the Labour government, in some respects Edwardes was a very Thatcherite figure. Just before he went to British Leyland, and while he was still managing director of the battery company Chloride, he was one of the ten businessmen the Confederation of British Industry consulted before providing the Conservative Party with discreet advice about what a Conservative government might do during its early days in office. On the whole the advice was cautious. In particular, businessmen were reluctant to do anything that might risk conflict with the trade unions. Edwardes, though, was more radical than most of his colleagues about economic policy in general and the need to weaken trade unions in particular – ominously, in view of what was to follow, Edwardes also appeared to take it for granted that a Conservative government would wish to 'lower interest rates'.[14] Thatcher's ministers recognized: 'Edwardes and his style of management ... is widely identified with the very policies of tough management and economic reality which we ourselves advance.'[15]

Edwardes liked to preen himself in the mirror of an admiring press to the annoyance of both trade unionists and managers at Longbridge. In January 1978 Edwardes sent a telex to the latter telling them that they should ignore the aggressive statements that he had made to a newspaper.[16] He could not afford to be seen as too close to the government if he wanted to maintain any chance of working with the trade unions. He made ostentatious attacks on government economic policy, particularly high interest rates, and claimed that the high value of sterling was damaging exports. He told the CBI conference of 1981 that if North Sea oil was pushing up the pound the government should 'leave the bloody stuff in the ground'. Like many men who relish the idea of being seen as 'tough talkers', Edwardes was nervous when it seemed that his tough words might provoke tough action from others. A Conservative MP conveyed a pitiful message from Edwardes to Thatcher in 1983:

> He told me that he was coming to a reception that the Prime Minister was giving and that he was unsure of his relationship with her. He said that he had to do things, or strike attitudes, in order to appear independent and non-political to the Trade Unions. He said that if he had not done that, he would not have been able to do much with BL. He also hoped that the Prime Minister had not taken offence at anything in his recent book.
>
> He told me that he was a strong supporter of the Government and a great admirer of the Prime Minister. I got the impression that he wanted to mend any broken fences.[17]

The Thatcher government's relations with British Leyland were also complicated by another man who talked tougher than he acted: Secretary of State for Industry Keith Joseph. When the Conservative Party was in opposition from 1975 to 1979, Joseph had been a passionate exponent of the need to restore the free market. He had attacked government subsidies to large car manufacturers: 'For every job preserved in British Leyland, Chrysler and other foci of highly-paid outdoor relief, several jobs are destroyed up and down the country.'[18]

However, some around Joseph knew that, once in government, he was unlikely to live up to his proclaimed radicalism. This was partly because he was a gentle person who often backed away from the consequences of his own proposals and because he suffered from a fatal propensity to understand the force of his opponents' argument. It was also because the Conservative Party was constrained by both economics and politics. In economic terms, it hoped to sell off state assets, such as British Leyland, but knew that doing so might in the short term mean granting them subsidies that might render them more efficient and thus more attractive to buyers. In political terms, Joseph knew that closing large factories would produce spectacular increases in unemployment in areas that – unlike, say, Newcastle – were not irrecoverably lost to the Conservative Party. The party was to win both Selly Oak and North-field, Birmingham seats that contained large numbers of car workers, in the 1979 election. The two big British Leyland plants – at Longbridge and at Cowley in Oxford – were particularly important: Geoffrey

Howe, the shadow Chancellor, wrote that local Tories feared that Oxford would become 'the Jarrow of the 1980s'.[19]

The government and Edwardes acted out a pantomime of mutual independence. The former sought to persuade the public that British Leyland was an independent entity being led back to commercial viability. A meeting at Downing Street in April 1980 about a strike at Leyland agreed: 'It was important for the government not to be drawn into public controversy at this stage about the dispute. Ministers should take the line that it was a matter for management to settle.'[20]

In practice, the government could hardly have left management free to settle things at Leyland even if it had wished to do so because the company would have gone bankrupt without state support. In public, ministers talked about managerial autonomy. In private, their advisers were brutal. Alfred Sherman, a would-be Svengali to right-wing Tories, had told Joseph in 1977 that British Leyland was a political creation and

> a political creation can only be politically dismembered . . . This job cannot be . . . realistically left to management . . . A Conservative government which seriously wishes to introduce change should be giving its managerial appointees a lead, not hiding behind their skirts.[21]

Private documents often reiterated that the government was the 'owner' of Leyland. John Hoskyns, the head of the Number 10 Policy Unit, wrote in April 1980: 'The one person that we have never taken advice from, as owners of the business, is the man we hired to run it – Edwardes himself.'[22] However, Hoskyns's subsequent comments suggested that listening to Edwardes did not necessarily mean accepting his advice, and indeed he thought that a 'sceptical tone' in communications with the managing director would be useful: 'if that upsets Edwardes too bad'.[23]

Behind the scenes, many Conservatives did not want British Leyland to survive at all. They discussed seeking the kind of advice that might be provided by a merchant bank. In plain English, this meant considering sale or dissolution. At times, they hoped that it might be bought by one of its foreign competitors. Both the government and Edwardes himself conducted secret negotiations that might have involved the sale of all or part of British Leyland. At times, ministers and their advisers considered breaking up the company into smaller units, a few of which might be able to survive on their own, or simply delivering 'the coup de grace to a company for which most people's patience is long exhausted'. This last opinion was expressed by Keith Joseph who, having swung away from the radicalism of opposition to support for the company during his early time in government, had swung back by January 1981: 'I have changed to the view that we should grasp the nettle now and accept the dissolution of BL.'[24]

There was much hypocrisy in the attitudes of prominent Conservatives to labour relations at British Leyland. In public, they insisted that the company had a future if its workers and their trade unions were 'realistic'. In private, however, some hoped that negotiations with the trade unions would fail and that this failure might bring the company down: 'If the present TGWU action precipitates the end, then the odium for BL's downfall will be firmly on that union – no bad thing.'[25]

Alongside the hypocrisy was real uncertainty. However things may have appeared to the population of Birmingham, the Conservatives had not come to power intending to destroy British industry. On the contrary, they anticipated that British economic revival would mean imitating the countries of continental Europe – especially France and Germany – which were industrial economies. There was much talk of the need to get away from Britain's 'anti-industrial culture' – supposedly imparted by schools and universities that encouraged young people to read too much E.M. Forster – and to revive British engineering. The Conservatives also assumed, until they broke the National Union of Mineworkers in 1985, that they would have to live with a strong trade union movement – they knew that many trade unionists had voted Conservative in 1979.

For these reasons, some Conservatives did hope for some of the time that Edwardes might succeed at Leyland. One project was particularly important: a new model, the Mini Metro, which was launched with much fanfare in 1980. The Metro sought to draw on the past of the British motor industry and that brief period in the 1960s when small British cars – being used by the associates of Michael Caine to rob Italian banks, or driven by John Lennon – had seemed glamorous. It was also the last expression of British economic nationalism. The motor industry had suffered from Britain's entry into the European Economic Community in 1972 and the consequent removal of tariff protection against foreign competition. In 1976, for the first time, Britain imported more cars than it exported. Edwardes banned foreign models from the British Leyland car park – thereby compelling some of his managers to arrive at work in the small vehicles their wives usually used for shopping. Advertisements featured the white cliffs of Dover and showed the new car pushing back the hordes of European automotive invaders in a scene that was unfortunately reminiscent of the opening credits of *Dad's Army*. Ostentatious patriotism sat oddly with attempts by Leyland to control its costs by buying components abroad or by using the threat of buying abroad to force down the prices charged by its local suppliers.

The Metro also brought an attempt to change labour relations at the Longbridge factory. The New West Works was built for the production of the Metro. Those who were transferred to working on the new model were selected by managers who were looking for 'flexibility'. When managers could not get sufficiently 'co-operative' employees from the existing staff at Longbridge, they recruited workers from areas of high unemployment, such as Liverpool and Scotland, and in some cases hired young workers. Trade unionists with long memories would have recognized some of the tactics that Herbert Austin had used in the 1930s.[26]

Michael Edwardes also sought a new order in industrial relations across the whole company. In truth, the problems of the British car industry were complicated and long term. It is not clear that any manager could have solved them. However, the image of Leyland as having been destroyed by strikes brought about by political extremists was so well entrenched that Edwardes himself may have come to believe it. He certainly understood that acting tough with shop stewards would get him credit from the government at a time when he was not in a position to deliver more concrete results. The press had created a perfect target for Edwardes in the person of Derek Robinson or 'Red Robbo'. Robinson (who had been born in 1927 and begun work at Longbridge during the war) had been Etheridge's deputy and succeeded him as convenor. Like Etheridge, and unlike the vast majority of workers at Longbridge, he was a Communist, but he was less shrewd, charismatic and experienced than Etheridge. In 1980, Robinson put his name to a pamphlet attacking the management's strategy at Leyland. When he refused to withdraw this, Edwardes sacked him.

The sacking was unfair and, except in terms of press coverage, pointless. Whatever he may have said, in practice Robinson was as moderate and pragmatic as Etheridge. When one of his Trotskyite rivals claimed that he had only ever started one strike, Robinson insisted that he had started two[27] – which would have accounted for an average afternoon of industrial disputes at Longbridge. Robinson often tried to smooth things over. In 1973, he had attempted to persuade a group of setters complaining about unpaid training that they 'resume normal working' before discussions.[28] One of his union colleagues recalled the frequency with which Robinson had been hauled out of bed at two or three in the morning to try to settle matters when part of the night shift walked out.[29] Ron Savage described one of the numerous occasions when the company had recourse to Robinson as an intermediary with strikers:

> eventually Robinson agreed to speak to Wheeler [the shop steward] on the phone and told Wheeler in no uncertain terms to get back to work and that the Works Committee would tell them what to do and what not to do and not the unofficial committee of the Sheet Metal Workers on West Works.[30]

Savage also recognized that Robinson was sometimes the least enthusiastic striker in his own shop: 'Robinson himself is on strike although I am sure this is because his position depends on him being a shop steward from the toolroom and he will have to abide by the majority decision.'[31]

Robinson made an easy target partly because he had alienated his own immediate colleagues in the toolroom, skilled men who expected their pay to be higher than that given to less privileged workers. His union, the AEU, was notably unenthusiastic about the demonstrations that followed Robinson's dismissal. There was another oddity in all this. Edwardes was not hostile to every kind of worker demand. Indeed, when workers struck to safeguard their differentials (i.e. to ensure that skilled men would be paid more than the less skilled), Edwardes was privately sympathetic. Roy Fraser led such a strike in the Cowley plant at Oxford in 1978. Edwardes wrote: 'His aspirations for higher relative pay to recognize skills were music to my ears.'[32]

UNEMPLOYMENT

The battles at Longbridge were fought out against the background of rising unemployment. This rise could be traced back to the 1970s. Unemployment levels in Birmingham at the beginning of the decade were almost insignificant by later standards, but they had an effect precisely because they hit a city that had so little recent experience of joblessness. In April 1971, there were 22,243 unemployed people in Birmingham – compared to 14,666 a year previously. David Perris, the forty-one-year-old secretary of the Birmingham Trades Council said: 'There is a whole generation – my generation – who do not know what it's like to be unemployed. We are beginning to find out.'[33]

Birmingham had not yet become the place of long-term, large-scale unemployment that it was to be in the early 1980s but it had ceased to be the place where workers could expect to move from one job to another overnight that it had been in the early 1960s. This required all sorts of uncomfortable adjustments. Those who had been laid off were forced to take jobs at lower wages – £15 per week rather than £20 for a labourer; £20 rather than £28 for a skilled man. Workers were not yet faced with the prospect of years on the dole but they had to ask themselves if they were willing to stay out of work for eight weeks to earn something close to their previous wage or whether they should settle for whatever was on offer.[34]

In 1977 Paul Willis published a book – *Learning to Labour: How Working-Class Kids Get Working-Class Jobs* – about rebellious lads at a secondary modern school in 'Hammertown', a pseudonym for Smethwick. Though beautifully evocative, it was an unsentimental work. Willis did not draw an admiring picture of his subjects, who were racist, violent and crude, and he did not imagine that the lives ahead of them were likely to be attractive ones. He presented them as victims of a system that funnelled them towards a lifetime of tedium in factories. However, the book acquired a curious and unintended significance. Willis had begun his research career in the late 1960s, and seems to have undertaken his fieldwork in the early 1970s. He was careful to locate his subjects in terms of place – to outline Smethwick's heavily working-class population and the role of industry in the town. He was, though, strangely indifferent to time and there was a Sisyphean quality to his work – as though a part of the working class would for ever be condemned to repeat the same routine. It was a routine that would involve the same pointless bravado, as boys got drunk at lunchtime on their last day at school, followed by the same start of working life at a foundry or on a building site – sometimes literally on the following day. By the time the book was published, however, the world that he described was beginning to totter. By the time a feminist colleague, Christine Griffin, published a riposte to him (dealing with working-class girls in Birmingham) the life of the school leaver was already likely to be governed by the various government-sponsored temporary work experience schemes rather than conventional jobs.[35]

The boys studied by Willis had to endure lectures by careers officers but most of them were already working part time before they left school. Their own sense of adult masculinity went with the idea that they understood the world of factories and building sites better than any official would ever do. Adult men did not like getting jobs through labour exchanges – perhaps because such places aroused ancestral memories of the 1930s. Only newly arrived immigrants, who had no connections in the city, willingly endured the humiliation of having some man, or worse some woman, behind a desk telling them what job they might or might not be able to do. The senior area manager at the Department of Employment said: 'many people regard walking into an exchange as an admission of defeat ... the stigma attaches not so much to being without a job as to having one found for you'.[36]

Even men who held on to their jobs could be painfully aware that the economy was changing. Alan Morris, born in 1931 in Tyseley, started work at fourteen: 'there were plenty of jobs about ... hundreds ... the headmaster sorted you out'. Not wanting to defer his National Service, he refused to take an apprenticeship, but, in spite of this, he found interesting, highly skilled work. From 1953 to 1955 he worked at the Jaguar plant in Coventry (commuting from Birmingham on his motorbike). He earned over £16 a week – at a time when his father, a skilled tool maker, was making £11. Jaguars were glamorous and the need to provide customized vehicles for film stars and 'a Texan oil millionaire' meant that the work was interesting: 'We were the kings.' In 1955, he got a job at Rover in Solihull. Here the work was more routine and, especially when he was building Land Rovers, often required brute force to manipulate heavy and outdated tools. But his job seemed secure. The spectacular money that men had sometimes made from piece work was replaced by the more stable incomes of the measured day rate. He got a mortgage, bought a house, moved to Solihull, partly to be nearer the factory but mainly to be nearer the good schools that might save his own children from factory work. He was the classic affluent worker – keen on kitchen improvements and on his car, which he used for pleasure rather than getting to work. By the time he was interviewed in 1983, the world was turning dark. He did not think that wages were keeping up with prices. He believed that the unions were too political and he had started to vote Tory: 'my father would turn in his grave'. For the first time in his life, he could not take a job for granted and this chilled him: 'I would rather rob a bank than go down the social security.'[37]

Unemployment hit different groups in different ways. Middle-class teenagers (or at least those with 'A levels') found that the simplest way to get a job was to leave the city, or avoid returning to it after university. The Clash's *London Calling* (released in 1979) had an unintended significance in such circles. The middle-aged – those who had been used to secure work and for whom retirement was still a long way off – were gripped by uncomprehending horror. Frank Skinner had left school about the same time as the boys studied by Paul Willis when employment was still relatively easy – though, perhaps because he was seeking a white-collar job, he accepted official advice: 'teenagers who needed a job went to the Youth Employment Centre'. After two years in the drawing office at Hughes-Johnson, he returned to full-time education and would eventually find his way to fame, fortune and a smart house by Hampstead Heath. For a time, however, he was thrown back to the Job Centre and he observed a distinction among his companions there:

> The men fell into two groups: the younger ones, with tattoos and lumber-jack coats, also chain-smoking, mainly roll ups, and the middle aged, who had always worked but fallen victim to international economics and other stuff they didn't understand. These guys always wore a suit and tie for their appointment, as if to say 'I shouldn't really be here. It's just temporary, I'm sure.' Over the years, I watched their suits and their optimism slowly grow threadbare. Most of those men never worked again.[38]

The young men with tattoos and roll-ups were probably not as insouciant as they pretended. Most had grown up expecting to work. They regarded physical labour as part of masculine identity and, in more practical terms, anticipated that earning money would mean they could become husbands and fathers. The subjects of Willis's research – still really children – referred to their girlfriends as the 'missus'. Ten years after his initial research, Willis published an article. This time it was not about work but about unemployment, which he defined as 'The Final Inequality'. He was now primarily concerned with people (his critics would have said still mainly men) between the ages of sixteen and twenty-four and with the ways in which work related to other things:

> Most importantly, perhaps, the wage is still the golden key (mortgage, rent, bills) to a personal household separate from parents and separate from work, from Production. The home is the main living embodiment of the (especially male) labourer's 'freedom and independence' from Capital – apart from wage labour of course, which is the price for the independence of the separate home. But this price really does purchase something. The household is an area of privacy, security and protection from the aggression and exploitation of work, from the patriarchal dependencies of the parental home, from the vicissitudes of the market place. The separate home is still a universal working-class objective and the promise, at least, of its warmth and safety more than offsets the risks and coldness of work. Waged work is still the key to its opposite. No wages is no key to the future.[39]

Some of those at the end of their careers had a relatively benign experience of the economic slowdown. Most firms had developed, with prodding from the unions, policies that decreed that 'last in' should be 'first out'. Since stability of employment had often been the thing that workers prized most (and that white workers were likely to get), many men had been with the same employer for decades. In the 1980s, some of these relatively privileged workers changed their strategy. Instead of seeking to hold on to their jobs at all costs, they began to trade in their years of service for early retirement deals. A man who had seen his children through school and acquired a decent house (either a property that he owned outright or one of the better council houses) had no particular reason to go on enduring the factory.

A political scientist compared British Leyland with the Fiat factory in Italy. She concluded that the former accepted 'rationalization' because many of the shop stewards were well-established workers who knew their own jobs would be safe.[40] The argument is plausible but it sits oddly with her own statistics since the number of shop stewards at Longbridge declined sharply during this period. It is possible that Leyland found ways to comb out shop stewards – particularly as they moved the production of the Mini Metro to New West Works. On the other hand, it is possible that shop stewards simply gave up in despair and withdrew from any explicit role in labour relations. It also seems likely that some shop stewards actively sought early retirement and perhaps even used their position to secure it. The Trotskyite Frank Henderson believed that the early 1980s at Longbridge saw a 'deliberate destruction of memory' as older workers were bought out with retirement deals and sometimes replaced by seventeen-year-olds.[41]

Many managed to hold out until they could blend redundancy into early retirement. John Taylor signed on the dole at the age of nineteen in 1979 when he was turned down for a place on the BA course at Birmingham School of Art. His father was angry: 'Dad had been made redundant – he liked to call it taking early retirement – at fifty-seven, and . . . we would be signing on for state benefits together.'[42] History does not record what Taylor *père* said when John's art school band evolved into a pop group so successful that its members could buy Ferraris as casually as most men of their age bought bags of chips.

Because unemployment rates increased so quickly, there could be sharp differences even among siblings. Ali and Robin Campbell, who founded UB40, had been born in the late 1950s. They never really worked after they left Moseley School of Art – though they did some black economy jobs, a little drug dealing and, when the social security office became particularly awkward, spent nine weeks on the night shift at Cadbury. Their older brother had left a grammar school in 1969 and undertaken an engineering apprenticeship. He gave this up in 1972 because he could earn £40 a week on a building site rather than £15 a week as an apprentice. He was out of work as soon as the downturn came – though he might have survived, presumably taking early retirement when the Longbridge plant closed in 2005, if he had completed his apprenticeship.[43]

HANDSWORTH REVOLUTION

The effects of unemployment in Birmingham intersected with the effects of racial division. The position of non-white people in the labour market had always been insecure. They were hired because other workers were unavailable. Partly because they had usually been hired last, they were usually the first to be laid off. Most importantly, they had rarely benefited from the network of informal contacts that were so important to white working-class people when it came to finding employment. Young

Pakistani men suffered worst from unemployment in Birmingham. They did not, though, become an object of great official concern – at least not until they became associated with a broader anxiety about Islamic terrorism after 2001. Large numbers of Asian women and children came to Birmingham. This meant that young Asian men were likely to live in families. They were probably less visible on the streets than they had been in the 1960s. Unemployment was sometimes concealed by family support – which contributed to a belief (particularly on the part of the Thatcher government) that Asians were independent and entrepreneurial. Teachers and social workers were often dismissive of the abilities of Asian children in the 1970s and 80s but they apparently assumed that such children were obedient, submissive and 'unproblematic'.

Young West Indian men, by contrast, did arouse much interest in Birmingham in the 1970s. Not all of this interest was unfavourable. Even racist white boys often listened to ska and reggae. In fact, Jamaican music came to play an important part in white culture in Birmingham. UB40 played an approximation of reggae – though their members were all white. Two Tone Records was founded in 1979 to promote a blend of black and white musical styles. The label was based in Coventry but its most commercially successful band was the Beat from Birmingham.

Reggae music was associated with Rastafarianism, a religion that had originated in Jamaica in the 1930s and attributed divine status to Haile Selassie, emperor of Ethiopia. Rastafarians were highly visible because they wore dreadlocks. They aroused interest from the police because they smoked marijuana. They also aroused interest from fashionable sections of the left because aspects of their theology – and particularly their propensity to reject the corrupt society of 'Babylon' – seemed to hint at a political radicalism. The Birmingham band Steel Pulse released their first album, *Handsworth Revolution*, in 1978. Its cover showed symbols of modernity (perhaps particularly associated with post-war Birmingham), such as cars and high-rise buildings, decaying as nature (or a verdant variety of nature that might be associated with Jamaica) reclaimed the city. Probably both sides made too much of Rastafarianism. Smoking dope, listening to reggae and having a flamboyant hairstyle did not necessarily imply a coherent set of religious beliefs – and in any case these practices were hardly confined to West

Indians. Equally, using the word 'Babylon' did not really mean a rejection of consumerism or capitalism. Indeed, some young West Indian men were very attached to that icon of post-war Birmingham: the car. The Handsworth riots of 1985 were partly sparked by an argument about a parking ticket.

Relations between young West Indian men and the police reached their nadir in the first half of the 1980s. The West Midlands police were almost entirely white, mostly male, poorly educated and hard-drinking. Some had apparently become convinced that young black men, Rastafarians in particular, accounted for much of the crime in the area and this produced some unpleasant confrontations – a ten-year-old boy said that he had been stopped on suspicion of possessing stolen goods because he was carrying Christmas presents.[44]

There were riots in Handsworth in 1981 and 1985; their roots lay in both high levels of unemployment and police harassment. Handsworth itself, which had been represented by a Conservative MP until 1974, became, along with Brixton in South London, a sort of shorthand for racial tension. In a strange way, Handsworth was separated in the popular imagination from Birmingham: the former seemed gritty and exciting at a time when the latter felt banal. Sociologists noticed that young black people in Birmingham often associated themselves with Handsworth even when they lived in other parts of the city. Some mixed-race children, raised in white neighbourhoods, moved to Handsworth in search of their roots.[45] Handsworth Songs, a film about the Handsworth riots produced in 1985 by the London-based Black Audio Film Collective, barely alluded to Birmingham, though it reproduced much footage from the 1964 documentary The Colony, which had been located in Birmingham but had not mentioned Handsworth.

In truth, Handsworth came to stand for divisions that could be uncomfortable for the British left. Radicals still used the term 'black' to encompass all non-white people. But different communities (especially Asian ones) increasingly thought of themselves as separate – particularly perhaps because various kinds of government funding were directed on the assumption that such communities were distinct. The only people to die in the Handsworth riots were two Pakistani subpostmasters who burned to death in their shop – the killing does not seem to have been intentional but many felt that it illustrated the hostility between racial groups.

Above all, the 1970s and 80s were marked by a generational conflict among West Indians. First-generation West Indians had often been seen by white commentators as 'easy going' in their family relations, but they were often authoritarian when dealing with their children. West Indian parents were sometimes dismayed by the poor discipline they associated with British schools. They were also often devout Christians. The West Indians interviewed for *The Colony*, all clean-cut and smartly dressed, made much of the Bible. They seemed to regard Rastafarianism, which some of them had encountered in Jamaica, with amusement. Most importantly, their lives sometimes revolved around a hope that they, and especially their children, would eventually integrate into mainstream British society. West Indian children born in Birmingham and, perhaps especially, those who had been brought to the city as children, had fewer illusions. Their parents had placed great faith in education but the schools to which West Indian children went were often poor. Sometimes they had to move school to fit in with their parents' changes in employment. Non-white parents rarely understood the education system as well as white ones (even working-class white ones) did. In the mid 1960s, non-white children made up 4.2 per cent of the secondary school population of Birmingham but just 0.7 per cent of the pupils at academically selective schools.[46] Academic education might not have seemed very important in the booming employment market of the time, but it mattered a good deal ten or fifteen years later as work, especially unskilled factory work, became harder to get. Teachers and careers advisers showed all sorts of racial bias. They were particularly prone to assume that non-white children would be unsuitable for office work – which was another reason why non-white young people were particularly hard hit by the decline in manual employment.

White commentators talked of the 'West Indian community' but, in truth, young West Indians could feel as disconnected from their families as from the rest of society. A high proportion of young West Indian men in Handsworth (this was less true of women) had been ejected from their own home – which partly accounted for the fact that they were so visible on the streets.[47] Rastafarianism was as much a rebellion against the religion of their parents as it was directed against white society: second-generation West Indians sometimes reinvented their own identity in ways that marked a break with their parents. Birmingham West Indians interviewed on television in the 1960s had generally spoken standard English;

young men interviewed in the 1980s often spoke patois – again, this seems to have been less true of women.[48] Some noted that even the sons of families that came from other islands affected a Jamaican dialect.[49] Jamaica – associated with reggae and Rastafarianism – was now the fashionable island, just as Handsworth was the fashionable district.

Some young men fantasized about escaping from Britain altogether. In spite of Rastafarianism's ostensible link with Ethiopia, very few of them considered going to Africa – though the Handsworth band Jungleman did flirt briefly with the idea of moving to Ghana.[50] Young West Indians in the 1980s were probably less likely than their parents to assume that black culture must mean African culture. James Hunte, who had come to Birmingham in the 1960s, and who had stood against the mainstream candidates in the 1977 Ladywood by-election, campaigned in the late 1970s for voluntary repatriation of West Indians (he himself returned to Barbados in 1987). A black travel agent recalled many enquiries about migration to the West Indies in the period from 1979 to 1983 – reaching a peak of fifty in one week in 1982.[51] Many of the enquiries were associated with unemployment. But going 'back' to Jamaica, which had plenty of problems of its own, was easier said than done. Practically none of those who enquired actually went.

WHITE GHETTOS

The role that Handsworth came to assume in the public imagination sometimes occluded the wider experience of the Birmingham working class. Large-scale unemployment bit first and most deeply in the inner city. By September 1983, more than 40 per cent of the population was unemployed in Deritend, Handsworth, Duddeston, Small Heath and Soho.[52] But unemployment spread to some of the housing estates that were further removed from the centre of the city. After 1974, Chelmsley Wood and Kinghurst were technically part of affluent Solihull but both had unemployment rates of over 20 per cent from the late 1970s.[53]

The big new council estates were especially hurt by unemployment because they had been designed at a time when full employment was taken for granted. Nothing epitomized the change more starkly than the Castle Vale estate. Conceived in the mid 1960s, it was closely linked to Birmingham industry and had been built on top of the aerodrome that had served the great Spitfire factory during the Second World War. The estate was devastated by the economic downturn. In 1971, employment rates in Castle Vale were higher than in the city as a whole; by the late 1980s, unemployment on the estate was 28 per cent – about twice the average for the city. Eventually, a third of those who lived in Castle Vale were 'economically inactive', meaning that they were neither employed nor looking for work, and the population of the estate had dropped by over 40 per cent in twenty years.[54]

Castle Vale was in some ways more of a ghetto than Handsworth. There were plenty of reasons why a middle-class person might go to Handsworth – some of them taught at the local grammar school. There was practically no reason why a middle-class person, except those who were specifically charged with addressing social problems, would go to Castle Vale. Inhabitants of the neighbourhood later recalled an almost dystopian world of drug dealers, gangs with baseball bats and an occasion when a television was apparently thrown out of the window of a tower block on to a police car. It is hard to know how true these stories were; few outsiders felt inclined to find out. In 2000, Alex Henshaw, the former test pilot from the Castle Bromwich factory, was invited to unveil a memorial to the Spitfire and those who had manufactured the plane. When he saw the state of the area surrounding the memorial, he almost turned around.[55] White youths in Castle Vale had something in common with the largely Asian youths in Alum Rock. In both cases, their neighbourhoods had become so associated with deprivation that some felt that their address alone would prevent them from being offered employment.[56]

BIRMINGHAM POLITICS IN THE 1980s

What happened to politics in Birmingham during the 1980s? Other cities – Liverpool, Sheffield, London – established themselves as bastions of a radical anti-Thatcherite left. Local councils in many parts of Britain in the 1980s behaved as though they were running guerrilla insurgencies against the policies of central government. Matters were less clear-cut in Birmingham. For one thing, the Conservative Party remained influential in the city. It lost control of the council in 1979 but regained it for two years in May 1982. The Conservatives consistently

won almost half of Birmingham's parliamentary seats – exactly half of
them in 1983. By contrast, in 1983 they won none of Liverpool's six
seats and only one of Sheffield's six.

Birmingham Conservative MPs were not a distinguished group.
David Bevan had poor relations with his constituency association in
Yardley. A charitable obituarist wrote that he had a boisterous character in spite of being a teetotaller; Tory Central Office thought he was a
drunk.[57] Jill Knight in Edgbaston seemed as though she had been geneti-
cally engineered by an alien scientist whose knowledge of humanity was
entirely derived from reading the *Daily Telegraph*. Anthony Beaumont-
Dark, in Selly Oak, was a comic character who was once so carried
away by his own eloquence that he spat his false teeth across the gang-
way of the House of Commons.

There was a recognizable current of Birmingham Toryism in the
1980s. The city's Conservative MPs were usually supporters of Margaret Thatcher on social policy. They wanted strict controls on immigration,
and the liberal views that some of them had paraded in the 1960s, when
such views were likely to be well received by the national leadership of
their party, were now forgotten. They were also stern when it came to
sexual morality – Jill Knight was behind Clause 28 of the Local Government Act 1988, which made it illegal for local councils to 'promote
homosexuality'. On the other hand, they were rarely supporters of
monetarism. In common with Birmingham industrialists, they worried
about the effects of high interest rates and a highly valued currency.
They wished to restrain foreign competition, especially for motor
manufacturers.

Even after Roy Jenkins left Birmingham, in 1974, and the Labour
Party, in 1979, Birmingham's Labour MPs were more substantial figures than their Conservative opponents. Roy Hattersley was only briefly
a cabinet minister (for prices and consumer protection from 1976 to
1979) but was on the Labour front bench during its long years in opposition and became its deputy leader in 1983. Jeff Rooker, who represented
Perry Barr, was an active back bencher who was to enter government in
1997. Clare Short had grown up in the city (though she moved away to
attend university and then work as a civil servant). She entered Parliament, as MP for Ladywood in 1983, relatively young and later attained
ministerial office.

The Labour Party in Birmingham was right-wing. Three local MPs moved out of the party altogether. Woodrow Wyatt became an open supporter of Margaret Thatcher. Brian Walden, who resigned as MP for Birmingham Ladywood in 1977 to become a television interviewer, was more discreet in the expression of his opinions but provided Thatcher with a good deal of tacit support. Roy Jenkins was one of the founders of the Social Democratic Party in 1981. He was supported by George Canning, who had been his constituency agent and also Lord Mayor of Birmingham, and by Jim Cattermole (a Labour organizer in the West Midlands).

The most important feature of the Birmingham Labour party, though, was not the famous people who left it but the fact that some more obscure figures with similar ideas stayed in the party and fought. Clive Wilkinson, the leader of Birmingham Council, signed an initial expression of support for the Social Democratic Party, though he did not in the end leave the Labour Party. Raymond Carter (MP for Northfield from 1970 to 1979) was also privately sympathetic to the SDP though he stayed in the Labour Party because he thought it could change.[58]

Men like Wilkinson and Carter turned out to be right. They and their allies did manage to keep control of the Birmingham Labour Party. The Trotskyite Militant Tendency was weak in the city (though strong in Coventry) and even the politics of Tony Benn exercised little appeal. Most of the city's Labour MPs were social democrats even after the defection of Roy Jenkins had made them wary of using that term. The deselection in 1983 of John Sever – who had replaced Brian Walden as MP for Ladywood after a by-election in 1977 – was a rare and short-lived example of strength on the part of the Labour left in Birmingham. But Clare Short, who replaced Sever, did not turn out to be very left-wing in the long run.

What made the Labour right in Birmingham immune to the kind of politics that pushed Ken Livingstone, David Blunkett and Derek Hatton to the fore in other cities? One answer to this may be class. Birmingham did not have the middle-class radicals who dominated the Left in London. The very fact that the council was often run by Conservatives – and always run by conservatives – may have prevented it from creating a constituency of left-wing public sector workers. Race also played an important role in Birmingham politics. Non-white people had been largely excluded from the Birmingham Labour Party, or at least from positions of influence in it, during the 1960s. In the 1970s, they became more politically active. One might have expected this to have benefited the far left – the Communist Party had often been more sympathetic to immigrants than the mainstream parties, and inside the Labour Party it was usually the left that took most interest in race. However, non-white members of the Labour Party (or at least those who spoke in their name and exercised influence in the party) were often not interested in the left. Some alleged that the Birmingham Labour Party had come to revolve around a Tammany Hall politics in which right-wing Labour MPs could depend on support from immigrants, especially Asians, in return for help with practical matters (particularly with regard to immigration cases). One party member recalled:

> When the party was going through its changes in the seventies and the left was emerging as a political force, some of the right-wing chose to recruit people from the ethnic community as a way of sustaining their position. I think if you were a moderate councillor in 1977 in a ward like Soho what you would do is talk to a couple of 'community leaders' and say that you were under threat and the community leader would recruit thirty people from within the community.[59]

The right of the Labour Party sometimes seem to have taken Asian party members for granted. One Labour official breezily referred to a couple of his supporters as 'Khan 1' and 'Khan 2'.

The Birmingham Labour Party was not simply a vote-gathering machine, though, and its relations with non-white groups in the city were not entirely cynical. Clare Short had worked with organizations to help disadvantaged black youngsters in Handsworth before her election as MP. The striking feature of Birmingham Labour politics was that the left, when it eventually organized, found it easier to do so around race than around class. The Birmingham party, culturally progressive but almost entirely untouched by Marxist – some would have said socialist – influence, was well suited to fit in with the rebranding of Labour launched by Tony Blair in the 1990s. In the 1997 election that brought Blair to power, every single Birmingham constituency returned a Labour candidate. The party's victory in the city was more complete than that of 1945. Edgbaston – the homeland of the Birmingham upper-middle class and a constituency that had, in effect, been held by the Conservatives since Joseph Chamberlain's break with the Liberal Party in 1885 – returned its first ever Labour MP.

Raymond Mason produced one of the most beautiful images of Birmingham with *Birmingham In Memoriam*, an oil painting of 1958 that was intended to capture the red-brick city, which was being replaced with concrete. When he had become more famous, Mason was commissioned to produce a sculpture to commemorate the centenary of Birmingham being granted the status of a city (in 1889) and to stand outside the newly built Convention Centre. Personally, I thought that the resulting work looked a parody of socialist realism produced by the makers of Wallace and Gromit. Eventually, a teenager set it on fire – though this seems to have been an accident rather than an act of aesthetic criticism. The blackened ruin that stood for a time was more interesting than the original.

14

Citizens of Somewhere?

If you believe you are a citizen of the world, you are a citizen of nowhere.

Theresa May, Conservative Party Conference,
Birmingham 2016

They [Muslim men] *were only ever two questions away from having their Britishness questioned: 'Where are you from?' 'Birmingham.' 'No, I mean where are you really from?'*

Kamran, youth worker in Birmingham, interviewed 2010[1]

In 2016, Theresa May, the newly appointed Prime Minister, gave a speech to the Conservative Party Conference in Birmingham. It was inspired by her chief of staff, Nick Timothy, who had grown up there. The speech's reference to 'citizens of nowhere' was, at least ostensibly, directed at the wealthy and privileged – Theresa May made much of tax evasion, of employers who preferred hiring foreign workers to training British ones and of 'celebrities' who refused to denounce terrorism. More generally, the speech seemed designed to illustrate the rebellion by 'deep England' against the rootless cosmopolitanism of the metropolitan elite.

The notion that Birmingham was a citadel of patriotism appeared to evoke the protectionist, working-class Toryism of Joseph Chamberlain – much lauded by Timothy – and perhaps also the more discreetly expressed admiration that many anti-European Tories felt for Enoch Powell. A few in Birmingham were still indiscreet in their expressions of admiration for Powell and Nigel Hastilow, who had edited the *Birmingham Post* from 1993 to 1999, had stood down as a Conservative parliamentary candidate after writing that Powell had been right about immigration.

Birmingham was not quite the place that Conservatives sometimes imagined it to be. For one thing, it was not Conservative. In 2015, nine Birmingham constituencies returned Labour MPs; Sutton Coldfield was the only island of Toryism within the city limits. The result was repeated in 2017. In fact, Birmingham was a more solidly Labour city in the twenty-first century than it had been at any previous point in its history. In view of the frequency with which New Labour was alleged to have broken with the provincial working class, it is worth noting that Labour's breakthrough in Birmingham had come under the leadership of Tony Blair. As for leaving the European Union, Birmingham voted in favour, but by the narrowest of margins (50.4 per cent) – even narrower than the margin at national level. Far from being unified against the 'metropolitan elite' on this matter, Birmingham was sharply divided. In three constituencies (Yardley, Northfield and Erdington) all four wards voted to leave; in two (Hall Green and Ladywood) all four voted to stay. Elsewhere there were large differences within single constituencies. In the Perry Barr constituency, almost 70 per cent of those in Oscott voted to leave; almost 65 per cent of those in Lozells and East Handsworth voted to stay.

CITIZENS OF THE WORLD?

The notion of Birmingham as a symbol of rootedness was strange for an obvious reason: it was a city of migrants. More particularly, immigration from overseas had transformed Birmingham since 1945 – so much so that the city was expected to become 'majority minority' (that is to say a place in which only a minority of the population would identify as white British) by 2025. However, referring to the 'black and ethnic minority' population of Birmingham could be deceptive. By 2016, the Birmingham population included a large group of East Europeans, who had come to the city as economic migrants, and another group from Africa, the Middle East and the Balkans, who had come as political refugees. The latter group included Bosnians, Albanians, Iraqis and Iranians. It also included thousands of Somalis, who often arrived in Birmingham having spent time in Sweden, Denmark and the

Netherlands. The immigrants of the late twentieth and early twenty-first centuries raised questions in the minds of Birmingham's more settled population with parents or grandparents from overseas. A young Asian woman from Small Heath said: 'With regard to new migrants, in a sense I kind of understand how white people felt when our grandparents came to England . . . Similarly, I know a lot of Asian people that are not happy about new migrants.'[2]

Early immigration had often involved 'zones of transition' through which all immigrants passed on their arrival, but increasingly Birmingham was subdivided as particular ethnic groups settled in particular neighbourhoods. Sometimes this meant that the psychological geography of Birmingham only partly corresponded with its real social make-up. Handsworth was widely associated with West Indian culture and was described by some as the 'black capital' of the city though the largest racial group in the area was Asian in origin. There were moments of violent conflict between Asians and those of Afro Caribbean descent – particularly in 2005, when false rumours spread that a black girl had been raped by Asian men, and in 2011, when three Asian men were killed protecting their property during riots. Somalis, being both dark-skinned and largely Muslim, sometimes got caught in the crossfire between communities. A young Bangladeshi man said of them: 'I think white people just mistake them for black people.'[3] Another Asian claimed to have heard Afro Caribbeans say: 'Somalians are not proper black.'[4]

Sometimes relations between communities involved a deliberate and playful hybridity. Observers were particularly struck by this quality among Asian youths. One wrote:

> Some of the guys . . . negotiate a series of identities . . . At home they'll be respectful Muslim boys, at school they will probably be conscientious students, but on the street they'll be listening to Tupac Shakur, and wearing New York street clothes, speaking a kind of mash of patois and Bengali and Brummie.[5]

Another suggested: '[I]ts just street culture, just another identity that they hold onto on the streets but when they're home they have another identity and when they're at school they have another identity.'[6] A Bangra group, playing music with origins in the Punjab, named themselves B21 in homage to the Handsworth postcode. More generally, a group of

Indian musicians blended Indian styles of dress and performance with those derived from reggae. The most famous of these stars was Steven Kapur (born in 1967), who performed under the name Apache Indian. Gursharan Singh Chana, whose family had moved from Uganda to Handsworth in the early 1970s, became a journalist who documented and commented on his neighbourhood, under the name 'Boy Chana', in his spare time from working as a bank clerk.

The fact that a large proportion of Birmingham's Asian population were Muslims provoked excited reaction in the United States. Steven Emerson, a commentator on the US network Fox News, said in 2015: 'In Britain, it's not just no-go zones, there are actual cities like Birmingham that are totally Muslim where non-Muslims just simply don't go in.' In fact, about 20 per cent of the population of Birmingham was Muslim and there were plenty of areas of the city in which Muslims were a small, and sometimes uncomfortable, minority. An ethnologist studying the white working class (as seen from a pub on a Birmingham council estate) noticed a shift in racist language – 'Pakis', blamed for coming 'here' to 'live off the state', became 'Muslims' after the Al Qaeda attacks in the United States of September 2001.[7] The Birmingham police installed surveillance cameras in the early twenty-first century, which were placed with remarkable frequency along the routes in and out of areas with a heavily Muslim population.[8]

Young men from Muslim backgrounds were the objects of concern to the authorities but many of them in Birmingham had complicated views of their own identity. Talking about the closure of the last pub on the Alum Rock Road, at least one Muslim man seemed to suggest that he had some sympathy for white people who felt that their culture was at stake in this 'last bastion'.[9] Some were devout and some associated their background with political beliefs. However, 'political Islam' might mean things that had nothing to do with a challenge to the British state. A 'jihad' in Small Heath was actually a campaign against litter on the streets. Dick Atkinson, a left-wing community activist who had emerged from the student protests of 1968, made common cause with Muslim leaders to have prostitutes removed from the streets of Balsall Heath. Young men joined a demonstration against an Israeli incursion into Lebanon – which aroused anxiety on the part of the police even though the British government had itself condemned the incursion.

Birmingham Muslims were often divided by geographical origins. This did not simply mean that those from Pakistan, India and Bangladesh might have a different sense of where they came from and speak different languages. Gujarati Muslims who had come straight from India were different from those who had arrived in Birmingham after their families had lived in Malawi for a generation or so. The former worshipped at the large new mosque in Trinity Road that was named for a time after Saddam Hussein, because the Iraqi president had given money for its construction. The latter worshipped at a separate mosque nearby, while Muslims from the Indian state of Bihar were building their own mosque within a quarter of a mile of the first two. As children, 'Gujis' distinguished their play areas from those they described as 'Muslims', by which they meant Pakistanis and Bangladeshis. Different origins could produce hostility: 'We had an Asian community in school but then there was a Pakistani community, Bengali community and consequently there used to be kick offs all the time between one group and another.'[10]

Different groups of young men had an increasing sense of a unified identity as time went on – perhaps just because they had grown older or perhaps because political events gave them a stronger sense of religious unity. Even then Muslims sometimes found defining themselves to be an awkward process. Of Muslim men interviewed by Arshad Isakjee, only two (both of whom had spent their early childhood in India) did not regard themselves as 'British', but this did not mean that the remainder always felt comfortable with their nationality. One said: 'I wouldn't say I belong to Britain. But I wouldn't see where else I belong'; another recalled his visits to family in Pakistan: 'But you go there and they call you anglesee – you come here and they call you Paki. It's a bit like being hit like a tennis ball from one place to another.'[11]

NEW BIRMINGHAM

Those who knew Birmingham might have felt that the building in which the Prime Minister delivered her speech of 2016 did not fit easily with her message. Few constructions symbolized gleaming, rootless anomie better than the International Convention Centre. It had been built in the 1980s, with the intention of reviving the city's economy, but had raised eyebrows among Thatcherite ministers because its construction broke rules about the amount of spending local government was allowed to undertake. The left wing of the Labour Party group on Birmingham City Council had also objected to the Convention Centre because they believed that it would divert money from projects – such as those to improve schools or public housing – that might have a more obvious benefit to ordinary residents of Birmingham.[12] The Convention Centre fitted into a more general drive to engage with a certain internationalism. Far from being a place that emphasized its status as 'somewhere', a part of central Birmingham had been designed by architects who assumed that its most important purpose was to provide a meeting place for those who came from elsewhere – particularly those who came from outside Britain. Most visitors arrived at New Street station, which had been rebuilt to funnel arriving passengers into the Bull Ring shopping centre, also redesigned in 2003 to provide a wide range of high-end shops under a single roof. Those who attended conferences and meetings in Birmingham were likely to associate it with soporific afternoons watching PowerPoint presentations and listening to speeches about corporate vision. The high point of the Convention Centre's brief history had come in 1998 – the year in which it hosted both the Eurovision Song Contest and the meeting of the G8 group of industrialized countries. Those who watched Tony Blair lead heads of government and state in a singalong of 'All You Need Is Love' probably felt that the first of these occasions was less cringe-making than the second.

The International Convention Centre stood in the middle of the city – the council was keen to counter the sense that had grown in the 1970s that Solihull was the real centre of business in the West Midlands. The site had once been occupied by houses and workshops. John Baskerville, the printer, had lived there; after his death his house was burned down in the Church and King riots of 1791. After the First World War, the area had been renamed 'Civic Square'. It had been the focus of an attempt to build new amenities – museums and an opera house – designed to revive the dynamism of nineteenth-century Birmingham. The most important legacy of these ambitions was the Hall of Memory, finished in 1925, to commemorate Birmingham men who had been killed in the Great War. Even this was scaled down for lack of funds – as were plans to rebuild Civic Square again after the Second World War. The new designs of the 1980s made little reference to the area's previous history. Civic Square was renamed 'Centenary Square'. This was a nod to the centenary of Birmingham being granted the status of city in 1889 – though this change had meant little at the high point of Birmingham's late-Victorian self-confidence and had never been considered as important as the earlier incorporation of Birmingham, the anniversary of which had been celebrated with much pomp in 1938.

The Convention Centre was part of a more general attempt to 'brand' Birmingham around the end of the twentieth century. Much of this branding felt contrived. The city centre was divided up into 'quarters' that owed more to reports by consultants than to local tradition. A Chinese Quarter was structured around a pagoda on Holloway Circus that had been donated by the Wing Yip supermarket group in 1998 – though there was not really any particular Chinese settlement in the area. Next to the Chinese Quarter was the Gay Village, which was also a deliberate creation by city authorities rather than being – like its model in Manchester – an area that sprang up naturally. In the 1950s, Birmingham planners had taken the motorized cities of the American Midwest as their model; now they looked to parts of Manhattan and hoped that a celebration of gritty urban life would draw in the young, creative and entrepreneurial.

Sometimes it seemed that Birmingham was inventing a past that was at odds with what many people must have remembered. The Cultural Quarter in East Birmingham sought to open the area to 'creative industries' but doing so involved knocking down the Railway pub – an unattractive modern building but one that had once provided a venue for local rock bands.[13] The revival of the St Patrick's Day Parade, after the Good Friday Agreement in Northern Ireland in 1998, involved a celebration of Irish identity that said nothing about the bitter legacy of the Birmingham pub bombings, which had caused the parade to be suspended for twenty-five years and which were still a source of agonizing memories for many in Birmingham. The Balti triangle of restaurants around the Ladywood Road was often treated as a treasured part of Birmingham's 'heritage' – though cheap Indian restaurants had often been built on self-destructive competition among proprietors who could force down prices by relying on cheap family labour.[14] In any case, the majority of the restaurants had closed by 2015.

BENEFIT STREETS

The construction of buildings such as the Convention Centre illustrated sharp divisions. Civic leaders often conceived of Birmingham as prosperous and, in every sense of the word, 'mobile'. This was not an entirely unrealistic view. Birmingham was not as rich as London or Edinburgh but average incomes were higher than in most provincial cities. There were, however, pockets of deep deprivation and Birmingham contained a large proportion of the areas in the country with the worst unemployment. In September 2018, the parliamentary constituency with the worst unemployment rate in Britain was Ladywood. Four other Birmingham constituencies – Hodge Hill, Erdington, Perry Barr and Hall Green – came close behind. Hartlepool, in third place, was the only parliamentary constituency that matched the unemployment rates in the worst parts of Birmingham and all these places were now worse than traditional centres of unemployment such as Jarrow or West Belfast.

The National Debtline, established to provide advice to people about managing debts, was based in Birmingham. Politicians who wished to demonstrate their concern about poverty visited the city. David Willetts, Conservative shadow Minister for Work and Pensions and a native of Birmingham, spent a night in a council house in Quinton in 2002. He was upstaged when enterprising journalists arranged for Jackie Douglas, a single mother from the same estate, to visit London for the first time in her life.[15] The Channel 4 series *Benefits Street*, first broadcast in 2014, concerned James Turner Street in Winson Green, where nine tenths of residents were said to live on state benefits.

Those who entered the Birmingham job market without experience or qualifications often found themselves in precarious positions. They got jobs but rarely kept them – either because the jobs were temporary or because they were so unrewarding that they offered no incentive to stay. One young man told an interviewer:

I've had loads of jobs, probably over thirty jobs [he had been, among other things, a window cleaner, an estate agent and a worker at

Cadburys] but I've never stuck at them or anything ... the jobs I've gone into, it's just for the money really and I've never really enjoyed them.

Most of those who got jobs did so through personal contacts. One had worked as a plasterer for his brother-in-law in Kingstanding and another from the area had done the same job for a friend of his mother's. A woman from King's Norton had worked as a cleaner with her boy-friend's mother and another had been employed in a Kingstanding nightclub where her brother was manager.[16] In the booming economy of the 1960s, personal contacts had often helped part of the working class to get well-paid jobs but now the best employment was accessible only through formal applications and dependence on personal contacts for jobs locked some people into deprivation. It meant that they were unlikely to move beyond their own network of acquaintances. Often it also meant that they were tied to their own neighbourhoods. The ability to travel made it easier to get employment, but relatively few young people from the most deprived estates had access to cars. Matters were made more complicated by poor public transport. It was said that buses did not stop on one estate because the drivers anticipated various kinds of trouble – drunkenness, disputes over fares or simply women trying to manoeuvre prams – from the kinds of passengers who were likely to get on there.[17]

Some of the most deprived in Birmingham lived their whole lives in small areas – sometimes spending most of their time within a five-minute walk of their home. One woman claimed never to have left her council estate except occasionally to go shopping in the local high street and once to go on a school trip.[18] Some – especially non-white young men – felt relatively safe in a neighbourhood that they knew but feared violence if they moved out of it. In earlier years, Birmingham had been a city of people who travelled and particularly people who commuted to work. But by the twenty-first century there were young people who had few associations outside the areas in which they grew up. Osman, a man of Pakistani origin who had moved from Small Heath (an area with a large Pakistani population) to Hodge Hill (an area that was by Birmingham standards unusually white), regarded himself as having been moulded by a knowledge of Birmingham beyond the neighbour-hood of his birth that was unusual in his milieu: 'I went to Cadbury

College, it was a forty-five-minute bus ride. I went to Aston university, so I was always travelling.'

THE POLITICS OF NOSTALGIA

Politics – particularly voting to leave the European Union – was not related to poverty in a simple way. Shard End was the Birmingham ward that voted most heavily in favour of leaving (8,127 to 2,617). But, though it was among the 10 per cent most deprived wards in the country, it was not by any means the most deprived ward in Birmingham (it was twelfth out of sixty-nine). Most of the Birmingham wards that were more deprived than Shard End voted to remain.

Areas of Birmingham that voted to leave the European Union in 2016 were rarely characterized by absolute levels of deprivation. The citadels of Brexit were those large estates built between the 1930s and the 1960s that had been designed to accommodate workers for the industries that flourished in the mid twentieth century. The populations of these estates were relatively old. Such estates were associated with a strong sense that things had once been better or, perhaps most importantly, that things had once seemed as though they were going to get better. Moving to Kingstanding in the 1930s or Castle Vale in the 1960s had usually been associated with the promise of a better life. Houses there were more comfortable and better appointed than in the older parts of the town. The estates had once been populated by families with young children and by those who had apparently secure jobs in Birmingham factories. From the 1970s onwards the mood had changed. There were fewer jobs and fewer young people. Some who came to such estates were now those who did not have much choice – particularly political refugees housed by the authorities.

The Northfield constituency, especially the Longbridge ward within it, was revealing in this respect. Northfield had once seemed synonymous with the car plant. It had drawn workers from as far afield as Wolverhampton but those who lived close to the factory were a privileged fraction of the working class. Privileged for the simple reason that they did not have to endure long journeys to work but also privileged because they usually had good quality council housing at a time when such housing was mainly occupied by white people – Longbridge had started to employ a significant number of non-white people by the 1970s but they generally commuted from areas such as Handsworth.

Employment at Longbridge declined sharply. In the late 1960s, there had been 25,000 workers there; a decade later it was 20,000; by 1997, there were 13,000 and in 2005 the plant effectively closed, meaning that the remaining 6,300 workers lost their jobs. On the whole, the closure of the factory did not plunge former workers into poverty. Within less than a year, 4,000 of them had found jobs, nine tenths of which were full-time. A few were now better paid, but the majority were worse off. After three years, wages for former Longbridge workers, adjusted for inflation, were more than £5,000 per year lower than they had been at Longbridge. Executives had mostly increased their pay, as had those at the very bottom of the wage hierarchy, but the great mass of semi-skilled and skilled workers earned less. In addition to this, most jobs were less secure. Some former Longbridge workers had had more than one job in the three years since they left the plant. Some were self-employed or worked for agencies. The highest wages, as far as manual workers were concerned, went to those who had taken jobs in construction – but such jobs, closely tied to particular projects, often seasonal and difficult to sustain for workers over a certain age, were almost always insecure. Furthermore, many found employment a long way from Longbridge and a long way from their homes. Most former Longbridge workers travelled over sixteen miles to work. Northfield had moved from being an area that drew in workers from the rest of Birmingham to being one from which people travelled to work elsewhere.

In absolute terms, former Longbridge workers were not badly off. Most of them, nine tenths of those who left the factory in 2005, now owned their own houses. Home ownership in the area was much more common than it had been at the height of the post-war boom. All the same, the area around Longbridge was marked by a sense of decline. For much of the post-war period, wages at the factory had increased faster than inflation and workers who embarked on a career there assumed that they would be better off at the end of their working life than their parents had ever been. By the early twenty-first century, this expectation of progress had gone.

A graduate student wrote a work of 'psychogeography' about Longbridge in 2011. He felt that there was something mocking about the promises that the area seemed to make to its inhabitants. According to the local authorities, Longbridge was to be integrated into a 'central technology corridor' that would run south from the city centre through the university and into Worcestershire. Education was essential to this vision. Bournville College now stood where the car factory had once been. But its presence – 'like a stranded liner washed up in the last wave of New Labour spending' – seemed incongruous.[19] The college had been founded in 1913 by the Cadbury family, who were seeking to promote inter-class harmony and educational opportunity at the time when Herbert Austin was trying to break unions at Longbridge. It had migrated to the Bristol Road and then moved into Longbridge. One assumes that at least some ex car workers must have felt that there was something undignified about the fact that their former place of employment now bore a name that was mainly associated with confectionery.

The hope invested in high technology sat uneasily with the fact that Northfield's population was older and less well educated than that of the city as a whole. Many of the students at Bournville College came from other parts of Birmingham. Many of them were also non-white (the college's most distinguished alumna was Preet Gill, the Sikh woman who became MP for Edgbaston in 2017) at a time when Northfield remained mainly white. It sometimes felt as though separate worlds existed side by side. Veterans of the track at Longbridge frequented the four working men's clubs that could still be found within easy distance of Longbridge station while students scuttled down a windswept road to McDonald's and Subway – the first pioneering outposts of a glamorous retail centre that developers had promised to build in the area.

Events leading up to the closure of Longbridge had a political resonance. The Rover Group – the name for the branch of what had been British Leyland that owned the Longbridge plant – was sold, first to British Aerospace in 1988 and then to the German firm BMW in 1994. BMW, having failed to revive the company, decided in 2000 to sell or close it. Alchemy, a private equity group based in London, offered to buy part of it, though it was no secret that such a purchase would have meant many job losses. An alternative proposal was put forward by the Phoenix Venture Holdings. Phoenix was led by John Towers, a former Rover executive, and appeared to have deeper roots in Birmingham than Alchemy. Its bid became associated with a campaign to 'save Longbridge', which was orchestrated by the *Birmingham Evening Mail* and drew 50,000 people to a rally in Cannon Hill Park.

Eventually Phoenix bought the Rover Group plant for £10. It was said that the deal was sealed during a conversation between the key mover behind the Phoenix group, and a government minister during a taxi journey from Longbridge to the station. The Phoenix consortium lasted for five years, but the Longbridge factory was effectively closed in 2005. Some of those involved in Phoenix made handsome returns on their modest investment. A report commissioned by the Department of Trade and Industry criticized the Phoenix consortium, and some of those involved in it were subsequently forbidden from acting as company directors.

The campaign to save Longbridge, and its eventual failure, fed a diffuse anti-Europeanism that had great influence in parts of Birmingham. The mood was reflected in letters to the *Evening Mail* in 2000:

> There must be a number of old chaps, who on reading the *Mail* headlines wonder why on earth we bothered . . . The European Community appears hell bent on the destruction of Great Britain, in waging economic warfare – not least in sending us their unwanted so-called asylum seekers. Enough is enough. (*Evening Mail*, 17 March 2000)
>
> Did we British really win the war . . . ? I believe that our 1939 enemy will definitely have won if we allow our currency to die. The Germans are not going to win this war. The Government should renationalise Rover now. (*Evening Mail*, 23 March 2000)
>
> Where the Luftwaffe failed to bring Longbridge to its knees, a handful of men from Munich have done so. (*Evening Mail*, 30 March 2000)[20]

Parties that expressed hostility to the European Union – and which often associated this with a broader dislike of foreigners – gained influence in Northfield. The Referendum Party won 3.2 per cent of votes in the constituency in 1997 (the national vote for the party was 2.6 per cent); the British National Party won 5.5 per cent of Northfield votes in 2010 (the national figure was 1.9 per cent). The share of the vote of the United Kingdom Independence Party in Northfield peaked at 16.7 per cent in 2015 (the national vote was 12.6 per cent). Northfield was one of the three Birmingham constituencies in which all wards voted to leave the European Union in 2016. The campaign to save Rover was apolitical, as it drew support from local politicians of various parties, but it sometimes involved hostility to 'London' as well as Europe, and more specifically to the Prime Minister of the day, Tony Blair. In the 2019 general election, when many northern constituencies voted Conservative for the first time, Northfield was the only Birmingham constituency to swing to the Tories.

The political mood of Northfield was one of regret for a vanished past but it was also one that raised questions about when that past might have been. Some Conservatives, who had felt no affection for Longbridge workers during the factory's most productive years, supported the plan to save the car plant. Defence of Longbridge rarely involved much reference to the strikes and union power that were seen to have characterized the plant in the 1960s and 70s.

There was a blind spot in Birmingham's nostalgic evocation of its past and this concerned the post-war period. Council estates were not regarded with much affection even by those who had once been excited to move to them. The turbulent labour relations of the 1960s and 70s were not remembered favourably even, and perhaps especially, by the workers who had gone on strike.

In fact, the kind of industry that had characterized much of Birmingham for most of the twentieth century – large-scale factories – simply disappeared from view in the early twenty-first century. The wonderful collection on 'Fort Dunlop Remembered' assembled by Chris Jukes was a rare example of a work that recalled the life associated with a large factory, but Jukes was painfully aware that the kind of 'job for life' that he had once expected had disappeared. The most striking account in his collection was provided by Maria Duffey, who had worked at the Fort as an employee of a call centre, long after tyre production had ceased there.[21]

Some factories, notably Longbridge, were eventually demolished. Strangely, the most famous one in the city – the Cadbury plant at Bournville – disappeared from view, even though it continued to operate. This had once been a particularly visible workplace. The public were encouraged to tour the production line and the sporting facilities around the works often drew in outsiders – generations of children learned to swim at the Linden Road baths. But Cadbury changed. The family became less and less associated with the business and power shifted from Bournville to London. In 2012, the American food company Kraft took the business over. The family were entirely displaced. People still visited Bournville but they no longer saw the production line and instead came to Cadbury World – a sort of diabetic Disneyland in which families were encouraged to ride the Crunchie rollercoaster and take a trip on an airship piloted by the 'Caramel Bunny'.

If industry was referred to at all in twenty-first century Birmingham, it was often an eighteenth- and nineteenth-century industry of small workshops. The jewellery quarter in central Birmingham became a focus for much discussion of the city's industrial past – though jewellery had actually ceased to play much of a role in the city's economy by 1900. A workshop – originally established in the late nineteenth century but abandoned during the recession of 1981 – was restored as 'the workshop that time forgot'.

The relation of twenty-first-century Birmingham to its own past is illustrated above all by one man: Carl Chinn. Chinn is a historian of the city but, rather like William Hutton in the eighteenth century, has become a historical actor as well as a writer of history. He was born in Birmingham in 1956. His father and grandfather were bookmakers, which meant that until the early 1960s they were operating outside the law. It also meant that they lived among the working class without being workers themselves. Chinn joined the family business but, when this was sold, he went to Birmingham University, wrote a PhD and became a lecturer and eventually a professor, until 2015. But he was always much more than this. His post was in 'community history', which meant that it was partly funded by the council and that he spent much time talking to people outside the academic world and encouraging them to record their own memories. He presented a programme on West Midlands Radio (from 1994 to 2013) and wrote a column for the Birmingham *Evening Mail* (from 1994 until 2016).

Most of all Chinn is a cultural entrepreneur of extraordinary energy. He has written dozens of books and prefaced dozens more by Birmingham authors. He has been commissioned to write official histories of local institutions. In recent years, he has led tours of the city's points of historical interest, produced podcasts, and written for websites. He has also become a performer – singing songs that evoke aspects of Birmingham's past, though as far as one can tell the songs are recent compositions rather than ones that were ever sung in Birmingham.

Chinn transcends conventional frontiers. Much of his history has been a dialogue in which listeners to his radio show or readers of his columns were encouraged to contribute their own versions of history. Two things pervade his writing. The first is fierce affection for a certain vision of his native city. The words 'brum' and 'brummies' recur continuously in his writing. The second feature is work. He has written of Birmingham as the 'workshop of the world' and his history of women is subtitled: 'they worked all their lives'. 'Hard-working' is one of Chinn's favourite terms of approbation. He also celebrates the working class, writing largely about people who are poor and derive their income from manual labour. His PhD was supervised by Dorothy Thompson, a distinguished scholar of Chartism, and one assumes Chinn must have met her husband, E.P. Thompson, the most famous historian of the British working class.

Unlike the Thompsons, Chinn is not a Marxist. He was a member of the Social Democratic Party in the early 1980s but then broke away from it and fought the 1983 general election in the Sparkbrook constituency as an 'independent Social Democrat' who stood for the imposition of import tariffs and the restoration of the death penalty. He obtained 281 votes – coming bottom of the poll and just below the Revolutionary Communist candidate. Since then, he has not made explicit party-political interventions. He has, though, frequently campaigned on local issues, particularly against factory closures, and was discussed as a potential mayor of the West Midlands region – a suggestion that was generously, or mischievously, put forward by Roy Hattersley, the victorious Labour candidate in Sparkbrook in 1983. Chinn's definition of working class is rarely associated with political militancy. He was the most flamboyant of the local figures behind the campaign to save the Longbridge factory. The book that he co-authored on this campaign was sympathetic to trade unionists and contained a moving passage on the dismissal of Derek Robinson (see chapter 13). All the same, one suspects that some of the older shop stewards at the factory would have raised an eyebrow at the fact that it was dedicated to the memory of Herbert Austin.[22] Chinn has been particularly interested in the history of women and, so far as one can tell, many of his readers are women – a group that were at least until recently less likely than men to be part of an organized left.

Chinn obviously has an extraordinary capacity for hard work but his life intersects with a period in which work ceased to be at the heart of

Birmingham's identity. He was born into the post-war boom when it was hard for anyone in Birmingham to stay unemployed for more than a couple of weeks. But his entry into academic life occurred at the moment when the city's unemployment increased spectacularly. At times it seems as though much of his writing is an elegy for an industrial Birmingham that ceased to exist in the early 1980s. It is an elegy that sometimes involves a certain studied vagueness about what industrial work actually meant. Quite often, it is glimpsed indirectly through the prism of domestic life – in one of his songs, a worker is having a 'swill' to wash off the swarf before going out drinking. There is little direct discussion of factory production lines, trade unions or strikes. Often it is as though the work being recalled is that of the nineteenth-century workshop rather than the late twentieth-century factory. Chinn presented even the campaign to save Longbridge in terms that seemed to owe more to pre-industrial craft traditions than to a production line: 'we are a folk talented in the taking of metal and forging and fashioning it into things of beauty and usefulness'.[23]

A part of Birmingham's recent history seemed lost in a kind of blind spot in the early twenty-first century. There were vast numbers of popular books on Birmingham's past – Brewin Books, based on an industrial estate in Redditch, specialized in the evocation of 'old Birmingham' and at one time had 150 titles in print. Alton Douglas, a television actor who had mainly been known for appearing in *Crossroads*, turned his hand to local history and produced thirty books. However, these works all tended to recall a period before 1945 (the war itself was quite a major topic). They were not exactly nostalgic – many were blunt about the poverty and even the brutality of much of life in working-class quarters of Birmingham – but they were sentimental in that they usually implied that such lives had redeeming virtues.

Two popular representations of Birmingham history were particularly resonant. The first came in the autobiographical novels of Kathleen Dayus – published from 1982 onwards – which described the extraordinarily difficult life of a woman born into the jewellery quarter in 1903 and her struggles to establish herself after the death of an alcoholic first husband in the 1920s – struggles that entailed handing her children to a Barnardo's Home. Dayus lived to be almost a hundred but her books focused on the period of her life before her second marriage (to a bookmaker) in 1946 and, because she worked in an archaic sector of the Birmingham economy, they often appeared to look back even further into the nineteenth century.

The second and very famous representation of the Birmingham past came in the television series *Peaky Blinders* – which was first broadcast in 2013. Derivative, ludicrously implausible and badly written, it was a huge international success. The most striking features of the series, though, sometimes involved not the fights but the scenes set in places of work – as though industry in Birmingham had come to feel more exotic than gangsters or spies. Some of it was filmed in the Black Country museum and the effect was, once again, to make Birmingham in the age of the Austin factory and the Dunlop works look as though it was dominated by Victorian workshops.

Conspicuously missing from all this was much reference to the rapid growth of the two or three decades after the war. The period of full employment (which meant, particularly, the 1950s and early 60s) or of rapid improvement in working-class living standards (which meant the late 1960s and early 70s) was largely ignored except in terms of bitter references to the damage done to communities by new buildings and roads. Post-war immigration sometimes seemed to fit awkwardly into a certain view of Birmingham's past. The city's most prominent popular historians are emphatically not racist, and Chinn especially has always gone out of his way to engage with Birmingham's ethnic diversity. All the same, one suspects that, at least for some readers, nostalgia about 'old Birmingham' was likely to mean nostalgia for white Birmingham.

There was a paradox in all of this. The audience for popular history looks to have been relatively old. It was largely composed of people who would have been adults for much of the post-war period. This was a generation that had often found work in large factories and often moved to new housing estates. Now their lives revolved partly around sepia-tinted photographs of working-class streets in central Birmingham – streets that they, or their parents, had left decades ago and which were now largely inhabited by people who had come to Britain in the relatively recent past.

Some of the contradictions of Birmingham's relations with its past, and perhaps its present too, were incarnated in the sculpture (commissioned in 1988 and completed in 1991) that stood outside the International Convention Centre. It was created by Raymond Mason, who was born in Birmingham in 1922. His father was a taxi-driver and mechanic; his maternal grandfather was a publican. Mason had grown up in Wheeleys Lane in Ladywood – he described it later as 'an adorable little working-class street' – and lived opposite a factory. He left Birmingham – drawn away first by a brief period of naval service in the Second World War, then by studies at art school and finally by his decision, in 1946, to move to Paris, where he spent most of the rest of his life. His departure owed something to his asthma, which meant that he was literally allergic to industrial Birmingham.

Mason returned briefly to Wheeleys Lane as Birmingham was about to launch into a period of frenetic building:

> The last time I really went back to Birmingham was in 1958 when my mother died and I discovered that my native city was dying as well ... After the funeral, I went back to my childhood home to sell the furniture and close everything up. The week had been rainy but I managed to finish several watercolours of the street, of the factory and of the area around. It was an absolute need. The bulldozers had already demolished the houses that I knew. Towards Lee Bank Hill everything was now a wasteland. Gone was my grandfather's pub. Gone was my past.
>
> The last evening before my return to Paris, I went to see the scene again. It had rained all day but now the clouds parted and suddenly a great sunset embraced the old red-brick city. I thought that when the sun had gone down finally, the moon of modern times would rise, and that everything would have the whiteness of reinforced concrete.
>
> On my return to Paris, I painted this moving scene in oils. In memory of my old town. It carries the date and the title 'In Memoriam', but not wanting to be that alone, no signature.

Mason was a celebrated artist by 1988 and Birmingham City Council commissioned him to create the sculpture to stand outside the Convention Centre.

It would have been hard to think of any building that better incarnated the moonscape of concrete modernity that Mason had so disliked in 1958 than the International Convention Centre but he justified his acceptance of the commission with these words:

> They tore the heart out of Birmingham ... When I was asked to do a monument I said yes – if I could evoke the city they had taken down ...

> When I think about it ... all my work has been devoted to my own
> class ... The possibility of evoking the Birmingham workman was
> irresistible.[24]

Mason's monument was entitled 'Forward' – a reference to the slogan that Birmingham had adopted on its incorporation in 1838. It was
made of fibreglass and depicted a factory and a group of workers. The
monument was curiously untethered to any particular time. The factory
looked as though it might date from the early twentieth century, some
of the workers appeared to be dressed in the style of the nineteenth century. A car seemed to allude to Birmingham's motor industry – though
that industry had flourished at the moment that Mason had once
described as the city's death. The figures depicted were all white – a fact
that was underlined and mocked by the Bangra singer Bally Jagpal, the
cover of whose 1997 album *Live and Direct* featured a photograph of
'Forward' with a middle-aged Indian woman sitting on the edge of the
plinth, framed by two large speakers from a sound system.

In 2003 the statue was transformed. A sixteen-year-old boy set it on
fire – apparently, he had been playing with matches, rather than intending an act of arson or aesthetic criticism. Briefly, the charred and
blackened remains could be seen before the whole thing was demolished. There was something about this sooty ruin that seemed more
evocative than the bland sculpture that had been destroyed. Apart from
the obvious racial dimension – every figure in the monument had been
given a dark complexion – it recalled the days when classically minded
Birmingham residents had labelled the smoke-blackened classical façade
of the town hall the 'black Parthenon'. Bizarrely, postcard sellers
reported that pictures of the monument now acquired a strange appeal
and sold better than most depictions of structures that still existed.

Conclusion

> It is still good ... to come here and taste the mature atmosphere of ages of civilization. England is so rich with riches of the past that nothing the living can do can destroy the vast wealth of accumulated tradition over the years. Take no notice of the living. We can elevate ourselves learning from the dead. They must have had an open mind so as to fight against the barriers surrounding them looking at these machineries that were invented by these great men of Birmingham. I think and I feel that they must have had an open mind to fight against the barriers surrounding them. Nothing can destroy the vast wealth of accumulated tradition.

These are the words spoken by the West Indian bus conductor Victor Williams as he walks around the Birmingham Science Museum – looking at statues of Boulton and Watt, men identified with what might now be labelled the 'Midlands Enlightenment' – in Philip Donnellan's documentary *The Colony*. Writing this book, I have often felt haunted by *The Colony*. Perhaps this is partly because the film and I are more or less contemporaries – we are both almost sixty. Partly it is because the film and the documents that its producers accumulated provide such an astonishingly rich source about the lives of people, especially West Indians, in Birmingham in the early 1960s. I have come, however, to think that Donnellan was using the film to provoke a wider reflection about Britain. Indeed, the film turned the conventions of its time on their head – looking at 'the English problem' through the eyes of immigrants rather than looking at the 'coloured problem' through the eyes of white people. The film is also fascinating to the historian because it does things that historians are not allowed to do. It proceeds by juxtaposition and suggestion rather than by argument. We see fleeting images and hear quotations but neither are explained. Much of it is set up in the form of discussions that never reach a conclusion and the most important voice in discussions – that of the producer himself – is one that we never hear.

By contrast, a history book has to conclude and the monologue from Victor Williams raises an awkward question. Does Birmingham have a history at all? Does the town of the late eighteenth century (let alone the village of the Middle Ages) have anything in common with the city of the twentieth and twenty-first centuries? *The Colony* evokes Birmingham's past with shots of statues of notables from the eighteenth and nineteenth centuries but the city has been so transformed by new roads and new buildings that few of those statues remain where they were first placed. Some have disappeared entirely and the city has seemed in recent years to find it difficult to hit on any physical memorial that might sum up its history.

Of course, rapid change *is* Birmingham's history – perhaps to a greater extent than many care to admit, Britain's history too. The late Sir Geoffrey Elton might seem an incongruous person to cite in this context – since he was a historian who worked on a period, the sixteenth century, when Birmingham barely existed and on a man, Thomas Cromwell, who apparently only mentioned Birmingham once and obliquely. Elton, a German-speaking Jew from Czechoslovakia who had arrived in Britain as a refugee in the late 1930s, once remarked that the British were almost unique among European nations because they had so *little* sense of the past. They were fascinated by pageantry and the more colourful vestiges of a certain kind of past but their own country had been formed by sharp ruptures.[1]

In fact, the first rupture in Birmingham's history came during the period studied by Elton and involved the marriage of Elizabeth, the widow of the last man to hold the title 'Birmingham', with the miller Askrigge. Thereafter, Birmingham was largely independent of, and sometimes hostile to, aristocracy. Birmingham figures sometimes worked with aristocrats (as Boulton did in the eighteenth century) and were sometimes in conflict with them – as the governors of King Edward's School were in conflict with Sir Thomas Holte and his allies in the seventeenth century or as, in a more Pooteresque fashion, Norman Tiptaft, the Lord Mayor during the Second World War, was in conflict with the Earl of Dudley. Mostly, though, Birmingham was, perhaps more than anywhere else in Britain, the home of an autonomous and self-confident bourgeoisie, people who saw no reason to defer to those who had been born into grander circumstances than themselves. There is much debate about whether the city was marked by as much social mobility as some of its citizens suggested but the mere fact that they wanted to make such claims is itself revealing. Birmingham was a place in which people boasted about having been born poor rather than one in which they hunted down impressive ancestors. Those who sought aristocratic patronage did so because they associated it with some distinct commercial or political advantage rather than because they regarded it as prestigious for its own sake. William Hutton expressed things with characteristic pungency when he commented on authors who sought to improve their own status by dedicating their work to distinguished people: 'When an author is too heavy to swim of himself, it serves as a pair of bladders, to prevent his sinking.' Aristocrats came to Birmingham in the late nineteenth century after Joseph Chamberlain's alliance with the Conservative Party, but men like Evelyn Cecil (the nephew of the third Marquess of Salisbury), who sat for the constituency of Aston Manor from 1900 until 1929, never quite seemed at home in the city – they had the air of medieval princes sent as hostages to guarantee an alliance with a rival court.

Indifference to aristocracy went together with a certain attitude to the Anglican Church. In statistical terms Birmingham was not a particularly Nonconformist town and King Edward's School, for many years the most important single institution in the city, was a bastion of Anglicanism. However, some Nonconformists – Unitarians and Quakers – exercised an influence that surpassed their comparatively limited numbers. Unitarians in particular saw themselves as an intellectual and moral elite even, and perhaps especially, when their religion excluded them from the country's best-known educational institutions. The religious climate of Birmingham was not marked by the moralistic fervour that might be associated with Wesleyanism but by a dry, ironic scepticism – a mood that made collaboration with free-thinkers easy. Opposition to 'establishment' in all its various senses was to be a consistent feature of Birmingham thinking from Priestley in the eighteenth century to Kenneth Tynan in the twentieth.

Birmingham fortunes – judged against those of Liverpool or Glasgow, let alone London – were modest but in a curious way this underwrote the autonomy of a group that remained distinctively middle class. When the middle classes were distracted from business, it was generally by public service in their own city rather than by the search for prestige outside it. British economic history is often presented as culminating in the triumph of London over the provinces and of finance/ international trade over industry. Birmingham does not fit neatly into this analysis. It is true that some local businesses, most notably that of the Kenricks, declined, but others rose. Far from being distant representatives of a London establishment, two of Britain's clearing banks – Lloyds and the Midland – were founded in Birmingham and preserved close links with the city's industrialists, sometimes loaning them money when it might have been prudent not to do so.

The fact that the Birmingham middle classes were independent of the aristocracy and that they were, at least for a time, radical about constitutional and religious matters does not mean that they were radical about social matters or that they were always allied with the Birmingham working classes. On at least two occasions – the Priestley riots of 1791 (when a Church and King mob attacked a part of the town's propertied classes) and the Bull Ring riots of 1839 (when Chartist rioters were put down at the instigation of the Birmingham middle classes) – there had been violent division between the two.

The single figure who best encapsulated the autonomy of the Birmingham bourgeoisie was Joseph Chamberlain and it is hard to overstate what a radical figure he was – a man who began his political career as a republican and finished it as an atheist, who was never a member of the established Church and who regarded aristocratic titles with open derision. Chamberlain has a strange effect on the history of Birmingham – attracting vast amounts of attention but also underwriting the idea that the whole drama of Birmingham's existence can be reduced to the period of Chamberlain's public life, which ran from about 1868 until 1914. Historians sometimes write as though there was nothing before Chamberlain but the penny-pinching triviality of local politics as conducted in the Woodman Tavern, and nothing after him but the slow decline of the Chamberlain dynasty, followed after 1945 by the physical and political destruction of the structures that had grown up under Chamberlain's aegis.

The sense that Birmingham was eclipsed in the twentieth century was tied in a strange way to the last stage of Joseph Chamberlain's career when his thinking revolved around empire. Those who study empire tend to focus on port cities and above all on the imperial metropolis in

London. In *Pax Britannica* James Morris imagines someone at the end of the nineteenth century standing on the bridge in St James's Park from which could be seen Horse Guards, the Colonial Office and the India Office.[2] Of course, Joseph Chamberlain was installed in the Colonial Office then but even his official biographer sees his time there mainly through London eyes.

Looking at Birmingham reminds us of the economic currents of empire, which sometimes seemed to run against political ones. Birmingham Nonconformists, most notably the Quaker Galton family, who manufactured guns, combined explicit opposition to slavery with commercial relations with those who conducted the slave trade. As late as the 1960s, Birmingham gunsmiths remarked that their relations with clients in India were sometimes closer than their relations with neighbouring workshops in Birmingham. They looked back wistfully to the last time of prosperity their trade had enjoyed during the wars of decolonization of the 1950s, when shotguns were used for 'police work' in Kenya and Malaya.[3]

Birmingham was the capital city of a certain view of empire. This was a view that emphasized economic benefits and, for all the imperial pageantry that surrounded Queen Victoria's Diamond Jubilee, it was economics that underlay Joseph Chamberlain's approach to Empire. It was an approach that revolved around Africa, Australasia and North America. India – associated with the spectacle and grandeur that so appealed to George Nathaniel Curzon or Winston Churchill – counted for little in Birmingham. Chamberlain once remarked that he was not interested in being Secretary of State for India because he was insufficiently 'cosmopolitan', by which he appeared to mean that he had no interest in the exoticism that so fascinated some of his compatriots. Leo Amery, MP for Sparkbrook and in many ways the heir to Joseph Chamberlain, had been born in India and was the last but one Secretary of State for India, but never visited the subcontinent in his adult life.

Norman Tiptaft (1883–1970) was a Birmingham notable who became Lord Mayor of the city in 1941. Attempting to revive his family jewellery business, he went on two international tours – one in 1929 and one in 1931. The places that he visited – India, Burma, Siam, Malaya, China, Japan and Canada on his first trip and the West Indies, Central America and Canada on his second – were largely part of the

British Empire. Tiptaft's world, however, was a long way from that of Government House or the memsahibs who scrutinized the military and civil lists to establish the hierarchy of importance among the guests at their bridge parties. Tiptaft was concerned with shops and salesmen and with his relentless battle against native guides who might seek to swindle him. He wrote about empire in interesting terms:

> The fact is, we have a certain section of India drawn from the idle-rich county-family, pitchforked into various jobs and they are not much use to the old county as remittance men. They are utterly useless parasites.[4]

Of course this relation between Birmingham and empire was to change drastically. As Roy Hattersley, MP for Sparkbrook, wrote of Birmingham in 1979, 'The old empire is closer to the mother country than ever before.'[5] Immigrants from the West Indies and the Indian subcontinent came to the city in the 1950s and 60s. Empire House, once the headquarters of the Birmingham Conservative Party, still stands, now somewhat dilapidated, in Neville Chamberlain's old constituency of Ladywood. Ladywood was one of the first constituencies in England to have a primarily non-white electorate. Since 2010 it has been represented in Parliament by Shabana Mahmood. Philip Donnellan, more sentimental about empire than he might have cared to admit, initially entitled his documentary on West Indians in Birmingham 'Mother Country' and suggested that many of them had come to Birmingham because of some residual loyalty instilled in them in their youth. Reading the original interviews with the people portrayed in Donnellan's film, one is struck by exactly the opposite sense. Non-European immigrants were interested in Birmingham for the same reason that Birmingham people had been interested in the British Empire: economics. Almost all immigrants saw it primarily as a place to find work and earn money.

The understandable fascination with Chamberlain and with Victorian Birmingham has had a curious effect on the historiography of Birmingham. It became the second largest city of Britain in 1911 and yet it is at this precise moment that historians often lose interest in it. The death of Joseph Chamberlain (in 1914) is assumed to have brought the end of a certain social model with which Birmingham had been associated. Many write as though the whole of the twentieth century was just an extended coda. This, though, was the very period in which the Birmingham economy boomed and in which the city made the greatest contribution to the British economy as a whole. Birmingham in the twentieth century or, to be more precise, Birmingham in the period that lasted more or less continuously from the First World War until the mid 1970s, was marked by rapid growth and prosperity.

In many ways Birmingham was *the* industrial city of twentieth-century Britain. It was the place where new industries – particularly those associated with motor cars – were most obviously important. It, more than anywhere except London, was the city that drew in migrants. Birmingham's prosperity was closely tied to that of Britain as a whole. An economic history published in 1940 suggested that Birmingham 'could not have fallen into a general decline, unless the whole of England had declined with it'.[6] The book went to press a year on 6 May, but its assertion about the Birmingham economy acquired an unintended significance since, in the second half of 1940, Britain's fortunes did indeed depend in more than a purely economic sense on the Spitfires coming out of Castle Bromwich.

There were particular features of the Birmingham economy that help explain both its success and the fact that it features so little in the British self-image. First, Birmingham's prosperity often fostered a lack of sentimentality in its population. People came to the city to work and often thought of it as having no other attractions except, particularly in the inter-war period, the networks of pubs and cinemas that helped well-paid workers spend their wages. People go on thinking of themselves as Scots or Irish for generations after their families have left those places and some describe themselves as Geordies or Scousers even when they have lived in South East England since they were eighteen. But inhabitants of Birmingham sometimes hesitate to describe themselves as 'brummies' even when they have lived in the city for years. This was true of the West Indians interviewed by Donnellan, who discuss at length whether it is possible to be a 'black brummie'; true of the second-generation Irish and even true of Dick Etheridge – the convenor at the Longbridge factory who never forgot he had been born in the Black Country and sometimes talked of 'Broomies' as though he regarded them as an alien race.

Secondly, the British view of industrialization often revolves around a single dramatic change – an invention or the discovery of a rich coal seam – that throws up a new industrial society that, within a generation or two, then begins to decline. Philip Donnellan was obsessed with economic decline and portrayed the Birmingham of the early 1960s as though it was a primarily Victorian town that could no longer live up to past glories. In fact, of course, the Birmingham economy was booming at the very moment that he made films about it (though it is true that West Indians were often excluded from the most modern factories).

But Birmingham did not decline until quite recently. The Frenchman Léon Faucher pointed out in 1844 that Birmingham was different from other industrial towns. The difference lay in the fact that Birmingham was 'the work of time': 'There is nothing there that resembles those giant cities improvised in less than half a century by the [spinning] jenny and the steam machine . . . the industrial ground forms little by little as a result of superimposed layers.'[7] Metallurgy and light engineering lent themselves to this kind of adaptation, which meant that businesses and workers moved relatively smoothly from one kind of production to another as circumstances changed – a process that can be seen as late as the 1930s when skilled workers from the declining gun trade of central Birmingham found jobs in the shadow factories making aircraft.[8]

The crescendo in Birmingham's economic growth came after the Second World War. This was also a moment when Birmingham seemed to fit into a particular kind of political pattern. The Labour Party was strong in the city, having struggled to establish itself during the long period of Chamberlainite hegemony but it was not completely dominant and had to share power at local level with the Conservatives. The Labour Party in Birmingham was also always a relatively right-wing one – social democratic rather than democratic socialist, to adopt the language of the 1980s.

Of course, Birmingham's prosperity did not last and the continuous adaptation that had marked the city's industry up to 1940 came to an end – partly because central government began to discourage new industries from setting up in the city, so that Birmingham became chained to the car industry like a galley slave chained to his oars. Decline was all the more marked because it happened so quickly in the 1970s and then, very fast indeed, in the early 1980s. That substantial proportion of the Birmingham population that had sought refuge in the city during the slump of the early 1930s must have had a horrible sense of recognition as, in less than a decade, Birmingham became a place of mass unemployment.

As far as much of Britain, and indeed much of the world, is

concerned, one result of the 1980s and its aftermath was to make historians look more sympathetically at the post-war years. The three
decades after the Second World War were often described as a 'golden
age'. Birmingham plays a curious role in all this. On the one hand, it
would be hard to think of anywhere that better incarnated post-war
growth, full employment and social democracy – the very things that
are now remembered so wistfully. But few people feel wistful about
Birmingham in the 1950s and 60s. Even after the downturn of 1981
Birmingham nostalgia was often focused on a more distant, and partly
imaginary, past of nineteenth-century workshops rather than twentieth-
century factories. Birmingham, perhaps more than anywhere in Western
Europe, was associated with the underside of economic growth. It was
a centre of racial tension and a centre too, by the 1970s, of frequent
strikes that looked to be beyond the control of the unions and to discon-
cert even the very people who were going on strike. Most of all, the
physical structure of post-war Birmingham was recalled without nostalgia. Birmingham residents in the 1960s and 70s were intensely conscious
that they lived in a man-made city – in the sense that it was dominated
by artificial structures – but also a city that seemed, in the words of one
journalist, to have been enslaved by its own creation – as though cars,
motorways and high-rise buildings had become ends in themselves
rather than means of providing for needs.

The drama of rapid growth in the first three quarters of the twentieth
century and rapid decline for a decade or so afterwards is over now.
Many of the structures that caused such offence in the 1970s have been
knocked down. Some features of the present-day city centre would per-
plex someone who arrived in a time machine from 1975. Trams, once
regarded as the epitome of archaic Victorian backwardness and finally
banished in the 1950s, are back on the city streets. The classical façade
of the Curzon Street station – closed for years and surrounded by the
grimy streets of Digbeth – has been exposed again by the building work
for the new high-speed train line from Birmingham to London.

In the last few decades, Birmingham has become a less distinctive
place. It has adjusted to the end of large-scale industry and become a
city of modest prosperity – though one that still has pockets of severe
unemployment and deprivation. In some ways, it is now a more tolerable place to live – less polluted, more racially integrated – than it was
just thirty or forty years ago. It is still the second largest city in England,

but on a global scale it is nothing special. There are thirty cities in China alone that have populations of over a million and many of those have grown from almost nothing in the 1980s. Ordinariness, though, confers its own importance. Our histories of cities and perhaps our histories *tout court* are often focused on capitals, political centres and places that are full of grand buildings. Birmingham reminds us that most people's lives do not revolve around such things. Birmingham is not an ancient place rooted in the Church and State and not a city that has been moulded by natural features. Perhaps it is a place that deserves to be described by the phrase that was once beloved of so many of its most eminent citizens: 'self-made'.

Appendix I. Size of Birmingham by Area and Population, 1801–1981

Year	Size area in hectares	Population
1801	3,437	70,670
1811	3,437	85,753
1821	3,437	106,722
1831	3,437	146,986
1841	3,437	182,922
1851	3,437	232,638
1861	3,437	296,076
1871	3,437	343,787
1881	3,437	400,774
1891	5,115	478,113
1901	5,115	522,204
1911	27,645	840,202
1921	17,645	919,444
1931	20,699	1,002,603
1951	20,699	1,112,685
1961	20,699	1,107,187
1966	20,881	1,064,220
1971	20,881	1,014,670
1981	26,430	1,006,527

Source: City of Birmingham, *Abstract of Birmingham Statistics*, 1979–1981

Appendix II. Growth of Birmingham since 1838 by Area

Date	Becoming or ceasing to be part of Birmingham	Hectares
Pre 1838	Birmingham Town	1,213
1838	Deritend Township	37
	Bordesley Township	761
	Duddeston/Nechells Township	374
	Edgbaston Parish	1,052
Birmingham Borough		3,437
1891	Balsall Heath Local Board District	184
	Saltley Local Board District	455
	Little Bromwich Hamlet	440
	Harborne Local Board District	599
Birmingham County Borough		5,115
1909	Quinton Parish	339
Birmingham County Borough		5,454
1911	Aston Borough Manor	388
	Handsworth UD	1,484

	Erdington UD	1,874
	Yardley RD	3,072
	King's Norton and Northfield UD	5,373
County Borough after 1911		17,645
1928	Part of Perry Barr UD	1,249
County Borough after 1928		18,894
1931	Part of Minworth Parish	239
	Part of Castle Bromwich Parish	690
	Part of Sheldon Parish	794
	Part of Solihull Parish	82
	County Borough after 1931	20,699
1964	Part of Solihull CB	1
	Part of Billesley Ward	–2
	Part of Sheldon Ward	Together with above
	Part of Hall Green Ward	–6
	County Borough after 1964	20,692
1966	Part of Aldridge UD	1
	Part of Bromsgrove RD	135
	Part of Halesowen MB	46
	Part of Meriden RD	7
	Part of Smethwick CB	3
	Part of Sutton Coldfield MB	44

	Part of West Bromwich CB	9
	Part of All Saints Ward	−11
	Part of Harborne Ward	−4
	Part of Perry Barr Ward	−1
	Part of Rotton Park Ward	−13
	Part of Sandwell Ward	−4
	Part of Soho Ward	−22
	Part of Stockland Green Ward	−1
	Birmingham County Borough after 1966	20,881
1974	Sutton Coldfield MB	5,549
	Birmingham Metropolitan District	26,430

Source: City of Birmingham, Abstract of Birmingham Statistics, 1979–1980

Key
CB County Borough
MB Metropolitan Borough
RD Rural District
UD Urban District

Appendix III. Population of Birmingham by Place of Birth, *1951, 1961, 1971*

		1951	1961	1971
UK	England	1,007,493	961,664	842,625
	Scotland	13,005	13,139	11,960
	Wales	25,457	21,560	17,280
	N. Ireland	8,251	11,379	11,375
	Other and not stated	600	3,554	370
Irish Republic		26,568	44,798	39,565
Ireland (part not stated)		1,530	2,784	5,300
Old Commonwealth	Australia	506	424	485
	Canada	909	792	725
	New Zealand	166	123	120
New Commonwealth	Africa	336	666	4,925
	Guyana	26	121	170
	Jamaica	345	12,017	19,385

	Trinidad and Tobago	37	144	280
	Other Caribbean	85	4,016	5,530
	India	2,205	4,801	17,885
	Pakistan	1,108	5,355	17,515
	Other Asian	606	1,796	2,250
Europe	France	391	319	320
	Germany	1,661	1,787	1,605
	Italy	392	945	1,000
	Poland	2,352	2,725	2,250
	Other European	2,546	2,243	2,215
Other countries and at sea		2,020	3,248	5,220
Birthplace not stated		13,457	5,604	3,930
Total		1,112,361	1,107,187	1,014,670

Source: Peter Ratcliffe, *Racism and Reaction: A Profile of Handsworth*

The figures do not add up perfectly because of errors in census data and because I have omitted certain very small categories.

Appendix IV. 'The Clearest and Most Overwhelming Evidence' – The Case of the Birmingham Six

The clearest and most overwhelming evidence that I have ever heard in a case of murder.

Mr Justice Nigel Bridge, when sentencing the Birmingham Six
at Lancaster Crown Court, 1975

We shouldn't have all these campaigns to get the Birmingham Six released if they'd been hanged. They'd have been forgotten and the whole community would be satisfied.

Lord Denning (former Master of the Rolls)
interviewed 1990[1]

Six men were convicted of the Birmingham pub bombings. They were Hugh Callaghan, Patrick Hill, Gerard Hunter, Richard McIlkenny, William Power and John Walker. Five of them were arrested in Lancashire as they travelled to Belfast. They were taken to a police station at Morecambe where they were subjected to forensic tests and interviewed by members of the West Midlands Police. Callaghan was arrested later in Birmingham.

The key evidence against the men was as follows:

First, some neighbours and colleagues of Walker said that they had seen odd deliveries to his house and that he had made suspicious comments at work. The judge said that this evidence would not in itself have been enough for conviction.

Second, Frank Skuse, a Home Office pathologist, said that he had found traces of explosives on the hands of two of the men, and fainter traces on the hands of a third.

Third, four of the men signed confessions. The police said that the two others had confessed orally. All men retracted their confessions and said that they had been given under duress. The defence sought to have the confessions ruled inadmissible but the judge refused this request.

In the mid 1980s, doubts were expressed about the safety of the convictions of the Birmingham Six. The Home Office weighed its options. The Home Secretary could simply have deployed royal prerogative to have the men pardoned or to shorten their sentences. He could have asked a lawyer to examine particular aspects of the evidence. He could have convened a public inquiry. He also had the option of referring the case back to the Court of Appeal. In a meeting with the Home Secretary, the Lord Chief Justice had said that cases should not be referred unless there was new evidence and officials anticipated, correctly as it turned out, that he might comment with asperity if the case of the Birmingham Six was referred back to him. Nonetheless the Home Secretary did refer the case to the Court of Appeal in 1987.

In January 1988, the Court of Appeal rejected the Birmingham Six's appeal against their convictions. Lord Lane, the Lord Chief Justice, said: 'the longer this case has gone on the more convinced this court has become that the verdict of the jury was correct'.

Three years later, the Birmingham Six were freed by the Court of Appeal. The Crown no longer claimed that the confessions and forensic evidence were reliable and recognized that the convictions were not 'satisfactory', but still argued that they were 'safe'. Ten years after their release, the Six were paid compensation, around £1 million each.

Judges found repeatedly against the Six. In their original trial, Mr Justice Nigel Bridge did not simply express his certainty of the men's guilt at the moment of sentencing. He also told the jury that he would not affect 'an Olympian detachment'. What this meant in practice was that he sneered at the accused and at those who presented evidence that might have helped their case. Sometimes he seemed to take over the job of conducting cross-examination for the prosecution – though he was fairly polite to the defence barristers, perhaps because he had discerned that they themselves were unconvinced of their clients' innocence. In 1976, the Court of Appeal, presided over by Lord Widgery, rejected an appeal by the Six against the verdict of their first trial. In

1977, the Six brought a civil case against the West Midlands and Lancashire Police for assault. This case took a long time to come to trial and the Court of Appeal intervened to stop it.

Birmingham MPs believed for many years that the Birmingham Six were guilty. Anthony Beaumont-Dark, Conservative MP for Selly Oak, particularly relished the chance that discussion of the case gave him to get his name in the papers. Roy Jenkins, MP for Stechford and a famously liberal Labour Home Secretary, was responsible for the Prevention of Terrorism Act that was passed just after the bombings – though he had come to accept by the 1980s that the Six ought to benefit from the scintilla of doubt that would justify an appeal. Roy Hattersley, MP for Sparkbrook, recognized that the means by which the Six had been convicted might not bear too much scrutiny, but even after this he continued for some time to think that they were probably guilty.

Officials at the Home Office also continued to believe in the men's guilt, even while conceding that the police might have behaved improperly. Indeed, the stronger the evidence that the original investigation had not been conducted properly, the more some officials worried about inquiries being reopened. They feared that men who were 'probably guilty' might be released. One of them wrote in December 1986:

> At the time of writing it is not possible to tell how much substance there will prove to be in the allegations that the police maltreated the six convicted men. If, as we fear, there is some substance in these claims, then the odds against their being acquitted on appeal will shorten considerably. And yet we have little doubt that the six men were involved, to a greater or lesser degree, in the pub bombings. There is a real possibility therefore that, because confessions may have been made under duress, six men who are, in our view, very probably guilty will have their convictions quashed and, as a result, have to be paid hundreds of thousands of pounds in compensation (some or all of which, it would be said, would find its way into the IRA's coffers).[2]

Officials also feared that a public inquiry into the case might reveal awkward facts about the police and other official bodies – presumably they were less worried that the Court of Appeal might raise questions about such matters:

[A]n inquiry would be bound to revive – probably to very little purpose – all the allegations which have been made of – variously – police malpractice, assaults by prison officers, defective scientific evidence, etc. Even if an inquiry's findings did not lend support to these allegations, the parading of them once more, more than 10 years after the event, would be bound to leave its mark and to create much bitterness and ill-feeling, particularly in the police service.

There would be a grave danger of an inquiry broadening out into areas such as the management of the Forensic Science Service, the safety of confessions made before PACE [Police and Criminal Evidence] requirements, liaison between the police and the intelligence agencies.[3]

Chris Mullin, a Labour MP with no links to Birmingham, was the most prominent figure who campaigned to prove the innocence of the Birmingham Six. He had that combination of characteristics – posh voice, scruffy appearance and left-wing views – that provokes fury in the British establishment. Policemen and officials hinted that his motives for taking up the case were, at best, mercenary. An official of Her Majesty's Inspectorate of Constabulary declared: 'The author of "Error of Judgement" will probably not be the last person to try and capitalize on the tragic events of 1974.'[4] The Chief Constable of the West Midlands wrote:

Chris Mullin himself is an individual of questionable motives. He has tried numerous and devious means to obtain interviews of police officers from this Force, both retired and still serving, who were involved with the Birmingham pub bombers; approaches which, incidentally, had not received official sanction, and his motives for the publication of such material at this late stage, almost 12 years after the event, must in itself be questionable.

. . .

I find the text of the extract from Mullin's book to be largely innuendo and mystification.

. . .

There is no doubt that the six men convicted of the Birmingham pub bombings were rightfully and lawfully convicted.

. . .

446

The kindest interpretation of Mr Mullin's intention in making the alleged disclosures might be that he is merely seeking pre-release publicity for his book. I do not need to labour less disingenuous motives for his behaviour.[5]

Mullin was vilified by some Tory MPs. John Patten, a minister at the Home Office, described a speech that he made to the House of Commons on the Birmingham Six as 'one of the worst and most wretched performances that I have ever heard in the House of Commons'.[6] The *Sun* ran the headline 'Loony MP Backs Bomb Gang'.

The notion that Mullin was motivated by either greed or sympathy for the IRA looks less plausible now. Investigation into parliamentary expenses revealed a man of almost monastic frugality – he had a black and white television at his Brixton flat. He liked Jeremy Corbyn, one of the few MPs who had been willing to help him in his campaign to free the Birmingham Six, but he gently suggested that it might be a good idea for his party to find a leader who stood a chance of winning a general election. Everything about Mullin's career suggests that he was a man of integrity and one whose judgement usually turned out to be good.

All the same, many people still believe that the Birmingham Six were guilty. Mullin had to be protected by bodyguards when he came to give evidence at an inquest into the victims of the bombings in 2019. In 1998, a former Tory MP, David Evans, paid libel damages to the Birmingham Six after he told a group of schoolchildren that they were guilty, but he had merely been unwise enough to say in public what many people said in private.

It might, therefore, be worth going through the case for and against the Six point by point. Many disparities in the prosecution evidence did not become clear until years after the first trial of the Six. There were, however, some features of the case that might have raised eyebrows even at the time.

Flaws in evidence presented by the prosecution at the first trial

First, the use of confessions as evidence might have seemed odd – even to those who accepted that the injuries the men had suffered in custody had not been inflicted during their interrogation by the police. Why would committed members of a ruthless terrorist organization confess to their crime just hours after having committed it?

Second, even those who accepted the prosecution evidence that two (or possibly three) of the suspects had traces of explosives on their hands might have wondered why none of the suspects had traces on their clothes and why there was no trace of explosives in the home of any of the men.

Third, the men's confessions appeared to bear more relation to what the police knew at the time of the interrogation than to what was later determined by investigators at the scene, and what the men who planted the bombs might have been expected to know.

Did the Birmingham Six support the IRA?

When the police arrested them, shortly after the Birmingham explosions, five of the six were on their way to attend the funeral of an IRA volunteer, James McDade, who some of them knew and who had blown himself up while trying to plant a bomb in Coventry. English law punishes acts rather than opinions. Being a supporter, or even a member, of the IRA was not a crime in 1974. There is a difference between expressing support for violent action and being willing to undertake it.

At first, the police alleged that the Birmingham Six were members of the IRA and held specific ranks. According to the confession attributed to Hugh Callaghan, he, Hill, McIlkenny and Power were lieutenants, Hunter was a captain and Walker was a brigadier. The IRA itself never put the Birmingham Six on its list of prisoners and the Six apparently received no help from the organization.

Assuming that in 1974 the police did believe the Six to be members of the IRA, there is uncertainty about when, and if, they abandoned this belief. In September 1986 Tom Meffen, the Deputy Chief Constable of the West Midlands, had a private meeting with Chris Mullin. He did not challenge Mullin's assertion that the Six were not members of the IRA and replied: 'We never said that they were.'[7] Around the same time, Chief Constable Geoffrey Dear wrote in a private report to the Home Office: 'As to their [the Six] being members of the IRA, several of them made such admissions and all admitted associations with James McDade.'[8]

If they were innocent, why did the Birmingham Six confess?

Billy Power confessed in the police station at Morecambe. Walker and McIlkenny confessed after the West Midlands Police had taken them back to the police station at Queens Road in Aston. Callaghan also confessed in Birmingham. Two men, Hunter and Hill, did not confess or, rather, they refused to sign confessions – the police insisted that they had made oral confessions. Significantly, the two who refused to sign were the ones with previous experience of police custody. The men later explained that they had confessed after brutal interrogation. They added that they had been beaten at Morecambe. One was told that a violent mob was surrounding his house in Birmingham and that the police would leave his wife and children to their fate if he did not cooperate. When brought back to Birmingham, the Six claimed that they were beaten further, threatened with dogs, and subjected to a mock execution with blank cartridges.

The men who signed confessions were terrified and confused. Walker was so agitated that he refused to be left alone with the duty solicitor who had been allocated to his case. He said later: 'I thought he was a policeman come to give me another beating. I wouldn't talk to him.' When asked to explain his black eye (this was the only injury that the police conceded the suspects had suffered while in their custody), Walker said that he had 'fallen' – though the police claimed that he had hit his head while being put in a car.

Photographs of the Six in custody apparently show them with bruises on their faces – though a medical expert consulted by the police in the mid 1980s insisted that the photographs were inconclusive and, for example, an apparent mark on the neck of Power might have been a 'love bite'.[9] A prison doctor and lawyers said they saw severe bruising on other parts of the men's bodies – though Mr Justice Bridge, at the trial of the Six, made it clear that he thought the doctor was merely covering for his colleagues in the prison service by pretending that the men had suffered injuries before they arrived at the jail.

There are three explanations of when and where the Six were beaten. The Home Office implied that the men were attacked by prison officers at Winson Green prison after they had been discharged from police custody. The prison officers claimed that the men had already been injured before they arrived at Winson Green. The Six themselves, however, were consistent in their claims that they had been beaten, both while in police custody and then again in prison.

In 1975, fourteen prison officers from Winson Green were charged with assaulting the Birmingham Six. All were acquitted after a trial in which the judge, Mr Justice Swanwick, expressed his distaste for the alleged victims. In reality, hardly anyone even pretended to believe that the Six had not been assaulted in prison. Winson Green was a brutal and badly run institution. A few years later, a coroner recorded a verdict of 'unlawful killing' on a man who died there – the prison officers who were prosecuted for his murder were acquitted after claiming that the man in their custody had suffered his fatal injuries by throwing himself against the cell walls.[10] With regard to the Birmingham Six, the Home Office accepted that, as a minister put it to Parliament: 'injuries to the men were caused while in Winson Green prison'.[11] It would have been hard for the Home Office to deny that the men had been assaulted in prison without admitting that they had been assaulted by the police who extracted their confessions.

Over the years, evidence came to light which seemed to support the Birmingham Six's claim that they had been assaulted in police custody. A cleaner at the police station at Morecambe recalled that at first they had been kept away from cells in which the suspects had been held but that, when they had been allowed in, they had seen blood on the walls. Two police officers who had been present at the station where the Six were held in Birmingham revealed that they had seen evidence of brutality.

The Birmingham Six looked like IRA men

As has been stressed, the Birmingham Six came from the same background as many IRA volunteers. They did not, however, behave like them. IRA men generally said nothing at their trial – though they sometimes made a political statement after conviction. The Six were tried with a man, Mick Murray, who behaved in exactly this way – which may have confused the jury. Mr Justice Bridge compared the behaviour of the Birmingham Six unfavourably to that of Murray: 'You may think that Murray's conduct in this trial has shown a certain measure of dignity which is totally absent from the conduct of some of his co-defendants.'[12] When such men were released after the Good Friday

Agreement of 1998, they discussed their terrorist careers without inhibition.

The Six protested their innocence at their trial and repeatedly since. They have never said anything after their release that even hinted that they had anything to do with the bombings. Though they were treated badly on their first arrival at Winson Green prison, thereafter the warders guarding them seem not to have been convinced that they were hardened terrorists. By the late 1980s, Walker – once alleged to have been a brigadier in the IRA – was allowed to receive unsupervised visits at Long Lartin prison, which was unusual for a man still nominally regarded as a Category A prisoner. Men in the same institution who were acknowledged as members of the IRA, even one who was within a month of the end of a fourteen-year sentence, were afforded no such treatment.[13] A Conservative minister at the Home Office told Parliament in 1986: 'I willingly concede that the behaviour of these men in prison has not been like many other IRA prisoners. There is no secret about that.'[14]

Is it possible that the police lied?

To those who know about revelations of police behaviour that followed, say, the murder of Stephen Lawrence in 1993 or the deaths at the Hillsborough football stadium in 1989, this may seem a naïve question. But in the 1970s and 80s, things were different. Peter Rawlinson, who had been Attorney General until a few months before the Birmingham pub bombings, had, as a young barrister, suggested in court that the police might have concocted a confession – 'It's all up. You bloody well know I done it' – that led to the execution of one of his clients. The judge had made it clear that he disliked this challenge.[15] Lord Denning stopped the civil action by the Six against the Lancashire and West Midlands Police on the following grounds:

> If the six men win, it will mean that the police are guilty of perjury, that they are guilty of violence and threats, that the confessions were invented and improperly admitted in evidence and the convictions were erroneous ... This is such an appalling vista that every sensible person in the land would say that it cannot be right that these actions should go any further.

In fact, the position of judges shifted over time as some police officers came forward to say that the Six had been ill-treated in custody. A former officer, Tom Clarke, who had been on duty at the Birmingham police station where the Six were held, said that he had seen evidence that the men were threatened with dogs. At the appeal hearing in 1987, counsel for the Crown argued that Clarke was an unreliable witness because he had been dismissed for having stolen money from a prisoner.

There was a particularly dramatic moment in the appeal hearing when Joyce Lynas gave evidence. She had been a police cadet on duty at the Birmingham station where the Six were held. She first testified that she had seen no brutality. But she then returned to court and said she wished to change her testimony. She had seen evidence that the Six were ill-treated. She explained that she had not previously revealed this because she felt under pressure to help her colleagues and also because she had received a sinister and anonymous phone call saying 'don't forget that you have children'.

Some thought that Joyce Lynas was a compelling witness because she had nothing to gain from changing her evidence. Her account suggested that there had not merely been improper behaviour by individual officers but that there had been a conspiracy to cover this up.

However, Igor Judge, the lead counsel for the Crown, drew attention to the fact that Lynas had lied on oath in her previous testimony and suggested that this invalidated anything she said. The judges shared this view. According to them, she was 'a witness not worthy of belief'. Eight years after the Appeal Court (civil division) under Denning dismissed a case brought by the Six on the grounds that it was inconceivable that police officers should lie, the Appeal Court (criminal division) under Lord Lane dismissed a case brought on behalf of the Six on the grounds that some police officers were obviously lying.[16]

In fact, there was much evidence that police officers in the West Midlands told lies. Internal disciplinary proceedings in the Birmingham force in 1972 had resulted in the punishment of seven officers for 'falsehood'.[17] Detective Sergeant Morton, one of the policemen who testified that the Birmingham Six had been delivered to Winson Green unharmed, was subsequently sentenced to a year in prison for assaulting a suspect in custody. Detective Superintendent George Reade of the West Midlands Serious Crime Squad conducted the first interrogations of the

Birmingham Six in Morecambe. At Christmas 1975 he led a raid on the house of Philip Buckley in Walsall. Buckley sued the police claiming that he had been punched, kicked and pushed downstairs. Reade gave evidence in court saying that no assault had occurred. The jury found against the police and awarded damages to Buckley.

In 1993, three detectives from the West Midlands – George Reade, Colin Morris and Terence Woodwiss – were prosecuted for perjury and conspiracy to pervert the course of justice in the case of the Birmingham Six. However, the judge – Mr Justice Garland – stopped the proceedings on the grounds that adverse publicity would make it impossible for the accused men to receive a fair trial.

The nature of the West Midlands Police Force

It is worth pointing out that concerns about the quality of the West Midlands force were not just expressed by left-wingers and did not merely relate to their treatment of the Birmingham Six. The reports of Her Majesty's Inspectorate of Constabulary (HMIC) are revealing – and might be even more revealing if parts of the report for 1974 had not been withheld. The West Midlands Police force was a relatively new creation in 1974. What had formerly been known as the West Midlands Force (responsible for policing in the area around Birmingham) had been merged with the Birmingham force and, though the new body took the name of the West Midlands, it was predominantly made up of people from the Birmingham force and based in that city. Most of the policemen who investigated the Birmingham Six were from the city and had previously belonged to the Birmingham, rather than West Midlands, force. However, George Reade, the most important of the officers in the presentation of the case against the Six, came from Walsall and had before the merger belonged to the West Midlands rather than the Birmingham force. HMIC also noted that a high proportion of crimes in the pre-merger West Midlands area were noticed only when suspects confessed to them.[18] As for the pre-merger Birmingham police, they seem to have enjoyed a comfortable relationship with prosecutors and judges. Even the Lord Chancellor's Office had been troubled by the extent to which Michael Argyle, a Birmingham Recorder known for his stiff sentences, 'hob-nobbed' with the police.[19]

The West Midlands Serious Crime Squad were particularly important in the investigation of the Birmingham bombing. An Assistant Chief
Constable of the West Midlands force justified the considerable resources
devoted to this squad on the grounds that it would have been impossible to catch the bombers without the 'intelligence' that it provided:
'without this knowledge, no other avenue of enquiry, including the
painstaking collection of evidence for forensic examination would have
led to the offenders'.[20] Members of the Serious Crime Squad were subsequently found to have misbehaved in other cases. New forensic
techniques demonstrated that members of the squad had repeatedly
added details to confessions after they had been signed. They were also
alleged to have assaulted prisoners and faked evidence. Chief Constable
Dearing disbanded the squad in 1989 – before the release of the Six and
at a time when he was still insisting on their guilt. No member of the
Serious Crime Squad was ever charged with an offence relating to their
improper methods, but it may give an idea of the culture in the unit that
one of its former members – Laurence Henry Shaw – was later convicted of armed robbery.

Forensic evidence

Frank Skuse, a Home Office forensic scientist, conducted tests on the
hands of the suspects soon after their arrest. He testified in court that
some of these revealed substances that could have come only from
explosives. Later it emerged that the substance in question was also
present in playing cards (the Six had been playing cards immediately
before their arrest). For reasons not directly related to the Birmingham
case, Skuse was required to take early retirement. When Granada television questioned his competence and/or integrity, he began a libel action
but then abandoned it.

Is it true that only left-wing troublemakers defended the Six?

Mullin and many of his supporters were on the left of the Labour Party.
However, a right-wing Tory MP, Sir John Farr, also concluded that the
Six were innocent and spoke out on their behalf. Douglas Hurd was
Conservative Home Secretary in the late 1980s and had previously
been Northern Ireland Secretary. He was a subtle politician with 'no

exaggerated respect for either police or judges'.[21] He was careful not to interfere in judicial matters, or to do anything that might offend the right wing of his party. Nonetheless, he referred the case to the Court of Appeal and his public remarks, even before the men's release, do not suggest that he was convinced of their guilt. The eventual release of the Six took place under a Conservative government.

Appendix V. The Colony

> *The intention was not to examine 'colour prejudice', it was certainly not our purpose to report on or review white people's feelings of superiority: that was frequently implied in one news broadcast after another, and in the routine programmes that almost entirely ignored the black minority. Our aim was to present what it felt like to be a West Indian, in Britain, in Birmingham, and to offer West Indians the chance to describe in their own way the feelings they had about Britain and the British.*
>
> Philip Donnellan, producer of *The Colony*[1]

> *Let's find a West Indian who'd do a truthful film about West Indians today.*[2]
>
> Philip Donnellan, letter to Huw Wheldon (BBC executive)

The Colony, the 1964 BBC documentary about West Indians in Birmingham, has had a huge influence – perhaps more so in recent years than at the time it was broadcast. Scenes from it were reproduced in subsequent films – such as the Black Audio Film Collective *Handsworth Songs*, which was made in response to the Handsworth riots of 1985. One should say, however, that, like many brilliant documentaries, this one included several sleights of hand. Those involved had complicated intentions, and those of the producer were not necessarily the same as those of the people who allowed themselves to be interviewed. Viewers who see the film now probably understand it in ways that are very different from how it would have been understood in 1964.

The film was directed by Philip Donnellan. Donnellan was, as his name suggests, of Irish origin but had actually been unaware of his background until late in life. His grandfather had come over during the potato famine and his father, commissioned in the army during the First World War, had adopted the manners of a middle-class Englishman. Donnellan himself, after an education at a minor public school, served as an officer during the Second World War and then, largely on account of his upper-class voice and manner, was recruited as an announcer by the BBC in London. He moved to Birmingham in 1948. Though he often talked of the need to make programmes about the city, he does not seem to have liked it much – he recalled arriving on 3 April 1948, when it was snowing. For most of the time that he worked in Birmingham, he actually lived away from the city – first in Warwick and then in Shropshire.

Donnellan moved into television and became a producer of documentaries. He also worked with Charles Parker, a radio producer who arrived in Birmingham in 1954. Parker, who undertook much of the sound recording for *The Colony*, was famous for making 'radio ballads' which concentrated on people who might not usually attract attention on the BBC and for his interest in folk music. Parker and Donnellan were particularly conscious of the relation between sound and image and the fact that the two sometimes seem oddly juxtaposed in *The Colony* is at least in part deliberate. The film's experimental quality also derives partly from the fact that its makers were using relatively new technology. Tape recorders had made it easier to interview people outside studios and easier to edit the resulting tracks. Light 16mm cameras made it easier to film in settings that might be made to look 'natural' – though the film is often deliberately not 'naturalistic'.

Donnellan had felt constrained by rigidly scripted programmes – which were a legacy of wartime censorship. He later claimed that *The Colony* was 'probably the first film the BBC made which allowed Caribbean people, West Indians, to speak about their own feelings absolutely untrammelled and undirected by a commentary, just to speak about their own feelings on film about the world that they had come into in Britain'.[3] *The Colony* was not exactly 'unscripted', though. Preserved in Birmingham Library are the notes on the planning of the film from 1963, transcripts of interviews with participants and a shot list detailing the scenes that were to be filmed.[4] It seems that the interviews with individuals were sometimes broadcast over the film. There were also filmed interviews (in which we see the interviewees as well as hear their voices) that involved people speaking in significant places or talking in groups. These were partly scripted in advance – in particular, the monologue delivered by Victor Williams as he walks around the Birmingham Science Museum was thought out before the producers had even decided which of their interviewees would feature in this scene. Unlike many documentaries of the time, there is no authoritative voice-over in which a single patrician narrator explains things (the role performed, for example, by Laurence Olivier in *The World at War*). The original script contains a kind of implicit voice-over, though, because notes alongside the interviews and/or plans for shots make it clear what impression is meant to be conveyed by each part of the film.

The film had a strange beginning. It started in November 1960 in Winson Green prison when Charles Parker interviewed Ezekial, who had been imprisoned for an assault on the former lover of the woman he lived with. Parker had met Ezekial while lecturing on folk music in the prison and had recorded him singing. It is not clear how Parker intended to use the interview and musical recordings, but Ezekial would not have fitted with the final form of *The Colony*, which emphasized the respectability of its subjects. Parker seems to have met Ezekial at the BBC headquarters in Portland Place in March 1964. Ezekial had left Birmingham by this time and it must have been hard to keep track of a man who moved around, was semi-literate and had no telephone. Ezekial wrote to Parker in October 1964: 'I never did hear nothing from you again.'

Parker apologized to Ezekial but the film had been planned as early as July 1963 and the producer must have been shooting it when Ezekial and Parker met in London – the schedule suggests that it was filmed between 17 February and 7 March 1964.

The Colony was first broadcast in June 1964. This was a year of high racial tension in Birmingham but the broadcast happened several months before the general election in which supporters of the Conservative candidate in Smethwick used racially charged terms and the film does not have much overt political content. Sometimes those who made it seem to have sought to convey an almost subliminal message. The original script anticipated a sequence of shots that would feature the word 'No': 'No parking' and 'No waiting' as well as 'No 57' on the front of a bus. It looked as if the producer was seeking to evoke the signs saying 'No coloured' that might be hung in the windows of Birmingham lodging houses – though, in fact, no interviewee alluded directly to such signs.

Comparing the final broadcast version with the original shooting notes, script and interviews conducted with individual West Indians, raises interesting questions. The final version alludes to the different islands of the West Indies but concentrates on Jamaica and shows a map of the island. The original proposal had also anticipated showing a map of Barbados and a succession of shots of a 'Jamaican face', a 'Barbadian face', etc. Some things that obviously matter to the interviewees are omitted from the final film. At one point, one of the West Indians alludes to having served in the forces. Stanley Crooke, another of the interviewees, asks him if he was in the air force during the war and he says that he was in the army during National Service (i.e. he was a post-war conscript). This is interesting because white British people so often assumed that black men had not been called up. It is also interesting to note that Crooke raises his eyebrows when told that someone had been in the post-war army – perhaps, though no one says so in so many words, some West Indians thought that the air force was better than the army and also that service in a war against fascism might be more admirable than post-war service with forces fighting colonial insurgencies. But the moment is brief. Perhaps Donnellan, a wartime commando, just did not take any references to peace-time soldiering seriously. The shooting script, however, reveals the tantalizing fact that the four West Indian men who were shown drinking and smoking together were talking 'mostly about the army'.

Many of those interviewed for *The Colony* had televisions and some alluded to the ways in which black people were presented in documentaries. Nevertheless, the press release for the film – it was publicized alongside an edition of *Gardeners' World* with Percy Thrower – made it clear that this was a film for a white audience:

> These people's forefathers were Africans. They went to the West Indies as slaves, interbred with our forefathers . . . worked the plantations that provided the wealth of our Empire, honoured our Queen, died in our wars. Now they are in our streets, they are our neighbours and their colony in Birmingham is an integral part of our life.

It was also clear from the original script notes that in a strange way the film was about white English people, even though they hardly featured in it. The original working title was 'Mother Country'. It was made at a time when British commentators were becoming obsessed with ideas of national decline. Donnellan was still obsessed with this topic when he was interviewed in 1991: '1865 to 1960. I mean it's a century of the steady decline in the attention of the managerial classes to the importance of maintaining industrial progress in Britain.'[5] The original treatment contained the question 'Does the White Englishman deserve to survive?' At one point in the script, an interviewee says: 'This isn't the England I'd expected. When I first saw the building I thought the whole place was factories . . . it looked backward . . . a country that was going backward with regard to the rest of the world.' At this point, a note opposite the interview says: 'Suddenly we see ourselves from the West Indies' point of view: old, decaying, a dying culture.' The film was originally intended to finish with West Indians filing up the gangplank onto a liner to return home. The script says: 'A man and his wife and family are going to Jamaica; for them the experiment has both succeeded and utterly failed. For us it has only failed.' Birmingham was presented as a city of grimy, Victorian buildings that seemed to incarnate national decline. Here the shot list reads simply: 'Effluent coming under arch on canal'.

The negative presentation of Birmingham, and to some extent Britain, is strange. West Indians may have expressed the desire to go home or the belief that their homeland was more attractive than industrial Britain but hardly any of them did return. As for the notion of Birmingham as symbol of decline, in the early 1960s it had a booming economy and full employment. Black immigrants had harder lives than white people and endured many humiliations but they were richer than they would have been in the West Indies and richer than the white working class of Birmingham would have been just a decade or so previously.

In retrospect, two things are striking about the assumptions behind *The Colony*. The first of these is the emphasis on decay and decline. One should remember that the filmmakers began their work in the same year that Harold Wilson delivered his 'white heat' speech about the virtues of technological modernization – and at a time when Wilson was still admired by left-wing intellectuals. On a local level, the emphasis on Birmingham as a symbol of a decayed Victorian past actually looks as though it might fit uncomfortably well with the assumptions that

Herbert Manzoni, the city engineer, made about urban development – assumptions that underlay the investment in roads and high-rise buildings that was already transforming Birmingham in the early 1960s. Secondly, Donnellan and Parker were interested in the culture of work but oddly uninterested in work itself – as though the folksongs that emerged from mines and fishing villages were more important than the labour through which miners and fishermen earned their living. *The Colony* features people at work but says remarkably little about matters such as economics – how much people got paid – or what actually happened in factories. The shot list alludes to people on a factory floor 'doing nonsensical things with bits of tin'.

The filmmakers wanted to present the differences between those drawn from the different islands in the West Indies. They emphasized that the islanders were separated by 'hundreds of miles of tropical sea' and that they had no more in common with each other than 'we have with Texans or French Canadians'. This emphasis is easier to understand when we recall that the film was made shortly after the West Indian Federation, promoted by Britain, had broken up. On the other hand, the producer did not directly address the hierarchy of pigmentation among West Indians – even though the original interviews frequently allude to this – or to sexual relations between the races – even though at least two of the male interviewees were married to white women. Religion plays a role in the documentary but some of the wilder statements of beliefs (at least one of the interviewees is a Seventh Day Adventist) did not make it into the final cut of the film. Those who read the original interviews may feel that the contradictions, ambiguities and uncertainties are the most interesting things about them. Some recall life in the West Indies in favourable terms but they also allude to the bitter strikes in Jamaica in 1938 and to the rise of Rastafarianism – neither of these feature in the final film and neither of them would fit neatly with its presentation of the West Indies as a place of bucolic innocence. In his original interview, but not in the version that appears in the film, Lloyd expressed active dislike for the intimacy of the society in which he had grown up: 'One thing I like about this country as opposed to Jamaica is that I walk down the street and I don't know anybody. It's so nice to be anonymous. It's a bind knowing everybody in the street.' Two of the interviewees talk approvingly of Britain as being 'civilized' but another says: 'Two words I don't like, one is civilization and the other is culture.

I'm afraid of these two words. The English in particular can't recognize any other culture but their own.'

In one important respect, the film appears to have confounded the original intention of its makers. Stan Crooke, the railway signalman from St Kitts, does not feature at all in the preliminary interviews. His interviews seem to have been recorded only during the filming itself – so that we never hear his voice without also seeing his face on screen. He was a particularly forceful character who expressed himself in memorable ways, and towards the end it feels almost as though he has hijacked the film. Instead of finishing, as the original script had suggested, with immigrants getting back on the boat at Southampton, it finished with Crooke at work. He is in the signal box at Selly Oak, which had been rebuilt in 1958. Since Selly Oak is between the Edgbaston campus of the university and Bournville this location does not quite fit with the film-makers' general view of Birmingham as a grimy industrial city, though the black and white film manages to confer a vaguely Victorian air on the scene. Crooke talks at considerable length with occasional pauses for thought. The words sound as though they are his own. It is towards the end of his monologue that he hints that life in the West Indies might actually not have been entirely idyllic and that there is an element of 'fantasy' in the usual portrayal of the Caribbean. He fears that West Indians might 'vegetate' if they do not free themselves from this fantasy and that this would be a bad thing for both them and 'the English'.

Notes

INTRODUCTION: THE 'WRONG KIND OF VULGARITY'

1. Kew National Archives (TNA), HO 186/2637, 'History of the Home Office Midland Civil Defence Region', dated 1 February 1947.
2. Christopher Dyer, 'Lords in a Landscape: The Berkeley Family and North-field (Worcestershire)', in Linda Clark (ed.), *The Fifteenth Century*, XIV: *Essays Presented to Michael Hicks* (2015), pp. 13–38.
3. H.V. Morton, *The Call of England* (1928), p. 176.
4. R.H. Hilton, *A Medieval Society: The West Midlands at the End of the Thirteenth Century* (1966).
5. Alexis de Tocqueville, *Journeys to England and Ireland*, edited J.P. Mayer (1958), p. 94.
6. Richard Hoggart, *An Imagined Life: Life and Times*, III: *1959–1991* (Oxford, 1992), p. 103.
7. Maiken Umbach, 'A Tale of Second Cities: Autonomy, Culture, and the Law in Hamburg and Barcelona in the Late Nineteenth Century', *The American Historical Review*, 110, 3 (2005), pp. 659–92.
8. G.M. Young, *Portrait of an Age* (2002, first published 1936), p. 130.
9. The changing status of Birmingham was remarked on in David Canna-dine's review of the last volume of the official history of Birmingham. David Cannadine, 'The "Best Governed City", Part Three', *The Historical Journal*, 19, 2 (1976), pp. 536–44. For a work that approaches Birmingham because it is seen as statistically representative, see Kenneth Newton, *Second City Politics: Democratic Processes and Decision-Making in Birmingham* (Oxford, 1976).
10. Morton did, though not in his best-known book, write many interesting passages about Birmingham, one of which I have cited in this chapter.
11. J.B. Priestley, *English Journey* (2018, first published 1934), p. 96.
12. Peter James and Richard Sadler, *Homes Fit for Heroes: Photographs by Bill Brandt, 1939–1943* (Stockport, 2004).
13. Frank Mort, *Capital Affairs: London and the Making of the Permissive Society* (2010).

14. Matt Houlbrook, *Queer London: Perils and Pleasures in the Sexual Metropolis, 1918–1957* (Chicago, 2005).
15. Lucien Febvre, Preface in Charles Bettelheim and Suzanne Frère, *Une Ville Française Moyenne: Auxerre en 1950* (Paris, 1950), p. xi.
16. Warwick University, Modern Records Centre, 1213/2/2/1, Albert Bennett, interview with Steven Tolliday 1–2 February 1981.

CITY LIMITS: A NOTE ON GEOGRAPHY

1. Ivor Davies, 'Urban Farming: A Study of the Agriculture of the City of Birmingham', *Geography*, 38, 4 (1953), pp. 296–303.
2. Henry Green, *Pack My Bag: A Self-Portrait* (1992, first published 1940), p. 234.
3. Harry Smith, 'Propertied Society and Public Life: The Social History of Birmingham, 1780–1832', DPhil, University of Oxford (2013).
4. David Parker and Christian Karner, 'Remembering the Alum Rock Road: Reputational Geographies and Spatial Biographies', *Midland History*, 36, 2 (2011), pp. 292–309.
5. Arshad Isakjee, 'Tainted Citizens: The Securitised Identities of Young Muslim Men in Birmingham', PhD, University of Birmingham (2013).
6. David Spencer and John Lloyd, *A Child's Eye View of Small Heath Birmingham: Perception Studies for Environmental Education*, University of Birmingham Centre for Urban and Regional Studies, Research Memorandum, 34 (Birmingham, 1974), p. 111.
7. John Taylor, *In the Pleasure Groove: Love, Death and Duran Duran* (2012), p. 54.
8. E.R. Dodds, *Missing Persons: An Autobiography* (Oxford, 1977), p. 93.
9. Stephen Games, *Pevsner – The Early Life: Germany and Art* (2010), p. 202.
10. Steven Bassett, 'Anglo-Saxon Birmingham', *Midland History*, 25, 1 (2000), pp. 1–27.
11. Warwick University, Modern Records Centre, 1213/2/2/1, Albert Bennett interview with Steven Tolliday, 1–2 February 1981.
12. Green, *Pack My Bag*, p. 237.
13. Karis Campion, 'Making Mixed Race: Time, Place and Identities in Birmingham', PhD, University of Manchester (2017).

1. MINUTE BEGINNINGS

1. Steven Bassett, 'Anglo-Saxon Birmingham', *Midland History*, 25, 1 (2000), pp. 1–27.
2. John Hunt, 'Families at War: Royalists and Montfortians in the West Midlands', *Midland History*, 22, 1 (1997), pp. 1–34. On the disputes of the

families around what is now Birmingham, see also Peter Coss, *Lordship, Knighthood and Locality: A Study in English Society, c. 1180–c. 1290* (Cambridge, 1991), pp. 277–280.

3. Paul Mohr, 'The de Berminghams, Barons of Athenry: A Suggested Outline Lineage from First to Last', *Journal of the Galway Archaeological and Historical Society*, 63 (2011), pp. 43–56.

4. William Hutton, *An History of Birmingham, to the End of the Year 1780* (Birmingham, 1781), p. 29.

5. Marie Fogg, *The Smalbroke Family of Birmingham, 1550–1749* (North Carolina, 2010).

6. Jacqueline B. Geater (ed.), *Birmingham Wills and Inventories, 1512–1603* (Stratford-upon-Avon, 2016), pp. 9 and 185–91.

7. Ibid., p. 14.

8. Ibid., pp. 135–7.

9. Ibid., pp. 222–3.

10. John Izon, *The Records of King Edward's School, Birmingham* (Oxford, 1974), pp. 85–94.

11. http://www.nationalarchives.gov.uk/pathways/citizenship/citizen_subject/docs/rastell_vintner.htm.

12. R. Helmholz, 'Clement Colmore (1550–1619)', *Ecclesiastical Law Journal*, 18, 2 (2016), pp. 216–21.

13. Conrad Gill, *Studies in Midland History* (Oxford, 1930), p. 146.

14. Bernard Capp, 'Healing the Nation: Royalist Visionaries, Cromwell and the Restoration of Charles II', *The Seventeenth Century*, 34, 4 (2019), pp. 493–512.

2. ENLIGHTENMENT BIRMINGHAM

1. Joseph Priestley, *Autobiography of Joseph Priestley*, edited by Jack Lindsay (this edn, Bath, 1970), p. 120.

2. William Hutton, *The Life of William Hutton Including a Particular Account of the Riots at Birmingham in 1791; to Which is Subjoined the History of His Family Written by Himself and Published by His Daughter: Catherine Hutton* (1816), p. 41.

3. Alan Parton, 'Poor-Law Settlement Certificates and Migration to and from Birmingham, 1726–1757', *Local Population Studies*, 38 (1987), pp. 23–9.

4. P. M. Jones, 'Industrial Enlightenment in Practice: Visitors to the Soho Manufactory, 1765–1820', *Midland History*, 33, 1 (2008), pp. 68–96.

5. Peter Jones, *Industrial Enlightenment: Science Technology and Culture in Birmingham and the West Midlands, 1760–1820* (Manchester, 2008), p. 36.

6. Eric Hopkins, 'Working-Class Housing in Birmingham during the Industrial Revolution', *International Review of Social History*, 31, 1 (1986), pp. 80–94.

7. Matthew Boulton, quoted in E. Robinson, 'Eighteenth-Century Commerce and Fashion: Matthew Boulton's Marketing Techniques', *The Economic History Review*, 16, 1 (1963), pp. 39–60.

8. Susan Whyman, *The Useful Knowledge of William Hutton: Culture and Industry in Eighteenth-Century Birmingham* (Oxford, 2018), p. 5.

9. Jones, *Industrial Enlightenment*, p. 28.

10. Jennifer Tann, 'Marketing Methods in the International Steam Engine Market: The Case of Boulton and Watt', *The Journal of Economic History*, 38, 2 (1978), pp. 363–91.

11. Jenny Uglow, *The Lunar Men: The Friends who Made the Future 1730–1810* (2002), p. 245.

12. Cited in William Hutton, *The History of Birmingham* (this edn, 1836), p. 412.

13. Conrad Gill, *A History of Birmingham, I. Manor and Borough to 1865* (Oxford, 1952), p. 71.

14. John Money, *Experience and Identity: Birmingham and the West Midlands, 1760–1800* (Manchester, 1977), p. 14.

15. John Money, 'Taverns, Coffee Houses and Clubs: Local Politics and Popular Articulacy in the Birmingham Area, in the Age of the American Revolution', *The Historical Journal*, 14, 1 (1971), pp. 15–47.

16. Robinson, 'Eighteenth-Century Commerce and Fashion'.

17. Uglow, *Lunar Men*, p. 218.

18. P. Minard, 'Le Bureau d'Essai de Birmingham, ou la Fabrique de la Réputation au XVIIIe Siècle', *Annales. Histoire, Sciences Sociales*, 65, 5 (2010), pp. 1117–46.

19. Robinson, 'Eighteenth-Century Commerce and Fashion'.

20. Val Loggie, 'Soho through the Eyes of John Philip', in Phillada Ballard, Val Loggie and Shena Mason (eds.), *A Lost Landscape: Matthew Boulton's Gardens at Soho* (Chichester, 2009), pp. 43–56.

21. Shena Mason, '"A Cheerful and Pleasant Spot": Matthew Boulton and Soho', in Ballard *et al.* (eds.), *A Lost Landscape*, pp. xi–xiv.

22. P.M. Jones, 'Industrial Enlightenment in Practice'.

23. Phillada Ballard, 'Made from the Barren Waste by Me: The Soho Landscape, 1757–94', in Ballard *et al.* (eds.), *A Lost Landscape*, pp. 1–22.

24. P.M. Jones, 'Industrial Enlightenment in Practice'.

25. Tann, 'Marketing Methods'.

26. Mahesh A. Kalra, 'The Birth of the "New" Bombay Mint, *c.* 1790–1830 – Matthew Boulton's Pioneering Contribution to Modernization of Indian Coinage', *Proceedings of the Indian History Congress*, 74 (2013), pp. 416–25.

27. Uglow, *Lunar Men*, p. 58.

28. https://www.autographauctions.eu/130713-lot-443-PRIESTLEY-JOSEPH-1733–1804-English-Theologian-Natural-Philosopher-Chemist-credited-with-the-d?auction_id=0&view=lot_detail.

29. Anthony Page, 'Rational Dissent, Enlightenment and Abolition of the British Slave Trade', *The Historical Journal*, 54, 3 (2011), pp. 741–72.

30. Catherine Hutton, *Reminiscences of a Gentlewoman of the Last Century: Letters of Catherine Hutton*, edited by Catherine Hutton Beale (Birmingham, 1891), p. 28, letter to Mrs Coltman, 25 December 1780. Catherine Hutton added: 'I do not, however, impute monotony and nonsense to Calvin, but to Mr P., one of his present disciples.'

31. D.I. Callaghan, 'The Black Presence in the West Midlands, 1650–1918', *Midland History*, 36, 2 (2011), pp. 180–94.

32. https://www.revolutionaryplayers.org.uk/sermon-on-the-slave-trade-by-dr-joseph-priestley/.

33. Page, 'Rational Dissent, Enlightenment and Abolition'.

34. Edward Thomason, *Memoirs during Half a Century*, 1 (1845), p. 23.

35. W.A. Richards, 'The Import of Firearms into West Africa in the Eighteenth Century', *Journal of African History*, 21, 1 (1980), pp. 43–59.

36. Clive Harris (ed.), *The History of the Birmingham Gun-Barrel Proof House, with Notes on the Birmingham Gun Trade* (Birmingham, 1946).

37. Page, 'Rational Dissent, Enlightenment and Abolition'.

38. Barbara Smith, 'The Galtons of Birmingham: Quaker Gun Merchants and Bankers, 1702–1831', *Business History*, 9, 2 (1967), pp. 132–50.

39. Money, *Experience and Identity*, p. 16.

40. Uglow, *Lunar Men*, p. 66.

41. Cited in Jack Lindsay, edited introduction to Priestley, *Autobiography of Joseph Priestley*, pp. 1–66, p. 24.

42. Hutton, *Reminiscences of a Gentlewoman*, letter to Mrs André, 25 August 1791, pp. 88–9.

43. Uglow, *Lunar Men*, p. 440.

44. Jonathan Atherton, '"Nothing but a Birmingham jury can save them": Prosecuting Rioters in Late Eighteenth-Century Britain', *Midland History*, 39, 1 (2014), pp. 90–109.

45. Hutton, *Reminiscences of a Gentlewoman*, letter to Mrs André, 25 August 1791, p. 87.

46. Ibid., letter to a friend, 21 July 1791, p. 84.

47. Atherton, '"Nothing but a Birmingham jury"'.

48. Hutton, *Reminiscences of a Gentlewoman*, cited in note by editor on Church and King riots of 1791, p. 71.

49. Ibid., letter to Sir Richard Phillips, 4 May 1816, p. 158.

50. Ibid., letter to Mrs André, 27 February 1794, p. 115.

51. Ibid.

3. REVOLUTIONARY BIRMINGHAM?

1. Catherine Hutton, *Reminiscences of a Gentlewoman of the Last Century: Letters of Catherine Hutton*, edited by Catherine Hutton Beale (Birmingham, 1891), letter to Sir Richard Phillips, 21 December 1814, p. 156.

2. James Bisset, *Memoir of James Bisset, Written by Himself*, edited by T.B. Dudley (Leamington, 1904), p. 76.

3. Thomas Clark, *A Biographical Tribute to the Memory of James Luckcock, Father of Sunday School Instruction in Birmingham* (Birmingham, 1835).

4. Harry Smith, 'Propertied Society and Public Life: The Social History of Birmingham, 1780–1832', DPhil, University of Oxford (2013).

5. R.B. Rose, 'Political History to 1832', in W.B. Stephens (ed.), *Victoria History of the Counties of England: A History of the County of Warwick*, VII: *The City of Birmingham* (Oxford, 1964), pp. 270–97, p. 273.

6. Cited in Boyd Hilton, *A Mad, Bad and Dangerous People? England, 1783–1846* (Oxford, 2006), p. 271.

7. Smith, 'Propertied Society and Public Life'.

8. Susan Thomas, 'George Edmonds and the Development of Birmingham Radicalism', PhD, University of Birmingham (2021).

9. *Hansard*, 24 November 1819, extract of letter from Mr Spooner, magistrate, to Lord Sidmouth, 5 July 1819.

10. Cited in ibid., 13 July 1819, Spooner to Sidmouth.

11. Quoted in Robert Walmsley, *Peterloo: The Case Reopened* (Manchester, 1969), p. 284.

12. Thomas, 'George Edmonds and the Development of Birmingham Radicalism'.

13. Carlos T. Flick, 'Thomas Attwood, Francis Place, and the Agitation for British Parliamentary Reform', *Huntington Library Quarterly*, 34, 4 (1971), pp. 355–66.

14. Eliezer Edwards, *Personal Recollections of Birmingham and Birmingham Men* (Birmingham, 1877), p. 4.

15. H. Miller, 'Radicals, Tories or Monomaniacs? The Birmingham Currency Reformers in the House of Commons, 1832–67', *Parliamentary History*, 31, 3 (2012), pp. 354–77.

16. Alexander Somerville, *The Autobiography of a Working Man* (1848).

17. D. Moss, 'A Study in Failure: Thomas Attwood, M.P. for Birmingham, 1832–1839', *The Historical Journal*, 21, 3 (1978), pp. 545–70.

18. Edwards, *Personal Recollections*, p. 42.

19. H.W.H. Lyttleton, cited in Phillada Ballard, 'A Commercial and Industrial Elite: A Study of Birmingham's Upper Middle Class, 1780–1914', PhD, University of Reading (1983).

20. Miller, 'Radicals, Tories or Monomaniacs?'

21. Edwards, *Personal Recollections*, p. 6.

22. Cited in Donna Taylor, 'Governance and Locality in the Age of Reform: Birmingham, 1769–1852', PhD, University of Birmingham (2019).

23. Thomas Milton Kemnitz, 'The Chartist Convention of 1839', *Albion: A Quarterly Journal Concerned with British Studies*, 10, 2 (1978), pp. 152–70.

24. Taylor, 'Governance and Locality in the Age of Reform'.

25. Denys P. Leighton, 'Municipal Progress, Democracy and Radical Identity in Birmingham, 1838–1886', *Midland History*, 25, 1 (2000), pp. 115–42.

26. Trygve R. Tholfsen, 'The Chartist Crisis in Birmingham', *International Review of Social History*, 3, 3 (1958), pp. 461–80.

27. David Cannadine, *Lords and Landlords: The Aristocracy and the Towns, 1774–1967* (Leicester, 1980), p. 156.

28. John R. Kellett, *The Impact of Railways on Victorian Cities* (1969), p. 131.

29. Ibid., p. 140.

30. Taylor, 'Governance and Locality in the Age of Reform'.

31. J.M. Moore, 'Reformation, Terror and Scandal: The 1853 Royal Commission into Abuses at Birmingham Prison', *Midland History*, 46, 1 (2021), pp. 82–100.

4. CHAMBERLAIN'S BIRMINGHAM

1. By the late nineteenth century, brewers were hostile to Liberal politicians, whom they associated with temperance campaigns. Chamberlain's move to alliance with the Conservatives, and his attempts to tone down the anti-drink campaigns of his associates, brought a partial reconciliation with the drink trade (see chapter 6) but none of the modern pubs that were built in inter-war Birmingham were named after members of the Chamberlain family.

2. Leslie Rosenthal, 'Joseph Chamberlain and the Birmingham Town Council, 1865–1880', *Midland History*, 41, 1 (2016), pp. 71–95.

3. Norman Tiptaft, *The City Father* (1925), p. 11.

4. Warwick Modern Records Centre, 1213/2/4/6, Dick Etheridge and Lily May Etheridge interview with Steven Tolliday, 13 January 1981.

5. Roy Hattersley, 'Birmingham', in Andrew Adonis and Keith Thomas (eds.), *Roy Jenkins: A Retrospective* (2004), pp. 51–8, p. 54.

6. Augustin Filon, 'Joseph Chamberlain et le Socialisme d'État', *Revue des Deux Mondes (1829–1971)*, 96, 2 (1889), pp. 393–427.

7. A French Resident in London (1879), cited in Phillada Ballard, 'A Commercial and Industrial Elite: A Study of Birmingham's Upper Middle Classes, 1780–1914', PhD, University of Reading (1983).

8. Peter Marsh, *Joseph Chamberlain: Entrepreneur in Politics* (1994), p. 142.

9. David Dutton, *Austen Chamberlain: Gentleman in Politics* (Bolton, 1985), p. 15.

10. Filon, 'Joseph Chamberlain et le Socialisme d'État'.

11. Cited in David Dutton, 'Unionist Politics and the Aftermath of the General Election of 1906: A Reassessment', *The Historical Journal*, 22, 4 (1979), pp. 861–76.

12. Filon, 'Joseph Chamberlain et le Socialisme d'État'.

13. Cited in Andrew Reekes, *The Birmingham Political Machine: Winning Elections for Joseph Chamberlain* (Birmingham, 2018), pp. 9 and 101.

14. Marsh, *Joseph Chamberlain*, p. 46.

15. Beatrice Potter Webb, *My Apprenticeship*, 1 (Cambridge, 1979, first published 1926), p. 127.

16. Ballard, 'A Commercial and Industrial Elite'.

17. E.P. Hennock, *Fit and Proper Persons: Ideal and Reality in Nineteenth-Century Urban Government* (1973), p. 172.

18. Loeb cited in Jules P. Gehrke, 'A Radical Endeavor: Joseph Chamberlain and the Emergence of Municipal Socialism in Birmingham', *The American Journal of Economics and Sociology*, 75 (2016), pp. 23–57.

19. Moisei Ostrogorski, 'The Introduction of the Caucus into England', *Political Science Quarterly*, 8, 2 (1893), pp. 287–316.

20. Ballard, 'A Commercial and Industrial Elite'.

21. Maureen Perrie, 'Hobby Farming among the Birmingham Bourgeoisie: The Cadburys and the Chamberlains on Their Suburban Estates, *c*.1880–1914', *The Agricultural History Review*, 61, 1 (2013), pp. 111–34.

22. Ballard, 'A Commercial and Industrial Elite'.

23. David Cannadine, 'The Calthorpe Family and Birmingham, 1810–1910: A "Conservative Interest" Examined', *The Historical Journal*, 18, 4 (1975), pp. 725–60.

24. R.A. Church, *Kenricks in Hardware: A Family Business, 1791–1966* (1969), p. 82.

25. Ballard, 'A Commercial and Industrial Elite'.

26. Phillada Ballard, '"Rus in Urbe": Joseph Chamberlain's Gardens at Highbury, Moor Green Birmingham, 1879–1914', *Garden History*, 14, 1 (1986), pp. 61–76.

27. Oliver Lodge, *Past Years: An Autobiography* (1931), p. 322.

28. E.R. Dodds, *Missing Persons* (Oxford, 1977), p. 112.

29. Rudolf Peierls, *Bird of Passage: Recollections of a Physicist* (Princeton: New Jersey, 1985), p. 212.

30. Catherine Hutton Beale, *Memorials of the Old Meeting House and Burial Ground, Birmingham* (Birmingham, 1882).

31. David Cannadine, *Lords and Landlords: The Aristocracy and the Towns, 1774–1967* (Leicester, 1980), p. 199.

32. Adrian Boult, *My Own Trumpet* (1973), p. 58.

33. Godfrey Winn, *Autobiography*, vol. 1: *The Infirm Glory* (1967), p. 25.

34. Rosenthal, 'Joseph Chamberlain and the Birmingham Town Council'.

35. Ballard, 'A Commercial and Industrial Elite'.

36. Ibid.

37. Helen Plant, '"Ye are all one in Christ Jesus": Aspects of Unitarianism and Feminism in Birmingham, *c.* 1869–90', *Women's History Review*, 9, 4 (2000), pp. 721–42.

38. Ibid.

39. Cited in Hennock, *Fit and Proper Persons*, p. 73.

40. Beale, *Memorials of the Old Meeting House*, p. 1.

41. Plant, '"Ye are all one in Christ Jesus"'.

42. Leonora Davidoff and Catherine Hall, *Family Fortunes: Men and Women of the English Middle Class, 1780–1850* (1987), p. 32.

43. Paula Bartley, 'Moral Regeneration: Women and the Civic Gospel in Birmingham, 1870–1914', *Midland History*, 25, 1 (2000), pp. 143–61.

44. Rosenthal, 'Joseph Chamberlain and the Birmingham Town Council'.

45. R.A. Wright, 'Liberal Party Organisation and Politics in Birmingham, Coventry, and Wolverhampton, 1886–1914, with Particular Reference to the Development of Independent Labour Representation', PhD thesis, University of Birmingham (1977).

46. Michele Shoebridge, 'The Women's Suffrage Movement in Birmingham and District, 1903–1918', MA dissertation, Wolverhampton Polytechnic (1983).

47. Plant, '"Ye are all one in Christ Jesus"'.

48. Ibid.

49. Chamberlain claimed that he had been persuaded to support women's suffrage by his colleague Charles Dilke – a claim that may have been rooted in the fact that he found it painful to recall his deceased wife.

50. Anderton quoted in Cannadine, 'The Calthorpe Family and Birmingham'.

51. Ostrogorski, 'The Introduction of the Caucus into England'.

52. Winn, *The Infirm Glory*, p. 25.

53. Leslie Rosenthal, 'Economic Efficiency, Nuisance, and Sewage: New Lessons from Attorney-General v. Council of the Borough of Birmingham, 1858–95', *The Journal of Legal Studies*, 36, 1 (2007), pp. 27–62. Leslie Rosenthal, *The River Pollution Dilemma in Victorian England: Nuisance Law versus Economic Efficiency* (Farnham, 2014).

54. Shane Ewen, 'Power and Administration in Two Midland Cities, *c.* 1870–1938', PhD, University of Leicester (2003).

55. H.V. Morton, *The Call of England* (1928), p. 176.

56. Asa Briggs, *History of Birmingham*, II: *Borough and City, 1865–1938* (Oxford, 1952), p. 81.

57. Alan Mayne, *The Imagined Slum: Newspaper Representation in Three Cities, 1870–1914* (Leicester, 1993).

58. Patricia Auspos, 'Radicalism, Pressure Groups, and Party Politics: From the National Education League to the National Liberal Federation', *Journal of British Studies*, 20, 1 (1980), pp. 184–204.

59. Ibid.
60. Cited in Wright, 'Liberal Party Organisation and Politics in Birmingham, Coventry, and Wolverhampton'.
61. Cited in Marsh, *Joseph Chamberlain*, p. 220.
62. Cited in Michael Dennis Blanch, 'Nation, Empire and the Birmingham Working Class, 1899–1914', PhD, University of Birmingham (1975).
63. Reekes, *The Birmingham Political Machine*, p. 101.
64. Speech at Birmingham, 15 May 1903.
65. Sir Harry Wilson, cited in J.L. Garvin, *The Life of Joseph Chamberlain*, III: *1895–1900* (1934), p. 10.
66. Garvin, *The Life of Joseph Chamberlain*, III: *1895–1900*, p. 15. In fact, Chamberlain had not been particularly enthusiastic about municipal electrification.
67. Ibid., p. 175.
68. Enoch Powell, speech, Dublin, late 1964.
69. Roger Ward, 'The Strange Death of Liberal Birmingham', *Journal of Liberal History*, 82 (2014), pp. 16–24.
70. Harold Macmillan, *The Macmillan Diaries*, II: *Prime Minister and After, 1957–1966*, edited by Peter Catterall (2004), entry for 11 January 1960, p. 534.
71. Alfred Gardiner, *Life of George Cadbury* (1923); Lowell Satre, *Chocolate on Trial: Slavery, Politics and the Ethics of Business* (Athens, Ohio, 2005); Catherine Higgs, *Chocolate Islands: Cocoa, Slavery and Colonial Africa* (Athens, Ohio, 2012).
72. Speech at Bingley Hall, 9 July 1906.
73. Dutton, *Austen Chamberlain*, p. 51.
74. Ibid.
75. Ibid., p. 90.

5. CLASSES WITHOUT CONFLICT?

1. Asa Briggs, *Victorian Cities* (this edn, 1968), pp. 186–7.
2. Moisei Ostrogorski, 'The Introduction of the Caucus into England', *Political Science Quarterly*, 8, 2 (1893), pp. 287–316.
3. Quoted in ibid.
4. Alexis de Tocqueville, *Journeys to England and Ireland*, edited J.P. Mayer (1958), p. 104.
5. Dennis Smith, *Conflict and Compromise: Class Formation in English Society, 1830–1914: A Comparative Study of Birmingham and Sheffield* (1982), p. 21.
6. Cited in Peter Marsh, *Joseph Chamberlain: Entrepreneur in Politics* (1994), p. 24.

7. E.P. Hennock, *Fit and Proper Persons: Ideal and Reality in Nineteenth-Century Urban Government* (1973), pp. 27 and 34.

8. R.A. Church, *Kenricks in Hardware: A Family Business, 1791–1966* (1969), pp. 54–5.

9. HMSO, *Children's Employment Commission, Second Report of the Commissioners: Trades and Manufactures* (1843), p. 19.

10. Church, *Kenricks in Hardware*, p. 55.

11. Patsy Davis, 'Green Ribbons: The Irish in Birmingham in the 1860s, a Study of Housing, Work and Policing', PhD, University of Birmingham (2003).

12. Douglas A. Reid, 'The Decline of Saint Monday, 1766–1876', *Past & Present*, 71, 1 (1976), pp. 76–101.

13. Walter Allen, *As I Walked Down New Grub Street* (1981), pp. 2–3.

14. Walter Allen, *All in a Lifetime* (1959), p. 43.

15. Michael Dennis Blanch, 'Nation, Empire and the Birmingham Working Class, 1899–1914', PhD, University of Birmingham (1975).

16. Carl Chinn, 'The Anatomy of a Working-Class Neigbourhood: West Sparkbrook, 1871–1914', PhD, University of Birmingham (1986).

17. Cited in Barbara Weinberger, 'Law Breakers and Law Enforcers, in the Late Victorian City: Birmingham, 1867–1877', PhD, University of Warwick (1981).

18. Timmins, cited in Dennis Smith, 'Paternalism, Craft and Organizational Rationality, 1830–1930: An Exploratory Model', *Urban History*, 19, 2 (1992), pp. 211–28.

19. William Hutton, *An History of Birmingham, to the End of the Year 1780* (Birmingham, 1781), p. 72.

20. Paul de Rousiers, *La Question Ouvrière en Angleterre* (Paris, 1895), pp. 1–12.

21. Susan Thomas, 'George Edmonds and the Development of Birmingham Radicalism', PhD, University of Birmingham (2021).

22. Clive Behagg, 'Myths of Cohesion: Capital and Compromise in the Historiography of Nineteenth-Century Birmingham', *Social History*, 11, 3 (1986), pp. 375–84.

23. Allen, *As I Walked Down New Grub Street*, p. 2.

24. Grace Holte, *The Girl from Guildford Street: Growing up in Working-Class Birmingham, 1957–1968* (Studley, 2018), p. 18.

25. Hutton, *An History of Birmingham*, p. 27.

26. W.P.H. Phillimore, *Some Account of the Family of Middlemore of Warwickshire and Worcestershire* (1901), p. 72.

27. D.C. Lloyd-Owen, 'Richard Middlemore (1804–1891)', *The British Journal of Ophthalmology* (February 1920), pp. 49–53.

28. Michele Langfield, 'Righting the Record? British Child Migration: The Case of the Middlemore Homes, 1872–1972', in Kent Fedorowich and Andrew

S. Thompson (eds.), *Empire, Migration and Identity in the British World* (Manchester, 2013), pp. 150–68.

29. On the creation of this title, see Kew, National Archives HO 45/11551.

30. Cited in Alan Fox, 'Industrial Relations in Nineteenth-Century Birmingham', *Oxford Economic Papers*, 7, 1 (1955), pp. 57–70.

31. Eliezer Edwards, *Personal Recollections of Birmingham and Birmingham Men* (Birmingham, 1877), p. 8.

32. Smith, *Conflict and Compromise*, p. 95.

33. F.E. Terry-Chandler, 'Compulsory Industriousness: Working Conditions and Exploitation in Birmingham during the Industrial Revolution', *Midland History*, 44, 1 (2019), pp. 71–84.

34. Jennifer Aston, 'Female Business Ownership in Birmingham 1849–1901', *Midland History*, 37, 2 (2012), pp. 187–206.

35. Cited in Mary Nejedly, 'Child Labour in an Industrial Town: A Study of Child Workers in Birmingham, 1750–1880', PhD, University of Birmingham (2019).

36. Belinda Leach, 'Grandma Page's Workshop: Outwork in Birmingham 1911–1914', *Oral History*, 22, 1 (1994), pp. 35–42.

37. H. Nockolds, *Lucas, The First 100 Years*, I: *King of the Road: 1875–1939* (1976), p. 137.

38. Ibid., p. 46.

39. James E. Vance, 'Housing the Worker: Determinative and Contingent Ties in Nineteenth-Century Birmingham', *Economic Geography*, 43, 2 (1967), pp. 95–127.

40. Ibid.

41. Nejedly, 'Child Labour in an Industrial Town'.

42. Ibid.

43. Ibid.

44. HMSO, *Children's Employment Commission 'Second Report of the Commissioners'*, p. 27.

45. Leonore Davidoff and Catherine Hall, *Family Fortunes: Men and Women of the English Middle Class, 1780–1850* (1987), pp. 128, 266 and 94.

46. Nockolds, *Lucas*, I, p. 14.

47. Henry Green, *Pack My Bag: A Self-Portrait* (1992, first published 1940), p. 234.

48. Asa Briggs, *History of Birmingham*, II: *Borough and City, 1865–1938* (Oxford, 1952), p. 13.

49. Church, *Kenricks in Hardware*, p. 263.

50. Davidoff and Hall, *Family Fortunes*, p. 267.

51. Vance, 'Housing the Worker'.

52. Terry Carter, *Birmingham in the Great War, 1914–1915: The First Eighteen Months of the War* (2016).

53. Initially Birmingham Corporation owned the tracks on which trams ran but private companies owned the trams. In 1904, as original agreements expired, the corporation took over the running of all trams.

54. Shane Ewen, 'Power and Administration in Two Midland Cities, *c.* 1870–1938', PhD, University of Leicester (2003).
55. Weinberger, 'Law Breakers and Law Enforcers'.
56. Fox, 'Industrial Relations in Nineteenth-Century Birmingham'. R.A. Church and Barbara M.D. Smith, 'Competition and Monopoly in the Coffin Furniture Industry, 1870–1915', *The Economic History Review*, 19, 3 (1966), pp. 621–41.
57. Jamie Scott, '"Labourism Revisited": W.J. Davis, Working-Class Culture, and Trade Unionist Politics in Birmingham, 1892–1906', *Midland History*, 38, 1 (2013), pp. 80–96.
58. Blanch, 'Nation, Empire and the Birmingham Working Class'.

6. NEW SOCIETY, 1911–38

1. Cited in Catherine Hall, 'Married Women at Home in Birmingham in the 1920's and 1930's', *Oral History*, 5, 2 (1977), pp. 62–83.
2. Brinley Thomas, 'The Influx of Labour into the Midlands 1920–37', *Economica*, 5, 20 (1938), pp. 410–34.
3. Charles Heath, *Service Record of King Edward's School Birmingham during the War, 1914–1919* (Birmingham, 1920).
4. Gregory James, 'The Chinese Mariners of the First World War', *Journal of the Royal Asiatic Society Hong Kong Branch*, 60 (2020), pp. 200–210.
5. http://www.whitefeatherdiaries.org.uk/let-politicians-fight.
6. Cadbury Brothers, *Bournville Works and the War 1914–1919* (Birmingham, 1919).
7. R.A. Church, *Kenricks in Hardware: A Family Business, 1791–1966* (1969), p. 147.
8. Lewis Johnman, 'The Large Manufacturing Companies of 1935', *Business History*, 28, 2 (1986), pp. 226–45.
9. Eric Hopkins, 'Working-Class Life in Birmingham between the Wars, 1918–1939', *Midland History*, 15, 1 (1990), pp. 129–50.
10. Warwick University, Modern Records Centre (MRC), MSS 356/7/2/28 i–iii, Paul Worms, Making Motors, Interview with Tom Brindley.
11. David Paulson, 'The Professionalisation of Selling and the Transformation of a Family Business: Kenrick & Jefferson, 1878–1940', *Business History*, 62, 2 (2020), pp. 261–91.
12. Church, *Kenricks in Hardware*, p. 211.
13. Adrian Cadbury interview with Niamh Dillon. *Food from Source to Salespoint* (2001–2003), British Library Sound & Moving Image, Catalogue reference C 821/122 © The British Library, reel 12.
14. Michael Rowlinson, 'The Early Application of Scientific Management by Cadbury', *Business History*, 30, 4 (1988), pp. 377–95.

15. Adrian Cadbury interview with Niamh Dillon. *Food from Source to Sales-point*, reel 4.

16. Robert Fitzgerald, 'Products, Firms and Consumption: Cadbury and the Development of Marketing, 1900–1939', *Business History*, 47, 4 (2005), pp. 511–31.

17. Richard Clay, 'The Painting of Frank Taylor Lockwood (1895–1961): Industrialized Iconoclasm as Seen from Birmingham's Suburbs'. Essay to be found on http://www.connectinghistories.org.uk/suburban-birmingham/suburban-birmingham-essays/.

18. Jo-Ann Curtis, 'Cadbury's Angels: the Depiction of Women and the Bournville Works'. Essay to be found on http://www.connectinghistories.org.uk/suburban-birmingham/suburban-birmingham-essays/.

19. Harold Nockolds, *Lucas, The First 100 Years*, 1: *The King of the Road: 1875–1939* (1976), p. 65.

20. Ibid., p. 321.

21. Warwick University, MRC, 1213/2/3/4, Bryn Charles interview with Steven Tolliday, 20 May 1981.

22. https://silodrome.com/austin-seven-stanley-edge/.

23. Roy Church, *Herbert Austin: The British Motor Car Industry to 1941* (1979), p. 84.

24. Frank Price, *Being There* (Leicester, 2002), p. 38.

25. Jim Simmons, *Soap Box Evangelist* (Chichester, 1972), p. 69.

26. Ruth Jane Procter, 'Infant Mortality: A Study of the Impact of Social Intervention in Birmingham, 1873–1938', MPhil, University of Birmingham (2011).

27. Alison Light, *Common People: The History of an English Family* (2014), pp. 38 and 59.

28. Clay, 'The Painting of Frank Taylor Lockwood'.

29. Hopkins, 'Working-Class Life in Birmingham Between the Wars'.

30. Michael Hunkin, 'Manors from Heaven: The Municipal Housing Boom and the Challenge of Community Building on a New Estate, 1929–1939'. Essay to be found on http://www.connectinghistories.org.uk/suburban-birmingham/suburban-birmingham-essays/.

31. Margaret Giles, 'Something that Bit Better: Working-Class Domesticity and "Respectability", 1919–1939', DPhil, University of York (1989).

32. Ibid.

33. Barry K. Hill, 'Women and Unemployment in Birmingham, 1918–1939', *Midland History*, 27, 1 (2002), pp. 130–45. DOI: 10.1179/mdh.2002.27.1.130.

34. Richard Etheridge, *Walking in the Shadow of a Political Agitator*, I: *Apprentice* (North Carolina, 2016).

35. Giles, 'Something that Bit Better'.

36. Mary Soutar, Edgar Wilkins and Philip Sargant Florence, *Nutrition and Size of Family: Report on a New Housing Estate, 1939* (Birmingham, 1942), p. 48.

37. Florence Lutwidge in Kingstanding Voices, https://kingstanding.wordpress.com/.

38. Hunkin, 'Manors from Heaven'.

39. Asa Briggs, *History of Birmingham*, II: *Borough and City 1865–1938* (Oxford, 1952), p. 250.

40. Walter Allen, *As I Walked Down New Grub Street: Memories of a Writing Life* (1981), p. 65.

41. Hall, 'Married Women at Home in Birmingham'.

42. Hill, 'Women and Unemployment in Birmingham'.

43. *Hansard*, 21 May 1935.

44. Kew National Archives (TNA), BT 70/48, 'Industrial Development Survey in 1935. Survey of Factories Established, Extended or Closed', reports by factory inspectors.

45. Hill, 'Women and Unemployment in Birmingham'.

46. Imperial War Museum Sound Archive (IWMSA), 20792, interview with Dilwyn Evans, reel 2.

47. Julia Laite, 'Immoral Traffic: Mobility, Health, Labor and the "Lorry Girl" in Mid Twentieth-Century Britain', *Journal of British Studies*, 52, 3 (2013), pp. 693–721.

48. Peter Scott, 'The State, Internal Migration, and the Growth of New Industrial Communities in Inter-War Britain', *The English Historical Review*, 115, 461 (2000), pp. 329–53.

49. Grace Holte, *The Girl from Guildford Street: Growing up in Working-Class Birmingham, 1957–1968* (Studley, 2018), p. 51.

50. MRC, 1213/2/1/4, Arthur Bate interview with Steven Tolliday, 27 January 1981.

51. MRC, 1213/2/2/4, Phil Blewitt interview with Steven Tolliday, 25 March 1981.

52. Leslie John Jones, *Three Times for a Jolly Welshman: An Autobiography of a Rhondda Exile* (Birmingham, 1984).

53. MRC, 1213/2/3/4, Bryn Charles interview with Steven Tolliday, 20 May 1981.

54. IWMSA, 16724, interview with Ernest Taylor.

55. Susannah Wright, 'The Work of Teachers and Others in and around a Birmingham Slum School, 1891–1920', *History of Education*, 38, 6 (2009), pp. 729–46.

56. TNA, Lab 23/60, Middlemore Emigration Homes, 64th Annual Report for 1936.

57. *Town Crier*, 5 February 1937, cited in R.P. Hastings, 'The Birmingham Labour Movement, 1918–1945', *Midland History*, 5, 1 (1979), pp. 78–92.

58. Norman Tiptaft, *The Individualist* (Birmingham, 1954), p. 105.

59. David Gutzke, *Pubs and Progressives: Reinventing the Public House in England, 1896–1960* (Dekalb, Illinois, 2006), p. 23.

60. Oxford, Bodleian Library, Conservative Party Archives (CPA), CCO1/8/286, Leddington, to J.P.L. Thomas MP, 26 February 1951: 'I think that the position is that Aston is quarrelsome with the Birmingham Unionist Association and indeed will have nothing to do with that organization. That is because the President, Mr Walter Scott, the Chairman, Mr Fred Smith, both prominent brewers . . . do not want to be absorbed into the Birmingham Unionist Association.'

61. Emily Cole, 'The Urban and Suburban Public House in Inter-War England', Historic England, Research Report number 4 (Portsmouth, 2015). https:// historicengland.org.uk/research/results/reports/4–2015.

62. Norman Tiptaft, *Inns of the Midlands* (Birmingham, 1951), p. 94.

63. Cole, 'The Urban and Suburban Public House'.

64. Hopkins, 'Working-Class Life in Birmingham'.

65. Henry Green, *Pack My Bag: A Self-Portrait* (1992, first published 1940), pp 23–4.

66. IWMSA, 10197, Edward Sturman.

67. Norman Tiptaft, *The City Father* (1925), p. 11.

68. Jeffrey Richards, 'The Cinema and Cinema-Going in Birmingham in the 1930s', in John K. Walton and James Walvin (eds.), *Leisure in Britain, 1780–1939* (Manchester, 1983), pp. 31–52.

69. Allen, *As I Walked down New Grub Street*, p. 58.

70. Kathleen Tynan, *The Life of Kenneth Tynan* (this edn, 1987), p. 25.

71. Patrick Higgins, *Heterosexual Dictatorship: Male Homosexuality in Post-War Britain* (1996), p. 218.

72. J. Richards, 'The Cinema and Cinema-Going in Birmingham in the 1930s'.

73. Paddy Scannell, 'Broadcasting and the Politics of Unemployment, 1930–1935', *Media, Culture and Society*, 2 (1980), pp. 15–28.

74. J.B. Priestley, *English Journey* (2018, first published 1934), p. 96.

75. Milennibrum Project, MS 2255/2/42, Bernard Loftus.

76. Louis MacNeice, *The Strings Are False: An Unfinished Autobiography* (1965), p. 138.

7. OLD POLITICS, 1911–38

1. *The Times*, 15 November 1922.

2. Austen Chamberlain, *The Austen Chamberlain Diary Letters: The Correspondence of Sir Austen Chamberlain with his Sisters Hilda and Ida, 1916–1937*, edited by Robert Self (Cambridge, 1995), letter to Ida, 18 November 1922, p. 201.

3. Norman Tiptaft, *The City Father* (1925), p. 78.

4. John Boughton, 'Working-Class Politics in Birmingham and Sheffield, 1918–1931', PhD, University of Warwick (1985).

5. Ibid.

6. Ibid.

7. Jim Simmons, *Soap Box Evangelist* (Chichester, 1972), p. 49.

8. Warwick University Modern Record Centre (MRC), MSS.356/7/2/28/i–iii, Paul Worms, 'Making Motors', interview with Tom Brindley. https://warwick.ac.uk/services/library/mrc/mss356_7_2_28_ii_side1.mp3.

9. Eric Hopkins, 'Working-Class Life in Birmingham between the Wars, 1918–1939', *Midland History*, 15, 1 (1990), pp. 129–50.

10. MRC, 1213/2/1/1, Alf Allen interview with Steven Tolliday, 28 January 1981: 'The attitude of management in those days, they used to send people out on a Friday lunchtime to come back to work on a Monday afternoon.'

11. Cited in Boughton, 'Working-Class Politics in Birmingham and Sheffield'.

12. HMSO, *Report of a Court of Enquiry into a Dispute between the Austin Motor Company Limited and Certain Workpeople, Members of the National Union of Vehicle Builders* (1953).

13. Worms, 'Making Motors', interview with Tom Brindley.

14. P. Searby, 'Great Dodford and the Later History of the Chartist Land Scheme', *The Agricultural History Review*, 16, 1 (1968), pp. 32–45.

15. MRC, 1213/2/5/1, George Evans interview with Steven Tolliday, no date.

16. MRC, 1213/2/1/1, Alf Allen interview with Steven Tolliday, 28 January 1981.

17. MRC, 1213/2/3/4, Bryn Charles interview with Steven Tolliday, 20 May 1981.

18. Boughton, 'Working-Class Politics in Birmingham and Sheffield'.

19. http://rowntree.exeter.ac.uk/items/show/597.

20. http://www.whitefeatherdiaries.org.uk/let-politicians-fight.

21. Kew National Archives (TNA), CAB 23/25/2, Cabinet meeting of 12 April 1921.

22. *The Times*, 4 December 1923.

23. TNA, CAB 24/128/49, 'Report on Revolutionary Organisations in the United Kingdom', Directorate of Intelligence, Home Office, 29 September 1921.

24. Shane Ewen, 'Power and Administration in Two Midland Cities, *c.* 1870–1938', PhD, University of Leicester (2003).

25. Allen Andrews, *The Prosecutor, the Life of M.P. Pugh: Prosecuting Solicitor and Agent for the Director of Public Prosecutions* (1968), pp. 41 and 17.

26. Adrian Boult, *My Own Trumpet* (1973), p. 49.

27. Keith Laybourn and David Taylor, *Policing in England and Wales, 1918–39: The Fed, Flying Squads and Forensics* (2011), p. 66.

28. TNA, HO 144/6898, statement of special constable Alfred James Gilmore, 16 July 1926. He reported having told his own trade union colleagues: 'there were some strikers (tramwaymen) who were doing duty [i.e. as special constables]'.

29. Simmons, *Soap Box Evangelist*, pp. 52–5.
30. Chamberlain, *The Austen Chamberlain Diary Letters,* Letter to Hilda Chamberlain, 12 March 1933, p. 423.
31. Austen Chamberlain, *Politics from Inside: An Epistolary Chronicle, 1906–1914* (1936), letter to Mary Chamberlain, 6 February 1914, p. 608.
32. *The Times*, 15 November 1922.
33. Frank Price, *Being There* (Leicester, 2002), p. 50.
34. Chamberlain, Politics from Inside, letter dated 7 May 1911, p. 337.
35. *The Times*, 19 March 1923.
36. Keith Feiling, *The Life of Neville Chamberlain* (1946), p. 80.
37. A.K. Chesterton, *Portrait of a Leader: Oswald Mosley* (1937), p. 54.
38. Cited in Boughton, 'Working-Class Politics in Birmingham and Sheffield'.
39. Neville Chamberlain, *The Neville Chamberlain Diary Letters*, III: *The Heir Apparent*, edited by Robert Self (Aldershot, 2002), entry for 15 October 1935 and entry for 4 July 1935, p. 156.
40. Ibid., IV: *The Downing Street Years, 1934–1940*, edited by Robert Self (Aldershot, 2005), letter to Ida, 5 August 1939, p. 438.
41. Ibid., letter to Ida, 17 November 1935, p. 162.
42. Ibid., letter to Ida, 19 October 1935, p. 157.
43. Ibid., letter to Ida, 4 July 1936, p. 199.
44. https://historicalpageants.ac.uk/featured-pageants/pageant-birmingham-1938/.

8. THE SECOND WORLD WAR IN BIRMINGHAM

1. Eric Armstrong, *A Birmingham Boyhood, 1923–40* (Stroud, 2015), p. 159.
2. Jean Debney, *The Dangerfields: Munitions & Memories* (Studley, 2001), p. 16.
3. David Thoms, *War Industry and Society: The Midlands, 1939–1945* (1989), p. 152.
4. Shane Ewen, 'Power and Administration in Two Midland Cities, *c.* 1870–1938', PhD, University of Leicester (2003).
5. Kew National Archives (TNA), HO 186/2637, 'History of the Home Office Midland Civil Defence Region', 1 February 1947.
6. Roy Church, *Herbert Austin: The British Motor Car Industry to 1941* (1979), pp. 138–40.
7. Imperial War Museum Sound Archive (IWMSA), 30001, Peter Ayerst.
8. IWMSA, 20055, Roy Deeley.
9. IWMSA, 30001, Peter Ayerst,
10. Alex Henshaw, *Sigh for a Merlin: Testing the Spitfire* (1990).
11. Thoms, *War, Industry and Society*, p. 49.

12. TNA, HO 186/2637, 'History of the Home Office Midland Civil Defence Region', 1 February 1947.

13. Thoms, *War, Industry and Society*, p. 37.

14. IWMSA 14932, Norman Edwards.

15. TNA, HO 192/1220, 'Ministry of Home Security: Factory Survey', Avery to Ministry of Home Security, 23 February 1942; Triplex undated reply to survey.

16. Rudolf Peierls, *Bird of Passage: Recollections of a Physicist* (Princeton, New Jersey, 2014), p. 149.

17. IWMSA, 11363, Ernest Withers.

18. Sabine Lee, 'Birmingham-London-Los Alamos-Hiroshima: Britain and the Atomic Bomb', *Midland History*, 27, 1 (2002), pp. 146–64.

19. Anthony Sutcliffe and Roger Smith, *History of Birmingham*, III: *1939–1970* (Oxford, 1974), p. 44.

20. Ibid.

21. Ibid.

22. Juliette Pattinson, '"Shirkers", "Scrimjacks" and "Scrimshanks"? British Civilian Masculinity and Reserved Occupations, 1914–45', *Gender and History*, 28, 3 (2016), pp. 709–27.

23. TNA, HO 192/1251, 'Birmingham Economic and Social Survey. Section S, Special Enquiry. Study of Selected Factories', ICI Witton Works, 8 December 1941.

24. TNA, HO 192/1240, letter from Farris and Sheldon, 4 February 1942.

25. Imperial War Museum (IWM), 6431, E.A. Dorking, 'Some Recollections of My Life During the Years 1930–1945'.

26. Sutcliffe and Smith, *History of Birmingham*, p. 44.

27. Harold Nockolds, *Lucas, The First 100 Years*, II: *The Successors* (1978), p. 77.

28. Ibid.

29. Adam Carey, 'Politics, Governance and the Shaping of Smethwick since 1945', MPhil, University of Birmingham (2016).

30. Debney, *The Dangerfields*, pp. 36–46.

31. http://www.bbc.co.uk/history/ww2peopleswar/stories/82/a4093382.shtml.

32. Debney, *The Dangerfields*, p. 69.

33. Sutcliffe and Smith, *History of Birmingham*, p. 43.

34. IWMSA, 5334, Gwendoline Stewart.

35. TNA, HO 192/1206, interview with Miss E. Lusty, 15 January 1942.

36. Ibid., interview with Miss Truscott, 8 January 1942.

37. Ibid., interview with Miss C.N. Harris, 13 January 1942.

38. Debney, *The Dangerfields*, p. 41.

39. TNA, HO 192/1206, interview with Miss Truscott, 8 January 1942.

40. Ibid., table attached to report by Hamilton Bayes to be presented to the Justices of the City on 24 January 1941.

41. John Rex and Robert Moore, *Race, Community and Conflict: A Study of Sparkbrook* (Oxford, 1967), p. 44.
42. TNA, HO 186/2637, 'History of the Home Office Midland Civil Defence Region', dated 1 February 1947.
43. Thoms, *War, Industry and Society*, pp. 108–9.
44. TNA, HO 192/937, report, signed Eric Bird, 2 August 1942.
45. IWMSA, 11580, Edward Ashill.
46. TNA, HO 192/1210, 'Birmingham Economic and Social Survey. Section G, Morale', signed PRB, 11 March 1942.
47. Ibid.
48. TNA, HO 192/1240, 'Psychological Effects of Raiding on Industrial Capacity', attached to note from Mr Abrams to Miss Hard, 1 April 1942.
49. Kieran Connell interview with Bob Willis, 27 March 2015, https://www.birmingham.ac.uk/Documents/college-artslaw/history/cccs/Interview-Transcripts/Bob-Willis.pdf.
50. TNA, HO 192/1208, *Birmingham News*, January 1941, cited in report on press.
51. TNA, HO 192/1198, 'History of Raids'.
52. TNA, HO 199/179, 'Air Raid Birmingham 20/11/1940', report, 20 November 1940, Home Security from Birmingham, BM GO HS.
53. TNA, HO 186/2637, 'History of the Home Office Midland Civil Defence Region', dated 1 February 1947.
54. Richard Overy, *The Bombing War: Europe, 1939–1945* (2013), p. 94.
55. Ibid., p. 160.
56. Colin Dobinson, *Fields of Deception: Britain's Bombing Decoys of World War II* (2000).
57. TNA, HO 186/2637, 'History of the Home Office Midland Civil Defence Region', dated 1 February 1947.
58. TNA, HO 199/156, Regional Commissioner Birmingham to Home Security Birmingham, 9 August 1940.
59. IWMSA 18772, Donald Thompson.
60. TNA, HO 196/19/273, Ministry of Home Security, Research and Experiments Department, 'Effects of the Birmingham Raid'.
61. Grace Holte, *The Girl from Guildford Street: Growing up in Working-Class Birmingham, 1957–1968* (Studley, 2018), p. 20.
62. IWMSA, 18729, Theresa Bothwell.
63. TNA, HO 192/1214, 'Statement of a Case by a Deputation Appointed by the Trades Council, Borough Labour Party and the Co-Operative Party to the City of Birmingham Emergency Committee', 6 September 1940, statement by Mr Simmons.
64. TNA, HO 196/19/273, Ministry of Home Security, Research and Experiments Department, 'Effects of the Birmingham Raid'.

65. TNA, HO 192/1188, Midland Red Report on Enemy Air Raids, by Mr Britisus, traffic manager.

66. TNA, HO 192/1210, 'Birmingham Economic and Social Survey. Section G, Morale', signed PRB, 11 March 1942.

67. Matthew Taylor, 'City Community and Sport in Birmingham during the Second World War', *Midland History*, 46, 2 (2021), pp. 246–60.

68. Eddie Fewtrell and Shirley Thompson, *King of Clubs: The Eddie Fewtrell Story* (Studley, 2007), p. 2.

69. TNA, HO 199/179, to Home Security from Birmingham, 23 November 1940, initialled WEC.

70. TNA, HLG 7/410, report by Manzoni, 17 January 1941.

71. TNA, HO 196/19/273, Ministry of Home Security, Research and Experiments Department, 'Effects of the Birmingham Raid'.

72. Gail Braybon and Penny Summerfield, *Out of the Cage: Women's Experiences in Two World Wars* (1987, 2013), p. 245.

73. TNA, HO 192/1251, 'Birmingham Social and Economic Survey', ICI, Kynoch Works.

74. Thoms, *War, Industry and Society*, p. 64.

75. TNA, CAB 65/9/3, meeting 4 September 1940.

76. Rex and Moore, *Race, Community and Conflict*, p. 71.

77. MRC, 1213/2/1/4, Arthur Bate interview with Steven Tolliday, 27 January 1981.

78. MRC, 1213/2/2/1, Albert Bennett interview with Steven Tolliday, 1–2 February 1981.

79. IWMSA, 11364, Ernest Withers.

80. MRC, 1213/2/4/6, Dick Etheridge and Lily May Etheridge interview with Steven Tolliday, 13 January 1981.

81. Denis Howell, *Made in Birmingham: The Memoirs of Denis Howell* (1990), p. 45.

82. MRC, 1213/2/1/4, Arthur Bate interview with Steven Tolliday, 27 January 1981.

83. P. Child, 'Blacktown, Mass-Observation, and the Dynamics of Voluntary Action in Mid-Twentieth-Century England', *The Historical Journal*, 63, 3 (2020), pp. 754–76.

84. MRC, 1213/2/1/4, Arthur Bate interview with Steven Tolliday, 27 January 1981.

85. Thoms, *War, Industry and Society*, pp. 74 and 69.

86. Norman Tiptaft, *The Individualist* (Birmingham, 1954), pp. 202–15.

87. Extract from *Birmingham Mail*, 16 March 1942, cited in report on press in HO 192/1208.

88. Tiptaft, *The Individualist*, pp. 169 and 176.

89. TNA, HO 192/1208, cited in report on press, *Birmingham Post*, 9 December 1940.
90. TNA, HO 192/1210, 'Birmingham Economic and Social Survey. Section G, Morale', signed PRB, 11 March 1942.
91. Ibid.
92. Ibid.
93. *The Times*, 5 July 1945.
94. HO 192/1206, interview with Miss Truscott, 8 January 1942.

9. MOTOR CITY, 1945–75

1. Matthew Parker, 'Making the City Mobile: The Place of the Motor Car in the Planning of Post-War Birmingham, *c*. 1945–1973', PhD, University of Leicester (2016).
2. Ibid.
3. Frank Hendriks, 'Cars and Culture in Munich and Birmingham: The Case for Cultural Pluralism', in Dennis Coyle and Richard Ellis (eds.), *Politics, Policy and Culture* (1994), pp. 51–69.
4. Simon Gunn, 'Ring Road: Birmingham and the Collapse of the Motor City Ideal in 1970s Britain', *The Historical Journal*, 61, 1 (2018), pp. 227–48.
5. David Lodge, *Quite a Good Time to Be Born: A Memoir, 1935–1975* (2015), p. 296.
6. J.M. Richard, *The Bombed Buildings of Britain: A Record of Architectural Casualties, 1940–41* (1942) concentrated on public buildings. It had around 200 illustrations depicting damage in Birmingham – they showed two churches and the market hall.
7. Richard Clay, 'The Painting of Frank Taylor Lockwood (1895–1961): Industrialized Iconoclasm as Seen from Birmingham's Suburbs'. Essay to be found on http://www.connectinghistories.org.uk/suburban-birmingham/suburban-birmingham-essays/.
8. David Spencer and John Lloyd, *A Child's Eye View of Small Heath Birmingham: Perception Studies for Environmental Education*, University of Birmingham Centre for Urban and Regional Studies, Research Memorandum, 34 (Birmingham, 1974), p. 31.
9. Kew National Archives (TNA), HO 186/2637, 'History of the Home Office Midland Civil Defence Region', 1 February 1947.
10. Tony Green, interviewed by Robert Wilkinson, 'An Oral History of Oral History', 2013, British Library Sound & Moving Image, Catalogue reference C 1149/31 © The British Library, reel 2.
11. Milennibrum Project, MS 2255/2/97, Joan Hart.
12. Maureen Smojkis, 'Out of the Shadows: Exploring the Lives of the Birmingham Polish', MPhil thesis, University of Birmingham (2014).

13. Grace Holte, *The Girl from Guildford Street: Growing up in Working-Class Birmingham, 1957–1968* (Studley, 2018), pp. 23 and 78.
14. *The Times*, 11 January 1964.
15. Gavin Stamp, *Britain's Lost Cities* (2007).
16. https://aghs.jimdofree.com/acocks-green-s-vulnerability/prefabs-updated/.
17. Phil Jones, 'The Suburban High Flat in the Post-War Reconstruction of Birmingham', *Urban History*, 32, 2 (2005), pp. 308–26.
18. Ibid.
19. John Boughton, *Municipal Dreams: The Rise and Fall of Council Housing* (2018), p. 111.
20. Ibid., pp. 108–9.
21. Ibid., p. 135.
22. Bernard Donoughue, *Downing Street Diary*, II: *With James Callaghan in No. 10* (2008), p. 296.
23. Frank Price, *Being There* (Leicester, 2002), p. 331.
24. Milennibrum Project, MS 2255/2/64, Carol Davis.
25. Quoted in Stacey Pethia, 'Reconstructing Communities: The Impact of Regeneration on Community Dynamics and Processes', PhD, University of Birmingham (2011).
26. Milennibrum Project, MS 2255/2/25, Paul Hill.
27. Frank Skinner, *Frank Skinner* (2001), p. 31.
28. Quoted in Pethia, 'Reconstructing Communities'.
29. Milennibrum Project, MS 2255/2/118, Jill Campbell.
30. Hazel Flett, 'Black Council Tenants in Birmingham', Working Papers on Ethnic Relations, 12 (1977).
31. Milennibrum Project, MS2255/2/76, Lester Burke.
32. Hazell Flett, Jeff Henderson and Bill Brown, 'The Practice of Racial Dispersal in Birmingham, 1969–1975', *Journal of Social Policy*, 8, 3 (1979), pp. 289–309.
33. Pethia, 'Reconstructing Communities'.
34. Milennibrum Project, MS 2255/2/46, Anita Stanton.
35. Brian Loasby, 'West Midlands Industrial Dispersal Projects', *Official Architecture and Planning*, 24, 8 (1961), pp. 357–64.
36. Ibid. Of fourteen companies that had moved from Birmingham to South Wales, five out of nine in metallurgy were dissatisfied with the move, while only two of five in other industries were.
37. *Hansard*, 21 March 1963.
38. W.T. Bowen, 'Re-Housing the Midlands Overspill', *Official Architecture and Planning*, 19, 11 (1956), pp. 555–8.
39. TNA, MAF 255/1075, Waldegrave to Henry Brook, 28 October 1960.
40. Bob West, 'Danger! History at Work: A Critical Consumer's Guide to the Ironbridge Gorge Museum', Birmingham Centre for Contemporary Cultural Studies, Occasional Papers (1985).

41. John Mawson and C. Skelcher, 'Updating the West Midlands Regional Strategy: A Review of Inter-Authority Relationships', *The Town Planning Review*, 51, 2 (1980), pp. 152–70.

42. TNA, EW 7/914, 'Written Evidence of the West Midlands Economic Planning Council to Committee on Intermediate Areas', attached to note from Thomas, 6 December 1967.

43. Ibid. Chair of Dawley Development Corporation to Sir Joseph Hunt, 14 June 1968. 'Birmingham Industries are not shaking loose from the city in sufficient number and, in any case, are not attracted by what Dawley had to offer. One can understand this to some extent as our road communications are very poor and, added to this, they have only to move some thirty or forty miles further north to attract all that a development area had to offer by way of financial inducements.'

44. John Boughton, 'Working-Class Politics in Birmingham and Sheffield, 1918–1931', PhD thesis, University of Warwick (1985).

45. Birmingham Education Committee, *Alderman Byng Kenrick. Tributes and Appreciations on his Retirement as Chairman of the Birmingham Educational Committee Expressed at a Meeting Held on the Twenty-Ninth Day of October and the Eighth Day of December 1943* (Birmingham, 1943), remarks by Professor Valentine.

46. Quoted in Parker, 'Making the City Mobile'.

47. Anthony Sutcliffe and Roger Smith, *History of Birmingham*, III: *1939–1970* (Oxford, 1974), p. 399.

48. Parker, 'Making the City Mobile'.

49. Birmingham did eventually come to have a higher rate of traffic accidents involving children than any other part of the country.

50. William Gissane and John Bull, 'A Study of 183 Road Deaths in and around Birmingham in 1960', *British Medical Journal*, 1, 5241 (1961), pp. 1716–20.

51. Parker, 'Making the City Mobile'.

52. Television interviews cited in ibid.

53. *The Times*, 20 April 1971.

54. 1971 census cited in Parker, 'Making the City Mobile'. The comparable figures for other cities were Sheffield 39 per cent, Leeds 35.5 per cent, Manchester 32 per cent, Newcastle-upon-Tyne 32 per cent.

55. Kaja Irene Ziesler, 'The Irish in Birmingham, 1830–1970', PhD, University of Birmingham (1989).

56. Adrian Cadbury interview with Niamh Dillon, *Food from Source to Salespoint* (2001–3), © The British Library, British Library Sound & Moving Image, Catalogue reference C 82/122 reel 4.

57. Skinner, *Frank Skinner*, p. 25.

58. Parker, 'Making the City Mobile', p. 117.

59. D. Bailey, C. Chapain, M. Mahdon, and R. Fauth, *Life after Longbridge: Three Years On: Pathways to Re-Employment in a Restructuring Economy* (2008), p. 19.

60. E.M. Davies, 'Changes in Car Ownership and Travel to Work Patterns in England and Wales between 1966 and 1971', *Transportation Science*, 13, 3 (1979), pp. 191–200.

61. Christine Griffin, *Typical Girls? Young Women from School to the Full-Time Job Market* (1985), p. 12.

62. Lawrence Black, 'The Lost World of Young Conservatism', *The Historical Journal*, 51, 4 (2008), pp. 991–1024.

63. Leslie John Jones, *Three Times for a Jolly Welshman: An Autobiography of a Rhondda Exile* (Birmingham, 1984), p. 50.

64. Holte, *The Girl from Guildford Street*, p. 72.

65. Peter Ratcliffe, *Racism and Reaction: A Profile of Handsworth* (1981), p. 129.

66. Kenneth Newton, *Second City Politics: Democratic Processes and Decision-Making in Birmingham* (Oxford, 1976), p. 238.

67. Ziesler, 'The Irish in Birmingham'.

68. David Adams and Peter Larkham, 'Walking with the Ghosts of the Past: Unearthing the Value of Residents' Urban Nostalgias', *Urban Studies*, 53, 10 (2016), pp. 2004–22.

69. Gissane and Bull, 'A Study of 183 Road Deaths'. In 1960, a baby was killed in its pram while its mother tried to pull it up over the kerb by a pedestrian crossing.

70. David Adams, 'Everyday Experiences of the Modern City: Remembering the Post-War Reconstruction of Birmingham', *Planning Perspectives*, 26, 2 (2011), pp. 237–60.

71. Parker, 'Making the City Mobile'.

72. Richard Hoggart, *An Imagined Life: Life and Times*, III: *1959–1991* (1992), p. 84.

73. Phillada Ballard, 'A Commercial and Industrial Elite: A Study of Birmingham's Upper Middle Class, 1780–1914', PhD, University of Reading (1983).

74. Asa Briggs, *History of Birmingham*, II: *Borough and City, 1865–1938* (Oxford, 1952), p. 140.

75. Hoggart, *An Imagined Life*, p. 84.

76. M.B. Stedman and P.A. Wood, 'Urban Renewal in Birmingham: An Interim Report', *Geography*, 50, 1 (1965), pp. 1–17. A.G. Sheppard Fidler, 'Post-War Housing in Birmingham', *The Town Planning Review*, 26, 1 (1955), pp. 25–47.

77. Price, *Being There*, pp. 208–9.

78. R. Lawton, 'The Daily Journey to Work in England and Wales: An Analysis of the Report on Usual Residence and Workplace, Census of England and Wales, 1951', *The Town Planning Review*, 29, 4 (1959), pp. 241–57.

79. Ratcliffe, *Racism and Reaction*, p. 221.

80. Paul Willis, *Learning to Labour: How Working-Class Kids Get Working-Class Jobs* (1977), p. 58.

81. Paul Panic, *I thought Solihull was for Snobs but these Punks Think Different: Punk/Mod Culture in 70–80s Solihull and Birmingham* (Birmingham, 2015).

82. William Dugdale, *Settling the Bill: The Memoirs of Bill Dugdale* (2011), p. 243.

83. Adrian Cadbury interview with Niamh Dillon, reel 1 and reel 20.

84. According to J.C. Loynton's excellent history of Solihull School, the late Mr Curry has now been rehabilitated.

85. City of Birmingham, *Abstract of Birmingham Statistics*, 1–3, 1931–1954, table 163, p. 127.

86. Milennibrum Project, MS 2255/2/118, Jill Campbell.

87. Hilda Khan, *Repercussions of Redundancy: A Local Survey* (1965), p. 233.

88. Ibid. See also the correspondence around the original report on which this book was based in National Archives, LAB 8/2795.

89. Graham Stevenson interviewed by Richard Stevens, Communist Party of Great Britain Biographical Project, British Library Sound & Moving Image, Catalogue reference C 1049/138 © The British Library, reel 2.

90. John Rex and Robert Moore, *Race, Community and Conflict: A Study of Sparkbrook* (Oxford, 1967). p. 92.

91. Jones, *Three Times for a Jolly Welshman*.

92. Ziesler, 'The Irish in Birmingham'.

93. Paul Willis, 'Human Experience and Material Production: The Culture of the Shop Floor', Centre for Contemporary Cultural Studies, Occasional Papers (1975).

94. Chris Jukes (ed.), *Fort Dunlop Remembered* (Studley, 2017).

95. Holte, *The Girl from Guildford Street*, p. 25. Grace Holte says that the politician was the Liberal Wallace Lawler, for whom her aunt worked. Lawler was just the kind of Tammany politician who got council houses for white working-class families. However, he was not elected to Parliament until 1972 and not elected to the council until 1962. There were no Liberals on Birmingham Council in 1956 when Grace's parents got their flat. I wonder whether the politician who intervened might in fact have been Denis Howell, who had lived in the same street as Grace's maternal grandmother until his election to Parliament in 1955.

96. Sutcliffe and Smith, *History of Birmingham*, p. 345.

97. Birmingham Central Library (BCL), 2565, diary of Roger Evans.

98. *The Times*, 27 February 1964.

99. Price, *Being There*, p. 97.

100. Denis Howell, *Made in Birmingham: The Memoirs of Denis Howell* (1990), p. 52.

101. HMSO, *Report of a Court of Enquiry into a Dispute between Austin Motor Company and Certain Workpeople, Members of the National Union of Vehicle Builders* (1953).

102. TNA, LAB 10/1168, note of meeting, Austin management, Engineering Employers' Federation and NUVB at Ministry of Labour under the chairmanship of Mr Maston, 24 June 1953.

103. Frank Henderson, *Life on the Track: Memoirs of a Socialist Worker* (2009), p. 48.

104. TNA, LAB 10/1168, note, dated 23 September 1953.

105. HMSO, *Report of a Court of Enquiry*.

106. Warwick University, Modern Records Centre (MRC), Papers of Dick Etheridge, MS 202/5/A/1/1, meeting, 16 February 1953.

107. MRC, 1213/24/6, Dick Etheridge and Lily May Etheridge interview with Steven Tolliday, 13 January 1981.

108. *The Times*, 2 January 1963.

109. MRC, 1213/2/2/4, Phil Blewitt interview with Steven Tolliday, 25 March 1981.

110. MRC, 697/1/1/3, Ron Savage, diary entry for 25 January 1974.

111. MRC, 1213/2/4/6, Dick Etheridge and Lily May Etheridge interview with Steven Tolliday, 13 January 1981.

112. MRC, 697/1/1, Ron Savage diary, 25 April 1973 and 27 April 1973.

113. Oxford Bodleian Library, Conservative Party Archive (CPA), CCO 2/2/8, 'West Midlands Area', signed 'ML', 12 March 1951.

114. CPA CCO 2/2/8, Ledingham to Thomas, 30 October 1951.

115. Sutcliffe and Smith, *Birmingham 1939–1970*, p. 215.

116. A.M. Potter, 'The English Conservative Constituency Association', *Western Political Quarterly*, 9, 2 (1956), pp. 363–75. D. Wilson, and M. Pinto-Duschinsky, 'Conservative City Machines: The End of an Era', *British Journal of Political Science*, 6, 2 (1976), pp. 239–44.

117. The fact that some of the last members of the great Birmingham families to be active in local public life were women went with the fact that female members of these families tended to be more left wing than their male relatives. Evelyn Crosskey (1893–1979), a descendant of the nineteenth-century Unitarian minister and of the Nettlefold family, was a Labour member of Birmingham Council from 1945 to 1971.

118. CPA, CCO 1/8/286, Aston to Ledingham, 2 June 1950; Ledingham to GD, 5 June 1950.

119. CPA, CCO 2/2/8, 'West Midlands Area', signed 'ML', 12 March 1951. 'In the past the Birmingham Unionist Association has not cooperated well with the Area, due to the personalities of the President, the Chairman and the late Chief Agent. The new Chief Agent, Tranter, has every wish to alter this. Despite the strong professional team in the City, the Organisation is not

first class by any means. The majority of the Agents and Constituency offices are centralized in Empire House – a very top heavy bureaucracy.'

120. CPA, CCO 1/14/345/347, 'City of Birmingham' from Galloway to COO, 31 December 1965.

121. Douglas Hurd, *Memoirs* (2003), p. 172.

122. Christopher Price interview with Emmeline Ledgerwood, *History of Parliament Trust* (2012), British Library Sound & Moving Image, Catalogue reference C 1503/39 © The British Library, track 3.

123. Roy Jenkins, *Twelve Cities: A Personal Memoir* (2002), p. 43.

124. Jenkins intervened to prevent Midland Waterways from building a sewage farm near the estates of the Duke of Devonshire. When the duke joined the Social Democratic Party, which Jenkins had helped found in 1981, Tories joked that he would bring a 'common touch to the party which Roy Jenkins so conspicuously lacks'.

125. Jim Simmons, *Soap Box Evangelist* (Chichester, 1972), p. 18.

126. Price, *Being There*, pp. 216–17.

127. Ian Popl, 'Roy Fisher's Mysticism', PhD, University of Manchester (2011).

128. Roy Fisher, *The Long and the Short of It: Poems 1955–2010* (Bloodaxe Books, 2012), www.bloodaxebooks.com.

129. David Spencer and John Lloyd, *A Child's Eye View of Small Heath Birmingham: Perception Studies for Environmental Education*, The University of Birmingham Centre for Urban and Regional Studies, Research Memorandum, 34 (Birmingham, 1974), p. 26.

130. Ibid.

131. Ibid., p. 22.

132. Ibid., p. 28.

133. Gunn, 'Ring Road'.

10. BIRMINGHAM IRISH, 1945–74

1. James Moran, *Irish Birmingham: A History* (Liverpool, 2010), p. 179.

2. Bridget Pugh, *Solid Citizens: Statues in Birmingham* (Sutton Coldfield, 1983).

3. Simon Jones, *Black Culture, White Youth: The Reggae Tradition from JA to UK* (1988), p. 128.

4. Birmingham Central Library (BCL), MS 4000/2/101, material collected for television programme *The Colony*.

5. Ibid.

6. John Rex and Robert Moore, *Race, Community and Conflict: A Study of Sparkbrook* (Oxford, 1967), p. 84.

7. Warwick Modern Record Centre (MRC), 1213/2/4/6, Dick Etheridge and Lily May Etheridge interview with Steven Tolliday, 13 January 1981.

8. Rex and Moore, *Race, Community and Conflict*, pp. 98–9.

9. Media Archive of Central England (MACE), Midlands Montage 23 July 1963, https://www.macearchive.org/films/midland-montage-23071963-travellers-sparkbrook.

10. Kaja Ziesler, 'The Irish in Birmingham, 1830–1970', PhD, University of Birmingham (1989).

11. Oliver Reilly, 'A Worker in Birmingham', *The Furrow*, 9, 4 (1958), pp. 217–24.

12. Ibid.

13. Ziesler, 'The Irish in Birmingham'.

14. Barry Hazley, 'The Irish in Post-War England: Experience, Memory and Belonging in Personal Narratives of Migration, 1945–1969', PhD, University of Manchester (2013).

15. Milennibrum Project, MS 2255/2/49, Georgina Mullen.

16. Rex and Moore, *Race, Community and Conflict*, p. 86.

17. Enda Delaney, *The Irish in Post-War Britain* (2007), p. 100.

18. Ian Jones, *The Local Church and Generational Change in Birmingham, 1945–2000* (Woodbridge, 2012), p. 28.

19. Daniel Cummings, *Rest and Be Thankful: Autobiography of a Belfast Missionary* (Newtownards, 2015).

20. Moran, *Irish Birmingham*, p. 168.

21. Reilly, 'A Worker in Birmingham'.

22. Ibid.

23. Cummings, *Rest and Be Thankful*, p. 309.

24. Paul Harrison in *New Society*, 1973, cited in Ziesler, 'The Irish in Birmingham'.

25. Ziesler, 'The Irish in Birmingham'.

26. Cited in ibid.

27. Henrietta Ewart, 'Caring for Migrants: Policy Responses to Irish Migration to England, 1940–1972', PhD, University of Warwick (2012).

28. Chris Mullin, *Error of Judgement: The Truth about the Birmingham Bombings* (this edn, 1990), p. 11.

29. Reilly, 'A Worker in Birmingham'.

30. A.H. Waterhouse and Diana H. Brabban, 'Inquiry into the Fertility of Immigrants', *The International Migration Digest*, 1, 2 (1964), pp. 152–66.

31. Norman Tiptaft, *Inns of the Midlands* (Birmingham, 1951), p. 99.

32. Rex and Moore, *Race, Community and Conflict*, p. 96.

33. Philip McCarvill, 'An Examination of Ethnic Identity: A Case Study of "Second Generation" Irish People in Birmingham', PhD, University of Warwick (2002).

34. Ibid.

35. MACE, Midland News, 18 August 1969. https://www.macearchive.org/films/midlands-news-18081969-interview-padraig-yeates.

36. Mullin, *Error of Judgement*, p. 2.
37. Roy Jenkins, *A Life at the Centre* (1991), p. 395.
38. MACE, 25 November 1974, https://www.macearchive.org/films/atv-today-25111974-birmingham-pub-bombings-brs-protest.
39. Sarah O'Brien, 'Negotiations of Irish Identity in the Wake of Terrorism: The Case of the Irish in Birmingham 1973–74', *Irish Studies Review*, 25, 3 (2017), pp. 372–94.
40. McCarvill, 'An Examination of Ethnic Identity'.
41. Mullin, *Error of Judgement*, p. 28.
42. Frank Henderson, *Life on the Track: Memoirs of a Socialist Worker* (2009), p. 72.
43. MRC, 697/1/4, Ron Savage diary, entries for 22–25 November 1974.
44. John Borland, Roy D. King, and Kathleen McDermott, 'The Irish in Prison: A Tighter Nick for "the Micks"?', *The British Journal of Sociology*, 46, 3 (1995), pp. 371–94.
45. MRC 697/1/5, Ron Savage diary, 6 January 1975.
46. O'Brien, 'Negotiations of Irish Identity'.
47. Ibid.
48. McCarvill, 'An Examination of Ethnic Identity'.
49. Laura O'Reilly, 'The Birmingham Pub Bombings, the Irish as a "suspect community" and the Memories of the O'Reilly Family', in Graham Dawson, Jo Dover and Stephen Hopkins (eds.), *The Northern Ireland Troubles in Britain Impacts, Engagements, Legacies and Memories* (Manchester, 2016), pp. 284–99.
50. Mullin, *Error of Judgement*, p. 217.
51. Raymond Carter, interviewed by Richard Stowell, *History of Parliament Trust*, 2013, British Library Sound & Moving Image, Catalogue reference C 1503/68 © The British Library, track 2.
52. O'Brien, 'Negotiations of Irish Identity'.
53. Philip Ullah, 'Rhetoric and Ideology in Social Identification: The Case of Second Generation Irish Youths', *Discourse and Society*, 1, 2 (1990), pp. 167–88.
54. Christine Griffin, *Typical Girls? Young Women from School to the Full-Time Job Market* (1985), p. 97.

11. NEIGHBOURS? NON-WHITE IMMIGRANTS TO BIRMINGHAM, 1945–75

1. Birmingham Central Library (BCL), MS 4000/2/101, material collected for television programme *The Colony*.
2. *The Times*, 15 May 1961.
3. BCL, MS 4000 2/101.

4. Karis Campion, 'Making Mixed Race: Time, Place and Identities in Birmingham', PhD, University of Manchester (2017).
5. BCL, MS 4000/2/101.
6. Ibid.
7. Ibid.
8. Ibid.
9. John Rex and Robert Moore, *Race, Community and Conflict: A Study of Sparkbrook* (Oxford, 1967), p. 100.
10. Campion, 'Making Mixed Race'.
11. Kenneth Newton, *Second City Politics: Democratic Processes and Decision-Making in Birmingham* (Oxford, 1976), p. 212.
12. Media Archive of Central England (MACE), Midland News, 20 August 1964, story number 6842, https://www.macearchive.org/films/midlands-news-20081964-explosion-house-destroyed-smethwick.
13. MACE, Midland News, 23 January 1964, story number 4976, https://www.macearchive.org/films/midlands-news-23011963-cold-railway-workers.
14. She appeared on a programme on BBC Midlands on 12 October 2012, interviewed by Satnam Rana. She mentioned something that was not alluded to in *The Colony* – that some employers simply would not take black people.
15. BCL, MS 4000/2/101.
16. *Birmingham Gazette*, cited in Kevin Searle, 'Mixing the Unmixables: The 1949 Causeway Green "Riots" in Birmingham', *Race and Class*, 54, 3 (2013), pp. 44–64.
17. Ibid.
18. Elizabeth Thomas-Hope, 'Hopes and Reality in the West Indian Migration to Britain', *Oral History*, 8, 1 (1980), pp. 35–42.
19. Geoffrey Goodman, *Bill Morris: A Trade Union Miracle* (2010), p. 40.
20. Milennibrum Project, MS 2255/2/74, Earl Barrow.
21. Rex and Moore, *Race, Community and Conflict*, p. 100.
22. Milennibrum Project, MS 2255/2/53, unnamed Kittian woman.
23. Campion, 'Making Mixed Race'.
24. Milennibrum Project, MS2255/2/12, Jossett Lynch. On people being struck by chimneys on their way to Birmingham, see also Thomas-Hope, 'Hopes and Reality in the West Indian Migration to Britain'.
25. Goodman, *Bill Morris*, p. 33.
26. BCL, MS 4000/2/101.
27. Ibid.
28. Ibid.
29. Ibid.
30. Ibid.
31. MACE, 'Look Around', 25 August 1961, https://www.macearchive.org/films/look-around-25081961-voluntary-exiles.

32. Peter Ratcliffe, *Racism and Reaction: A Profile of Handsworth* (1981), p. 248.
33. BCL, MS 4000/2/101.
34. Ibid.
35. Campion, 'Making Mixed Race'.
36. MACE, Midlands Montage, 16 September 1960. He spoke thus: 'A great deal of what passes for integration or is indeed the only integration that goes on at a rather deep level in a city such as this is that of girls, British girls and women either married to or, more often, living with single men from overseas. I know that this is a subject that is dangerous to talk about in public but I am casting no stones ... Sometimes those girls are able to do extraordinary things for racial integration.' https://www.macearchive.org/films/midland-montage-15091960-vicar-speaks-racial-integration.
37. Lydia Lindsey, 'The Split-Labor Phenomenon: Its Impact on West Indian Workers as a Marginal Working Class in Birmingham, England, 1948–1962', *The Journal of Negro History*, 78, 2 (1993), pp. 83–109.
38. BCL, MS 4000/2/101.
39. A.H. Waterhouse and Diana H. Brabban, 'Inquiry into the Fertility of Immigrants', *The International Migration Digest*, 1, 2 (1964), pp. 152–66.
40. Ibid.
41. Rex and Moore, *Race, Community and Conflict*, pp. 99–100.
42. Milennibrum Project, MS 2255/2/53, unnamed Kittian woman.
43. P. Davies, *Trapped: Unmarried West Indian Mothers in Handsworth* (Birmingham, 1983).
44. John R. Lambert, *Crime, Police and Race Relations: A Study in Birmingham* (Oxford, 1970), p. 259.
45. Ibid., p. 238.
46. Lenny Henry, *Who Am I, Again?* (2019).
47. Cited in Adam Carey, 'Politics, Governance and the Shaping of Smethwick since 1945', MPhil, University of Birmingham (2016).
48. Ratcliffe, *Racism and Reaction*, p. 17.
49. Paul Foot, *Immigration and Race in British Politics* (1965), p. 19.
50. MACE, 'Left, Right and Centre', 3 April 1978, https://www.macearchive.org/films/left-right-and-centre-03041978-immigration-control.
51. William Dugdale, *Settling the Bill: The Memoirs of Bill Dugdale* (2011), p. 258.
52. Rex and Moore, *Race, Community and Conflict*, p. 115.
53. Peter Williams, 'Building Societies and the Inner City', *Transactions of the Institute of British Geographers*, 3, 1 (1978), pp. 23–34.
54. I recall a South-African born acquaintance in Birmingham who sought an extension to their mortgage. The building society manager rang him up and asked him a long series of questions – 'Where were you born?'; 'Where do your family live?' Eventually, my acquaintance put the manager out of his

misery and said, 'I'm white.' The conversation ended and the extension was granted.

55. Oliver Reilly, 'A Worker in Birmingham', *The Furrow*, 9, 4 (1958), pp. 217–24.
56. *The Times*, 13 January 1965.
57. Rex and Moore, *Race, Community and Conflict*, p. 41.
58. Kieran Connell, 'Race, Prostitution and the New Left: The Postwar Inner City through Janet Mendelsohn's "Social Eye"', *History Workshop Journal*, 83, 1 (2017), pp. 301–40.
59. Foot, *Immigration and Race*, p. 14.
60. BCL, MS 4000/2/101.
61. MACE, 4 November 1965, https://www.macearchive.org/films/atv-today-04111965-racism-interview. The interviewee is not identified in this clip but his words are identical to those used by one of the interviewees in BCL, MS 4000/2/101.
62. BCL, MS 4000/2/101.
63. Kenneth Clarke, Nicholas Budgen and John Lenton, *Immigration, Race and Politics: A Birmingham View* (Bow Group Pamphlet, 1966).
64. MACE, 'The Start of a Career', https://www.macearchive.org/films/start-career.
65. Lindsey, 'The Split Labour Phenomenon'.
66. Milennibrum Project, MS 2255/2/74, Earl Barrow.
67. Hilda Khan, *Repercussions of Redundancy: A Local Survey* (1965), p. 75.
68. BCL, MS 4000/2/101.
69. Khan, *Repercussions of Redundancy*, p. 75.
70. R.A. Church, *Kenricks in Hardware: A Family Business, 1791–1966* (1969), p. 303.
71. MACE, Midland News, 25 March 1963, https://www.macearchive.org/films/midlands-news-25031963-jamaican-high-commissioner-visits-west-bromwich.
72. Cited in Foot, *Immigration and Race*, pp. 18–19.
73. Tony Green, interview with Robert Wilkinson, An Oral History of Oral History (2013), British Library Sound & Moving Image, Catalogue reference C 1149/31 © The British Library, reel 2.
74. Rex and Moore, *Race, Community and Conflict*, p. 121.
75. MACE, ATV Today, 22 February 1967, https://www.macearchive.org/films/atv-today-22021967-metal-closures-strike.
76. BCL, MS 2141/A/4/14, cutting from *Evening Mail*, 22 February 1967.
77. MACE, ATV Today, 22 February 1967, https://www.macearchive.org/films/atv-today-22021967-metal-closures-strike.
78. MACE, Midland News, 22 November 1968, https://www.macearchive.org/films/midlands-news-27111968-interview-shop-steward-smethwick.

79. MACE, Midland News, 22 November 1968, https://www.macearchive.org/films/midlands-news-22111968-white-workers-strike-smethwick-factory.

80. Carey, 'Politics, Governance and the Shaping of Smethwick'.

81. BCL, MS 4000/2/101.

82. MACE, Midland News, 23 May 1969, https://www.macearchive.org/films/midlands-news-23051969-pickets-west-bromwich-factory.

83. Goodman, *Bill Morris*, p. 40.

84. Church, *Kenricks in Hardware*, p. 303.

85. MRC, 697/1/5, Ron Savage diary, entries for 3–6 January 1975.

86. *The Times*, 20 January 1955.

87. *The Times*, 8 September 1966.

88. *The Times*, 29 November 1959.

89. Oxford Bodleian Library, Conservative Party Archive (CPA), CCO 1/14/345/347, Gallup Poll, March 1964 , attached to letter Geoffrey Lloyd to Alec Douglas-Home, 21 July 1964.

90. CPA, CCO 1/14/345/347, Eric [presumably Eric Tranter] to Galloway, 8 February 1963. Galloway forwarded the note to Conservative Central Office on 12 February with a more sceptical note of his own: 'The Coloured problem undoubted [*sic*] is serious in Birmingham; so is the general movement of population for other reasons, and therefore whilst undoubtedly there is a good deal to be said for Tranter's point, I cannot see why he can be quite so dogmatic that people have "left their residences in the Constituencies as a result of coloured immigration".'

91. CPA, CCO 1/14/345/347, Burman to Macleod, 5 June 1963.

92. *The Times*, 5 October 1964.

93. Clarke, Budgen and Lenton, *Immigration, Race and Politics*, p. 1.

94. Reginald Eyre, interviewed by Isobel White, *History of Parliament Trust* (2014), British Library Sound & Moving Image, Catalogue reference C 1503/95 © The British Library.

95. CPA, CCO 1/14/348/2, Hall Green by-election final report, signed Galloway, 6th May 1965: 'declining the invitation of the Press and other to embark on such problems as coloured immigration; he stuck to the economic factors'.

96. CPA, CCO 2/7/6, unattributed comments from a member of the West Midlands Area Committee, in response to questions from Ian Wallace in letter of 13 September 1968.

97. *The Times*, 9 March 1964.

98. Kenneth Newton, *Second City Politics: Democratic Processes and Decision-Making in Birmingham* (Oxford, 1976), p. 208.

99. Les Back and John Solomos, *Race, Politics and Social Change* (1995), p. 69.

100. *The Times*, 24 February 1966, Mr T.H. Jones previously a member of the Birmingham Immigration Control Association and now founder of the

Argus Britons' Rights Association, which was in turn affiliated to the Sussex Racial Preservation Society, said: 'I supported Peter Griffiths at the last election but I do not think that he has taken the stand that people expected of him.'

101. *The Times*, 24 July 1961.

102. MACE, Midland News, 10 May 1963, https://www.macearchive.org/films/ midlands-news-16051963-smethwick-vice-vigilantes.

103. *The Times*, 7 January 1965.

104. MACE, Midland News, 16 May 1963, https://www.macearchive.org/films/ midlands-news-16051963-smethwick-vice-vigilantes.

105. *The Times*, 9 March 1964.

106. Cited in Foot, *Race and Immigration*, p. 32.

107. *Hansard*, 16 July 1965.

108. MACE, ATV Today, 4 November/1964, https://www.macearchive.org/films/ atv-today-04111964-peter-griffiths-vox-pops.

109. MACE, Midland News, 10 November 1965, Story number 8254, https:// www.macearchive.org/films/midlands-news-10111965-interview-west-indian-and-pakistani-welfare-officers.

110. BCL, MS 4000/2/101.

111. Ibid.

112. *The Times*, 14 February 1969.

113. MACE, Midland Montage, 27 July 1961, https://www.macearchive.org/ films/midland-montage-27071961-smethwick-rent-strike.

114. BCL, MS 4000/2/101.

115. Ibid.

116. https://www.pebblemill.org/blog/the-colony-a-reflection-by-contributor-victor-williams-daughter-sandra/.

117. H. Ter Heide, 'West Indian Migration to Great Britain', *Nieuwe West-Indische Gids/New West Indian Guide*, 43 (1963–4), pp. 85–8. The author points out that men from Antigua refused to cut sugar cane (a low status occupation) on their own island but were willing to do it when they migrated to the Virgin Islands.

118. Rex and Moore, *Race, Community and Conflict*, p. 70.

119. MACE, ATV Today, 31 May 1965, https://www.macearchive.org/films/ atv-today-31051965-estate-bar-non-white-residents.

120. Olivier Esteves, *The 'Desegregation' of English Schools: Bussing, Race and Urban Space, 1960s–80s* (Manchester, 2018), pp. 94–100.

121. Milennibrum Project, MS 2255/2/118, Jill Campbell.

122. BCL, MS 4000/2/101.

123. Foot, *Immigration and Race in British Politics*, p. 44.

124. David Spencer and John Lloyd, *A Child's Eye View of Small Heath Birmingham: Perception Studies for Environmental Education*, University of

Birmingham Centre for Urban and Regional Studies, Research Memorandum, 34 (1974), p. 29.

125. Paul Willis, *Learning to Labour: How Working-Class Kids Get Working-Class Jobs* (1977), p. 36.

126. Laxmi Jamdagni, *Hamari Rangily Zindagi*, I: *Our Colourful Lives* (1980).

12. CULTURAL REVOLUTIONS

1. Kathleen Tynan, *The Life of Kenneth Tynan* (1987), p. 12.

2. Andrzej Panufnik, *Composing Myself* (1987), p. 268.

3. Claire Cochrane, *Shakespeare and the Birmingham Repertory Theatre, 1913–1929* (1993).

4. L.W. Conolly (ed.), *Bernard Shaw and Barry Jackson, Selected Correspondence of Bernard Shaw*, IV (2002), p. xi.

5. Walter Allen, *As I Walked Down New Grub Street: Memories of a Writing Life* (1981), pp. 57–8.

6. Louis MacNeice, *The Strings Are False: An Unfinished Autobiography* (1965), p. 130.

7. Allen, *As I Walked Down New Grub Street*, p. 37.

8. MacNeice, *The Strings Are False*, pp. 134–40.

9. E.R. Dodds, *Missing Persons: An Autobiography* (Oxford, 1977), p. 113.

10. Alekhine played in a chess tournament in Birmingham in 1926. It is not clear what brought Kerensky to Birmingham, though he had known Oliver Locker Lampson, Conservative MP for Handsworth from 1910 to 1945, during the latter's service on the eastern front during the First World War.

11. Stephen Games, *Pevsner – the Early Life: Germany and Art* (2010), p. 204.

12. W.H. Auden and T.C. Worsley, 'Education', *The Listener*, 8 December 1937, reprinted in Edward Mendelson (ed.), *W.H. Auden Prose*, I (2000), pp. 389–425.

13. Eric Ives, Diane Drummond, and Leonard Schwarz, *The First Civic University: Birmingham, 1880–1980 – An Introductory History* (Birmingham, 2000), p. 260.

14. Kew National Archives (TNA), KV 2/1833, letter from Chief Constable to Sir Vernon, 22 January 1938.

15. Allen, *As I Walked Down New Grub Street*, p. 48.

16. P. Child, 'Blacktown, Mass-Observation, and the Dynamics of Voluntary Action in Mid-Twentieth Century England', *The Historical Journal*, 63, 3 (2020), pp. 754–76.

17. Frank Price, *Being There* (Leicester, 2002), pp. 233–44.

18. Richard Hoggart, *An Imagined Life: Life and Times*, III: *1959–1991* (1992), p. 88.

19. Kieran Connell interview with Paul Hoggart, https://www.birmingham. ac.uk/Documents/college-artslaw/history/cccs/Interview-Transcripts/Paul-Hoggart.pdf.

20. Kieran Connell interview with John Ellis, https://www.birmingham.ac.uk/ Documents/college-artslaw/history/cccs/Interview-Transcripts/John-Ellis.pdf.

21. Kieran Connell interview with Bob Willis, https://www.birmingham.ac.uk/ Documents/college-artslaw/history/cccs/Interview-Transcripts/Bob-Willis.pdf.

22. Stuart Hall, with Bill Schwarz, *Familiar Stranger: A Life Between Two Islands* (2017), p. 235.

23. Frank Henderson, *Life on the Track: Memoirs of a Socialist Worker* (2009), p. 68.

24. Graham Denton, *The Odd Man Out: The Fascinating Story of Ron Saunders' Reign at Aston Villa* (2017), p. 18.

25. Laurie Hornsby, *Brum Rocked On* (Studley, 1999).

26. Eddie Fewtrell and Shirley Thompson, *King of Clubs: The Eddie Fewtrell Story* (Studley, 2007).

27. John Taylor, *In the Pleasure Groove: Love, Death, and Duran Duran* (2012), p. 84.

28. Leigh Michael Harrison, 'Factory Music: How the Industrial Geography and Working-Class Environment of Post-War Birmingham Fostered the Birth of Heavy Metal', *Journal of Social History*, 44, 1 (2010), pp. 145–58.

29. Grace Holte, *The Girl from Guildford Street: Growing up in Working-Class Birmingham, 1957–1968* (Studley, 2018), p. 122.

30. Birmingham Central Library (BCL), MS 4000/2/101, material collected for the documentary *The Colony*.

31. Ibid., 23 December 1963.

32. Milennibrum Project, MSS 2255/2/118, Jill Campbell.

33. Paul Willis, *Learning to Labour: How Working-Class Kids Get Working-Class Jobs* (1977), p. 38.

34. Patrick Higgins, *Heterosexual Dictatorship: Male Homosexuality in Post-War Britain* (1996), pp. 218–19.

35. Michael Layton, *Birmingham's Front Line: True Police Stories* (Stroud, 2016), digital edition, no pagination.

36. http://www.gaybirminghamremembered.co.uk/memories/Being%20the%20out%20gay%20Councillor.

37. Sandra Winn, 'The Developing Geography of AIDS: A Case Study of the West Midlands', *Area*, 20, 1 (1988), pp. 61–7.

38. TNA, BN 89/232, 'Poor Families in Birmingham', report apparently dating from the early 1970s.

39. http://gaybirminghamremembered.co.uk/memories/Birmingham%20Women%27s%20Liberation%20Conference%201978.

40. http://gaybirminghamremembered.co.uk/memories/Chaos%20and%20
hostility%20at%20the%20WLM%20Conference%2C%201978.

41. Paul Edmond, *Duran Duran Unseen, Photographs, 1979–1982,* written and
designed by Kasper de Graaf and Malcolm Garrett (Richmond, 2005), no
pagination.

13. SIGNING OFF

1. Thatcher Foundation Website (TFW), 104026.

2. Warwick Modern Record Centre (MRC), 1213/2/4/6, Dick Etheridge and
Lily May Etheridge interview with Steven Tolliday, 13 January 1981.

3. Ken Spencer, Andy Taylor, Barbara Smith, John Mawson, Norman Flynn,
and Richard Batley, *Crisis in the Industrial Heartland: A Study of the West
Midlands* (Oxford, 1986), p. 41.

4. Churchill College Cambridge, Thatcher Archive (THCR), 5,1,5,19 Duguid
to Lankester, 10 April 1980.

5. Spencer *et al., Crisis in the Industrial Heartland*, p. 55.

6. Media Archives of Central England (MACE), Summary of television programme from 1987, https://www.macearchive.org/films/central-choice-
defence.

7. Frank Watters, *Being Frank: The Memoirs of Frank Watters* (Barnsley, 1992).

8. Arthur Scargill, 'The New Unionism', *New Left Review*, 1, 92 (1975).

9. Frank Henderson, *Life on the Track: Memoirs of a Socialist Worker* (2009),
p. 66.

10. Raymond Carter, interview with Richard Stowell, *History of Parliament
Trust* (2013), British Library Sound & Moving Image, Catalogue reference
C 1503/68 © The British Library, track 2.

11. MRC, MS 697/1/1/1, diary of Ron Savage, 28 February, 29 February and 2
March 1972.

12. Henderson, *Life on the Track*, p. 69.

13. By the standards of white South Africa in the 1980s, Edwardes was a
liberal – though he was sympathetic to the limits on the government's capacity to change. He also urged the Conservative Party in 1977 that the 'Race
Relations act not be pressed too quickly if disruption is to be avoided'.

14. THCR, 2/6/1/21, Edwardes, 5 April 1977.

15. TFW, 130148, Joseph to Thatcher, 21 January 1981.

16. MRC, 697/1/13, Ron Savage diary, 6 January 1978.

17. TFW, 1511/2, John Patten to Ian Gow, 4 May 1983.

18. TFW, 110796, Joseph. 'Monetarism is not Enough', speech delivered at
Stockton, 5 April 1976.

19. TFW, 109768, Howe to Heseltine, 16 November 1976.

20. TFW, 116389, meeting at 10 Downing Street, 17 April 1980.

21. TFW, 111992, Sherman to Joseph, 9 November 1977.
22. TFW, 116391, Hoskyns to Thatcher, 17 April 1980.
23. Ibid.
24. TFW, 130148, Joseph to Thatcher, 21 January 1981.
25. TFW, 116388, Hoskyns to Thatcher, 16 April 1980.
26. Graham Willman and Paul Winch, *Innovation and Management Control: Labour Relations at BL Cars* (Cambridge, 1985), pp. 143–5.
27. Henderson, *Life on the Track*, p. 84.
28. Jack Saunders, *Assembling Cultures: Workplace Activism, Labour Militancy and Cultural Change in Britain's Car Factories, 1945–1982* (Manchester, 2019), p. 199.
29. Cited in ibid., p. 237.
30. MRC, 697/1/4, Ron Savage diary, 25 November 1974.
31. MRC, 697/1/8, Ron Savage diary, 9 April 1976.
32. Michael Edwardes, *Back from the Brink: An Apocalyptic Experience* (1983), p. 89.
33. *The Times*, 20 April 1971.
34. Ibid.
35. Christine Griffin, *Typical Girls? Young Women from School to the Full-Time Job Market* (1985).
36. *The Times*, 20 April 1971.
37. MRC, MSS 356/7/2/55, Paul Worms interview with Alan Morris.
38. Frank Skinner, *Frank Skinner* (2001), p. 201.
39. Paul Willis, 'Unemployment: The Final Inequality', *British Journal of Sociology of Education*, 7, 2 (1986), pp. 155–69.
40. Miriam Golden, 'The Politics of Job Loss', *American Journal of Political Science*, 36, 2 (1992), pp. 408–30.
41. Henderson, *Life on the Track*, p. 82.
42. John Taylor, *In the Pleasure Groove: Love, Death, and Duran Duran* (2012), p. 78.
43. Ali and Robin Campbell with Paul Gorman and Tim Abbot, *Blood and Fire: The Autobiography of the UB 40 Brothers* (2005), p. 36.
44. There was much discussion of the Birmingham police in the 1980s. John Brown published *Shades of Grey: A Report on Police – West Indian Relations in Handsworth* (1977). Some saw this work as excessively sympathetic to the police and published a riposte that drew on interviews with young black men. Derek Bishton and Brian Homer (eds.), *Talking Blues: Black Community Speaks about its Relationship with the Police* (Birmingham, 1978). Most revealing are the reports by Her Majesty's Inspectorate of Constabulary on the Birmingham and West Midlands Police in the 1970s (at which point most of those on duty would have been recruited). See also the autobiographical account by a thoughtful police officer: Michael Layton, *Birmingham's Front Line: True Police Stories* (Stroud, 2016), digital edition, no pagination.

45. Karis Campion, 'Making Mixed Race: Time, Place and Identities in Birmingham', PhD, University of Manchester (2017).

46. Kenneth Clarke, Nicholas Budgen and John Lenton, *Immigration, Race and Politics: A Birmingham View* (Bow Group Pamphlet, 1966), p. 10.

47. Ivan Henry Beresford, 'Homelessness and a Particular Response among Young West Indians in Handsworth Birmingham', MSocSc, University of Birmingham (1975).

48. Bishton and Homer (eds.), *Talking Blues*. Many of the young men interviewed for this collection spoke in patois but the women spoke standard English.

49. Danièle Joly, 'Ethnicité et Violence chez les Jeunes Antillais: Une Intervention Sociologique à Birmingham', *Cahiers Internationaux de Sociologie*, 105 (1998), pp. 383–413, http://www.jstor.org/stable/40690793.

50. Kieran Connell, *Black Handsworth: Race in 1980s Britain* (Berkeley, California, 2019), p. 115.

51. Ferdinand Dennis, *Behind the Frontlines: Journey into Afro-Britain* (1988), p. 101.

52. Spencer *et al.*, *Crisis in the Industrial Heartland*, p. 38.

53. Ibid., p. 133.

54. Stacy Pethia, 'Reconstructing Communities: The Impact of Regeneration on Community Dynamics and Processes', PhD, University of Birmingham (2011).

55. Alex Henshaw, *Sigh for a Merlin: Testing the Spitfire* (1990), p. 106.

56. Pethia, 'Reconstructing Communities'; David Parker and Christian Karner, 'Remembering the Alum Rock Road: Reputational Geographies and Spatial Biographies', *Midland History*, 36, 2 (2011), pp. 292–309. Job applicants from the Alum Rock Road were advised to say that they came from Saltley.

57. THCR, 6/2/4/59, note dated 19 July 1982: 'he has a drink problem'.

58. Raymond Carter, interviewed by Richard Stowell, *History of Parliament Trust*, 2013, British Library Sound & Moving Image, Catalogue reference C 1503/68 © The British Library, track 2.

59. Les Back and John Solomos, *Race, Politics and Social Change* (1995), p. 69.

14. CITIZENS OF SOMEWHERE?

1. Arshad Isakjee, 'Tainted Citizens: The Securitised Identities of Young Muslim Men in Birmingham', PhD, University of Birmingham (2013).

2. Kamaljeet Gill and Kjartan Sveinsson, *Passing the Baton: Inter-Generational Conceptions of Race and Racism in Birmingham*, Runnymede Report (2011).

3. Ibid.

4. C. Karner and D. Parker, 'Religion versus Rubbish: Deprivation and Social Capital in Inner-City Birmingham', *Social Compass*, 55, 4 (2008), pp. 517–31.
5. Ibid.
6. Gill and Sveinsson, *Passing the Baton*.
7. Susan Ann Jones, 'Women Can't Play Dominos: An Ethnographic Study of Working-Class Life in a Midlands Pub', PhD, University of Birmingham (2018).
8. A. Isakjee and C. Allen, '"A Catastrophic Lack of Inquisitiveness": A Critical Study of the Impact and Narrative of the Project Champion Surveillance Project in Birmingham', *Ethnicities*, 13, 6 (2013), pp. 751–70.
9. Isakjee, 'Tainted Citizens'.
10. Gill and Sveinsson, *Passing the Baton*.
11. Isakjee, 'Tainted Citizens'.
12. Patrick Loftman and Alan Middleton, 'Emasculating Public Debate and Eroding Local Accountability: City Promotion of Urban Development Projects in Birmingham', *Geographische Zeitschrift*, 89 (2001), pp. 85–103.
13. Libby Porter and Austin Barber, 'Planning the Cultural Quarter in Birmingham's Eastside', *European Planning Studies*, 15, 10 (2007), pp. 1327–48.
14. Elizabeth Buettner, '"Going for an Indian": South Asian Restaurants and the Limits of Multiculturalism in Britain', *The Journal of Modern History*, 80, 4 (2008), pp. 865–901.
15. *The Times*, 2 March 2002.
16. Alex Fenton, Peter Tyler, Sana Markkanen, Anna Clarke and Christine Whitehead, *Why Do Neighbourhoods Stay Poor? Deprivation, Place and People in Birmingham: A Report to the Barrow Cadbury Trust* (Cambridge, 2010).
17. Jones, 'Women Can't Play Dominos'.
18. Ibid.
19. Christopher Prendergast, 'A Birmingham Psychogeography: Continuity and Closure', PhD, University of Keele (2015).
20. Cited in David Parker and Paul Long, 'Reimagining Birmingham: Public History, Selective Memory and the Narration of Urban Change', *European Journal of Cultural Studies*, 6, 2 (2003), pp. 157–78, doi: 10.1177/1367549 403006002002.
21. Chris Jukes (ed.), *Fort Dunlop Remembered* (Studley, 2017).
22. Carl Chinn and Stephen Dyson, *'We Ain't Going Away!': The Battle for Longbridge* (Studley, 2000).
23. Cited in Parker and Long, 'Reimagining Birmingham'.
24. Tim Hall, 'Images of Industry in the Postindustrial City: Raymond Mason and Birmingham', *Ecumene*, 4, 1 (1997), pp. 46–68.

CONCLUSION

1. Geoffrey Elton, *The History of England: Inaugural Lecture Delivered 26 January 1984* (Cambridge, 1984), p. 28: 'The many people who confuse conservatism and pageantry with a sense of history will find this hard to believe, but it is a serious truth about the English in the mass that they know very little and care not greatly about their history.'
2. James Morris, *Pax Britannica: The Climax of an Empire* (this edn, 1979), p. 182.
3. Helen White and Rodger Trudgeon, 'Birmingham's Gun Quarter: A Skilled Trade in Decline', *Oral History*, 11, 2 (1983), pp. 69–83.
4. Norman Tiptaft, *The Man Who Went on Business* (1932), p. 37.
5. Roy Hattersley, 'Turbans, Bangles and Beards', *The Listener*, 8 November 1979.
6. C.R. Fay, *English Economic History, Mainly since 1700* (Cambridge, 1940), p. 181. Cited in Asa Briggs, *History of Birmingham*, II: *Borough and City, 1865–1938* (Oxford, 1952), p. 29. Fay's preface is signed 6 May. It is worth citing Fay's remarks in full: 'All through the nineteenth century Birmingham was in the industrial limelight alike in transport and industry, in the railway age and the automobile age and in the transition from iron to steel and from steel to alloys. The technical reason for this was this was a home of engineering in many forms, as well as the possessor of many trades. It could not have fallen into general decline unless the whole of England declined with it.'
7. Léon Faucher, 'Études sur L'Angleterre, VI: Birmingham', *Revue des Deux Mondes (1829–1971)*, 7, 2 (1844), pp. 161–91.
8. White and Trudgeon, 'Birmingham's Gun Quarter'.

APPENDIX IV. THE CASE OF THE BIRMINGHAM SIX

1. *The Spectator*, 18 August 1990.
2. Kew National Archives (TNA), HO 504/24, note by B.M. Caffarey, 9 December 1986.
3. Ibid.
4. Ibid., note by Bicknell, assistant to HMIC, 15 July 1986.
5. Ibid., Dear to Caffarey, 27 June 1986.
6. *Hansard*, 16 February 1988.
7. Chris Mullin, *Error of Judgement: The Truth about the Birmingham Bombings* (this edn, 1990), p. 267.
8. TNA, HO 504/24, Dear to Caffarey, 27 June 1986. See also the Early Day Motion submitted in the House of Commons on 30 April 1990, https://edm.parliament.uk/early-day-motion/1043/birmingham-six-no3.

9. TNA, HO 504/24, 'R v Hill and others. Report on photographs as requested by Miss Margaret Pereira, ... in letter dated 16th January 1986', illegible signature, 27 January 1986.

10. Richard Smith, 'Deaths in Prison', *British Medical Journal* (Clinical Research Edition), 288, 6412 (1984), pp. 208–12.

11. *Hansard*, 24 July 1986, David Mellor.

12. Chris Mullin, *Error of Judgement*, p. 204.

13. *Hansard*, 23 June 1986, question from Tony Banks.

14. Ibid., David Mellor.

15. Peter Rawlinson, *A Price Too High: An Autobiography* (1989), pp. 51–4.

16. Mullin, *Error of Judgement*, p. 307.

17. TNA, HO 287/1198, Birmingham City, Annual Inspection of the Force, inspection forms and notes, Appendix A. Discipline Summary of Proceedings.

18. TNA, HO 287/2526, Her Majesty's Inspectorate of Constabulary, Report on West Midlands Constabulary, 1974.

19. TNA, LCO 2/6813, to, or from, Lord Chancellor's Office, 12 July 1966.

20. TNA, HO 287/2527, Inspection of West Midlands Police by Mr R.G. Fenwick, 1975.

21. Douglas Hurd, *Memoirs* (2003), p. 356.

APPENDIX V

1. https://www.pebblemill.org/blog/the-colony-paul-long/.

2. Ieuan Franklin, 'Documenting the Social and Historical Margins in the Films of Philip Donnellan', *Revue LISA/LISA e-journal* [Online], XII, put online on 27 February 2014; accessed on 5 October 2021. URL: http://journals.openedition.org/lisa/5606; DOI: https://doi.org/10.4000/lisa.5606.

3. British Entertainment History Project, interview 206, Philip Donnellan, https://historyproject.org.uk/interview/philip-donnellan.

4. Birmingham Central Library (BCL), MS 4000/2/101.

5. The British Entertainment History Project, interview number 206. Donnellan alludes to Martin Weiner's work on British industrial decline.

Bibliography

PUBLISHED WORKS

Unless otherwise stated, place of publication is London.

Adams, David, 'Everyday Experiences of the Modern City: Remembering the Post-War Reconstruction of Birmingham', *Planning Perspectives*, 26, 2 (2011)

Adams, David, and Larkham, Peter, 'Walking with the Ghosts of the Past: Unearthing the Value of Residents' Urban Nostalgias', *Urban Studies*, 53, 10 (2016)

Allen, Walter, *All in a Lifetime* (1959)

—, *As I Walked Down New Grub Street: Memories of a Writing Life* (1981)

Andrews, Allen, *The Prosecutor, the Life of M.P. Pugh, Prosecuting Solicitor and Agent for the Director of Public Prosecutions* (1968)

Armstrong, Eric, *A Birmingham Boyhood, 1923–40* (Stroud, 2015)

Aston, Jennifer, 'Female Business Ownership in Birmingham 1849–1901', *Midland History*, 37, 2 (2012)

Atherton, Jonathan, '"Nothing but a Birmingham jury can save them": Prosecuting Rioters in Late Eighteenth-Century Britain', *Midland History*, 39, 1 (2014)

Auspos, Patricia, 'Radicalism, Pressure Groups, and Party Politics: From the National Education League to the National Liberal Federation', *Journal of British Studies*, 20, 1 (1980)

Back, Les and Solomos, John, *Race, Politics and Social Change* (1995)

Bailey, D., Chapain, C., Mahdon, M., and Fauth, R., *Life after Longbridge: Three Years On: Pathways to Re-Employment in a Restructuring Economy* (2008)

Ballard, Phillada, 'Made from the Barren Waste by Me: The Soho Landscape, 1757–94', in Phillada Ballard, Val Loggie and Shena Mason (eds.), *A Lost Landscape: Matthew Boulton's Gardens at Soho* (Chichester, 2009)

—, '"Rus in Urbe": Joseph Chamberlain's Gardens at Highbury, Moor Green Birmingham', *Garden History*, 14, 1 (1986)

Bartley, Paula, 'Moral Regeneration: Women and the Civic Gospel in Birmingham, 1870–1914', *Midland History*, 25, 1 (2000)

Bassett, Steven, 'Anglo-Saxon Birmingham', *Midland History*, 25, 1 (2000)

Beale, Catherine Hutton, *Memorials of the Old Meeting House and Burial Ground, Birmingham* (Birmingham, 1882)

Behagg, Clive, 'Myths of Cohesion: Capital and Compromise in the Historiography of Nineteenth-Century Birmingham', *Social History*, 11, 3 (1986)

Bettelheim, Charles, and Frère, Suzanne, *Une Ville Française Moyenne: Auxerre en 1950* (Paris, 1950)

Birmingham Education Committee, *Alderman Byng Kenrick. Tributes and Appreciations on his Retirement as Chairman of the Birmingham Educational Committee Expressed at Meetings Held on the Twenty-Ninth Day of October and the Eighth Day of December MCMXLIII* (Birmingham, 1943)

Bishton, Derek, and Homer, Brian (eds.), *Talking Blues: Black Community Speaks about its Relationship with the Police* (Birmingham, 1978)

Bisset, James, *Memoir of James Bisset, Written by Himself*, edited by T.B. Dudley (Leamington, 1904)

Black, Lawrence, 'The Lost World of Young Conservatism', *The Historical Journal*, 51, 4 (2008)

Borland, John, King, Roy D., and McDermott, Kathleen, 'The Irish in Prison: A Tighter Nick for "the Micks"?', *The British Journal of Sociology*, 46, 3 (1995)

Boughton, John, *Municipal Dreams: The Rise and Fall of Council Housing* (2018)

Boult, Adrian, *My Own Trumpet* (1973)

Bowen, W.T., 'Re-Housing the Midlands Overspill', *Official Architecture and Planning*, 19, 11 (1956)

Braybon, Gail, and Summerfield, Penny, *Out of the Cage: Women's Experiences in Two World Wars* (2013, first published 1987)

Briggs, Asa, *History of Birmingham*, II: *Borough and City 1865–1938* (Oxford, 1952)

—, *Victorian Cities* (this edn, 1968)

Brown, John, *Shades of Grey: A Report on Police–West Indian Relations in Handsworth* (1977)

Buettner, Elizabeth, "'Going for an Indian": South Asian Restaurants and the Limits of Multiculturalism in Britain', *The Journal of Modern History*, 80, 4 (2008)

Cadbury Brothers, *Bournville Works and the War 1914–1919* (Birmingham, 1919)

Callaghan, D.I., 'The Black Presence in the West Midlands, 1650–1918', *Midland History*, 36, 2 (2011)

Campbell, Ali, and Robin, with Paul Gorman and Tim Abbot, *Blood and Fire: The Autobiography of the UB40 Brothers* (2005)

Cannadine, David, *Lords and Landlords: The Aristocracy and the Towns, 1774–1967* (Leicester, 1980)

—, 'The "Best Governed City", Part Three', *The Historical Journal*, 19, 2 (1976)

—, 'The Calthorpe Family and Birmingham, 1810–1910: A "Conservative Interest" Examined', *The Historical Journal*, 18, 4 (1975)

Capp, Bernard, 'Healing the Nation: Royalist Visionaries, Cromwell, and the Restoration of Charles II', *The Seventeenth Century*, 34, 4 (2019)

Carter, Terry, *Birmingham in the Great War 1914–1915: The First Eighteen Months of the War* (2016)

Chamberlain, Austen, *The Austen Chamberlain Diary Letters: The Correspondence of Sir Austen Chamberlain with his Sisters Hilda and Ida, 1916–1937*, edited by Robert Self (Cambridge, 1995)

—, *Politics from Inside: An Epistolary Chronicle 1906–1914* (1936)

Chamberlain, Neville, *The Neville Chamberlain Diary Letters*, III: *The Heir Apparent, 1928–33*, edited by Robert Self (Aldershot, 2002)

—, *The Neville Chamberlain Diary Letters*, IV: *The Downing Street Years*, edited by Robert Self (Aldershot, 2005)

Chesterton, A.K., *Portrait of a Leader: Oswald Mosley* (1937)

Child, P., 'Blacktown, Mass-Observation, and the Dynamics of Voluntary Action in Mid-Twentieth-Century England', *The Historical Journal*, 63, 3 (2020)

Chinn, Carl, and Dyson, Stephen, *'We Ain't Going Away!': The Battle for Longbridge* (Studley, 2000)

Church, R.A., *Kenricks in Hardware: A Family Business, 1791–1966* (1969)

—, and Smith, Barbara M.D., 'Competition and Monopoly in the Coffin Furniture Industry, 1870–1915', *The Economic History Review*, 19, 3 (1966)

Church, Roy, *Herbert Austin: The British Motor Car Industry to 1941* (1979)

City of Birmingham, *Abstract of Birmingham Statistics*, vols. 1–3, *1931–1954* (1955)

Clark, Thomas, *A Biographical Tribute to the Memory of James Luckcock Father of Sunday School Instruction in Birmingham* (Birmingham, 1835)

Clarke, Kenneth, Budgen, Nicholas, and Lenton, John, *Immigration, Race and Politics: A Birmingham View* (Bow Group Pamphlet, 1966)

Cochrane, Claire, *Shakespeare and the Birmingham Repertory Theatre, 1913–1929* (1993)

Cole, Emily, 'The Urban and Suburban Public House in Inter-War England', Historic England, Research Report number 4 (Portsmouth, 2015), https://historicengland.org.uk/research/results/reports/4-2015

Connell, Kieran, 'Race, Prostitution and the New Left: The Postwar Inner City through Janet Mendelsohn's "Social Eye"', *History Workshop Journal*, 83, 1 (2017)

—, *Black Handsworth: Race in 1980s Britain* (Berkeley, California, 2019)

Conolly, L.W. (ed.), *Bernard Shaw and Barry Jackson, Selected Correspondence of Bernard Shaw*, vol. IV (2002)

Coss, Peter, *Lordship, Knighthood and Locality: A Study in English Society c. 1180–c. 1290* (Cambridge, 1991)

Cummings, Daniel, *Rest and Be Thankful: Autobiography of a Belfast Missionary* (Newtownards, 2015)

Davidoff, Leonore, and Hall, Catherine, *Family Fortunes: Men and Women of the English Middle Class, 1780–1850* (1987)

Davies, E.M., 'Changes in Car Ownership and Travel to Work Patterns in England and Wales between 1966 and 1971', *Transportation Science*, 13, 3 (1979)

Davies, Ivor, 'Urban Farming: A Study of the Agriculture of the City of Birmingham', *Geography*, 38, 4 (1953)

Davies, P., *Trapped: Unmarried West Indian Mothers in Handsworth* (Birmingham, 1983)

Debney, Jean, *The Dangerfields: Munitions & Memories* (Studley, 2001)

Delaney, Enda, *The Irish in Post-War Britain* (2007)

Dennis, Ferdinand, *Behind the Frontlines: Journey into Afro-Britain* (1988)

Denton, Graham, *The Odd Man Out: The Fascinating Story of Ron Saunders' Reign at Aston Villa* (2017)

Dobinson, Colin, *Fields of Deception: Britain's Bombing Decoys of World War II* (2000)

Dodds, E.R., *Missing Persons: An Autobiography* (Oxford, 1977)

Donoughue, Bernard, *Downing Street Diary*, II: *With James Callaghan in No. 10* (2008)

Dugdale, William, *Settling the Bill: The Memoirs of Bill Dugdale* (2011)

Dutton, David, 'Unionist Politics and the Aftermath of the General Election of 1906: A Reassessment', *The Historical Journal*, 22, 4 (1979)

—, *Austen Chamberlain: Gentleman in Politics* (Bolton, 1985)

Dyer, Christopher, 'Lords in a Landscape: The Berkeley Family and Northfield (Worcestershire)', in Linda Clark (ed.), *The Fifteenth Century*, XIV: *Essays Presented to Michael Hicks* (2015)

Edmond, Paul, *Duran Duran Unseen, Photographs, 1979–1982,* written and designed by Kasper de Graaf and Malcolm Garrett (Richmond, 2005)

Edwardes, Michael, *Back from the Brink: An Apocalyptic Experience* (1983)

Edwards, Eliezer, *Personal Recollections of Birmingham and Birmingham Men* (Birmingham, 1877)

Elton, Geoffrey, *The History of England: Inaugural Lecture Delivered 26 January 1984* (Cambridge, 1984)

Esteves, Olivier, *The 'Desegregation' of English Schools: Bussing, Race and Urban Space, 1960s–80s* (Manchester, 2018)

Etheridge, Richard, *Walking in the Shadow of a Political Agitator*, I: *Apprentice* (North Carolina, 2016)

Faucher, Léon, 'Études sur l'Angleterre, VI: Birmingham', *Revue des Deux Mondes (1829–1971)*, 7, 2 (1844)

Fay, C.R., *English Economic History, Mainly since 1700* (Cambridge, 1940)

Febvre, Lucien, preface in Charles Bettelheim and Suzanne Frère, *Une Ville Française Moyenne: Auxerre en 1950* (Paris, 1950)

Feiling, Keith, *The Life of Neville Chamberlain* (1946)

Fenton, Alex, Tyler, Peter, Markkanen, Sana, Clarke, Anna, and Whitehead, Christine, *Why Do Neighbourhoods Stay Poor? Deprivation, Place and People in Birmingham: A Report to the Barrow Cadbury Trust* (Cambridge, 2010)

Fewtrell, Eddie, and Thompson, Shirley, *King of Clubs: The Eddie Fewtrell Story* (Studley, 2007)

Filon, Augustin, 'Joseph Chamberlain et le Socialisme d'État', *Revue des Deux Mondes* (1829–1971), 96, 2 (1889)

Fisher, Roy, *The Long and the Short of It: Poems 1955–2010*, Bloodaxe Books, 2012, www.bloodaxebooks.com

Fitzgerald, Robert, 'Products, Firms and Consumption: Cadbury and the Development of Marketing, 1900–1939', *Business History*, 47, 4 (2005)

Flett, Hazel, 'Black Council Tenants in Birmingham', Working Papers on Ethnic Relations, 12 (1977)

—, Henderson, Jeff, and Brown, Bill, 'The Practice of Racial Dispersal in Birmingham, 1969–1975', *Journal of Social Policy*, 8, 3 (1979)

Flick, Carlos T., 'Thomas Attwood, Francis Place, and the Agitation for British Parliamentary Reform', *Huntington Library Quarterly*, 34, 4 (1971)

Fogg, Marie, *The Smalbroke Family of Birmingham 1550–1749* (North Carolina, 2010)

Foot, Paul, *Immigration and Race in British Politics* (1965)

Fox, Alan, 'Industrial Relations in Nineteenth-Century Birmingham', *Oxford Economic Papers*, 7, 1 (1955)

Franklin, Ieuan, 'Documenting the Social and Historical Margins in the Films of Philip Donnellan', *Revue LISA/LISA e-journal* [Online], XII, 1, (2014)

Games, Stephen, *Pevsner – The Early Life: Germany and Art* (2010)

Gardiner, Alfred, *Life of George Cadbury* (1923)

Garvin, J.L., *The Life of Joseph Chamberlain*, III: *1895–1900* (1934)

Geater, Jacqueline B. (ed.), *Birmingham Wills and Inventories, 1512–1603* (Stratford-upon-Avon, 2016)

Gehrke, Jules P., 'A Radical Endeavor: Joseph Chamberlain and the Emergence of Municipal Socialism in Birmingham', *The American Journal of Economics and Sociology*, 75 (2016)

Gill, Conrad, *Studies in Midland History* (Oxford, 1930)

—, *A History of Birmingham*, I: *Manor and Borough to 1865* (Oxford, 1952)

Gill, Kamaljeet, and Sveinsson, Kjartan, *Passing the Baton: Inter-Generational Conceptions of Race and Racism in Birmingham*, Runnymede Report (2011)

Gissane, William, and Bull, John, 'A Study of 183 Road Deaths in and around Birmingham in 1960', *British Medical Journal*, 1, 5241 (1961)

Golden, Miriam, 'The Politics of Job Loss', *American Journal of Political Science*, 36, 2 (1992)

Goodman, Geoffrey, *Bill Morris: A Trade Union Miracle* (2010)

Green, Henry, *Pack My Bag: A Self-Portrait* (1992, first published 1940)

Griffin, Christine, *Typical Girls? Young Women from School to the Full-Time Job Market* (1985)

Gunn, Simon, 'Ring Road: Birmingham and the Collapse of the Motor City Ideal in 1970s Britain', *The Historical Journal*, 61, 1 (2018)

Gutzke, David, *Pubs and Progressives: Reinventing the Public House in England, 1896–1960* (Dekalb, Illinois, 2006)

Hall, Catherine, 'Married Women at Home in Birmingham in the 1920's and 1930's', *Oral History*, 5, 2 (1977)

Hall, Stuart, with Schwarz, Bill, *Familiar Stranger: A Life Between Two Islands* (2017)

Hall, Tim, 'Images of Industry in the Postindustrial City: Raymond Mason and Birmingham', *Ecumene*, 4, 1 (1997)

Harris, Clive (ed.), *The History of the Birmingham Gun-Barrel Proof House, with Notes on the Birmingham Gun Trade* (Birmingham, 1946)

Harrison, Leigh Michael, 'Factory Music: How the Industrial Geography and Working-Class Environment of Post-War Birmingham Fostered the Birth of Heavy Metal', *Journal of Social History*, 44, 1 (2010)

Hastings, R.P., 'The Birmingham Labour Movement, 1918–1945', *Midland History*, 5, 1 (1979)

Hattersley, Roy, 'Turbans, Bangles and Beards', *The Listener*, 8 November 1979

—, 'Birmingham', in Andrew Adonis and Keith Thomas (eds.), *Roy Jenkins: A Retrospective* (2004)

Heath, Charles, *Service Record of King Edward's School Birmingham during the War, 1914–1919* (Birmingham, 1920)

Helmholz, R., 'Clement Colmore (1550–1619)', *Ecclesiastical Law Journal*, 18, 2 (2016)

Henderson, Frank, *Life on the Track: Memoirs of a Socialist Worker* (2009)

Hendriks, Frank, 'Cars and Culture in Munich and Birmingham: The Case for Cultural Pluralism', in Dennis Coyle and Richard Ellis (eds.), *Politics, Policy, and Culture* (1994)

Hennock, E.P., *Fit and Proper Persons: Ideal and Reality in Nineteenth-Century Urban Government* (1973)

Henry, Lenny, *Who Am I, Again?* (2019)

Henshaw, Alex, *Sigh for a Merlin: Testing the Spitfire* (1990)

Higgins, Patrick, *Heterosexual Dictatorship: Male Homosexuality in Post-War Britain* (1996)

Higgs, Catherine, *Chocolate Islands: Cocoa, Slavery, and Colonial Africa* (Athens, Ohio, 2012)

Hill, Barry K., 'Women and Unemployment in Birmingham, 1918–1939', *Midland History*, 27, 1 (2002)

Hilton, Boyd, *A Mad, Bad and Dangerous People? England 1783–1846* (Oxford, 2006)

Hilton, R.H., *A Medieval Society: The West Midlands at the End of the Thirteenth Century* (1966)

HMSO, *Report of a Court of Enquiry into a Dispute between the Austin Motor Company Limited and Certain Workpeople, Members of the National Union of Vehicle Builders* (1953)

—, *Children's Employment Commission, Second Report of the Commissioners: Trades and Manufactures* (1843)

Hoggart, Richard, *An Imagined Life: Life and Times*, III: *1959–1991* (Oxford, 1992)

Holte, Grace, *The Girl from Guildford Street: Growing up in Working-Class Birmingham, 1957–1968* (Studley, 2018)

Hopkins, Eric, 'Working-Class Housing in Birmingham during the Industrial Revolution', *International Review of Social History*, 31, 1 (1986)

—, 'Working-Class Life in Birmingham between the Wars, 1918–1939', *Midland History*, 15, 1 (1990)

—, 'Industrial Change and Life at Work in Birmingham 1850–1914', *Midland History*, 27, 1 (2002), pp. 112–29

Hornsby, Laurie, *Brum Rocked On* (Studley, 1999)

Houlbrook, Matt, *Queer London: Perils and Pleasures in the Sexual Metropolis, 1918–1957* (Chicago, 2005)

Howell, Denis, *Made in Birmingham: The Memoirs of Denis Howell* (1990)

Hunt, John, 'Families at War: Royalists and Montfortians in the West Midlands', *Midland History*, 22, 1 (1997)

Hurd, Douglas, *Memoirs* (2003)

Hutton, Catherine, *Reminiscences of a Gentlewoman of the Last Century: Letters of Catherine Hutton*, edited by Catherine Hutton Beale (Birmingham, 1891)

Hutton, William, *An History of Birmingham. To the End of the Year 1780* (Birmingham, 1781)

—, *The Life of William Hutton Including a Particular Account of the Riots at Birmingham in 1791; to Which is Subjoined the History of His Family Written by Himself and Published by His Daughter: Catherine Hutton* (1816)

—, *The History of Birmingham* (Birmingham, this edn, 1836)

Isakjee, A., and Allen, C., '"A Catastrophic Lack of Inquisitiveness": A Critical Study of the Impact and Narrative of the Project Champion Surveillance Project in Birmingham', *Ethnicities*, 13, 6 (2013)

Ives, Eric, Drummond, Diane K., and Schwarz, Leonard, *The First Civic University: Birmingham, 1880–1980 – An Introductory History* (Birmingham, 2000)

Izon, John, *The Records of King Edward's School, Birmingham* (Oxford, 1974)

Jamdagni, Laxmi, *Hamari Rangily Zindagi*, I: *Our Colourful Lives* (1980)

James, Gregory, 'The Chinese Mariners of the First World War', *Journal of the Royal Asiatic Society Hong Kong Branch*, 60 (2020)

James, Peter, and Sadler, Richard, *Homes Fit for Heroes: Photographs by Bill Brandt, 1939–1943* (Stockport, 2004)

Jenkins, Roy, *A Life at the Centre* (1991)

—, *Twelve Cities: A Personal Memoir* (2002)

Johnman, Lewis, 'The Large Manufacturing Companies of 1935', *Business History*, 28, 2 (1986)

Joly, Danièle, 'Ethnicité et Violence chez les Jeunes Antillais: Une Intervention Sociologique à Birmingham', *Cahiers Internationaux de Sociologie*, 105 (1998)

Jones, Ian, *The Local Church and Generational Change in Birmingham, 1945–2000* (Woodbridge, 2012)

Jones, Leslie John, *Three Times for a Jolly Welshman: An Autobiography of a Rhondda Exile* (Birmingham, 1984)

Jones, P.M., 'Industrial Enlightenment in Practice: Visitors to the Soho Manufactory, 1765–1820', *Midland History*, 33, 1 (2008)

—, *Industrial Enlightenment: Science Technology and Culture in Birmingham and the West Midlands, 1760–1820* (Manchester, 2008)

Jones, Phil, 'The Suburban High Flat in the Post-War Reconstruction of Birmingham', *Urban History*, 32, 2 (2005)

Jones, Simon, *Black Culture, White Youth: The Reggae Tradition from JA to UK* (1988)

Jukes, Chris (ed.), *Fort Dunlop Remembered* (Studley, 2017)

Kalra, Mahesh A., 'The Birth of the "New" Bombay Mint, *c.* 1790–1830 – Matthew Boulton's Pioneering Contribution to Modernization of Indian Coinage', *Proceedings of the Indian History Congress*, 74 (2013)

Karner, C., and Parker, D., 'Religion versus Rubbish: Deprivation and Social Capital in Inner-City Birmingham', *Social Compass*, 55, 4 (2008)

Kellett, John R., *The Impact of Railways on Victorian Cities* (1969)

Kemnitz, Thomas Milton, 'The Chartist Convention of 1839', *Albion: A Quarterly Journal Concerned with British Studies*, 10, 2 (1978)

Khan, Hilda, *Repercussions of Redundancy: A Local Survey* (1965)

Laite, Julia, 'Immoral Traffic: Mobility, Health, Labor and the "Lorry Girl" in Mid Twentieth-Century Britain', *Journal of British Studies*, 52, 3 (2013)

Lambert, John R., *Crime, Police and Race Relations: A Study in Birmingham* (Oxford, 1970)

Langfield, Michele, 'Righting the Record? British Child Migration: The Case of the Middlemore Homes, 1872–1972', in Kent Fedorowich and Andrew S. Thompson (eds.), *Empire, Migration and Identity in the British World* (Manchester, 2013)

Lawton, R., 'The Daily Journey to Work in England and Wales: An Analysis of the Report on Usual Residence and Workplace, Census of England and Wales, 1951', *The Town Planning Review*, 29, 4 (1959)

Laybourn, Keith, and Taylor, David, *Policing in England and Wales, 1918–39: The Fed, Flying Squads and Forensics* (2011)

Layton, Michael, *Birmingham's Front Line: True Police Stories* (Stroud, 2016)

Leach, Belinda, 'Grandma Page's Workshop: Outwork in Birmingham 1911–1914', *Oral History*, 22, 1 (1994)

Lee, Sabine, 'Birmingham-London-Los Alamos-Hiroshima: Britain and the Atomic Bomb', *Midland History*, 27, 1 (2002)

Leighton, Denys P., 'Municipal Progress, Democracy and Radical Identity in Birmingham, 1838–1886', *Midland History*, 25, 1 (2000)

Light, Alison, *Common People: The History of an English Family* (2014)

Lindsey, Lydia, 'The Split-Labor Phenomenon: Its Impact on West Indian Workers as a Marginal Working Class in Birmingham, England, 1948–1962', *The Journal of Negro History*, 78, 2 (1993)

Lloyd-Owen, D.C., 'Richard Middlemore (1804–1891)', *The British Journal of Ophthalmology* (February 1920)

Loasby, Brian, 'West Midlands Industrial Dispersal Projects', *Official Architecture and Planning*, 24, 8 (1961)

Lodge, David, *Quite a Good Time to Be Born: A Memoir, 1935–1975* (2015)

Lodge, Oliver, *Past Years: An Autobiography* (1931)

Loftman, Patrick, and Middleton, Alan, 'Emasculating Public Debate and Eroding Local Accountability: City Promotion of Urban Development Projects in Birmingham', *Geographische Zeitschrift*, 89 (2001)

Loggie, Val, 'Soho through the Eyes of John Philip', in Phillada Ballard, Val Loggie and Shena Mason (eds.), *A Lost Landscape: Matthew Boulton's Gardens at Soho* (Chichester, 2009)

Loynton, J.C., *A History of Solihull School 1560–2010* (Solihull, 2010)

Macmillan, Harold, *The Macmillan Diaries*, II: *Prime Minister and After, 1957–1966*, edited by Peter Catterall (2004)

MacNeice, Louis, *The Strings Are False: An Unfinished Autobiography* (1965)

Marsh, Peter, *Joseph Chamberlain: Entrepreneur in Politics* (1994)

Mason, Shena, '"A Cheerful and Pleasant Spot": Matthew Boulton and Soho', in Phillada Ballard, Val Loggie and Shena Mason (eds.), *A Lost Landscape: Matthew Boulton's Gardens at Soho* (Chichester, 2009)

Mawson, John, and Skelcher, C., 'Updating the West Midlands Regional Strategy: A Review of Inter-Authority Relationships', *The Town Planning Review*, 51, 2 (1980)

Mayne, Alan, *The Imagined Slum: Newspaper Representation in Three Cities, 1870–1914* (Leicester, 1993)

Mendelsøn, Edward (ed.), *W.H. Auden Prose*, I (2000)

Miller, H., 'Radicals, Tories or Monomaniacs? The Birmingham Currency Reformers in the House of Commons, 1832–67', *Parliamentary History*, 31, 3 (2012)

Minard, P., 'Le Bureau d'Essai de Birmingham, ou la Fabrique de la Réputation au XVIIIe Siècle', *Annales. Histoire, Sciences Sociales*, 65, 5 (2010)

Mohr, Paul, 'The de Berminghams, Barons of Athenry: A Suggested Outline Lineage, from First to Last', *Journal of the Galway Archaeological and Historical Society*, 63 (2011)

Money, John, 'Taverns, Coffee Houses and Clubs: Local Politics and Popular Articulacy in the Birmingham Area, in the Age of the American Revolution', *The Historical Journal*, 14, 1 (1971)

—, *Experience and Identity: Birmingham and the West Midlands, 1760–1800* (Manchester, 1977)

Moore, J.M., 'Reformation, Terror and Scandal: The 1853 Royal Commission into Abuses at Birmingham Prison', *Midland History*, 46, 1 (2021)

Moran, James, *Irish Birmingham: A History* (Liverpool, 2010)

Morris, James, *Pax Britannica: The Climax of Empire* (this edn, 1979)

Mort, Frank, *Capital Affairs: London and the Making of the Permissive Society* (2010)

Morton, H.V., *In Search of England* (1927)

—, *The Call of England* (1928)

Moss, D., 'A Study in Failure: Thomas Attwood, M.P. for Birmingham, 1832–1839', *The Historical Journal*, 21, 3 (1978)

Mullin, Chris, *Error of Judgement: The Truth about the Birmingham Bombings* (this edn, 1990)

Newton, Kenneth, *Second City Politics: Democratic Processes and Decision-Making in Birmingham* (Oxford, 1976)

Nockolds, Harold, *Lucas, The First 100 Years*, I: *The King of the Road: 1875–1939* (1976)

—, *Lucas, The First 100 Years*, II: *The Successors* (1978)

O'Brien, Sarah, 'Negotiations of Irish Identity in the Wake of Terrorism: The Case of the Irish in Birmingham 1973–74', *Irish Studies Review*, 25, 3 (2017)

O'Reilly, Laura, 'The Birmingham Pub Bombings, the Irish as a "suspect community" and the Memories of the O'Reilly Family', in Graham Dawson, Jo Dover and Stephen Hopkins (eds.), *The Northern Ireland Troubles in Britain: Impacts, Engagements, Legacies and Memories* (Manchester, 2016)

Ostrogorski, Moisei, 'The Introduction of the Caucus into England', *Political Science Quarterly*, 8, 2 (1893)

Overy, Richard, *The Bombing War: Europe, 1939–1945* (2013)

Page, Anthony, 'Rational Dissent, Enlightenment and Abolition of the British Slave Trade', *The Historical Journal*, 54, 3 (2011)

Panic, Paul, *I Thought Solihull was for Snobs (but these Punks Think Different): The Mell Square Musick Story, Punk/Mod Culture in 70s/80s Solihull and Birmingham* (Birmingham, 2015)

Panufnik, Andrzej, *Composing Myself* (1987)

Parker, David, and Long, Paul, 'Reimagining Birmingham: Public History, Selective Memory and the Narration of Urban Change', *European Journal of Cultural Studies*, 6, 2 (2003)

Parker, David, and Karner, Christian, 'Remembering the Alum Rock Road: Reputational Geographies and Spatial Biographies', *Midland History*, 36, 2 (2011)

Parton, Alan, 'Poor-Law Settlement Certificates and Migration to and from Birmingham, 1726–1757', *Local Population Studies*, 38 (1987)

Pattinson, Juliette, '"Shirkers", "Scrimjacks" and "Scrimshanks"? British Civilian Masculinity and Reserved Occupations, 1914–45', *Gender and History*, 28, 3 (2016)

Paulson, David, 'The Professionalisation of Selling and the Transformation of a Family Business: Kenrick & Jefferson, 1878–1940', *Business History*, 62, 2 (2020)

Peierls, Rudolf, *Bird of Passage: Recollections of a Physicist* (Princeton, New Jersey, 1985)

Perrie, Maureen, 'Hobby Farming among the Birmingham Bourgeoisie: The Cadburys and the Chamberlains on Their Suburban Estates, *c.*1880–1914', *The Agricultural History Review*, 61, 1 (2013)

Phillimore, W.P.H., *Some Account of the Family of Middlemore of Warwickshire and Worcestershire* (1901)

Plant, Helen, '"Ye are all one in Christ Jesus": Aspects of Unitarianism and Feminism in Birmingham, *c.* 1869–90', *Women's History Review*, 9, 4 (2000)

Porter, Libby, and Barber, Austin, 'Planning the Cultural Quarter in Birmingham's Eastside', *European Planning Studies*, 15, 10 (2007)

Potter, A.M., 'The English Conservative Constituency Association', *Western Political Quarterly*, 9, 2 (1956)

Price, Frank, *Being There* (Leicester, 2002)

Priestley, Joseph, *Autobiography of Joseph Priestley,* edited by Jack Lindsay (this edn Bath, 1970)

Priestley, J. B. *English Journey* (2018, first published 1934)

Pugh, Bridget, *Solid Citizens: Statues in Birmingham* (Sutton Coldfield, 1983)

Ratcliffe, Peter, *Racism and Reaction: A Profile of Handsworth* (1981)

Rawlinson, Peter, *A Price Too High: An Autobiography* (1989)

Reekes, Andrew, *The Birmingham Political Machine: Winning Elections for Joseph Chamberlain* (Birmingham, 2018)

Reid, Douglas A., 'The Decline of Saint Monday, 1766–1876', *Past & Present*, 71, 1 (1976)

Reilly, Oliver, 'A Worker in Birmingham', *The Furrow*, 9, 4 (1958)

Rex, John, and Moore, Robert, *Race, Community and Conflict: A Study of Sparkbrook* (Oxford, 1967)

Richards, Jeffrey, 'The Cinema and Cinema-going in Birmingham in the 1930s', in John K. Walton and James Walvin (eds.), *Leisure in Britain, 1780–1939* (Manchester, 1983)

Richards, J.M., *The Bombed Buildings of Britain: A Record of Architectural Casualties, 1940–41* (1942)

Richards, W.A., 'The Import of Firearms into West Africa in the Eighteenth Century', *Journal of African History*, 21, 1 (1980)

Robinson, E., 'Eighteenth-Century Commerce and Fashion: Matthew Boulton's Marketing Techniques', *The Economic History Review*, 16, 1 (1963)

Rose, R.B., 'Political History to 1832', in W.B. Stephens (ed.), *Victoria History of the Counties of England: A History of the County of Warwick*, vol. VII: *The City of Birmingham* (Oxford, 1964)

Rosenthal, Leslie, 'Economic Efficiency, Nuisance, and Sewage: New Lessons from Attorney-General v. Council of the Borough of Birmingham, 1858–95', *The Journal of Legal Studies*, 36, 1 (2007)

—, *The River Pollution Dilemma in Victorian England: Nuisance Law versus Economic Efficiency* (Farnham, 2014)

—, 'Joseph Chamberlain and the Birmingham Town Council, 1865–1880', *Midland History*, 41, 1 (2016)

Rousiers, Paul de, *La Question Ouvrière en Angleterre* (Paris, 1895)

Rowlinson, Michael, 'The Early Application of Scientific Management by Cadbury', *Business History*, 30, 4 (1988)

Satre, Lowell, *Chocolate on Trial: Slavery, Politics and the Ethics of Business* (Athens, Ohio, 2005)

Saunders, Jack, *Assembling Cultures: Workplace Activism, Labour Militancy and Cultural Change in Britain's Car Factories, 1945–1982* (Manchester, 2019)

Scannell, Paddy, 'Broadcasting and the Politics of Unemployment, 1930–1935', *Media, Culture and Society*, 2 (1980)

Scargill, Arthur, 'The New Unionism', *New Left Review*, 1, 92 (1975)

Scott, Jamie, '"Labourism Revisited": W.J. Davis, Working-Class Culture, and Trade Unionist Politics in Birmingham, 1892–1906', *Midland History*, 38, 1 (2013)

Scott, Peter, 'The State, Internal Migration and the Growth of New Industrial Communities in Inter-War Britain', *The English Historical Review*, 115, 461 (2000)

Searby, P., 'Great Dodford and the Later History of the Chartist Land Scheme', *The Agricultural History Review*, 16, 1 (1968)

Searle, Kevin, 'Mixing the Unmixables: The 1949 Causeway Green "Riots" in Birmingham', *Race and Class*, 54, 3 (2013)

Sheppard Fidler, A.G., 'Post-War Housing in Birmingham', *The Town Planning Review*, 26, 1 (1955)

Simmons, Jim, *Soap Box Evangelist* (Chichester, 1972)

Skinner, Frank, *Frank Skinner* (2001)

Smith, Barbara, 'The Galtons of Birmingham: Quaker Gun Merchants and Bankers, 1702–1831', *Business History*, 9, 2 (1967)

Smith, Dennis, *Conflict and Compromise: Class Formation in English Society, 1830–1914: A Comparative Study of Birmingham and Sheffield* (1982)

—, 'Paternalism, Craft and Organizational Rationality, 1830–1930: An Exploratory Model', *Urban History*, 19, 2 (1992)

Smith, Harry, 'William Hutton and the Myths of Birmingham', *Midland History*, 40, 1 (2015)

—, Bennett, Robert J., and van Lieshout, Carry, 'Entrepreneurship in Birmingham and Manchester, 1851–1911: A Tale of Two Cities?', *Midland History*, 45, 3 (2020)

Smith, Richard, 'Deaths in Prison', *British Medical Journal* (Clinical Research Edition), 288, 6412 (1984)

Somerville, Alexander, *The Autobiography of a Working Man* (1848)

Soutar, Mary, Wilkins, Edgar, and Sargant Florence, Philip, *Nutrition and Size of Family: Report on a New Housing Estate, 1939* (Birmingham, 1942)

Spencer, David, and Lloyd, John, *A Child's Eye View of Small Heath Birmingham: Perception Studies for Environmental Education*, The University of Birmingham Centre for Urban and Regional Studies, Research Memorandum, 34 (1974)

Spencer, Ken, Taylor, Andy, Smith, Barbara, Mawson, John, Flynn, Norman, and Batley, Richard, *Crisis in the Industrial Heartland: A Study of the West Midlands* (Oxford, 1986)

Stamp, Gavin, *Britain's Lost Cities* (2007)

Stedman, M.B., and Wood, P.A., 'Urban Renewal in Birmingham: An Interim Report', *Geography*, 50, 1 (1965)

Stephens, W.B. (ed.), *Victoria History of the Counties of England: A History of the County of Warwick*, VII: *The City of Birmingham* (Oxford, 1964)

Sutcliffe, Anthony, and Smith, Roger, *History of Birmingham*, III: *1939–1970* (Oxford, 1974)

Tann, Jennifer, 'Marketing Methods in the International Steam Engine Market: The Case of Boulton and Watt', *The Journal of Economic History*, 38, 2 (1978)

Taylor, John, *In the Pleasure Groove: Love, Death, and Duran Duran* (2012)

Taylor, Matthew, 'City Community and Sport in Birmingham during the Second World War', *Midland History*, 46, 2 (2021)

Ter Heide, H., 'West Indian Migration to Great Britain', *Nieuwe West-Indische Gids/New West Indian Guide*, 43 (1963–4)

Terry-Chandler, F.E., 'Compulsory Industriousness: Working Conditions and Exploitation in Birmingham during the Industrial Revolution', *Midland History*, 44, 1 (2019)

Tholfsen, Trygve R., 'The Chartist Crisis in Birmingham', *International Review of Social History*, 3, 3 (1958)

Thomas, Brinley, 'The Influx of Labour into the Midlands 1920–37', *Economica*, 5, 20 (1938)

Thomas-Hope, Elizabeth, 'Hopes and Reality in the West Indian Migration to Britain', *Oral History*, 8, 1 (1980)

Thomason, Edward, *Memoirs during Half a Century* (1845)

Thoms, David, *War Industry and Society: The Midlands, 1939–1945* (1989)

Tiptaft, Norman, *The City Father* (1925)
—, *The Man Who Went on Business* (1932)
—, *Inns of the Midlands* (Birmingham, 1951)
—, *The Individualist* (Birmingham, 1954)
Tocqueville, Alexis de, *Journeys to England and Ireland*, edited J.P. Mayer (1958)
Tynan, Kathleen, *The Life of Kenneth Tynan* (1987)
Uglow, Jenny, *The Lunar Men: The Friends who Made the Future 1730–1810* (2002)
Ullah, Philip, 'Rhetoric and Ideology in Social Identification: The Case of Second Generation Irish Youths', *Discourse and Society*, 1, 2 (1990)
Umbach, Maiken, 'A Tale of Second Cities: Autonomy, Culture, and the Law in Hamburg and Barcelona in the Late Nineteenth Century', *The American Historical Review*, 110, 3 (2005)
Vance, James E., 'Housing the Worker: Determinative and Contingent Ties in Nineteenth-Century Birmingham', *Economic Geography*, 43, 2 (1967)
Walmsley, Robert, *Peterloo: The Case Reopened* (Manchester, 1969)
Ward, Roger, 'The Strange Death of Liberal Birmingham', *Journal of Liberal History*, 82 (2014)
Waterhouse, A.H., and Brabban, Diana H., 'Inquiry into the Fertility of Immigrants', *The International Migration Digest*, 1, 2 (1964)
Watters, Frank, *Being Frank: The Memoirs of Frank Watters* (Barnsley, 1992)
Webb, Beatrice Potter, *My Apprenticeship*, 1 (Cambridge, 1979, first published 1926)
West, Bob, 'Danger. History at Work: A Critical Consumer's Guide to the Ironbridge Gorge Museum', Birmingham Centre for Contemporary Cultural Studies, Occasional Papers (1985)
White, Helen, and Trudgeon, Roger, 'Birmingham's Gun Quarter: A Skilled Trade in Decline', *Oral History*, 11, 2 (1983)
Whyman, Susan, *The Useful Knowledge of William Hutton: Culture and Industry in Eighteenth-Century Birmingham* (Oxford, 2018)
Williams, Peter, 'Building Societies and the Inner City', *Transactions of the Institute of British Geographers*, 3, 1 (1978)
Willis, Paul, 'Human Experience and Material Production: The Culture of the Shop Floor', Centre for Contemporary Cultural Studies, Occasional Papers (1975)
—, *Learning to Labour: How Working-Class Kids Get Working-Class Jobs* (1977)
—, 'Unemployment: The Final Inequality', *British Journal of Sociology of Education*, 7, 2 (1986)
Willman, Graham, and Winch, Paul, *Innovation and Management Control: Labour Relations at BL Cars* (Cambridge, 1985)
Wilson, D., and Pinto-Duschinsky, M., 'Conservative City Machines: The End of an Era', *British Journal of Political Science*, 6, 2 (1976)

Winn, Godfrey, *Autobiography, vol. 1: The Infirm Glory* (1967)

Winn, Sandra, 'The Developing Geography of AIDS: A Case Study of the West Midlands', *Area*, 20, 1 (1988)

Wright, Susannah, 'The Work of Teachers and Others in and around a Birmingham Slum School, 1891–1920', *History of Education*, 38, 6 (2009)

Young, G.M., *Portrait of an Age* (2002, first published 1936)

SERIAL PUBLICATIONS

Hansard
The Spectator
The Times

UNPUBLISHED DISSERTATIONS

Ballard, Phillada, 'A Commercial and Industrial Elite: A Study of Birmingham's Upper Middle Class, 1780–1914', PhD, University of Reading (1983)

Beresford, Ivan Henry, 'Homelessness and a Particular Response among Young West Indians in Handsworth Birmingham', MSocSc, University of Birmingham (1975)

Blanch, Michael Dennis, 'Nation, Empire and the Birmingham Working Class, 1899–1914', PhD, University of Birmingham (1975)

Boughton, John, 'Working-Class Politics in Birmingham and Sheffield, 1918–1931', PhD, University of Warwick (1985)

Campion, Karis, 'Making Mixed Race: Time, Place and Identities in Birmingham', PhD, University of Manchester (2017)

Carey, Adam, 'Politics, Governance and the Shaping of Smethwick since 1945', MPhil, University of Birmingham (2016)

Chinn, Carl, 'The Anatomy of a Working-Class Neigbourhood: West Sparkbrook, 1871–1914', PhD, University of Birmingham (1986)

Davis, Patsy, 'Green Ribbons: The Irish in Birmingham in the 1860s, a Study of Housing, Work and Policing', PhD, University of Birmingham (2003)

Ewart, Henrietta, 'Caring for Migrants: Policy Responses to Irish Migration to England, 1940–1972', PhD, University of Warwick (2012)

Ewen, Shane, 'Power and Administration in Two Midland Cities, *c.* 1870–1938', PhD, University of Leicester (2003)

Giles, Margaret, 'Something That Bit Better: Working-Class Domesticity and "Respectability", 1919–1939', DPhil, University of York (1989)

Hazley, Barry, 'The Irish in Post-War England: Experience, Memory and Belonging in Personal Narratives of Migration, 1945–1969', PhD, University of Manchester (2013)

Isakjee, Arshad, 'Tainted Citizens: The Securitised Identities of Young Muslim Men in Birmingham', PhD, University of Birmingham (2013)

Jones, Susan Ann, 'Women Can't Play Dominos: An Ethnographic Study of Working-Class Life in a Midlands Pub', PhD, University of Birmingham (2018)

McCarvill, Philip, 'An Examination of Ethnic Identity: A Case Study of "Second Generation" Irish People in Birmingham', PhD, University of Warwick (2002)

Nejedly, Mary, 'Child Labour in an Industrial Town: A Study of Child Workers in Birmingham, 1750–1880', PhD, University of Birmingham (2019)

Parker, Matthew, 'Making the City Mobile: The Place of the Motor Car in the Planning of Post-War Birmingham, c. 1945–1973', PhD, University of Leicester (2016)

Pethia, Stacey, 'Reconstructing Communities: The Impact of Regeneration on Community Dynamics and Processes', PhD, University of Birmingham (2011)

Popl, Ian, 'Roy Fisher's Mysticism', PhD, University of Manchester (2011)

Prendergast, Christopher, 'A Birmingham Psychogeography: Continuity and Closure', PhD, University of Keele (2015)

Procter, Ruth Jane, 'Infant Mortality: A Study of the Impact of Social Intervention in Birmingham, 1873–1938', MPhil, University of Birmingham (2011)

Shoebridge, Michele, 'The Women's Suffrage Movement in Birmingham and District, 1903–1918', MA, Wolverhampton Polytechnic (1983)

Smith, Harry, 'Propertied Society and Public Life: The Social History of Birmingham, 1780–1832', DPhil, University of Oxford (2013)

Smojkis, Maureen, 'Out of the Shadows: Exploring the Lives of the Birmingham Polish', MPhil, University of Birmingham (2014)

Taylor, Donna, 'Governance and Locality in the Age of Reform: Birmingham, 1769–1852', PhD, University of Birmingham (2019)

—, 'To the Bull Ring! Politics, Protest and Policing in Birmingham during the Early Chartist Period', MRes, University of Birmingham (2014)

Thomas, Susan, 'George Edmonds and the Development of Birmingham Radicalism', PhD, University of Birmingham (2021)

Weinberger, Barbara, 'Law Breakers and Law Enforcers, in the Late Victorian City: Birmingham, 1867–1877', PhD, University of Warwick (1981)

Wright, R.A., 'Liberal Party Organisation and Politics in Birmingham, Coventry, and Wolverhampton, 1886–1914, with Particular Reference to the Development of Independent Labour Representation', PhD, University of Birmingham (1977)

Ziesler, Kaja Irene, 'The Irish in Birmingham, 1830–1970', PhD, University of Birmingham (1989)

KEW NATIONAL ARCHIVES

Department of Health and Social Security

BN 89/232

Board of Trade

BT 70/48

Cabinet Papers

CAB 23/25/2
CAB 65/9/3
CAB 24/128/49

Department of Economic Affairs

EW 7/914

Ministry of Health

HLG 7/410

Home Office

HO 45/11551
HO 144/6898
HO 186/2637
HO 192/1188
HO 192/1198
HO 192/1206
HO 192/1208
HO 192/1210
HO 192/1214
HO 192/1220
HO 192/1240

HO 192/1251
HO 192/937
HO 196/19
HO 199/156
HO 199/179
HO 287/1706
HO 504/24

The Security Service

KV 2/1833

Ministry of Labour

LAB 8/2795
LAB 10/1168
LAB 23/60

Lord Chancellor's Office

LCO 2/6813

Ministry of Agriculture and Fisheries

MAF 255/1075

BRITISH LIBRARY SOUND ARCHIVE

Adrian Cadbury interviewed by Niamh Dillon, *Food from Source to Salespoint*, 2001–2003, British Library Sound & Moving Image, Catalogue reference C 82/122 © The British Library

Raymond Carter interviewed by Richard Stowell, *History of Parliament Trust*, 2013, British Library Sound & Moving Image, Catalogue reference C 1503/68 © The British Library

Reginald Eyre interviewed by Isobel White, *History of Parliament Trust*, 2014, British Library Sound & Moving Image, Catalogue reference C 1503/95 © The British Library

Tony Green interviewed by Robert Wilkinson, *An Oral History of Oral History*, 2013, British Library Sound & Moving Image, Catalogue reference C 1149/31 © The British Library

Christopher Price interviewed by Emmeline Ledgerwood, *History of Parliament Trust*, 2012, British Library Sound & Moving Image, Catalogue reference C 1503/39 © The British Library

Graham Stevenson interviewed by Richard Stevens, *Communist Party of Great Britain Biographical Project*, British Library Sound & Moving Image, Catalogue reference C 1049/138 © The British Library

CAMBRIDGE, CHURCHILL COLLEGE ARCHIVES CENTRE. THATCHER ARCHIVE

THCR 2/6/1/21
THCR 5/1/5/19
THCR 6/2/4/59

BIRMINGHAM CENTRAL LIBRARY

MS 4000/2/101, documents collected for *The Colony*
MS 2565, diary of Roger Evans
MS 2141/A/4/14. Disputes and Discrimination in Employment

MILENNIBRUM PROJECT

The originals of these interviews can be consulted at the Birmingham Central Library. However, in almost all cases I have relied on the excellent summaries that are available with the online catalogue.

MS 2255/2/74 Earl Barrow
MS 2255/2/118 Jill Campbell
MS 2255/2/46 Anita Stanton
MS 2255/2/49 Georgina Mullen
MS 2255/2/53 unnamed Kittian woman
MS 2255/2/64 Carol Davis
MS 2255/2/25 Paul Hill
MS 2255/2/12 Jossett Lynch
MS 2255/2/76 Lester Burke
MS 2255/2/97 Joan Hart
MS 2255/2/42 Bernard Loftus

OXFORD, BODLEIAN LIBRARY
Conservative Party Archives

CCO 1/8/286
CCO 1/14/345/347
CCO 1/14/348/2
CCO 2/2/8
CCO 2/7/6

IMPERIAL WAR MUSEUM DOCUMENT COLLECTION

IWM 6431, E.A. Dorking, 'Some Recollections of My Life During the Years 1930–1945'

IMPERIAL WAR MUSEUM SOUND ARCHIVE

11580 Edward Ashill
30001 Peter Ayerst
18729 Theresa Bothwell
20055 Roy Deeley
14932 Norman Edwards
20792 Dilwyn Evans
5334 Gwendoline Stewart
10197 Edward Sturman
16724 Ernest Taylor
18772 Donald Thompson
11363 Ernest Withers

UNIVERSITY OF WARWICK MODERN RECORD CENTRE
Diaries of Ron Savage

697/1/1
697/1/3
697/1/4
697/1/5
697/1/8
697/1/13

PAPERS OF DICK ETHERIDGE

MS 205/5/A/1/1

INTERVIEWS CONDUCTED BY STEVEN TOLLIDAY

The original recordings and transcripts can be consulted at Warwick but I have
used the online versions.

MRC, 1213/2/1/1, Alf Allen, 28 January 1981
https://mrc-catalogue.warwick.ac.uk/records/TOL/2/1/1
MRC, 1213/2/1/4, Arthur Bate, 27 January 1981
https://mrc-catalogue.warwick.ac.uk/records/TOL/2/1/4
1213/2/2/1, Albert Bennett, 1–2 February 1981
https://mrc-catalogue.warwick.ac.uk/records/TOL/2/2/1
1213/2/2/4, Phil Blewitt, 25 March 1981
https://warwick.ac.uk/services/library/mrc/archives_online/speakingarchives/
1213-1-9_side_a.mp3
1213/2/3/4, Bryn Charles, 20 May 1981
https://mrc-catalogue.warwick.ac.uk/records/TOL/2/3/4
1213/24/6, Dick Etheridge and Lily May Etheridge, 13 January 1981
https://mrc-catalogue.warwick.ac.uk/records/TOL/2/4/6
1213/2/5/1, George Evans, no date
https://mrc-catalogue.warwick.ac.uk/records/TOL/2/5/1

INTERVIEWS CONDUCTED BY PAUL WORMS
FOR MAKING MOTORS

MSS 356/7/2/28, i–iii, Tom Brindley
https://warwick.ac.uk/services/library/mrc/mss356_7_2_28_ii_side1.mp3
MRC, MSS 356/7/2/55, Alan Morris
https://warwick.ac.uk/services/library/mrc/mss356_7_2_55_side1.mp3
https://warwick.ac.uk/services/library/mrc/mss356_7_2_55_side2.mp3

WEBSITES

Margaret Thatcher Foundation

https://www.margaretthatcher.org/

Gay Birmingham Remembered

http://www.gaybirminghamremembered.co.uk/

Media Archive of Central England

https://www.macearchive.org/

INTERVIEWS WITH PEOPLE ASSOCIATED WITH THE CENTRE FOR CONTEMPORARY CULTURAL STUDIES CONDUCTED BY KIERAN CONNELL

John Ellis
https://www.birmingham.ac.uk/Documents/college-artslaw/history/cccs/Interview-
   Transcripts/John-Ellis.pdf
Paul Hoggart
https://www.birmingham.ac.uk/Documents/college-artslaw/history/cccs/
   Interview-Transcripts/Paul-Hoggart.pdf
Bob Willis
https://www.birmingham.ac.uk/Documents/college-artslaw/history/cccs/
   Interview-Transcripts/Bob-Willis.pdf

OTHER SOURCES ON THE WORLD WIDE WEB

https://www.youtube.com/watch?v=N6xfzh3P_Y
http://rowntree.exeter.ac.uk/items/show/597
http://www.bbc.co.uk/history/ww2peopleswar/stories/82/a4093382.shtml
http://www.nationalarchives.gov.uk/pathways/citizenship/citizen_subject/docs/
   rastell_vintner.htm
http://www.whitefeatherdiaries.org.uk/let-politicians-fight
https://aghs.jimdofree.com/acocks-green-s-vulnerability/prefabs-updated/
https://historicalpageants.ac.uk/featured-pageants/pageant-birmingham-1938/
https://historyproject.org.uk/interview/philip-donnellan
https://mediaculturehistory.wordpress.com/2010/11/16/33608194/
https://silodrome.com/austin-seven-stanley-edge/
https://www.autographauctions.eu/130713-lot-443-PRIESTLEY-JOSEPH-
   1733–1804-English-Theologian-Natural-Philosopher-Chemist-credited-with-
   the-d?auction_id=0&view=lot_detail
https://www.pebblemill.org/blog/the-colony-a-reflection-by-contributor-
   victor-williams-daughter-sandra/

https://www.pebblemill.org/blog/the-colony-paul-long/

https://www.revolutionaryplayers.org.uk/sermon-on-the-slave-trade-by-dr-joseph-priestley/

https://www.search.connectinghistories.org.uk/Details.aspx?&ResourceID=1402&PageIndex=1&SearchType=2&ThemeID=42

Clay, Richard, 'The Paintings of Frank Taylor Lockwood (1895–1961): Industrialized Iconoclasm as Seen from Birmingham Suburbs'. Essay to be found on http://www.connectinghistories.org.uk/suburban-birmingham/suburban-birmingham-essays/

Curtis, Jo-Ann, 'Cadbury's Angels: The Depiction of Women and the Bournville Works'. Essay to be found on http://www.connectinghistories.org.uk/suburban-birmingham/suburban-birmingham-essays/

Hunkin, Michael, 'Manors from Heaven: The Municipal Housing Boom and the Challenge of Community Building on a New Estate, 1929–1939, Suburban Birmingham: Spaces and Places, 1880–1960'. Essay to be found on http://www.connectinghistories.org.uk/suburban-birmingham/suburban-birmingham-essays/

https://kingstanding.wordpress.com/

Acknowledgements

I am grateful to my agent, James Pullen, and my editor, Simon Winder, who supported a somewhat idiosyncratic project with great enthusiasm. Rebecca Lee saw the book through the press with her usual efficiency and good humour. This is the fourth of my books to be edited by Bela Cunha. Authors whose prose has been sharpened by Bela's rigour and whose egos have been salved by her kindness will understand why I was so keen to obtain her service again. Archivists at Birmingham Central Library, the Warwick Modern Records Centre and the Bodleian Library in Oxford were extraordinarily helpful. I owe particular debts to Anabel Farrell in Oxford and Martin Sanders in Warwick. The Conservative Party kindly authorized me to quote from their archives, and staff at the BBC, particularly Samantha Blake, went to great lengths to allow me to quote from the material that was assembled for the documentary *The Colony*. I am also grateful to Sara Parker and Julia Johnson for their help with this matter.

Credits for pictures are given separately but I am particularly grateful to Janet Mendelsohn and Marc Levitt for the quick and gracious way in which they responded to my request to use one of Janet's extraordinary photographs. I also owe a great deal to Andrew Milton, who took a number of photographs of Birmingham on my behalf. I am also grateful to Fiona Audley of the *Irish Post* for her help in tracing one of the excellent photographs by Brendan Farrell.

I am grateful to Curtis Brown for permission to quote from David Lodge's *Changing Places* and to Bloodaxe Books for permission to quote from the poems of Roy Fisher.

David Gottlieb, Jon Parry and Paul Readman provided useful advice about aspects of this book. David Edgerton was, as always, a stimulating interlocutor. David Carpenter, Helen Parr and Munro Price read the whole manuscript and made many helpful suggestions. Talita Ilacqua and Tom Kelsey did much to sustain my morale.

This is a highly personal book and my greatest debts are personal ones – to my mother and father, Susan and Joe, to my sister, Katie Vinen, and to my brother-in-law, Richard Wheater. Above all, I owe more than I can say to Alison Henwood and to our children – Emma and Alex.

Index

economy, 265–8; post-war politics,
275–9; pub bombings (1974),
299–305; immigration and race
relations, 309–48, 408–11; post-
war cultural life, 353–60;
newspapers, 359; intelligentsia,
359–60; post-war decline, 360–65;
bands, 365–9, 371–3; sexual
revolution, 369–71; unemployment
(1980s), 377, 389–94; 1980s
politics, 399–402; unemployment
(twenty-first century), 414–16;
historiography, 421–5, 432–3
Birmingham, Edward de, 7
Birmingham, manor of, 6, 10
Birmingham, William de, 7
Birmingham airport, 261
Birmingham Chamber Music
Society, 358
Birmingham Cinema Committee,
171–2
Birmingham City (football club),
170
Birmingham Conservative Party,
276–8, 336, 399–400
Birmingham Council, 243
Birmingham Daily Mail, 179
Birmingham family, 7
Birmingham Fire Brigade, 206
Birmingham Hampden Club, 51
Birmingham Higher Education
Association, 93
Birmingham Immigration Control
Association, 341
Birmingham International station, 261
Birmingham Labour Party, 184–8,
228–31, 278–9, 282, 339,
400–402, 434
Birmingham Law Society, 138
Birmingham Liberal Association
(BLA), 95, 100–101, 104
Birmingham Liberal Unionist
Association, 104

Birmingham Political Union (BPU),
47, 53–4, 58, 59
Birmingham Polytechnic, 362
Birmingham Post, 69, 108, 276–7, 359
Birmingham Railway Carriage and
Wagon Company, 210
Birmingham Repertory Theatre, 354,
361
Birmingham School Board, 100
Birmingham School of Art, 97
Birmingham Screw Company, 76
Birmingham Six, 300, 303–4, 443–55
Birmingham Small Arms Company
(BSA), 149, 211, 218–19
Birmingham Town Hall, 98, 202
Birmingham University, 87, 238–9,
355–6, 361–5
Birmingham Women's Suffrage
Society, 94
Birmingham Young Conservatives,
256–7
Bishop Vesey's grammar school, 10
Bisset, James, 49–50
Black, Patrick, 372
Black Country, xxvi, 162, 342
Black Horse pub, Northfield, 169
Black Sabbath (band), 367, 368
Black Sabbath Bridge, *350–351*
Blackburn, Raymond, 233
Blair, Tony, 408, 412, 420
Blewitt, Phil, 274
Blitz, in Birmingham, 211
Bloomer, William, 161
Boer War (1899–1901), 107
bomb sites, 239
Bonar Law, Andrew, 192, 194
Bondfield, Margaret, 169
Bordesley, 59
Boscovich, Roger Joseph SJ, 39
Bothwell, Theresa, 221
Boult, Adrian, 88
Boulton, Matthew, 23, 26–32, 34–6,
38, 41, 42–3, 50–51, 57, 123, 128

Finney, Donald, 341, 342
First World War, 140, 148–9
Fisher, Bartholomew, 42
Fisher, Roy, xxv, 161, 280
Fitz Ansculf, William, 6
'Five Miles Act', 88
Florence, Philip Sargant, 356–7, 358
Foley, Maurice, 291
football, 170
Forster, William, 100
Fort Dunlop (factory), 150, 180, 268, 420
Fothergill, John, 29
Fowler, Norman, 277
Franco-Prussian War (1870–71), 76
Fraser, Antonia, 232n, 259
Fraser, Roy, 389
French, Field Marshal Sir John, 149
French Revolution, 35–6, 47
French Revolutionary Wars, 48–9
Frisch, Otto, 212
Futurist, The (cinema), 171

Galloway, Jack, 278
Galton, Mary Anne, 84
Galton, Samuel, 37
Galton, Samuel Tertius, 84
Galton family, 37, 43, 84, 431
Gangsters (TV series), 372
Garland, Mr Justice, 453
Garner, Fred, 155
Garvin, James Louis, 109–10
Gaskell and Chambers (company), 211
Gaynor, Anthony, 299
Geach, Charles, 61–2, 128, 139
General Election (1945), 231–3
General Electric (GEC), 150, 180
General Strike (1926), 177, 184, 186
Gibbons, Steve, 366–7, 372
Gibbs, Alan, 335
Giehse, Therese, 171, 355
Gill, Preet, 418
Gillott, Joseph, 81, 114

Gillott's pen factory, 135
Girdler, Captain Robert, 15
GKN (company), 139, 150
Gladstone, William Ewart, 97, 101, 102, 103–4
Golden Hillock secondary school, 347
Goldsbrough, Francis, 169
Gordon Walker, Patrick, 341–2
Gough, Henry, 21
Gough family, 85, 129
grammar schools, 269–70
Gravelly Hill see Spaghetti Junction
Great Dodford, 182–3
Green, Henry, xxvii, xxx, 137, 138, 169–70
Green, Tony, 239, 331
Greenwood, Arthur, 197
Greer, Germaine, 361
Greisbroke, Henry, 9
Grenville, William, 41
Grey, Charles, 2nd Earl Grey of Fallodon (Lord Grey), 53
Grieve, Percy, 261
Griffin, Christine, 305, 390
Griffiths, Peter, 309, 339–41, 342, 343, 348
gun manufacture, 37, 431
Gurden, Harold, 343

Hackett, General Sir John, The Third World War (1982), xv
Hall, Stuart, 310, 363, 364, 371, 378
Hall Green, 414
Hallas, Eldred, 186
Halward, Leslie, 355, 359
Hampson, John, 355, 358
Handsworth, xxv, 147, 248, 259, 322, 334, 336; and racial division, 394–8
Handsworth Songs (film, 1985), 396, 456
Hannon, Sir Patrick, 232
Hansom, John, 202
Harborne, 13, 219, 331